Blockchain Fundamental Analysis for Digital Asset Investors

A Guide to Minimizing Risk and Maximizing Returns

Paul Garvey

Apress®

Blockchain Fundamental Analysis for Digital Asset Investors: A Guide to Minimizing Risk and Maximizing Returns

Paul Garvey
Sugar Land, TX, USA

ISBN-13 (pbk): 979-8-8688-1550-8 ISBN-13 (electronic): 979-8-8688-1551-5
https://doi.org/10.1007/979-8-8688-1551-5

Managing Director, Apress Media LLC: Welmoed Spahr
Acquisitions Editor: Shivangi Ramachandran
Development Editor: James Markham
Editorial Assistant: Jessica Vakili

Cover designed by eStudioCalamar

Distributed to the book trade worldwide by Springer Science+Business Media New York, 1 New York Plaza, New York, NY 10004. Phone 1-800-SPRINGER, fax (201) 348-4505, e-mail orders-ny@springer-sbm.com, or visit www.springeronline.com. Apress Media, LLC is a Delaware LLC and the sole member (owner) is Springer Science + Business Media Finance Inc (SSBM Finance Inc). SSBM Finance Inc is a **Delaware** corporation.

For information on translations, please e-mail booktranslations@springernature.com; for reprint, paperback, or audio rights, please e-mail bookpermissions@springernature.com.

Apress titles may be purchased in bulk for academic, corporate, or promotional use. eBook versions and licenses are also available for most titles. For more information, reference our Print and eBook Bulk Sales web page at http://www.apress.com/bulk-sales.

Any source code or other supplementary material referenced by the author in this book is available to readers on GitHub. For more detailed information, please visit https://www.apress.com/gp/services/source-code.

If disposing of this product, please recycle the paper

*To my amazing wife, Ariel—**this book is dedicated to you**. Thank you for putting up with all the early mornings, late nights, and weekends I spent working on it. I know it meant sacrificing time together, and I can't tell you how much I appreciate your patience and support through it all. I couldn't have done this without you. This book exists because of you—my deepest gratitude and love.*

Table of Contents

About the Author

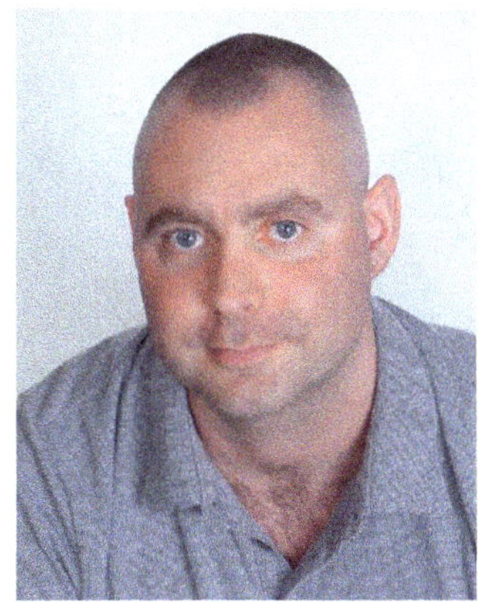

Paul Garvey's journey into blockchain began from an unconventional angle—not through tech or information technology, but through a career in mechanical engineering. With a degree in mechanical engineering, and years of experience as a rotating equipment engineer, Paul applies the same deep-engineering discipline and analytical mindset to blockchain that he once used to solve complex machinery problems.

Since first discovering the technology in 2016, Paul has immersed himself in blockchain and digital assets through self-study, seminars, books, courses, and hands-on investing. Today he helps newcomers cut through the noise by focusing on the core fundamentals that make or break a project, sharing clear, data-driven insights through articles, talks, and mentoring.

His technique simplifies investment decisions while reducing financial risk by focusing on real fundamentals that can make or break a project, making it easier.

About the Technical Reviewer

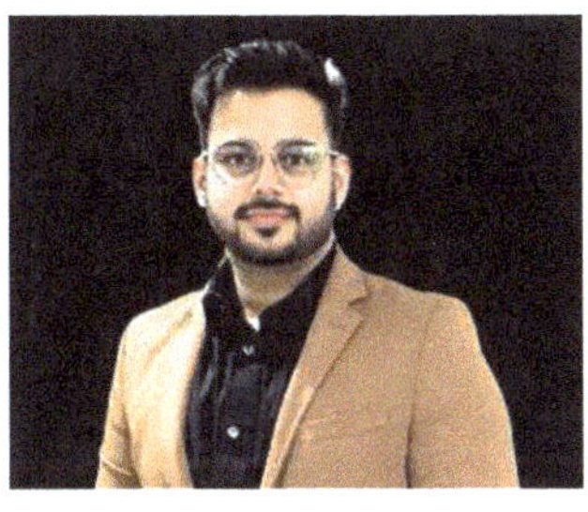

Pranav Burnwal is a serial entrepreneur and technology leader with over eight years of expertise in blockchain and more than a decade in full-stack development. As a 4x founder, he has a proven track record of building innovative products across multiple domains, including Web3, education technology, and digital identity. Pranav has successfully secured multiple rounds of funding for his ventures, demonstrating strong business acumen alongside technical leadership. Recognized as a thought leader and educator in the blockchain space, he is passionate about driving technological innovation and mentoring the next generation of engineers. Outside of work, Pranav enjoys traveling, sparring, bike rides, and artisanal coffee.

Acknowledgments

I am forever grateful to the Apress team. Shivangi Ramachandran, my acquisitions editor, recognized the manuscript's potential, got the ball rolling during the introduction and contract stage, and stayed helpful from start to finish. Sowmya Thodur, production team lead, kept every piece moving with calm efficiency. James Markham, development editor, provided guidance and suggestions that were second to none, refining every rough edge. Jessica Vakili, editorial assistant, along with Welmoed Spahr, managing director, and the rest of the behind-the-scenes crew, worked tirelessly to shape the manuscript into its final form.

Beyond the Apress team, my deepest thanks go to Pranav Burnwal, our technical reviewer. His sharp eye, expert insights, and relentless feedback elevated the content in ways that wouldn't have happened without him.

To my family and my wife, Ariel, thank you for always having my back, believing in me, and keeping my spirits up when I was completely buried in this project and struggling to see the light at the end of the tunnel.

And a big thanks to Uncle Mike—your weekly check-ins on the book kept me going throughout the entire journey. Knowing you cared about the progress made all the difference!

This book wouldn't exist without all of you. Thank you.

Preface

Pitfalls with Digital Asset Investing

Since you have purchased this book, you might already have some experience investing in digital assets, have no experience, or perhaps know someone who's dabbled in it and made anything from minor to significant profits. Sadly, for most people, regardless of the hype and numerous success stories of people becoming millionaires and billionaires overnight, most individuals who invest in digital assets lose money at the hands of experienced investors or fraudsters. This is due to a variety of reasons, including poor fundamental analysis skills, bad timing of the market, lack of experience, being influenced by hype, being subjected to scam assets "projects," little to no profit taking, not understanding the associated risks, uncontrolled emotions, or simply not knowing why you are investing in the first place. Unfortunately, this lack of overall experience results in much guesswork, emotional decision-making, or blind trust in hype.

When selecting a digital asset for investment, it is essential that the investor evaluate the fundamental aspects of the project to help increase profitability while decreasing the risk of financial loss. Seeking a second opinion from reputable investors, influencers, or other experts in the field is not necessarily bad. In fact, it is encouraged and often seen as a positive aspect when the thoughts and opinions of others align with yours, signaling confluence and adding additional validity to one's fundamental analysis. However, relying entirely on other people's reviews may generate short-term luck in the crypto markets. Still, it does not suffice for a long-term success strategy and will ultimately end in tears. The issue is that when investors can't evaluate a crypto project themselves, they are potentially inheriting unwanted risk, as the faith of their hard-earned money is in the hands of others—this is a clear path to financial ruin. Therefore, from a fundamental aspect, it is vital that investors understand the project, the core fundamentals, and how value is generated. Evaluating "crypto" projects is a skill developed over time—the more time and effort exerted, the faster and more efficiently one will identify high-fundamental projects for investment while filtering out poor, weak, and scam projects.

Additionally, unlike traditional markets, the digital asset world is plagued with fraudulent projects trying to take investors' money without the intention of ever providing value. These scam projects pour most of their money into devious marketing strategies to lure in new, inexperienced investors, hide the truth, and flee with their money. Additionally, because the blockchain world is still unregulated in most countries, it is very difficult to track down the individuals responsible.

Another important point to note is that, unlike traditional markets, most investments in the blockchain world are 'self-directed' investments. In conventional markets—including IRAs or traditional 401k accounts—less experienced investors can invest in exchange-traded funds (ETFs) and other financial instruments, including mutual funds, index funds, or professionally managed portfolios, where financial and economic experts guide investment decisions. However, because the digital asset class is not yet regulated (at the time of writing this book), there is little to know about investment options like that of traditional markets—outside of a bitcoin spot ETF. Therefore, the investor is directly responsible for research, fundamental analysis, and decision-making when selecting digital asset investments for their asset portfolio—adding an extra layer of complexity and risk.

Purpose of This Book

Without a proper strategy and evaluation process, digital asset investors are far more likely to lose money than accumulate wealth. To address this, this book presents a detailed evaluation process focusing on the fundamental aspects of typical blockchain-based projects. This fundamental evaluation process's core objective is maximizing profits while reducing investor risk.

The key blockchain fundamental elements for crypto projects that investors need to analyze are broken down and discussed, covering a specific set of elements:

1) ***Project Documentation (Whitepaper/Litepaper)***
2) ***Core Offering (Product/Service)***
3) ***End-User Experience***
4) ***Blockchain Architecture***
5) ***Token Design and Use Case***
6) ***Tokenomics***
7) ***Financial Metrics***
8) ***Project Team***
9) ***Project Roadmap***
10) ***Project Codebase***
11) ***Incentivization and Rewards***
12) ***Community and Social Media***
13) ***Funding and Partnerships***

These core fundamental elements equip investors with the knowledge to make well-informed strategic decisions while helping to avoid common mistakes, such as investing in scams or projects with poor or worthless use cases. When performing a fundamental analysis, investors should look to disqualify projects rather than approving them for investment—the approval and disqualification criteria for each fundamental element are discussed in detail.

It is important to note that this book is not a "get rich quick" solution, nor does it guarantee success. It is highly advised to run from anyone who tries to sell or pitch something that guarantees massive returns, as such claims often lead to disappointment or financial loss. Experienced investors know that ninety-nine percent of the time, it is hard work, time, dedication, patience, and the willingness to accept and learn from your and other people's mistakes that form the foundation for a long-term profitable investor. Before continuing with this book, this must be understood and accepted to avoid false promises or misconceptions.

For those who accept the challenge, the content within this book serves as a platter of information that teaches how to evaluate blockchain projects and *the basis* of *blockchain technology*. While there are definitely no "safe bets" when investing within the blockchain world, by the end of this book, you will be equipped to make an educated and informed investment decision. No more solely relying on influencers, hype, and wild speculation.

How to Use This Book

Understanding this book's concepts and evaluation techniques requires little to no prior experience or knowledge of blockchain technology—all it takes is the commitment and willingness to learn. However, some sections of this book may seem a little daunting at first, triggering thoughts such as, "*How long does it actually take to analyze just one project?*" and "*Is there really a need for this for an analysis this deep*?" As with most things, if investing in digital assets is a new experience, evaluating a project at the beginning may take longer than someone who has a prior background in blockchain and experience with digital assets.

Spending adequate time learning how to evaluate a project's fundamental strengths and weaknesses not only helps investors increase profits but also builds a valuable skill set in fundamental analysis that remains yours for life. This helps to identify high-profit potential projects at the infant stage before the masses. Nothing compares to confidently conducting your own fundamental analysis—as the saying goes in the crypto world, #DYOR (Do Your Own Research).

The following is a guide to help you navigate this book most efficiently.

1) **Learn the Essentials**

   Read each section carefully while taking adequate time to understand the technology and fundamental aspects involved.

2) **Stick to the Steps**

   At the end of each fundamental section is a set of "Action Items" designed as a step-by-step guide to help investors evaluate the fundamental element discussed in each section. These steps should be strictly adhered to for best results.

3) **Build Your Ranking System**

   It is strongly recommended that investors generate a personalized system for recording the results that works for them. This can be in a text or Excel file. There is no right or wrong way to do it; everyone has their own preference. However, unless you are keen on sharing your findings with others, the fundamental analysis results are only visible to you; therefore, select a system that works best for you. I prefer using a simple Microsoft Excel file, with the key fundamental elements listed as row headers and their corresponding evaluation details in the columns.

4) **Write Notes That Work**

   Note that this book does not utilize a numerical rating system for scoring the fundamental aspects of a project. Although it has somewhat worked in the past, experience has proven that the results are not as quantifiable as they may seem, and not everyone has the same perspective on how well the project performs in certain areas. For example, it is hard to numerically rate how strong a use case is, team members' backgrounds and credibility, or project roadmap elements such as vision and milestone feasibility. However, feel free to use a numerical system when taking notes and recording the results for each fundamental evaluation section. Also, consider using a ranking system such as *poor, fair, strong, or excellent*—again, use whatever system works best for you.

5) **Dig Deeper When Required**

   If you come across a section that's hard to understand, take some time to do extra research online. While the chapters don't directly build on one another, it's still important to fully grasp the fundamental elements before moving on to the next chapter.

6) **Verify Official Channels**

   Sometimes, accessing all the key project information for fundamental evaluation can prove a tedious task. If this happens, it is recommended to reach out to the project team or trusted members of the community. However, proceed with extreme caution and ensure you only contact them through the project's official channels, which should be accessible via their website.

7) **Stick to the Facts**

   An effective and accurate evaluation of a blockchain project requires interdisciplinary skills. Therefore, try to refrain from letting hype influence your analysis. Stick to the facts and always use your best judgment.

8) **Push Through the Tech**

   Try not to get bogged down when encountering areas that seem very technical in nature. Although it may be hard to see, with hard work, dedication, and a positive attitude, these areas will become second nature to you as time progresses.

9) **Think with Logic, Not Emotion**

   Be aware of your mindset when conducting an analysis; emotion can easily lead you to qualify for a project for investment. Remember, always look for ways to disqualify a project instead of approving it for inclusion in your portfolio. This approach ensures that only truly strong, fundamentally sound projects make it into your portfolio.

Conventions Used in This Book

To accommodate simplicity, various terms and phrases are used throughout the book. These are as follows:

1) For simplicity and ease of writing, blockchain-based projects, whether actual blockchain infrastructures or token-based decentralized applications (dApps), are called "projects" or more often 'crypto' projects.

2) The term "red flag" is a warning sign or indication of potential problems, risks, or issues that require deeper research or where one should avoid investing altogether—depending on where and how the term is used in context.

3) At the beginning of each section is an "Evaluation Objective," which details the fundamental objective to be evaluated as part of the investor's analysis. The action steps to achieve the evaluation objective are detailed at the end of each section.

4) *The acronym "DYOR" means* "Do Your Own Research." This means that investors should do their own research before investing. The responsibility is on the investor, not anyone else.

5) Technology evolves rapidly, meaning some of the technologies referenced in example projects may have been updated or replaced. Financial data can also change frequently, and reference links may be altered or moved. However, the fundamental evaluation techniques outlined in this book remain timeless and should not be significantly impacted by these changes.

6) Throughout this book, you will find specific notices designed to highlight important information; these notices include

   a. **PRO TIP** - Practical advice or actionable insights to help you make better investment decisions.

   b. **FACT** - Key pieces of information or important details that every investor should know.

   c. **CAUTION** - When evaluating a project, you should be aware of warnings about potential risks, red flags, or issues.

Contacting the Author

You can contact me, Paul Garvey, through the below outlets:

Follow me on LinkedIn: `https://www.linkedin.com/in/paul-garvey-eng/`

Follow me on X: `https://x.com/PaulsCryptoCall`

Visit my website: `https://garveypaul.com/`

Disclaimer

This book is for informational purposes only and does not constitute legal, financial, or investment advice. The author is not a licensed financial advisor, and nothing herein should be interpreted as a recommendation to buy, sell, or hold any asset. All investment decisions are made at the reader's own risk. The author and publisher disclaim any liability for losses or damages resulting from the use or misuse of this content.

Cryptocurrency markets are volatile, and past performance is not indicative of future results. Examples of projects, cryptocurrencies, decentralized applications (dApps), or tokens are provided solely for educational purposes and do not represent endorsements. Readers are urged to conduct independent research and consult professionals before making financial decisions.

CHAPTER 1

Introduction to Blockchain Technology

As per Imran Bashir in his book *Mastering Blockchain*, a blockchain can be defined as "a peer-to-peer, distributed ledger that is cryptographically secure, append-only, immutable (extremely hard to change), and updateable only via consensus or agreement among peers." In simple terms, a blockchain is an ever-growing secure record-keeping database of transactions that have taken place between two network participants (parties). This database—known as a distributed ledger—logs blocks of data containing information, known as metadata, about each transaction being added to the blockchain in chronological order upon verification of each block.

Fact A blockchain is a decentralized, immutable digital accounting system that records "who owns what" and maintains all state changes over time.

Blockchain is a type of distributed ledger technology (DLT). This decentralized-distributed network can be either public or private and is made up of computers (also called nodes) that store information electronically. These nodes coordinate and interact with one another to achieve a specific outcome. The most common type of information

P. Garvey, *Blockchain Fundamental Analysis for Digital Asset Investors*,
https://doi.org/10.1007/979-8-8688-1551-5_1

stored is transactional data such as the sender and beneficiary addresses, type, quantity, value of assets, and time and date of the transaction. The blockchain's task and objective is to efficiently gather, record, and transfer digital information in a trustless and secure manner. Network participants typically consist of anyone who interacts with the network, such as senders, receivers, and "miners" who help validate and process blocks of transactions on the blockchain.

One of the key advantages of the blockchain is that it operates on a decentralized peer-to-peer (P2P) network that does not require any centralized authorities to accommodate the transfer of assets or information. For example, participants can send digital assets (and information) to one another for a small fee without needing a bank, government agency, or third-party application to help process and secure the transaction. Transactions on the blockchain are sent from one side of the world to another in a few seconds to a minute, versus one to three days with conventional banking systems. There is no limit to the value of digital assets that can be transferred at any time. Additionally, unlike traditional banking systems, there is no requirement to explain the source of the funds, the purpose of the transaction, or to whom the funds are being sent. However, it is advised to keep an account of all transactional data for tax purposes. An array of online software can help investors with this task, e.g., CoinLedger, Koinly, TokenTax, and CoinTracking.

Another core aspect and major benefit of blockchain technology is that it operates in a trustless manner, which means that unlike a typical bank, participants sending assets do not need to know or trust the individuals, known as *miners,* who verify and process the transactions on the network. This is achieved through *consensus mechanisms* where miners are incentivized (typically with crypto assets) to reach a consensus on whether the block of transactions is either valid or invalid.

Blockchain Key Characteristics

Contrary to what many new people in the crypto realm may think, blockchain technology has a deeper meaning than simply a technology that offers a byproduct, digital investment assets. Blockchains exhibit key characteristics that make them unique and attractive in today's world. These are briefly discussed in the following sections.

Decentralization

Unlike traditional ledgers or databases controlled by a central authority (e.g., banks and governments), a blockchain is distributed across a network of computers called nodes. Each transaction initiated on the network, either sending and receiving digital or other information, is executed among peers and not reliant on a central authority. Therefore, the network cannot be shut down, as the power and responsibility are distributed across all nodes on the network. Additionally, this distributes consensus participation across nodes on the network, though influence may vary depending on the consensus mechanism (e.g., mining power in PoW), which also helps to facilitate transaction verification.

Immutability

Immutable means something that will never change or cannot be changed. With respect to blockchain technology, immutability refers to the inability of recorded data—transactional or other—to be manipulated, modified, or deleted once recorded on the blockchain network. This is achieved through a combination of *cryptographic hash functions* and unique consensus mechanisms that help secure block data and link the blocks in a chain structure, hence the "blockchain." The deeper the blocks, the harder it is for the data to be altered, making it highly secure. However, there are rare and unlikely events that may occur, such as a 51% attack, where if hackers take control of at least 51% or more of the network's computational power, they will have the ability to manipulate past block data.

Transparency

Transactional data on the blockchain is entirely traceable all the way back to the genesis block—the first recorded block on a blockchain. This, in turn, creates transparency, as all transactions are visible and verifiable, thus generating a high level of trust and integrity.

Anonymity/Pseudonymity

Blockchain technology offers both *anonymity* and *pseudonymity* to network participants. Blockchains geared toward privacy, e.g., Zcash (ZEC) and Monero (XMR), provide complete anonymity and untraceable transactions, thus hiding user identity on the network. Meanwhile, blockchains such as bitcoin and Ethereum are classified as pseudonyms. On a pseudonymous blockchain, all transactions are public and traceable, meaning that, although a user's identity is not directly revealed, their public address can often be linked with their identity. On the other hand, traditionally, banks are neither anonymous nor pseudonymous because a user's account number is directly linked to their identity.

Auditability

Auditability in blockchain refers to the ability to verify and trace every recorded transaction on-chain through an immutable reference point. This reference point is imprinted into every node throughout the blockchain network, allowing for precise traceability. At any given point in time, this makes each and every transaction ever made on a public blockchain completely auditable, which, in turn, enhances the verification of data integrity and authenticity without a central authority, promoting security and trust across the network.

Autonomy

"Autonomy" comes from ancient Greek and means "self-legislation" or "self-governance." Individuals can have full self-control and self-govern, e.g., their assets, identity, the right to speak, the right to vote, etc. Through the core characteristics of blockchain technology, such as decentralization, immutability, security, traceability, transparency, and privacy, users can experience autonomy, thus eliminating any requirement, restriction, or control from central authorities.

bitcoin

bitcoin is the world's first digital decentralized currency payment system that operates on a secure, peer-to-peer blockchain, enabling trustless transactions without the need for intermediaries. Because bitcoin is not backed or governed by any government or legal entity, it is seen as one of the most disruptive creations in recent history. bitcoin was created in 2009 by a pseudonym by the name of Satoshi Nakamoto and is defined as a "purely peer-to-peer version of electronic cash that would allow online payments to be sent directly from one party to another without going through a financial institution."

The word itself, "bitcoin," has a lot of history. bitcoin is commonly spelled with the capital letter "B". However, using a lowercase letter "b" (as on `www.bitcoin.org`) signifies that there is no centralized entity that can or is controlling the network. bitcoin is spelled with a lowercase "b" throughout this book.

The creation of bitcoin did not happen accidentally. It happened because of an urgent need to disengage from controlling centralized authorities and traditional online payment methods, whereby some form of financial institution was required to accommodate any exchange between two parties.

Fact bitcoin utilizes the Secure Hash Algorithm (SHA)-256 to generate a cryptographic hash of the data stored in each block on the blockchain. This works by converting the data in the block into a 256-bit hexadecimal number. This hex number captures and contains all the transaction details and connections to the chain's previous blocks.

Outside of financial profit, the primary purpose of these centralized financial entities was to eliminate the issue of double spending, which arises from computing issues, resulting in spending the same money twice. However, bitcoin remarkably solves the problem of double spending by providing an electronic payment system that, unlike financial institutions, does not rely on trust. Instead, bitcoin uses cryptography, a cryptographic mechanism that enables transactional confirmation and maintainability of a universal ledger (the blockchain) cash monetary system. Double spending is explored in more detail in the section "Double Spending" in Chapter 6, "Blockchain Architecture."

Note: bitcoin is referenced throughout this book because it is the most widely known digital asset and most notable proof-of-work (PoW) based blockchain. Some references address bitcoin's scalability issues, but these are purely for context and do not diminish the asset in any way. bitcoin is a revolution of technology that has revolutionized the global financial sector by introducing a decentralized, transparent, and secure asset, successfully bringing autonomy and financial freedom to people around the world.

Cryptography

Most people reading this book may have sent or received digital assets. However, what happens on the back end makes these transactions possible—without the aid of traditional banking or third-party applications. Blockchains rely on cryptographic algorithms and economic incentives to ensure the integrity and legitimacy of every transaction or state change. In this section, asymmetric cryptography technology is discussed step-by-step, including how private keys, public keys, and public addresses are utilized in the cryptographic process.

bitcoin has been in circulation since 2009; however, the technology has been in the making for decades through the field of cryptography. The term "*cryptography*" has Greek roots, which means "secret writing." It is the science that protects information and makes it incomprehensible to those who intercept it so that it can be read and understood only by the recipient. There are two types of cryptographic encryption: *symmetric encryption* and *asymmetric encryption*. For this book, only asymmetric encryption is discussed, as it plays a central role in blockchain verification and identity mechanisms, particularly through public-private key cryptography. However, it is essential to understand the key components that make this possible: *cryptographic keys*.

Cryptographic Keys

In cryptography, a cryptographic key is digital data represented by a string of characters used within an encryption algorithm. Their primary purpose in blockchain is to digitally sign transactions and verify ownership, ensuring data integrity and authenticity between users. The types of cryptographic keys used in the blockchain world consist of a ***private key***, a ***public key***, and a ***public address***. This section discusses the creation of cryptographic keys, their core functionality, and their purpose. This also builds the foundation of asymmetric encryption, which will be discussed in more detail in the subsequent section.

Private Key

A private key, also known as a secret key, is a cryptographic variable used with an algorithm to sign transactions and prove ownership in a blockchain network. The corresponding public key is used to verify that digital signature, ensuring the transaction was authorized by the rightful owner. A public address, derived from the public key through a hashing process, is used to receive funds and can be shared openly. In blockchain technology, private keys are essential for securing access to digital assets and authorizing actions on-chain. They must be kept secure, as anyone with access to the private key can control the associated wallet and its contents. Figure 1-1 shows an image from bitaddress.org, where users can quickly generate a set of cryptographic keys in a paper wallet format.

Figure 1-1. *Generation of a bitcoin private key and public address. The public key has also been generated behind the scenes (compliments of `https://www.bitaddress.org/bitaddress.org-v3.3.0-SHA256-dec17c07685e1870960903d8f58090475b25af946fe95a734f88408cef4aa194.html`)*

Pro Tip The private key should be kept in a very safe place that only the owner knows—hence why it is called a private key. In the unfortunate event that someone gains access to your private keys, they have the power to steal all of your assets.

The relationship between the private key, the public key, and the public address can be seen in Figure 1-2. Creation of the keys starts with the Private Key (k)—k, short for key—where the key is generated randomly using *cryptographically secure pseudorandom number generators (CSPRNG)*. These generators are often initialized by a human source of randomness, where users may be asked to wiggle their mouse around for a few seconds until the generator reaches 100%—this is how the keys are created in the example from Figure 1-2.

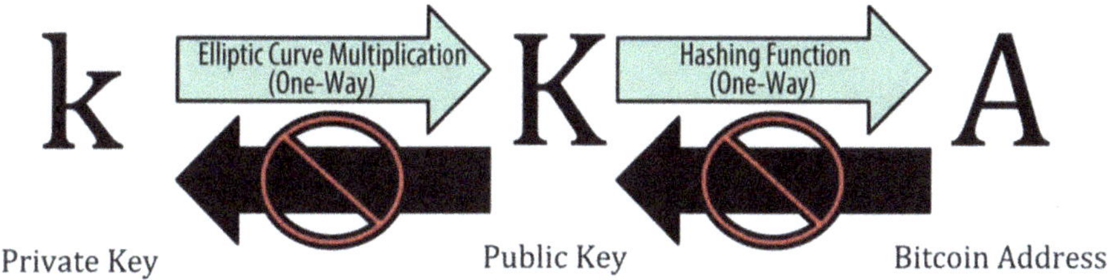

Figure 1-2. *Generation architecture of a private key, public key, and public address (compliments of `https://www.oreilly.com/library/view/mastering-bitcoin/9781491902639/ch04.html`)*

Public Key

In asymmetric cryptography, the public key is used to decrypt messages, thus only allowing the individual to use the corresponding and cryptographically linked public key. The public key also has an essential role in transaction processing (e.g., bitcoin transaction) to help verify that the digital signature came from the corresponding private key, thus authenticating that the sender is the rightful owner of the assets being sent on-chain.

As per Figure 1-2, the Public Key (K) is created and derived from the Private Key (k) using Elliptic Curve Cryptography (EEC), a unidirectional cryptographic function. The private and public keys are cryptographically and mathematically linked together at the time of creation and enable secure communications and transfer of data from one party to another without the need for sharing any private and secret detail such as their private key.

Public Address

A public address can be considered equivalent to a typical bank account number. It is used to receive digital assets. The public address is typically shared by anyone who wants to send you digital assets. However, caution should be exercised, as it may be used to link with one's identity.

Per Figure 1-2, the public address (A) (e.g., bitcoin wallet address) is created and derived from the public key through a one-way hashing function.

Asymmetric Encryption

Asymmetric Encryption, or Public key Cryptography, is a cryptographic method for encrypting and decrypting data. For example, Bob and Alice both have a set of Public and Private Keys. If Bob wanted to send Alice a decrypted message, he would first type the message in a standard readable language (e.g., English). Then, using Alice's **Public Key**, he would encrypt that message, turning it into an unreadable, scrambled text called *ciphertext*. When Alice receives the *ciphertext,* she uses her **Private Key** to decrypt Bob's message, thus converting it to its original form, English. It is important to note that if Bob lost his Private Key, he could never decrypt Alice's message. Figure 1-3 shows an example of asymmetric encryption—Bob on the left and Alice on the right.

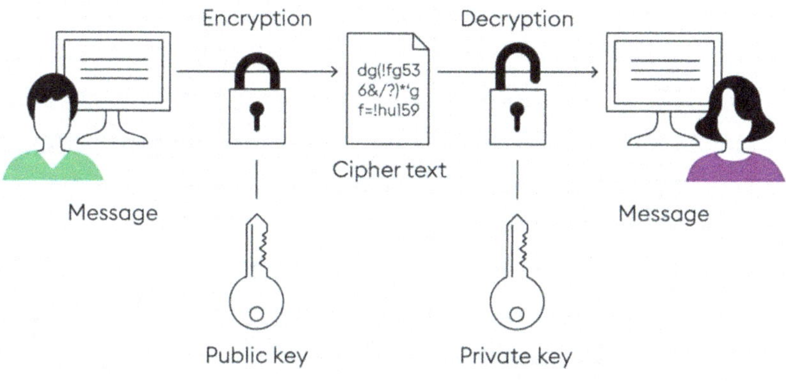

Figure 1-3. *Asymmetric encryption (compliments of `https://www.bitpanda.com/academy/en/lessons/what-is-asymmetric-encryption/`)*

Asymmetric Encryption with Respect to Blockchain

Asymmetric cryptography in blockchain is not used in the traditional sense to "encrypt" and "decrypt" data. Instead, the significant and key advantage of asymmetric encryption in blockchain is the introduction of the *digital signature*. Digital signatures provide integrity using asymmetric cryptography and primality, which are used to authenticate if the sender is the rightful owner of the assets being sent (e.g., bitcoins). This technology is widely utilized in various protocols for authentication purposes and has proven very trustworthy and secure.

Think of a digital signature as a stamp that proves and authenticates that the sender is the true owner of the digital assets before the sender broadcasts the transaction to the network. When creating a digital signature, the entire message or transaction data is not signed directly. Instead, a *hash function* generates a condensed and unique version of the message called a *digest* (or footprint). This digest is a hash of the full transaction data as defined by the blockchain protocol. It includes details such as the sender's and receiver's public addresses, the asset being sent, the date, time, transaction fee, and other relevant fields. The *digest* is then encrypted with the sender's private key to create the digital signature.

When spending digital currency (e.g., bitcoin), the sender starts by showing their **public key** and a **digital signature** that has been encrypted with their **private key**. This information is propagated through the bitcoin network, where full nodes verify the digital signature to confirm the sender is authorized to transfer the funds. When this transaction reaches the recipient, the digital signature is verified using the sender's public key, which provides access to the *digest.* The recipient then creates their own *digest* from the received message by using the same hash function that the sender used to generate their *digest.* If they match, the signature is confirmed as authentic and signifies that the transaction has not been tampered with.

This unique technology allows for the signing, encryption, and verification of messages, thus providing high security. Asymmetric encryption also ensures that the ownership of one's digital assets cannot be faked, forged, or spent if ownership rights cannot be verified. This technology does not just secure transactions. It is also used to confirm ownership by validating the digital signature using the owner's public key, making it a unique, reliable, and versatile technology for digital signatures and encryption. Asymmetric encryption is an incorruptible, easily verifiable, essential ingredient for blockchains.

Recap of the Cryptographic Keys and Their Role in Asymmetric Encryption and a Typical bitcoin Transaction

Private Key Characteristics and Functionality

- Generated at random through *cryptographically secure pseudorandom number generators (CSPRNG).*
- Signs transactions that can be verified using the corresponding public key.
- *Verifies digital asset ownership (through digital signature).*
- *Provides access to one's funds stored on the blockchain.*
- *Should be hidden and kept safe at all times.*
- *Advised to keep a backup of the private key in a safe and secure place.*

Public Key Characteristics and Functionality

- Utilizing Elliptic Curve Cryptography (ECC) technology, the *public key* is mathematically derived from the *private key* using elliptic curve multiplication.
- *Used to encrypt messages.*
- *Used by miners during transaction processing and authentication to help verify that the digital signature came from the corresponding private key.*
  - The Public Key is not always shown to the wallet owner by default, especially in basic wallet interfaces, but it can typically be accessed or derived, particularly in HD wallets and multi-signature setups. *When processing a transaction, the Public Key is used behind the scenes to help with the verification process.*

Public Address Characteristics and Functionality

- Utilizing Elliptic Curve Cryptography (ECC) technology, the *public address* is derived (hashed) from the *public key*.
- *Equivalent of a typical bank account number used to receive digital assets.*
- *Typical visible and freely shared with anyone who wants to send you digital assets. However, caution should be exercised, as it may be used to link with one's identity.*

Web3

Web3 was coined by Dr. Gavin James Wood, the co-founder of Ethereum and creator of Polkadot, Kusama, Parity Technologies, and the Web3 Foundation, where Mr. Wood envisioned a transparent and decentralized web that is not controlled by central entities, and the power handed back to the rightful owners, the users.

Web3 can be described as a new emerging internet technology centered on the core principle of decentralization. Through JavaScript-based libraries (e.g., Web3.js, Next.js, Ether.js, and Truffle Suite) and APIs (Application Programming Interface), Web3 bridges the gap. It establishes connections between blockchains (including smart contracts, decentralized applications (dApps), and the Internet). This enables ownership opportunities and enables trustless cryptographic secure transactions for all Web3 and network participants.

Evolution of the Web

To truly understand Web3, it is worth going back in time and exploring the main concepts, features, and limitations of Web1 and Web2.

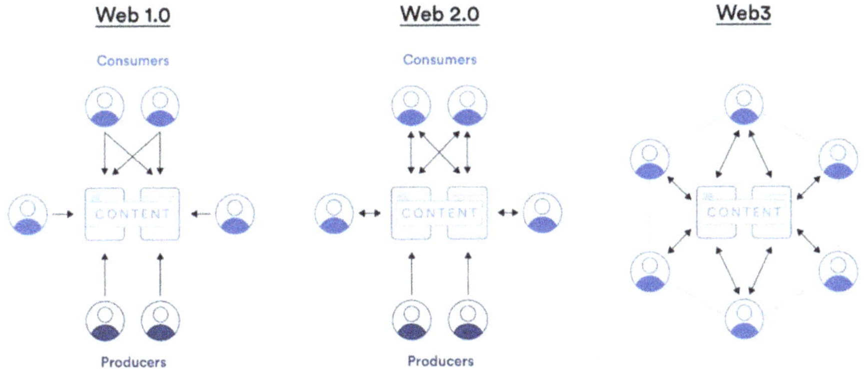

Figure 1-4. *Interactions between content consumers and producers on Web 1.0, 2.0, and Web (compliments of* `https://chain.link/education/web3`*)*

Web1

Web1, also known as the *Static Web*, was the first version of the web that was ever created; it existed from 1991 to the early 2000s. It was designed to allow groups of readers to access information, content, and facts more efficiently. This was the first time users saw and experienced a worldwide digital network. Web1 saw the introduction of three fundamental concepts that helped form the backbone of today's internet. These are as follows:

1) **HTML (Hyper Text Markup Language)** – HTML is the standard markup language used to structure content on the web. HTML code is converted and visually displayed on the web page through browsers such as Chrome and Firefox. Web1 saw the introduction of URLs, making it possible for users to browse the web by entering the web address into their browser.

2) **URL (Unique Address for Webpages)** - A URL is simply an online address to resources and information on the web.

3) **HTTP (Hypertext Transfer Protocol)** - HTTP forms the foundation of the web, where it is used to load webpages using hypertext links. An application layer protocol transfers information between networked computers and servers.

Fact The first-ever web page went live on August 6, 1991. It was created by Tim Berners-Lee and provided information about the World Wide Web project, such as how to use hypertext to access documents and data on the Internet. First web page URL: `https://info.cern.ch/hypertext/WWW/TheProject.html`

Web1 operated in a peer-to-peer fashion that allowed individuals—with the technical knowledge—to host web pages on a server and push the information online—all without censoring and controlling centralized entities. The Web1 era displayed static (HTML) web pages, which could not be altered. Users could only search and view information online via web browsers; hence, it is classified as a one-way "read-only" web. Additionally, online interaction was practically nonexistent, and it was technically challenging to create online content, making it non-user-friendly.

Although controversial, another issue was that Web1 protocols were *stateless*, meaning the HTTP protocol did not maintain session state by default. Features like cookies—which enable user recognition, session memory, and personalized experiences—were introduced later, making early web interactions rigid and impersonal. Therefore, it was impossible for a simple "Welcome back" message to appear, with no shopping cart functionality or customization on any website or application. Due to this, there was no financial incentive for developers or creators to build any platforms or online stores as we know them today. These factors, along with technical barriers to content creation, resulted in a significant content generation challenge for Web 1.0.

Web2

Web2, also known as the "*Interactive Web,*" was coined in 1999 by Darcy DiNucci, an information architecture consultant. Web2 represents the current version of the internet that is familiar to most users today. While Web1 focused solely on reading, Web2 shifted to user experience and User-Generated Content (UGC), opening up a whole new world of user interaction, participation, and contribution—earning the title "read-write" web. This created many opportunities, generating a more dynamic Internet where users could become consumers and creators.

In the early 2000s, with the ability to store, analyze, and interpret user data using cookies, Web2 exploded with giants such as Amazon, Microsoft, eBay, and Google. As a result, this marked the beginning of internet shopping as we know it today. Over time, many brick-and-mortar stores shut their doors due to the influx of online shoppers. Additionally, through the birth and growth of social media platforms such as X, Facebook, and Instagram, users could interact with one another, create content, and share it with the rest of the world in seconds. The creation of these Web2-based companies, from small to large, changed the way the world interacted with one another. Developers were now in demand and had massive financial incentives to build websites, platforms, and applications for themselves or other companies.

Web2 saw the introduction and upgrades of various fundamental elements that helped Web2 flourish—these are as follows:

- **JavaScript** - It is a scripting language that enables developers to implement complex features, allowing web pages to display and control dynamically updating content such as multimedia, animated images, interactive maps, and 2D/3D graphics through APIs and libraries.
- **Cascading Style Sheets (CSS)** - It is an easy-to-design language that helps developers place the finishing touches on a website to enhance the *"look and feel"* of the web page. This includes text color, font style, layout designs, paragraph spacing, column sizes, etc.
- **HTML5** - It introduced the ability to store data locally on the user's device. This allows content to be delivered faster and more securely, thus enabling a smoother and more consistent experience for web users and developers.
- **HTTPS** - It is a protocol that secures communication and data transfer between a user's web browser and a website. Although introduced during Web1, HTTPS became widely adopted in Web2 as the need for secure online transactions and data privacy grew.

Although Web2 had many benefits for users and companies, it did not come without disadvantages. As Web2 progressed, large entities discovered that they could retain more customers by subjecting them to targeted ads based on their customer profile and including set preferences. This caused ethical issues regarding the exploitation of user data and concerns with data tracking, data ownership, and censorship breaches of user data. In summary, Web2 companies, especially large technology companies, were able to gather and exploit personal user data for financial gain. The users have no control over their data after it is entered for specific purposes online.

Furthermore, because Web2-based user data is stored in large, centralized server silos, the risk of hacking and data breaches is also a major concern. User data is bought and sold for large sums of money, making it very lucrative and a target for hackers. However, even with this known risk of a data breach, governments and power entities still prefer centralization because they can intervene, control, and shut down programs and websites if they don't like what they see.

Centralized entities such as Facebook, Instagram, and TikTok also have the power and control to shut down user accounts after users unknowingly violate internal community rules. In most cases, the user can do nothing to reverse the decision. This also applies to centralized banks, where user bank accounts can be suspended, funds frozen, or transactions canceled.

Web3

Web3, also known as the decentralized Internet, solves many of the problems associated with Web2. Think of Web3 as an open-to-all, trustless, permissionless network primarily built on three core elements: cutting-edge computing, artificial intelligence, and decentralized data networks. World Wide Web inventor Tim Berners-Lee initially coined Web 3.0, the **Semantic Web,** where he envisioned an intelligent, autonomous, and open Internet that uses artificial intelligence (AI) and machine learning (ML) to act as a "global brain" and process content conceptually and contextually. For this reason, Web3, often called the "**read-write-execute"** web, allows users and machines to read, write, and interact with content on a peer-to-peer network to aid a more efficient, autonomous, and decentralized personal user experience. This Web interaction and utilization stage moves users from centralized platforms like Facebook, Google, or X and toward decentralized, nearly anonymous platforms.

It is important to note that the term "Web3" is often used broadly and undefinedly. According to the Oxford Learner's Dictionary, Web3 is defined as *"the third stage of development of the internet that is supposed to be more decentralized (with no central control or permission needed from a central authority) and make more use of artificial intelligence."* It is common to hear Web3 being used to label decentralized applications (e.g., Web3 dApps) with a certain aspect of truth. However, more specifically, Web3 is an emerging third version of the Internet utilizing APIs and JavaScript-based libraries such as Web3.js, Next.js, Ether.js, and Truffle Suite (for the Ethereum blockchain) to establish the connection between blockchains, dApps, and the Internet. Through this connection, the decentralized benefits of blockchain technology are leveraged, with dApps being the byproduct of Web3 technology (hence, Web3 dApps), allowing users to interact and avail of these benefits. (Note—Web3, the decentralized Internet, is greatly supported by these libraries and APIs, which help simplify and accelerate development.) Furthermore, these libraries, APIs, and blockchain technology cannot function without the Internet. Thus, a combined effort of these technologies provides a gateway to a more secure, transparent, and user-empowered digital future.

Decentralization

Web3 deviates from traditional Web2's centralized data storage silos by utilizing distributed ledger technology (DLT) to enable data storage across multiple nodes on the network. This significantly increases the level of security because, unlike centralized storage systems, in the case of an attack, there is no single point of failure; therefore, if one node fails, the network is unaffected. Protocols such as InterPlanetary File System (IPFS) majorly contribute to the decentralized web by facilitating decentralized file sharing and data storage on a peer-to-peer (P2P) network.

Trustless

Through Web3 dApps, network participants can send and receive payments (native coins or cryptographic tokens) to one another without the necessity of centralized banking systems or financial applications like on Web2. Moreover, unlike traditional banks, Web3 facilitates the execution of transactions on the blockchain network in a trustless manner, meaning senders or receivers do not need to know or trust the network nodes verifying the transactions.

Ownership and Governance Rights

In the world of Web3, digital rights are another fundamental aspect integrated into its core vision. When an individual purchases a digital asset on the blockchain (on-chain), they are the rightful owners of that asset and hold the digital rights to that asset. Digital rights, or ownership rights, are implemented at the application layer and supported by blockchain protocols, ensuring trusted and certified ownership of digital assets. Digital ownership is expressed through digital signatures tied to the assets and stored in the "*Web3 tree τ*" (Figure 1-5)—a conceptual framework for understanding the structure and organization of Web3. The *Web3 tree τ* emphasizes the integration of *digital rights exchange* into internet protocols at the application layer.

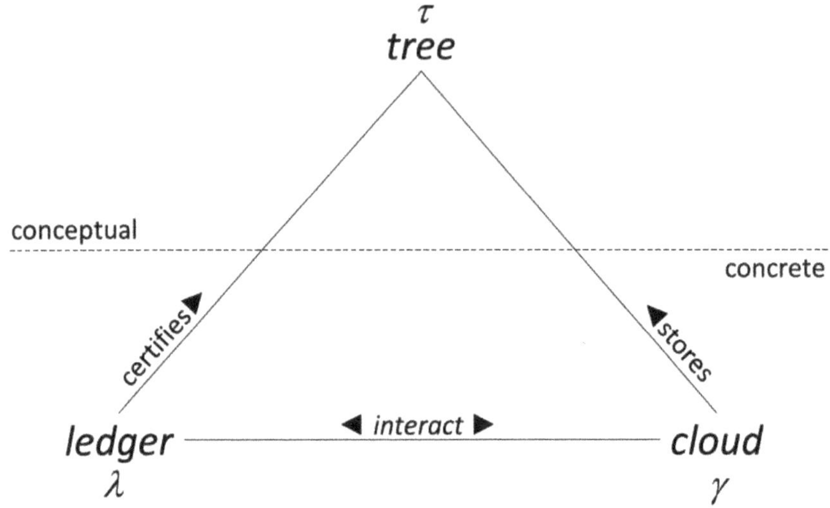

***Figure 1-5.** Web3 fundamental components: tree, ledger, and cloud (compliments of "Towards a Foundation of Web3" by Ahto Buldas, Dirk Drahiem et al.)*

As discussed, Web3, at its core, lies in the concept of digital ownership and rights of digital assets on-chain. By purchasing native coins, tokens, or NFTs, users can gain access to features, governance rights, or a stake in a Web3 protocol, dApp, or ecosystem—depending on the token's design. Users can store, control, and manage these assets in a way that is similar to owning physical possessions. In contrast to Web2, where the user's personal data is exploited by centralized entities for profits, Web3 enables users to own asset rights, where they can own a stake and potentially generate profits. Furthermore, ownership now goes beyond coins: Web3 lets users hold provable rights to videos, music, books, NFT artwork, and even real estate via government-backed title-deed NFTs such as **Dubai Land Department's Prypco Mint**. Users can take control of their digital lives through the power of Web3 and blockchain technology.

Digital ownership rights establish ownership of an individual's assets on-chain and are also integral to the decentralized decision-making processes—known as *Web3 governance*. Web3 governance may grant token holders voting power and referendum participation, but this depends on the token's design—many tokens offer no vote, and voting weight is usually proportional to the amount held or staked, not shared equally. Unlike traditional centralized systems where a single entity (e.g., government or corporations) makes decisions, Web3 projects rely on a more inclusive, fair, community-driven, and transparent decision-making approach.

Permissionless

Web3 aims for a permissionless, open-source architecture: any user may interact with blockchains or dApps without approval from a central authority. Where access limits exist, they are defined transparently in smart-contract code or by DAO votes—not imposed unilaterally by a platform owner. By contrast, Web2 applications can revoke user access at will. Further details on permissionless blockchains and open-source software are discussed in the section "Permissionless and Permissioned Blockchains" in Chapter 6, "Blockchain Architecture," and the section "Open and Closed Source Software" in Chapter 12, "Project Codebase," respectively.

Figure 1-6 represents the evolution of the web generated by Fabric Ventures.

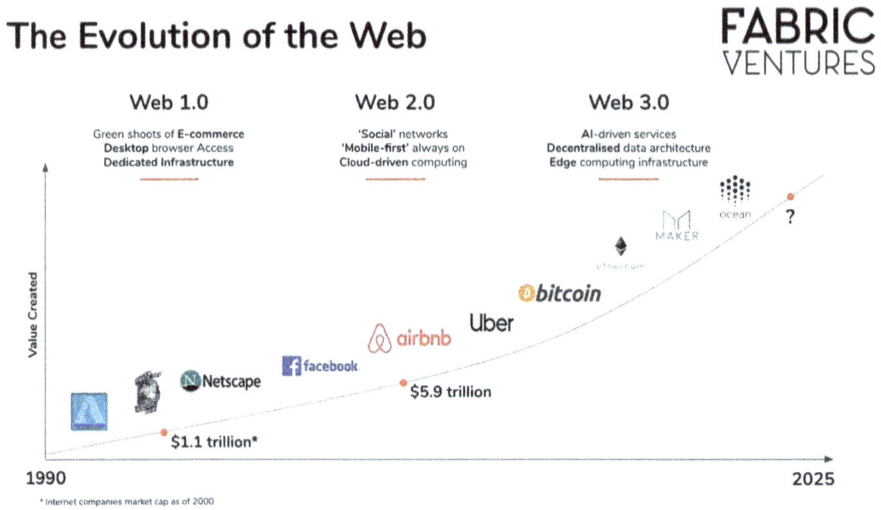

***Figure 1-6.** The Evolution of the Web (compliments of `https://medium.com/fabric-ventures/what-is-web-3-0-why-it-matters-934eb07f3d2b`)*

Summary of Web Evolution

The web's evolution from Web1 to Web3 marks a significant shift from static pages (Web1) to interactive social media (Web2) and now to a decentralized, blockchain-based Web3, emphasizing user control and privacy. This evolution has transformed how we interact with the internet, data, and assets, and, more importantly, how they are controlled. Table 1-1 summarizes the most critical differences between Web1, Web2, and Web3.

Table 1-1. *Comparison of the webs*

Web Evolution			
Aspect	**Web1**	**Web2**	**Web3**
Classification	Read-only static web	Read-write interactive web	Read-write-execute, also known as read-write-own (through digital assets and tokenization, users can own part of the network)
Fundamentals	Static web pages (HTML, URL, HTTP)	Dynamic content (JavaScript, HTML5, CSS3, HTTPS)	Decentralized, peer-to-peer distributed ledger technology, blockchain, artificial intelligence (AI), machine learning
Purpose/ Interactivity	Information only; reading of articles, webpages	Social networking, user-generated content, e-commerce	Decentralized applications (dApps), smart contracts, metaverse worlds, ownership rights, autonomy
System Architecture	Decentralized, self-hosting servers	Centralized servers	Decentralized infrastructure, blockchain, permissionless
Currency/ Payments	None	Fiat payments via digital processors (PayPal, Visa, Mastercard, etc.)	Native digital currencies and tokens

(*continued*)

Table 1-1. *(continued)*

Web Evolution			
Aspect	**Web1**	**Web2**	**Web3**
Autonomy (Data/Asset)	Limited flexibility, read and download of data only. Centralized entities control assets.	Create, share, and distribute content—data and assets controlled by centralized entities.	Self-governing of user data, self-identity, and asset management, interaction without the need for intermediaries
Immutability	Content can be easily altered or deleted	Content can be moderated or removed by platforms	Immutable records on the blockchain
Censorship	Little to no censorship	Centralized platform moderation—content can be removed or restricted	Protocol-level censorship resistance; any blocking must be coded or DAO voted
Trust Model	Trust in website owners and self-hosting servers	Trust in centralized entities, corporations	Trustless consensus algorithms
Security	Basic security measures, prone to attacks	Security risk, single point of failure	Enhanced security through decentralization and consensus mechanisms

(continued)

Table 1-1. *(continued)*

Web Evolution			
Aspect	**Web1**	**Web2**	**Web3**
Scalability	Limited scalability due to cost and technical hurdles	Enhanced scalability through large, centralized storage silos	Scalability issues through distributed networks, layer-2 solutions
Governance	Controlled by website owners or admins	Controlled by centralized entities, corporations, and platform owners	Community-driven governance, decentralized decision-making
Privacy	No user interaction—negligible privacy concerns	Centralized data collection: privacy depends on the platform—controls exist, but user tracking is common	Confidentiality and anonymity are enhanced through cryptographic protocols
Monetization	Practically none	E-commerce, subscription services, influencer monetization	Tokenization, decentralized finance (DeFi), mining, staking
Environmental Impact	Negligible impact	Increased energy consumption due to data centers	Significant energy consumption, but shifting toward more energy-efficient consensus mechanisms

Blockchain Applications

Blockchain offers more than just digital currencies and a new class of investment assets. Blockchain technology enables immutable, transparent transactions that secure digital information without the need for a central authority, fostering trust in decentralized storage solutions and peer-to-peer interactions. By offering secure, decentralized solutions for transactions, data management, and a trustless environment, blockchain empowers companies to enhance efficiency and explore new avenues to innovative products and services that were impossible in traditional markets. These innovations are built on decentralized applications (dApps), which are directly accessible to the public.

Table 1-2 shows some of the core and most popular applications of blockchain technology in today's world. As time progresses, more blockchain use cases and applications are emerging. Blockchain technology is expected to continue to advance, resulting in an ever-growing number of new applications and use cases.

Table 1-2. *Blockchain applications examples*

Popular Blockchain Applications		
Application	**Description**	**Examples**
Digital Asset Transfer	Peer-to-peer transactions where users can send and receive digital assets	bitcoin, Ethereum, XRP
Wallets/Key-Management Tools	Store private keys, sign transactions, and connect to dApps	MetaMask, Trezor, Trust Wallet
Digital Payment	Pay for goods or convert fiat ↔ crypto through integrated payment apps	BitPay, Lightning Network
Digital Identity Verification	Secure decentralized verification and authenticity of user credentials	KILT Protocol
Smart Contracts	Smart contracts are digital contracts stored on the blockchain that automate on-chain agreements, workflows, and financial transactions. Eliminates the need for intermediaries or central entities.	Ethereum, Solana, Binance Smart Chain
Asset Tokenization Non-Fungible Tokens (NFTs)	Asset tokenization is the process of converting the value of an asset (real-world assets (RWA), intellectual property, etc.) into digital tokens known as Non-Fungible Tokens (NFTs). This aids fractional ownership and generates liquidity, traceability, and audibility.	Centrifuge.io, OpenSea, Dapper Labs

(continued)

Table 1-2. *(continued)*

Popular Blockchain Applications		
Application	**Description**	**Examples**
Decentralized Finance (DeFi)	Financial technology that utilizes blockchain technology to provide peer-to-peer financial services without the need for banks or other intermediaries. Truly decentralized applications eliminate the need for intermediaries or central entities.	Uniswap, Aave, Compound, Curve, MakerDAO
Internet of Things (IoT)	Internet of Things (IoT) refers to a network of connected devices and technology that facilitates communication between devices themselves and the cloud. Combined with blockchain technology, IoT enables these devices to send data to private (or public) blockchain networks to create tamper-resistant records of shared transactions.	IBM Blockchain
Decentralized Gaming and Metaverse	Decentralized gaming and metaverse ecosystems utilize blockchain technology and smart contracts to store essential gaming data in a decentralized manner that contributes additional security, privacy, player control, and fairness.	Sandbox, Star Atlas, Decentraland, Sorare

(continued)

Table 1-2. *(continued)*

Popular Blockchain Applications		
Application	**Description**	**Examples**
Healthcare	Blockchain technology complements healthcare by improving patient data security, privacy, and interoperability. This is achieved by offering a decentralized, tamper-resistant method to record transactions, enhance data integrity, and streamline processes across diverse stakeholders.	Akiri, MedicalChain, Avaneer Health
Government	Blockchain technology positively impacts various government sectors such as foreign aid, law enforcement, record keeping, payroll tax collection, central banking and government smart contracts, and tracking of vaccinations, loans, and student grants.	Ankr, Kaleido, Burstiq, Voatz, Follow My Vote
Media	Blockchain technology solves many of the pain points in the media industry, such as data privacy, royalty payments, and intellectual property piracy.	Steemit, Open Music Initiative, Madhive
Supply Chain Management	Blockchain technology revolutionizes supply chain management by enhancing transparency, traceability, and efficiency, reducing costs, and combating counterfeiting and unethical sourcing practices.	Chain.io, DHL, Slync.io

CHAPTER 2

Investing in Digital Assets

A digital asset is an asset that is created and stored in a digital—binary format and contains monetary or personal value in the form of usage or ownership rights. Digital images, photos, documents, videos, and audio files are considered "assets" because they hold monetary and personal values. Digital assets have recently expanded to the blockchain world by introducing digital currencies and various types of cryptographic tokens.

Digital assets are an integral part of the digital economy, with their management and security being critical for individuals, businesses, and governments. On public blockchains, each tokenized digital asset carries unique on-chain metadata that makes it easily discoverable and verifiably distinct. Additionally, any usage rights attached to a tokenized asset—such as reproduction, resale, or use as DeFi collateral—are set off-chain by the asset's legal owner and therefore vary across jurisdictions. Depending on the permissions granted with the crypto asset, holders may also have the opportunity to vote in referendums through predetermined governance structures. Many Web3 dApps require users to hold their native tokens in order to utilize many features and operations within the application. For example, most DeFi dApps require users to purchase and stake a specific number of tokens to earn income from DeFi activities, including liquidity

P. Garvey, *Blockchain Fundamental Analysis for Digital Asset Investors*,
https://doi.org/10.1007/979-8-8688-1551-5_2

mining, lending, or borrowing. On the flip side, in-built restrictions are embedded in digital assets. These may include copying and sharing restrictions, feature restrictions, and limited issuance privileges.

Terminology such as crypto, coins, tokens, and altcoins is widely misused in the blockchain realm. See the following explanations for clarity.

1) **Coins** - Also known as cryptocurrencies or crypto, are native to Layer 1 blockchains and act as a currency (digital money) for online payments, used to reward miners, and for network transaction fees.

    - Examples: ETH, BTC, SOL

2) **Cryptographic Tokens** - A "token," often mislabeled as a "crypto token," does not have its own native blockchain; instead, it is created on an existing network—*typically a Layer-1 chain, though tokens can also be deployed on Layer-2 solutions.* They serve a variety of use cases, including utility, governance, security, and non-fungible tokens (NFTs). These tokens are used to interact with Web3 dApps.

    - Examples: LINK, UNI, MKR, USDT, USDC

3) **Altcoins** - An altcoin, or alternative coin, is any other cryptocurrency (coin) and blockchain outside of bitcoin. This term originated from bitcoin being the first blockchain and cryptocurrency, with all other blockchains as alternatives to bitcoin.

Fact All cryptocurrencies and tokens are digital financial assets for which ownership and transfers of ownership are guaranteed by a cryptographic decentralized protocol.

Why Invest in Digital Assets?

People invest in digital assets for diverse reasons—potential price appreciation, access to decentralized services, portfolio diversification, and participation in emerging technology. Similar to traditional assets, people invest with the hope that the asset's value will rise and, in turn, generate profits. As with traditional markets, digital asset investing has benefits and drawbacks.

Benefits of Digital Asset Investing

Investing in digital assets as an alternative asset class has many great benefits. These are as follows:

Access Rights and Permissions
Although potential profit is the standard investment motivator, many investors purchase digital assets for permission and access rights to participate in various protocol operations and features. This may include voting rights to help steer a project they believe could benefit themselves or the greater good of the community or economy. Beyond mere financial gains, other motivators include access and participation rights to engage popular DeFi financial tools, such as providing liquidity, token-backed collateral loans, and lending activities.

Innovation and Future Potential
From a high-level economic view, blockchain with digital assets is considered a unique transformational technology that positively contributes to many sectors, including banking, healthcare, supply chains, and government-related processes. As a result, investors' eyes are turning to digital assets for an alternative investment that has the potential to become mainstream in the not-so-distant future.

Store of Value

Similar to gold in traditional markets, many digital asset investors are attracted to the potential long-term store of value and a hedge against inflation. bitcoin is often referred to as "digital gold." Recently, bitcoin and other popular digital assets have outperformed gold multiple times, yet their higher volatility means the long-term store-of-value advantage is still debated.

Autonomy

Autonomy is one's right to self-govern, to have independence or freedom. Many people's desire to invest in digital assets stems from the direct ownership and control of their holdings without interference from intermediaries or central entities. When assets are kept in self-custodied wallets on a decentralized blockchain, confiscation by authorities is technically difficult without the holder's cooperation; tokens held by centralized or regulated custodians do not share this protection. Therefore, this adds a layer of personalized protection over investors' funds.

Trading Days and Time Flexibility

Unlike conventional markets, digital asset markets operate 24/7, offering the flexibility to purchase and sell assets anytime, including weekends and holidays. This enables traders and investors to react faster to global events.

No Day Trading Requirements

Digital asset traders do not require a minimum account balance to trade on any centralized or decentralized exchange. On the other hand, for traditional markets, the pattern day trader (PDT) rule applies. The PDT rule states that traders and investors require a minimum balance of $25,000 in their day trading account if they execute four or more day trades over five business days using a margin account, provided the number of day trades represents more than 6% of their total trades in the margin account for that same five-business day period.

Drawbacks of Digital Asset Investing

Benefiting from digital asset investment does not come without drawbacks. Investors must be fully aware of the associated risks, which can help them make wiser investment decisions.

Digital Asset Storage

While innovative, the decentralized nature of cryptocurrencies introduces significant risks, including theft, scams, and the loss of funds due to forgotten passwords or stolen devices. Due to security concerns, lack of control and privacy, and the added counterparty risk of centralized-exchange (CEX) wallets, many investors are reluctant to keep their funds there. Instead, many investors opt to access their funds through cold-storage devices where they can completely self-govern their assets. Although this storage method significantly lowers the risk of cyberattack theft, the onus is on individuals to keep wallet access codes safe. If proper protective measures are not in place and the access codes are lost, stolen, or misplaced, there is a high possibility that the investor will never retrieve their funds.

Liquidity Challenges

Outside the very largest assets, mid-cap tokens such as Ankr (ANKR) or Ocean Protocol (OCEAN)—each trading only about $0.6-14 million a day—can face significant slippage when larger orders hit the market. Whether one experiences liquidity challenges largely depends on the size of the order, the exchange where the order is placed, and the liquidity provisions corresponding to the time of trade execution. However, as a general rule of thumb, for the average retail investor, small market capitalization projects—with under $20 million daily volume—may experience slippage when executing trades.

Lack of Regulation

At the time of writing this book in 2024, although some progress is being made, the digital asset markets are still largely unregulated. There is a common debate about whether enforced regulation will positively or negatively impact digital asset markets. One predicted benefit of regulated digital markets is reducing fraud, scams, and market manipulation. With little effort, the current concern is that fraudsters can create a project and launch it on a selection of decentralized exchanges without any form of official vetting. As a result, many investors fall victim to the scam and lose their funds. Therefore, it is critical that the investor has the skills to identify and disregard scam projects.

High Volatility

Digital asset markets are highly volatile with wild fluctuations compared to traditional market assets. Depending on one's experience level, this can lead to substantial profits or losses.

Skepticism

Despite the fundamental core benefits of blockchain technology, the digital asset markets are often speculative, with many skeptics predicting a bubble and a collapse of the digital markets. For this reason, many people are reluctant to invest in digital assets.

Investment Analysis

Investment analysis is a comprehensive process and a broad term used to capture various investment evaluation methods. This process involves thorough research that aims to help investors determine how an investment is likely to perform based on many key factors, including market trends, economic indicators, financial data, profit margins, earnings reports, entry price, exit price, etc. Whether you are an individual investor or a top-tier hedge fund manager, understanding the investment analysis process is essential for making informed investment decisions for all asset types, including digital assets, stocks, ETFs, bonds, commodities, and real estate.

Key Objectives of Investment Analysis Techniques

- *Determination of an asset's suitability to a specific investor.*
- *Predicting the future performance of the asset.*
- *Evaluating risk, returns,* yield potential, and price movements.
- *Evaluating and creating an overall financial strategy.*
- *Assessing the relationship between asset correlations.*
- *Competitor evaluation.*
- *Evaluation of industry sectors and economic trends.*

Digital Asset Investment Analysis Techniques

Investors use many different investment analysis techniques to evaluate various investment assets. There are two primary investment analysis techniques for digital assets: *fundamental analysis* and *technical analysis.* Although fundamental and technical analysis techniques aim to minimize risk and maximize profits, each method serves a different purpose, analyzing the investment from various angles and perspectives.

Note that technical analysis is outside the scope of this book. However, it is recommended that investors research and learn the basics of technical analysis because it can provide valuable insights into market trends, price movements, and trading patterns, helping to complement their fundamental analysis skills and make more informed investment decisions.

Fundamental Analysis

Fundamental Analysis (FA) is a method used by investors to determine the actual or "fair market" value of an asset, such as a stock or digital asset. The overall aim is to determine if the asset's intrinsic value is higher or lower than its current market price and what effect the fundamental qualities will have on the asset's future price. This is achieved by evaluating the company's health by studying an array of fundamental factors. For example, to analyze a stock, an investor studies the company's balance sheets, income statements, and cash flow statements, combined with the economic, market, industry, and sector conditions a company operates in and its financial performance in terms of revenue.

Fact Fundamental analysis is a technique that evaluates the core elements of a project to determine if its current price is overvalued or undervalued with respect to its market price and to predict whether these elements will positively or negatively influence the asset's future price.

Fundamental Analysis in the World of Digital Assets

Fundamental evaluation of blockchain projects is a process that involves examining various aspects of a project to determine if the project's fundamental value—estimated from on-chain metrics, tokenomics, and overall project health—is higher or lower than its current market price per coin (or token) and to help predict its future potential for success or failure. Unlike equity markets, there is no single formula (such as a P/E ratio or discounted-cash-flow model) for digital-asset valuation; analysts weigh a basket of quantitative and qualitative indicators to judge whether a token appears over- or undervalued. Given the digital asset markets' highly volatile and competitive nature, conducting fundamental analysis is imperative for achieving long-term success and sustainability.

The fundamental evaluation of traditional assets somewhat differs from the evaluation of digital asset investments. Fundamental evaluation of traditional assets focuses on financial and economic data, including financial statements, market trends, and other quantifiable information that can be used to assess an asset's performance and potential growth. However, the fundamental evaluation of digital asset elements includes but is not limited to token design, blockchain architecture (scalability, security, decentralization), ecosystem, regulation, project team, community engagement, roadmap, and the programming languages used for construction. This fundamental analysis also includes tokenomics, which reveals the token's role and distribution within the ecosystem, incentives for users, and the overall economic model that supports value creation and distribution among stakeholders.

Fundamental analysis is achieved by researching various sources of information, such as whitepapers, litepapers, various other technical papers, blog articles, code reports, project websites, social media, forums, and on-chain metric data websites. Table 2-1 outlines the core fundamental elements when evaluating projects within the crypto realm.

Table 2-1. *Digital asset's core fundamental elements*

Key Blockchain Project Fundamental Elements	
Evaluation Metric	**Description**
Project Documentation	Indicates a project's technical, financial, and operational aspects through technical papers known as whitepapers, litepapers, and other related documents. This also provides insight into the project's transparency, commitment, and deliverables.
Core Offering	Evaluates the core use case, product, service, and practical applications offered. It outlines the problems solved and the corresponding benefits.

(*continued*)

Table 2-1. *(continued)*

Key Blockchain Project Fundamental Elements	
Evaluation Metric	**Description**
End-User Experience	Evaluates the functionality, accessibility, and satisfaction provided by the product or service. It considers how well the platform meets user needs and ensures a smooth and intuitive interaction.
Blockchain Architecture	Assesses the structural design and level of scalability, interoperability, and decentralization. Evaluates other architectural essentials, including consensus mechanisms, governance design, and public, private, hybrid, and consortium blockchains.
Token Design	Examines incentive mechanisms that direct token accrual (rewards) to users, validators, and core contributors, supporting long-term project sustainability and growth.
Tokenomics	Evaluates the supply mechanics, distribution model, vesting schedules, token types, and standards.
Financial Metrics	Evaluate various on-chain and off-chain financial metric data, including market capitalizations, liquidity, trading volume, transaction volumes, active addresses, transfer volumes, hash rates, realized capitalizations, etc., to assess network health, activity, and growth.
Project Team	Analyzes the team's experience, expertise, qualifications, track record, and achievements in the blockchain sector.
Project Roadmap	Evaluates the project's roadmap with respect to the team's vision, planned goals and objectives, and milestones to determine feasibility and strategic alignment.

(continued)

Table 2-1. *(continued)*

Key Blockchain Project Fundamental Elements	
Evaluation Metric	**Description**
Project Codebase	Assesses the project's development performance and developer activity, including Git code commits, audit reports, open issues, open-source software licensing, programming languages utilized, and other relevant metrics.
Incentivization and Rewards	Examines the incentives and rewards offered to developers, validators, and users for participating, interacting, or adding value to the network or decentralized application.
Community and Social Media	Assesses the project's social community engagement, popularity, moderator quality, and other social activity metrics.
Funding and Partnerships	Evaluates the project's funding sources and the track record or reputation of its backers, including private and institutional investors. For public sales, it examines key factors like token pricing, soft and hard caps, and fair launch and premine models.

Benefits of Fundamental Analysis

Evaluating the core fundamentals of any project within the crypto world offers many benefits, including valuable insight that guides investors to make more informed investment decisions:

1) **Informed Investment Decisions** - Allows investors to predict a project's future viability and sustainability.

2) **Strategy and Portfolio Requirements** - Allows investors to determine which digital assets meet and align with their strategy and portfolio requirements, e.g., low-to-medium to high-risk investments.

3) **Comparative Analysis** - Allows investors to compare competitors within the same sector with the same use case and value proposition to determine whether a project is undervalued.

4) **Risk Assessment** - Helps investors understand the associated risks involved, such as poor use cases, an inexperienced team, unrealistic milestones, weak partnerships, and code issues that will affect the project's future success and stability.

5) **Eliminates Fraudulent Investments** - Performing fundamental analysis significantly lowers and, in most cases, entirely reduces the chances of investing in fraudulent projects or scams.

6) **Independent Research** - Possessing the skills to conduct your own research enables investors to make investment decisions with firsthand, non-biased information. This results in more informed and rational decision-making, free from the noise and emotional swings that can dominate social media platforms and influencer content.

Technical Analysis

Technical analysis (TA), also known as *charting*, is a method short- and long-term traders and investors use to identify future patterns and trade setups. TA is achieved by analyzing statistical trends and patterns from historical data such as price action and volume. Traders use TA as an edge to analyze opposing selling and buying forces resulting from supply and demand that dictate an asset's price.

Some may agree that TA is less reliable in digital asset markets due to the extreme volatility and, therefore, deemded it more effective in traditional markets that operate under normal conditions, with high volume and liquidity. There is truth in this statement. Digital assets with low market capitalization tend to suffer from low volume and liquidity. As a result, even the smallest buying and selling forces tend to generate false signals and send price action on an unpredictable rollercoaster. However, the more popular, well-known digital assets generally have much deeper liquidity, making them less susceptible to extreme volatility and therefore offering more reliable price forecasts. Moreover, inexperienced traders are advised not to trade extremely low market capitalization assets; instead, they should only exercise strong fundamental analysis for investment purposes.

There are literally thousands of on-chart data analysis tools and indicators that provide insightful information about trends and price patterns that help investors spot potential opportunities. TradingView is probably the most common price-action analysis platform that offers up-to-the-minute market data, including price quotes, volume, and indicators, to help traders respond to market movements. Day and short-term traders frequently use technical analysis to devise strategies and time their buying and selling activity. Figure 2-1 shows a typical TradingView setup with BTC/USD as the trading pair. The chart shows two very common indicators, Exponential Moving Averages (EMAs) and the Stochastic.

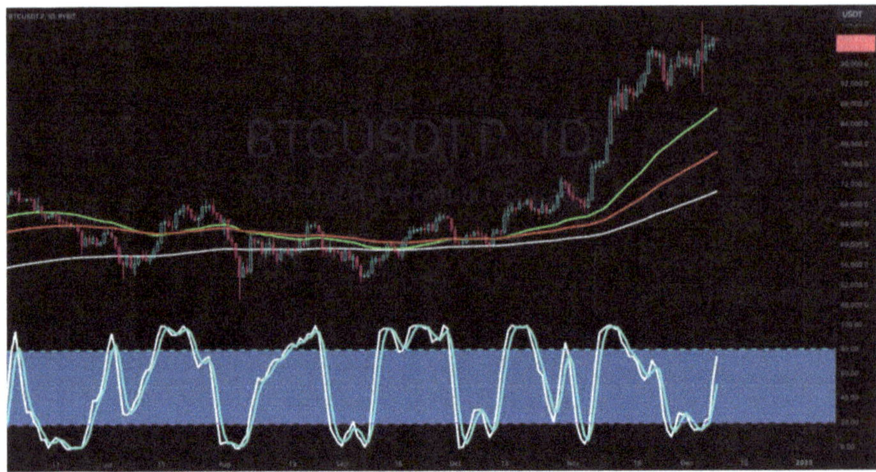

Figure 2-1. *BTC/USD with exponential moving averages (EMA) 50, 100, and 200 and Stochastic RSI indicators (compliments of* `https://www.tradingview.com/x/JF5aL89N/`*)*

Exponential Moving Averages (EMAs)

Exponential moving averages (EMAs) are technical indicators that track a financial instrument's average price over time. As the name suggests, a moving average (MA) represents the asset's average price based on the selected MA time length. However, EMAs slightly differ from MAs, whereby EMAs place greater weight and significance on the most recent data points. For example, Figure 2-1 shows three EMAs: the 200 EMA (white line), the 100 EMA (red line), and the 50 EMA (green line). The 50 EMA shows the average price of BTC based on the last 50 days, with more weight on price action data closer to the current price. The 100 EMA, 200 EMA, and all EMA time lengths follow the same structure—this is why EMAs are often referred to as the *exponentially weighted moving average.*

Stochastic

The stochastic oscillator is a momentum indicator that compares a specific closing price of a security with its price range over a designated period. By altering this period or applying a moving average to the results, the oscillator's responsiveness to market changes can be modified. Its purpose is to create trading signals for overbought and oversold conditions, using a scale that ranges from 0 to 100. As the oscillator signal moves into the 70 to 100 zone, the asset is deemed *overbought,* meaning that momentum is more likely to shift downward, decreasing the price per coin. Opposingly, when the oscillator signal moves into the 30 to 0 zone, the asset is deemed *oversold,* meaning that momentum is more likely to shift upward, increasing the price per coin. It is important to note that the stochastic oscillator is a reactive indicator. A reactive indicator confirms market trends based on past price data, and it does not predict future movements but instead reflects changes that have already occurred in the market.

Competitor Analysis

As of writing this book, there are over 16,300 active crypto projects, leading to significant competition across various niches, including decentralized finance (DeFi), blockchain infrastructures, nonfungible tokens (NFTs), metaverse, Internet of Things (IoT), gaming, and more. Like traditional companies, investing in crypto projects requires heavy competitor analysis and scrutiny. Some might argue that this is even more critical due to the unregulated and volatile nature of the crypto market. Therefore, conducting competitor analysis is essential before investing in any crypto project.

Although innovations and use cases appear regularly, most of the projects on the market are another variation of an existing idea. It is vital to distinguish between project teams that add actual value versus teams that produce a product whose features and technology are identical to an already existing project. Typically, these copycat teams are only after short-term gains and abandon the project. The end goal of competitor analysis is to determine if a particular project has a significant fundamental advantage over its competitors, as this will help reduce risk and maximize profits. Identifying competitors and understanding their strengths and weaknesses will allow the investor to make more informed decisions based on the project's fundamentals and gaps in the market.

Competitor analysis will be executed against each fundamental element discussed throughout this book. Once you understand a specific category's core concepts and fundamentals, performing ongoing evaluations from the same category and competitor analysis can be executed more efficiently. Furthermore, when investing in a category (e.g., DeFi, IoT, and infrastructure) for the first time, it is advised to identify the leaders (by market capitalization) in that specific category and evaluate and study why they are the highest-performing projects. Determine what fundamental qualities they have that stand out from the rest. This will provide a solid fundamental foundation to evaluate other similar projects. For example, for blockchain infrastructure projects (e.g., Ethereum, Polkadot, and MINA), attractive fundamentals included the ability to scale with demand, interoperability, transaction processing speed, decentralization, governance, ease of use, developer-friendliness, social following, etc. For DeFi projects, desirable fundamentals include smart contract reliability, liquidity, interoperability with other ecosystems, security, robust tokenomics and sustainable revenue models, a highly experienced team with a great reputation, and financial backing from known angel and private equity firms.

Pro Tip It is a good sign when a new blockchain start-up company openly lists its competitors and identifies how their project is superior. This type of transparency builds trust and directly addresses any investor concerns.

How to Identify and Evaluate Competitors

Follow these action steps to identify, compare, and evaluate competitors within the crypto space.

1) **Identify the Competitors**

   There are many ways to identify competitors. They are as follows:

   a) Real-time crypto data analytics platforms are the most common way to identify competitors; these include CoinMarketCap, CoinGecko, and AlphaGrowth.io. Visit any one of these platforms and filter by category. For example, Figure 2-2 shows an image from AlphaGrowth.io displaying the decentralized exchanges (DEX) by market capitalization. Users can also analyze important metrics such as revenue, total value locked (TVL), number of users, volume and X, Telegram, and Discord followers—all these are discussed in the applicable sections throughout this book.

#	Project ^	Category	TVL ^	1d Change ^	7d Change ^	30d Change ^	MCap ∨	Price ^
1	Uniswap Labs	Services					$5,756,493,934	$7.64
2	Injective	Bridge	$32,224,657	-0.28%	2.49%	3.57%	$3,183,746,021	$32.56
3	Aerodrome	DEX	$664,736,206	0.69%	2.30%	5.01%	$1,532,044,745	$2.15
4	Curve DEX	DEX	$2,100,989,056	1.22%	15.37%	27.61%	$1,457,843,317	$1.16
5	Raydium	DEX	$2,438,619,809	3.53%	3.32%	47.48%	$1,431,809,196	$4.91
6	PancakeSwap AMM	DEX	$1,502,481,066	0.30%	11.51%	20.38%	$1,211,818,944	$4.12
7	1inch Network	DEX Aggregator	$7,118,154	-1.16%	10.82%	49.07%	$823,840,618	$0.59
8	BabyDogeSwap	DEX	$2,499,570	5.14%	11.20%	17.78%	$673,528,865	0.0_8$41
9	WOOFi Swap	DEX	$18,954,650	5.43%	9.91%	40.62%	$632,233,066	$0.33
10	0x	Tooling					$631,661,850	$0.74

Figure 2-2. *Top decentralized exchanges (DEX) by market capitalization (compliments for `https://alphagrowth.io/projects/top-dex-projects-on-all-by-market-cap-value`)*

b) Visit the Telegram and Discord channels of the project being evaluated and keyword search "competitor"—this sometimes provides additional insight into potential competitors researched by the community.

c) Review the project whitepaper to verify if the team mentioned any of their competitors. Often, teams will compare their technology, features, and other fundamental aspects to those of competitors, highlighting why they believe their product is superior—of course, never assume they are correct. Always do your own research.

d) Make a note of some of the top competitors with respect to their market capitalization and any other significant findings during the analysis.

2) **Research Competitors**

   a) Review their websites and documentation from the previously generated list of competitors, specifically their whitepaper.

   b) Scan for fundamentals such as product use case, value proposition, architecture, features, team, tokenomics, etc. *(Note—these fundamental elements are discussed in detail throughout this book; refer to these sections when performing your analysis.)*

   c) Visit YouTube and search for reviews that some credible influencers (i.e., channels with clear expertise, transparent sponsorship disclosures, and consistently high viewer engagement) may have done on some of the competitors. Note that although YouTube is helpful, you should always validate the information provided with your own research.

3) **Project Comparison**

   Compare competitor fundamentals against the initial project you are interested in investing in. If it helps, generate a table on Microsoft Excel (or equivalent) to analyze all the fundamental data found during the analysis.

4) **Analyze the Results**

   a) Analyze the results to determine if the project is still worth investing in. Maybe one of its competitors is fundamentally outperforming it?

b) Evaluate against the following questions:

   i) Is there anything unique, something that stands out?

   ii) Do any of the projects seem like replicas? New startups that completely copy another project with no competitive edge or advantage are unlikely to have long-term success and longevity.

   iii) Did the project whitepaper outline its competitors? If so, did it detail how the project plans to outpace them?

   iv) Is the project outperforming its competitors with respect to:

      - Sophisticated architecture (e.g., modular layers, built-in sharding, or native roll-up support)?

      - Advanced technology (benchmark the project against the latest breakthroughs—check fresh whitepapers, dev forums, and roadmaps to see if it's staying current)?

      - Additional functionality and features (e.g., native AMM/order books, smart liquidity routing, DAO governance tools, programmable fee & reward splits, gas-less transactions, integrated oracles)?

      - Incentives (e.g., sustainable yields, fair fee rebates, rewards designed for long-term users)?

- Ecosystem strength (solid developer tooling and libraries, cross-chain asset bridges, broad wallet/exchange support, deep liquidity)?
- Other edge factors (regulatory compliance and licenses, proven security audits, standout partnerships, and overall brand reputation)?

5) **Take Notes and Document Your Findings in Your Own Style**

6) **Combine the Findings with Other Sections of the Fundamental Evaluation Process**

PART I

Start of Blockchain and Digital Asset Evaluation

Core Fundamental Analysis Elements

This section begins the systematic evaluation process for blockchain and digital asset projects. The following elements form the foundation of analysis that investors must apply to every project:

1. ***Project Documentation (Whitepaper/Litepaper)***
2. ***Core-Offering (Product/Service)***
3. ***End-User Experience***
4. ***Blockchain Architecture***
5. ***Token Design and Use Case***
6. ***Tokenomics***
7. ***Financial Metrics***
8. ***Project Team***

9. ***Project Roadmap***
10. ***Project Codebase***
11. ***Incentivization and Rewards***
12. ***Community and Social Media***
13. ***Funding and Partnerships***

CHAPTER 3

Project Documentation

Each crypto project typically has an array of technical and non-technical documentation with a combined primary purpose of informing stakeholders about the product or service offering, the problem it solves, and the underlying blockchain technology and mechanics that make it possible—think of it as an informative marketing tool that completely describes the product from every aspect.

This chapter discusses critical project documentation such as the whitepaper, litepaper, and other technical papers. The overall objective of the investor is to utilize the project documentation to help evaluate whether the project is worth investing in.

Many different types of project-specific documents help describe and define practically every fundamental aspect of a project. However, the whitepaper is the most important and comprehensive document investors utilize during a fundamental evaluation. Therefore, the whitepaper, along with the litepaper—a simplified and shortened version of the whitepaper—are the two primary documents discussed in detail in this chapter.

Nevertheless, being familiar with other technical and less common project documents such as the *Yellowpaper*, *Mauvepaper*, *Beigepaper*, and *Flashpaper* is helpful—see Table 3-1. Despite the titles suggesting specific colors, like "Yellowpaper," these documents don't necessarily adhere to those color schemes and, in most cases, are standard black and white. In most circumstances, crypto projects stick to the standard whitepaper and litepaper with little deviation from the other technical papers.

P. Garvey, *Blockchain Fundamental Analysis for Digital Asset Investors*,
https://doi.org/10.1007/979-8-8688-1551-5_3

Table 3-1. Types of blockchain technical papers

Blockchain Technical Papers			
Document Type	**Purpose/Description**	**Example**	**Links**
Whitepaper	A comprehensive document that outlines a blockchain project's vision, technology, and objectives, serving as a blueprint for its structure, goals, and potential use cases. Also, in funding rounds as part of a sales pitch to stakeholders.	Ethereum Whitepaper	https://ethereum.org/669c9e2e2027310b6b3cdce6e1c52962/Ethereum_White_Paper_-_Buterin_2014.pdf
Litepaper	Provides a shortened high-level summary of the whitepaper that is easier to read and understand—hence, the name "lite" paper is often referred to as a "lightpaper."	Polkadot Litepaper: An Introduction to Polkadot	https://polkadot.network/Polkadot-lightpaper.pdf
Yellowpaper	Provides in-depth technical details of a company's product or service.	The Ethereum Yellowpaper	https://gavwood.com/paper.pdf

Mauvepaper	Provides in-depth information on a blockchain project's architecture. Mauvepapers are less common than whitepapers but offer more detailed insights than a whitepaper. Often aimed at more advanced users or stakeholders seeking a deeper understanding of the project's technical and economic aspects.	Nebulas Mauvepaper: Developer Incentive Protocol	`https://www.nebulas.io/docs/NebulasMauvepaper.pdf`
Beigepaper	The beigepaper is a simplified version of the yellowpaper.	An Ethereum Technical Specification	`https://cryptopapers.info/assets/pdf/eth_beige.pdf`
Flashpaper	A concise document that quickly presents a blockchain project's core fundamentals. It offers a high-level overview for readers who want a quick summary without extensive technical detail.	Aavenomics	`https://docs.aave.com/aavenomics/flashpaper`

Other Technical Documentation

Projects may also provide additional technical documents as applicable. Most of these documents are technical tutorials that guide developers when running nodes, creating decentralized applications (dApps) on the network, doing dApp integrations, setting up APIs, staking, and many more. Most projects provide such technical documentation; however, unfortunately, the quality of the documentation ranges from project to project. These documents must be to a standard that developers can use and follow easily with little help from the project team, as this can sometimes be highly inefficient and can often hinder the project's growth. The issue is that most investors do not have developer experience, so it is hard to evaluate such documents. If you find yourself in this category, check on the project's developer forum—typically accessible from the project website—for the overall sentiment and if there are many complaints regarding the quality of the documentation.

Whitepaper

Evaluation Objective: Evaluate a project whitepaper, ensuring its legitimacy and quality while assessing the potential value of the offered product or service.

The term "whitepaper" originated with the British government, and one of the earliest examples is the *Churchill White Paper of 1922*. This document was a type of position paper or industry report published by a UK government department. The term "white-paper" itself was derived from the color of the cover, which was, of course, white.

The first cryptocurrency whitepaper was the bitcoin whitepaper (Figure 3-1), which is known to be written by its creator, Satoshi Nakamoto, in 2008. Since then, thousands of whitepapers have been written by blockchain-based companies, independent development teams, DAOs, and individual developers, each claiming their product, service, or technology is the future. However, as investors, it is crucial to understand that no matter how attractive an investment opportunity looks, every project is not a winner; in fact, very few are in comparison to the number of projects in existence. Therefore, cutting out the "noise" and projects with poor fundamentals is essential to help identify high-quality, profitable investments.

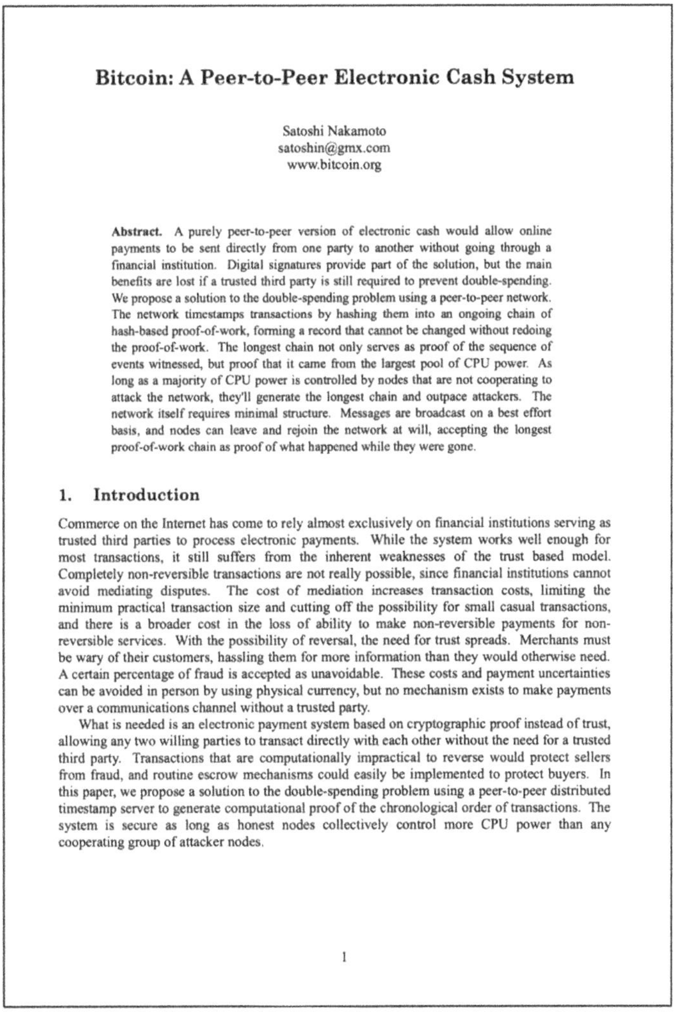

Bitcoin: A Peer-to-Peer Electronic Cash System

Satoshi Nakamoto
satoshin@gmx.com
www.bitcoin.org

Abstract. A purely peer-to-peer version of electronic cash would allow online payments to be sent directly from one party to another without going through a financial institution. Digital signatures provide part of the solution, but the main benefits are lost if a trusted third party is still required to prevent double-spending. We propose a solution to the double-spending problem using a peer-to-peer network. The network timestamps transactions by hashing them into an ongoing chain of hash-based proof-of-work, forming a record that cannot be changed without redoing the proof-of-work. The longest chain not only serves as proof of the sequence of events witnessed, but proof that it came from the largest pool of CPU power. As long as a majority of CPU power is controlled by nodes that are not cooperating to attack the network, they'll generate the longest chain and outpace attackers. The network itself requires minimal structure. Messages are broadcast on a best effort basis, and nodes can leave and rejoin the network at will, accepting the longest proof-of-work chain as proof of what happened while they were gone.

1. Introduction

Commerce on the Internet has come to rely almost exclusively on financial institutions serving as trusted third parties to process electronic payments. While the system works well enough for most transactions, it still suffers from the inherent weaknesses of the trust based model. Completely non-reversible transactions are not really possible, since financial institutions cannot avoid mediating disputes. The cost of mediation increases transaction costs, limiting the minimum practical transaction size and cutting off the possibility for small casual transactions, and there is a broader cost in the loss of ability to make non-reversible payments for non-reversible services. With the possibility of reversal, the need for trust spreads. Merchants must be wary of their customers, hassling them for more information than they would otherwise need. A certain percentage of fraud is accepted as unavoidable. These costs and payment uncertainties can be avoided in person by using physical currency, but no mechanism exists to make payments over a communications channel without a trusted party.

What is needed is an electronic payment system based on cryptographic proof instead of trust, allowing any two willing parties to transact directly with each other without the need for a trusted third party. Transactions that are computationally impractical to reverse would protect sellers from fraud, and routine escrow mechanisms could easily be implemented to protect buyers. In this paper, we propose a solution to the double-spending problem using a peer-to-peer distributed timestamp server to generate computational proof of the chronological order of transactions. The system is secure as long as honest nodes collectively control more CPU power than any cooperating group of attacker nodes.

1

Figure 3-1. *First-page bitcoin whitepaper (compliments of `https://bitcoin.org/bitcoin.pdf`)*

So, what exactly is a whitepaper? A whitepaper is a crucial document generated by the project team that provides stakeholders with technical and non-technical information relating to the project. It identifies the problem and, more importantly, the solution to that problem. A whitepaper encompasses crucial aspects that ultimately define the entire project and what it offers, including the core purpose, functionality, use case, value proposition, design and architecture, tokenomics, and the roadmap—at a minimum. Depending on the team and project, some whitepapers are more detailed and inclusive than others.

Whitepapers are a strategic way to present valuable, in-depth information that meets target audiences' needs—explaining the project's purpose, technology, and value proposition. Furthermore, a whitepaper is a means to promote the project and the value being offered. For example, crypto projects typically require funding to bring the vision and core product to life. The whitepaper is utilized during funding rounds, and it is presented by the project team to private equity firms, institutions, angel investors, and retail investors—through public offerings—to help educate and seek investment. The whitepaper is the primary reference point when it comes to project documentation. It is typically found through the project's official website as a .pdf download—this is by far the safest place to search for the whitepaper.

Fact Ethereum, a smart contract platform, is another excellent example of a whitepaper—`https://ethereum.org/en/whitepaper/`

Whitepaper Content List

A high-quality whitepaper will include valuable information that details the purpose of the product or service, what it is solving, the value proposition, the technology, the architecture, the token design, the incentives, the team, the tokenomics, the funding, the vesting schedules, the roadmap, and relevant legal considerations. It is important to note that the project roadmap is often released as a separate document and/or produced later than the whitepaper. The project roadmap is explored in Chapter 11, "Project Roadmap."

The following is a list of content that should be included in every whitepaper as standard.

1. ***Product/Service Description***
    a. ***Problem Being Solved***
    b. ***The Solution***
    c. ***How Does It Operate***
2. ***Value Proposition***
3. ***Technology***
    a. ***System Architecture***
    b. ***Blockchain Type***
    c. ***Consensus Mechanism/Operation***
    d. ***Explorer Details***
4. ***Token***
    a. ***Purpose of the Token***
    b. ***Token Type/Standard***
5. ***Tokenomics***
    a. ***Token Supply***
    b. ***Inflationary/Deflationary/Fixed Supply***
    c. ***Token Allocation Details***
    d. ***Vesting Schedule Details***

6. ***Funding and Partnerships***
    a. ***Details of Seed, Private, ICO, and IDO Rounds***
    b. ***List of Current Investors***
    c. ***List of Current Partnerships***
7. ***Reward/Incentives***
8. ***Roadmap/Vision***
    a. ***Accomplished Milestones***
    b. ***List of Future Milestones***
    c. ***Timelines for Future Milestones***
9. ***Legal Legislation/Documentation***
10. ***References/Sources/Foot Notes***
11. ***Disclaimer***

Whitepaper Benefits

Whitepapers are a rich source of insight, and consistently reading them can help investors in the following ways:

- **Technical Evaluation** - Whitepapers provide insights into the core project's fundamentals, helping readers understand the critical aspects of the project.
- **Technical Knowledge** - Whitepapers are packed with technical insights—and often economic or governance details—that can meaningfully expand your blockchain knowledge.

- **Investment Decisions** - Whitepapers provide the data to help you evaluate projects, resulting in wiser investment decisions.
- **Technical Confidence** - Whitepapers get more straightforward to understand the more you read them.
- **Scam Projects** - Whitepapers help you to quickly identify scam projects.
- **Risk Assessment** - Whitepapers paint a realistic picture of what the project offers and, in turn, allow the investors to see associated risks, limitations, and challenges the project may face.
- **New Opportunities** - Whitepaper newfound knowledge and understanding can lead to new doors and opportunities in the blockchain sector.
- **Comparative Analysis** - By reading multiple whitepapers, investors can compare projects based on their objectives, technology, and strategies. This comparison can help identify key differentiators and potential opportunities.

Caution The whitepaper is the single most critical document for digital asset investors. At a very minimum, no investment should be made without reading the project whitepaper and understanding what you are investing in.

Whitepaper Styles

Whitepapers come in a variety of styles. Some whitepapers are only a few pages long and highly visual, with many images. They can be read within thirty minutes to an hour or two. It is strongly advised not to invest in projects that generate whitepapers of this caliber. They are most likely scams, have an extremely poor use case, or suffer from a severe lack of funding—either way, it is not worth inheriting that level of risk.

On the opposite end of the spectrum, complex projects, or projects that hold a lot of value, typically generate quite detailed and lengthy whitepapers with heavy technical verbiage throughout. These whitepaper styles range from a few pages long to over one hundred pages. Whitepapers like these typically contain a lot of technical content that new investors may not understand and can seem somewhat daunting at first glance. However, whitepapers of this quality provide vital information integral to the fundamental evaluation process and any digital asset investment decision. Investors need to be highly vigilant when analyzing a whitepaper. It is very common for project teams to add a lot of "fluff" to whitepapers, beefing them up, with the sole intention of tricking investors into thinking that the product or service is something more than it is. This "fluff" often contains the history of bitcoin, current blockchain-related news, general information about blockchain technology, or similar unrequired information—this is a red flag. The whitepaper should be clear, free from fluff, and strictly focus on the product or service offered by the project. No exceptions.

Polkadot Network is a robust, advanced blockchain network. Figure 3-2 shows the first page of the Polkadot Network whitepaper.

POLKADOT: VISION FOR A HETEROGENEOUS MULTI-CHAIN FRAMEWORK
DRAFT 1

DR. GAVIN WOOD
FOUNDER, ETHEREUM & PARITY
GAVIN@PARITY.IO

Abstract. Present-day blockchain architectures all suffer from a number of issues not least practical means of extensibility and scalability. We believe this stems from tying two very important parts of the consensus architecture, namely *canonicality* and *validity*, too closely together. This paper introduces an architecture, the *heterogeneous multi-chain*, which fundamentally sets the two apart.

In compartmentalising these two parts, and by keeping the overall functionality provided to an absolute minimum of *security* and *transport*, we introduce practical means of core extensibility in situ. Scalability is addressed through a divide-and-conquer approach to these two functions, scaling out of its bonded core through the incentivisation of untrusted public nodes.

The heterogeneous nature of this architecture enables many highly divergent types of consensus systems interoperating in a trustless, fully decentralised "federation", allowing open and closed networks to have trust-free access to each other.

We put forward a means of providing backwards compatibility with one or more pre-existing networks such as Ethereum. We believe that such a system provides a useful base-level component in the overall search for a practically implementable system capable of achieving global-commerce levels of scalability and privacy.

1. Preface

This is intended to be a technical "vision" summary of one possible direction that may be taken in further developing the blockchain paradigm together with some rationale as to why this direction is sensible. It lays out in as much detail as is possible at this stage of development a system which may give a concrete improvement on a number of aspects of blockchain technology.

It is not intended to be a specification, formal or otherwise. It is not intended to be comprehensive nor to be a final design. It is not intended to cover non-core aspects of the framework such as APIs, bindings, languages and usage. This is notably experimental; where parameters are specified, they are likely to change. Mechanisms will be added, refined and removed in response to community ideas and critiques. Large portions of this paper will likely be revised as experimental evidence and prototyping gives us information about what will work and what not.

This document includes a core description of the protocol together with ideas for directions that may be taken to improve various aspects. It is envisioned that the core description will be used as the starting point for an initial series of proofs-of-concept. A final "version 1.0" would be based around this refined protocol together with the additional ideas that become proven and are determined to be required for the project to reach its goals.

1.1. **History.**

- 09/10/2016: 0.1.0-proof1
- 20/10/2016: 0.1.0-proof2
- 01/11/2016: 0.1.0-proof3
- 10/11/2016: 0.1.0

2. Introduction

Blockchains have demonstrated great promise of utility over several fields including "Internet of Things" (IoT), finance, governance, identity management, web-decentralisation and asset-tracking. However, despite the technological promise and grand talk, we have yet to see significant real-world deployment of present technology. We believe that this is down to five key failures of present technology stacks:

Scalability: How much resources are spent globally on processing, bandwidth and storage for the system to process a single transaction and how many transactions can be reasonably processed under peak conditions?

Isolatability: Can the divergent needs of multiple parties and applications be addressed to a near-optimal degree under the same framework?

Developability: How well do the tools work? Do the APIs address the developers' needs? Are educational materials available? Are the right integrations there?

Governance: Can the network remain flexible to evolve and adapt over time? Can decisions be made with sufficient inclusivity, legitimacy and transparency to provide effective leadership of a decentralised system?

Applicability: Does the technology actually address a burning need on its own? Is other "middleware" required in order to bridge the gap to actual applications?

In the present work, we aim to address the first two issues: scalability and isolatability. That said, we believe the Polkadot framework can provide meaningful improvements in each of these classes of problems.

Modern, efficient blockchain implementations such as the Parity Ethereum client [17] can process in excess of 3,000 transactions per second when running on performant consumer hardware. However, current real-world blockchain networks are practically limited to around 30 transactions per second. This limitation mainly originates from the fact that the current synchronous consensus mechanisms require wide timing margins of safety on the expected processing time, which is exacerbated by the

1

Figure 3-2. *First page of Polkadot Networks whitepaper (compliments of file:///Users/paulgarvey/Dropbox/Mac/Downloads/Polkadot-whitepaper.pdf)*

Recently, crypto projects have leaned towards a more professional, dynamic, and visual approach instead of a traditional whitepaper format. The purpose of this is to aid in the efficient displaying and updating of fundamental data and general project information. Figure 3-3 displays a screenshot from the Moonbeam Networks landing page for technical documentation, showcasing essential fundamental data available for developers, investors, and network participants, including building applications, node setup, native tokens, and other related resources.

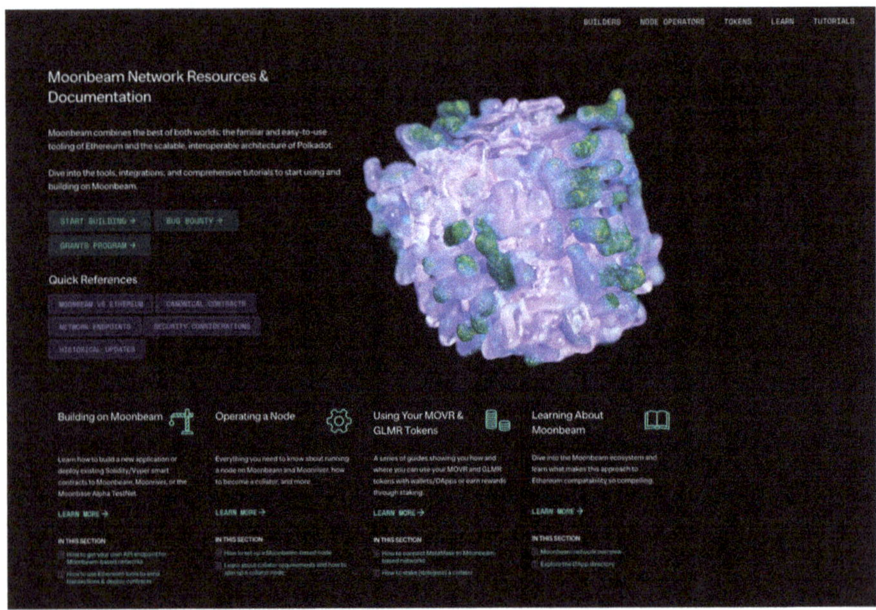

***Figure 3-3.** Moonbeam Network resources and documentation (compliments of `https://docs.moonbeam.network/`)*

Figure 3-4 shows Moonbeam's learning page, where anyone can research practically any aspect of the project, such as details on its network, sister network "Moonriver Network," testnets, the team's vision, technological infrastructure, including the programming languages used, native tokens, open-source licensing detail, and much more.

Blockchain networks like Moonbeam are constantly improving, adding features and updates to keep up with the fast-changing environment and ensure users have a smooth and efficient experience. Implementing constant updates and new feature developments in a traditional whitepaper format is possible but very inefficient for both the project team and end-users—each new revision can add an extra layer of confusion in projects that iterate rapidly, while slower-moving networks may be fine with periodic updates. Thus, it makes sense for projects like Moonbeam to construct a system that provides the best user experience with a constant flow of updated information.

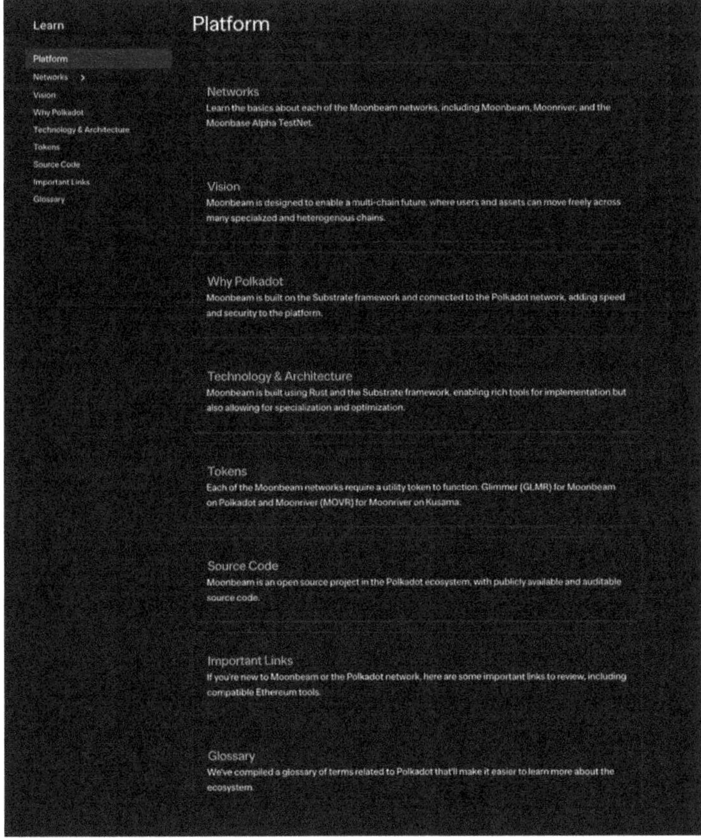

Figure 3-4. *Moonbeam Network platform—fundamentals (compliments of `https://docs.moonbeam.network/learn/platform`)*

Whitepaper Editions

Depending on the project, some traditional whitepapers may undergo many publication revisions due to constant project updates. As projects progress and technology advances, whitepaper updates are necessary. However, unlike the online "dynamic" whitepaper interfaces—like Moonbeam Network—traditional whitepapers require updating of the actual whitepaper document. As updates are made, new whitepaper publication dates are issued, or the changes are tracked through Git commit history and release tags. Therefore, always check that you have the correct and latest edition of the whitepaper in question before starting the evaluation process.

When a whitepaper is updated, it typically includes changes such as new features, technical improvements, governance models, and general enhancements. However, investors should always verify whether the project team is making significant changes to the core fundamentals. This could involve steering the core product or service and its use case in a completely different direction, significantly deviating from the original design. Changes of this magnitude warrant thorough investor research to ensure the team is transparent about the reasons for the pivot and offers a clear, evidence-based rationale rather than merely chasing trends. Note that it is not necessarily bad if the team wants to adapt and tweak their product to suit the changing times. However, these changes should be accompanied by a solid, reasonable justification from the project team, clearly explaining their reasons.

Whitepaper References

Whitepaper references are invaluable for investors, providing hidden insights into the author's credibility. As expected from any published paper, book, or high-quality article, references should be cited only from reliable sources. The author's credibility is at stake when citing from Wikipedia, other whitepapers, or other questionable websites. Figure 3-5 shows a snapshot from the Polkadot Network whitepaper showing references from quality sources.

REFERENCES

[1] The specs for libp2p and associated submodules. `https://github.com/libp2p/specs`.
[2] Webassembly. `http://webassembly.org/`, 2016.
[3] Adam Back, Matt Corallo, Luke Dashjr, Mark Friedenbach, Gregory Maxwell, Andrew Miller, Andrew Poelstra, Jorge Timon, and Pieter Wuille. Enabling blockchain innovations with pegged sidechains. 2014.
[4] Krista Bennett, Christian Grothoff, Tzvetan Horozov, Ioana Patrascu, and Tiberiu Stef. Gnunet-a truly anonymous networking infrastructure. In *In: Proc. Privacy Enhancing Technologies Workshop (PET*. Citeseer, 2002.

Figure 3-5. *References section from the Polkadot Networks whitepaper (compliments of `https://polkadot.network/whitepaper/`)*

Unfortunately, investors unknowingly or deliberately skip the reference section of a whitepaper—a major mistake. Investors must check to see if the whitepaper author has cited material from credible sources such as books, peer-reviewed journal articles, and academic databases such as Google Scholar. It is common for credible authors to have published online articles on reputable websites. Although these may be deemed valuable, the author should cross-check the team's credibility, experience, and qualifications using LinkedIn alongside verifiable signals such as GitHub activity, published research, and conference records.

Whitepaper Footnotes

Footnotes can enhance a whitepaper's credibility by allowing authors to cite sources, clarify terms, and substantiate claims, signaling that adequate research supports the argument. Footnotes are used for many things, including defining a term, providing backup for a number, date, or statistic, explaining a topic, or stating a controversial view. They are located at the bottom of the page in the footer section, hence, "footnotes." Figure 3-6 shows an example of a footnote from the Polkadot Networks whitepaper explaining a "long-range 'nothing-at-stake' attack" denoted by the number four—in superscript—in the main body text.

POLKADOT: VISION FOR A HETEROGENEOUS MULTI-CHAIN FRAMEWORK DRAFT 1 6

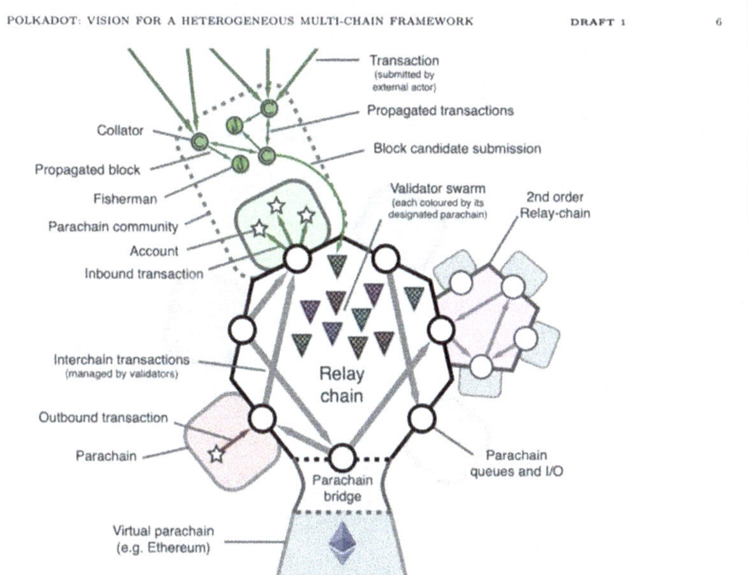

FIGURE 2. A summary schematic of the Polkadot system. This shows collators collecting and propagating user-transactions, as well as propagating block candidates to fishermen and validators. It also shows how an account can post a transaction which is carried out of its parachain, via the relay-chain and on into another parachain where it can be interpreted as a transaction to an account there.

funds coming from a token base expansion (up to 100% per year, though more likely around 10%) together with any transaction fees collected. While monetary base expansion typically leads to inflation, since all token owners would have a fair opportunity at participation, no token-holder would need to suffer a reduction in value of their holdings over time provided they were happy to take a role in the consensus mechanism. A particular proportion of tokens would be targeted for the staking process; the effective token base expansion would be adjusted through a market-based mechanism to reach this target.

Validators are bonded heavily by their stakes; exiting validators' bonds remain in place long after the validators' duties cease (perhaps around 3 months). This long bond-liquidation period allows future misbehaviour to be punished up until the periodic checkpointing of the chain. Misbehaviour results in punishment, such as reduction of reward or, in cases which intentionally compromise the network's integrity, the validator losing some or all of its stake to other validators, informants or the stakeholders as a whole (through burning). For example, a validator who attempts to ratify both branches of a fork (sometimes known as a "short-range" attack) may be identified and punished in the latter way.

Long-range "nothing-at-stake" attacks[4] are circumvented through a simple "checkpoint" latch which prevents a dangerous chain-reorganisation of more than a particular chain-depth. To ensure newly-syncing clients are not able to be fooled onto the wrong chain, regular "hard forks" will occur (of at most the same period of the validators' bond liquidation) that hard-code recent checkpoint block hashes into clients. This plays well with a further footprint-reducing measure of "finite chain length" or periodic reseting of the genesis-block.

5.3. **Parachains and Collators.** Each parachain gets similar security affordances to the relay-chain: the parachains' headers are sealed within the relay-chain block ensuring no reorganisation, or "double-spending", is possible following confirmation. This is a similar security guarantee to that offered by Bitcoin's side-chains and merge-mining. Polkadot, however, also provides strong guarantees that the parachains' state transitions are valid. This happens through the set of validators being cryptographically randomly segmented into subsets; one subset per parachain, the subsets potentially differing per block. This setup generally implies that parachains' block times will be at least as long as that of the relay-chain. The specific means of determining the partitioning is outside the scope

[4]Such an attack is where the adversary forges an entirely new chain of history from the genesis block onwards. Through controlling a relatively insignificant portion of stake at the offset, they are able to incrementally increase their portion of the stake relative to all other stakeholders as they are the only active participants in their alternative history. Since no intrinsic physical limitation exists on the creation of blocks (unlike PoW where quite real computational energy must be spent), they are able to craft a chain longer than the real chain in a relatively short timespan and potentially make it the longest and best, taking over the canonical state of the network.

Figure 3-6. *Footnote from page six of Polkadot Networks whitepaper (compliments of* `https://polkadot.network/whitepaper/`*)*

Since the footnotes are smaller and less noticeable than the text in the main body, authors sometimes insert specific statements that can favor the project team but are harmful to the investor. For those with prior experience investing in digital assets, it is no surprise that some projects are not fully transparent and cannot be trusted. Therefore, they are more likely to conceal essential information within the footnotes to avoid legal action. There was one instance where the whitepaper's author had verbiage in a footnote specifying that the project's team had unrestricted control over the project's treasury. It is essential that investors take the time to read the footnotes, as this can save a lot of time and money.

Best Way to Approach a Whitepaper

For those who have already *encountered* one or more whitepapers, you may agree that they were initially intimidating, intense, complicated to read, and difficult to understand. However, do not let this discourage you. As with any other challenge, this is just a stumbling block that time and commitment will help you overcome. Whitepapers must be read from start to finish. The more whitepapers you read, the more that "technical jargon" will make sense to you. Eventually, you will gain the skills to quickly identify the critical information and red flags that help distinguish between winning and losing investments.

Simple Steps to Becoming a Whitepaper Master

1) **Daily Commitment** - Commit to reading a few pages of a whitepaper daily—even for fifteen minutes.

2) **Progression** - Although it may seem obvious, avoid moving to the following line or paragraph without understanding the previous one.

3) **Research** - Look up anything you don't understand on Google or YouTube before proceeding. Over time, you'll gain speed, and everything will begin to make sense.

4) **Key Points** - Highlight or note key points or items requiring further investigation.

5) **Keep Informed** - Read books on blockchain technology. "*Mastering Blockchain*" by Imran Bashir is an informative book that deep dives into distributed ledgers, consensus protocols, smart contracts, decentralized applications, digital assets, and much more.

For those who have never read a whitepaper before, it is advised to read the following:

1) **bitcoins Whitepaper** - `https://bitcoin.org/bitcoin.pdf`

2) **Ethereum's Whitepaper** - `https://ethereum.org/en/whitepaper/`

3) **Polkadot's Whitepaper** - `https://assets.polkadot.network/Polkadot-whitepaper.pdf`

It's advisable to start by studying the bitcoin, Ethereum, and Polkadot whitepapers because understanding these foundational documents makes grasping other whitepapers significantly easier. This is because these whitepapers combined provide the foundational detail and lay the groundwork for understanding how many other blockchains operate with respect to layered architectures, consensus mechanisms, and verification processes.

Action Steps

Follow these steps to evaluate a project whitepaper, ensuring its legitimacy and quality while assessing the potential value of the offered product or service.

1) **Locate the Whitepaper**

   Locate the whitepaper through official links via the project website.

2) **Initial Thoughts**

   When reading the whitepaper, what are your first thoughts considering the below criteria?

   a) First, has the project been provided with a whitepaper? (If not, it is a red flag.)

   b) Is the whitepaper very short and packed with images, with little verbiage regarding the product or service? (If so, abandon the evaluation.)

   c) Is the whitepaper full of "fluff" as a filler? (Long, convoluted explanations and lots of unnecessary "waffle" are major red flag.)

3) **Product or Service Offering**

   How did the product or service offering sound considering the below criteria:

   a) Does the whitepaper immediately state the purpose of the product, service, and value offering at the beginning of the document? If so, what is it?

b) Does the product or service sound exciting or boring?

c) Do you think many people would benefit from the offered product or service?

d) What is your overall feeling about the project?

e) Does it stand out?

f) Is there anything special about it?

g) Does it sound exactly like another project, you know? If so, what advantage or edge does this project have? (if any)

h) Is there something about it that you think will make it successful?

4) **Whitepaper Quality Checks**

Analyze the Whitepaper against the following quality checks.

a) Is the whitepaper laid out in a way that is easy for the reader to follow?

b) Is it structured and formatted in a professional manner?

c) Have the whitepaper references been cited from legitimate sources such as books, journal articles, Google Scholar, reputable authors, etc.? (Unreliable authors and random websites are red flags.)

d) In the whitepaper footnotes, is there any harmful verbiage that may affect stakeholders in the short or long term?

   e) Are there clear, precise headings and subheadings?

   f) Are there contradictions or discrepancies?

   g) Proper use of grammar, punctuation, and spelling?

   h) Are the images used of high quality?

   i) Are the pages numbered correctly?

5) **Take Notes and Document Your Findings in Your Own Style**

6) **Combine the Findings with Other Sections of the Fundamental Evaluation Process**

Evaluation of the Results

The condition of the whitepaper is an excellent measure of the team's competence, attention to detail, product potential, and overall project quality. Suppose the whitepaper lacks information or is of poor quality. In that case, it is advised to act on the side of extreme caution and carefully reconsider whether to continue with the rest of the fundamental evaluation process. If the project has no whitepaper, ideally you should abandon the evaluation; however, if other verifiable materials exist—audited smart-contract code, detailed GitHub architecture docs, or third-party security reports—you may proceed, but only with heightened caution.

Litepaper

Evaluation Objective: Evaluate a project litepaper, ensuring its legitimacy and quality while assessing the potential value of the offered product or service.

The litepaper is simply a concise, less intense, simplified version of the whitepaper. It is generally less technical and easier to understand, and in most cases, it is significantly shorter than a whitepaper. The purpose of the litepaper is to provide stakeholders with a more digestible overview of the project's fundamental value offering in a short amount of time.

The litepaper is evaluated much like the whitepaper but is given less weight in the overall fundamental rating. The reason is that the litepaper is vague as per design, and no investment should be made based on the litepaper alone. Nevertheless, if the project supplies a litepaper, it should be compared against the whitepaper for technical confluence and quality checks.

It is important to note that in the early stages of a project lifecycle, the litepaper may be the only paper available, as the whitepaper may still be in development. However, this is not uncommon—especially for projects still refining their architecture—and should be clarified with the team. It is strongly suggested that investors should not invest based on the litepaper—the whitepaper rules. If the project has launched, and no whitepaper is available, it is advised not to invest. Figure 3-7 shows a screenshot of the *table of contents* from the Polkadot Networks litepaper.

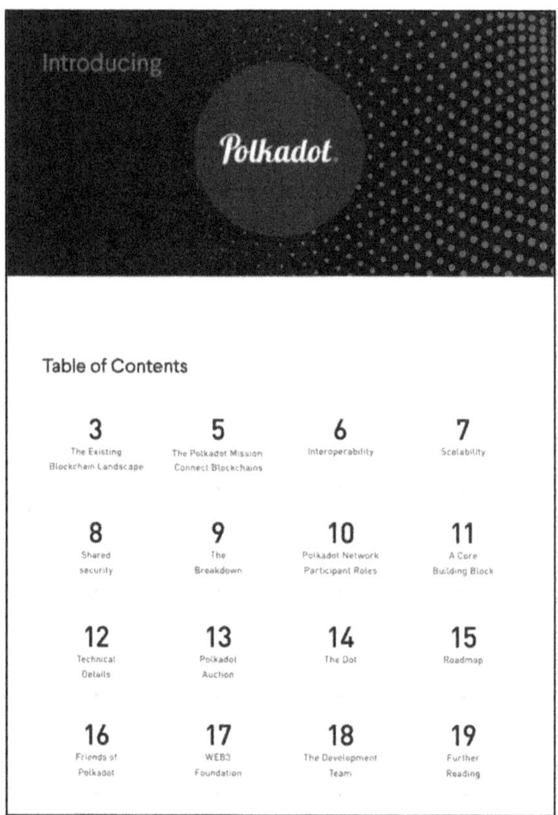

Figure 3-7. *Polkadot Network litepaper (compliments of* `https://github.com/w3f/polkadot-light-paper/blob/master/Polkadot-lightpaper.pdf`*)*

Most projects have a whitepaper and a litepaper. It is good practice to read both papers and confirm if they are in sync with one another. Also, checking the issued date and ensuring you have the latest edition is good practice. Scan for any contradictions that may raise red flags. Remember, investors should seek reasons to disqualify a potential investment rather than seeking reasons to justify it. It is important to note that some projects may not even have a litepaper—this is not a red flag or something to be concerned with. Like the whitepaper, the roadmap is not always included and will likely be presented in a separate document.

Although the information will not be as dense as in the whitepaper, it is common for litepapers to share the same headings and subheadings, but this can vary from project to project. Following is a generic table of contents list for a litepaper.

1. ***Product/Service Description***
    a. *Problem being solved*
    b. *The solution*
    c. *How does it operate*
2. ***Value Proposition***
3. ***Technology***
    a. *System architecture*
    b. *Blockchain type*
    c. *Consensus mechanism/operation*
    d. *Explorer details*
4. ***Token***
    a. *Purpose of tokens*
    b. *Token type/standard*
5. ***Tokenomics***
    a. *Token supply*
    b. *Inflationary/deflationary/fixed supply*
    c. *Token allocation details*
    d. *Vesting schedule details*

6. ***Funding and Partnerships***
    a. *Details of seed, private, ICO, and IDO rounds*
    b. *List of current investors*
    c. *List of current partnerships*
7. ***Reward/Incentives***
8. ***Roadmap/Vision***
    a. *Accomplished milestones*
    b. *List of future milestones*
    c. *Timelines for future milestones*
9. ***Legal Legislation/Documentation***
10. ***References/Sources/Footnotes***
11. ***Disclaimer***

Action Steps

Follow these steps to evaluate a project litepaper, ensuring its legitimacy and quality while assessing the potential value of the offered product or service.

The litepaper is evaluated much like the whitepaper but is given less weight in the overall fundamental rating. The reason is that the litepaper is vague as per design, and no investment should be made based on the litepaper alone. Nevertheless, if the project supplies a litepaper, it must be evaluated against the whitepaper for technical confluence and quality checks.

(Note—some of the evaluation checks below may have already been executed if the whitepaper has been evaluated before the litepaper.)

1) **Locate the Litepaper**

   Locate the whitepaper through official links via the project website.

2) **Initial Thoughts**

   When reading the litepaper, what are your first thoughts considering the below criteria?

   a) First, has the project provided a litepaper?

   b) Is the litepaper very short and packed with images, with little verbiage regarding the product or service? (If so, abandon the evaluation.)

   c) Is the litepaper full of "fluff" as a filler? (Long convoluted explanations and lots of unnecessary "waffle" are major red flag.)

3) **Product or Service Offering**

   How did the product or service offering sound considering the below criteria?

   a) Does the litepaper immediately state the purpose for the product, service, and value offering at the beginning of the document? If so, what is it?

   b) Does the product or service sound exciting or boring?

   c) Do you think many people would benefit from the offered product or service?

   d) What is your overall feeling about the project?

   e) Does it stand out?

   f) Is there anything special about it?

   g) Does it sound exactly like another project, you know? If so, what advantage or edge does this project have? (if any)

   h) Is there something about it that you think will make it successful?

4) **Litepaper Quality Checks**

   Analyze the litepaper against the following quality checks.

   a) Is the litepaper laid out in a way that is easy for the reader to follow?

   b) Is it structured and formatted in a professional manner?

   c) Have the litepaper references been cited from legitimate sources such as books, journal articles, Google Scholar, reputable authors, etc.? (Unreliable authors and random websites are red flags.)

   d) In the litepaper footnotes, is there any harmful verbiage that may affect stakeholders in the short or long term?

   e) Are there clear, precise headings and subheadings?

   f) Are there contradictions or discrepancies?

g) Proper use of grammar, punctuation, and spelling?

h) Are the images used of high quality?

i) Are the pages numbered correctly?

5) **Take Notes and Document Your Findings in Your Own Style**

6) **Combine the Findings with Other Sections of the Fundamental Evaluation Process**

Evaluation of the Results

Although important, the litepaper does not carry as much weight as the whitepaper. However, it is still advised to check if the litepaper is in good condition with clear, precise, and easy-to-understand information of good quality throughout. If the project team does not have a litepaper, it is not necessarily harmful, as many great projects do not have a litepaper.

CHAPTER 4

Core Offering

In the blockchain realm, a core offering refers to the project's primary product or service to the end users. This offering is developed through the application of blockchain technology, leveraging key attributes like decentralization, security, transparency, immutability, and traceability to enhance its value.

Fact This core offering is what differentiates the project from others and is a critical element in defining its value proposition and appeal to end-users and investors.

As with traditional centralized companies, if a crypto project does not offer a good product or service, its likelihood of long-term success is near zero—just like any investment tied to that project. Therefore, it is vital that the core product, its use case (what it does), and its value proposition (what value it provides) are thoroughly evaluated.

Fundamentals Discussed in This Chapter:

- Product Use Case and Value Proposition
- Minimum Viable Product (MVP)
- Product Testing
- Live on Mainnet
- Founding Year

P. Garvey, *Blockchain Fundamental Analysis for Digital Asset Investors*,
https://doi.org/10.1007/979-8-8688-1551-5_4

Product Use Case and Value Proposition

Evaluation Objective: Determine if the project has a strong product use case value proposition with genuine market demand.

The product or service is the most critical aspect of any crypto project. Think of it as a car's engine; without it, the car cannot move; therefore, it is deemed worthless to anyone who needs to get from A to B. Similarly, a crypto project that lacks a valuable, practical product is considered useless. As history has proven, although rare, there are rare exceptions to this rule. For example, the meme token DOGE made extraordinary gains where the price per token is entirely driven by the community and popular, influential figures like Elon Musk—despite the token's use case being largely limited to low-fee tipping and micro-transactions, offering little intrinsic utility relative to its market value.

When writing this book, there were over 32,600 crypto projects with hundreds of different types of products and services. Some of the popular product categories are decentralized exchanges (DEX), decentralized finance (DeFi), logistics/supply chain, digital currency (e.g., bitcoin), nonfungible tokens (NFTs), identity management, decentralized gaming, and decentralized blockchain infrastructures where decentralized applications (dApps) are built on.

Each product or service has a specific use case and end-user value derived from that use case. The terms "product use case" and "value proposition" are often used interchangeably and inaccurately. Despite their similarities, these terms have distinct meanings that investors should clearly understand. To illustrate, here's an explanation of each term using Uniswap—a decentralized exchange (DEX) application—as an example.

Case Study—Uniswap (Product/Service, Use Case, and Value Proposition)

Product (or Service) Definition

A product or service refers to the creation of any application, platform, or technology developed using blockchain technology. These products or services aim to provide specific functionalities or solutions, typically utilizing the benefits of blockchain technology, including decentralization, transparency, security, immutability, and traceability.

Service Offering (Uniswap)

Uniswap is a decentralized exchange (DEX) built on the Ethereum blockchain. Uniswap operates on an automated market-making (AMM) model, allowing users to swap ERC-20 tokens without the necessity of or interference from third-party intermediaries. It also accommodates projects that need to launch their token quickly, cheaply, and efficiently with adequate liquidity.

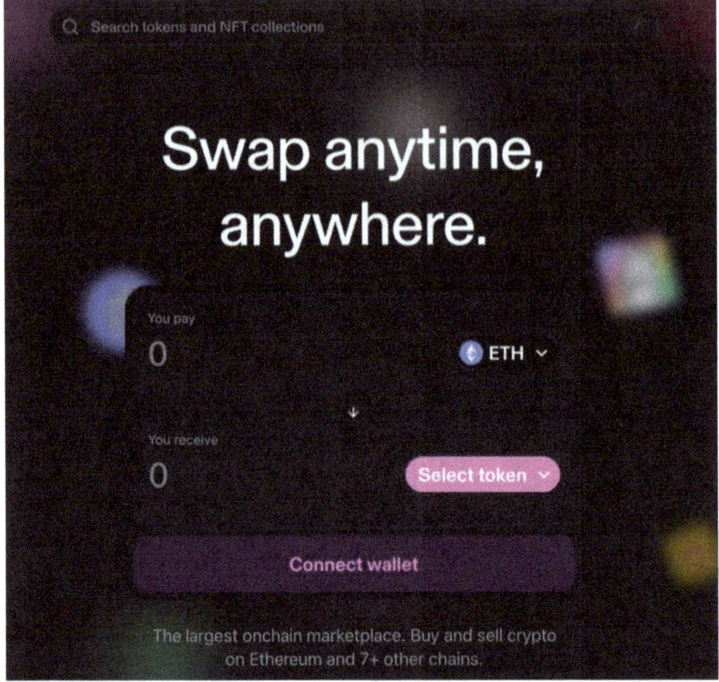

Figure 4-1. *Uniswap decentralized exchange interface (compliments of `https://app.uniswap.org/`)*

Use Case Definition

A use case refers to a specific situation where the product (or service) can be used and how it is used. In other words, what particular functions and tasks are executed to solve the initial problem?

Use Case (Uniswap)

Uniswap has multiple use cases, including:

- **Digital Asset Trading** – On the Uniswap DEX, digital asset holders can swap digital assets (coins, tokens, NFTs) with one another in a decentralized manner without any interference from third-party intermediaries.

- **Liquidity Mining -** On the Uniswap interface, users can provide liquidity for asset traders by depositing token pairs (or coins) such as ETH/USDT into a liquidity pool with other liquidity providers (LPs). In return for providing liquidity, these liquidity providers (LPs) earn trading fees generated by the pool.
- **Digital Asset Launch** - Project teams and individuals have the functionality to launch ERC-20 tokens on Uniswap's DEX and provide immediate liquidity for the desired trading pairs. This is attractive for projects because of the simplified listing process, immediate liquidity and trading, and low listing costs.

Value Proposition Definition

A product's value proposition defines the unique value offered to its end users. It focuses on the specific factors that attract and entice the end-users to avail the product or service. The value proposition varies depending on the project and end-user requirements. Additionally, the level of value that a product offers is closely linked to the level of investment it attracts—the greater the value delivered, the more significant the investment is likely to be made.

Value Proposition (Uniswap)

Uniswap provides many in the following ways:

- **Decentralized Trading with Restrictions** - Uniswap's primary value lies in their Automated Market Maker (AMM) model, which allows anyone throughout the globe to trade digital assets without the protocol-level country/location restrictions that typically bind centralized exchanges—though the official Uniswap frontend may geofence users in certain jurisdictions.

- **Token Launch** - Similar to restriction-free trading, projects can list (i.e., add liquidity for) their ERC-20 token on the DEX without centralized third-party interference.
- **Revenue-Sharing Proposal** - Through Uniswap's governance "revenue sharing proposal," all those who stake and delegate their UNI tokens will be rewarded by receiving a distribution of the protocol's income earned from exchange fees. This offering provides additional value and direct financial incentives for all UNI token holders.

In summary, the product (or service) refers to the application, platform, or technology developed using blockchain technology; the use case is how the product is used; and the value proposition is the unique value offered to its end-users.

Product Use Case, Value Proposition, and Associated Market Demand

The product's use case is one of the most critical aspects, and its operation directly impacts a project's long-term success and longevity. However, a strong use case must stem from a genuine market need, ensuring that the product the project team offers is legitimate and market-relevant. There needs to be a demand for the product; otherwise, it will not gain traction, and therefore, investment cannot be justified. When a product offers an in-demand, strong, well-designed use case that meets current market demand, it becomes a key growth driver.

While some crypto projects genuinely address real-world problems or make an existing process more efficient, saving time and money for companies, others do not. The truth is that most crypto projects fail and become a distant memory. It is relatively easy to launch a crypto project with a poor product or, worse, a fraudulent promise of a product that does not exist. The goal of the individuals behind these poor use case or scam projects is to lure in investors with slick marketing, misleading claims, and broken promises to secure their money. Once investments have been made and the hype is over, the team starts to fade into the shadows with investor capital. In the end, investors are left holding digital assets that are now completely worthless or worth only a fraction of the initial price per token or coin, with little to no chance of price recovery.

Evaluating the Product Use Case, Value Proposition, and Associated Market Demand

The product and its use case are the heart of a crypto project; without them, there is no value, project, or reason for investing. Therefore, it is the responsibility of the investors to perform adequate research and checks to evaluate the product and its use case to ensure legitimacy, market demand, and appeal to potential users or investors.

Table 4-1 shows Polkadot Network and a fictitious (dummy) project named MysticMania, evaluating both based on their respective product use cases. This evaluation aims to determine if the product use case is strong, legitimate, provides actual value, and has market demand. Investors are advised to use this evaluation procedure or generate a similar system for the same purpose and requirements. Most of the fundamental information required for the analysis can be found in the project whitepaper, project website, related official blog articles, real-time crypto, and CoinMarketCap.com. CoinMarketCap.com is a popular digital asset real-time market data platform that many investors rely on for accurate and reliable information, such as digital asset price tracking and exchange data. CoinMarketCap is used extensively as a research tool to help identify new potential investments. For a recent tutorial, visit CoinMarketCap's official YouTube page: `https://www.youtube.com/watch?v=165M98Vaa5I`.

***Table 4-1.** Product use case, value proposition, and market requirement analysis of Polkadot and MysticMania (dummy/fictitious project)*

	Product Use Case, Value Proposition, and Market Demand Evaluation	
Evaluation Metric	**Polkadot Network**	**MysticMania (Dummy Project)**
Product or Service	An open-source, Web3, decentralized, multi-chain, scalable infrastructure that enables the creation of different blockchains, their operation, and communication with one another.	A decentralized crypto wallet application where users are incentivized with native tokens for securing their digital assets via the dApp.
Use Case	Blockchain Creation and Operation: Enables users to utilize Polkadot's parachain framework to build, launch, and operate custom-built, robust, decentralized blockchains that cater to the needs and requirements of the customer.	Provision of rewards alone is not considered a use case.

Does the Use Case Provide Actual Value? How?	Yes **Interoperability**—High level of interoperability within its parachain network, sister chain, Kusama, and other blockchain ecosystems, significantly increasing end-user value. **Scalable**—Polkadot is highly scalable. This is achieved through economic and transactional scalability by using a shared set of validators to secure multiple blockchains and distributing transactions across these parallel blockchains, allowing for efficient handling of high transaction volumes and stable fees. Additionally, an upcoming scaling upgrade, known as elastic scaling, is still in development and will allow parachains to produce and validate multiple blocks per Relay Chain block, enabling higher throughput and faster transaction processing once deployed. A highly scalable blockchain increases overall user efficiency with faster and cheaper transactions, contributing value to the entire ecosystem. **Governance**—Polkadot uses a sophisticated, on-chain governance approach where the network's stakeholders make all decisions directly on the blockchain. The DOT token is at the heart of the Polkadot governance structure, enabling DOT holders and direct interaction with proposals set forth by the community. The three bodies of on-chain governance in Polkadot are the DOT Holders, the Council, and the Technical Committee, who work with one another to ensure order and efficient decision-making and progression of the network.	No Provision of rewards alone does not provide any value. Plenty of projects provide rewards as standard.

(*continued*)

Table 4-1. (continued)

Product Use Case, Value Proposition, and Market Demand Evaluation		
Evaluation Metric	**Polkadot Network**	**MysticMania (Dummy Project)**
What Problem Is Being Solved?	Polkadot Network solves many issues plaguing decentralized blockchains, including lack of interoperability, scalability issues, high energy consumption, security issues, and poor on-chain governance structures.	MysticMania does not solve any problem.
Can the Problem Be Solved Using Traditional Centralized Methods Instead of Blockchain Technology?	No Polkadot users demand the benefits of decentralization that centralized systems fail to provide. These benefits include a trustless operating blockchain, high security (no single point of failure), transparency, open-source, anonymity, high availability, decreased corruption, and bureaucratic burdens with decentralized governance.	Yes Traditional banking and third-party financial applications provide interest-bearing accounts that serve the same purpose.
Is the Use Case Strong Enough to Attract Users or Clients?	Yes There is a high demand for powerful blockchain infrastructures where users can build custom blockchains. Polkadot Network's popularity has gradually grown since its launch in 2020, where many customers have bidding wars for a chance to win one of Polkadot's parachain slots.	No MysticMania does not have a valid use case. Other projects provide legitimate use cases in addition to reward offerings as standard practice.

Do Other Projects with Similar Product Use Cases Have High Market Capitalizations Listed on CoinMarketCap.com?	Yes This is a popular and in-demand product use case. There are many other infrastructure-based projects on CoinMarketCaps.com's top 100 projects ranked by market capitalization, some of which include Ethereum, Solana, Injective Protocol, Near Protocol, MINA Protocol, and BNB Chain.	No Incomparable because most projects offer rewards as standard.
Does a Blockchain or dApp-Based Solution to This Problem Make Sense?	Yes A decentralized infrastructure with an exact use case and provision of the same value is not possible without blockchain technology.	No The proposed use case can be achieved with traditional banking systems.
Does the Product Use Case Add Value to the Blockchain Ecosystem?	Yes High-level interoperability between Polkadot's parachains and other ecosystems (including Ethereum through Moonbeam Network—Ethereum Virtual Machine (EVM)/increased liquidity and asset transfer between ecosystems/full on-chain Governance.	No Does not contribute any value to the ecosystem.

(continued)

Table 4-1. *(continued)*

Product Use Case, Value Proposition, and Market Demand Evaluation		
Evaluation Metric	**Polkadot Network**	**MysticMania (Dummy Project)**
Is the Use Case Solid Enough That the Company Will Have Long-Term Success?	Yes Lots of projects can be built on Polkadot. Polkadot remains one of the most advanced infrastructures, and the future looks promising.	No The proposed use case does not provide any value; therefore, there is a very low chance of the project succeeding.
Verdict	*Sophisticated, decentralized infrastructure with a valid use case that adds extreme value to users and the entire blockchain ecosystem.* *High market requirement—solves genuine problems.* *The Polkadot Network is a unique decentralized infrastructure, deserving a continued fundamental evaluation to determine its investment potential.*	*A project that rewards customers for holding digital assets in a dApp wallet. Provides no value—receiving rewards is not a use case (there needs to be some function or service that offers some form of value).* *No market requirement—does not solve any problem.* *MysticMania is not unique or worth an investment.*

Action Steps

Follow these action steps to determine if the project has a strong product use case, value proposition, and genuine market demand.

1) **Research the Product Use Case and Value Proposition**

   Read the project's whitepaper, blog articles, public code repositories (e.g., GitHub commit history), and any other relevant technical information from the project's website to gain a sufficient understanding of the product use case and value proposition. This is critical because it provides a foundation for the rest of the fundamental evaluation process. Reach out to the project team if clarity or further information is required.

2) **Evaluate the Product Use Case and Value Proposition**

   Using Table 4-1 as a template, evaluate the project's product use case and value proposition.

3) **Take Notes and Document Your Findings in Your Own Style**

4) **Combine the Findings with Other Sections of the Fundamental Evaluation Process**

Evaluation of the Results

Avoid investing in any project that fails to deliver a strong product use case that provides actual value and has a genuine market requirement. While initial hype may or may not generate short-term profits, the project is ultimately destined for failure.

Minimum Viable Product (MVP)

Evaluation Objective: Determine if the project team has an MVP (at minimum) available for testing.

A minimum viable product (MVP) is a product with the minimum necessary features required to validate an idea or concept and meet the initial needs of end-users. The core advantage of an MVP is that it provides a way to test an idea in real market conditions with minimal resources before fully developing and launching a complete product. Moreover, an MVP allows a company to showcase its product to potential stakeholders at the early stages of development. In the crypto world, this could be dApps (decentralized applications) targeting different sectors, including decentralized finance (DeFi), gaming, non-fungible tokens (NFTs), the metaverse, or dApps for identity-focused infrastructures such as KILT Protocol.

MVPs are used at the early stages of a project lifecycle and, in most cases, take the form of a simple dApp, SDK, protocol module, or other demonstrable component. Projects that have already launched with a *token generation event (TGE)*—which involves creating new tokens and selling them to investors and supporters—are highly likely to have an MVP at a very minimum. Ideally, they should have a beta version or even a final working product. In most circumstances, already established projects have a full working product; however, they may require an MVP to test new application features or product services.

An MVP is critical for several reasons, including:

- **Building End-User Base** - An MVP enables the project to enter the market quickly, gain a competitive edge, and start building a user base.

- **Market Validation** - An MVP allows for testing a product or service in a real-world setting and receiving feedback. This allows the project team to validate their concept with real users and gather valuable feedback before committing to a full-scale launch.
- **Technical Feasibility** - Developing an MVP helps identify and tackle technical challenges early, including basic smart-contract functionality and initial integration work; more complex items—such as custom consensus logic or full cross-chain interoperability—are typically prototyped in later iterations.
- **Security Concerns** - An MVP allows developers to identify and fix potential security flaws, code vulnerabilities, bugs, and glitches before they escalate into more serious issues.
- **Regulatory Compliance** - An MVP helps identify potential regulatory hurdles and challenges upfront, thus ensuring the final product complies with applicable laws and regulations.
- **Investment** - An MVP can help provide a tangible proof-of-concept that attracts stakeholders.
- **Community Building** - Releasing an MVP helps attract early stakeholders and community members who can provide valuable feedback and contribute to the project's development, success, and longevity.
- **Traction** - An MVP is a magnet for early adopters, boosting initial traction, which is critical for the project's future growth and success.

Pro Tip Always visit the project's social media channels, such as Telegram, X, Discord, and Reddit, to help gauge the broader community's perception of the product.

MVP, Beta Importance for Investors

When investing, investors must check if the project has an active MVP or a beta version. An MVP is always released before a beta. While an MVP is the first and initial saleable version of the product with minimum features, the beta version is an almost final version released to a more significant number of people to try under real conditions. The core objective of the beta is to identify any remaining bugs or defects before a final polished version is released. Investors need to verify if the team, at a minimum, has an MVP released for testing—this is critical for the following reasons:

- **Reduced Risk** - An MVP significantly reduces the chance that the project is a scam.
- **Verified Progress** - An MVP proves the team's commitment and technical abilities by pushing beyond the conceptual phase toward a working product.
- **Validation** - An MVP validates the initial concept and assumptions of usability.
- **End-User Testing** - An MVP allows a selected group of end-users, typically community members, to test the product and offer back real-world feedback and insights about the product's features and useability.
- **Future Potential** - An MVP provides valuable insight into product potential to disrupt the market.

Fact It is more desirable if a beta version or the final product is released, as this indicates that the team has progressed past the MVP phase.

Action Steps

Follow the steps below to determine if the project, at a minimum, has released an MVP or beta model available.

1) **Determine If an MVP, Beta, or Final Working Product Is Available**

   Visit the project's website to verify if an MVP, beta, or final product is available. This will usually be a simple dApp, SDK, protocol module, or other demonstrable component the end-user can interface with the product or service. The link to the dApp is typically indicated with a button labeled "*Launch App*" (or similar) and is found on the home page of the project website.

2) **Take Notes and Document Your Findings in Your Own Style**

3) **Combine the Findings with Other Sections of the Fundamental Evaluation Process**

Evaluation of the Results

Without an MVP, beta, or full working product, it is advised not to proceed with an investment. The reason for this is that without a demonstrable proof-of-concept, the associated risk increases significantly, compounded by the potential threat of fraudulent activities.

Product Testing

Evaluation Objective: Verify whether their core product has undergone or is currently undergoing testing by the team and community.
Product testing is integral to the project's product development phase, success, and longevity. Once an MVP has been developed, it must be thoroughly tried and tested before its official release. This helps and aids the delivery of a safe and efficient product, thus increasing customer satisfaction and user experience.

Considering that the vast majority of dApps within the blockchain realm are financially oriented, it is imperative that such dApps are thoroughly tested before digital assets with real monetary value are utilized. Therefore, the project team must thoroughly test their product and provide clear demonstrations to the community to prove the concept and verify functionality.

It is highly admirable that the MVP has progressed to the beta phase. During the beta phase, the community can thoroughly test the functionality of the core beta model. Execution of this phase is critical for investors, as it proves the team has been working diligently to deliver the product that has been promised. Moreover, the beta testing phase is a significant core deliverable deemed a vital milestone on project roadmaps. Reaching the beta phase significantly lowers the chances of the project being a scam while considerably enhancing the team's credibility and overall value.

Once a working product has been established, it is highly recommended that every investor test the beta model's core features and functionality. This will provide first-hand information and direct feedback that may help with other aspects of the overall fundamental evaluation. However, in the interest of safety, caution should be exercised when interacting with any monetary-based decentralization application.

To help eliminate any financial damage, it is recommended that no digital assets other than testnet tokens with no monetary value should be used to interact with such dApps—especially a dApp that is still in the testing phase.

Pro Tip It is recommended that the audit and security audit of a dApp/product's code be validated before interaction, as it would be unfortunate to lose assets due to a coding glitch while testing a new DeFi liquidity mining protocol.

Testnet

A "***testnet***" is the term given to a safe ***"sandbox"*** *environment* where the core product (e.g., dApp or blockchain) is *tested and experimented* on before it is pushed to Mainnet—more on Mainnet later in the next section. Testnets are risk-free and secure alternative blockchains that are near separate deployments that replicate mainnet configurations and tooling of the original mainnet or live blockchain. Both developers and community members use testnets to help prepare the product for official release on the mainnet. They help protect the project code on Mainnet from any potential vulnerabilities or damage caused by untested features.

For example, consider a scenario where the project team has developed a new decentralized exchange (DEX) where users can buy and sell digital assets. Before the official launch, the team needs to ensure the product DEX is completely safe to use; thus, they need to identify and fix any harmful bugs or glitches that may be financially detrimental to users. To achieve this, an alternate blockchain—testnet—is deployed as a separate network configured to resemble the original mainnet blockchain. This helps protect users during beta testing while also protecting the true mainnet where the DEX will be officially launched. During the testing phase, testnet tokens, also known as dummy tokens, are issued to the community for use when testing. This adds an extra layer of security that allows the development team and the community to safely interact with the DEX without losing any money. Once all bugs, glitches, and code vulnerabilities have been identified and fixed, associated updates are pushed to the mainnet. After the project team is satisfied that all changes and updates have been implemented, the dApp should be ready and safe for use with tokens with real monetary value.

Pro Tip Early community members participating in the testing phase are often rewarded for their efforts and contributions. This presents a fantastic opportunity to gain exposure to new startup projects that may be valuable in the future.

Testnet Advantages

- **Risk-Free Testing Environment** - Provides a safe environment where the project code is safely tested and experimented with without damaging the product. This may include testing new features, updates, smart contracts, and applications without the risk of losing real funds or causing disruptions on the mainnet. Also, developers can stress-test the blockchain network to determine how it handles high traffic or transactional volume.
- **Cost Effective** - Since testnet tokens have no real value, developers can perform extensive testing without incurring the high costs of using real digital assets.

- **Removal of Bugs and Vulnerabilities** - Utilizing a testnet helps identify and fix bugs, vulnerabilities, and other issues before deploying changes to the mainnet, improving the overall security of the blockchain application.
- **Community Engagement** - Testnets help promote community engagement with the product by allowing the community to participate in early testing and provide feedback on any issues found, with the possibility of being rewarded for their efforts.
- **Code Updates** - New code updates can be safely implemented and experimented on the testnet before going live on the mainnet.
- **Innovation** - By enabling a safe haven for experimentation, testnets promote innovation where radical new ideas can be tested and refined before they are implemented on the mainnet.

Pro Tip Projects with a strong group of early beta testers are a fantastic sign of a project's credibility and acceptance.

Testnet Examples

Ethereum has several testnets with different names and features. As per Ethereum's official website, there are two maintained public testnets for Ethereum: Goerli and Sepolia.

- **Goerli Testnet** - Ethereum's first cross-client testnet for Ethereum smart contract development. Allows for testing in a safe environment with all mainnet features but without gas fees. However, Goerli is being phased out and is moving entirely to the Sepolia testnet.

- **Sepolia Testnet** - A stable Ethereum testnet that merged from Proof of Work (PoW) to Proof of Stake (PoS) along with the Ethereum mainnet. Sepolia is the recommended default testnet for Ethereum and serves developers with the infrastructure to deploy and test Solidity smart contracts and application development. Sepolia ETH—a testnet-only token explicitly issued for testing purposes—is used for gas on the Sepolia testnet.

Blockchain Explorers

A blockchain explorer—or a ***block explorer***—is a web-based tool to view and track for transactional data, including addresses, tokens, smart contracts, source codes, wallet addresses, prices, and other activities on a blockchain in real time. Most people mainly use blockchain explorers to check the status of a specific transaction, e.g., pending, unconfirmed, or confirmed. Developers utilize block explorers, particularly testnet block explorers, for many reasons, including verifying transactional and block data such as metadata, gas fees, gas limits, block confirmations, transaction times, and other miscellaneous data.

Each unique blockchain infrastructure typically provides a mainnet block explorer plus separate explorer(s) for each testnet the chain runs. The type of explorer used depends on the current stage of the blockchain project's development. For example, when a blockchain is still under development, all transactions will be done on the testnet and verified on the testnet block explorer. On the other hand, when the development and testing phases are complete, all live transactions are done on the mainnet and verified using the mainnet block explorer. After launching on the mainnet, developers may continue utilizing the testnet to test new features and upgrades. These are verified on the testnet explorer before being deployed to the mainnet. Figure 4-2 shows Ethereum's mainnet block explorer named EtherScan, displaying market, financial, and recent transaction data from a DeFi project called MakerDAO.

Fact In many cases, the testnet, mainnet, and corresponding block explorers are often utilized simultaneously. In a circumstance like this, the primary product may be complete and live on the mainnet, and in parallel, the team could be working on and testing upgrades and new features on the testnet before they push the code to the mainnet.

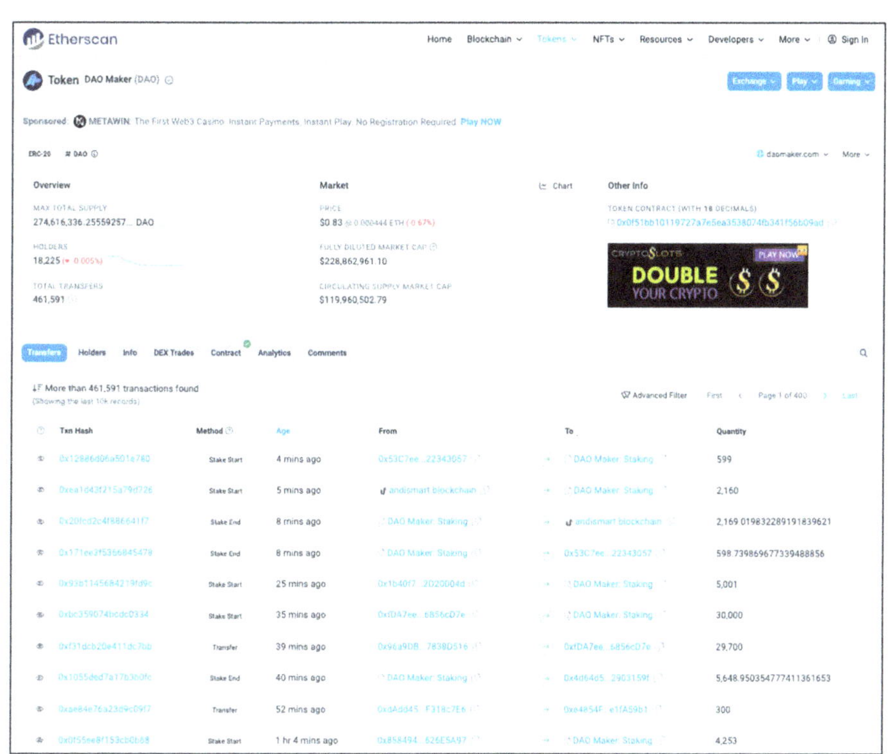

Figure 4-2. *Ethereum's Mainnet Block explorer showing "MakerDAO" on Ethereum's mainnet (compliments of* `https://etherscan.io/token/0x0f51bb10119727a7e5ea3538074fb341f56b09ad`*)*

Each transaction on the block explorer is identified by a *transaction* hash, often abbreviated as "Txn Hash." Each time a transaction is initiated on the blockchain, a new hash is automatically calculated. Each transaction hash contains information related to that specific transaction, including the status of whether it failed or was successful, the initiator and receiver address, the type of assets being sent, the timestamp, the transaction fee, and the gas price.

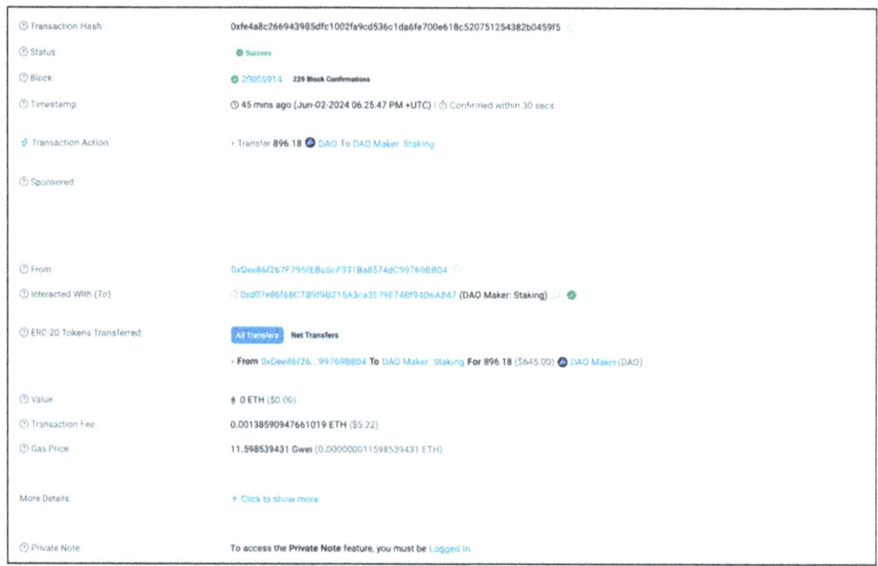

Figure 4-3. *Transactional data for the "MakerDAO" transaction (tnx hash ending in 59fg) displayed on Ethereum's mainnet block explorer Etherscan (compliments of `https://etherscan.io/tx/0xfe4a8c266943985dfc1002fa9cd536c1da6fe700e618c520751254382b0459f5`)*

Pseudo-anonymous

Most transactions on the blockchain are seen as ***pseudo-anonymous***. This means that if an individual's public *pseudonym* (wallet) address is ever linked to their identity, everything they ever wrote under that pseudonym will now be connected to them. This could happen in many ways—for example, using a public address for payments, tips, or donations, or linking the address to a KYC-verified account on a centralized exchange. It is also important to note that transactions on the blockchain are traceable all the way back to the *genesis block,* where the first transactions were executed on the blockchain. Therefore, if privacy is a concern, keeping public addresses and your identity safe and out of the public's view is advised.

Testnet Block Explorer

As previously stated, every testnet has its own independent and corresponding block explorer, which is used to view and analyze transactions, blocks, addresses, and other activities on the testnet. Figure 4-4 shows **Polkadot's Westend TestNet Block Explorer**.

The latest "blocks"—bundles of transactions—are shown on the left, while the latest single transaction transfers are visible on the right-hand side. Take note of when the latest blocks and transactions were executed, 8 seconds ago and 33 minutes ago, respectively. This data is extremely beneficial to investors for the following reasons:

- **New Product Testing Phase Activity** - For projects in their early phase, analyzing TestNet transactions will provide critical data on whether the team has started testing, stopped testing, or is still in their testing phase. It is admirable to see a steady flow of recent transactions spaced a few seconds to a few minutes apart, as this proves that the team is still working in the background and has not abandoned the project.

- **Continuous Improvement for Established Products** - For projects that are already established, like the Polkadot Network, it is desirable to see ongoing activity on the TestNet throughout the block explorer in the form of recent transactions. This indicates that while a full working product is already available, Polkadot (in this example) is still working diligently in the background on possible new features, upgrades, fixing of potential bugs or vulnerabilities, etc.

Fact A testnet block explorer offers the same information and features as a mainnet block explorer but is explicitly designed for a testnet blockchain instead of a mainnet blockchain.

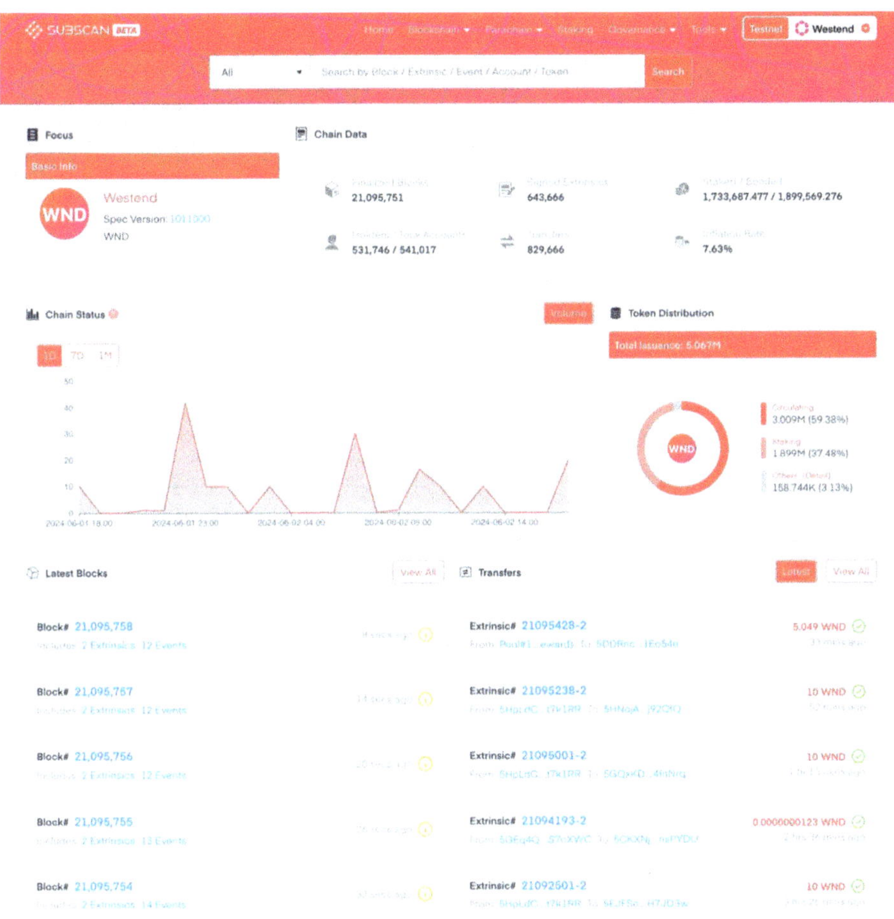

Figure 4-4. *Polkadot's Westend testnet block explorer by SubScan (compliments of* `https://westend.subscan.io/`*)*

The testnet the project team utilizes during the testing phase will depend on the blockchain infrastructure (e.g., Ethereum, Polkadot, Solana, MINA) on which the dApp is built. However, if the product itself is an entirely new blockchain, the team will create and use their own new testnet and testnet block explorer. For example, Moonbeam Network—a Layer 1 blockchain built on Polkadot, a Layer 0 blockchain—created its own testnet called Moonbase Alpha—see Figure 4-5.

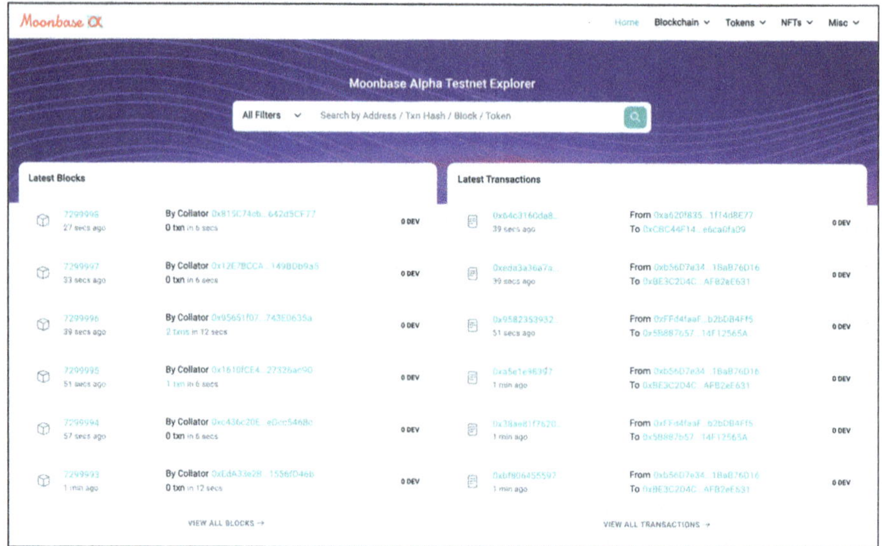

***Figure 4-5.** "Moonbase Alpha" block explorer from Moonbeam Networks TestNet named Moonbase Alpha (compliments of `https://moonbase.moonscan.io/`)*

Pro Tip Whether a project is established or still in development, always check for transactions on their TestNet block explorer. Projects with a continuous and constant flow of transactions are highly admirable, as they indicate that the project team is still working diligently in the background.

Action Steps

For well-established projects with a large following and a sizeable market capitalization, there is no requirement to check the status of the primary product testing phase. However, for early-stage projects, verifying whether their core product has undergone or is currently undergoing testing by the team and community is highly recommended for investors.

Follow these steps to verify whether their core product has undergone or is currently undergoing testing by the team and community.

1) **Determine If an MVP, Beta, or Final Working Product Is Available**

   Visit the project's website to verify if an MVP, beta, or final product is available. This will usually be a dApp so the end-user can interface with the product or service. The link to the dApp is typically indicated with a button labeled "*Launch App*" (or similar) and is found on the home page of the project website.

2) **Project Roadmap—Product Testing Schedule**

   Check the project roadmap for the dates allocated for the product testing phase.

   a) Have the team already completed their testing phase for the core product?

   b) When is testing due to begin?

   c) If the testing has not been finished according to previous timelines, request the team supply valid explanations for the project's delay.

3) **Analyze Testnet Transactions**

   Determine the name of the testnet and the corresponding testnet block explorer that the team has and will be utilizing for testing their product or service.

   a) **New Product Testing Phase Activity** - Check for testnet "explorer" transactions to verify if the product testing phase has started or been completed. It is admirable to see a constant flow of recent transactions, a few seconds to a few minutes apart, on the testnet block explorer.

   b) **Continuous Improvement for Established Products** – Verify if the team is working diligently in the background on new upgrades, features, and potential bug fixes by identifying a recent and continuous flow of TestNet transactions on the testnet block explorer.

4) **Take Notes and Document Your Findings in Your Own Style**

5) **Combine the Findings with Other Sections of the Fundamental Evaluation Process**

Evaluation of the Results

It is a positive sign if the product has already been officially released or, at a minimum, has passed the testing phase with positive feedback from the community. However, proceed cautiously if the project team has not yet started or completed the initial testing phase. Treat it as a potential red flag when the team repeatedly misses testing milestones, shows no Testnet activity, **and** offers no clear communication or revised timeline. It is common for new startups to be in the development stage for some time, and it is not necessarily a red flag if a project has not yet completed its product testing phase. However, more research is needed to better understand the project's progress and potential.

During the testing phase, it is common for the community to encounter multiple glitches and bugs in a product or service, which in most cases is a dApp or some form of customer interface. The primary purpose of this phase is to identify and resolve these issues. There is no major cause for alarm provided the development team acknowledges and addresses feedback and concerns from the community.

Live on Mainnet

Evaluation Objective: Determine if the project code (product) is live on the mainnet.

The mainnet is the primary blockchain network where real transactions occur, and coins or tokens with actual economic value are used instead of testnet tokens (dummy tokens), which are solely for testing purposes. The term *"live on the mainnet"* is often used in the blockchain space to describe when a blockchain protocol is fully developed, tested, and deployed on the mainnet for public use. Once the project team is confident that the protocol is in good working order, the code will be deployed on the mainnet using the finalized, audited codebase. All transactions are then broadcasted on the live network, verified, and recorded on a distributed ledger technology (blockchain). At this stage, users can participate in various tasks like verifying transactions—through mining—executing smart contracts, and interacting with decentralized applications (dApps) using real monetary value tokens.

When a project goes live on mainnet—also known as livenet—it is now running on the mainnet (live network). The testing phase is over by this stage, and all identified bugs and glitches should have been addressed. It is considered a significant project milestone for the project team when their product goes live on the mainnet. This indicates that the team has researched, developed, tested, and deployed the product for actual world use. Furthermore, it tells the community that the team is now more trustworthy, as they deliver on their promises.

Investors need to confirm if the project code is live on the mainnet. This is crucial because projects with their core product tested and officially deployed tend to carry slightly lower investment risk. Furthermore, it allows investors to examine and test out the final product, providing a deeper understanding of its overall features and value offering.

How to Determine If Project Code (Product) Is Live on the Mainnet

The fastest way to determine if project code is live on the mainnet is first to confirm that the team has a working product and then, using the mainnet block explorer, verify if a recent and continuous flow of transactions is visible. Also, most block explorers show the total number of transactions initiated on the blockchain, which tends to be millions. Figure 4-6 shows the recent transactions and the total number of transactions for the Ethereum blockchain on Ethereum's mainnet block explorer, Etherscan.

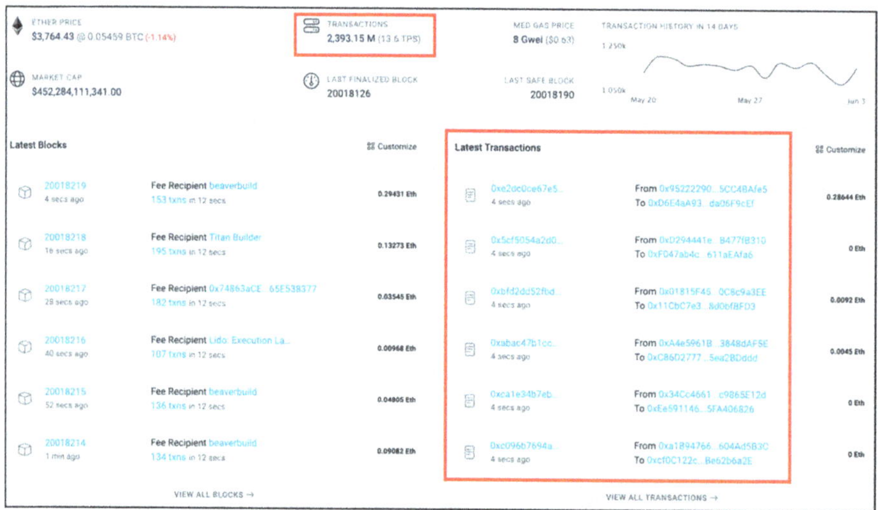

Figure 4-6. *Ethereum's mainnet block explorer, Etherscan, showing recent transactions on the Ethereum network every few seconds and the total number of on-chain transactions—2,393.15-m transactions executed (compliments of* `https://etherscan.io/`*)*

For dApp and token-based projects that are built on top of a blockchain network, the total number of transactions and recent transactions can be found by simply locating the smart contract address of the token on any crypto-asset price-tracking website such as

CoinMarketCap.com or CoinGecko.com and then plugging it into the mainnet block explorer for the network it is built on.

For example, Figure 4-7 shows an image from CoinMarketCap, highlighting the smart contract address of Chainlink—an oracle-based communication and information transfer project. Chainlink's smart contract address can be copied from CoinMarketCap and pasted into Etherscan (Figure 4-8), which displays Chainlink's recent transactions and total transaction count.

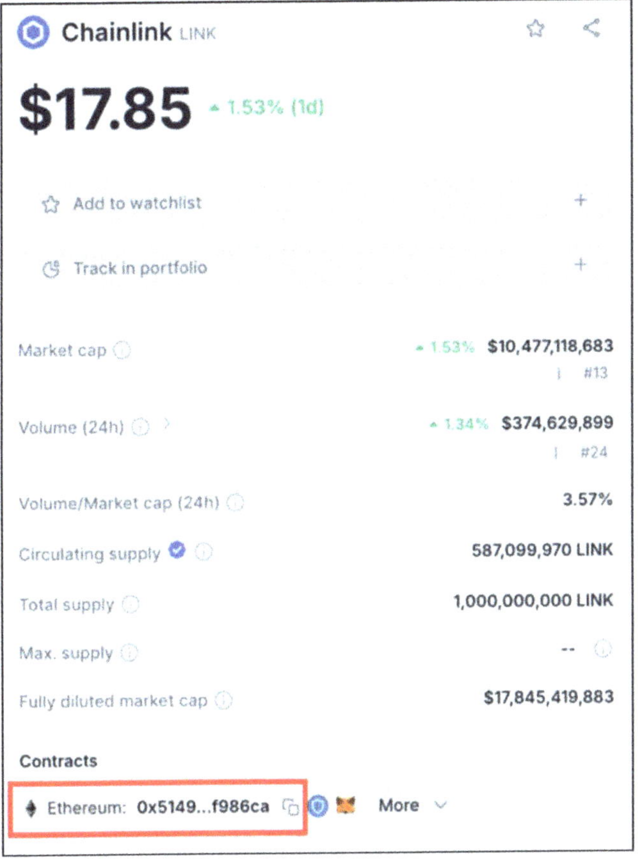

***Figure 4-7.** Screenshot from CoinMarketCap.com showing data and contract address for Chainlink (compliments of `https://coinmarketcap.com/currencies/chainlink/`)*

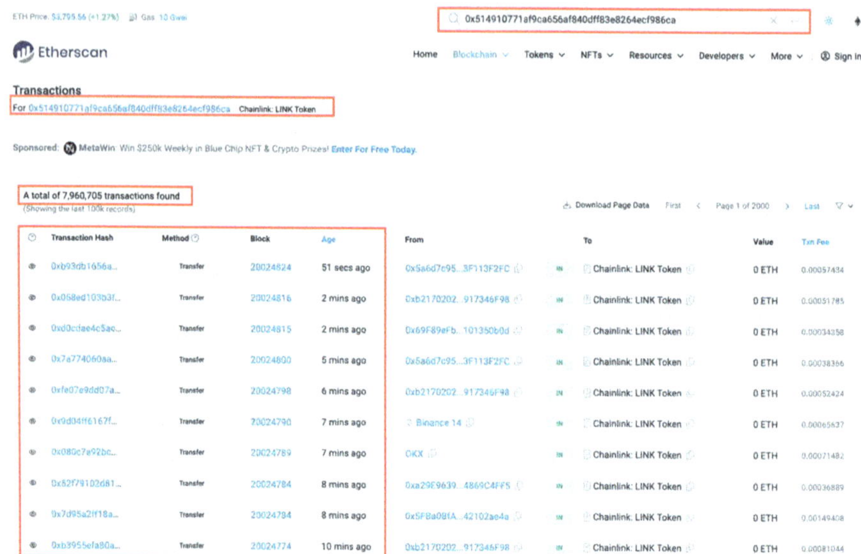

Figure 4-8. *Etherscan, Ethereum's mainnet block explorer, displays Chainlink's recent transactions with timestamps ranging from a few seconds to minutes ago, along with the total number of on-chain transactions executed—7.9 million in total (compliments of `https://etherscan.io/txs?a=0x514910771af9ca656af840dff83e8264ecf986ca`)*

As previously mentioned, investing in a project whose product is fully deployed on the mainnet typically carries less risk compared to one still in the testing phase. However, there may be legitimate and concerning reasons why a project may not be live yet:

Legitimate Reasons:

1. The team is adhering to the roadmap and mainnet launch dates.

2. The team has run into more issues during the testing phase than expected.

3. Additional features or innovations added to the project scope.

Reasons for Concern:

1. The project team has abandoned the project.
2. Bad management or leadership.
3. Understaffed.
4. Lack of funding.

Action Steps

Follow the steps below to determine if the project code (product) is live on the mainnet.

1) **Determine If the Project Is Live on the Mainnet**

   As described in this section, verify if the project has gone live by:

   a) First, verify if the project has a working product.

   b) Secure the project's contract address via a reputable crypto asset price tracking website like CoinMarketCap.

   c) Using the contract address, analyze the level of transactional activity on the mainnet block explorer.

      i) Is the transaction count at least a million or above? As a rough guide, projects showing fewer than about one million on-chain transactions are generally still in an early-growth phase; use this figure only alongside other adoption metrics (active addresses, TVL, and developer commits). The higher the transactions, the more attractive.

   d) Contact the project team through official support channels for further confirmation or support if required.

2) **Roadmap "Live on Mainnet" Date Analysis**

   Locate the project roadmap through the official website and identify the dates the project is scheduled to go live on the mainnet. Analyze against the following criteria.

   (Note that the project roadmap is discussed in detail in Chapter 11, "Project Roadmap").

   a) Has the "live or mainnet" date passed? If so, has the project gone live on the mainnet?

   b) If the mainnet dates have passed and the project is not live, then consider the following:

      i) Has the team provided any legitimate reason why the project roadmap is behind schedule? A project could be delayed for several reasons, including new additions of features and innovations, ongoing development, lack of funding, understaffing, poor management, many bugs and vulnerabilities, scams, project abandonment, etc.

      ii) What condition is the community sentiment in?

3) **Take Notes and Document Your Findings in Your Own Style**

4) **Combine the Findings with Other Sections of the Fundamental Evaluation Process**

Evaluation of the Results

It is highly admirable if the project is live on the mainnet. However, as with every new startup, it may take some time before all testing is accomplished and updates implemented. Therefore, it is acceptable if the project is not yet live on the mainnet as long as the team continues to prioritize the "live on mainnet" milestone on their project roadmap. Remember, a mainnet launch is encouraging, but it does not, by itself, guarantee the project's maturity or trustworthiness.

Founding Year

Evaluation Objective: Determine the founding year of the project to gauge its credibility, ensure its technology remains up-to-date, and verify the authenticity of the team's claims.

The founding year of a blockchain project is a vital piece of information for investors for several reasons. Projects that are only a few months old may carry higher risk because they have had little time to build a verifiable track record. On the other hand, a blockchain project that is, e.g., seven or eight years old may still be utilizing old, outdated technology, thus carrying increased risk. In such a case, investors are advised to conduct adequate research to ensure that the project updates its product and overall system where applicable. Checking the project roadmap for upcoming milestones is a good starting point.

Furthermore, project teams sometimes try to increase their credibility by providing fictitious information, such as the number of years they have been developing and working on the project. For these reasons, it is essential to verify the team's honesty and the company's founding year. The founding year of a project can be verified by several methods, including checking the domain-registration date, reviewing the first commits and release tags in public code repositories, and confirming when company pages were created on LinkedIn or Platform X.

Figure 4-9 shows an image of the domain registration detail for Moonbeam Network on a domain age checker website called Duplichecker.com. As shown, Moonbeams' domain was registered on November 14, 2019, roughly 5 years ago—when writing this book.

Domain Name	Domain Created on	Age	Domain Updated on	Domain Expiration Date
moonbeam.network	2019-11-14 16:38:042019-11-14 15:38:04		2024-10-16 01:39:222024-10-11 01:39:08	2025-11-14 16:38:04

***Figure 4-9.** Moonbeam Network domain registration year (compliments of `https://www.duplichecker.com/domain-age-checker.php`)*

Figure 4-10 displays a snapshot from Ethereum's LinkedIn page, the About section, indicating that the company was founded in 2014. Most projects have a LinkedIn page showing the year they were founded. Note—if a project does not have a LinkedIn profile, this is considered strange and a possible red flag, especially if there are no sources to evaluate the team members—this is explored in more detail in Chapter 10, "Project Team."

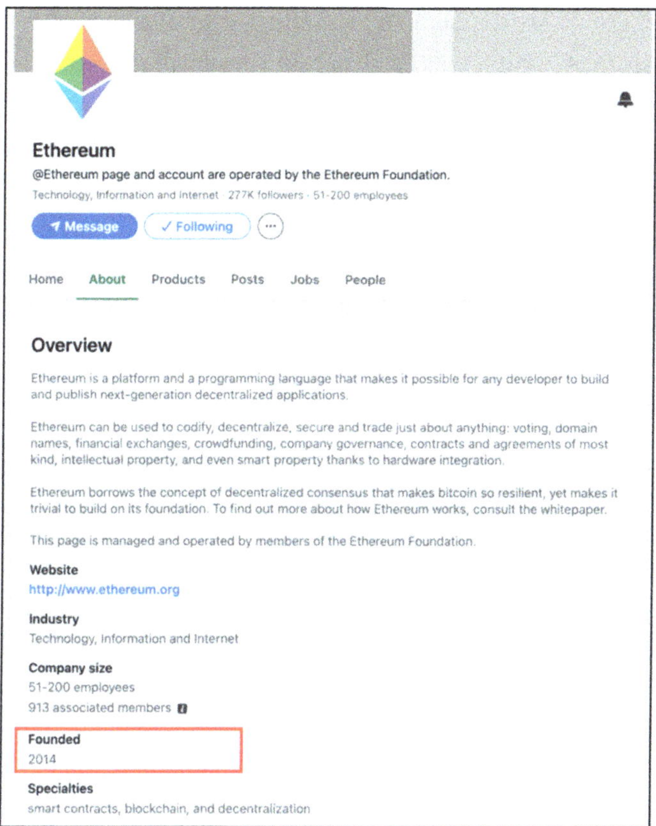

Figure 4-10. *Ethereum founded year—2014 (compliments of `https://www.linkedin.com/company/ethereum/about/`)*

Fact Given the high number of blockchain projects that collapse within a year of launching, teams with several years of experience developing the core product present significantly lower investment risk than those with only a few months of work behind them.

Another good way to check the founding year of a project is to check the year their profile on X was established. Out of all the social platforms available, X is one of the most popular for crypto, where nearly all projects have a presence and are used as primary sources to interact with the community. When a profile is set up in X, it locks the date the project joined the platform. Although the join date itself cannot be edited, accounts can occasionally be purchased and rebranded—an uncommon but real possibility—so treat the date as supportive evidence rather than definitive proof. Figure 4-11 shows Moonbeam Network, which joined X in **January 2020**.

***Figure 4-11.** Moonbeam Network, joined date (compliments of `https://x.com/MoonbeamNetwork`)*

Action Steps

Follow these steps to determine the founding year of the project to gauge its credibility, ensure its technology remains up-to-date, and verify the authenticity of the team's claims.

1) **Verify Domain Registration Year**

   Determine the year the project's domain was registered using the following steps.

   a) Visit the project's official website and copy the URL address.

   b) Visit a website named Duplichecker at `https://www.duplichecker.com/domain-age-checker.php`

   c) Paste the project domain URL into the "Domain Age Checker" box and select "Check Domain Age." This provides the year the domain was registered.

2) **Verify X Join Year**

   Determine the year the project set up their company profile on X using the following steps.

   a) Visit the project's official website.

   b) Locate and project X, the social media icon.

   c) On X, underneath the project's banner, it shows the year the project joined the platform.

3) **Verify LinkedIn Join Year**

   Determine the year the project set up their company profile on LinkedIn using the following steps.

   a) Visit the project's official website.

   b) Locate the hyperlink to the company's LinkedIn profile.

c) Navigate to the "About" section,

d) The founding year will be displayed at the bottom of the "About" section.

Evaluation of the Results

In most cases, the results should indicate that the domain and social profiles were created around the same time—unless the domain was purchased from someone else, which would be considered less likely. Nevertheless, this information should be used to help verify the team's credibility regarding how long they have been working on the product.

For example, deeper investigation is required if the team claims a major product release is just two months away, the token is already trading on exchanges, but the domain registration and social platform join dates are only a few weeks or months old—this raises concerns and possible red flags. On the other hand, if the project was founded seven years ago, a deeper evaluation of the technology, product, and market demand is vital to ensure they have updated their technology, product offering, and overall system to help them remain competitive.

CHAPTER 5

End-User Experience

End-user experience (UX) is a critical factor that directly impacts user adoption, long-term success, and growth of projects within the crypto space. It comprises the entire user journey and satisfaction when interacting with decentralized applications (dApps), wallets, exchanges, documentation, and other related aspects. Factors including transaction speed, gas costs, customer support efficiency, and geographic accessibility limitations also impact end-user experience. Projects that allocate adequate time and resources to delivering a seamless, intuitive, and secure UX ensure that users can easily navigate their user interface regardless of their technical expertise. This also entails providing all users with clear and concise onboarding instructions to eliminate any confusion when interacting with the product in any degree or form, thus enhancing user adoption.

This section evaluates the end-user experience with respect to various aspects of interaction with the final product. A smooth, intuitive, and efficient end-user experience is essential, as it directly impacts user retention. While a high user retention rate indicates that a significant proportion of users continue to use a product or service over a given period, a low user retention rate suggests that many users stop using the product or service shortly after starting. An expanding user base often correlates with a project's growth and perceived value and can influence coin price, but the relationship is not guaranteed, so it is good practice to cross-check it against fundamentals such as protocol revenue, token-supply changes, and developer activity.

P. Garvey, *Blockchain Fundamental Analysis for Digital Asset Investors*,
https://doi.org/10.1007/979-8-8688-1551-5_5

The end-user experience is vital for investors. A seamless, well-designed product that provides ease of use, self-explanatory interfaces, and fast and efficient customer support directly boosts user adoption and retention rates—vital indicators of a project's potential for growth and profitability. Projects that attract and maintain a broad user base are highly desirable for investors, as they signify a sustainable business model and market demand. A positive end-user experience can enhance the reputation and credibility of a crypto project while reducing investor risk. Furthermore, a polished, professional-looking UI is generally a stronger positive signal of legitimacy than a rough MVP interface and often indicates that the team is dedicated to delivering the highest-quality user experience to end users; however, UI quality alone isn't conclusive—some credible early-stage projects still ship with bare-bones design, so it's important to remain vigilant. These critical factors, coupled with a flawless end-user experience, can also lead to higher user engagement, thus contributing to increased value and return on investment.

The following sections explore various areas where end-users interact with the product, the team, and other factors that enhance or limit end-user experience and interaction.

Fundamentals Discussed in This Chapter:

- Product Application UI/UX
- dApp Usability and Functionality Assessment
- Transaction Speed and Cost
- End-User Customer Support and Communication
- Digital Asset Exchanges

Product Application UI/UX

Evaluation Objective: Evaluate whether the project website, dApp, or other interface offers high-quality UI/UX.

User interface (UI) and user experience (UX) are two critical aspects of product development that incorporate various types of products, such as apps, interfaces, and project websites within the blockchain sector. Although these terms are often used interchangeably, they are very different concepts.

UI refers to the look, feel, and interactivity of a web page or dApp. It considers interactive elements such as buttons, icons, and dropdown menus. Color scheme, font selection, and typography are also considered to help bring it all together. It is said that UI builds an emotive connection between users and products. On the other hand, UX refers to the overall experience a user has when interacting with a product, service, system, or application. The designer is responsible for ensuring that the product interface's design, interactive content, and layout are enjoyable, easy to navigate, self-explanatory, and easy for the user to use. Another responsibility of the designer is to understand what activities the end-user will execute to refine the corresponding customer interactions, remove friction points, and minimize the required steps to complete these tasks. Additionally, a good UX highlights the product's value to clarify the capabilities and benefits to the customers.

UI/UX for Blockchain

Most crypto projects offer *some* user-facing interface—whether their own dApp, a command-line tool, or integrations in third-party wallets—to let users interact with the product. Typically, the user-facing front end is a web or mobile application hosted on traditional servers, while it interacts with decentralized smart contracts that live on the blockchain. Each project creates and customizes its dApp for the specific product or service being offered. Each dApp interface differs wildly with respect to the type of project or service being offered.

Figure 5-1 shows an image of Moonbeam Networks—a smart contract platform for building cross-chain connected applications—dApp interface. Moonbeams dApp allows users to connect their decentralized wallets and participate in operations such as staking, governance referendums, asset management, cross-chain transfers, and various other related activities.

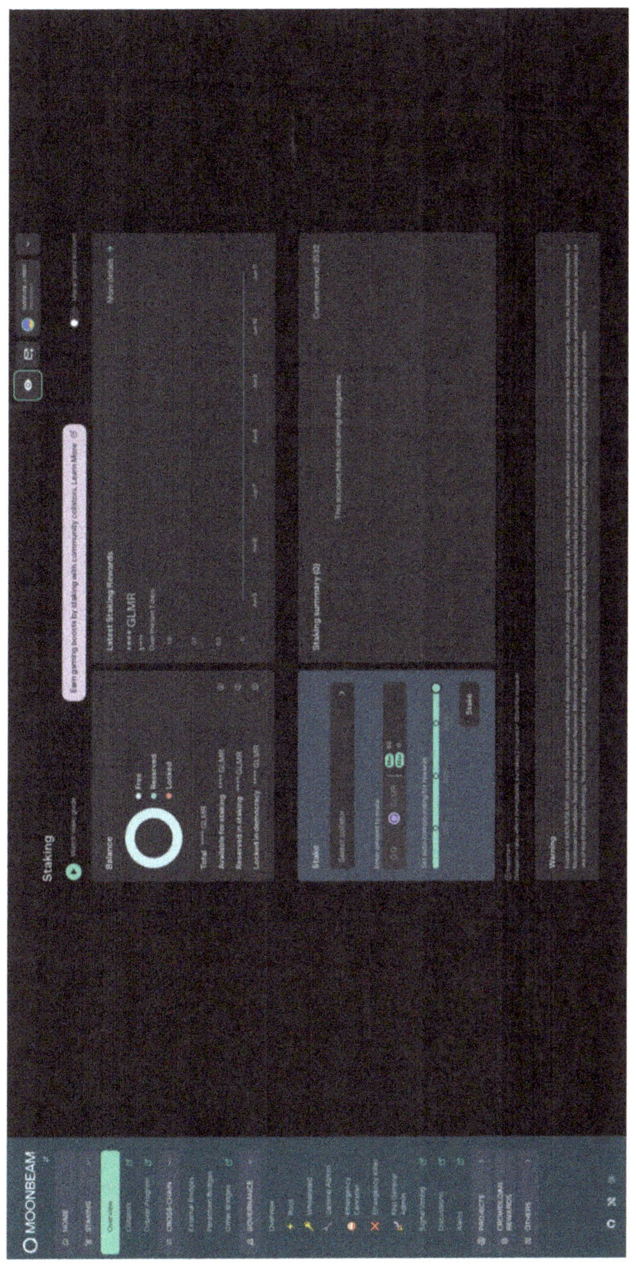

Figure 5-1. *Moonbeam Networks dApp interface (compliments of* `https://apps.moonbeam.network/moonbeam/staking`*)*

The UI of Moonbeam's dApp looks clean and modern, and it has an optional dark theme that is visually appealing. The blend of contrasting colors throughout the dApp makes the primary features stand out. The framework and overall layout are incredibly simplistic, self-explanatory, and easily accessible in design—users select options from the left-hand side menu, and the selection is displayed on the center screen interface. Additionally, the dApp is responsive on all screen sizes and devices, promoting a seamless user experience.

Moonbeams UX design significantly reduces friction for the end-user by incorporating intuitive one-click options and clear labels, and it categorizes each selection for easy navigation. On their main "staking overview" dashboard, the user's staking details are the primary focus, providing a comprehensive overview of staking risk, balance, status, rewards earned, and validator performance. Another attractive feature is interactive elements such as sliders that enable users to control the percentage of staking rewards to be compounded. Users can also see their staking rewards in real time over a given period. Furthermore, when using the dApp, load times are consistently fast, enhancing customer experience and satisfaction.

Project Website

UI/UX also applies to project websites. Typically, the project website is one of the first "go-to" for investors for information about the project, with links to the whitepaper, dApp, social media channels, and other related information on the project. First impressions matter; therefore, it is vital that the project website has excellent UI/UX design.

UI/UX Investor Analysis Skills

Investors do not need UI/UX experts to determine if the project dApp or website has good UI/UX. From using various software, applications, and websites in our day-to-day lives, most people subconsciously have a good sense if a website or dApp looks poor, cheap, awkward to use, and counterintuitive versus a sleek, easy-to-use, self-explanatory, visually appealing design. Unfortunately, first impressions of a poor and below-average UI/UX-designed website or dApp are carried through to every other aspect of the project, including the product and team's performance. Opposingly, good UI/UX leaves positive, lasting impressions with new customers and end-users, resulting in an increasing user base and increased interest among investors. Therefore, it is essential that the project has a modern-looking dApp and website with good UI/UX.

Caution If a company is reluctant to spend money on a professional website where they showcase their product, it makes you wonder what other areas they are cutting corners on, too. Additionally, if you personally struggle to navigate the project's website, dApp, or wallet, treat it as a potential red flag and validate the issue by checking feedback from users with different experience levels.

Action Steps

Follow these steps to evaluate whether the project website, dApp, or another interface offers high-quality UI/UX.

1) **Evaluate the dApps UI/UX Design**

   Evaluate the UI/UX of the MVP, beta, or final working product.

   a) Visit the project's official website to find the product interface, typically a dApp. This could be an MVP, a beta version, or the final product.

   b) Analyze the product's UI/UX using the same approach applied in the Moonbeam Network example.

      i) Is the interface intuitive and easy to navigate?

      ii) Is there a flow of colors and fonts in the design that is visually consistent and professional looking?

      iii) Is there a nice range of features that enhance usability, such as sliders, dropdowns, or buttons?

      iv) Does the system provide clear and helpful feedback when mistakes are made? Are there clear error alerts or notices?

      v) Does the product work well on both desktop and mobile devices?

      vi) Does it load quickly?

2) **Evaluate the Project Website UI/UX**

   Using the same UI/UX methodology, analyze the UI/UX qualities of the official project website.

3) **Take Notes and Document Your Findings in Your Own Style**

4) **Combine the Findings with Other Sections of the Fundamental Evaluation Process**

Evaluation of the Results

If the project website, dApp, or any other interface has poor UI/UX, it's not a good sign. Poor UI/UX may result from a lack of funding, an inexperienced team, poor management, or poor-quality control. Regardless of the reason, deem a project with bad UI/UX an early warning sign calling for additional research and careful monitoring before any investment is considered.

dApp Usability and Functionality Assessment

Evaluation Objective: Evaluate a dApp's usability and functionality to determine if it is reliable and user-friendly.

The usability and functionality of a decentralized application (dApp) are of the highest importance for the success and adoption of any project. Suppose a dApp is poorly designed, glitchy, and unreliable. In that case, it can potentially drive away users and result in financial loss if digital assets with monetary value are used for interaction—severely damaging the company's reputation. Therefore, it is always a good idea to test the dApp's functionality before investment to see if it works as promised—especially if this is a promising new startup that has seen limited real-world user testing so far.

When test running a dApp's useability and functionality, it is important to use testnet tokens—if the project is still in the product testing phase—otherwise, test with tokens with monetary value but the lowest amount possible to help minimize losses. This allows investors to check how well the app performs, how responsive it is, and how easy it is to use. A smooth and user-friendly experience is a good sign that the project is solid and has real value, while glitches or usability problems might be a red flag for potential risks. Remember, if you struggle to use the dApp—and similar issues are reported by users with varying experience levels—treat it as a red flag (unless the dApp is clearly in its MVP or beta phase).

Action Steps

Follow these steps to evaluate a dApp's usability and functionality to determine if it is reliable and user-friendly.

1) **Test the dApp's Usability and Functionality**

   Explore the dApps features, test running the actual product, and evaluate against the following criteria.

   a) Were any glitches or unexpected errors encountered?

   b) Did the product work as expected?

   c) How responsive and fast was the application? Were there any noticeable delays?

   d) Was there anything that seemed annoying or caused an unpleasant experience?

2) **Take Notes and Document Your Findings in Your Own Style**

3) **Combine the Findings with Other Sections of the Fundamental Evaluation Process**

Evaluation of the Results

If the dApp was easy to use and run smoothly, consider it a great sign the project is on the right track. However, if glitches, errors, delays, or bugs are encountered, assume a red flag and do not invest until the project team has explained and resolved issues or doubts. Nevertheless, exercise extreme caution and do not invest if you are unsatisfied.

Transaction Speed and Cost

Evaluation Objective: Determine if a project offers fast transactions and low gas costs that align with its practical use case requirements.
When a car moves from A to B, the two primary metrics are how long the journey takes and the cost of gas. Similarly, transactions on the blockchain are evaluated using two key metrics: transaction speed can mean (1) the time to first block inclusion or (2) the time to finality after N confirmations—about 12 blocks on Ethereum and 6 on bitcoin—and gas cost, which is the fee required to execute the transaction on the network. Transaction speed and cost are critical to customer experience. Companies and network participants are discouraged from using blockchains with high fees and slow transactions, especially when they have a selection of other blockchains with fast transaction processing times and low gas costs.

In this section, transaction speed and costs are discussed, along with the reasons why factors such as these are so crucial, as they directly impact end-users' experience, businesses, and investors.

Transaction Speed

Transaction speed is crucial in blockchain design and end-user experience for the following reasons.

- **Real-Time Transaction Speed for dApps** – Many dApps require near-instantaneous transactions, such as decentralized finance (DeFi), trading, gaming, and IoT. Slow transaction speeds can limit the types of applications built on a blockchain. Additionally, slow transaction times and fluctuating gas costs often result in unsuccessful transactions on decentralized exchanges (DEX).
- **Business Operations** – Most businesses utilizing the blockchain require fast transaction processing for their day-to-day operations. For example, supply chain management and payroll systems rely on timely financial transactions to support integral operations and the needs of their customers.
- **User Experience** – Slow transaction speeds can lead to a poor user experience and frustration that may discourage them from reusing that network.
- **Competitiveness** – Blockchains offering fast transaction speeds are more admirable than slower ones, thus attracting more users and developers to the platform.
- **User Retention** – Without fast transaction speeds, the network will likely see a decline in user retention.

It is important to note that the required transaction speed of a blockchain network depends on its specific use case. For example, bitcoin—which operates on a **proof-of-work** (PoW) consensus mechanism—is primarily designed as a store of value coupled with online digital currency payments. Since bitcoin's primary purpose is to provide a secure and decentralized store of value, ultra-fast transaction speeds are not deemed critical. However, other use cases such as DeFi, decentralized exchanges, gaming, and similar applications rely on fast, near-instant transactions to maintain an efficient and smooth end-user experience. These applications often utilize faster consensus mechanisms like Proof-of-Stake (PoS) to meet the performance demands of their users—more on consensus mechanisms in the section "Consensus Mechanisms" in Chapter 6, "Blockchain Architecture."

Transaction "Gas" Cost

In the blockchain realm, "gas" is the term for transaction fees required to pay miners or validators for the computational power needed to process and validate transactions on the network. The *gas* fee is paid using the native token of the blockchain being utilized for the transaction. For example, when using the Ethereum blockchain, the fee is paid in gwei (gigawei), which are tiny fractions of ETH—one gwei is one-billionth of one ETH.

Similar to transaction speed, the consensus mechanism utilized is the primary variable affecting gas costs. PoW-based blockchains—because of the amount of computational power required—have higher transaction fees than PoS-based blockchains or similar technology, where transactions are verified in a cost-efficient manner. Furthermore, the cost of gas will differ depending on the network traffic and congestion. Fluctuations in network traffic can be influenced by various factors, such as the time of day, major events, project-related news, updates on interest rates, or activity from prominent influencers.

The money generated from transaction costs serves many essential functions on the network. It incentivizes miners to secure the network by validating and processing transactions. It also discourages network abuse by making it costly for attackers to flood the system with spam. Additionally, for bitcoin, transaction fees increasingly subsidize miner revenue as block rewards fall after each halving; other networks with perpetual or variable inflation may rely less on fees for long-term security.

Why Low Gas Costs Matter

- **Accessibility** – Low gas costs make the blockchain more accessible to users.
- **Trading** – Low gas costs attract traders on various decentralized exchanges (DEX).
- **Affordability** – Low gas costs make participating in the blockchain more affordable for users, which helps boost user adoption.
- **Encourages Development** – Low gas costs encourage developers to build more complex and innovative applications on the blockchain, as they don't have to worry as much about the cost of transactions and smart contract execution.
- **User Growth** – Low transaction costs encourage more (and smaller) transactions, which in turn attract additional users, amplifying network effects and ecosystem growth.

Fact Consensus mechanisms are protocols utilized by blockchain networks to agree on the validity of transactions and to prevent double spending, ensuring all nodes maintain a consistent copy of the ledger.

How to Check Transaction Speed and Gas Cost

Transactional speed and gas cost can be typically found by searching for coin or token "Gas Tracker" websites online. For example, transactional speed and gas cost for Polygon (MATIC) are shown in Figure 5-2. Typically, when initiating a transaction on-chain, users have the option to pay higher fees for faster transaction processing. On Polygon, gas-tracker tiers such as 30 gwei ("Fast") and 31 gwei ("Rapid") illustrate that a small fee bump *can* speed up confirmation during network congestion, but the effect is minimal when traffic is low.

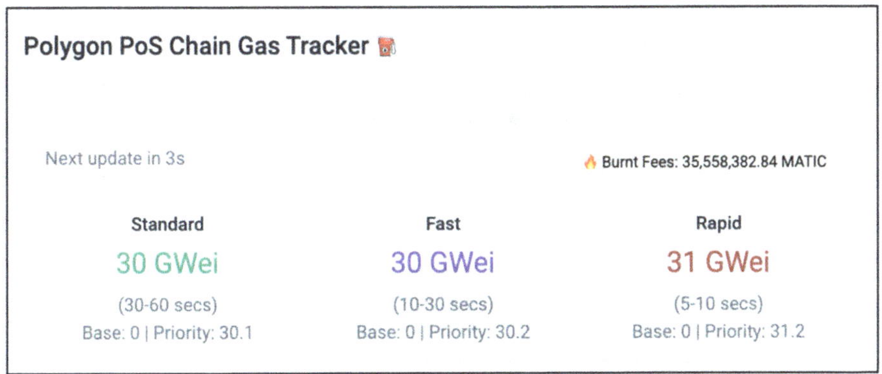

Figure 5-2. *Polygon's transaction speed and gas price in real-time (compliments of* `https://polygonscan.com/gastracker/`*)*

For convenience, there are many online gwei/USD calculators that display/convert gwei to USD and vice versa. Figure 5-3 shows an online gwei/USD calculator from Coinbrain.com, calculating 31 gwei to be worth $0.24.

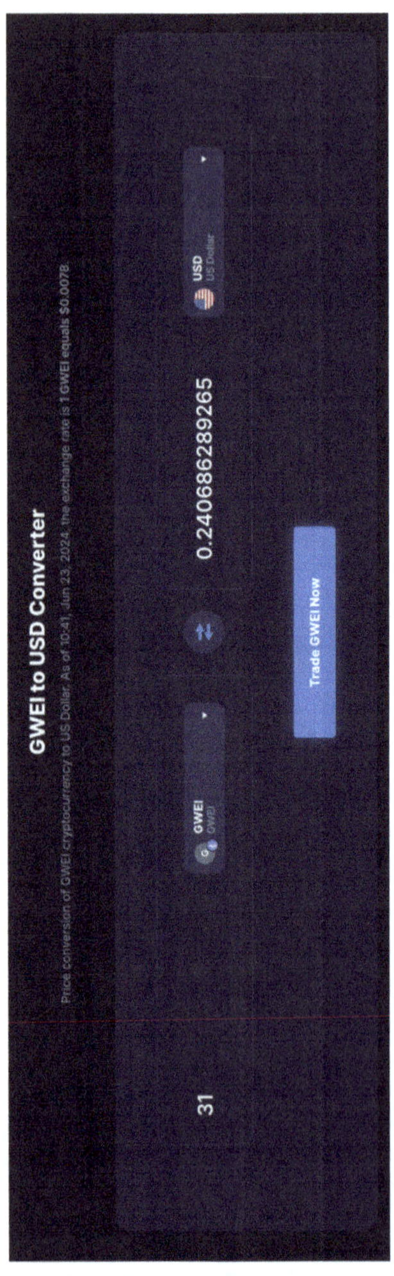

Figure 5-3. *gwei to USD Converter with calculation displaying the cost of 31 gwei as $0.24 USD (compliments of* `https://coinbrain.com/converter/eth-0x29e683aeafd03bb6c02055c3ca8b6edb4bb9bae5/usd`*)*

As a comparison to PoS-based protocols, Figure 5-4 is from YCharts.com, showing bitcoin's average transaction cost of $3.93 over three years. Additionally, Figure 5-5 from Blockchain.com shows bitcoin's median confirmation time of 10 minutes over three years. It is clear that PoW-based blockchains, such as bitcoin, have considerably slower transaction times with higher transaction costs than PoS protocols, as in the case of Polygon.

Fact Layer 2 protocols, like the Lightning Network for bitcoin (BTC), use micropayment channels to enhance blockchain scalability. They enable faster and more cost-efficient transactions by processing them off-chain while maintaining security.

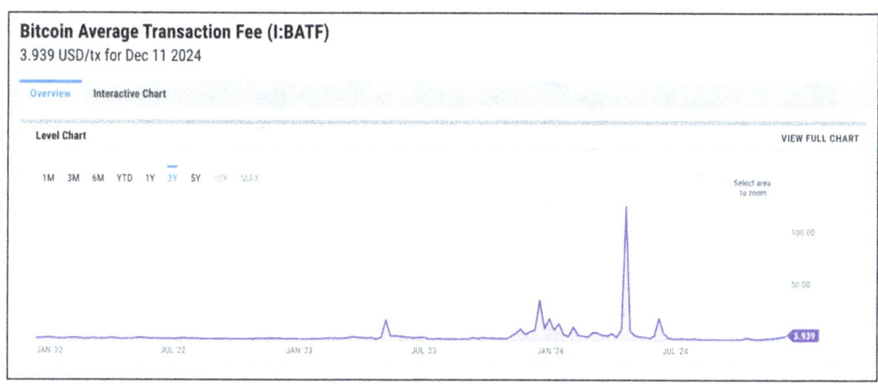

Figure 5-4. *bitcoin's average transaction cost over a three-year period is $3.93. (compliments of `https://ycharts.com/indicators/bitcoin_average_transaction_fee`)*

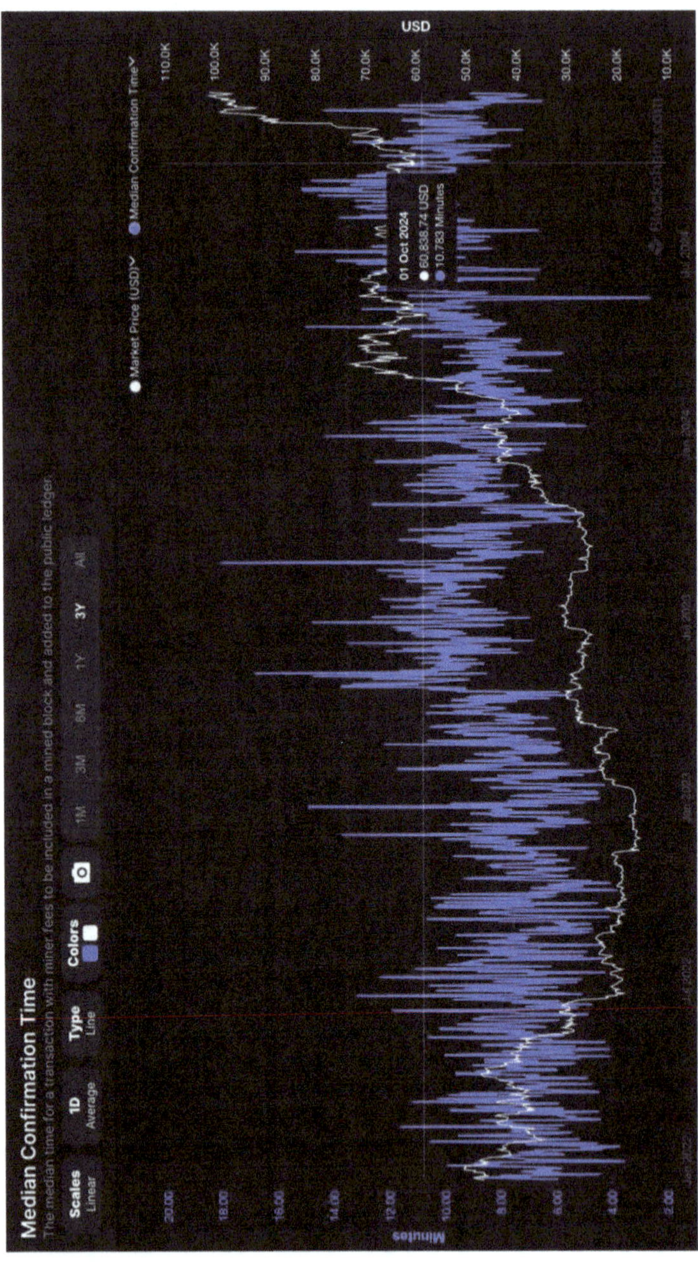

Figure 5-5. *bitcoin's median confirmation time of 10 minutes over a three-year period (compliments of* `https://www.blockchain.com/explorer/charts/median-confirmation-time`*)*

Investor Analysis of Transaction Speed and Gas Cost

Unfortunately, there is no straightforward answer that indicates the best transaction speed and gas costs. Near-instant transactions with free gas are the ideal outcome for end-user experience. However, as investors, this mindset is not practical, as it will exclude many potentially worthwhile investment opportunities—not to mention that miners and validators need to be paid for work done on the network without solely relying on newly minted coins as payment. Use cases like gaming, trading, DeFi platforms, and decentralized exchanges (DEXs) benefit from ultra-fast transaction speeds and minimal gas fees. No participant wants to wait ten minutes for an in-game purchase or close a decentralized exchange trade. However, outside of these high-frequency, real-time use cases, ultra-fast speeds are admirable but not always entirely essential.

While it is easy to get consumed and caught up in transaction speed and gas costs, most modern blockchains—especially those complemented with Layer 2 (L2) protocols—can process transactions in seconds or, at worst, within a minute or two. Therefore, most individuals taking advantage of a blockchain or dApp with a practical use case do not wait ten minutes for a transaction to clear unless they are specifically on a legacy PoW network. Most other blockchains, including layer two protocols that are either Proof-of-Stake (PoS), Delegated Proof-of-Stake (DPoS), or newer consensus models, typically achieve transactions from 5 to 60 seconds, which is considered good enough for most applications.

With respect to gas costs, for networks like Ethereum, fees fluctuate depending on the level of network traffic and congestion, sometimes with USD ranging from a few cents to a few dollars. As an investor, the primary focus is not just on the cost of fees at a specific moment—it is more important to predict if they are suitable for the use case in question. For example, if you want to invest in a gaming project, evaluating if the fees are low, stable, and fast enough to provide a smoother and more efficient gaming experience is advised. On the other hand, if a lending platform was being evaluated, a 60-second delay or a small fee might not matter at all. Nevertheless, that is not to say that instant transactions are more admirable than a 60-second wait time; it is just that they may not be as critical, depending on the use case.

Action Steps

Follow these steps to determine if a project offers fast transactions and low gas costs that align with its practical use case requirements.

1) **Determine the Transaction Speed and Gas Cost**

   a) Search for the network's gas price and transaction speed by performing a quick online search. For an example using Ethereum, browse keywords such as "*Ethereum's gas price and transaction speed native tracker*"—see Figure 5-6 for reference.

   b) If available, it is good practice to seek an average gas price through the "*heat map*"—see Figure 5-7 for reference.

   c) Advanced option—if you run your own node (or use a public RPC gateway), you can fetch the current gas price directly via the network's native API call—for Ethereum, for example, `eth_gasPrice` returns the value in wei.

***Figure 5-6.** Ethereum's gas prices with associated transaction speeds (compliments of `https://etherscan.io/gastracker`)*

***Figure 5-7.** Seven-day historical oracle gas price (compliments of `https://etherscan.io/gastracker#chart_gasprice`)*

2) **Evaluate Transaction Speed and Gas Cost Against Use Case**

   Determine if the transaction speed and gas cost align with the use case as discussed and the examples provided in this chapter. Additionally, evaluate against the following criteria.

   a) Does the project's speed and cost align with its purpose?

   b) Is the network's transaction time fast enough? If it's not under 1 minute, double-check if it makes sense for the dApp users.

   c) Be cautious of projects overselling "zero-fee" claims.

3) **Competitor Analysis**

   Check how the project's transaction speed and gas costs stack up against competitors to see if it offers better value for its purpose.

4) **Take Notes and Document Your Findings in Your Own Style**

5) **Combine the Findings with Other Sections of the Fundamental Evaluation Process**

Evaluation of the Results

If the results show that the transaction fees and gas costs are unsuitable for the use case requirements and operability, it is advised not to invest.

End-User Support and Communication

Evaluation Objective: Determine if the project team has adequate customer and communication support strategies.

Customer support and communication play a vital role in the blockchain industry for both the project team and end-users. New and complex technologies are constantly being introduced within the blockchain world; therefore, having reliable support and transparency is key to building trust. End-users rely on the project team's help to solve issues, provide direction guidance, and answer technical and non-general questions about the product or service. The team is also responsible for keeping the end-users informed with updates like platform upgrades, roadmap changes, new partnerships, and other important news about the product or service.

Why Is Customer Support and Communication

Customer support and communication from the project team are important for the following reasons:

- **Transparency** - Consistent updates on platform developments, security issues, and policy changes to maintain user trust.
- **Engagement** - When the project team actively participates in community discussions and interviews and responds to user inquiries, it helps generate and maintain a strong, growing community.
- **Education** - Provision of resources to the community, such as product tutorials, articles, and webinars on safe practices and blockchain technology, to help educate users.

- **Feedback** - Communication is essential for collecting and acting on user feedback to improve the product or services and address concerns from the community.
- **Social Media** - Maintaining an active presence on social platforms like X, YouTube, Telegram, and Discord keeps users updated while promoting positive community sentiment.

Evaluating a Project's End-User Support and Communication Strategies

Evaluate a project's level of end-user support and communication strategies against the following metrics criteria.

1) **Multi-channel Support** - People prefer different platforms, so the project team should be present on key social media channels. At a minimum, they should have a presence on X, YouTube, and Discord.
    - **Task -** Review the project's social or support channels and note typical response times (both peak and off-peak hours).
2) **Support Coverage** - Because crypto markets run 24/7, projects should aim for support that spans multiple time zones (e.g., staggered moderators or rotating shifts). Full round-the-clock coverage may be unrealistic for very small or early-stage teams, but long daylight gaps in responsiveness can still be a red flag.
    - **Task -** Visit the project's social media channels and any other support channels offered and analyze the times the team was responsive to the community and end-user.

3) **Quality of Responses** – The quality of support responses from the project team is vital and should be helpful, provide clarity, and be professional at all times.

   - **Task** – Analyze the team responses to user queries across the project's various social media channels. Were the responses helpful to the user?

4) **Response Time** – The project team should answer user queries and questions in a timely fashion. This helps with user retention and satisfaction.

   - **Task** – Measure the average response time from the project team **or active community moderators** to user questions through various support channels. Faster responses mean more efficient and timely help. For community-run projects, a response within a few hours is considered strong, while sub-hour replies remain exceptional.

5) **User Tutorials** – It is essential that platform and dApp tutorials are always available to users. This entails the installation process, onboarding instructions, operating guidelines, critical aspects that require caution, potential bugs, malfunctions, glitches, and anything else that enhances user retention and satisfaction.

   - **Task** – Visit the project website and confirm that dApp and platform tutorials are available.

6) **Project, Project, and dApp Updates** - It is imperative that the project team communicate various project, platform, and dApp updates in a timely manner. This also includes security updates on issues that may be harmful to users.

   - **Task -** Visit the project's social media channels and any other support channels offered and verify if the project team is posting regular updates. Are there any adverse reactions from the community regarding the lack of communication and updates?

Action Steps

Follow the steps below to determine if the project team has adequate customer and communication support strategies.

1) **Effective Customer Support and Communication Strategy Evaluation**

   Execute the tasks outlined in the *"Evaluating a Project's End-User Support and Communication Strategies" section.*

2) **Take Notes and Document Your Findings in Your Own Style**

3) **Combine the Findings with Other Sections of the Fundamental Evaluation Process**

Evaluation of the Results

It is not a deal breaker if the project team falls short on one of the six key end-user support and communication metrics discussed in this chapter. However, if there's a consistent pattern of weak performance across multiple aspects, exercise extreme caution—be aware of a possible red flag.

Digital Asset Exchanges

Evaluation Objective: Determine if the investment asset is listed on a tier-one exchange to confirm its credibility, legitimacy, liquidity, and accessibility for investors.

Digital asset exchanges are platforms where users trade digital assets, such as cryptocurrencies, tokens, and other assets, such as Non-Fungible Tokens (NFTs). These exchanges serve as a marketplace that connects users looking to buy or sell their digital assets, often using traditional fiat currency or other digital assets as a means of exchange.

As the digital asset market continues to grow, the role of digital asset exchanges has become increasingly important. These platforms provide essential infrastructure for the expanding digital asset ecosystem, allowing worldwide investors access to a wide range of digital assets. Therefore, understanding the dynamics of digital asset exchanges and the importance of asset listings on major platforms is essential for investors looking to reduce investment risk. A digital asset exchange's main key roles and functions are as follows.

- Providing a secure and user-friendly platform for trading digital assets.
- Establishing market prices through supply and demand dynamics.
- Offering liquidity by matching buyers and sellers.
- Facilitating the storage of digital assets through wallets.
- Providing features such as staking, leverage/margin trading, and other passive income strategies.
- Implementing regulatory compliance measures.

- Conducts a listing review—although standards vary by centralized exchange, and some CEXs will list projects primarily for an upfront fee, so diligence depth can differ.
- Providing access to trading tools, data, and analytics.

Types of Digital Asset Exchanges

There are two primary types of digital asset exchanges: ***centralized*** and ***decentralized.*** Although both exchange types serve the same purpose, they differ and function in different ways. Investors need to understand the core differences of each type to help identify project popularity, risk, and potential future growth.

Centralized Exchanges (CEX)

Examples: Coinbase, Bybit, Kraken, Kucoin
Total CEXs: 253 (at the time of writing this book)
A centralized exchange (CEX) is a digital asset trading platform where users can buy, sell, and trade digital assets with centralized companies such as Coinbase. These exchanges function as intermediaries, facilitating transactions between buyers and sellers while maintaining control over user funds and transactions.

Centralized exchanges typically offer visually appealing, user-friendly interfaces, a wide range of trading pairs, and high liquidity levels, making them popular among investors. However, they also require users to trust the exchange with their assets and personal information, which may expose them to security risks and privacy concerns. While some centralized exchanges are financially backed and insured, others are not. Therefore, you must check if the centralized exchange they want to avail of is insured before use so that you are protected, and your stolen assets will be refunded if an attack occurs.

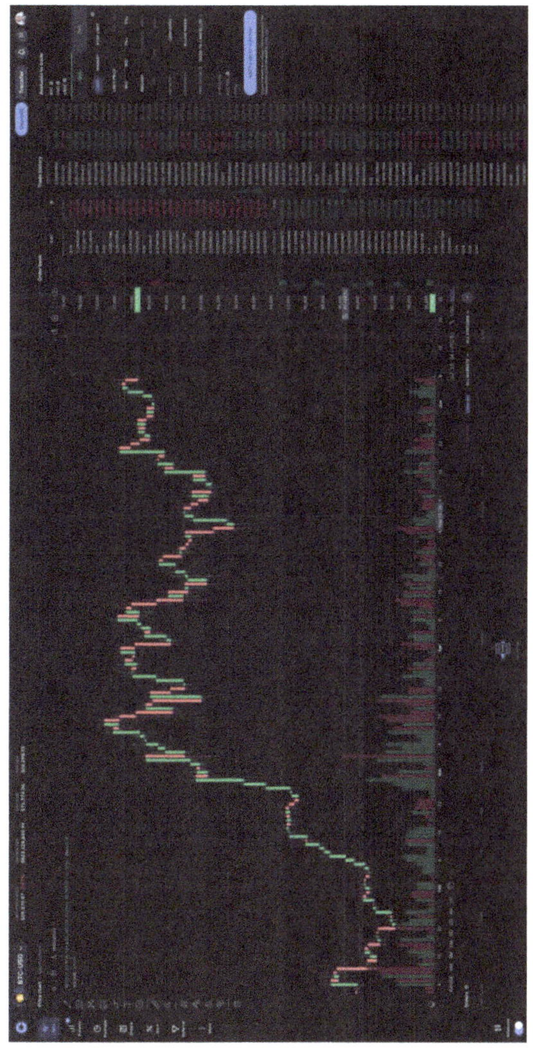

Figure 5-8. *Coinbase centralized exchange (compliments of* `https://www.coinbase.com/advanced-trade/spot/BTC-USD`*)*

Decentralized Exchanges (DEX)

Examples: Uniswap, dYdX, PancakeSwap

Total DEXs: 492 (at the time of writing this book)

A decentralized exchange (DEX) is, in essence, a decentralized application (dApp) that enables users to trade digital assets peer-to-peer without relying on a central authority or intermediary. DEXs utilize blockchain technology and smart contracts to facilitate peer-to-peer transactions between buyers and sellers, enabling users to connect their wallets and maintain control over their assets and private keys. Another core advantage of DEXs is that there are no geographical restrictions; therefore, investors can freely invest in any asset on the DEX without any limitations or user verification process.

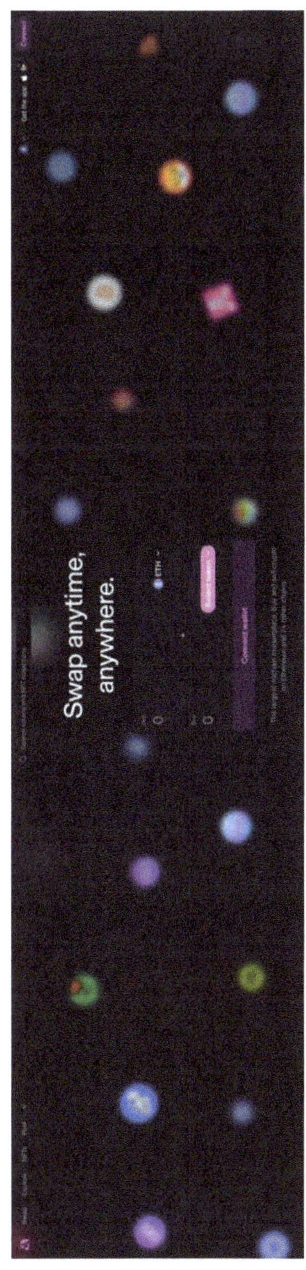

Figure 5-9. *Uniswap decentralized exchange (DEX) (compliments of* `https://app.uniswap.org/`*)*

Centralized and Decentralized Exchanges Compared

As discussed, CEXs and DEXs represent two distinct approaches to trading digital assets. Each type of exchange offers a unique set of features and trade-offs, catering to different investor needs. By analyzing these differences, investors can make informed decisions when selecting the most suitable trading platform for their specific requirements and investment goals.

Table 5-1. *Centralized and decentralized exchange comparison*

Centralized Versus Decentralized Digital Asset Exchanges		
	Centralized Exchanges (CEX)	**Decentralized Exchanges (DEX)**
User Interface	User-friendly interfaces and trading tools.	Improving usability with more intuitive designs is still generally more complex than CEX.
User Experience	Comprehensive customer support and user-friendly interfaces.	Limited or no customer support; users must manage issues independently.
Liquidity	High liquidity levels due to a large user base.	Increasing liquidity through innovations like liquidity pools and aggregators.
Trading Pairs and Fiat Support	Wide range of trading pairs, including fiat currencies.	Limited trading pairs and fiat support but improving via fiat on/off ramps and cross-chain protocols.

(*continued*)

Table 5-1. (*continued*)

Centralized Versus Decentralized Digital Asset Exchanges		
	Centralized Exchanges (CEX)	**Decentralized Exchanges (DEX)**
Multi-chain Asset Accessibility	Assets are easily traded with each other across multiple blockchains.	Rapid advancements in multi-chain trading via bridges and interoperable blockchains—but note that many bridges are semi-centralized and have become frequent hack targets.
Features	Advanced trading tools and charting features.	Limited user features but growing adoption of advanced tools like limit orders and analytics.
Security	Enhanced security measures, but risk due to centralization—single point of failure.	Reduced risk of hacks and breaches due to decentralization.
Regulatory Compliance	Adhere to regulatory requirements through KYC and AML processes.	Enhanced privacy and resistance to censorship.
Asset Control	Custodial—Users do not have full control of their digital assets.	Non-custodial—Users retain control of private keys and assets.

(*continued*)

Table 5-1. (*continued*)

Centralized Versus Decentralized Digital Asset Exchanges		
	Centralized Exchanges (CEX)	**Decentralized Exchanges (DEX)**
Privacy & Anonymity	Requires disclosure of personal information.	Allows for more anonymous trading, though some DEXs are integrating compliance tools.
Performance & Scalability	Fast transactions and overall speed (transactions processed through a centralized server)	Slower transaction speeds due to blockchain scalability issues, but Layer 2 solutions improve speed.
Transaction Fees	Fee schedules can be attractive for high-volume traders, though some Layer-2 or optimized-chain DEXs now match or even undercut CEX pricing.	Higher fees on congested blockchains; reduced fees on optimized chains or Layer 2.
Centralization Risks	Vulnerable to hacks, security breaches, and regulatory actions.	More resistant to these risks due to decentralization.
Transparency	Lack of complete transparency, with users sometimes receiving their transaction hash only after a successful transfer or withdrawal.	Higher level of transparency due to blockchain technology.
Examples	Binance, Coinbase, Gemini, Kraken, KuCoin.	Uniswap, SushiSwap, PancakeSwap, Curve, 1 inch, Balancer.

Benefits of Top-Tier CEX Listings

Although many advantages are associated with DEXs, asset listings on a top-tier centralized exchange have distinct advantages. One significant benefit is the increased liquidity, as top-tier centralized exchanges often aggregate larger trading volumes—though liquidity still varies by exchange and specific trading pair. This enables faster transactions and reduced-price slippage, leading to a smoother end-user and trading experience for investors.

Another significant advantage is the increased visibility and credibility of the asset. Investors often see top-tier centralized exchanges as more legitimate and trustworthy—the more substantial and reputable the exchange, the greater its credibility and visibility. Major tier-one exchanges execute a thorough vetting process on projects before listings are approved. This vetting process typically involves evaluating fundamentals such as the project's whitepaper, product or service, project team, infrastructure, current volume (if already listed), regulatory compliance, and overall market potential. This evaluation process enables CEXs to filter out potential scams or low-quality projects, protecting investors from possible losses. This process also attracts more users and investors to the token, contributing to its growth and adoption.

Transactions on top-tier CEXs are often faster and cheaper than those on main-chain DEXs; however, it's important to note that in recent times Layer-2 and other optimized DEXs have begun to match—or even exceed—CEX performance for certain pairs. On centralized exchanges, trades are matched off-chain, and the exchange later batches withdrawals for on-chain settlement—avoiding per-trade gas costs while still relying on the blockchain for final settlement. Furthermore, many top-tier exchanges offer tiered fee structures, meaning the more you trade, the lower the fees. For example, platforms like Binance or Kraken provide discounts for large-volume traders or those using platform-native tokens (e.g., BNB on Binance).

Considering all these factors, it is a considerable advantage for an asset to be listed on a DEX and a reputable, credible top-tier CEX. The end-user experience is enhanced by dual visibility, as CEXs offer fast transaction speed, low fees, ease of use, and project credibility. At the same time, DEXs provide transparency, worldwide accessibility, decentralized security, and self-custody.

Pro Tip Never invest in a project without confirming the correct token name, ticker symbol, and, most importantly, its contract address on CoinMarketCap. This particularly applies to tokens being purchased on decentralized exchanges, where thousands of fraudulent representations of legitimate tokens are sold to inexperienced investors.

Top-Tier CEX Asset Verification

Because of the numerous benefits of a top-tier CEX listing, it is recommended that investors verify whether the digital asset is approved and listed on a reputable top-tier exchange. This can be achieved with a few simple steps.

1) **Check the Asset's CEX Listings**

    a) Use the search bar at the top of CoinMarketCap's (`https://coinmarketcap.com/`) homepage to search for the project's token using the project's name or ticker symbol. See the example of the Polkadot Network in Figure 5-10.

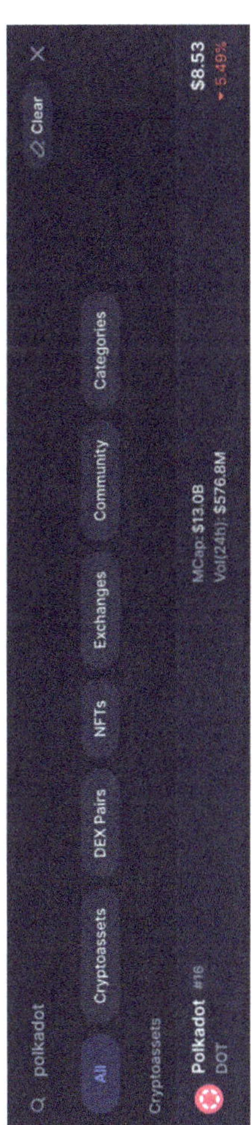

Figure 5-10. *Asset search bar at the top of the CoinMarketCap webpage (compliments of* `https://coinmarketcap.com/`*)*

b) Verify the token's details are correct by double-checking the project name ticker symbol and visiting the website link and social media. Also, take note of the contract address—this is crucial to avoid confusion with similarly named tokens or potential scams.

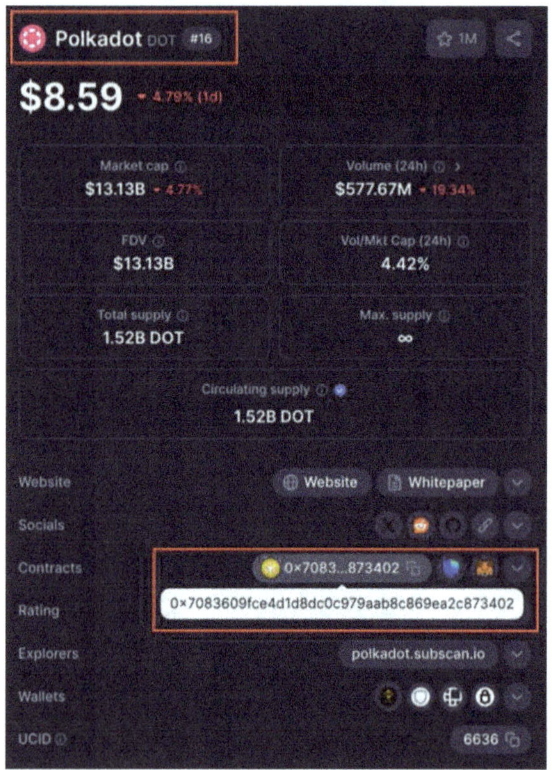

Figure 5-11. *Polkadot Network "DOT" coin and project details (compliments of `https://coinmarketcap.com/currencies/polkadot-new/`)*

c) Navigate to the "Market" tab to view a list of exchanges where the token is listed and the respective trading pairs available in each exchange. See the example of the Polkadot Network in Figure 5-12.

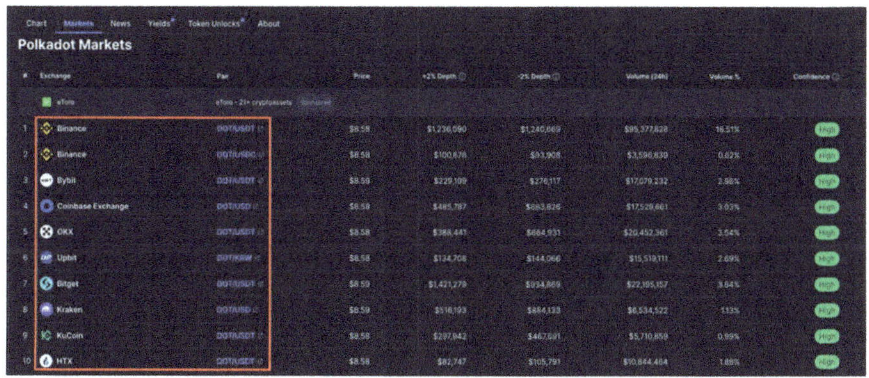

Chart | Markets | News | Yields | Token Unlocks | About

Polkadot Markets

#	Exchange	Pair	Price	+2% Depth	-2% Depth	Volume (24h)	Volume %	Confidence
	eToro	eToro - 21+ cryptoassets						
1	Binance	DOT/USDT	$8.58	$1,236,090	$1,240,669	$95,377,828	16.51%	High
2	Binance	DOT/USDC	$8.58	$100,678	$93,908	$3,596,839	0.62%	High
3	Bybit	DOT/USDT	$8.59	$229,109	$276,117	$17,079,232	2.98%	High
4	Coinbase Exchange	DOT/USD	$8.58	$485,787	$683,826	$17,529,661	3.03%	High
5	OKX	DOT/USDT	$8.58	$388,447	$664,931	$20,452,361	3.54%	High
6	Upbit	DOT/KRW	$8.58	$134,708	$144,066	$15,519,111	2.69%	High
7	Bitget	DOT/USDT	$8.59	$1,421,279	$934,869	$22,195,157	3.84%	High
8	Kraken	DOT/USD	$8.59	$516,193	$884,133	$6,534,522	1.13%	High
9	KuCoin	DOT/USDT	$8.58	$297,942	$467,691	$5,710,859	0.99%	High
10	HTX	DOT/USDT	$8.58	$82,747	$105,791	$10,844,484	1.88%	High

Figure 5-12. *Polkadot Network, available digital asset exchange platforms (compliments of* `https://coinmarketcap.com/currencies/polkadot-new/`*)*

2) **Identify Highly Ranked Tier-1 Digital Asset Exchanges**

a) From the CoinMarketCap home page, on the top menu bar, select "*Exchanges*" to view the most highly ranked exchanges in terms of traffic, liquidity, trading volumes, and confidence in the legitimacy of trading volumes reported. For instance, on CoinMarketCap's spot-exchange leaderboard, Binance is presently ranked #1 by reported trading volume, with Bybit and Coinbase appearing next on the list.

b) Investors can also view the ranking of the top derivative, decentralized, and lending platforms.

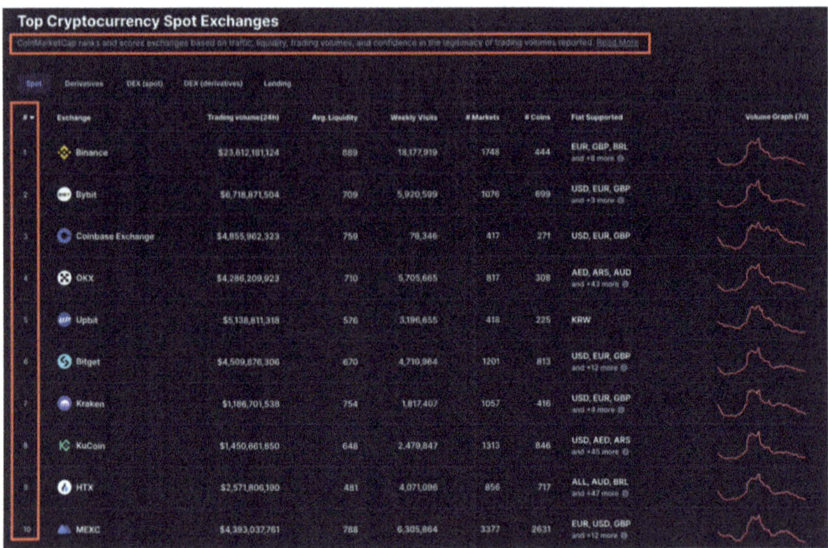

Top Cryptocurrency Spot Exchanges

CoinMarketCap ranks and scores exchanges based on traffic, liquidity, trading volumes, and confidence in the legitimacy of trading volumes reported. Read More

Spot | Derivatives | DEX (spot) | DEX (derivatives) | Lending

#	Exchange	Trading volume(24h)	Avg. Liquidity	Weekly Visits	# Markets	# Coins	Fiat Supported	Volume Graph (7d)
1	Binance	$23,612,181,124	889	18,177,919	1748	444	EUR, GBP, BRL and +8 more	
2	Bybit	$6,718,871,504	709	5,920,599	1076	699	USD, EUR, GBP and +3 more	
3	Coinbase Exchange	$4,855,962,323	759	78,346	417	271	USD, EUR, GBP	
4	OKX	$4,286,209,923	710	5,705,665	817	308	AED, ARS, AUD and +43 more	
5	Upbit	$5,138,811,318	576	3,196,655	418	225	KRW	
6	Bitget	$4,509,876,306	670	4,710,964	1201	813	USD, EUR, GBP and +12 more	
7	Kraken	$1,186,701,538	754	1,817,407	1057	416	USD, EUR, GBP and +4 more	
8	KuCoin	$1,450,661,650	648	2,479,847	1313	846	USD, AED, ARS and +45 more	
9	HTX	$2,571,806,190	481	4,071,096	856	717	ALL, AUD, BRL and +47 more	
10	MEXC	$4,393,037,761	788	6,305,864	3377	2631	EUR, USD, GBP and +12 more	

Figure 5-13. *Top highly ranked centralized digital asset exchanges from CoinMarketCap (compliments of* `https://coinmarketcap.com/rankings/exchanges/`*)*

3) **Compare Asset Markets to Top-Tier Exchanges**

   a) Verify if the exchanges that, e.g., the Polkadot Network "DOT" coin, are among the top-ranked CEXs on CoinMarketCap. It indicates high credibility and legitimacy if they appear in the top tier. For example, Polkadot's "DOT" is listed in nine of the top ten ranked exchanges, indicating strong credibility.

Action Steps

Follow the steps below to determine if the investment asset is listed on a tier-one exchange to confirm its credibility, legitimacy, liquidity, and accessibility for investors.

1) **Verify If the Asset Is Listed on a Top-Tier Exchange**

   Follow the steps outlined in the "*Top-Tier CEX Asset Verification*" section to verify if the asset is listed on top-tier centralized exchanges.

2) **Take Notes and Document Your Findings in Your Own Style**

3) **Combine the Findings with Other Sections of the Fundamental Evaluation Process**

Evaluation of the Results

When a digital asset is listed on a major tier-one digital exchange, it significantly enhances a project's visibility, credibility, and liquidity, attracting more investors and helping with the growth and adoption of the asset within the ecosystem.

Suppose an investor is interested in a specific digital asset not listed on any reputable exchange. In that case, it is important to exercise on the side of caution and avoid investing unless a green light is achieved after a full fundamental evaluation is carried out. This particularly applies to new start-up projects in their initial stages that may have failed or are still undergoing a rigorous vetting process executed by the tier-one exchange. Therefore, it is important to be aware that these projects carry extra risk and chances of poor liquidity.

The choice of exchange, whether a centralized, decentralized, low-tier, or high-tier exchange, depends on the risk level the investor is comfortable with. Understanding the associated risks thoroughly is essential before making any investment decisions.

CHAPTER 6

Blockchain Architecture

In this chapter, the architectural design of a blockchain project is analyzed. Blockchain architecture can be described as the design of the structural infrastructure that governs the core operation and interaction of participants on a peer-to-peer network. The same principle applies to a traditional business where embedded systems and procedures dictate day-to-day operations, manufacturing processes, marketing strategies, business development, and so on. The setup and design of these systems directly affect end-user experience, efficiency, profitability, and the reputation of the company.

In terms of blockchain technology, the architectural design affects scalability, interoperability, network congestion, transaction times, transaction speed, transaction cost, functionality, and security. For this reason, the architectural design of a company using blockchain technology is imperative to the project's success. The aim is to have a fast, efficient, high-performing, multi-feature blockchain with impressive interoperability features.

Fundamentals Discussed in This Chapter:

- Blockchain Architecture Layers
- Blockchain Trilemma
- Public, Private, Hybrid, and Consortium Blockchains

P. Garvey, *Blockchain Fundamental Analysis for Digital Asset Investors*,
https://doi.org/10.1007/979-8-8688-1551-5_6

- Permissionless and Permissioned Blockchains
- Anonymity and Privacy Enable Blockchains
- Governance
- Cross-Chain Interoperability

Blockchain Architectural Layers

Evaluation Objective: Assess the value and potential of Layer 0, 1, 2, or 3 blockchain projects, as well as any dApp built on top of these blockchains.

Blockchain layers are simply different levels, or layers, of a system stacked on top of each other and work together toward the overall goal of making the underlying blockchain function more efficiently. Multiple blockchain and protocol layers are often required because blockchains are imperfect and difficult to scale with the growing demand, resulting in network congestion, poor usability, slow transaction processing times, and high gas costs—frustrating to end-users.

Each layer complements the one below it, creating a more efficient system by adding new capabilities or improvements. These layers are denoted as L0 for Layer Zero, L1 for Layer 1, L2 for Layer 2, and L3 for Layer 3. Together, these layers improve the overall end-user experience and aim to meet the requirements of traditional companies that want to optimize their business through blockchain technology. Blockchain companies strive to design a robust blockchain system that can freely scale without any limitations. Unfortunately, at the time of writing this book, most blockchains cannot achieve this without the help of layered protocols.

It is worth noting that not every blockchain is multi-layered. There are plenty of blockchains that do not rely on L2s or L3s for support. In some cases, network traffic is minimal, making additional scaling layers unnecessary. A new or less popular blockchains may also lack the user base to justify such development. Furthermore, some blockchains are designed with advanced native scalability and interoperability features, eliminating the need for external layers. For example, Polkadot leverages its Relay Chain and parachains to achieve scalability and high throughput, bypassing the need for L2 or L3 solutions entirely.

By understanding blockchain layers, investors can make informed investment decisions. The first part of this section discusses the difference between the four architectural layers—L0 to L3—followed by an evaluation procedure, examining layers as standalone ecosystems for investment purposes.

Blockchain Layer Overview

The easiest way to introduce blockchain layers is by comparing them to different aspects of a building—see the following analogy for reference.

Layer 0 Blockchains - *The Foundation*
L0 provides the foundational infrastructure on which everything else is built. It also helps connect multiple blockchains, allowing them to communicate and transfer assets and information between one another.

Layer 1 Blockchain - *The Building*
L1 is the main blockchain protocol that operates independently or on top of an L0. This layer accommodates transaction execution, verification, and on-chain activities and operations.

Layer 2 Protocols - *The Utilities (AC, Water, Electricity, etc.)*
L2 is an optimization layer whose main job is to improve the efficiency of L1, helping to free up the L1 base layer, allowing it to scale and reduce transaction costs.

Layer 3 Protocols - *Advanced Features (Smart Systems)*
L3—built on top of L2—provides additional functionality, performance, and interoperability for dApps and blockchain infrastructure.

Table 6-1. Blockchain layered architectural structure

Layer 3 (L3) Protocols (e.g., Orbs Network)
Layer Two (L2) Protocols (e.g., Immutable X, Lightning Network)
Layer One (L1) Blockchains (e.g., Ethereum, Binance Chain, Moonbeam, Cardano, bitcoin)
Layer Zero (L0) Blockchains (e.g., Polkadot, Cosmos)

Layer Zero Blockchains

Examples: Polkadot Network, LayerZero, Cosmos Network
Layer Zero (L0) blockchains can run their own native chains and simultaneously serve as a foundational layer that higher systems—such as Layer 1 networks, Layer 2 solutions, sidechains, and dApps—build on while still operating independently. They provide the underlying security and enable frictionless cross-chain interoperability that facilitates the communication and seamless exchange of data and assets for all blockchains and platforms built on top. L0 strives to provide a one-time solution to tackle industry-known issues such as scalability and interoperability between blockchains, thus aiming to provide users with a seamless experience across multiple networks. Additionally, L0's allows developers to build innovative, custom-made, scalable blockchains and dApps with enhanced transaction speed, on-chain governance, interoperability, staking and privacy features, etc.

The Polkadot Network is an excellent example of an L0 blockchain that provides "parachain" infrastructure (Figure 6-1) that possesses a true multi "para"-chain application environment where enhanced scalability and cross-chain interoperability provide frictionless communication between and seamless data transfer across the multi-ecosystem network and beyond.

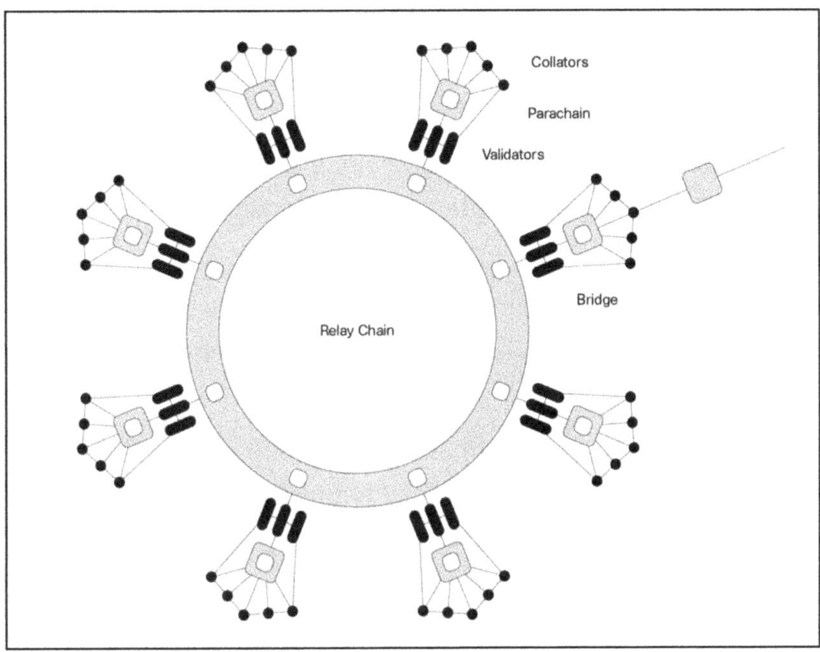

Figure 6-1. *Polkadot Network parachain architecture (compliments of `https://guide.kusama.network/docs/polkadot-v1/`)*

Core Components of Polkadot's Blockchain Infrastructure

Figure 6-1 shows Polkadot's overall architecture and corresponding components. Polkadot's Relay Chain—represented as a ring—acts as the main chain of the system and is surrounded by multiple parachains connected to it. Each parachain communicates with one another through the relay chain. The functionality of each core component of Polkadot's architecture (as outlined by Polkadot Network) is as follows:

- **Relay Chain** - The heart of Polkadot, responsible for the network's shared security, consensus, and cross-chain interoperability.
- **Validators** - Secure the Relay Chain by staking DOT, validating proofs from collators, and participating in consensus with other validators.
- **Parachain** - Sovereign blockchains that can have their own tokens and optimize their functionality for specific use cases.
- **Collators** - Maintain shards by collecting shard transactions from users and producing proofs for the validator.
- **Bridges** - Allow parachains and parathreads to connect and communicate with external networks like Ethereum and bitcoin.
- **Parathreads** - Similar to parachains but use a pay-as-you-go model; rather than locking up DOT for a long-term slot lease, a parathread pays a small fee each time it submits a block, so projects with sporadic activity avoid the higher cost of continuous connectivity.

Layer One Blockchains

Examples: Ethereum, BNB Chain, Moonbeam Network
Layer one (L1) blockchains, also known as *base layers,* provide a blockchain-based foundation on which developers can build all types of services, products, and software applications. L1s are typically standalone blockchain infrastructures that provide and utilize their own consensus method for securing the network. They rely on cross-chain bridges and other cross-chain interoperability methods to communicate with other

blockchains and ecosystems. A prime example of an L1 blockchain is Ethereum, which hosts thousands of dApps offering a wide range of products and services. Notable examples of these dApps include Uniswap, Aave, and OpenSea.

Although L1s are most often standalone infrastructures, they are sometimes supported and, in some ways, secured and supported by the underlying layer-zero network. As previously discussed, any L1 built on top of an L0 inherits admirable benefits such as cross-chain interoperability, enhanced security, and the potential to build custom-built L1 blockchains with ease of use.

Moonbeam Network is an excellent example of an L1 blockchain built on the Polkadot Networks L0 decentralized, secure, and scalable parachain infrastructure. Many dApps, including SushiSwap, Band Protocol, and Curve, are built on the Moonbeam Network. However, these dApps benefit from the security of Moonbeam and Polkadot's blockchain infrastructures, allowing for enhanced cross-chain "multi-ecosystem" interoperability, scalability, decentralized governance features, and low cost and rapid transaction processing.

Layer Two Protocols

Examples: Immutable, Lightning Network, Polygon zkEVM

A Layer 2 (L2) is a collective term for another blockchain or off-chain protocol solution layered on top of the underlying L1 blockchain. L2s are designed to address parent L1 blockchain issues such as network congestion, poor scalability, slow transaction speeds, high transaction fees, and overall poor user experience. This is achieved by scaling the underlying L1 blockchain by improving the throughput—the amount of work that can be processed from one location to another at any given time—and transaction processing speed.

L2 protocols work by batching and validating large batches of transactions off-chain before they are returned and processed on the parent blockchain. This removes and reduces the work an L1 blockchain must do as part of a typical consensus and transaction processing process. It is important to note that L2 protocol solutions derive security from their parent L1 blockchain.

Immutable X is a Layer 2 protocol on Ethereum that boosts throughput without sacrificing security or decentralization by using StarkWare's ZK-STARK-based *validium* system: batches of transactions are compressed into *"validity proof"* form and posted to Ethereum for final verification, while the data themselves are held off-chain. The proof is then sent to the Layer 1 parent blockchain (Ethereum) for processing. This technology is a combination of NFT-specific exchange, proof logic, and rollup technology developed by StarkWare. Immutable's cutting-edge Layer 2 NFT trading protocol allows for more than 9,000 NFT transfers, trades, and mints per second.

Another example of a Layer Two protocol is the bitcoin Lightning Network. The Lightning Network creates a second layer on top of the bitcoin blockchain that uses user-generated micropayment channels to aid faster and cheaper transactions without changing the block size.

Layer Three Protocols

Examples: *Orbs Network*

Layer three (L3) protocols—an emerging, loosely defined class built atop L2 solutions—aim to add extra functionality, interoperability, and performance for dApps and underlying blockchain infrastructure. They also offer application-specific functionalities with highly customizable options and security features for each dApp. Like L2 protocols, L3's protocols inherit and take advantage of the security of the underlying L1 blockchain, e.g., the Ethereum blockchain.

An example of an L3 is Orbs Network, a blockchain infrastructure designed for a broad range of on-chain DeFi applications—not just advanced trading. Orbs enhance DeFi functionality by supplying tools for aggregated liquidity, algorithmic and limit orders, decentralized derivatives, and other finance-focused modules.

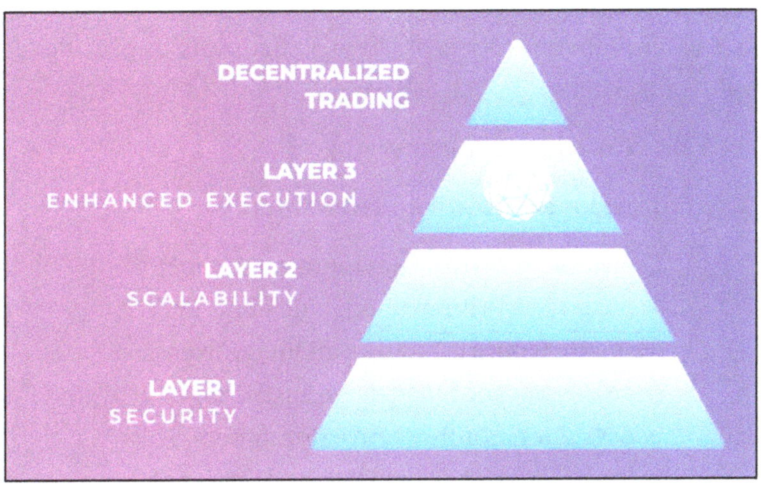

Figure 6-2. *Orbs—Layer 3 for decentralized trading*

Blockchain Layer "Ecosystem" Evaluation

When investing in Layer Zero (L0), Layer One (L1), Layer Two (L2), and Layer Three (L3) blockchains, it is beneficial if they are evaluated as ecosystems versus individual projects. A blockchain ecosystem is an interconnected network of on-chain blockchain-based applications, participants, and technologies built around a specific blockchain protocol. Instead of a single GDP-style metric, treat a blockchain ecosystem like an economy and examine multiple indicators—network activity, developer engagement, total value locked (TVL), and on-chain revenue—to gauge its capacity for value creation and innovation. Each ecosystem should be assessed as if it were a "country" to determine the overall health and value of the network under specific blockchain-focused evaluation criteria.

Although very important, the value of the blockchain ecosystem is not just about the technology, such as interoperability, scalability, and level of decentralization. The underlying value of a blockchain ecosystem is a result of and should be evaluated against such criteria as developer growth and retention, infrastructure technology strength, on-chain competition, and synergistic software clusters. The following sections detail how to evaluate a blockchain network ecosystem, with examples provided for each evaluation criterion.

1) **Value Creation Efficiency**

    a) **Developer Growth and Retention**

    Developer growth and retention are vital for an ecosystem's innovation, efficiency, and strength. Figure 6-3 shows an image from `DeveloperReport.com` detailing the top ecosystem's monthly active developers. This is further broken down into the number of full-time and total developers, indicating, as a percentage, if the number of developers has increased or decreased over one to two years. Investors can further manipulate this table to view the highest increase and decrease of developers per ecosystem.

Top Ecosystems Monthly Active Developers

	Full-Time Developers			Total Developers		
Ecosystem	JUL-01 2024	1y %	2y %	JUL-01 2024	1y %	2y %
Ethereum	2,788	-10%	-10%	8,865	-18%	-31%
Base	889	+14%	-	3,991	+52%	-
Polygon	834	-26%	-33%	2,877	-33%	-45%
Polkadot	761	-18%	-22%	2,414	-13%	-20%
Arbitrum	712	-20%	-6%	2,530	-10%	0%
Cosmos	683	-15%	-12%	2,272	-10%	-11%
Solana	664	-8%	-22%	2,856	+14%	-24%
Scroll	649	+4%	+23%	2,429	+14%	+12%
BNB Chain	556	-21%	-31%	2,015	-22%	-41%
Avalanche	496	-10%	-17%	1,706	-9%	-12%
Optimism	466	-23%	-20%	1,707	-14%	-13%
Bitcoin	358	-18%	-21%	1,246	-7%	-16%

Figure 6-3. *The top ecosystem's monthly active developers (compliments of `https://www.developerreport.com/`)*

Pro Tip View the "Developer Report" generated by Electric Capital to gain detailed insight into the developer metrics for the top ecosystems.

---

b) **Infrastructure Technological Strength**

Infrastructure accessibility and ease of use of features and dApps, such as decentralized wallets and various browser extensions for buying, selling, and trading digital assets, are critical to support the growth of an ecosystem. The number of software applications in a specific niche for a particular ecosystem can be easily obtained by visiting `AlphaGrowth.io`.

Choose the desired ecosystem and dApp type from the dropdown menu to display the number of dApps for that specific niche in the selected ecosystem. As an example, Figure 6-4 shows the details and the number of decentralized wallet applications for the Ethereum blockchain—a total of 62 at the time of writing this book.

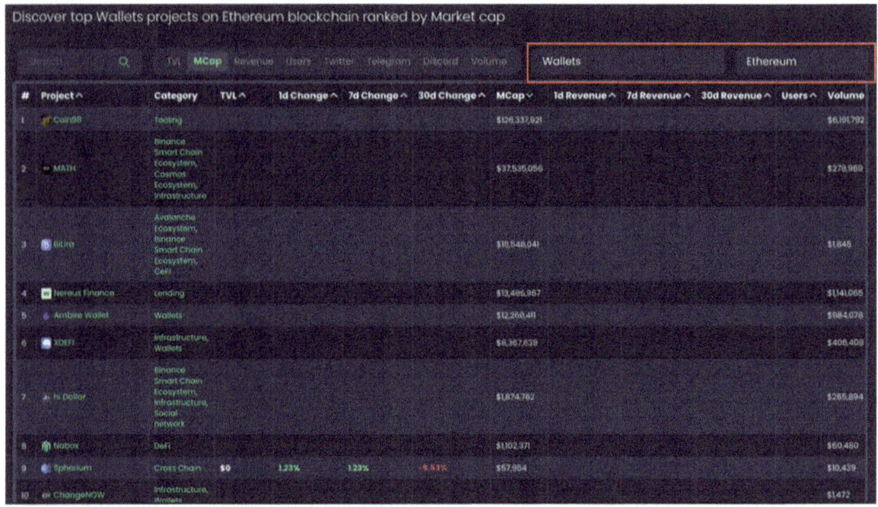

Figure 6-4. *Top wallets on the Ethereum blockchain ranked by market capitalization (compliments of `https://alphagrowth.io/projects/top-wallets-projects-on-ethereum-by-market-cap-value`)*

Pro Tip Because Ethereum is the oldest and most mature smart-contract platform, boasting the longest track record and a broad dApp ecosystem, it is advised to compare all findings against Ethereum under the same analysis parameters. This will provide a good indication of how equipped the infrastructure's technological strength is compared to Ethereum.

In addition to decentralized wallets and various types of browser extensions, it is imperative that an ecosystem has adequate developer software and learning-based coding applications with supporting documentation for new creators joining the ecosystem—a quick and easy check can help determine this. For example, a simple browser check for Ethereum's developer tools helped locate Ethereum's learning tools on Ethereum.org (`https://ethereum.org/en/developers/learning-tools/`). Ethereum's learning portal contains dozens of applications where newcomers can learn to write code and deploy in a test environment—see Figure 6-5. Furthermore, there is a significant amount of supporting documentation available for Ethereum, catering to a wide range of expertise from beginner to advanced. This includes categories such as introductions, fundamentals, smart contracts, and a variety of tutorials.

Outside of the developer software and documentation available through Ethereum.org, many websites provide learning tools, environments, and supporting documentation to help newcomers learn Ethereum's native language, Solidity. Use Ethereum as a baseline because it's been around the longest and offers plenty of developer tools and guides.

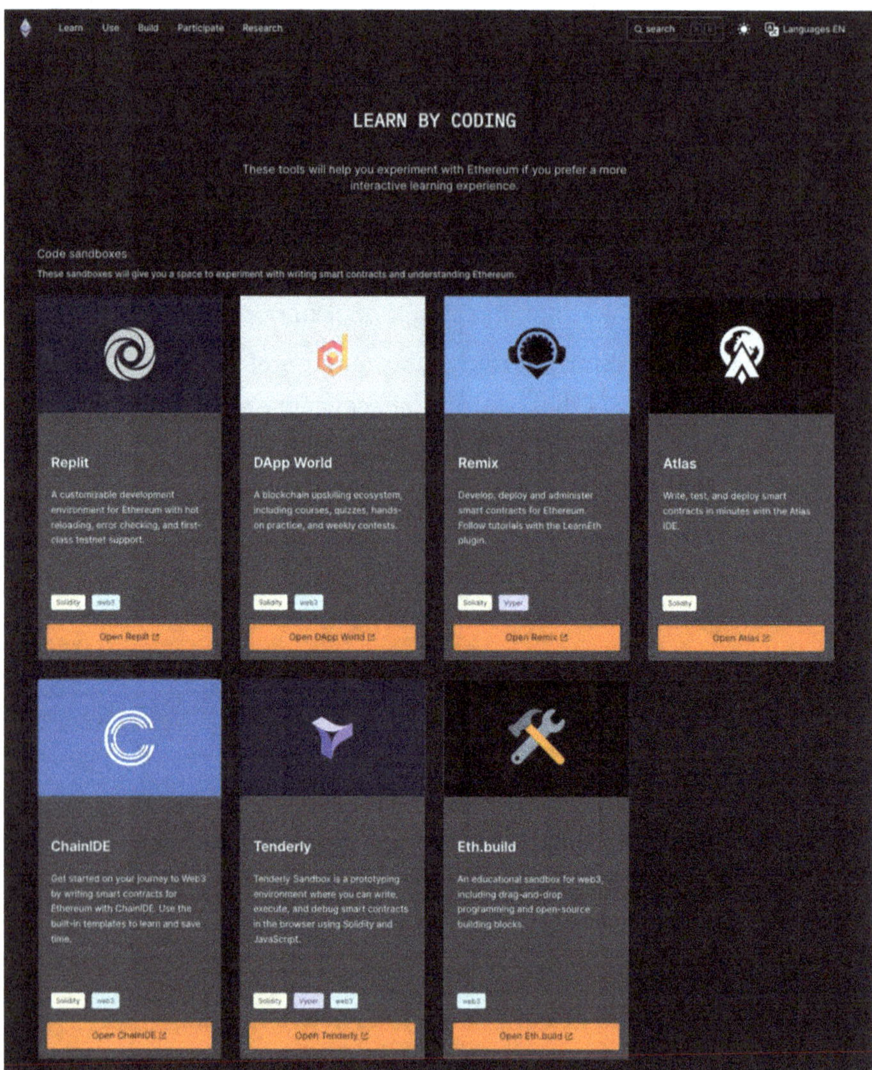

Figure 6-5. *Ethereum's learning portal containing dozens of applications where newcomers can learn to write code and deploy in a test environment (compliments of `https://ethereum.org/en/developers/learning-tools/`)*

2) **On-Chain Competition and Synergy**

   a) **On-Chain Competition**

      To support and nurture a growing ecosystem, there must be adequate competition between dApps of the same niche in one ecosystem. Without direct competition of software applications providing the same product or service, it creates an unwanted monopoly, hindering innovation, leading to stagnation in development, higher costs for users, and a poor and inefficient ecosystem.

      The most efficient way for investors to check for the on-chain competition is to visit `AlphaGrowth.io`, filter for the required ecosystem, and filter again for the specific product or service offered. For example, Figure 6-6 shows an image from `AlphaGrowth.io` (`https://alphagrowth.io/projects/top-dex-projects-on-binance-smart-chain-by-tvl`) where all decentralized exchanges (DEX), 369 DEXs in total, are built on Binance Smart Chain. The high DEX count on BSC shows plenty of activity; however, it's important to note that many of these projects are simple forks with low volume, so verify quality and real usage in addition to the headline data.

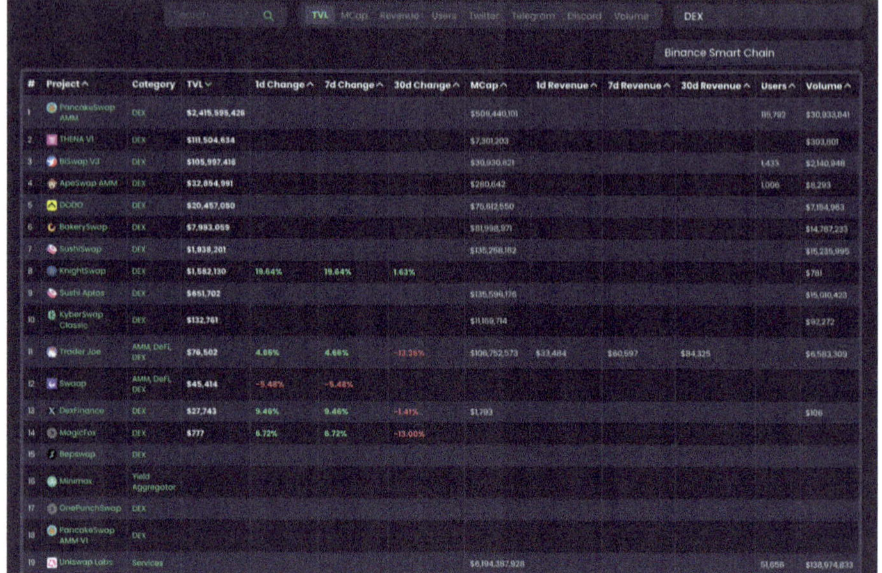

TVL MCap Revenue Users Twitter Telegram Discord Volume DEX

Binance Smart Chain

#	Project	Category	TVL	1d Change	7d Change	30d Change	MCap	1d Revenue	7d Revenue	30d Revenue	Users	Volume
1	PancakeSwap AMM	DEX	$2,415,595,426				$509,440,101				115,792	$30,933,841
2	THENA V1	DEX	$111,504,634				$7,301,203					$303,801
3	BiSwap V3	DEX	$105,997,416				$30,930,821				1,433	$2,140,948
4	ApeSwap AMM	DEX	$32,854,991				$280,642				1,006	$8,293
5	DODO	DEX	$20,457,080				$75,612,550					$7,184,963
6	BakerySwap	DEX	$7,983,059				$81,998,971					$14,787,233
7	SushiSwap	DEX	$1,938,201				$135,298,182					$15,235,995
8	KnightSwap	DEX	$1,582,130	19.64%	19.64%	1.63%						$781
9	Sushi Aptos	DEX	$651,702				$135,596,176					$15,010,423
10	KyberSwap Classic	DEX	$132,761				$11,169,714					$92,272
11	Trader Joe	AMM, DeFi, DEX	$76,502	4.66%	4.66%	-13.35%	$106,752,573	$33,484	$60,597	$84,325		$6,583,309
12	Swaap	AMM, DeFi, DEX	$45,414	-5.48%	-5.48%							
13	DexFinance	DEX	$27,743	9.46%	9.46%	-1.41%	$1,793					$106
14	MagicFox	DEX	$777	6.72%	6.72%	-13.00%						
15	Bepswap	DEX										
16	Minimax	Yield Aggregator										
17	OnePunchSwap	DEX										
18	PancakeSwap AMM V1	DEX										
19	Uniswap Labs	Services					$6,194,387,928				51,656	$138,974,833

Figure 6-6. *DEXs available on Binance Smart Chain (369 in total at the time of writing this book) (compliments of `https://alphagrowth.io/projects/top-dex-projects-on-binance-smart-chain-by-tvl`)*

b) **On-Chain Synergy**

Every crypto project has a specific product or service offering that creates value for users and customers—this is known as the value proposition. Like traditional centralized companies, blockchain-based projects often integrate and complement each other's products and services to enhance customer value. These projects typically exhibit synergy and are often within the same or similar sectors. Additionally, when working together, they can achieve a greater value output than they would by operating independently.

For an ecosystem to thrive and reach its full potential, it must incorporate a diverse range of crypto projects from various sectors that support each other's growth. There are dozens of types of potential crypto project combinations that have potential synergy with one another, including DeFi dApps with gaming, NFTs with DeFi, stablecoins with DeFi, DeFi with real-world asset tokenization applications, various combinations of L1s, L2s, and L3s, and DEXs and layered blockchains, as in the case of Sushi and ZetaChain, in which, through Sushi's integration with ZetaChain, users can swap native BTC across as many as 30 blockchain networks, though the feature relies on cross-chain messaging and is being rolled out in stages. It is the investor's responsibility to confirm that the ecosystem they are investing in—whether in an L0, L1, L2, or L3—features a diverse range of project types, with many projects within each category to drive long-term growth and synergy. This principle also applies when investing in a dApp-based project within an ecosystem. A large, thriving ecosystem with a diverse selection of dApps working in synergy provides a blooming environment for the project to grow to its full potential. Without a thriving ecosystem, the potential growth of any dApp can be significantly hindered. The most effective way for investors to verify this information is by visiting AlphaGrowth.io, where they can filter results based on whether they are investing in a dApp or a layered blockchain project—examples of each are provided for reference.

Layer "Ecosystem" Blockchain Project Investment

To check if an L0, L1, L2, or L3 ecosystem has a diverse selection of project types with a substantial number of projects within each selection type, visit AlphaGrowth.io and filter for the project you want to invest in. Review the specified project categories within that ecosystem, including the number of projects within each category. For example, Figure 6-7 shows some of the projects built on Cosmos Network, a layer zero blockchain, with the category of each project within the Cosmos ecosystem shown in the second column. It is also feasible to filter by category if desired. Always compare the results to popular and elite ecosystems.

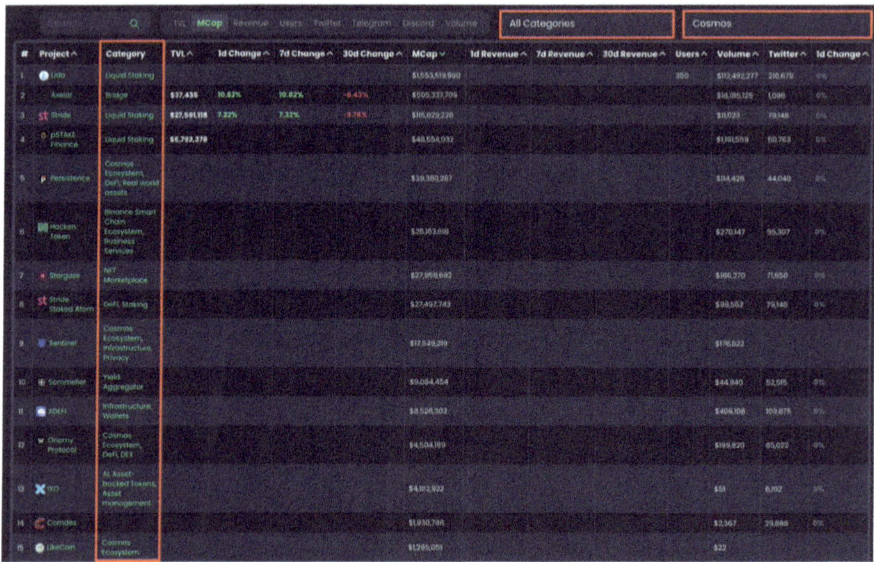

#	Project	Category	TVL	1d Change	7d Change	30d Change	MCap	1d Revenue	7d Revenue	30d Revenue	Users	Volume	Twitter	1d Change
1	Lido	Liquid Staking					$1,553,519,990				350	$112,492,277	216,679	0%
2	Axelar	Bridge	$37,435	10.82%	10.82%	-6.43%	$505,337,709					$16,095,125	1,098	0%
3	Stride	Liquid Staking	$27,591,118	7.32%	7.32%	-3.78%	$115,029,220					$11,023	79,148	0%
4	pSTAKE Finance	Liquid Staking	$6,793,379				$48,554,032					$1,191,559	50,763	0%
5	Persistence	Cosmos Ecosystem, DeFi, Real world assets					$39,380,267					$114,426	44,040	0%
6	Hacken Token	Binance Smart Chain Ecosystem, Business Services					$28,163,818					$270,147	95,307	0%
7	Stargaze	NFT Marketplace					$27,959,682					$166,270	71,650	0%
8	Stride Staked Atom	DeFi, Staking					$27,497,743					$99,562	79,148	0%
9	Sentinel	Cosmos Ecosystem, Infrastructure, Privacy					$17,549,219					$176,622		
10	Sommelier	Yield Aggregator					$9,084,454					$44,940	52,515	0%
11	XDEFI	Infrastructure, Wallets					$8,526,302					$406,108	109,875	0%
12	Onomy Protocol	Cosmos Ecosystem, DeFi, DEX					$4,504,189					$199,820	65,022	0%
13	IXO	AI, Asset-backed Tokens, Asset management					$4,182,922					$51	6,192	0%
14	Comdex						$1,930,786					$2,367	29,888	0%
15	LikeCoin	Cosmos Ecosystem					$1,295,051					$22		

Figure 6-7. *Projects built on Cosmos Network with corresponding project categories (compliments of* `https://alphagrowth.io/projects/top-all-projects-on-cosmos-by-market-cap-value`*)*

Decentralized Application (dApp) Investment

When investing in a dApp, investors must first determine the ecosystem (blockchain network) of which the dApp is a part. A large, thriving ecosystem with a wide selection of dApps working in synergy with one another provides a blooming environment, enabling the project (dApp) to grow to its full potential. Opposingly, an ecosystem with poor diversity, coupled with a low number of projects within the network, will hinder the growth of any project within the ecosystem. Figure 6-8, from AlphaGrowth.com, shows a DeFi project named Aave, which shows all the blockchains Aave is available on, highlighted in the red box.

Once the name of the ecosystem the dApp resides in is established, then evaluate the ecosystem as per the steps previously outlined in *"Layer 'Ecosystem' Blockchain Project Investment."* If the dApp is within a thriving ecosystem, it has higher chances of success than the same dApp in an ecosystem with poor diversity and a low project number count.

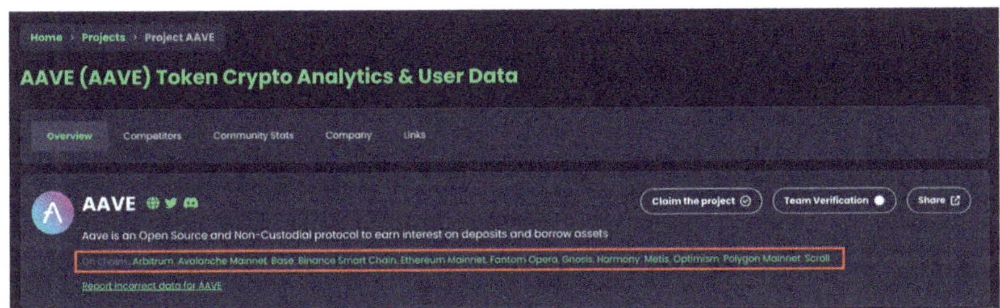

Figure 6-8. *Aave (DeFi project) showing all available chains (ecosystems) Aave is on (compliments of `https://alphagrowth.io/aave`)*

Action Steps

Follow the steps below to assess the value and potential of Layer 0, 1, 2, or 3 blockchain projects and any dApp built on top of these blockchains.

1) **Identify the L0, L1, L2, or L3 Ecosystem for Evaluation**

2) **Evaluate the Ecosystem as Described in the Section** "Blockchain Layer 'Ecosystem' Evaluation"

3) **Take Notes and Document Your Findings in Your Own Style**

4) **Combine the Findings with Other Sections of the Fundamental Evaluation Process**

Evaluation of the Results

Suppose the results from the evaluation indicate a poor ecosystem. In that case, it is advised to take note of your findings and perform the analysis again later to determine if there are signs of progress. There may be a situation where the project is a new startup and may need time to gain traction. Regardless, investing in a miniature ecosystem with only under one hundred projects is risky unless it excels in every other aspect of the full fundamental analysis.

Blockchain Trilemma

Coined by Vitalik Buterin, the creator of Ethereum, the *blockchain trilemma* points out that the three critical elements that characterize a blockchain—*decentralization*, *security*, and *scalability*—cannot perfectly coexist. Developers keep refining protocols to balance decentralization, security, and scalability, but at present some trade-off is always required; as a blockchain's user base grows, one of the three elements is inevitably affected. In most cases, if a blockchain is highly secure and scalable, then decentralization is affected, or if a blockchain is decentralized and secure, scalability is affected. This is one of the most challenging obstacles to overcome with blockchain technology and directly impacts the end user. The key challenge is to achieve scalability, security, and decentralization simultaneously.

An example of this is the Ethereum blockchain. While Ethereum is highly secure and close to being completely decentralized, it suffers massive scalability issues. The battle to combat the blockchain trilemma issue is ongoing. Ongoing research—such as roll-ups, sharding, and modular designs—continues to chip away at the trilemma, though a complete solution is still uncertain. Polkadot Network's relay chain and parachain design improves scalability and interoperability, yet this comes with its own decentralization trade-offs—so the trilemma is eased, not fully solved.

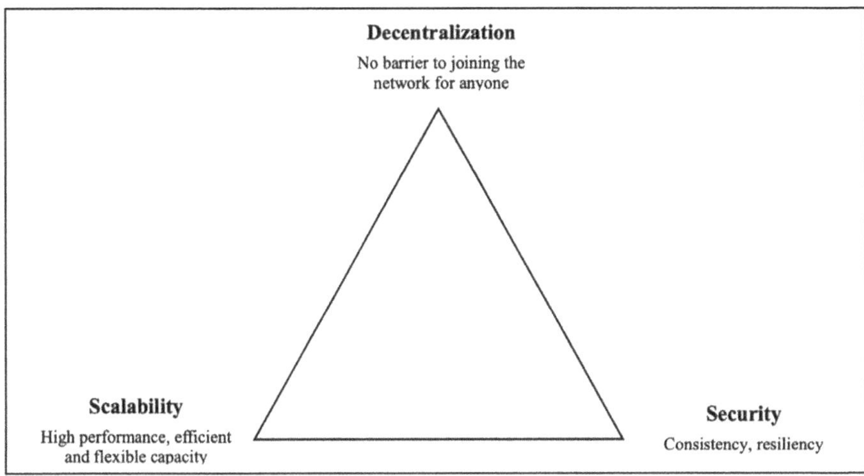

Figure 6-9. *Blockchain Trilemma*

Before investing in a blockchain-based project, it's essential to understand its limitations and challenges regarding scalability, security, and decentralization. These aspects can significantly affect the project's profitability, usability, and overall performance. The following sections discuss each of the three characteristics of the Blockchain Trilemma—decentralization, scalability, and security—and highlight the potential risks and key items to examine before investing.

Decentralization

Evaluation Objective: Determine if a project exhibits centralized traits that could undermine its performance, security, and long-term success or sustainability.

This section covers centralized systems, decentralized systems, and Distributed Ledger Technology (DLT). Investors need to understand the basics of this technology, as it is the backbone of blockchain technology. The long-term dangers of projects implementing specific centralization processes are discussed. It is imperative that these centralized processes, such as online storage, governance structures, and mining clusters, do not jeopardize the long-term security and performance of the product or service offered. Additional centralized factors impacting decentralization are also discussed, equipping investors with valuable insights into potential pain points to evaluate before investing.

When a new company decides which decentralized or centralized network to elect, there is no right or wrong answer. It solely depends on the type of business, specifications, and operational requirements. Crypto projects are mainly decentralized; however, the level of decentralization varies from project to project. Many projects have a strong centralized aspect with respect to governance, which dictates the entire operation and direction of the blockchain. This means a central authority decides on factors such as staking, vesting, token allocations, fees, mining rewards, and inflation and deflation rates.

One of the biggest perks of decentralization is that it creates transparency and gives real power—like voting rights—back to the community. However, when parts of a project are centralized, it defeats the whole purpose. If you are investing in decentralized digital assets, it's important to look closely at how decentralized they are. Check if any centralized aspects could impact the project's security, performance, or long-term success.

Table 6-2 details the structure of centralized, decentralized, and distributed systems. For simplicity, centralized systems are examined first, then moving on to decentralized and distributed systems, including decentralized distributed ledger technology.

Table 6-2. *Centralized, decentralized, and distributed communication systems*

Centralized, Decentralized, and Distributed Communication Systems		
Centralized	**Decentralized**	**Distributed**
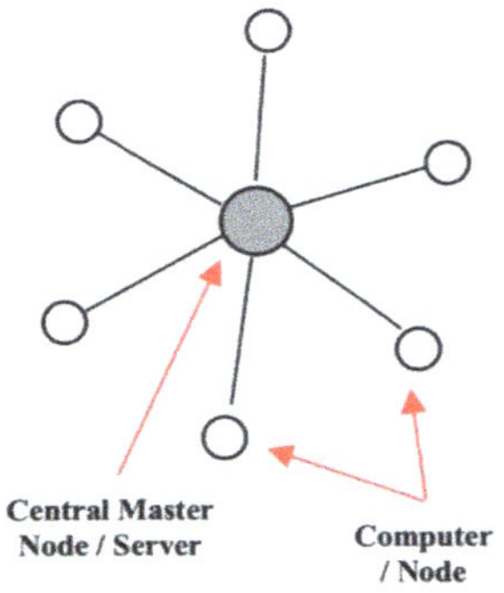 Central Master Node / Server Computer / Node	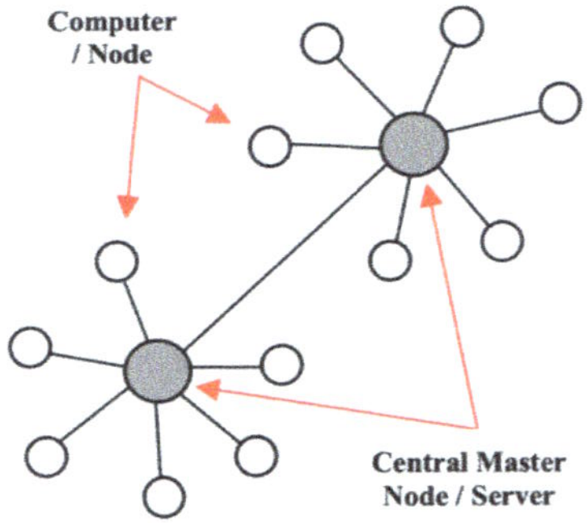 Computer / Node Central Master Node / Server	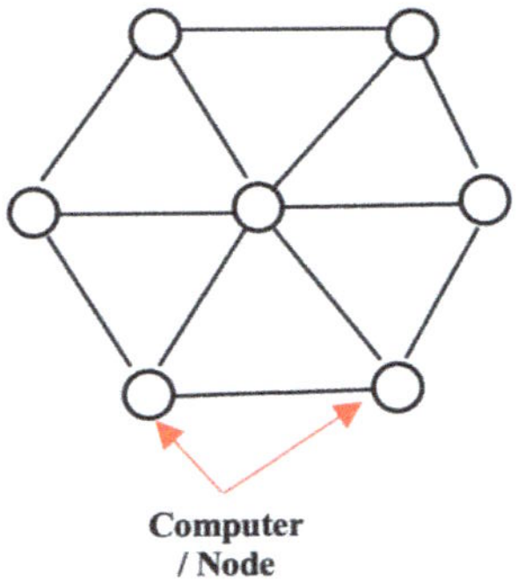 Computer / Node
Advantages • Simple, rapid deployment • Affordable maintenance • Consistency • Dedicated resources • Quick updates • Great UI/UX	**Advantages** • Increased flexibility/scalability • Faster performance • Enhanced privacy • High availability • Autonomy/self-governance • Promotes individual freedoms • Reduces power asymmetries	**Advantages** • Extreme fault tolerance • Speed and scalability • Enhanced transparency • Increased reliability and availability • Improved performance

(continued)

Table 6-2. (*continued*)

Centralized, Decentralized, and Distributed Communication Systems		
Centralized	**Decentralized**	**Distributed**
Disadvantages	**Disadvantages**	**Disadvantages**
• Increased downtime risks • High dependency on network connectivity • Higher security risks • Limited scalability • Less possibility of data backup	• High maintenance costs • Coordination issues • Increased downtime risks if main servers all crash • High-security risks • Limited scalability	• High maintenance costs • Coordination issues • Sometimes challenging to achieve consensus

Centralized Systems

Central networks are the most common type of system used today. They are a type of network configuration where participants go through a single central authority in order to communicate with one another. The central authority handles, stores, and processes user data; access is typically permission-based and restricted to approved parties rather than open to everyone on the network. As per Table 6-2, the central authority is known as a *central master node or server*. Connected to the master node are several standard nodes (computers), often called client nodes. Client nodes connect to the main server and can submit data requests instead of performing them directly.

In a centralized network, only known and identified parties can transact on the network. Therefore, all transactions or requests from client nodes can be audited. A simple audit can identify any bad actors on the network who are acting maliciously. With respect to governance, the entire network is governed and controlled by the owners or central authority. Network participants have little to no rights or influence over the structural changes or direction of the network. All user rights are controlled by the central governing authority and are typically limited.

It is important to note that in a centralized system, all network participants (clients) cannot communicate directly with one another without the help of the central server, which is also known as a master node. If the central node were to fail, then the system would break and could cause serious issues such as security breaches and system downtime—this is known as a single point of failure. This single point of failure is attractive to hackers, and if breached, the data can easily be exploited by malicious actors on the network.

An example of a centralized system is `Dropbox`, whereby each user communicates and is connected through a central master node. Let's assume Bob wants to share a document with Alice via Dropbox. He would first invite Alice to view the document by sharing a Dropbox link (or equivalent method). When Alice clicks on the link, she will connect to the Dropbox main server (master node), where Bob has stored and saved the document. Centralized systems are the most common type of system adopted in organizations where a client sends a request to a company server and receives the response. Other types of centralized systems include traditional banks, centralized databases, AWS, YouTube, Reddit, IBM, and Wikipedia.

Decentralized Systems

As per the Merriam-Webster dictionary, *decentralization* can be defined as the process by which the activities of an organization, particularly those regarding planning and decision-making, are distributed or delegated away from a central authoritative location or group. An important factor of a decentralized system is that each network node has a vote in the case of a governance referendum. Furthermore, there is no single entity, or master node, that receives and responds to requests. As per Table 6-2, there are at least two master nodes in a decentralized network. These master nodes can communicate with one another, enabling all nodes—also known as peers—on the network to communicate with each other. Most decentralized networks use a peer-to-peer (P2P) architecture—nodes talk directly to one another without a single master—but some projects adopt federated or hybrid models that still distribute control away from one central entity.

Take a traditional cloud storage system, for example. In a centralized system, when individuals upload and save data to the "cloud," it is sent and saved on a server farm called a data center. Data centers contain thousands of servers and hard drives that store our information. Unfortunately, this system has many flaws. The organizations that own these cloud storage systems have complete control of customer data—or assets—and sometimes, this data is exploited for profits. In addition, data centers are a single point of failure, meaning that if something were to happen to this data center, such as a destructive fire, a virus, a cyberattack, or the internet stopped working for whatever reason, customer data would be in grave danger.

Decentralization addresses the problems commonly found in centralized systems. A powerful core element of decentralization is that information is spread across many nodes—often via a distributed ledger in blockchain systems, though other decentralized designs may use federated storage or gossip protocols. This means that a decentralized system is not dependent on a single master node or point of failure, like a centralized system. Thus, decentralization is a type of network redundancy that ensures fewer entities do not control the network. This is one of the key factors and benefits of decentralization. If a bad actor tries to corrupt a node, the attempt is rejected by the rest of the network unless the attacker controls a majority of its consensus resources—e.g., over 51 percent of total hash power in a **proof-of-work** chain, or a supermajority of staked tokens in a **proof-of-stake** network—conditions that are economically and technically hard to achieve.

Through on-chain governance, decentralization allows network participants—network nodes and token holders—to vote in on-chain referendums that help direct and control the blockchain's operations. Decentralization is an essential property of public open-source blockchain networks where participants can read, write data, and contribute to consensus without authorization.

A decentralized blockchain also provides the ability to validate transactions and smart contracts without the need for a trusted authority, e.g., a bank. It creates censorship resistance, as no central authority can govern and dictate what happens with your digital property. This is one of the primary reasons why, in recent times, much focus has been placed on decentralized systems over centralized systems. For example, through decentralized finance, people have rights and permissions to govern and control their assets without any interference from centralized entities—this is known as *autonomy*, which is the right to self-govern one's assets. In addition, unlike centralized systems, decentralization provides benefits and features such as transparency, efficiency, cost savings, development of trusted ecosystems, and, in some cases, privacy and anonymity.

Centralized Versus Decentralized Systems

There has been much debate over centralized versus decentralized systems. User requirements play a major role for companies when deciding to run with centralized or decentralized networks for business operations, with some even going hybrid. There may be cases whereby using a decentralized network may not make sense or be adequate for the requirements and specifications required by the central authority. However, despite current scalability and power consumption issues, decentralized systems advance daily and have significant advantages over traditional centralized systems. Table 6-3 highlights the pros and cons of centralized and decentralized networks.

Table 6-3. *Centralized versus decentralized systems*

Traditional Centralized Systems Versus Public Decentralized Blockchains		
Feature	**Centralized Systems**	**Decentralized Systems**
Ownership	Service Provider	All Users
Architecture	Client/Server	Decentralized distributed technologies
Security	Can be highly secure when well-designed, but relies on one administrative domain	Reduces single points of failure, yet introduces new attack surfaces and coordination risks
High availability	Yes (via redundancy, load balancing, and failover mechanisms)	Yes

(continued)

Table 6-3. *(continued)*

Traditional Centralized Systems Versus Public Decentralized Blockchains		
Feature	**Centralized Systems**	**Decentralized Systems**
Fault tolerance	Yes (achieved via redundant servers, backups, and automated failover)	Yes
Collusion resistance	Basic, because it's under the control of a group or even a single individual	High resistance, as a consensus algorithm, ensures defense against adversaries
Application Architecture	Single application	Application replicated across all nodes on the network
Trust	Consumers have to trust the service provider	No mutual trust required
Cost to consumer	Typically higher (provider fees or subscriptions)	Often lower, but can spike with network-based fees (e.g., gas); cost varies by use case
Anonymity	Generally limited (identity or KYC is often required; a few services offer partial pseudonymity)	Protocol-dependent; most are pseudonymous rather than fully anonymous
Privacy	No	Yes (but in most cases, not transactional data)
Transparency	No	Yes
Governance/Voting Rights	No	Yes

(continued)

Table 6-3. *(continued)*

Traditional Centralized Systems Versus Public Decentralized Blockchains		
Feature	**Centralized Systems**	**Decentralized Systems**
Latency	Low latency, direct communication minimizes delays	Higher latency due to distributed consensus
Energy Costs	Low energy costs	Higher, especially in proof-of-work (PoW) systems

Distributed Ledger Technology

Distributed ledger technology (DLT) is a type of technological infrastructure that allows for simultaneous access, validation, and recording and updating across a networked database of interconnected nodes (computers). Think of it as a decentralized record-keeping system where several spread-out parties—nodes—collectively work together to execute specific tasks and maintain a shared database known as a ledger. When a data change is proposed, the network first reaches consensus; once agreement is achieved, the new information is committed and replicated across all nodes, ensuring every copy of the ledger remains identical.

In a distributed ledger network, data is shared among peer nodes to accomplish a specific task, such as securing data, reaching consensus, enhancing processing power or bandwidth, or establishing a global structure with no central authority. The concept of DLT has been utilized for decades in industries such as healthcare for storing medical records, supply chain management for tracking shipments and providing transparency to customers, and in the financial system for cross-border payments, trade finance, and streamlining processes such as clearing and settlement.

In a distributed system, the network nodes and computational resources tend to be geographically distributed. This allows each node across the network to process and access data equally. With respect to the decision-making process, nodes participate in consensus according to the rules of the system—for example, some networks give every node one vote, while others weight voting power by stake, reputation, or designated roles. One of the major advantages of DLT is that it is highly fault-tolerant, meaning that the systems will continue to operate without interruption when one or more of its components fail. This makes DLT very secure and reliable.

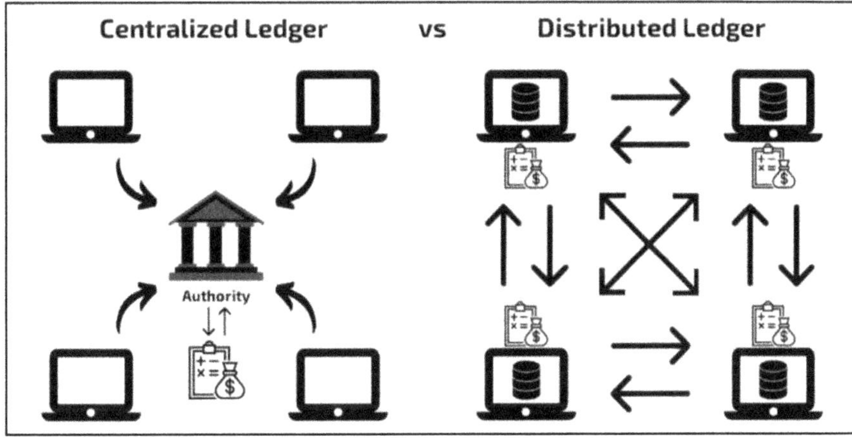

Figure 6-10. *Centralized ledger versus distributed ledger (compliments of* `https://imiblockchain.com/blockchain-vs-distributed-ledger-technology/`*)*

It is important to note that, unlike centralized systems, a distributed ledger is decentralized, meaning it has no single point of failure (master node)—see Figure 6-10 for reference. This significantly decreases the risk of system failure and attacks, as the data is spread out and shared among the nodes on the network versus being stored and controlled by a central authority.

Blockchain and Distributed Ledger Technology (DLT)

Blockchain technology and distributed ledger technology (DLT) are intertwined but different. DLT is an umbrella term that describes any system that relies on a shared database to process, record, and verify transactions in a shared network—which can be public (open) or permissioned/private, depending on the use case. DLT has various forms, with the blockchain utilizing a specific type of DLT implementation where "blocks" of data are organized linearly. Each block has a timestamp and a link to the block that came before it, creating a chain of blocks—hence the name "blockchain."

Fact Another type of DLT is directed acyclic graphs (DAG), a decentralized data structure that uses topological ordering, where each node is directed toward a single direction and no cycles exist, enabling faster transactions and scalability in blockchain systems—e.g., Fantom blockchain utilizes DAG technology.

While all blockchains are a type of distributed ledger, not all distributed ledgers are blockchains. Blockchains distinctly differ from DLT in several different ways.

Table 6-4. The key differences between blockchain and DLT

Differences Between Blockchain and Distributed Ledger Technology		
Feature	**Blockchain**	**Distributed Ledger Technology (DLT)**
Definition	A type of DLT where data is stored in linearly linked blocks and secured using cryptographic hashes.	A decentralized record-keeping system where several nodes collectively work together to execute specific tasks and maintain a shared database.
Structure	Organized in a linear linked chain of blocks, where each block contains transactional data.	Can be organized in various structures, such as a block-based chain, DAGs (Directed Acyclic Graphs), or other configurations.
Immutability	Highly immutable; once data is written to a block, it is very difficult to alter.	Varies: some DLTs may allow changes or modifications under certain conditions.
Transparency	Typically, public and transparent.	Can be public, private, or permissioned, with varying degrees of transparency.
Efficiency	Often less efficient due to scalability issues.	Can be more efficient, especially in permissioned or private settings.
Use Cases	Commonly used for cryptocurrencies, smart contracts, and public ledgers.	Broad applications include supply chain management, healthcare, finance, and more.
Scalability	Typically suffers from scalability issues, especially with PoW-based consensus mechanisms.	Generally, more scalable, as different DLTs can be optimized for performance and efficiency.

(*continued*)

Table 6-4. (*continued*)

Differences Between Blockchain and Distributed Ledger Technology		
Feature	**Blockchain**	**Distributed Ledger Technology (DLT)**
Security	Highly secure due to cryptographic techniques and decentralization.	Security varies; while decentralization provides robustness, some DLTs might prioritize speed over security.
Flexibility	Less flexible; it follows a strict chain of blocks, which can limit its adaptability.	More flexible, as different structures and protocols can be employed to meet specific customer needs.

The most common blockchain that adopts DLT is bitcoin. bitcoin utilizes *decentralized public distributed ledger technology* where nodes across the bitcoin network reach consensus, record, share, track, and synchronize transactions across a shared ledger. For bitcoin nodes to reach consensus across its distributed ledger, it is sufficient that the nodes agree among themselves and define the transactional data—as per the protocol design—that shall be included in the shared database. In bitcoin, each transaction is bundled into a block, and the block header contains a cryptographic hash that links it to the previous block—creating an immutable chain of records.

True Decentralization

Blockchain technology can exist under different varying levels of decentralization. Typically, crypto projects are classified as decentralized. However, in reality, there are various centralized aspects to every project. Often, projects integrate centralized processes to aid operation and other custom requirements that are not feasible or hard to accomplish in a decentralized manner. Therefore, although the underlying node structure of a crypto project is decentralized, most projects are not entirely decentralized.

Despite honest efforts, it is extremely difficult to achieve true decentralization. Take Coinbase, for example, where its stablecoin, USDC, is essentially classified as centralized finance (CiFi) as it is backed one-for-one by the US dollar and issued and managed by Circle—a single corporate issuer operating under US regulatory oversight. Additionally, Coinbase is owned and backed by a centralized entity named Coinbase Global, Inc. Many cryptocurrency projects have centralized development teams that write and maintain the code instead of publicly allowing anyone to contribute to the code and direction of the project. Governance is often centralized, with key decisions—such as upgrades or protocol changes—made by a select group within the project rather than involving the broader community through transparent voting processes.

Increased *layers of centralization* impact the security of a decentralized blockchain. It threatens the uncensored nature of the decentralized blockchain and causes roadblocks to mainstream adoption. The core underlying value of blockchain technology is that it is "trustless," meaning that you don't have to trust a third party: a bank, a person, or any intermediary that could operate between you and your digital asset transactions or holdings. When introducing various centralized layers, this "trustless" factor is depleted, causing blockchain users to now "trust" individuals or centralized authorities (e.g., centralized software, servers, and operating teams) when using the product or service. This generates a single point of failure and targeted malicious acts, which counteract the entire value and beneficial aspects that blockchain technology possesses. Each and every centralized layer introduced into a "decentralized" crypto project increases the potential for attack, exploitation, and failure.

Fact Crypto projects with an extremely high level of decentralization are nearly impossible to regulate, as no identifiable individual or institution can be coerced or sanctioned. This means central authorities can't shut it down, e.g., bitcoin.

Centralized Factors That Affect Decentralization

Investors have an important role in investigating whether the level of centralization in a crypto project has or will damage the project's performance and long-term success. It can be noted that most projects have some degree of centralized traits and still do well. However, projects that rely on many centralized processes expose investors to single-point technical failures, insider control over funds, and the possibility of sudden regulatory intervention, so the likelihood of your investment being harmed is much higher.

Factors That Affect the True Decentralization

1) **Token Distribution/Consensus Power**

   The security of the project is a risk if a small number of individuals or institutions own the majority share of the token supply. If most of the token supply is centralized among a small number of token holders, they have the power to manipulate major decisions easily through governance voting. This is a major threat for projects using PoS (proof-of-stake) consensus mechanisms. A project's native tokens must be spread out evenly among holders to evenly distribute consensus power. Note that some

PoS chains—e.g., Cardano's Ouroboros protocol—embed safeguards such as randomized leader selection and stake delegation to limit the influence of large stakeholders.

2) **Mining Power Distribution**

   Mining node distribution refers to how mining power (hash rate) and the validation of transactions are spread across different participants in a blockchain network. Nodes play a critical role in verifying transactions and maintaining network security. A well-distributed, global network of mining power and nodes increases the level of decentralization, significantly reducing the probability of a single entity taking control of the network, thus reducing the chances of a **51% Attack**—more detail on this in the section "51% Attack."

3) **Governance Structure**

   Governance is the process of making and implementing decisions within an organization, system, or network. There are three primary types of governance structures: centralized, decentralized, and a hybrid model (both centralized and decentralized traits). Blockchain governance is explored in the section "Governance."

   a) **Centralized Governance Model** - In a centralized governance structure, decision-making authority is concentrated within the project team or a small group of stakeholders. This small group makes all the decisions, sets policies, and enforces rules. Typically, any changes must be manually implemented on-chain, which involves manual labor from developers.

b) **Decentralized Governance Model** – Decentralized "on-chain" governance models distribute decision-making power across a broader group of participants, handing voting power back to the network of nodes and stakeholders. These decisions are often implemented automatically on-chain (depending on the blockchain's features and functionality). This model promotes a fair, transparent, and democratic voting system over which no single entity has control. An example of a decentralized governance model is bitcoin.

c) **Hybrid Governance Model** – Most hybrid "off-chain" governance models consist of centralized and decentralized elements where the community and stakeholders can vote. The votes are collected by the project team, where they are counted, and results are posted publicly. Although this type of model hands the power back to the community and stakeholders, it severely lacks transparency, as the votes cannot be visibly tracked on-chain, with no option but to trust the project team, to be honest.

4) **Infrastructure, Storage, and Operations**

Blockchain infrastructure processes are foundational elements that help build, support, and maintain the development of a decentralized ecosystem, making it useable for end-users. These processes include native and third-party wallets, decentralized storage, and decentralized exchanges (DEXs), allowing users to buy and sell digital assets without intermediaries. This removes the requirement for relying on centralized applications and services. Although challenging, a truly decentralized infrastructure should not rely on centralized services and applications, as this increases centralized risk, especially when compounded together.

One of the more critical centralized aspects that many crypto projects utilize is centralized cloud storage. Using traditional centralized cloud storage systems is risky because the reliance on centralized servers—a single point of failure—makes them a prime target for cyberattacks. A hack could result in network distribution, privacy breaches, data loss, loss of community trust, and a damaging effect on one's investment.

a) **Storage** - Data such as a blockchain's transaction history should be stored using decentralized solutions to ensure true decentralization. For example, decentralized services like Akash Network and IPFS (InterPlanetary File System) should be utilized instead of centralized services like Amazon Web Services (AWS).

b) **Website Front End** - The front end of websites is typically hosted on centralized servers. Developers can utilize decentralized services like Akash Network and IPFS to host their front-end website data.

c) **Centralized Exchanges** - Centralized exchanges risk being shut down or hacked. However, using CEXs is a tricky obstacle to avoid, as they significantly influence an asset's visibility and accessibility. However, for long-term storage of crypto assets, it is strongly recommended that investors store their asset holdings on cold storage devices such as Trezor or a Ledger.

5) **Developers and Backers**

Having a small, concentrated number of individuals, developers, and institutions in charge of development and operations can harm the project's performance, security, and longevity. This is important for the following reasons.

a) ***Longevity*** - If anything happened to the core team (various team members, developers, backers), the project would die, become bankrupt, or be severely affected in multiple other ways. The more unaffiliated individuals, developers, and institutions involved in the cryptocurrency project, the higher the level of decentralization it possesses, thus reducing unwanted risk.

b) ***Security*** - When a small group of individuals, developers, and institutions runs the project, it is more likely to be hacked or compromised by internal and external bad actors.

Effects of Layered Infrastructure on Decentralization

The decentralization of a blockchain project or dApp is often directly influenced by the degree of decentralization of the layered infrastructure it relies on. Take Centrifuge, for example, which is built on the Polkadot Network. Polkadot is paving the way for the most decentralized layer zero protocol, so Centrifuge inherently benefits from these decentralization features. While Centrifuge still possesses the ability to control and customize its decentralization aspects, analyzing the underlying layered infrastructure is a solid starting point for understanding its decentralization potential.

Action Steps

When investing in a crypto project, it is advised to gauge what level of decentralization the project possesses. Exercising this task will help investors identify any centralized layers that can either increase the risk of attack or harm the long-term longevity and success of the project—and your investment. Remember, it is challenging for a project to be completely decentralized; however, the closer it is to being completely decentralized, the safer it is from any centralized attack, manipulation, or failure.

Follow these steps to determine if a project exhibits centralized traits that could undermine its performance, security, long-term success, or sustainability. Please refer to the section "Centralized Factors that Affect Decentralization" for more details.

Most, if not all, of the answers to the following evaluation steps are typically found in the whitepaper, project websites, and official blog articles. If there are any unknowns, please contact the project team and the community through the company's official contact channel and verified social media channels.

1) **Token Distribution/Consensus Power**

   a) Determine if the supply is evenly spread out across asset holders. It is a red flag if most of the supply is concentrated among a few individuals, institutions, and/or team members.

      i) Check the whitepaper for information on token supply allocation. Here, you will find the distribution allocation percentages for the team, investors, and community (more on token supply is in Chapter "Token Economics and Design").

      ii) Use applicable block explorers (e.g., Etherscan or BscScan) to verify wallets containing larger quantities of the token supply.

      Alternatively, a quick search on `Google.com` will work also. For example, just type "Moonbeam largest wallets" into Google to search Moonbeam Network's top wallet holders. The first link will bring you to the following page, which shows Moonbeam top holders. Always verify URLs before processing.

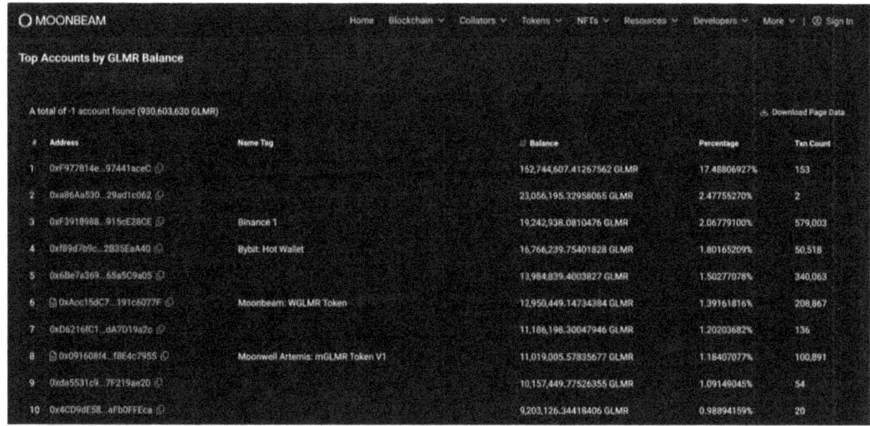

MOONBEAM

Top Accounts by GLMR Balance

A total of -1 account found (930,603,630 GLMR)

#	Address	Name Tag	Balance	Percentage	Txn Count
1	0xF977814e...97441aceC		162,744,607.41267562 GLMR	17.48806927%	153
2	0xa86Aa530...29ad1c062		23,056,195.32958065 GLMR	2.47755270%	2
3	0xF3918988...915cE28CE	Binance 1	19,242,938.0810476 GLMR	2.06779100%	579,003
4	0xf89d7b9c...2B35EaA40	Bybit: Hot Wallet	16,766,239.75401828 GLMR	1.80165209%	50,518
5	0x6Be7a369...65a5C9a05		13,984,839.4003827 GLMR	1.50277078%	340,063
6	0xAcc15dC7...191c6077F	Moonbeam: WGLMR Token	12,950,449.14734384 GLMR	1.39161816%	208,867
7	0xD6216fC1...dA7D19a2c		11,186,198.30047946 GLMR	1.20203682%	136
8	0x091608f4...f8E4c7955	Moonwell Artemis: mGLMR Token V1	11,019,005.57835677 GLMR	1.18407077%	100,891
9	0xda5531c9...7F219ae20		10,157,449.77526355 GLMR	1.09149045%	54
10	0x4CD9dE58...aFb0FFEca		9,203,126.34418406 GLMR	0.98894159%	20

***Figure 6-11.** Top accounts by GLMR balance (compliments of `https://moonscan.io/accounts`)*

2) **Mining Power Distribution**

   If no publicly available mining distribution map exists, contact the project team directly for the data. Note that this information is sometimes problematic to find depending on the network, especially if it is not a popular network. Refer to the section "51% Attack" for a more detailed evaluation.

3) **Infrastructure, Storage, and Operations**

   a) Review the project's website, whitepaper, official blog articles, and dApp to identify any centralized components in its infrastructure, storage, or operations (if any).

   b) Extreme caution is to be exercised if the project team avails of centralized storage instead of decentralized storage applications such as Akash Network and IPFS (InterPlanetary File System).

4) **Governance Structure**

   a) Review the project whitepaper and other technical documentation to determine if the team has implemented a centralized, decentralized, or hybrid governance model. Blockchain governance is explored in more detail and evaluated in the section "Governance."

5) ***Developers and Backers***

   a) Are many unaffiliated individuals, developers, and institutions involved in the project? There are multiple checks you can do for this:

      i) Check the company website for a list of all backers and investors.

      ii) Go to GitHub, check the number of developers, and check if the project is open-sourced. More on this in Chapter 10, "Project Team."

      iii) Check the company page on LinkedIn to view all those internally involved with the project.

6) **Take Notes and Document Your Findings in Your Own Style**

7) **Combine the Findings with Other Sections of the Fundamental Evaluation Process**

Evaluation of the Results

The fewer centralized processes the project team uses for the main product or service, the higher the level of decentralization that is typically achieved. Using centralized processes isn't necessarily a red flag, but projects that mostly or entirely use decentralized software processes tend to possess higher levels of security and attraction among investors.

Scalability

Evaluation Objective: Determine if a blockchain project has strong scalability qualities, directly impacting the scalability of any dApps built on it.

In recent years, blockchains have experienced immense popularity and growth. However, this has come at a cost, and a critical design issue has been identified: their inability to scale under increased load. At the time of writing, scalability is considered the bottleneck of the blockchain infrastructure. Anyone who has sent digital assets on-chain has likely dealt with frustratingly slow transaction processing times, high gas fees, and poor user experience due to network congestion—a symptom of a blockchain's limited scalability. But what exactly does blockchain scalability mean?

Blockchain scalability refers to a blockchain's ability to scale and maintain user efficiency under increased load. Taking this a step further, blockchain scalability defines a blockchain's ability to support high transactional throughput while allowing for continuous growth to support increasing blockchain participants. It is important to note that blockchain scalability is primarily measured by its *throughput* rate and *latency*.

Throughput

For blockchain technology, *throughput* is the average measure of how many transactions can be processed at any given time. Throughput is measured in **transactions per second** (TPS) or can also be measured in Transactions Per Minute (TPM). It reflects a blockchain's ability to process a specific number of transactions within a given timeframe.

The number of transactions per block and the time between blocks impact the throughput of a blockchain. For example, a new bitcoin block is generated roughly every ten minutes (600 seconds), where, on average, about 4000 transactions are processed during this timeframe. TPS is calculated by dividing the number of transactions by the number of seconds. Therefore, bitcoin's TPS is 6.67 TPS (4000/600). Many elements affect a blockchain's TPS rate, such as latency, block size and time, consensus mechanism, and scalability solutions. All these elements are explained in this section.

As discussed, the TPS indicates how many transactions the blockchain can process at any given time. When a blockchain grows in popularity, the number of users increases exponentially. For most blockchains, when this happens, the rated TPS becomes inadequate as the number of transactions waiting to be processed exceeds the maximum TPS of the blockchain. When this happens, the network becomes congested, causing poor user efficiency. The reason for this is not simply a poor TPS. Another factor is *latency,* which is a vital element for scalability.

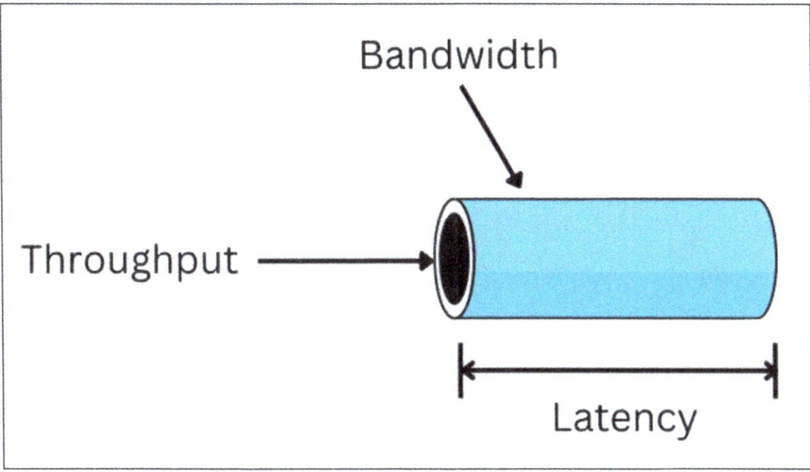

***Figure 6-12.** Representation of throughput, bandwidth, and latency (compliments of `https://shardeum.org/blog/latency-throughput-blockchain/`)*

Latency

Latency—often called block inclusion time—is the period from broadcast to the first block confirmation, whereas finality marks the point that block becomes irreversible. These can differ; on Ethereum, inclusion averages ~12 s, while full finality takes ~13 min (two epochs). Unlike TPS, which is essentially the number of transactions that can be processed at any given time, finality includes the complete process from the transaction request, including transactions in a block, broadcasting to the network nodes, block validation, and addition of the block to the blockchain.

While a high throughput rate is essential to enable a system to handle a large volume of transactions efficiently, the ultimate objective is to achieve low latency to ensure rapid transaction processing and a seamless user experience. Although hard to achieve, this balance between throughput and latency is crucial for blockchain scalability. Many factors affect latency and throughput, including consensus mechanisms, bandwidth, network congestion, and self-imposed scaling limits, e.g., setting a max block size to enhance security.

Fact bitcoin's first confirmation arrives in about 10 minutes, but economic finality is usually counted after six confirmations (~60 minutes). Moonbeam reaches probabilistic finality in ~1 minute, while Fantom's Lachesis protocol finalizes blocks in 1–2 seconds.

The scalability issue is seen when sending assets on the bitcoin blockchain. Since bitcoin cannot scale—at least not without the help of sidechains or L2s, e.g., the Lightning Network—it frequently becomes congested when a high volume of users execute transactions. This has a massive impact on performance, affecting user experience in terms of long transaction processing times and increased transaction fees.

Bandwidth

In the context of blockchain, *bandwidth* refers to the amount of data that can be transmitted or processed by the network over a specific time (bits/sec). Bandwidth is crucial because it limits the number of operations a user or network node can perform within a given timeframe. For example, think of bandwidth as a highway with a maximum and limited number of lanes. In blockchain, this limitation is vital to maintain stable network operations, prevent overloads, and ensure transaction security.

Blockchain Scalability Terminology

Table 6-5 shows the primary factors and common terminology associated with blockchain scalability. Note that although all these factors are essential and directly affect a blockchain's ability to scale, some items, such as smart contract complexity, energy consumption, cost, block size, and network load, are deemed overkill for most digital asset investors. Therefore, they are not included in this book's overall fundamental evaluation strategy. However, it is good to know these factors and their ability to hinder blockchain scalability, performance, and user efficiency.

Table 6-5. *Blockchain scalability terminology (compliments of Blockchain and the related issues: a review of current research topics: Journal of Management Analytics: Vol 5 , No 4 – Get Access (tandfonline.com))*

Blockchain Scalability Terminology		
Number	**Factor**	**Description**
1	Transaction Throughput	This implies the total number of transactions the protocol may handle in one second—measured in transactions per second (TPS). High transactional throughput is admired, provided it does not impact decentralization or security.
2	Latency	This is the time from transaction broadcast until it is first included in a block (block-inclusion latency). Measured in seconds or milliseconds. Finality—the point at which the block becomes irreversible—is a separate metric.
3	Storage	Refers to the total space/capacity a blockchain can consume.
4	Block Size	Ideally, block size strikes a balance—larger blocks boost capacity but slow propagation, increasing orphan-block risk.
5	Smart Contract	Smart contract complexity can cause delays in processing times.
6	Computation Energy	This indicates if the algorithm (or the utilizing system) consumes significant energy for block mining. Depending on the type of consensus mechanism, some blockchains consume more energy and time for mining and transaction verification.

(continued)

Table 6-5. *(continued)*

		Blockchain Scalability Terminology
Number	**Factor**	**Description**
7	Network Load	This implies the number of transactions being carried by the network. Network congestion is a result of increased load on the blockchain.
8	Cost Issue	This implies the total cost associated with verifying a transaction in the blockchain.
9	Number of Nodes	This refers to the total number of nodes available in the blockchain network. A high number of network nodes increases decentralization, but depending on the consensus mechanism used, the effect on time-to-consensus is protocol-specific—some designs (e.g., Avalanche or Algorand) sustain low-latency finality even with thousands of validators.
10	Consensus Model	A consensus mechanism represents the process of approving/verifying blockchain transactions.

Consensus Mechanisms

Consensus mechanics can be considered the core of blockchain architecture in which scalability thrives. They are a vital part of blockchain technology and play a significant role in guaranteeing blockchain networks' security, decentralization, and scalability. As outlined in *"Systematic literature review of challenges in blockchain scalability," Khan D* states that twenty journal papers highlighted the consensus mechanism as the second most discussed factor concerning public blockchain scalability. These cleverly designed consensus mechanisms are also related to a blockchain's throughput, which is also associated with the overall performance of a blockchain.

What Is a Consensus Mechanism?

A consensus mechanism is a system protocol that dictates how transactions are processed, verified, and added to the blockchain. When a network participant initiates a transaction on the blockchain, the transaction is Broadcasted to the network nodes and placed inside virtual *blocks* with other transactions. Using an already-defined consensus mechanism, these blocks of transactions are verified by network nodes and added to the blockchain, block by block. Consensus mechanisms are also responsible for blockchain security and integrity across the entire network. They are available in many different types and forms, each impacting a blockchain's throughput, overall performance, and security.

The two most common types of consensus mechanisms are proof-of-work (PoW) and proof-of-stake (PoS). Both consensus mechanisms operate on a decentralized peer-to-peer network without the need for any trusted authority. Other commonly used consensus mechanisms are Delegated Proof-of-Stake (DPoS) and Proof-of-Authority (PoA). Some networks instead employ DAG-based data structures together with separate consensus algorithms (e.g., Avalanche).

Proof-of-Work (PoW)

Proof-of-Work (PoW) is a consensus algorithm used in blockchain networks to confirm transactions and add new blocks to the blockchain. While *mining* refers to the specific activity where miners compete with one another to solve a mathematical problem (puzzle) based on a particular set of transactions, PoW serves as a general framework outlining the rules and procedures for validating transactions on the network. The underlying logic facilitates the functioning of decentralized systems such as bitcoin.

Fact Based on Digiconomist's bitcoin Energy Consumption Index (April 2025 snapshot), the network burns roughly 600 kWh per on-chain transaction—about what the average US household uses in 20 days. Actual consumption per transaction fluctuates with hashrate, block occupancy, and miner-hardware efficiency.

When a network participant initiates a transaction, it is placed in a *mempool, also known as a* memory pool, with other unconfirmed transactions. A mempool—stored on each node—can be described as a virtual waiting room where unconfirmed and pending transactions are held until a *miner* processes them to be added to the next block. Mempool data is sent across all nodes on the bitcoin network. Nodes select unconfirmed transactions from the mempool and place them inside an unconfirmed block.

Fact In bitcoin's early days, mining ran on ordinary CPUs and later GPUs; today, profitable mining demands application-specific integrated circuit (ASIC) rigs. Running a full bitcoin node, however, still only requires off-the-shelf hardware with enough storage and bandwidth.

Through the transaction validation process outlined by the PoW (proof-of-work) consensus mechanism, each node that has an unconfirmed block races against each other to be the first one to solve a mathematical puzzle and hence, "confirm" and verify if the block they are working on is valid. This verification and the transactional record-keeping process are known as mining—the "work" in "proof-of-work." The mathematical puzzle, which uses transactional data, is highly complex and depends on a block target and the block nonce that is encoded in the unconfirmed block. The first node to solve the puzzle provides the "proof-of-work" and earns the right to assemble the next block, typically selecting the highest-fee transactions from the mempool before committing it to the chain. Additionally, the first miner who solves the puzzle wins a reward. In the case of bitcoin, miners are incentivized with newly mined BTC—hence the term "mining"—and also receive money, in the form of BTC, from transaction fees as a reward for processing transactions on the network. This incentivization in the form of mining rewards is a means to keep nodes from acting maliciously.

Fact As bitcoin heads toward its hard cap of 21 million coins (block subsidy ends around 2140), miners will depend mainly on transaction fees; by 2040 the subsidy will already be below 0.2 BTC per block.

Once the block is confirmed, it is broadcasted to all network participants, re-confirmed, and further validated by other nodes on the network. This adds stability and security to the block, making it harder to be tampered with. The confirmed block is linked—referenced—to the previous "parent" block's *hash*, forming a *chain of blocks*, hence the *blockchain*. This *hash* is generated by a mathematical cryptographic hashing algorithm called the "Secure Hash Algorithm" (*SHA-256)* and stored in each block's header. The sequence of hashes linking each block to its parent creates a chain—the blockchain—going back to the first block, the *genesis block*.

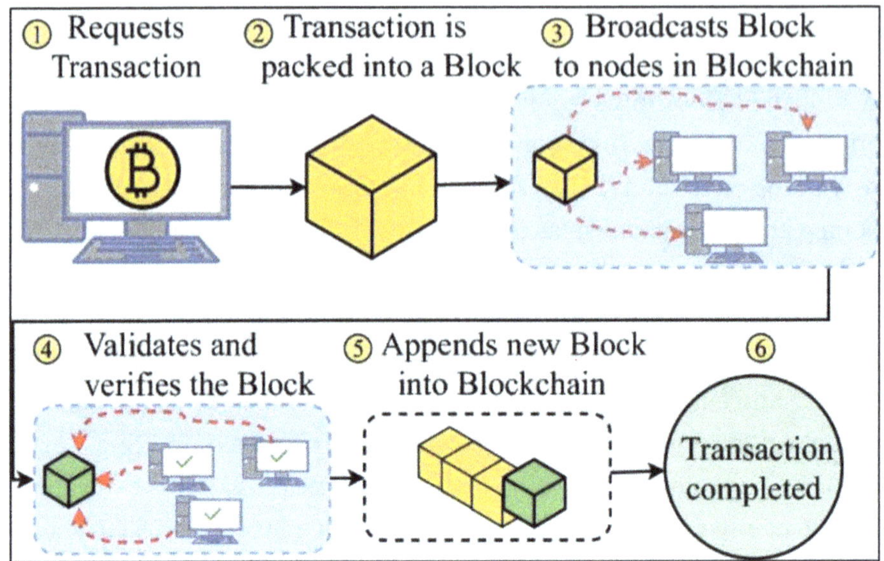

Figure 6-13. *Typical cryptocurrency transaction (compliments of*`https://link.springer.com/content/pdf/10.1007/s10586-021-03301-8.pdf`*)*

Fact Mining and proof-of-work (PoW) are related concepts—while mining is the process of using computing power to solve complex mathematical problems and validate new transactions on a blockchain, proof-of-work (PoW) is the consensus mechanism that requires miners to do this work and compete with each other to create new blocks and earn rewards.

If a malicious actor attempts to compromise a network by changing the block's confirmed data, e.g., a month ago, all the block hashes up to that point would have to agree and change. This is highly unlikely to happen due to the amount of computational power required. Furthermore, the bitcoin blockchain is considered an *immutable*—unable to be changed—

chain of back-linked blocks that store transactional data. The deeper the blocks, the more immutable the blocks become. In the unlikely event of something like this occurring, attackers would have to control over 51% of the bitcoin network mining hash rate—this is known as the 51% Attack. Although possible, it is doubtful that this will ever occur. This is what makes the blockchain so secure and why it is considered *immutable*.

A typical block on the bitcoin network contains specific information; see the below table.

Table 6-6. *Typical bitcoin block data*

Typical bitcoin Block Data		
Field	**Size**	**Description**
4 bytes	4 bytes	The size of the block, in bytes
Block Header	80 bytes	Several fields from the block header
Transaction Counter	Variable (1-9 bytes)	Total number of transactions in the block (including the *coinbase* transaction)
Transactions	Variable	The transactions in the block

Factors Behind Increased Network Traffic

Proof-of-work (PoW) based networks, such as bitcoin, are notorious for congestion. Network congestion is caused by a high volume of transactions resulting from various factors such as blockchain popularity, economic news, big crashes, or even when high-profile people (e.g., Elon Musk) post on social media about a particular project. This can leave network participants waiting for lengthy periods to process their transactions. To speed up processing times, users often pay higher transaction fees to network miners to prioritize their transactions.

Proof-of-Stake (PoS)

Proof-of-stake (PoS) is a consensus mechanism to validate incoming transactions and add them as new blocks on the blockchain. PoS and PoW are both operated by network participants instead of a central authority, and both serve the same purpose and end goal; however, the transaction verification process is very different.

Miners are known as ***validators in a PoS system.*** Validators pledge *to "stake"* their tokens or coins in a smart contract on the blockchain. Validators are selected through schemes that weight stake size (and sometimes stake duration) while adding randomness or rotating committees—Ethereum's beacon chain, for instance, draws proposers via a RANDAO lottery; proposing a block is often called minting (or forging). Validators have a higher chance of being selected with an increased number of coins staked, which entails locking them up through a validator process. An example of a project that utilizes this method is the Ethereum blockchain. Rewards in the form of newly minted coins native to the PoS blockchain are issued to validators for work done during the validation process. Validators can grow in power the longer they have spent validating transactions and increasing their number of pledged tokens for staking.

PoS maintains security and good behavior by penalizing malicious validators who are improperly validating harmful or fraudulent data. If a validator is found to be misbehaving, some or even all of their entire stake could be penalized. In terms of energy, PoS is more energy-efficient and scalable than PoW; however, it can be more susceptible to centralization and attacks by wealthy nodes. Table 6-7 concisely summarizes and compares PoW versus PoS consensus mechanisms.

Table 6-7. PoW versus PoS

PoW Versus PoS	
Proof-of-Work (PoW)	**Proof-of-Stake (PoS)**
Block creators are known as miners.	Block creators are known as validators.
Slow transaction processing and verification.	Fast transaction processing and verification.
High Cost. Expensive equipment (ASIC) and energy are needed for the mining process.	Low Cost. Stake (coins or tokens) is the main requirement; validation can run on consumer-grade hardware.
Not energy efficient—miners compete against each other.	Energy efficiency—validators selected at random.
Difficult to scale.	Easier to scale.
Robust security due to expensive upfront requirements.	Network control can be bought.
Miners receive block rewards.	Validators receive transaction fees as rewards.
Potential of a 51% attack.	Resistant to 51% attacks—grouped validators can be removed by the community.

Other Types of Consensus Mechanisms

Outside of PoW and PoS, there are several other consensus methods used in blockchain technology, including the following:

- **Nominated Proof-of-Stake (NPoS)** - It is a variation of proof-of-stake (PoS) where token holders nominate validators to secure the network. These validators earn rewards for creating new blocks. Their rewards are based on their quantity stake and reputation.

- **Proof-of-Authority (PoA) -** It is a consensus mechanism typically utilized in private and permissioned blockchains where a limited number of authorized validators are allowed to validate transactions.
- **Directed Acyclic Graphs (DAG)** - A transaction-ordering data structure, not a consensus mechanism. Networks such as IOTA, Hedera, and Avalanche store transactions in a DAG and run a separate consensus layer on top. The parallel graph layout lets many validators append transactions at once, boosting throughput and lowering latency compared with a single linear chain.
- **Practical Byzantine Fault Tolerance (PBFT) -** It is a consensus algorithm that provides high fault tolerance, ensuring the blockchain can function even if some nodes fail or act maliciously. It is typically used in permissioned and private blockchains where only trusted nodes are granted access.
- **Delegated Proof-of-Stake (DPoS)** - It is a consensus mechanism where token holders vote to elect a small group of delegates who validate transactions and create new blocks on their behalf. Prominent DPoS networks include EOS, Tron, and Bitshares.

Most Scalable Consensus Mechanism

It is challenging to identify the most efficient and scalable consensus mechanism, as many factors as the type of blockchain, whether it is public, private, permissioned, permissionless, centralized, or decentralized. Additionally, the specific purpose of the blockchain may require a particular type of consensus mechanism to cater to the product or service. However, PoW-based blockchains (e.g., bitcoin)—due to the work and computational power and work required—are deemed highly secure but the least efficient.

Many consensus mechanisms discussed, such as PoS, NPoS, and DPoS, are considered faster and more scalable than PoW-based blockchains. bitcoin is in a league of its own, so it is tough to compare PoW against PoS (or similar) based projects. Projects such as DeFi, DEXs, gaming, IoT, etc. that require extremely fast and low-cost transactions typically avoid using a PoW-based consensus mechanism; instead, a PoS or similar variation is adopted. For example, before Ethereum transitioned from PoW to PoS, transactions on Uniswap—especially during periods of high user volume—were extremely high, with some transactions costing hundreds of dollars and coupled with long processing times. With Ethereum's PoS consensus mechanism, transaction processing times and costs have significantly been reduced.

Scalability Improvement Solutions

To overcome scalability issues, a blockchain must possess the capability to increase its computational *throughput* and lower its *latency* as more demand is generated. However, achieving this typically comes at a cost. As per the Blockchain Trilemma, decentralization and security are jeopardized as a blockchain's scalability increases. Indeed, it would be possible to achieve much higher throughput and lower latency by sacrificing decentralization and security. For example, reducing the number of consensus-participating full nodes can raise throughput because fewer validators need to exchange messages. However, trimming the full-node set lowers decentralization and overall security; with fewer validators controlling a larger share of power, the probability of a 51% attack rises. (Light or SPV clients are not part of this calculation since they don't vote in consensus.)

Fortunately, ongoing scaling solutions are being developed with the primary goal of helping to scale the mainchain (parent chain), e.g., Ethereum, while striving to maintain decentralization and security. For ease of comprehension, scaling solutions are broken out into two primary groups: *first-layer scaling solutions* and *second-layer scaling solutions*.

First- and Second-Layer Scaling Solutions

Blockchain scaling solutions are classified into two primary categories: first- and second-layer scaling solutions. Layer one scaling solutions enhance performance by altering the parameters of the blockchain system, which focus on consensus mechanisms, network, and data structure of blockchain (e.g., sharding, which divides state and transaction processing across coordinated shard chains that still share security with the main chain block size, block and block time, and block compression).

In contrast, layer two scaling solutions, typically known as off-chain solutions, are built (layered) on top of the existing first layer. These solutions proposed scaling mechanisms that operate outside of the main L1 blockchain but communicate and interact with it for various reasons, including the transfer of assets and transactional data and to ensure blockchain security and integrity. L2 scaling solutions include sidechains, rollups, state channels, payment channels, and Plasma chains.

Horizontal and Vertical Scaling Solutions

First- and second-layer scaling solutions are further organized and classified into two groups: *horizontal and vertical scaling.*

Horizontal scaling, also known as scaling out, involves adding more nodes to the network, thus increasing the throughput and capacity of the underlying L1 blockchain. This is the most popular type of scaling solution due to its ability to handle increased demand without significantly altering the existing L1 blockchain architecture. Additionally, horizontal scaling provides greater flexibility and easier upgrades than vertical scaling methods, ensuring the network can meet current and future demands. Some drawbacks to horizontal scaling include added complexity; rollups execute transactions off-chain but post data and cryptographic proofs back to L1. While they inherit the base chain's security, optimistic rollups impose a challenge window that can delay final withdrawals. Horizontal scaling solutions are complex, resulting in higher costs and the potential for data inconsistency in distributed systems. Additionally, horizontal scaling can introduce additional latency, as requests need to be routed to the appropriate node.

On the other hand, vertical scaling solutions are a more traditional approach that focuses on increasing the capacity and power of existing resources (e.g., nodes). This is achieved by upgrading the hardware or adding more resources to a single node. This allows for more processing power and memory for a single blockchain, thus improving throughput and reducing latency. One drawback to vertical scaling is that each node on the system has limitations regarding how much it can be vertically scaled. Once this limit is reached and the system still requires additional scalability, layer two scaling solutions become viable. Note, in recent times, many teams have shifted away from pushing L1s to scale vertically and instead deploy L2 horizontal solutions, which can grow capacity without forcing every node to upgrade its hardware.

Breaking it down, vertical and horizontal scaling can be simplified in terms of a busy restaurant. To cope with the additional growth, vertical scaling can be implemented where more chairs can be added to existing tables. For example, two extra chairs are added to every table in the restaurant, increasing the number of people from four to six per table—this is known as vertical scaling, whereby existing hardware (or software) is altered to accommodate and deal with additional demand. Alternatively, a horizontal scaling strategy is implemented when vertical scaling is no longer adequate and cannot deal with the queues of people standing outside the restaurant waiting for seats. In this case, a horizontal scaling solution entails adding additional tables on the restaurant floor so that everyone can sit and eat simultaneously without any long wait times. Horizontal scaling would also include opening additional restaurants and expanding the business. The same concepts apply to the scaling of blockchains, with horizontal scaling being the most popular due to the high volume of users on the networks.

Table 6-8 shows the popular first and second layer, horizontal and vertical scaling blockchain solutions.

Table 6-8. First- and second-layer blockchain scaling

First- and Second-Layer Blockchain Scaling Solutions					
Layer Solution	**Scaling Category**	**Solution Type**	**Function/Operation**	**Advantages**	**Disadvantages**
First Layer Solutions	Vertical	Block Size and Time	Updating the blockchain code to increase the block size Example: Bitcoin Cash	– Increases throughput – Reduces transaction cost	– Slower block propagation, higher orphan-block risk. – Leads to centralization issues
	Vertical	Consensus Mechanisms	Updating the consensus mechanism—e.g., PoW → PoS—can boost throughput, but it's a major architectural overhaul that can take years (see Ethereum's Merge). Example: Ethereum	– Energy efficient – Scalability – Less specialized hardware	– Centralization risk – Potential lower security
	Horizontal	Sharding	Works by dividing blockchain networks into smaller parts (shards). Each shard processes its own transactions, coordinating consensus across shards through a beacon (root) chain. Example: Zilliqa	– Increases throughput due to parallel processing of shards – Improved transaction speed – High scalability – Reduced node storage, as each node needs only to store and process the data of a single shard	– Security risk if only one shard is compromised – Cross-shard transactions introduce complexity and transaction delays

(continued)

Table 6-8. (*continued*)

First- and Second-Layer Blockchain Scaling Solutions					
Layer Solution	**Scaling Category**	**Solution Type**	**Function/Operation**	**Advantages**	**Disadvantages**
	Horizontal	Directed Acyclic Graph (DAG)	A non-linear data structure where multiple blocks can be added to the blockchain simultaneously. Example: IOTA, Fantom	– High throughput – Removes the need for miners – Low transaction fees – Fast Transactions	– Security issues: vulnerable to attacks, e.g., double spending – Underdeveloped: in its early stages with unexplored limitations
	Vertical	Segregated Witness (SegWit)	Increases block capacity by splitting a transaction into two parts, allowing more transactions per block. Separating the signatures from the main transaction data makes the transaction ID unchangeable, addressing the issue of transaction malleability. Example: bitcoin, Litecoin	– Increases block size, thus increasing the throughput – Increases network capacity as a result of increased block size – Fixes the transaction malleability issue of creating a new transaction's identifier (*id*) for an existing transaction	– Potential to cause hard forks – Centralization issues – Compatibility and adoption—backward-compatible; old addresses still work, and new bech32 addresses make transactions cheaper. – Limited adoption unless all nodes need to support the upgrade

	Vertical	Block Compression	Sends compact blocks (BIP-152) that skip transactions the peer already holds, cutting relay bandwidth. Examples: Compact Block Relay (BIP-152), Erlay (BIP-330)	– Lowers bandwidth usage – Increases throughput – Reduces the size of blockchain data	– High computational overhead – High Complexity
Second-Layer Solutions (off-chain solutions)	Horizontal	Zero-nowledge (ZK) Rollups	Operates by batching a large number of transactions together, generating a "*validity proof*" of those transactions called a ZK-STARK. The proof is then sent to the Layer 1 parent blockchain (e.g., Ethereum) for processing. Example: Immutable	– Reduces the workload of the parent chain – High potential throughput and low latency – Reduced transaction fees – Very fast withdrawal period – High proof publishing cost per batch, but low amortized on-chain cost per transaction.	– High complexity – High off-chain computational cost for generating ZK proofs
	Horizontal	Optimistic Rollups	Operates by executing transactions off-chain (L2) and only publishing transaction data and a new state root on-chain (L1). These rollups assume that transactions are valid unless challenged, hence the term "optimistic." Examples: Arbitrum, Optimism	– Reduces the processing load on Layer 1, thus increasing scalability – Low transaction fees – Low complexity – Low off-chain computational costs	– Long and complex dispute resolution process – Long wait for asset withdrawals – High pre-transaction on-chain cost

(continued)

Table 6-8. (continued)

First- and Second-Layer Blockchain Scaling Solutions					
Layer Solution	**Scaling Category**	**Solution Type**	**Function/Operation**	**Advantages**	**Disadvantages**
	Horizontal	Side Chains	Operates by transferring, processing, and verifying transactions on a pegged sidechain that runs parallel to the mainchain. After transactions are processed, the sidechain's own validators finalize the block and periodically post a checkpoint to the mainchain for bridging and dispute resolution. Example: Polygon PoS	– Reduces the load on the mainchain – Faster and cheaper transaction processing due to increased throughput – Enables interoperability between different blockchains – Allows for experimentation with new features without risking the security of the mainchain.	– Security issues: may not have the same level of security as the mainchain – Sidechains add more complexity to the blockchain network

Horizontal	Plasma	Developed by Vitalik Buterin and Joseph Poon, Plasma chains are a scalable solution framework where there are several chains called "child chains" that are connected and pointing back to the parent chain. Child chains can further spawn into more sub-chains, creating blockchains within blockchains. Child chains are rooted using a smart contract on the parent chain, and users can achieve asset transfer between the Plasma chain and the Ethereum main chain via the root. These child chains verify transactions (off-chain) but are then settled on the parent chain (e.g., Ethereum). Additionally, child chains derive some security from the parent "root" chain, making them secure. Examples: Loom Network	– Offers high throughput and low cost per transaction. – Highly customizable to suit specific use cases – Reduces load on Ethereum Mainnet by moving computation and storage off-chain – More secure than sidechains, as their security is derived from the parent "root" chain	– Does not support general computation, e.g., cannot run smart contracts – Attention is required to ensure the security of one's funds – Relies on one or more operators to store and serve data upon request. – Delayed withdrawals – Potential to congest the mainchain if too many users try to exit at the same time

(continued)

Table 6-8. *(continued)*

First- and Second-Layer Blockchain Scaling Solutions					
Layer Solution	**Scaling Category**	**Solution Type**	**Function/Operation**	**Advantages**	**Disadvantages**
	Horizontal	State Channels	Works by processing multiple transactions off-chain. It provides a secure, cost-effective, and private environment for unlimited interactions before finalizing them on the blockchain. The concept of "state" signifies the state of the blockchain at a particular moment, while "channel" is where the communication takes place. Users mostly communicate with each other off-chain and only interact with the underlying blockchain to open the channel, close the channel, or settle potential disputes between participants. Plasma technology is used in projects including Ethereum and Polygon	– High transaction throughput by reducing load on the mainchain – Near-instant transactions – Private transactions – Low transaction fees – Ideal for microtransactions and recurring payments	– High upfront cost – High complexity – Dispute handling can be cumbersome, often requiring interaction with the main chain – Requires participants to be online during the channel closure to prevent malicious behavior – Less transparency can lead to longer disputes – Pre-funding required

Horizontal	Payment Channels	It operates by enabling two participants to conduct numerous transactions off-chain, reducing the load on the main blockchain. The process involves two on-chain transactions: one to create and fund a smart contract (opening the channel) and another to reclaim the funds (closing the channel). Example: Lightning Network	– Extremely low transaction fees – Near-instant transactions – Very low latency – Private transactions	– Payment channel only – Requires two parties to be online at the same time – Limited capability, only handles the channel's native asset (e.g., BTC on Lightning) – Pre-funding required – Dispute handling can be cumbersome and often requires interaction with the main chain

Pro Tip Be cautious of new blockchain projects that claim to have developed advanced technology solving scalability issues. Often, these tests are conducted in a testnet environment, not under real-world conditions on a mainnet. Make sure to do thorough research to verify their claims.

How to Measure Blockchain Scalability Performance

Many factors affect blockchain scalability, such as throughput, bandwidth, latency (finality), consensus mechanism, transaction per second (TPS), number of nodes, energy consumption, and block size. Analyzing all these factors together provides a clear understanding of how scalable a blockchain really is. However, for the purpose and requirement of this fundamental evaluation, it is considered excessive and not deemed necessary. Instead, for this fundamental evaluation, investors should focus on metrics such as the type of consensus mechanism identified, throughput rate measured in transactions per second (TPS), and block time, which is the average amount of time it takes miners to verify a block of transactions and add it to a blockchain.

1) **Consensus Mechanism**

   Determine the type of consensus mechanism used, e.g., PoW, PoS, DPoS, PoA, etc. (if the project employs a DAG data structure, identify the separate consensus algorithm layered on top). For dApps, this will be the consensus mechanism adopted by the underlying blockchain.

   a) Compare the consensus mechanism used against the one utilized by high-performing competitors with the same product or service.

b) If a different consensus mechanism is used, investigate the reasons why. In the end, using a different consensus mechanism is acceptable if the proper team has proper justification and proof, and it has been successful on other projects.

It does not make sense to have a PoW consensus mechanism, e.g., for a decentralized exchange or a gaming dApp, where high throughput and low latency are deemed necessary to handle the high volume of transactions.

c) Suppose the consensus mechanism is based on new and untested technology. In that case, conducting thorough research or considering postponing investment until the technology has been successfully demonstrated in a real-world environment is highly recommended.

2) **Throughput and Block Time**

Determine the blockchain's throughput rate in transactions per second (TPS) and the corresponding block time. This information for most blockchains is available at Chainspect.com/dashboard.

a) If a dApp, check the blockchain the project is built on. This information should be clearly visible on the whitepaper, the company, and social channels.

b) Ideally, a high TPS with low block time is admirable. As a reference, bitcoin has a TPS of 6.77tx/s with a block time of 9m 44s over a 30-day average—see Figure 6-14 for reference. Although bitcoin is the world's most popular and powerful decentralized digital asset, its TPS and block time—without the help of Layer 2 scaling solutions—are considered poor and unsuitable for most projects requiring a high transactional volume.

c) On the other hand, Polygon's TPS (37.85 tx/s) with a block time of 2.18s is shown in Figure 6-15 and is considered highly admirable for most projects launched today.

d. When researching TPS and block time, it is advised to always compare it to well-known, popular competitors with high market capitalizations.

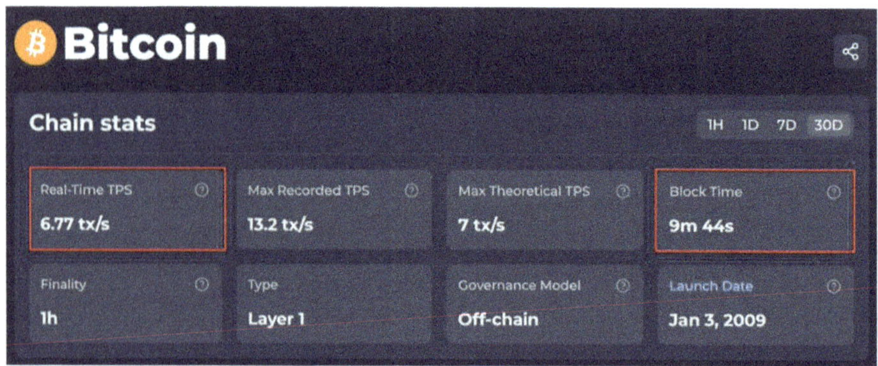

Figure 6-14. *bitcoin scalability performance metrics over a 30-day average (compliments of* `https://chainspect.app/chain/bitcoin`*)*

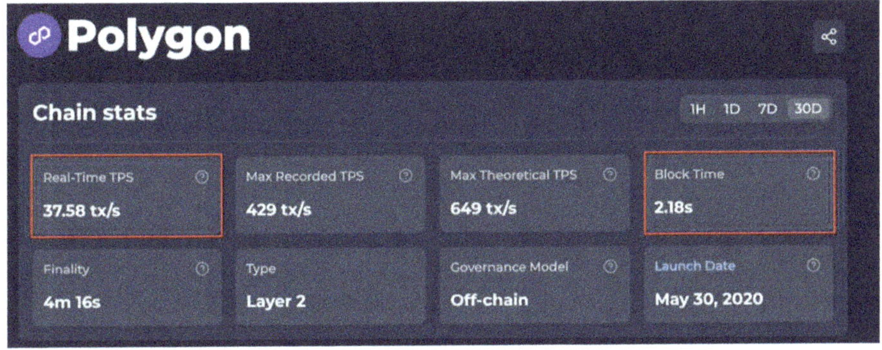

Figure 6-15. *Polygon scalability performance metrics over a 30-day average (compliments of* `https://chainspect.app/chain/polygon`*)*

Fact Blockchains with a high TPS rate and low block time have performed well when exposed to high transactional volume situations. Furthermore, these blockchains suffer less congestion and have lower gas fees than projects with a low TPS and high block time.

Action Steps

Follow these steps to determine if a blockchain project has strong scalability qualities, directly impacting the scalability of any dApps built on it.

1) **Assess Blockchain Scalability**

   Using the steps outlined in the "*How to Measure Blockchain Scalability Performance*" section, analyze the chain's consensus mechanism, throughput, and block time to determine its scalability potential and efficiency.

2) **Take Notes and Document Your Findings in Your Own Style**

3) **Combine the Findings with Other Sections of the Fundamental Evaluation Process**

Evaluation of the Results

Suppose the blockchain's TPS and block time performance are poor compared to high-performing competitors. In that case, it is advised to proceed with caution until the rest of the fundamental evaluation is complete. Investors should strongly consider not investing in the project depending on how poor the TPS and block time performance are.

Security

Evaluation Objective: Identify security threats to blockchain projects and implement measures to protect the network and your digital assets. Blockchain technology is known for its robust security features that help secure and protect data against a wide array of attacks. The security is achieved through a combined effort of asymmetric cryptography, consensus mechanisms, and decentralization that offer safe and robust protection for network participants. However, as with most systems, some caveats compromise the security of blockchains and, in turn, jeopardize investors' digital asset investments. These threat factors include 51% attacks, double-spending, contentious hard forks or chain-reorganization attacks, vendor attacks, end points, denial-of-service (DoS), and *Sybil* attacks. Additionally, human factors from the project team, including poor implementation practices and overall incompetency, can compromise the blockchain project's integrity.

Important Security Check for Investors

As discussed, there are many ways a blockchain, or dApp, can be attacked and exploited for money in the form of on-chain digital assets. These different types of attacks are outlined in this section, as it is beneficial for investors to be aware of and understand them. However, it is challenging for investors or even the project team to predict if a project will undergo an attack. In most cases, it is only after an attack that previously unnoticed flaws or vulnerabilities in the system are exposed. Therefore, the primary focus in this section outlines the steps and actions investors have control of and how to implement them to help secure their digital assets from attack.

51% Attack

A 51% attack, in the context of proof-of-work (PoW) based blockchain, refers to a situation where an entity or group gains control of more than 50% of a network's mining power—also known as the hash rate. This should not be confused with a group of individuals owning more than 51% of the supply of a particular asset. Many projects have suffered a 51% attack, including Bitcoin Gold (2018 & again in 2020), Ethereum Classic in 2019, and Verge in 2018.

When a 51% attack occurs, attackers control enough hash power to find valid nonces—and thus new blocks—faster than honest miners, letting them extend a private chain and overrule honest blocks. This allows attackers to decide which block is permissible, thus preventing new transactions from gaining confirmations and stopping transactions between network participants.

With control over most block mining, attackers can reorganize the chain—forking below previously confirmed blocks—to double-spend their own transactions. However, attackers can only double-spend transactions for which they hold a valid signature, and the attack is profitable only if they succeed in invalidating a payment yet still receive a non-reversible product or asset. (For a step-by-step explanation of 51% chain reorganizations and double-spends, see A. Antonopoulos, *Mastering Bitcoin*, 2nd ed., ch. 10 "Mining and Consensus," pp. 270–273.)

However, transactions that have been locked in and confirmed before the start of the 51% attack are extremely difficult to change. Furthermore, the longer transactions have been confirmed on-chain, the more immutable they are, making it nearly impossible to manipulate these permanent transactions.

Fact Attackers cannot reverse other people's transactions on the network or prevent users from broadcasting their transactions to the network. In addition, a 51% attack cannot create new assets, steal assets from unrelated parties, or alter the functionality of block rewards.

Likelihood of a 51% Attack

A 51% attack, although possible, is a very challenging, complicated, and expensive task, with the likelihood of success decreasing as the network expands with additional mining nodes. Firstly, they need control of over 50% of the network and create an alternate blockchain—a fork of the original blockchain—that would eventually be accepted at a specific point in time and then exceed the hash rate of the original chain.

To even have a chance to achieve this, e.g., the bitcoin network, thousands of *application-specific integrated circuit machines* (ASIC) mining machines are required, costing about roughly $10,000 per ASIC machine. Not as many ASIC machines would be needed for 51% of attacks on smaller networks; however, the cost of the equipment required may outweigh the benefits of the attack. Furthermore, outside of cost, attackers must control 51% of the network's hashing power and introduce the altered blockchain at an exact time. Attackers would have to keep up with the block creation rate or get their alternate chain inserted before the "honest" blockchain network creates valid new blocks. Failure to do this will result in a failed 51% attack.

51% Attack on Proof-of-Stake Networks

For a 51% attack to occur on a proof-of-stake (PoS) based network, the attackers must own 51% of the staked native asset (e.g., staked ETH). Although this is possible, it is somewhat unlikely for this to happen to larger market capitalization projects. Additionally, "*slashing*," a penalty mechanism, would detect and punish validators who act maliciously or against the network's interests by automatically "slashing" or confiscating the attacker's staked assets, resulting in substantial financial loss.

Consensus Mechanisms

Selecting a consensus mechanism is a complex task because they have different qualities, advantages, and disadvantages that suit different use cases. Regarding security, each consensus mechanism offers distinct methods of protecting the network from attacks, but they also come with specific vulnerabilities. Table 6-9 shows the most common consensus mechanisms and their associated pros and cons in terms of security.
It is beneficial for investors to possess a basic understanding of these mechanisms to better understand the security risks before investing.

Table 6-9. Consensus mechanisms security qualities and drawbacks

Consensus Mechanisms—Security Qualities and Drawbacks		
Consensus Mechanism	**Advantages**	**Disadvantages**
Proof-of-Work (PoW)	High security.	– Although unlikely, there is potential for a 51% attack. – Smaller networks are at risk of mining centralization.
Proof-of-Stake (PoS)	Resistant to 51% attacks if staked assets are well-distributed.	– Potential for "Nothing at Stake" attacks on the network if little to no coins are staked. – May be susceptible to centralization risks if small groups of people stake large amounts.
Delegated Proof-of-Stake (DPoS)	Security can be maintained even with a small group of trusted delegates.	– Centralization risk due to a small number of delegates controlling the network. – Risk of malicious attacks through delegate collusion.
Nominated Proof-of-Stake (NPoS)	– Enhances decentralization and security by allowing nominators to select validators they trust. – Reduces the risk of collusion as nominators can switch validators.	– Network security depends on staking distribution and the behavior of nominators and validators. – Risk of centralization if a few validators accidentally or maliciously receive disproportionate nominations. – Potential for "Nothing at Stake" attacks on the network if little to no coins are staked.

(*continued*)

Table 6-9. (*continued*)

Consensus Mechanisms—Security Qualities and Drawbacks		
Consensus Mechanism	**Advantages**	**Disadvantages**
Practical Byzantine Fault Tolerance (PBFT)	High fault tolerance, ensuring security even if some nodes are acting maliciously	– Vulnerable to Sybil attacks if there is a small number of nodes – Not scalable for large, public networks, potentially reducing security in larger settings.
Directed Acyclic Graph (DAG)	High transaction throughput while maintaining security in certain conditions.	– Susceptible to man-in-the-middle (MITM) attacks. – Complexity in maintaining security due to lack of a linear blockchain structure.
Proof-of-Authority (PoA)	High security with a limited number of trusted validators.	– Centralization risk as validators are pre-approved, making the system more vulnerable to attack.

Double Spending

A 51% attack can trigger an issue known as *double-spending*. In a traditional banking context, this happens when a reconciliation flaw lets the same funds be spent twice: for example, imagine Bob has $1,000 in his bank account and sends $400 to Alice. If the banking network works properly, Bob's balance falls to $600 and Alice's rises to $400; if the ledger fails to update, Bob's balance remains $1,000 while Alice still receives $400, allowing Bob to spend that $400 again—i.e., double-spending.

The introduction of blockchain with distributed-ledger technology (DLT) and bitcoin's proof-of-work (PoW) consensus mechanism has solved the issue of double-spending. It works by a peer-to-peer network of nodes, each verifying transactions broadcasted to the network. The network nodes work together to agree on whether the transactions are valid or invalid. If a transaction is deemed invalid, it will not be processed, thus eliminating the double-spending problem.

Fact Note that digital assets are not stored in wallets or any decentralized digital asset storage application. Digital assets are stored on-chain. Digital wallets only provide an interface to access the funds when the asset holder enters their applicable security keys and password, thus verifying they are the owner of the assets.

Forking

Like traditional centralized businesses and applications, blockchains require updates to increase performance and fix any occurring issues. In the crypto space, these updates can sometimes lead to what is known as a "fork." In open-source crypto projects, a *fork* happens when miners and network participants cannot reach a unanimous consensus regarding new proposed changes and upgrades to the protocol. A protocol is a combined set of specific rules that all nodes in the network follow. A protocol has many different purposes and functions, including

- Maintaining decentralization by eliminating the need for a central authority, distributing control across the entire network, and defining key parameters such as block size and miner rewards
- Ensuring the safe, efficient, and reliable data transfer across the network

- Maintaining and controlling security
- Operations of the consensus mechanism
- Networking functions
- Interoperability

Unfortunately, due to blockchain design limitations and disagreement among miners and network participants, these protocol upgrades cannot be incorporated without sometimes splitting the blockchain into two separate blockchains, each following its own independent protocol and community. The transactional history is shared and continues from one blockchain to another, but each blockchain goes in different directions. The process of forking varies depending on the blockchain's architecture and use case, and forks are generally categorized into two types: **soft forks** and **hard forks**.

Soft and Hard Forks

As previously stated, a "fork" occurs when miners and network participants cannot reach a unanimous consensus regarding new proposed changes and upgrades to the protocol. There are two types of forks: a soft fork and a hard fork—see a comparison of these fork types in Table 6-10.

Table 6-10. *Hard and soft forks compared*

	Blockchain Soft and Hard Forking	
	Soft Fork	**Hard Fork**
Definition	A soft fork is a backward-compatible upgrade to the protocol software.	A hard fork is a non-backward-compatible change to the protocol software that often results in a permanent split in the blockchain.
Forking (splitting)	No permanent split in the blockchain is necessary.	A permanent split in the blockchain is necessary.
Compatibility	Old nodes are still compatible with new nodes, meaning that nodes running older protocol versions can still validate new transactions.	The new nodes do not recognize the old nodes as valid. The old nodes will continue maintaining the original chain while the new nodes will operate and maintain the other "forked" blockchain.
Fork Awareness	When a soft fork happens, the old nodes are made aware that the consensus rules have changed.	When a Hard-fork happens, all nodes on the network are requested to make changes and upgrade to the new protocol. The nodes that do not upgrade will continue to operate and remain on the existing chain.
Protocol Changes	A new protocol is compatible with the old protocol. Old nodes will recognize the new blocks as valid.	A new protocol is not compatible with the old protocol. Old nodes do not recognize the new blocks as valid.

(*continued*)

Table 6-10. *(continued)*

Blockchain Soft and Hard Forking		
	Soft Fork	**Hard Fork**
Forking Affects	Soft forks generally cause less disruption, but they can still introduce major features or critical fixes.	Hard forks are more disruptive and typically are used for significant changes.
Miner's Responsibility	Miners can mine without upgrading, but if they don't follow the tighter soft-fork rules, their blocks may be rejected—so in practice they upgrade to avoid wasting work.	Miners must update their protocol to keep participating in the mining process.
Token Holders	Token holders are not affected.	Token holders on the old chain are usually granted tokens on the new one as well because they share the same history.
Example	Segregated Witness (SegWit) bitcoin protocol update	Bitcoin Cash

The forking of a blockchain project is extremely hard to predict and, in most cases, completely unpredictable in the early stages of the project lifecycle. A decision to fork tends to form as the chain matures and community members deem new requirements, upgrades, and updates necessary.

Fact Through advanced technology, infrastructure projects like Polkadot Network do not require forking in order to upgrade and update their blockchain.

Dangers with Hard Forking

The primary issue with forking is that it poses serious security threats; these include:

- When a blockchain project undergoes a hard fork and splits into two separate blockchains and cryptocurrencies—one crypto for each chain—it initially results in fewer miners and nodes. This, in turn, lowers the computing power for each blockchain. If any alliance of bad actors combines forces and controls more than 50% of the network, a 51% attack can occur, thus making the project extremely vulnerable to double-spending and fraudulent activity.
- When a blockchain forks, a 1:1 copy of the crypto tokens is produced and copied to the new "forked" chain. To claim their new tokens, holders must prove ownership of their assets by signing with their private keys. This presents an opportunity for scammers to pose as authority figures or team members, asking you to click on fraudulent links and stating, "Claim Your Tokens Here." They intend to gain access to your private keys to steal your funds.

- For both soft and hard forking, the time surrounding the fork and the price per coin are typically highly volatile; therefore, it is advised not to buy or sell your assets unless you are experienced and have a strategy and plan in place.

Sybil Attacks

The most challenging attack in permissionless blockchains is the Sybil attack, in which malicious actor(s) (nodes) create several fake identities to gain a disproportionately large influence on the network. The Sybil attack aims for these malicious nodes to fool the blockchain network into thinking their identity is genuine and legitimate. If they succeed in doing so and have enough malicious nodes on the network, they can use that influence against honest nodes for their benefit.

Fact The term "Sybil" comes from a 1973 novel by Flora Schreiber, which features a character named Sybil who has an identity-related medical issue and often operates with multiple identities.

Dangers of a Sybil Attack

An attacker could act maliciously in a voting referendum through on-chain governance by using multiple fake identities to outvote legitimate nodes. Moreover, attackers have the potential to intercept and analyze sensitive user data like IP addresses, compromising users' privacy and security. Sybil attacks can also compromise the integrity of a blockchain, leading to potential loss of funds, privacy breaches, and corrupted transaction data. They can also cause problems like refusing to receive or transmit blocks and blocking other network users. A Sybil attack in blockchain can also lead to *denial-of-service* (DoS) attacks.

Fact In 2020, the privacy-focused Monero blockchain was a victim of a Sybil attack that lasted ten days. Although unsuccessful due to Monero's community and diligent developer team, the attacker aimed to deanonymize platform transactions.

Denial-of-Service Attacks

A denial of service (DoS) attack targets to disrupt the availability of the network, server, or application and prevents legitimate requests from being executed. A DoS attack works by the attacker sending a flood of requests, thus overloading the victim's server to the point that it can't handle the load. It is important to note that sending requests can be legitimate and fraudulent (spam). Nevertheless, the DoS attack depletes the server's CPU or network's ability to operate normally and slows down transaction throughput, preventing the timely validation of legitimate transactions.

Fortunately, due to the decentralized nature of blockchain technology, including the protective attributes of consensus mechanisms, many DoS attacks are preventable. However, DoS attacks, primarily a variant named *distributed denial-of-service* (DDoS), are still prominent attacks in the blockchain realm. As the name suggests, a DDoS attack is a large, distributed type of DoS attack that affects a whole network of network participants, e.g., the blockchain. When this happens, attackers send spam transactions to the blockchain that fill up the block data, thus hindering legitimate transactions from being added to the chain. As a result, all legitimate transactions will end up in the mempool, waiting for the next block, but will not be added due to system failure. A new type of DoS attack, a blockchain denial-of-service (BDoS), has emerged, where PoW-based blockchains are attacked. BDoS attacks corrupt the mining reward incentive mechanism, where the attacker invests resources to incentivize rational miners to stop mining, potentially halting the blockchain.

Fact The Solana blockchain suffered multiple DDoS attacks in **January 2022**, causing it to go offline for approximately four hours.

Blockchain Investor Endpoint Security

Blockchain investor endpoint security refers to the protection measures designed to protect crypto investors when interacting with the blockchain and protect their digital assets from attackers. Attackers affect investors by intercepting the blockchain itself, resulting in hacking and stealing the chain's native assets. Attackers also directly attack investors by taking advantage of poor investor security measures and fraudulent links.

This section focuses on protecting the investor from attackers. Devices that access the blockchain, digital asset wallets, online and offline security, and other miscellaneous safety precautions and protective measures are discussed. Table 6-11 outlines these essential key protective measures for blockchain investors.

Table 6-11. *Blockchain Investor End-Point Security Protective Measures*

Blockchain Investor Endpoint Security Protective Measures	
Item Description	**Investor Action**
Paper Notebook for Login Details	Storing a digital asset wallet and crypto exchange login and password details in a notebook instead of an online password manager adds a layer of safety. Always create a paper backup in case the original backup gets accidentally lost or destroyed.
Two-Factor Authentication (2FA)	Download, install, and implement the Google Authenticator Application (or similar high-ranking authenticator software) on your cellular device, tablet, or computer. Using 2FA when accessing crypto exchanges or digital asset wallets is essential.

(*continued*)

Table 6-11. *(continued)*

Blockchain Investor Endpoint Security Protective Measures	
Item Description	**Investor Action**
Passwords	Ensure created passwords are long and secure using plenty of random letters, numbers, and special characters. Always store passwords in a paper notebook and keep a secure offline backup.
Security Updates	Ensure internet security is installed and updated on all devices, preventing hackers from attacking. Set alarms once a month to scan your computer for potential malware. It is also advised to consider keystroke encryption software.
Login Details	Creating a new unique email address for every new crypto exchange account opened is advised. This makes it difficult for attackers to access all asset accounts if compromised.
URLs	Unfortunately, many scams and "look-alike" fraudulent websites use identical front-end displays and similar URLs to those of reputable exchanges. The sole intention of these attackers is to fool people into entering their login details so that they can steal their digital assets. Always double-check URLs to ensure that you are accessing the correct website. Additionally, bookmark the URLs as an extra safety precaution.
Private Key Management	Safely storing your private keys is of the utmost importance. There are many ways to store your private keys, including paper wallets, hardware wallets, steel seed capsules, steel seed wallets, and many others. For most investors, the choice of storage depends on your level of interaction with your cryptocurrency assets. However, storing private keys and associated passwords in a notepad with a paper copy is strongly advised.

(continued)

Table 6-11. *(continued)*

Blockchain Investor Endpoint Security Protective Measures	
Item Description	**Investor Action**
Third-Party Wallet Applications	Using third-party wallet application providers to store digital assets is not recommended unless the team behind the wallet application has a flawless and credible reputation.
Cell Phone Security	Ensure that your cellular device is protected by reputable internet security software and is password protected at all times. Additionally, if the device is lost or stolen, ensure the phone's data can be erased remotely. Always keep your phone number private.
Custodial Services	Custodial services involve a third party (typically an exchange) holding the user's private keys. Here, the asset owner is required to trust the custodial provider to keep their assets secure. If it is deemed necessary to use custodial services, it is advised only to use reputable custodial services insured against an attack. These include the Coinbase and Gemini exchanges.
Non-Custodial Software Wallets	Non-custodial services give users full control and responsibility over their private keys. This allows for greater security and privacy, but full responsibility and technical fallsback on the asset owner. Only use non-custodial software wallets if absolutely necessary. Although you have complete control of your private keys, your assets are at risk if your device is hacked. Popular non-custodial software wallets include Atomic Wallet, MetaMask, and Exodus wallet providers.

(continued)

Table 6-11. (*continued*)

Blockchain Investor Endpoint Security Protective Measures	
Item Description	**Investor Action**
Cold (hardware) Wallet Storage	A cold storage wallet is a physical, offline, digital asset storage wallet not connected to the internet. It provides very high-level security. Always ensure the cold wallet is updated with the latest software from an authentic manufacturer link or website. Additionally, do not have any cold-storage access codes stored on your cellular device or computer connected to the internet. Examples of hardware wallets are Trezor and Ledger.
Virtual Private Network (VPN)	Using a VPN redirects your internet traffic to disguise your IP address, which makes it very difficult for attackers to track your exact location. In addition, a VPN encrypts the information you send through the internet, stopping anyone who wants to intercept your information. This applies to every web interaction, including signing in and out of crypto exchanges. VPN examples include NordVPN, ProtonVPN, and Surfshark.
Phishing Links	Phishing links are fraudulent links sent by attackers to investors to steal investor information, including login details and passwords, to steal your digital assets. These links are typically sent via email or through social media. Always assume a received link is fraudulent. Never click on a link without verifying it is from a trusted source by checking the email address. Hover over the link to see and determine if the URL is genuine. If you did make a specific request to a provider, disregard the email/link immediately.

(*continued*)

Table 6-11. (*continued*)

Blockchain Investor Endpoint Security Protective Measures	
Item Description	**Investor Action**
Digital Asset Transactions	Before initiating a transaction, it is recommended to double-check and ensure the correct receiving address has been entered. If an incorrect receiving address was used for the transaction, the sent funds are lost forever. As a safety precaution, and especially for people new to crypto, it is advised to send a small amount first to confirm the transaction was successful.
Passing/Death	As a precaution, in the event of your death, it is recommended to write down instructions on how to access your digital asset funds. This should also include all passwords, recovery seeds, codes, phrases, names of wallets, exchanges, associated URLs, etc.

Action Steps

It is extremely difficult for investors to foresee if a cryptocurrency project will suffer an attack or security breach. The attackers typically expose flaws and weak points in a cryptocurrency project. However, adhering to the following precaution and protective measures is recommended to eliminate or significantly reduce the likelihood of significant financial loss and ensure a more secure investment experience.

Please note that the following security checks and precautions exclude all security threats concerning the project "code" or programming languages. Threats that arise from "code" issues are covered in Chapter 12, "Project Codebase."

1) **51% Attacks**

   Statistically speaking, it is doubtful that the cryptocurrency project will suffer a 51% attack. However, below are two protective measures to protect investor assets.

   a) **Low Market Capitalizations –** Low market cap coins (e.g., coins under $10m MC) are at the most risk of a 51% attack; therefore, extreme caution is recommended when investing in these coins. Mitigate risk by limiting exposure to low market capitalization, less-established crypto projects.

   b) **PoW Consensus Mechanisms** – PoW-based projects are more susceptible to 51% attacks compared to other types of consensus mechanisms. For example, adopting a DPoS consensus mechanism (or similar variant) reduces the risk of a 51% attack, as the delegates or elected representatives can remove malicious or conspiring validator nodes suspected of planning a 51% attack. Always research and evaluate the pros and cons of a project's consensus mechanism prior to investing.

2) **Forking**

   If a "forking" situation arises, protect yourself through the following precautions:

a) Carefully read and become familiar with all the documentation about the upcoming fork. Ensure the project team provides the information about the fork, and it comes from legitimate sources, e.g., the company website's official project blog.

b) Do not deviate from the step-by-step procedure outlined by the team to protect and secure investor assets at the time of the fork.

c) Do not fall victim to fraudulent emails containing scam hyperlinks. Check the URL to ensure it is from the company site. If you are in doubt, contact the project team via official communication channels.

3) **Blockchain Investor Endpoint Security**

   Investors are recommended to adhere to the precautions and protective measures in Table 6-11 to promote safe interaction with the blockchain and protection of one's digital assets from attackers.

4) **Take Notes and Document Your Findings in Your Own Style**

5) **Combine the Findings with Other Sections of the Fundamental Evaluation Process**

Evaluation of the Results

As discussed, predicting if a crypto project will be subjected to a future attack is very difficult. However, once investors adhere to the precautions and protective measures outlined, the chances of losing one's assets are significantly reduced.

Public, Private, Hybrid, and Consortium Blockchains

Evaluation Objective: Determine if the project operates on a public blockchain to ensure it offers the transparency, immutability, and trustless nature that helps reduce risk compared to other blockchain types.

Blockchains types are classified into four main categories: *public, private, hybrid, and consortium blockchains*. Each blockchain type has its own purpose and associated pros and cons. There is no right or wrong type of blockchain; it solely depends on the blockchain requirements, functionality, and use case. However, public blockchains are more popular among investors because of high decentralization, security, transparency, immutability, and no requirement for trust among nodes or private entities. Table 6-12 outlines and compares the core differences between *public, private, hybrid, and consortium blockchains.*

Table 6-12. Public, private, hybrid, and consortium blockchain properties

	Blockchain Classifications			
Properties	**Public blockchain**	**Private blockchain**	**Hybrid blockchain**	**Consortium blockchain**
Determination of consensus	All miners	An organization	Multiple consensus models (organization-driven)	Selected, pre-approved nodes
Read permission	Public	Public or private	Public or private	Public or private
Immutability	Close to full immutability	Can be tampered with	Partly immutable (depends on public/private rules)—can be tampered with	Partly immutable (governance-based)—can be tampered with
Efficiency	Low (depends on scaling solutions)	High	High	High
Decentralization	Yes	No	Partly centralized	Partly centralized
Consensus process	Permissionless	Permissioned	Permissioned	Permissioned

(continued)

Table 6-12. (*continued*)

	Blockchain Classifications			
Properties	**Public blockchain**	**Private blockchain**	**Hybrid blockchain**	**Consortium blockchain**
Advantages/Benefits	Immutable, transparent, trustless, pseudonymous, decentralized	Privacy, scalability, speed, access control, performance, governance control	Flexibility and customization, high security and scalability, enhanced privacy, increased regulatory compliance	Decentralized, access controls, collaboration friendly, configurable (often negligible) transaction cost
Disadvantages/Issues	Poor scalability (improving with Layer 2s), low TPS, high energy consumption (with PoW), not suitable for holding sensitive data (no permission functionality available)	Trust involved, partly decentralized, lack of transparency, controlled governance, interoperability issues	Transparency, cost, governance complexities, interoperability issues	Lack of transparency, complexity, partly decentralized, maintainability, infrastructure costs, interoperability issues
Use Cases	Web3 dApps interaction, cryptocurrency/token investing, document validation	Supply chains—retail, healthcare, financial services, private asset ownership	Retail, supply chains, banking, real estate	Food tracking, banking, payments, research
Examples	bitcoin, Ethereum	Hyperledger, Quorum (kaleido.io)	XDC Network	R3

Public Blockchain

A *public blockchain* is an open, permissionless, transparent, and decentralized blockchain ledger. It allows all network participants to check and verify transactions on the blockchain and participate in the consensus process. Every participant in a public blockchain network can contribute to the control mechanism, agreeing on a single state of the data without needing a trusted third party. Unlike private blockchains, public blockchains are as close to immutable as possible, meaning it is extremely difficult to tamper with the blockchain. Each user has access to historical and contemporary records and, if they meet the protocol's requirements, can run a mining (or validator) node. Public blockchains have a higher decentralized level than that of private and consortium blockchains. Examples of public blockchains are bitcoin and Ethereum.

Advantages of a Public Blockchain

- **Decentralization** - Public blockchains are decentralized, meaning they operate without a central authority, providing greater transparency and resilience to the network.
- **Transparency** - Transactions on public blockchains are transparent and open to all participants, increasing trust and reducing the risk of fraud.
- **Immutability** - Transactions on public blockchains are immutable, meaning they cannot be altered or deleted, making them highly secure.
- **Incentivization** - Public blockchains use incentives like cryptocurrencies to encourage participants to validate transactions and maintain the network in a non-malicious manner.

- **Accessibility** – Public blockchains are open to anyone, regardless of their geographic location or financial status, providing equal access to the network.

Disadvantages of a Public Blockchain

- **Scalability** – Public blockchains can suffer congestion because capacity does not grow linearly with users; however, Layer-2 solutions (rollups, channels) increasingly mitigate this limit.
- **Privacy** – Public blockchains are transparent, meaning that transactions are visible to all participants, which can be a disadvantage for organizations dealing with sensitive information.
- **Regulatory Challenges** – Some public blockchains' lack of central authority and anonymity features can pose regulatory challenges.

Overall, public blockchains offer significant benefits regarding transparency, security, and accessibility but also have limitations, such as scalability, privacy, and regulatory challenges. These factors should be considered when determining whether a public blockchain is the right solution for a particular use case.

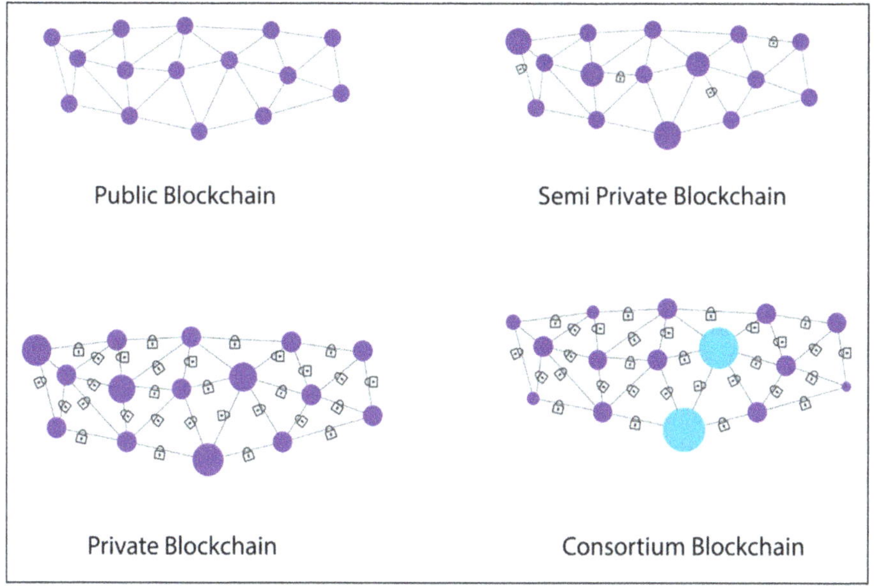

Figure 6-16. *Public, private, hybrid, and consortium blockchain architectural structure (compliments of `https://komodoplatform.com/en/academy/blockchain-technology-types/`)*

Private Blockchain

A *private* blockchain is a centralized distributed ledger that operates as a closed "database catering to organizational privacy requirements." In a private blockchain, the nodes are restricted from the public, and only those with permission rights from the organization can run a full node, make transactions, or validate/authenticate the blockchain changes. The participant's identity and credentials must be authenticated, verified, and authorized before mining rights are granted. Additionally, due to various strict policies within organizations, it is not uncommon for nodes to be denied access even if all their credentials are in order. Once a node has been granted access, the owner has the right to revoke access or override, edit, or delete any transactional data that has been executed and added to the ledger. Private blockchains are typically smaller than other blockchain types and are operated by organizations that want to execute smart contracts with high security and speed.

A private blockchain is a **permissioned** distributed ledger that operates as a closed database catering to organizational privacy requirements. In a private blockchain, nodes are restricted from the public, and only those with permission from the organization can run a full node, make transactions, or validate/authenticate ledger changes. The participant's identity and credentials must be authenticated, verified, and authorized before validator privileges are granted; many private chains dispense with proof-of-work mining altogether and instead use permissioned consensus algorithms such as PBFT or Raft. Additionally, strict internal policies may still deny nodes access even when their credentials are in order. Once a node has been granted access, the owner can revoke rights or override, edit, or delete transactional data already written to the ledger. Private blockchains are typically smaller than other blockchain types and are operated by organizations that need high-speed, high-security smart-contract execution. An Example of a private blockchain is Corda. An example of a private blockchain is Hyperledger Fabric.

Fact Although private, hybrid, and consortium blockchains may benefit organizations that want to utilize the benefits of blockchain technology while remaining private, they are not considered immutable, meaning the blockchain transactional history can be tampered with and reversed. Additionally, they introduce a "trust" factor affecting transparency, contradicting the core benefits of blockchain technology.

Advantages of a Private Blockchain

- **Privacy** - Depending on company requirements, private blockchains are more private than public blockchains, as they allow only authorized participants to access and view data.
- **Scalability** - Private blockchains can handle more transactions per second (TPS) than public blockchains, making them faster and more efficient.
- **Governance Control** - Private blockchains enable organizations to have more control over the governance of the network, allowing them to set their own rules and standards and make decisions without any interference.

Disadvantages of a Private Blockchain

- **Centralization** - Private blockchains are more centralized than public blockchains because they are owned and operated by a single organization or consortium of organizations.
- **Security** - A private blockchain network is centralized, increasing the risk of attack. Private blockchains have fewer nodes or members, making them more vulnerable to a security compromise.
- **Limited Transparency** - Private blockchains have limited transparency, as they only allow authorized participants to access and view data, which can limit trust and increase the risk of fraud.

- **Trust** - Since private blockchain nodes are centralized, achieving trust in the system is difficult.
- **Interoperability** - Private blockchains can be challenging to integrate with other systems and blockchains, making it difficult to achieve interoperability.
- **Dependency** - Private blockchains depend on the infrastructure and resources provided by the organization or consortium that owns and operates them.

Hybrid Blockchain

A *hybrid* blockchain (aka a semi-private blockchain) combines characteristics of public and private blockchains, typically public and private, where multiple users are given permissions and abilities. The idea behind a hybrid blockchain is to take advantage of the benefits of each type of blockchain while minimizing its limitations. For example, a public blockchain is known for its transparency and immutability, but it may not be suitable for handling sensitive data or providing privacy. On the other hand, a private blockchain offers more control over data privacy and access, but it lacks the transparency and security of a public blockchain.

Fact In a hybrid blockchain, transactions and records are typically not made public; however, they can be validated (if required) by granting access via a smart contract.

In a hybrid blockchain, the public blockchain records transactions that need to be transparent and publicly visible, while the private blockchain stores sensitive information that must remain confidential. These two blockchains are connected via a communication layer, enabling secure and seamless information exchange between them. Hybrid blockchains are becoming increasingly popular as they balance the benefits of public and private blockchains, making them suitable for a wide range of use cases, including retail and highly regulated markets such as the banking sector. XDC Network is a hybrid chain: its public ledger anchors transactions for transparency, while private sub-networks handle sensitive data—demonstrating how a single platform can deliver both public and permissioned functionality.

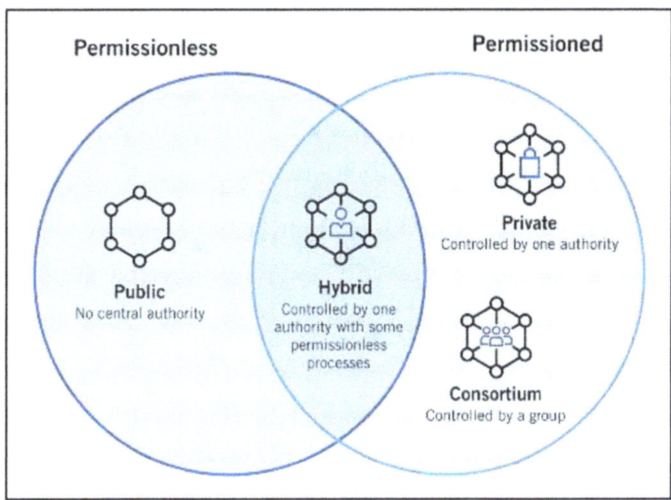

***Figure 6-17.** Hybrid blockchain (compliments of `www.simplilearn.com`)*

Advantages of a Hybrid Blockchain

- **Flexibility** - A hybrid blockchain can be customized to fit specific use cases that require the functionality and benefits of both private and public blockchains.

- **Scalability** - A hybrid blockchain is partly centralized, which allows it to scale as per demand, allowing for high transaction volumes and sensitive data storage.
- **Privacy** - A hybrid blockchain can offer enhanced privacy for sensitive data by using a private blockchain for specific information.
- **Compliance** - Hybrid blockchains can be designed to comply with specific regulations or industry standards.

Disadvantages of a Hybrid Blockchain

- **Transparency** - Hybrid blockchains restrict access to certain information on the network.
- **Complexity** - Hybrid blockchains can be more complex to design, develop, and maintain than single blockchain solutions.
- **Cost** - Hybrid blockchain solutions can be more expensive due to the additional development and maintenance required.
- **Governance** - The governance structure of a hybrid blockchain can be more complex, requiring careful coordination between the public and private blockchains.
- **Interoperability** - Interaction and communication with different blockchains can be challenging, limiting the effectiveness of a hybrid blockchain solution.

Consortium Blockchain

A consortium blockchain—also called a federated blockchain—falls between public and private models: it is permissioned yet jointly governed by multiple independent organizations. However, it differs from a typical hybrid and private blockchain because it is not owned by a single entity or individual. Instead, it involves various organizational members working together on a decentralized network. It also differs in functionality because transaction data are submitted by several member organizations and validated only by their pre-approved nodes, not by the open public. It selects nodes from a public or private branch of the blockchain to handle the verification and consensus process. The data in a consortium blockchain can be open or private and be noted as partly decentralized. Examples of consortium blockchains are Hyperledger, Hashed Health, and R3.

Fact A consortium blockchain is classified as a permissioned blockchain because only selected nodes are authorized to have read and write permissions. Access groups can be controlled and limited, thus eliminating the risks that come with just one entity controlling the network on a private blockchain.

Advantages of a Consortium Blockchain

- **Decentralization** - Consortium blockchains are decentralized, meaning they operate without a central authority, providing greater transparency and resilience to the network.
- **Access Controls** - Consortium blockchains allow only authorized participants to access and view data, providing enhanced privacy and security.

- **Governance** - Consortium blockchains provide more control over the governance of the network, as organizations can set their own rules and standards.
- **Collaboration** - Consortium blockchains encourage collaboration between organizations, promoting data sharing and resources.
- **Transactions** - Fast transaction speed with little to no transaction fee required.

Disadvantages of a Consortium Blockchain

- **Transparency** – Less transparent than public blockchains.
- **Complexity** - Consortium blockchains can be more complex to design, develop, and maintain than single blockchain solutions.
- **Dependency** - Consortium blockchains depend on the infrastructure and resources provided by the organizations that own and operate them.
- **Infrastructure Cost** - Implementing a consortium blockchain solution can be expensive due to the additional development and maintenance required.
- **Maintainability** - Upgrading the blockchain is a long and tedious task requiring every member's permission.
- **Consensus** - Chances of frequent disputes between the member organizations.

Top of Form

What Does All This Mean for Investors?

Public blockchains *generally* present the lowest operational risk for retail investors. The public open-source nature promotes a high level of transparency, which is one of the core benefits of blockchain over traditional centralized companies. Most blockchain-based projects launched are public and open-source, with only a minute few comprising private, hybrid, or consortium blockchains. That said, enterprises are increasingly deploying private or consortium networks to enable deeper, domain-specific collaboration among trusted parties.

Due to their non-transparent and semi-transparent nature, private and hybrid blockchains tend to carry high risks for investors. Moreover, most investors are not interested in these types of blockchains because of the level of trust involved, coupled with the fact that block data, can be modified only through authorized governance processes, and any edits are logged for auditability. While consortium blockchains offer fast transaction speed, they are also semi-private, introducing the "trust" factor and suffering from limited public transparency—though authorized members typically have full access to the ledger.

Action Steps

Follow the steps below to determine if the project operates on a public blockchain to ensure it offers the transparency, immutability, and trustless nature that helps reduce risk compared to other blockchain types.

1) **Verify Blockchain Type**

   Verify, with the aid of the whitepaper, if the project is utilizing a public, private, hybrid, or consortium-type blockchain.

   a) If a public blockchain type is adopted, move to the next part of the overall evaluation.

b) If a private, hybrid, or consortium blockchain is utilized, it is recommended that more research be conducted into why, with the preferable option of passing on the investment.

2) **Take Notes and Document Your Findings in Your Own Style**

3) **Combine the Findings with Other Sections of the Fundamental Evaluation Process**

Evaluation of the Results

It is strongly recommended to gravitate toward public blockchains when investing because private, hybrid, or consortium-type blockchains carry too much risk for investors.

Permissionless and Permissioned Blockchains

Evaluation Objective: Determine if a blockchain is permissionless to ensure it offers full transparency, decentralized governance, and open participation.

Blockchains can be further classified as either *permissioned* or *permissionless*. Permissionless or permissioned refers to how blockchains are governed regarding user access, transparency, verification, and decentralization. Both types have their benefits and drawbacks; however, for several reasons, permissionless blockchains tend to be the more attractive choice for investors.

The most significant difference between permissionless and permissioned blockchains is that, unlike a permissioned blockchain, a permissionless blockchain has no restrictions and allows for open participation, where anyone can run a node and attempt to validate blocks; voting power is determined by hash power (PoW) or staked coins (PoS), not by prior approval. A permissioned blockchain governs the consensus by restricting the access of the consensus protocol to the selected few governing nodes, which can often result in an increased level of centralization and malicious behavior. Because permissioned blockchains require network nodes to trust the governing nodes to reach consensus, they deviate from the core "trustless" principle that defines blockchain technology.

Fact A permissioned blockchain doesn't have to be private—access can be restricted to vetted participants while transaction data, state proofs, or even a read-only API remain publicly visible, blending selective membership with open transparency.

It is important to note that, by definition, a permissioned blockchain is not obligated to be private in nature. A permissioned blockchain can also be a public blockchain but with regulated access. Let's assume bitcoin, a public permissionless blockchain, decided to become a public permissioned blockchain. This can be achieved by introducing an access control layer to the top of the bitcoin blockchain that verifies the identity of a user and then allows access to the blockchain—although there is no chance of this ever happening with bitcoin. Table 6-13 outlines and compares permissionless and permissioned blockchains.

Fact most public blockchains are permissionless, meaning public nodes can freely join the network without permission. Each node on the network has full read and write permissions.

Table 6-13. Permissionless versus permissioned type blockchains

Permissionless Versus Permissioned Blockchains		
	Permissionless	**Permissioned**
Description	A permissionless blockchain is an open public blockchain, meaning anyone can run a node and participate in the consensus validation.	A permissioned blockchain is a closed network. Network participants must be granted permission to participate in the consensus validation.
Uses	Digital asset trading, crowdfunding, insurance, decentralized finance, gaming NFTs, donations, distributed file storage, and many more.	Typically used by organizations to manage supply chains, internal voting, create contracts, verify payment between parties, etc.
Consensus Mechanism	Typically, use proof-of-work (PoW) or proof-of-stake (PoS), where anyone can participate in transaction validation.	Typically, proof-of-authority (PoA) or practical byzantine fault tolerance (PBFT) is used, where only a pre-approved set of nodes (validators) can validate transactions.
Traits/ Characteristics	Fully decentralized Trustless Transparent	Partly decentralized Trusted Partly transparent
Blockchain Development	Open sourced	Closed to public/developed by a closed group of selected developers.
Scalability	Issues with scalability	More scalable than permissionless but with a higher level of centralization.

(continued)

Table 6-13. *(continued)*

Permissionless Versus Permissioned Blockchains		
	Permissionless	**Permissioned**
Energy	Fluctuating energy costs depend on the consensus mechanism utilized.	More energy efficient
Transaction Speed	Generally slower than permissioned blockchains.	Faster than permissionless
Governance	Decentralized governance structure (Governed by consensus-based protocols.)	Centralized governance structure (Not governed by consensus-based protocols—Decisions are made on a central, predefined level by network members.)
Security	High security due to a high level of decentralization. The possibility of collusion by bad actors within the network is reduced.	Not as secure as permissionless blockchains, the security relies on the integrity of its internal members (nodes).

What Does This Mean for Investors?

As per Table 6-13, permissionless and permissioned blockchains have specific pros and cons. However, *permissionless blockchains* are much preferred by investors over permissioned blockchains for the following reasons.

- **Transparency** – Permissionless blockchains are fully transparent, meaning all users can access transactional data on the network. Transparency is essential to incentivize users to trust the blockchain network.

- **Verification Process** - Permissive blockchains allow the public an opportunity to participate in the verification process known as *mining*. No permission rights or authorization is necessary.
- **Monetary and Utility Benefits** - Permissionless blockchains allow anyone to purchase native coins, which can be used for various on-chain utilities (transactions, governance activities, etc.) on the network and may also hold monetary value.
- **Decentralization** - Permissionless networks are decentralized, resulting in higher security and community trust.

Action Steps

Follow these steps to determine if a blockchain is permissionless to ensure it offers full transparency, decentralized governance, and open participation.

1) **Verify If a Permissioned or Permissionless Blockchain**

   Locate the project whitepaper and search for verbiage about permissions. Typically, every blockchain whitepaper has this called out. It may also be discussed in the technical help documents for node setup. Reach out to the project team if in doubt.

   a) If the project being evaluated is a dApp, determine the underlying blockchain layer it is built on and then continue to determine if it is of permissionless or permissioned type.

2) **Take Notes and Document Your Findings in Your Own Style**

3) **Combine the Findings with Other Sections of the Fundamental Evaluation Process**

Evaluation of the Results

If the blockchain is permissioned, it carries unnecessary risks that make it less attractive for investment. Most investors are drawn to cryptocurrency projects because of the financial benefits linked to permissionless blockchains. Therefore, it is recommended to focus on permissionless blockchain projects, which offer a higher potential for financial growth.

Anonymity- and Privacy-Enabled Blockchains

Evaluation Objective: Determine if a project offers identity protection and privacy features that keep your data safe and allow for secure, anonymous interactions.

Protecting user privacy has been a major concern for people for decades. Outside of the dangers of user data being stored in centralized silos, which are subject to a single point of attack, user data can also be exploited and sold by large corporations for a profit. Gathering and sharing user data among corporations turns companies into powerful monopolies, making it extremely difficult for smaller companies to compete. When user data is sold, it is bundled into smaller groups and sold to other companies for target campaigns—a never-ending privacy battle for users and their data. Furthermore, online users are frequently required to provide sensitive information, such as social security numbers, passports, driving licenses, and birth certificates, to prove their identity, which has led to hackers getting access to this data, resulting in the data being manipulated and used in fraudulent activities.

How Does Blockchain Help Protect User Data?

Blockchain technology protects user data against the threats listed above, thus helping to maximize user privacy and pseudonymity. This is achieved through the unique decentralization properties that accommodate the safe, decentralized data storage on a peer-to-peer network. Unlike traditional centralized data servers, blockchain leverages its decentralized structure and robust verification mechanisms to store and replicate user data, eliminating the risk of a single point of failure.

It is important to note that not all cryptocurrency projects possess complete user privacy and anonymity qualities. Most cryptocurrency projects are "*pseudonymous,*" meaning users interact with the blockchain using an alter identity known as a *public address*. This public address provides user privacy and shields their true identity from the general public. However, a user's pseudonymity can be compromised if people can link their identity and public address together. An example of this would be if a user posted their public address on a website or social media as a payment method, accepting donations, or interacting on a centralized exchange. Once people match your name to your public address, they can quickly determine what assets you hold by entering your public address into the block explorer (e.g., Etherscan for Ethereum).

All *pseudonymous* blockchain transactions are deemed traceable and can be tracked on the blockchain explorer. However, this level of transparency has given rise to concerns regarding privacy and the potential for surveillance. As a result, specific blockchains that focus on privacy were created. These blockchains counteract traceability by utilizing privacy-enabled features that prevent other users from viewing your transactional history and assets. The *Monero* blockchain is an example of a privacy-enabled blockchain. While privacy-focused blockchains like Monero provide excellent anonymity and privacy features, they are somewhat disliked by regulators and law enforcement because they are exploited for illegal activities, such as money laundering or financing illicit operations.

Identity and Data Protection

The difference between *anonymity* and *pseudonymity* is that anonymity enables users to operate or speak in a way that makes them completely unidentifiable. In contrast, pseudonymity allows users to be identified by a chosen name or identifier, which conceals their true identity. Blockchain projects like Kilt Protocol and Mina Protocol offer true anonymity and identity privacy. These blockchains allow users to interact anonymously online and remove the requirement to submit identity-related documents such as a passport or driving license to verify their identity.

Figure 6-18 shows a snapshot of the KILT Protocol wallet that allows users to interact anonymously with various services online. Through Kilt's unique technology, once users verify their identity, they can sign up and register for many websites and services without having to prove their identity again with highly personal information. For example, upon registering for a centralized digital asset exchange, instead of the user submitting their passport, driving license, and proof of residential address, they would verify their identity by submitting a cryptographic "*proof*," which essentially would validate—or invalidate—the user's identity.

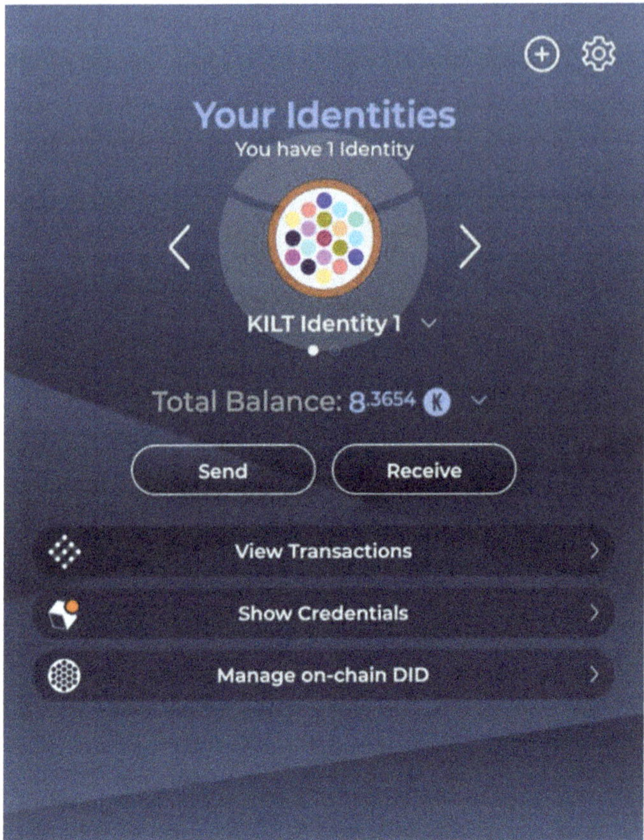

***Figure 6-18.** Kilt protocol—Sporran identity wallet (Chrome extension) (compliments of `https://www.kilt.io/`)*

What Does This Mean for Investors?

Privacy-enabled blockchains such as Pirate Chain and KILT Protocol are relatively new but are becoming more popular as time progresses. The average person strives for higher security and protection of their data and identity when interacting with online and offline services. Given that most crypto projects do not offer privacy features, they are not crucial when investing. Furthermore, privacy blockchains offering identity protection are a specific niche. Therefore, when investing in a project offering identity privacy, it is advised to only compare and evaluate against similar projects within the same niche.

Pro Tip Outside of investment purposes, protecting your privacy is of the utmost importance, which everyone should have the right to. As such, exploring projects such as KILT Protocol may be worthwhile.

Action Steps

Follow these steps to determine if a project offers identity protection and privacy features that keep your data safe and allow for secure, anonymous interactions.

1) **Determine If the Project Possesses Privacy and Identity Protection Features**

   From the Protect Whitepaper, determine if the project offers privacy and/or identity protection features.

2) **Take Notes and Document Your Findings in Your Own Style**

3) **Combine the Findings with Other Sections of the Fundamental Evaluation Process**

Evaluation of the Results

Privacy and identity protection are specialized areas that do not impact the core evaluation of projects outside this niche.

Governance

Evaluation Objective: Determine if a blockchain uses on-chain governance to ensure a fair, transparent process that benefits from decentralization and automated decision-making.

Given the importance of blockchain governance, an entire book could be dedicated to the subject alone. However, as per the scope of this book, the key points of blockchain governance are discussed. Governance refers to the structures and processes that ensure accountability, transparency, responsiveness, stability, inclusiveness, empowerment, and broad-based participation. More specifically, blockchain governance comprises a set of rules and processes that help regulate a blockchain's direction and core functionality, including the overall architecture, upgrades, and new features. The whitepaper generally details valuable information about a project's blockchain governance model.

It is common for blockchains to incorporate governance functionality into their native coin or token. An example of this is seen with the Polkadot Networks, native coin, and DOT. As part of Polkadot's governance model, DOT holders can lock up their DOT if they want to participate and vote in Polkadot's public referendums.

Like every country needs to govern itself with laws, regulations, and new changes, this principle also applies to blockchain-based companies. However, institutional, private, and retail investors typically share differing interests and perspectives on what is best for the blockchain network. To rectify these issues, effective governance is essential to foster compromise, equality, and mediation among all parties involved. Through blockchain governance, digital asset holders have the opportunity to vote on important decisions that ultimately affect the long-term success and longevity of the project.

A clear, maintainable, efficient blockchain governance structure must be implemented to help enhance a project's success and community spirit. The lack of blockchain governance can result in many issues, including hard and soft fork splits, division of communities, code vulnerabilities, and loss of community and investor interest, all of which affect the long-term success and longevity of the project. Robust decentralized governance can help *mitigate* these issues by providing a frictionless on-chain voting process that lets participants contribute to protocol decisions.

When designing, operating, and managing a blockchain, important decisions are made in a wide range of architectural areas. These decisions, typically voted upon through governance, are critical to the blockchain's success. As per Evrim Tan, *"Blockchain Governance" in the Public Sector,* a typical framework clusters nine types of governance decisions, which are as follows:

1) **Infrastructure architecture**
2) **Application architecture**
3) **Interoperability**
4) **Decision-making mechanism**
5) **Incentive mechanism**
6) **Consensus mechanism**
7) **Organization of governance**
8) **Accountability of governance**
9) **Control of governance**

Blockchain Governance Models

Participation through blockchain governance is primarily achieved through two main types of governance models: ***on-chain governance*** *and* ***off-chain governance.*** Note some blockchains also adopt a hybrid governance model where elements of both on-chain and off-chain governance are combined, allowing for a balance between decentralization and efficiency. It enables network participants to vote on key decisions (on-chain) while allowing a centralized party or parties to make certain decisions quickly and efficiently when needed (off-chain). However, in the interest of simplicity and fundamental evaluation requirements, this section solely focuses on on-chain and off-chain governance models.

Off-Chain Governance

As the name suggests, with off-chain governance, all decisions, public discussions, proposals, and collectively agreed-upon updates are made off-chain in a centralized manner. Off-chain governance often relies on informal processes such as mailing-list debates, GitHub pull requests, or improvement-proposal frameworks (e.g., Ethereum's EIPs). While the core team usually coordinates the discussion and tallies sentiment, final changes still depend on broad community acceptance—miners, validators, and users must upgrade their software for any decision to take effect.

On-Chain Governance

Through an on-chain governance system, all the formal proposal and voting phases are recorded on-chain, while discussion happens off-chain and implementation is carried out by the core team. Unlike an off-chain governance structure, on-chain governance is online only; however, a small group, or board, of developers manages, coordinates, and helps reach consensus between the stakeholders (if required). In an on-chain structure, stakeholders comprise miners, developers, and asset holders.

Figure 6-19 shows Polkassembly—an open-source premier platform for governance and collaboration in the Polkadot ecosystem—where users can view and engage in Moonbeam Network's on-chain governance processes.

Fact Polkadot's native token, DOT, plays a key role in on-chain activities such as governance, staking, and bonding, allowing stakeholders to participate in the network's operation and decision-making process.

Figure 6-19. Polkassembly is an open-source platform where users can view and engage in Moonbeam Network's on-chain governance processes (compliments of `https://moonbeam.network/tutorial/participate-in-moonbeam-governance-with-polkassembly/`)

During an on-chain public vote, developers propose changes called *improvement proposals* through code updates. Each stakeholder has the opportunity to either accept or reject the proposed change. Stakeholders use their private keys for verification and submission. Many networks employ token-weighted voting (the more native coins you hold, the greater your voting power); for example, a participant with 10 000 coins carries more weight than one with 2 000. Other protocols adopt one-validator-one-vote, quadratic, or reputation-based schemes. This provides an incentive to investors who have a genuine interest in the blockchain projects success. Additionally, some cryptocurrency projects reward participants for taking part in governance referendums.

Off-Chain Versus On-Chain Governance

Table 6-14 outlines the distinct differences between on-chain and off-chain governance models. Use it as a general guide rather than a project-by-project verdict—each protocol tweaks the rules in its own way, so no single description fits all cases. For context, on-chain setups include Polkadot Network, Tezos, and Decred, while off-chain processes drive bitcoin's BIP and Ethereum's EIP.

Table 6-14. *On-chain versus off-chain blockchain governance*

Comparison of Off-Chain Versus On-Chain Blockchain Governance		
	Off-Chain Governance	**On-Chain Governance**
Definition	Governance rules and decisions occur outside the protocol through forums, calls, and improvement drafts.	Governance rules and decisions are embedded in protocol code and executed by smart contracts.
Formality and Structure	Informal, norm-driven. Forums, developer meetings, and improvement drafts guide changes without legally binding rules.	Formal, rule-driven. Smart-contract procedures define who can propose, how to vote, and how thresholds are tallied.

(*continued*)

Table 6-14. (*continued*)

Comparison of Off-Chain Versus On-Chain Blockchain Governance		
	Off-Chain Governance	**On-Chain Governance**
Transparency	Opaque in comparison—discussions and decisions happen off-chain (e.g., on mailing lists or calls), which can make the process less transparent or even "hidden" to outsiders.	Transparent by design—all proposals, votes, and outcomes are recorded on the public ledger, allowing anyone to audit the governance process in real time.
Decision-Making Process	Decisions emerge via social consensus and offline agreement. If accepted, they are implemented through software updates that network participants choose to run.	Decisions are made via on-chain voting mechanisms. Stakeholders (e.g., token holders) vote on proposals through the blockchain.
Trust Requirements	Trust in people is required. Since governance operates off the ledger, stakeholders must rely on core developers, miners, or foundation leaders to honor consensus and implement decisions.	Trust in the protocol—decisions are enforced by code and distributed consensus, reducing reliance on any single individual.

(*continued*)

Table 6-14. *(continued)*

Comparison of Off-Chain Versus On-Chain Blockchain Governance		
	Off-Chain Governance	**On-Chain Governance**
Upgrade Mechanism	Software updates driven by community agreement. Community-agreed software releases roll out upgrades; users choose to install them, and if too many refuse the update, the chain can split.	On-chain proposals and code amendments are decided within the system. Token holders vote on proposals; once a change passes, the protocol auto-applies it—no off-chain wrangling required (in most circumstances).
Adaptability	Flexible—rules aren't hard-coded, so the community can bend or add them when needed, though debate can drag.	Rigid—rules are baked into code; consistent but hard to change quickly without a new on-chain vote.
Incentives	No native token rewards: participation hinges on reputation, community goodwill, or other off-chain perks because governance sits outside the protocol's incentive layer.	Embedded token rewards or staking bonds motivate voters and directly link governance actions to the network's economic outcomes.
Stakeholder Participation	Open discussion but unofficial—anyone can weigh in, yet a small core of developers and miners usually decides, limiting wider influence.	Inclusive by design but uneven—any token holder can vote, but if turnout is low and large holders dominate, this raises decentralization concerns (although some protocols have protection against this).

(continued)

Table 6-14. (*continued*)

Comparison of Off-Chain Versus On-Chain Blockchain Governance		
	Off-Chain Governance	**On-Chain Governance**
Consensus Method	Rough consensus—no fixed vote count; agreement is gauged informally, so decisions can be fuzzy and drag on when opinions split in some circumstances.	Formal votes—majority or supermajority rules give quick, clear results, but token weighting can tilt power toward big holders (although some protocols have protection against this).
Complexity	High social complexity—governance is scattered across chats and forums, unstructured, and hard to audit.	High technical complexity—smart-contract code is heavy to build, yet once live, it's fully on-chain and easy to audit.
Automation and Execution	Manual—developers push updates; nodes opt in, but the manual nature often results in delays or errors.	Automated—protocol self-executes approved changes (though some protocols still require limited manual steps).

Fact Powered by a Wasm-based runtime, the Polkadot Network can enact forkless upgrades—on-chain governance votes swap in new code, adding features or fixing bugs without the disruption of a hard fork.

What Does This Mean for Investors?

The topic of blockchain governance is far from unique, but there are still a lot of opinions about whether blockchains are better suited to off-chain or on-chain governance models. There are arguments for both on-chain and off-chain model types. One important aspect is that, similar to decentralization enabling autonomy, on-chain governance enables all stakeholder voices to be heard in a trustless, transparent manner, thus allowing "the people" to self-govern the direction of the blockchain. All stakeholders should have the opportunity to vote and influence the direction and success of the blockchain through an equal and transparent process, not just high-end network investors and investment entities.

It can be argued that the benefits of on-chain governance are on a case-by-case basis depending on the type of blockchain and the types and severity level of the decisions to be made. More specifically, the question is whether the benefits of human decision-making (off-chain) outweigh the benefits of on-chain code-based rule decision-making made through an on-chain automated process. Although the on-chain governance process still relies on the thoughts and decisions made by all stakeholders, there is no heavy human interaction and discussion as per traditional off-chain systems, which could either have a negative or positive effect.

Moving forward and toward a fairer and more decentralized world, gravitating closer to a complete on-chain governance model is somewhat logical, considering the array of benefits it has over traditional off-chain governance processes. Although some kinks remain, progress has been made in massive strides, and a decentralized, equal, efficient, and transparent governance process is now upon us. A blockchain with such on-chain governance features can be seen as an advantage, majorly contributing to the overall advancement and success of the blockchain.

Action Steps

Follow these steps to determine if a blockchain uses on-chain governance to ensure a fair, transparent process that benefits from decentralization and automated decision-making.

1) **Determine the Type of Governance Structure Implemented**

    a) Identify if the blockchain utilizes an on-chain or off-chain governance model from the project whitepaper. Reach out to the project team for further clarification (if required).

    b) For dApps, the underlying blockchain strongly influences the governance process adopted. Research the blockchain on which the dApp is built, and review whether it adopts an on-chain or off-chain governance model.

2) **Take Notes and Document Your Findings in Your Own Style**

3) **Combine the Findings with Other Sections of the Fundamental Evaluation Process**

Evaluation of the Results

Blockchain infrastructures with full on-chain governance technology are significantly more advanced than blockchains that rely on traditional off-chain models. Long-term investing in fundamentally strong projects with full on-chain governance technology is admirable. Whether a project entirely or partially implements this technology is less important; knowing that the underlying infrastructure incorporates on-chain governance features at their disposal is a major fundamental advantage.

However, investors should not be discouraged if the project possesses an off-chain or partly centralized (hybrid) governance protocol, provided there is a solid, near-transparent voting system in place that includes the community. This should be combined with some form of guarantee that a single group does not make final decisions for people.

Cross-Chain Interoperability

Evaluation Objective: Evaluate the network's level of cross-chain interoperability.

Cross-chain interoperability simply refers to a blockchain's ability to freely communicate with other blockchains, thus aiding a frictionless transfer of information, assets, and data with one another. With the correct cross-chain interoperability protocol solution, any economic activity on one blockchain can be represented on another blockchain. Spreading economic activity from one blockchain to another will, in turn, unlock a giant blockchain ecosystem that enables the frictionless free flow of data and assets—this is the overall goal. However, this is not easily achieved.

Imagine the destruction if banks across the globe failed to communicate with one another. The transfer of money would cease, causing complete chaos. Similarly, imagine if *Gmail* could not communicate with *Outlook* or *Yahoo*, the entire system would crash, causing catastrophic inefficiency in communication. The same principle also applies to blockchain networks. Unlike humans, most blockchains cannot naturally communicate (talk) with one another; however, a few—such as Cosmos, which ships with IBC, and Polkadot, whose XCM format lets its parachains exchange messages—are purpose-built for native cross-chain communication. Although this issue isn't unique to blockchain—many tech products mature in isolated silos—the ecosystem still struggles to scale because most networks grow inside their own independent silos. There are many different ways blockchains can be constructed, each satisfying and tailoring a wide range of applications; due to this, they have little in common with each other. There is an array of different blockchains, all competing with one another with varying levels of scalability, decentralization, security, privacy, programmability, and interoperability. However, no universal blockchain protocol satisfies the entire blockchain ecosystem. This blockchain tribalism leads to a significant duplication of efforts, with many developers opting to deploy their smart contracts on multiple blockchains, further dividing communities and introducing UI hurdles.

Take bitcoin, for example; due to bitcoin's specific protocol, programming language, and architecture design, bitcoin cannot freely communicate with, e.g., Ethereum. More specifically, the assets and transactions documented and stored on bitcoin's network cannot be easily represented on other blockchains. The same principle applies to the majority of blockchains: due to their independent system protocols, programming languages, consensus mechanisms, architecture design, and other influencing factors—such as the ever-evolving advancement of blockchain features and requirements—blockchains cannot communicate in a frictionless manner. Due to this barrier, data, information, and native and derivative assets from a specific blockchain cannot be transferred organically. Although collaboration is clearly visible, each network aims to grow its own independent ecosystem to claim the "throne." New innovative architectural designs strive to satisfy interoperable issues; however, currently, there is no one-size-fits-all solution.

Interoperability Solutions

The value of a blockchain is limited to its ability and level of interoperability to communicate with other ecosystems. Interoperability between blockchains unlocks a huge amount of liquidity and utility. To enhance these capabilities, blockchain networks are desperately trying to overcome interoperability issues with various techniques—these techniques are discussed in the section.

1) **Cross-Chain Bridges**

   Cross-chain bridges—essentially software applications—"bridge" the gap, enabling the transfer of cryptocurrency, wrapped tokens, non-fungible tokens (NFTs), or other digital assets between blockchain networks. Token bridges work by locking or burning tokens via a smart contract on a source chain and unlocking or minting tokens via a separate smart contract on the destination chain. Cross-chain bridges are not limited to any network. However, because most token bridges rely on a small—often centralized—validator set or multi-sig, any flaw in the bridge contracts or in either connected chain makes them prime targets for hacks. There are many types of token bridges available; the three main ones are as follows:

   a) **Burn and Mint** - Burn tokens on the source chain, then reissue the same tokens by minting them on the destination chain.

   b) **Lock and Mint** - Lock tokens in a smart contract on the source chain, then wrapped versions of the tokens are minted on the destination chain, often referred to as bridged assets, or vice versa.

   c) **Lock and Unlock** - Lock tokens on the source chain, then unlock the same tokens from a liquidity pool on the destination chain. These types of token bridges usually attract liquidity on both sides of the bridge via incentive programs such as revenue sharing.

Fact Binance Bridge is a popular cross-chain bridge. It enables the transfer of assets from Ethereum to the Binance Smart Chain (or vice versa). Additionally, it allows users to convert crypto tokens into formats compatible with Binance Chain and BSC.

2) **Wrapped Tokens**

   Wrapped tokens are digital assets that represent other assets, such as cryptocurrencies or traditional assets like gold or real estate. Wrapped tokens help facilitate asset transfer and interoperability between blockchains of different protocols. It is important to know that wrapped tokens are not actually transferred between networks. Instead, the original tokens are locked on the source chain while a custodian or bridge contract mints an equivalent wrapped token on the destination chain. bitcoin (BTC), for example, can be used on the Ethereum blockchain as *"wrapped"* BTC, *WBTC*. This unlocks a new world of smart contract dApps and features such as DeFi (decentralized finance) for bitcoin holders.

3) **Sidechains**

   The purpose of a sidechain is to combat scalability issues affecting the parent L1 blockchain. Sidechains achieve this by relieving the computational load off the mainchain, thus freeing up throughput and allowing the mainchain to handle a higher volume of transactions. Additionally, it is common for sidechains to host thousands of dApps, freeing up the mainchain and overall ecosystem.

A sidechain can be public or private, with each sidechain possessing its own token, protocol, consensus mechanism, and security—unlike L2s that derive security from the parent mainchain. Sidechains are independent blockchain networks that connect to a parent blockchain, or mainnet, through a *two-way peg*.

The two-way bridge (often called a two-way peg) lets users lock assets on the mainnet while minting or unlocking their equivalent on the sidechain, so value can move between the two networks without a traditional custodian. Polygon PoS is a popular example of a sidechain. It runs parallel to the Ethereum blockchain and provides a separate network that increases bandwidth for transactions, lowering fees and increasing throughput compared to Ethereum. Figure 6-20 shows the architecture for Ethereum (rootchain/mainchain) and Polygon PoS (sidechain) with Plasma checkpoint nodes to aid transaction validation. The following process outlines how digital assets are transferred from a mainnet (parent chain) to a sidechain or vice versa.

a) Digital assets are not actually transferred from chain to chain; instead, once a smart contract (transaction) has been executed and validated, the protocol locks the digital assets on the mainnet while unlocking the same amount on its sidechain, or vice versa.

b) In order to achieve this, an *off-chain process* is also required, the purpose of which is to transfer data between the mainnet and sidechain.

c) Once the smart contract has been executed, it sends a signal to the mainnet (parent chain), which triggers the off-chain process to "relay" the transactional information to the sidechain, thus verifying the transaction.

d) The funds are then released on the sidechain, allowing users to move digital assets across both blockchains.

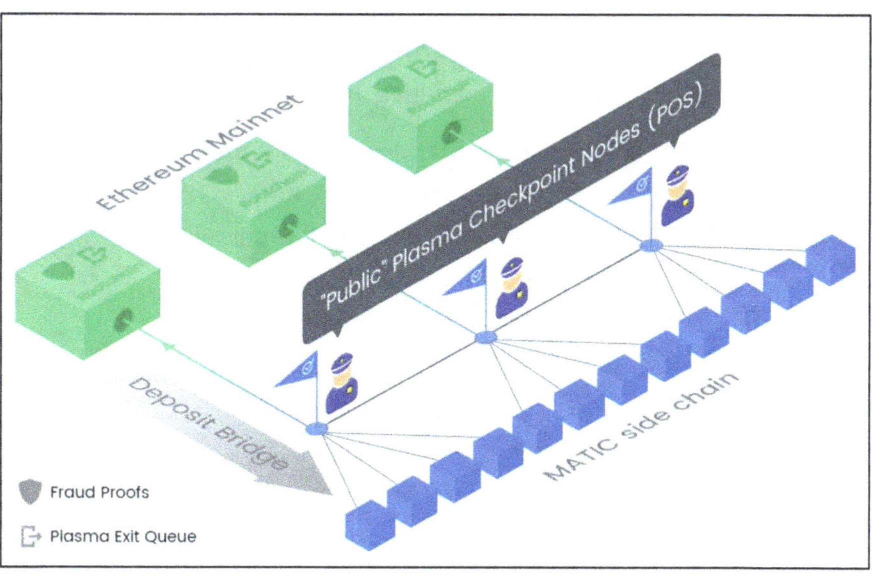

Figure 6-20. *Polygon (MATIC)/Ethereum sidechain (compliments of Polygon Matic—`https://polygon.technology/polygon-pos`)*

Fact Sidechains typically have their own consensus protocols that complement the mainnet by improving typical issues such as high transaction fees, privacy, and security.

---

4) **Blockchain Routers**

   Blockchain routers help improve interoperability between multiple blockchain networks by enabling the communication and exchange of data between them. Like a typical router, blockchains can possess routing features, which, according to the communication protocol, analyze and transmit communication requests, dynamically maintaining a topology structure of the blockchain network.

   An example of a blockchain router is the Router Protocol. Router Protocol architecture allows contracts on one chain to interact with other contracts securely and decentralized. This is achieved by validating state changes on the source chain (Router Protocol) and the target chain (e.g., Ethereum). In doing so, Router Chain can write custom logic to trigger events in response to these external state changes. Furthermore, applications on the Router chain can leverage a trustless network of relayers to update states on external chains directly from the Router chain.

5) **Hash-Locking Technology**

   Hashed TimeLock Contracts (HTLC) are a type of cross-chain interoperability standard that enables cross-chain atomic operations such as *hashed time-locks*. HTLCs ensure that any transfer between two nodes can be completed through a payment channel typically mediated by a smart contract (or native script on non-programmable chains like bitcoin).

Fact Atomic swaps can be defined as the cross-exchange of digital assets whereby one asset can be exchanged for another without a third party or centralized intermediary, e.g., a decentralized exchange.

First used by the Lightning Network, HTLCs are extremely smart in design. See a simplified HTLC process of a BTC/ETH transaction between Alice (sender) and Bob (receiver):

a) Alice hashes a secret code to obtain *hash-lock* $\mathbf{h_1}$ and create a *time lock* t_1.

b) Using the hash and times locks created, Alice creates a smart contract $\mathbf{c_a}$, where she locks her fund's assets (e.g., 2 BTC) and sends the corresponding hash value to Bob.

c) When Bob receives Alice's hash value (random number), he can view and confirm that Alice has her asset (2 BTC) time-locked.

d) Bob then uses Alice's hash-lock $\mathbf{h_1}$ and his own time lock $\mathbf{t_2}$ and creates smart contract $\mathbf{c_b}$, where he locks his assets (3 ETH). It is critical that Bob's $\mathbf{t_2}$ (time) *is less than Alice's* $\boldsymbol{t_1}$ *so that Bob has adequate time to claim his assets from Alice.*

e) Alice unlocks Bob's funds from contract $\mathbf{c_b}$, thereby revealing the secret code.

f) Bob uses the revealed secret to unlock Alice's funds from contract c_a.

Note Once Bob and Alice have verified both assets, ownership is transferred, and transactional data is stored on each blockchain network. However, if Bob and Alice do not verify the assets within the time-lock period, both assets revert to the original sender—automatically via contract expiry on programmable chains or via a pre-signed refund transaction on bitcoin.

---

6) **Notary Schemes**

Notary schemes are an interoperability solution that facilitates the transfer of assets between network participants on different blockchains—in other words, they simplify the tasks of cross-chain transactions. Unlike sidechains, notary schemes are not an extension of a parent chain. Instead, they are third parties who manage the entire process and must be trusted to act honestly, introducing a centralized trust assumption. This third party (notary) can access both accounts (Blockchains A and B). It essentially acts as a middleman who verifies when an event has occurred on Blockchain (A) and then feeds this information to the second Blockchain (B).

The process works by:

1) **User (1)** - Sends assets from Chain (A) to Notary.

2) The Notary locks and confirms the digital assets sent from User (1).

3) The Notary transfers the digital assets from its account to User (2) on target Chain (B).

There are two types of notaries:

- ***Single-Signature Notary*** - A cross-chain interoperability solution where a single node—selected by a notary group or system—collects, validates, and confirms data or asset transfers between blockchains. While this setup is very efficient, it introduces centralization risks, as the entire process relies on a single validator—a single point of failure.

- ***Multi-Signatory Notary*** - As the name suggests, in a multi-stage notary system, the data collected from the source chain (A) must be verified by multiple notary nodes who have to reach a consensus of over two-thirds or more of the nodes involved. This model enhances security and reduces centralization risks by distributing validation across multiple nodes.

7) **Oracles**

Oracles are a unique technology that connects off-chain (real-world) data with on-chain data, and most operate in an off-chain or hybrid setup that relays information between chains. In doing so, Oracles feed information to blockchains that can be set by triggers, allowing smart contracts to execute a specific task when a real-world input or output is received. Furthermore, Oracles can also be used internally on-chain, enabling interoperability between multiple blockchains, known as ***cross-chain oracles.*** Chainlink, a trusted Oracle-based leader in the blockchain industry, defines cross-chain oracles as a technology that "*can read and write information between different blockchains, enabling interoperability for moving both data and assets between blockchains, such as using data on one blockchain to trigger an action on another or bridging assets cross-chain so they can be used outside the native blockchain they were issued on.*" Oracles provide Web3 with the core technology to connect to new and existing legacy systems, data sources, and advanced calculations.

8) **Independent Blockchain Solutions**

A direct form of interoperability is rooted in blockchains, specifically and architecturally designed to facilitate interoperability between different blockchains, enabling them to communicate and share information seamlessly. Several independent blockchain projects currently strive to provide interoperability that eases communication and data and asset transfer between a magnitude of different blockchains and ecosystems—two primary examples are Polkadot Network and Cosmos Network.

a) Polkadot Network is a heterogeneous multichain with the most sophisticated and advanced interoperable technology, consisting of relay chains, parachains, parathreads, and bridges. Polkadot enables cross-blockchain transfers of any type of data or asset, not just tokens. Polkadot uses a unique technology called Cross-Consensus Message Format (XCM). XCM cannot actually send messages between systems. It is a format for how message transfer should be performed, thus enabling all blockchains (parachains and parathreads) within the Polkadot ecosystem to connect, send, and receive data and assets to one another internally without using bridges (bridges are used to connect non-Polkadot external networks, e.g., bitcoin and Ethereum). The core of Polkadot's technology is the relay chain, which provides a unified consensus and security guarantee for the entire system, with the parachains sharing the security guarantee from the relay chain. This type of technology sets the standard for future blockchains and their interoperability features. Kusama (Polkadot's Canary network) possesses and operates the same architectural design as the Polkadot Network.

b) Cosmos Network is a decentralized network of independent blockchains designed to solve scalability and interoperability issues. The heart of the technology is the Cosmos Hub, which connects these blockchains, or "zones," using the Inter-Blockchain Communication (IBC) protocol—see Figure 6-21. IBC enables secure communication and the transfer of digital assets and data between IBC-compatible chains. Together with the Tendermint consensus algorithm—a Byzantine Fault Tolerant (BFT) protocol that keeps the network secure and running smoothly, even if some nodes fail or act maliciously—Cosmos creates a seamless, scalable ecosystem for cross-chain transactions.

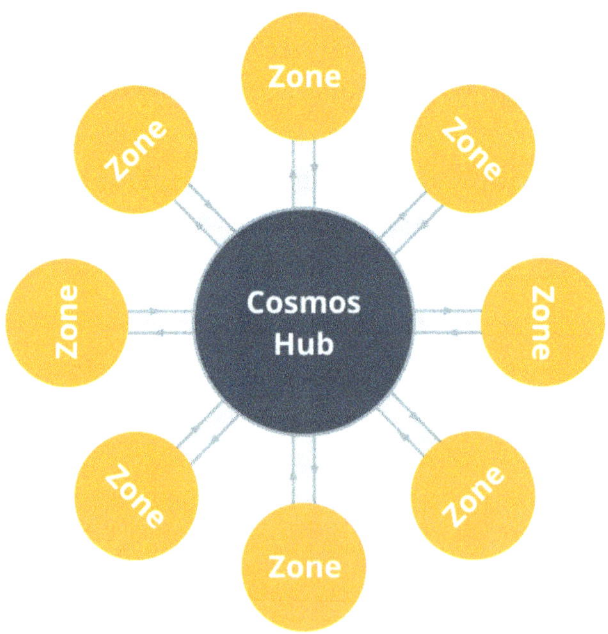

Figure 6-21. *Cosmos hub blockchain architecture (compliments of* `https://cointelegraph.com/learn/what-is-cosmos-a-beginners-guide-to-the-internet-of-blockchains`*)*

Benefits of Cross-Chain Interoperability

There are many reasons cross-chain interoperability is highly valued. Some of these may even be deemed critical to optimize user efficiency and contribute to the success of a network. In this section, the main benefits of cross-chain interoperability are outlined. *Notably, the absence of these benefits can highlight limitations in a blockchain network's interoperability, which may ultimately impact its value and future success.*

- **Cross-Chain Asset Transfer** – Blockchain interoperability aids the transfer of assets from different blockchains across multiple blockchain networks. This broadens and strengthens the entire blockchain ecosystem, providing more flexibility, efficiency, and interconnectivity between network participants.
- **Cross-Chain Self-sovereign Identity** – Enabling blockchain users to securely own and control their identity on a single blockchain while, through interoperability, presenting that identity across multiple blockchain networks of their choice. This is achieved by anchoring user credentials on one blockchain (*with an Identity Provider, e.g., KILT Protocol*) that possesses a high level of interoperability with other blockchain networks. Users can then use their credentials outside their primary blockchain without significant effort.
- **Network Effects** – The term "network effects" was first coined by Robert Metcalfe (*Metcalfe's Law),* the co-inventor of Ethernet, in the early 1980s. Metcalfe observed that as more devices were connected to a network, the value of the network to each user increased exponentially. In the context of blockchain,

network effects are significant as they are amplified by the increasing number of users on the network. As more people use a blockchain network, it creates a virtuous cycle of increasing value and enhanced user interaction, thus underpinning the value of many cryptocurrencies and decentralized applications.

- **Service and Innovation** – A more extensive user base also promotes more significant interaction between users on the network, leading to the development of new applications, services, and use cases. As more developers and entrepreneurs explore the possibilities of the blockchain, it creates a snowball effect of innovation and investment that can lead to even more adoption and value creation.
- **Security** – A growing user base enhances the network's overall security and reliability. As each user helps to validate and verify transactions, the network becomes more decentralized and resistant to manipulation or fraud. This, in turn, attracts more users and strengthens the network effects even further.

- **Liquidity** – Blockchain interoperability is crucial in enhancing liquidity in the DeFi ecosystems. Interoperability increases liquidity in DeFi ecosystems by enabling the efficient transfer of assets between different networks, reducing fragmentation, and improving market efficiency. This enables DeFi platforms to connect with more liquidity sources, expanding their access to a broader range of assets and markets. With blockchain interoperability, DeFi protocol users can seamlessly transfer assets between different networks, providing users with more trading opportunities and increasing market depth. This creates a more interconnected ecosystem where users can efficiently trade their assets and access a more diverse range of financial products and services. Furthermore, DeFi platforms heavily rely on liquidity to function effectively, as the availability of funds determines the prices of assets and the efficiency of the trading process.

- **Enhanced Functionality** – Blockchain interoperability can allow for new use cases, applications, and innovations by combining the technology of multiple ecosystems into one. This, in turn, helps overcome the limitations of a single blockchain network. For example, developers can leverage the strengths of numerous blockchain networks to create a more high-tech, robust, and efficient dApp ecosystem. Additionally, developers can create and run dApps with combined multi-chain functionality that can handle large-scale transactions, complex data structures, and multiple types of digital assets.
- **Multi-Chain Token Swaps** – Interoperability plays a major key role in allowing users to swap assets from different blockchain networks easily—this is known as an *atomic swap*. Atomic swaps, also called *atomic cross-chain trading*, refer to exchanging cryptocurrencies and tokens between different blockchain networks.
- **Collaborations and Partnerships** – Blockchain interoperability allows protocols from various chains to connect with one another and share data and resources, which helps form new partnerships and collaborations.

Investors Check for Blockchain Interoperability

When investing, it is essential to remember that a blockchain's, or dApps, future value is underpinned by its level of interoperability to communicate with other blockchains. If a blockchain network cannot easily interact with different networks—at a minimum, the main blue-chip networks (bitcoin, Ethereum, Polkadot, etc.)—then its growth and performance are hindered in many ways. Small networks that are relatively new, and the associated dApps built on these networks, are at the highest risk if they cannot avail of the substantial and essential ingredients such as increased liquidity, multi-chain trading, atomic swaps, new innovations and collaborations, cross-chain asset transfer, optimized network effects, and more.

There are many blockchain interoperability solutions that blockchain networks implement to connect and communicate with one another. These solutions include cross-chain bridges, sidechains, wrapper tokens, notary schemes, hash-locking, blockchain routers, and oracles. It is in the investor's best interest to identify and understand the interoperability methods utilized by the network in question. More importantly, this check will highlight concerns or limitations around the blockchain's inability to connect with other chains.

Review the Project Documentation

To begin, review the project documentation, including the whitepaper, official blog articles, and other related technical papers and articles found through the project website or other reliable sources for verbiage on interoperability solutions. Additionally, perform multiple searches on your preferred browser for the chain's interoperability solutions—be sure to enter lots of keywords, including cross-chain bridges, sidechains, wrapper tokens, notary schemes, hash-locking, blockchain routers and oracles, etc. This will help expose any interoperable features the blockchain has to offer. Moreover, reaching out to the project and development teams through official channels will provide significant insight. Also, always verify the information provided by asking the team for reference URLs for official articles or project documentation.

Unfortunately, unless the blockchain is interoperability-focused, the project whitepapers sometimes won't detail specific interoperability techniques they plan to use to connect to other chains. Or, if verbiage was initially provided, the likelihood of it being uploaded is slim. However, these checks are essential and are recommended as a good starting point. Many projects will display links to recent material, technical articles, and documentation that are often more updated than the whitepaper—depending on if it is regularly updated. It is always worth thoroughly exploring the project website, deep diving, and scanning all available links.

Accessing Interoperability via Focused Blockchains

Underlying blockchain infrastructures that offer native in-built interoperability solutions are the most effective type of interoperable solution. Suppose the blockchain is designed with interoperability in mind. In that case, its architecture will be clearly detailed and explained in the project whitepaper and associated technical documentation, often accompanied by architecture drawings and illustrations to help simplify the heavy technical verbiage. For a better understanding, search on YouTube for explanation videos, as they usually help break it down and explain blockchain architectures visually and simplistically. Additionally, the developer portal—generally through the Projects Discord channel—is another excellent place to seek technical explanations.

Once a good understanding of the interoperable designed infrastructure is achieved, evaluate it considering the criteria below:

1) **Native Interoperable Architectural Design**

    a) How does blockchain interoperable architectural design operate? How does it work?

b) How does the blockchain infrastructure connect with other blockchain ecosystems?

c) Are other blockchain interoperable solutions (e.g., bridges, wrapped tokens, sidechains, etc.) used in the design but outside the core in-built interoperable infrastructure design?

2) **Usability and Complexity**

a) Does the interoperable blockchain infrastructure make it easy or difficult for other blockchains to connect?

b) If multi-interoperable solutions are utilized as part of the design, does this add an extra layer of complexity for the user or developer?

c) Is it easy to send assets cross-chain?

d) Are major digital asset Web3 wallets, such as MetaMask, TrustWallet, etc., supported?

3) **Ease of Compatibility**

a) What is the level of compatibility with existing mainstream token standards such as ERC-20, ERC-721, etc.?

b) Does it currently support token standards from major blue-chip networks?

c) Are there bridges or wrapping mechanisms to interact with Ethereum-based assets?

d) Does the platform offer non-technical, user-friendly functionality for migrating or operating existing tokens across multiple chains?

e) WASM enables developers to write smart contracts in languages like Rust or C++, simplifying onboarding and offering faster, safer execution than Ethereum's EVM.

    i) Does the blockchain support WASM-based smart contracts?

    ii) Can it run contracts built for other WASM-compatible blockchains?

4) **Security**

    a) Are there any known past security threats or weak points with any interoperable solutions implemented?

5) **Current Ecosystems**

    a) Is the blockchain interoperable with popular blue-chip ecosystems like Ethereum, Polkadot, and Solana?

    b) What other ecosystems is it interoperable with?

    c) How many ecosystems is it interoperable with in total?

6) **Reputation**

    a) Does the interoperable infrastructure have a good track record?

    b) How does the community feel about it?

    c) Any negative or positive feedback?

    d) Are there any significant items of concern that stand out?

7) **Project Support**

   a) Does the developer documentation to integrate projects or cross-chain asset transfer features look straightforward and easy to follow?

   b) Is the developer portal active with visible, fast, and informative responses?

8) **Competitors**

   a) How does it overall compare to competitors?

   b) Does it have more or less connected ecosystems?

   c) Is it easier or more difficult to move assets cross-chain?

   d) Are there any other significant observations indicating poor or high-quality interoperable architectural design?

Accessing All Other Forms of Interoperability Solutions

Outside of blockchains that offer native in-built interoperability solutions, there are many interoperability solutions that blockchain networks implement to connect and communicate with one another. These solutions include cross-chain bridges, sidechains, wrapper tokens, notary schemes, hash-locking, blockchain routers, and oracles. It is in the investor's best interest to identify and understand the interoperability methods being utilized. This will help provide valuable insight to measure the level and ease of interoperability with other chains. More importantly, this check will highlight potential concerns or limitations around the blockchain's inability to connect with different networks, resulting in poor cross-chain asset transfer. Once the types of cross-chain interoperability solutions have been identified, it is time to ensure they are sufficient and allow for growth through other ecosystems.

Once you have a good understanding of the interoperable solutions being used, evaluate them based on the criteria below:

1) **Interoperable Solutions Adopted**
   a) What are the types of interoperable solutions used, such as cross-chain bridges, sidechains, wrapper tokens, notary schemes, hash-locking, blockchain routers, oracles, or other types?
   b) How do they operate?
   c) Is there more than one type of interoperable solution used? If so, what is the reason for this?
2) **Usability and Complexity**
   a) Does the interoperable blockchain solution make it easy or difficult for other blockchains to connect?
   b) Is it easy to send assets cross-chain?
   c) Are major digital asset Web3 wallets like MetaMask, TrustWallet, etc. supported?
3) **Ease of Compatibility**
   a) What is the level of compatibility with existing mainstream token standards such as ERC-20, ERC-721, etc.?
   b) Does it currently support token standards from major blue-chip networks?

c) Are there bridges or wrapping mechanisms to interact with Ethereum-based assets?

d) Does the platform offer non-technical, user-friendly functionality for migrating or operating existing tokens across multiple chains?

e) WASM enables developers to write smart contracts in languages like Rust or C++, simplifying onboarding and offering faster, safer execution than Ethereum's EVM.

i) Does the blockchain support WASM-based smart contracts?

ii) Can it run contracts built for other WASM-compatible blockchains?

4) **Security**

a) Are there any known past security threats or weak points with any interoperable solutions implemented?

5) **Current Ecosystems**

a) Is the blockchain interoperable with popular blue-chip ecosystems like Ethereum, Polkadot, and Solana?

b) What other ecosystems is it interoperable with?

c) How many ecosystems is it interoperable with in total?

6) **Reputation**

a) Does the chain have a good track record with these interoperable solutions?

   b) How does the community feel about it?

   c) Any negative or positive feedback?

   d) Are there any significant items of concern that stand out?

7) **Project Support**

   a) Does the developer documentation to integrate projects or cross-chain asset transfer features look straightforward and easy to follow?

   b) Is the developer portal active with visible, fast, and informative responses?

8) **Competitors**

   a) How does it overall compare to competitors?

   b) Does it have more or less connected ecosystems?

   c) Is it easier or more difficult to move assets cross-chain?

   d) Are there any key signs of good or bad design in the interoperability solutions?

Assessing Blockchain Interoperability Using Crypto Asset Market Data and Price Tracking Websites

As a final step in evaluating a project's interoperability, investors should determine how many native coins or tokens are represented, locked, or minted across other networks. The broader the spread of native coins (e.g., ETH) or tokens (e.g., UNI) across multiple networks, the better the indication of the project's interoperability—especially when those cross-chain representations are issued or formally endorsed by the project's core team rather than created ad hoc by users—which boosts growth potential and adoption for both the project and interconnected chains. On the other hand, a fictitious blockchain project, Capticious Network, with the native coin "XYZ," represented on a single network, signifies a severe lack of interoperability between the Capticious and other blockchain networks.

Figure 6-22 shows two screenshots from CoinMarketCap.com. The image on the left highlights Ethereum and the other networks (marked within the red boxes) where Ethereum's "ETH" coins are locked or represented. There are currently fourteen different networks on which ETH coins are present or represented, indicating a high level of interoperability for Ethereum across multiple blockchain ecosystems. Additionally, any of the fourteen connected networks interoperable with such a large ecosystem as Ethereum inherit cross-chain benefits, including liquidity, multi-chain trading, atomic swaps, etc. In comparison, a network with native coins only locked on minted on one or two other networks is considered poor.

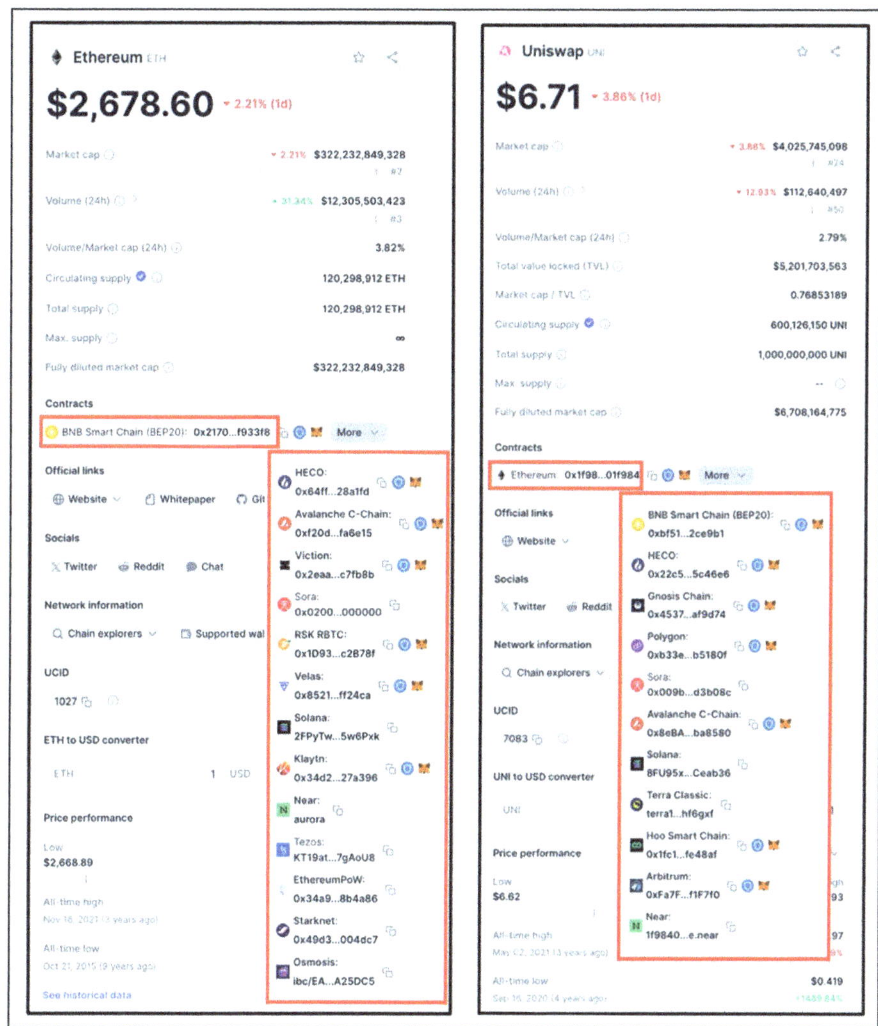

Figure 6-22. *Ethereum's "ETH" coins secured on other blockchains, and Uniswap "UNI" tokens secured on different blockchain networks (compliments of `https://coinmarketcap.com/currencies/ethereum/` and `https://coinmarketcap.com/currencies/uniswap/`)*

The image on the right-hand side of Figure 6-22 highlights Uniswap, a decentralized exchange (DEX) that allows users to trade crypto assets without a centralized third party. The ecosystems in which Uniswap's "UNI" tokens are present or represented are indicated inside the vertical red box. The primary network, Ethereum, on which Uniswap is built, is shown inside the horizontal red box. Note that UNI tokens are available on twelve networks, including the native network, Ethereum. This indicates that UNI is a popular token that seamlessly integrates across multiple networks, enhancing accessibility, usability, and adoption. Outside of the token's popularity, many cross-chain representations are created by third-party bridges or community initiatives rather than the core Uniswap team; a token's integration with other chains is due to the underlying blockchain infrastructure's in-built interoperable features, combined with various interoperable solutions discussed in this chapter.

Action Steps

Follow the steps below to determine a blockchain level of interoperability.

1) **Determine the Level of Interoperability**
   Execute the activities discussed in the section titled "Investor Checks for Blockchain Interoperability."

2) **Take Notes and Document Your Findings in Your Own Style**

3) **Combine the Findings with Other Sections of the Fundamental Evaluation Process**

Evaluation of the Results

When investing in new, smaller blockchain networks, it is recommended to ensure that the network has adequate interoperability with larger ecosystems (e.g., Ethereum, bitcoin, Avalanche, Polkadot, Cosmos, Solana, Binance, Tron, etc.). Similarly, when investing in a particular dApp, it is imperative that the dApp is built on a blue-chip blockchain or, at a minimum, a smaller ecosystem with adequate interoperability with some of the bigger and more popular ecosystems.

CHAPTER 7

Token Design and Use Case

Token design is a critical aspect that directly impacts a project's chance of success. The design of a token dictates how it functions within an ecosystem. It incorporates the specific characteristics and rules that dictate how, when, and where a token can be used, whether it's for transactions, governance, or representing ownership in a project. Each time a token is being designed for a specific use case, it is up to the designer and the project team to decide how the token will be utilized within the platform and the broader ecosystem. Its utility will heavily depend on the design and functional requirements within the project's dApp and use case.

For digital asset investors, token design provides valuable insight that helps evaluate the potential of a blockchain project. While a project with a token that has high fundamental qualities can signal long-term sustainability, a poorly designed token with little to no value can have a negative impact on the project. Therefore, it is essential to investigate whether the token has a legitimate use case within the ecosystem, one that cannot be solved with traditional centralized companies. Another critical aspect of token design is token accrual mechanisms. Token accrual mechanisms are specifically designed strategies that are built into the token design that aim to increase the utility and demand of the token over time. These methods and strategies include staking distributions,

P. Garvey, *Blockchain Fundamental Analysis for Digital Asset Investors*,
https://doi.org/10.1007/979-8-8688-1551-5_7

buyback-and-burn, fee rebates, governance rewards, and many more. The better the quality of the token's accrual mechanisms, the more appealing the token becomes to investors.

The first half of this chapter provides background on the various types of digital assets, such as cryptocurrencies, tokens, and altcoins. Additionally, the various types of tokens are discussed, and common token standards are presented, before breaking down the essential elements of token design, providing investors the knowledge and skills to help gauge the inner value of a token's design.

Fundamentals Discussed in This Chapter:

- Cryptographic Tokens, Cryptocurrency, and Altcoins
- Token Standards
- Token Design
- Token Accrual Process and Mechanisms

Cryptographic Tokens, Cryptocurrency, and Altcoins

Cryptographic tokens, cryptocurrencies, and altcoins are all digital assets secured by cryptographic technology, math-based algorithms to secure and protect data, ensuring it stays private and authentic during digital transactions.

Although not intentional, terms such as tokens, cryptocurrency (coins), and altcoins are widely misused by investors. In short, a cryptocurrency (e.g., BTC and ETH)—also known as a coin—operates on and is native to its own blockchain. On the other hand, a token (e.g., UNI and LINK) is created on an existing blockchain and serves various functions within decentralized applications (dApps). Lastly, altcoins, or alternative coins (cryptocurrency), are essentially any other coins outside of bitcoin. In this section, cryptographic tokens, cryptocurrency, and altcoins are in more detail.

Cryptocurrency

A cryptocurrency—also known as a "coin"—is a native *protocol coin* that is issued directly by the blockchain protocol on which it runs, which is why it is often referred to as a blockchain's native currency. bitcoins, the native coin BTC, is a prime example and notably the most well-known cryptocurrency. BTC holds real monetary value that can be traded in centralized and decentralized exchanges as well as used as a form of payment for goods and services online. However, the core purpose and functionality of cryptocurrency *coins,* also called ***built-in coins,*** is to secure the blockchain network. Native coins pay the fees that make spam attacks expensive, reward miners/validators for block production, and cover other on-chain costs, so they're essential to the network's security and day-to-day operation. They can also be used as a store of value and a medium of exchange.

Fact Native coins (e.g., BTC and ETH) are issued by—and integral to—their own base chains, whereas utility tokens are typically issued *on* an existing chain; coins can be wrapped (e.g., WBTC) to gain DeFi functionality on other networks.

Another example of a coin is Ether (ETH), which serves as the native coin for the Ethereum blockchain. Thousands of cryptocurrency projects and their users, built on top of the Ethereum network, utilize ETH to pay fees and complete transactions on the network. ETH is used to incentivize good behavior, secure the network, cover transaction costs, and reward miners for computational work performed. Additionally, ETH is used by developers to pay the associated fee for deploying smart contracts on the Ethereum blockchain.

Altcoins

Altcoins, which is short for *alternative coins (cryptocurrency)*, are referred to by investors as all cryptocurrencies outside of bitcoins, BTC. This includes a magnitude of coins from blockchains such as Polkadot, Ethereum, Solana, Avalanche, BNB Smart Chain, Fantom, and many more. Alternative blockchains aim to provide more value in terms of functionality and scalability for users, though some choose to trade off a degree of decentralization for higher throughput or other features. An example of this is the Ethereum blockchain, where advanced programmable smart contract capabilities have unlocked extreme value for users and provided solutions for many businesses that now utilize blockchain technology to lower operating costs, build trust, and give back rights to their customers.

Cryptographic Tokens

Cryptographic tokens—digital assets issued on existing blockchains—are a key building block for many Web3 applications and are secured by the underlying distributed ledger. They can represent anything from digital assets to specific permissions, whether in the real world, digital space, or even legal agreements. Tokens, or application-type tokens, are created on top of existing blockchain Layer 0 and Layer 1 networks such as Polkadot Network and Ethereum. In contrast to the native coins (e.g., BTC) that typically represent a (digital) currency, tokens represent a variety of transferable and countable goods such as digital and physical assets, shares, votes, memberships, loyalty points, and other utilities.

Cryptographic tokens are issued by deploying smart-contract code on the blockchain (e.g., ERC-20 or ERC-721 contracts on Ethereum). Cryptographic tokens are stored, recorded, and managed on the blockchain using distributed ledger technology. However, a token's security and validity rely on both the base-layer consensus (which orders transactions) and the verification logic embedded in its smart-contract code (e.g., ERC-20 or ERC-721) that enforces balances, transfers, and supply.

A crypto token can serve multiple purposes, offering functionality that goes far beyond simple value transfer. For example, its utility spans across various sectors, enabling tokenization of real-world and digital assets, granting and managing permissions, supporting decentralized interactions, enabling payments, serving as a store of value, and even paying the gas fees that enable smart-contract execution and DeFi services.

Types of Tokens

Due to the disruptive impact of blockchain technology, companies are continuously exploring and generating new ways to take advantage of blockchain and its byproduct, cryptographic tokens. Blockchain and smart contract technology allow companies to program and customize cryptographic tokens to suit their individual needs and requirements. Cryptographic tokens allow for the creation of new companies that can be automated with respect to transaction data and record keeping on the blockchain. In this section, the primary types and categories of cryptographic tokens are discussed.

The main types of cryptographic tokens are as follows:

1. ***Utility Tokens***
2. ***Security Tokens***
3. ***Non-Fungible Tokens***
4. ***Wrapped Tokens***
5. ***Stable Tokens***

Utility Tokens

Decentralized applications (dApps) embed cryptographic tokens—commonly known as utility tokens—as a means of local payment that enables network participants and users to interact with the platform, including its specific products, services, and features. Think of a utility token as a ticket or coupon that can be cashed in, traded, or used to access a particular feature. Utility tokens offer at least one core primary purpose; however, some tokens are multi-functional—of course, this all depends on the sector and the project's team level of creativity. The operation of utility tokens, or platform tokens, is directly related to the token design architecture and functionality of the product or service offered. Utility tokens may grant users access to specific features, enable voting on governance proposals, be used as collateral in DeFi projects, or be used to pay transaction fees within the ecosystem. For instance, Uniswap's UNI token, which is primarily used as a governance token, allows holders to participate in Uniswap's governance referendums, where they can vote on upgrades and the direction of the dApp.

Security/Equity Tokens

Security tokens (STO) can be considered the digital, Web3 version of financial securities. They represent transferred ownership of a stake in a company. Similar to purchasing equity shares (stocks) in a traditional company—where ownership reflects the firm's assets and any outstanding debt—when an individual buys a security token, they are essentially buying a share of the cryptocurrency company.

Security tokens resemble equity shares: holders obtain a proportional claim on the firm—including its assets, liabilities, and any dividend-like cash flows. However, unlike utility tokens, security tokens do not encounter the extreme volatility that some digital asset investors are attracted to. Instead, security tokens accrue in value from an increase in the core proposition of the company itself.

In the United States, security tokens are regulated by the US government and the US Securities and Exchange Commission (SEC). Due to these regulations, security tokens are subject to a high level of scrutiny, which can be a nightmare for new cryptocurrency startups. For this reason, cryptocurrency projects tend to stay clear of security tokens and gravitate towards utility tokens instead.

The US Supreme Court uses the *Howey Test* to determine whether a transaction under the Securities Act of 1933 and the Securities Exchange Act of 1934 qualifies as an "investment contract." If a transaction qualifies as an "investment contract," that transaction is then considered a security. The sale or offering of cryptocurrency tokens is what the *Howey Test* examines when deciding whether a token should be treated as a security (versus a utility token or similar). Examples of security tokens are tZero and Blockchain Capital.

Non-Fungible Tokens

Non-fungible tokens (NFTs) have become extremely popular since the first ever NFT named Quantum (Figure 7-1) was created in 2014 by a digital and media artist called Kevin McCoy. But what is an NFT, and what purpose does it serve? Before NFTs are discussed, it is beneficial to understand the difference between a fungible and a non-fungible token.

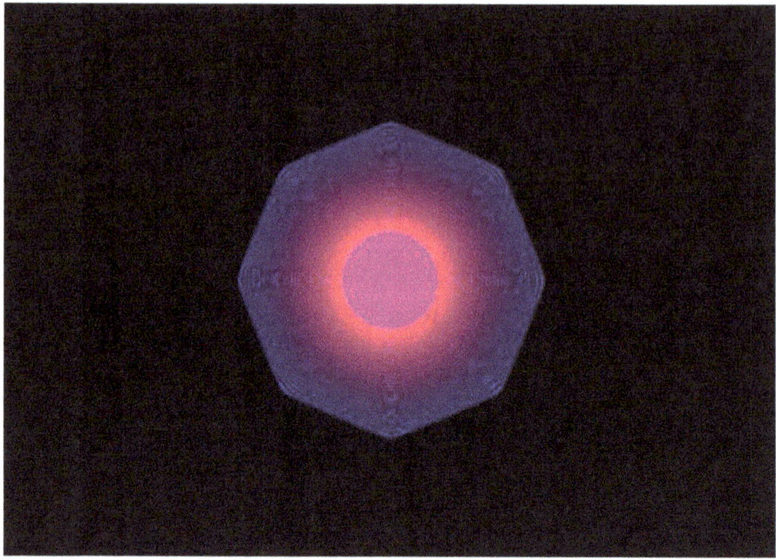

Figure 7-1. *Quantum NFY (compliments of Kevin McCoy)*

As per the Merriam-Webster dictionary, the definition of *"fungible"* is *"being something (such as money or a commodity) of such a nature that one part or quantity may be replaced by another equal part or quantity in paying a debt or settling an account."* With respect to cryptocurrency, take bitcoin, for example, one unit of BTC (1 BTC) can be equally swapped for another unit of BTC without any gain or loss (excluding transaction fees) because each unit of bitcoin represents equal value at any given time. More specifically, one BTC can be divided into equal parts (e.g., quarters) and swapped for the same proportion without any gain or loss. Most currencies—both on- and off-chain—are designed to be fungible, though some stablecoins or wrapped tokens can temporarily lose fungibility if they de-peg or face liquidity constraints. Leaving aside geographical financial economic benefits, one USD carries equal value in New York as it does in any other state in the United States. Similarly, each unit of a cryptocurrency is equal and interchangeable with another unit of the same currency, i.e., 1 ETH can be swapped for 1 ETH, or 1 SOL for 1 SOL, without any gain or loss.

Table 7-1. *Fungible versus non-fungible tokens*

	Digital Asset Kinds	
	Fungible Tokens	**Non-Fungible Tokens**
Attributes	Identical and interchangeable	Unique and non-interchangeable
Value Exchange	Can be exchanged 1:1 (e.g., 1 ETH for 1 ETH)	Cannot be exchanged 1:1 (e.g., NFTs represent unique assets)
Divisibility	Divisible into smaller units (e.g., 1 ETH can be divided into gwei, or $20 can be exchanged for two $10 bills)	Not divisible (e.g., an NFT or a driver's license cannot be broken into smaller parts)

Non-fungible tokens (NFTs) are not fungible, meaning they are not interchangeable as they do not carry equal value. Unlike fungible tokens, NFTs cannot be divided or merged and are uniquely identifiable in nature by their publicly verifiable on-chain unique id and pre-programmed characteristics. They are transferable, can optionally include rich metadata, and—via newer mechanisms such as ERC-1155 or fractional NFT vaults—can even be held in divisible or multi-copy forms.

As previously discussed, the first NFT was created in 2014; however, NFTs only started to become mainstream in 2017 with the release of CryptoKitties on the Ethereum blockchain. CryptoKitties was a unique collection of cat NFTs and was one of the first to use Ethereum's ERC-721 token standard. As with every NFT, each CryptoKittie NFT had its own unique id and characteristics. Additionally, the CryptoKitties collection has in-built functionality that enables holders with two or more CyptoKitties

NFTs to "breed" their NFT Kitties together, which generates a unique combination of the traits from each CryptoKittie. Initially driven entirely by the Ethereum blockchain, this technology was sparked and shaped by a worldwide surge of artists and developers, leading to thousands of new NFT collections in subsequent years.

NFT Use Cases

The revolutionary technology behind NFTs was specifically created to represent ownership over digital or physical assets; however, it has evolved from static art to a magnitude of use cases relating to the tokenization of off-chain and on-chain assets. This includes tokenizing of digital music, educational certificates, supply chain tracking using on-chain IoT (Internet of Things), copyright enforcement, gaming, loyalty programs, Know-Your-Customer (KYC) procedures, concert tickets, and nonprofit organizations. In the gaming industry, gamers can "mint" in-game NFT assets such as clothes, swords, hats, and shields with the option of holding or trading on a peer-to-peer (P2P) system. Innovative projects like Moonsama (built on Moonriver Network) launched the unique Moonsama NFT collection—see Figure 7-2 and Figure 7-3. Moonsama NFT holders can utilize their NFTs in the metaverse to gain rewards. Outside of the outstanding thought process, design, and uniqueness that projects like Moonsama possess, the overwhelming passion of the community can be considered another core driving force.

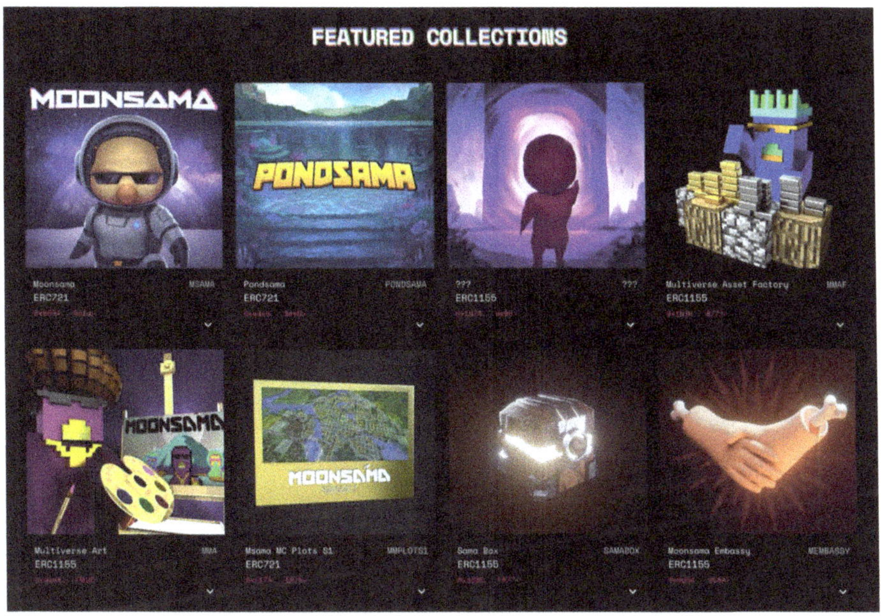

Figure 7-2. *Moonsama NFT marketplace (compliments of* `https://marketplace.moonsama.com/collections`*)*

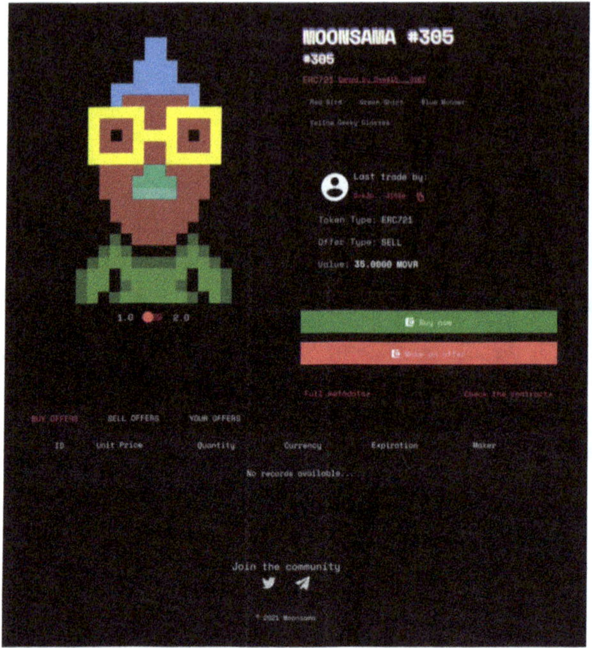

Figure 7-3. *Moonsama NFT (compliments of* `https://marketplace.moonsama.com/`*)*

NFTs also facilitate the tokenization of real-world assets, which is not feasible with fungible tokens, as they cannot digitally represent uniqueness. Centrifuge, which is built on the *Polkadot Network,* and *Altair,* on the *Kusama Network,* are the first protocols to bring real-world assets on-chain. This DeFi-based company enables *small- and medium-sized enterprises* (SMEs) or individuals to tokenize real-world assets such as invoices, royalties, high-value NFTs, real estate, or even a mortgage—and this is just the beginning. Investors provide the liquidity for these tokenized assets and, in return, are rewarded with stable on-chain rewards. Think of it like investing in real-world companies on-chain.

Wrapped Tokens

Wrapped tokens were proposed as a means to overcome the absence of communication between different blockchains. They are digital assets that represent native tokens from one blockchain on another, facilitating cross-chain interoperability. They are created by locking the original asset and minting a corresponding wrapped version, such as wrapped bitcoin (WBTC), on a different chain like Ethereum. This process enables assets like bitcoin to participate in decentralized finance (DeFi) applications, where they would otherwise be incompatible. Although wrapped tokens introduce benefits like liquidity, they also reintroduce trust issues since third-party custodians must manage the underlying locked assets.

Stable Tokens

Stable tokens are created to retain a consistent value, typically fluctuating by no more than approximately one percent on average. These tokens are typically pegged to fiat currencies (e.g., the US dollar), or in some instances, they are even pegged to commodities such as gold (e.g., Paxos Gold). Depending on the stable token, price stability is maintained through different methods. For example, while some stablecoins are supported by physical reserves (collateralized stablecoins), others use algorithms to regulate supply and demand (algorithmic stablecoins). Stable tokens are attractive for investors because they are considered a safe and steady store of value while waiting for an investment opportunity. Additionally, many stable tokens can be staked, allowing investors to earn staking rewards without worrying about price fluctuation.

Token Standards

Token standards can be described as a set of rules, conditions, and functions that allow the development of digital assets on different blockchain protocols. A token standard dictates how a token operates, including facilitating the interaction between blockchains, decentralized applications (dApps), and smart contracts. Many token standards exist to serve diverse purposes, including fungible and non-fungible assets, wallet integrations, on-chain and off-chain events, and multi-assets.

The most common token standard is Ethereum's ERC (Ethereum Request for Comment)—see Table 7-2 for other popular ERC token standards. Ethereum's *ERC-20* token standard is one of the most widespread and powerfully adopted standards. ERC-20 establishes a standard for fungible tokens such as USDT and DAI. This means that every token has the same characteristics, making each token identical in type and value. Before becoming a standard, an ERC must be reviewed, commented, and accepted by the community through an EIP **(Ethereum Improvement Proposal)**. Table 7-2 outlines the most common ERC token standards as defined by Ethereum.org. There are six primary functions that an ERC-20 compliant token standard must implement:

1. **totalSupply** - Returns the total supply of the token in circulation.

2. **balanceOf** - Returns the token balance of a specific account.

3. **transfer** - Transfers a certain number of tokens from the sender to a specific address.

4. **transferFrom** - Allows tokens to be transferred on behalf of another account, provided it has been approved

5. **approve** - Authorizes a spender to withdraw from the sender's account up to a specified value.

6. **allowance** - Returns the remaining number of tokens that a spender is allowed to transfer from the owner's account.

Table 7-2. *Common ERC cryptographic token standards*

Popular ERC Token Standards			
Token Name	**Token Code**	**Token Type**	**Use Cases**
Ethereum Request for Comment	ERC-20	Fungible	A standard interface for fungible (interchangeable) tokens, like voting tokens, staking tokens, or virtual currencies.
Ethereum Request for Comment	ERC-721	Non-fungible	A standard interface for non-fungible tokens, like a deed for artwork or a song. The ERC-721 standard specifies that every NFT has a globally unique id, is transferable, and can optionally include metadata.
Ethereum Request for Comment	ERC-777	Fungible	ERC-777 lets developers add extra features—via external *send/receive hooks*—such as mixer contracts for better privacy or optional key-recovery services, if integrated by the token's ecosystem. (ERC-77 improves on ERC-20 and is backward compatible.)
Ethereum Request for Comment	ERC-1155	Fungible/ Non-fungible	ERC-1155 allows for more efficient trades and bundling of transactions—thus saving costs. This token standard allows for creating both utility tokens (such as $BAT) and non-fungible tokens like VeeFriends.
Ethereum Request for Comment	ERC-4626		A tokenized vault standard designed to optimize and unify the technical parameters of yield-bearing vaults.

(*continued*)

Table 7-2. *(continued)*

Popular ERC Token Standards			
Token Name	**Token Code**	**Token Type**	**Use Cases**
Ethereum Request for Comment	ERC-1238	Fungible/ Non-fungible	Allows managing both fungible and non-fungible non-transferable tokens in one smart contract. An example of this is minting a badge and reputation points in one transaction.

Not all blockchains adopt Ethereum's token standards. In fact, most blockchain infrastructures generate a token standard specific to their blockchain requirements. BEP-20 is the token standard for Binance Smart Chain, similar to how TZIP-7 and TZIP-12 are for the Tezos blockchain. The increase in blockchain infrastructures has led to the generation of a lot of new token standards—some of these standards are outlined in Table 7-3.

Table 7-3. Common cryptographic token standards

Non-ERC Token Standards			
Token Name	**Token Code**	**Token Type**	**Use Cases**
Tezos Interoperability Proposal	TZIP-7	Fungible	Similar to the ERC-20, TZIP-7 implements token transfer operations and approvals for spending tokens from other accounts.
Tezos Interoperability Proposal	TZIP-12	Multi-asset/ Non-fungible	TZIP-12 (FA2) is a standard that was proposed to provide improved expressivity to contract developers to create new types of tokens, all while maintaining a common interface standard for wallet integrators and external developers.
Tezos Interoperability Proposal	TZIP-10	Wallet Interaction	TZIP-10 is a Tezos Improvement Proposal that specifies a standard way for dApps to interact with wallets.
NEO Enhancement Proposals	NEP-5	Fungible	Provides systems with a generalized interaction mechanism for tokenized smart contracts.
NEO Enhancement Proposals	NEP-11	Non-fungible	The standard for creating NFT contracts.
Binance Smart Chain Evolution Proposal	BEP-20	Fungible	BEP-20 is a token standard on Binance Smart Chain that extends ERC-20. BEP-20 defines how tokens can be spent, who can spend them, and other rules for their usage.

Tokenized Assets

Asset tokenization is an expansion of blockchain technology that enables tangible or intangible objects to be converted into digital assets (tokens) that can be bought, sold, and traded. Tokenization of an asset allows that asset to be broken into one or more digital tokens, enabling shared ownership among investors. Investors are free to digitally store, trade, and transfer their real or virtual assets without any central reliance or interference from a third party, entity, or intermediary, provided such transfers comply with the securities, property-transfer, or other relevant regulations in the jurisdictions involved. Refer to Table 7-4 for examples of both tangible and intangible assets that can be tokenized.

Table 7-4. *Examples of tangible versus intangible assets that can be tokenized*

Tangible Versus Intangible Assets	
Tangible Assets (Physical Assets)	**Intangible Assets (Virtual Assets)**
Real estate	Deeds
Vehicles	Patents
Equipment	Trademarks
Inventory	Copyrights
Art	Software
Precious metals (e.g., silver, gold, and platinum)	Licenses

Token Design and Use Case

Evaluation Objective: Evaluate whether the token's use case has a genuine and legitimate purpose by assessing its functionality, whether it actually solves a real-world problem, and its overall necessity within the ecosystem.

The design of a crypto token is integral to its product or service. Effective token architecture, focusing on design mechanisms and structure, is key for ensuring protocol security and investor profitability. The overall aim is to maximize the token's functionality and value, thus helping increase the price per token. Poor token designs with inadequate functionality and core purpose severely impact the success of any project. Innovative, multi-purpose token design mechanisms are crucial for meeting the needs of stakeholders and the protocol. Token demand rises when stakeholders see value in the product and the token itself. By the end of this section, investors will know how to assess whether a token has a legitimate, viable use case, with genuine purpose and strong accrual mechanisms.

If a token's purpose and functionality cannot be justified, the project is destined for failure—in other words, is it possible for users to operate a project's core product without a token? Without a valid token use case and confirmation that there is no other possible way for the project's core product to function with a utility token, investors should avoid investing. It is vital that the token has essential functionality that enables users and customers to avail of the product that otherwise cannot be achieved with traditional methods.

Traditional companies that are turning to blockchain technology to solve real-world problems—or making a system more efficient—are more likely to have a legitimate token use case and requirement compared to those who are creating a token with no genuine requirement. It is common for fraudulent companies to fabricate extremely poor token use cases and, through marketing, portray them as unique and attractive-looking investments, simply to fund-raise significant amounts of capital through Initial Coin Offerings (ICOs) and other similar public sale offerings. Therefore, it is vital for investors to possess the skills to identify and separate the poor fundamental and fraudulent token use cases from legitimate ones with decent and essential functionality.

For example, consider a car dealership that created the "CAR" token using Ethereum's smart contracts. When buying a car, customers have the option to pay for the car using CAR tokens—instead of fiat currency—to receive rewards for future purchases in return. At first glance, this may sound appealing; however, people already use cash to buy cars without issues and use traditional loyalty programs for rewards. Therefore, CAR token use case serves no legitimate purpose or functionality that cannot already be achieved using traditional methodologies. Unfortunately, this happens a lot in the blockchain world, and it is sometimes hard to identify. The truth is that most crypto projects fail in the first year, whether it is a scam from day one or because of an inexperienced team or lack of funding; it ultimately results in a poor fundamental use case with no hope of ever providing true value or gaining traction.

Evaluating Token Design

An entire book could be dedicated to token design, as it is a specialized field of its own. However, for the purpose of this fundamental evaluation, a simplified analysis is more than adequate. Table 7-5 shows two tokens, **Chainlink** (LINK) and a fictitious token, **HotelStay** (HTS), compared against each other under minimal but effective token criteria that help validate the legitimacy of the token design use case and functionality.

Table 7-5. Token design legitimacy

	Token Design Evaluation	
Token "Legitimacy" Criteria	**Chainlink (LINK)**	**HotelStay (HTS)**
Token Functionality/ Utility	– Used for payment of oracle services. For example, using a Chainlink oracle to fetch off-chain data requires paying with LINK. – Used as a form of incentive and collateral for maintaining data accuracy. When data providers submit information to smart contracts, if they provide inaccurate data, they risk losing their staked LINK. This incentivizes data providers to provide reliable data. – Rewards holders for staking LINK to help maintain network security. – LINK holders are expected to take part in decentralized, on-chain governance once the planned governance framework goes live.	– Used exclusively for hotel bookings. – Used as loyalty rewards.
Real-World Problem Solving	Bridges blockchain and external data sources.	– Does not address a unique problem. – Service works with existing traditional payment and loyalty systems.

(continued)

Table 7-5. (*continued*)

Token Design Evaluation		
Token "Legitimacy" Criteria	**Chainlink (LINK)**	**HotelStay (HTS)**
Token Necessity	– Essential for Oracle operations and network security.	– Unnecessary for platform functionality. – Can be replaced by traditional currencies.

As the results from Table 7-5 indicate, the LINK token has many essential functions and tasks that are essential for Chainlink's oracle service. The token is an integral and essential element of the overall operations and service provided by Chainlink—connecting external data sources to blockchains by providing real-world data to smart contracts. On the other hand, HotelStay does not solve an actual problem or make a traditional system more efficient, and as a result, there is no benefit of utilizing blockchain technology for hotel bookings. More specifically, the token, HTS, does not have significant functionality that justifies it being a "token," since fiat currency and traditional loyalty point systems achieve the same result. HotelStay's token, HTS, does not qualify as a legitimate token use case and is considered a major red flag.

Fact If a company has a very weak token use case, they may attempt to conceal critical details—this should be considered a warning sign. Reputable companies with legitimate use cases are transparent and provide ample information about their operations and the issues they aim to resolve.

Action Steps

Follow these steps to evaluate whether the token's use case has a genuine and legitimate purpose by assessing its functionality, whether it actually solves a real-world problem, and its overall necessity within the ecosystem.

1) **Token Design and Functionality**
   Review the official project documentation to gain a full understanding of the token's function, use case, purpose, etc.

2) **Evaluation of the Tokens' Legitimacy**
   Evaluate the tokens under the design criteria as specified in Table 7-5 (*real-world problem solving, token functionality/utility, and token necessity*).

3) **Additional Thoughts and Questions**

   a) Can the proposed use case be achieved using the traditional (off-chain) solutions?

   b) Has the team highlighted any significant benefits of implementing their product or service?

   c) Are there additional reasons for choosing on-chain over off-chain for this use case?

   d) Is it more or less expensive to avail of the product or service on-chain or off-chain?

   e) Is it easier and more user-friendly to use the same product or service on-chain or off-chain?

   f) Is it faster to use the same product or service on-chain or off-chain?

4) **Take Notes and Document Your Findings in Your Own Style**

5) **Combine the Findings with Other Sections of the Fundamental Evaluation Process**

Evaluation of the Results

After evaluating a token's legitimacy, and it is determined that the token does not qualify for a legitimate use case, it is advised to avoid making any form of size of investment. On the other hand, a fundamentally strong token with justified functionality is considered a green light for investors.

Token Accrual Processes and Mechanisms

Evaluation Objective: Determine if the project has effective token accrual processes and mechanisms in place to help ensure sustainable value growth and long-term investor demand.

Understanding token accrual processes starts with grasping the concept of value accrual—how a token ecosystem generates demand, sustains it over time, and captures that demand as tangible value. In the blockchain space, value accrual is about creating mechanisms that transform external usage or interest into lasting economic benefits within the protocol.

Understanding token accrual processes starts with grasping the concept of value accrual—how a token ecosystem creates and maintains demand over time and *transforms* that demand into *captured value*. In the blockchain space, captured value refers to the economic value that a protocol or token ecosystem retains within its system rather than letting it flow out. This occurs when the protocol or token creates a mechanism that converts external demand or usage into a sustainable form of internal value. For example, in a decentralized finance (DeFi) protocol, users often pay a protocol fee to access services—this fee (typically a slice of the transaction) can be "captured" by the protocol for redistribution or growth. This captured value can then be reinvested into the system, used to reward token holders, or stored in a treasury to fund future growth.

Breaking it down, value accrual starts with creating demand for the token, sustaining that demand over time, and—crucially—capturing part of the resulting economic activity (e.g., via fees, burns, or revenue sharing) so that it flows back to the token holders and the project.

Fact Price action alone does not indicate value accrual, and value can accrue without immediate price change. It's important for investors to focus on how a protocol captures, retains, and reflects value through demand, independent of price.

Token Accrual Processes and Mechanisms

Token accrual processes and mechanisms are the tools that drive value accrual by pairing real utility with demand-capture and scarcity mechanics (e.g., fees, burns, and staking locks), allowing the token to absorb a share of the network's economic activity over time. When speaking about creating and maintaining demand for a token, the processes and mechanisms outlined in this section are the "why" behind people wanting to hold or use the token over time. It is the investor's duty to understand how and whether the team is achieving value accrual. More specifically, verify that effective value accrual processes and mechanisms are utilized (if any).

Token Accrual Processes

There are three main types of token accrual processes; they are as follows:

- **Reinvestment in the Protocol**

  This process involves collecting a portion of the collected profits and reinvesting it back into the protocol. The funds are used to pay developers and other miscellaneous items that overall enhance the product or service. This strategy increases the value output and token accrual.

  A large proportion of the profits is often kept in the treasury. Any yield-generating deployment (e.g., staking and liquidity provision) should be diversified, capped, and approved by governance to avoid undue concentration risk. The treasury funds are maintained and only spent as required—this type of value accrual is from *future opportunity*. However, it is critical that the treasury is governed by the token holders and not solely by the project team. Note, in essence, this type of value accrual is indirectly provided to the token holders by making the protocol's treasury larger with increased future potential versus being provided directly to token holders in the form of economic benefits.

- **Governance Input**

  A fair, decentralized governance model is a key part of value accrual because it allows token holders to influence how a protocol captures and retains value over time—without this, all decisions are made by the project team, making it highly centralized and, in most cases, untrustworthy. This ability to guide the protocol's growth means investors are directly involved in value creation, not just hoping for price increases. Key governance areas that are critical are items related to core product and service and critical areas like profit distribution and reinvestment strategies. Decisions made through governance should have an overall goal of retaining value within the ecosystem.

- **Token Supply Management**

  Token supply management refers to how the token supply is managed, in terms of supply reduction and distribution. Note, this is not focusing on the initial token allocation of the entire supply at launch, but rather the reduction and distribution of the supply resulting from specific token accrual mechanisms. For example, depending on the token accrual mechanism, a proportion of the token supply may be burnt, therefore in theory creating higher demand for the remaining supply. Instead, a portion of transaction fees may be allocated to token holders proportional to their stake. It is important that the project team and stakeholders (through governance) are effectively managing and controlling the token supply with specifically designed token-accrual design mechanisms catering to the product and overall tokenomic structure. A real-world example is BNB on BNB Smart Chain, whose quarterly auto-burn mechanism permanently removes a portion of supply based on on-chain activity and revenue.

Token Accrual Mechanisms

Token accrual mechanisms are features within a blockchain protocol designed to create long-term value for a token by incentivizing holding and sustainable demand. They matter to investors because they help a token gain value over time, instead of buying and selling for a quick profit. These mechanisms are built into the protocol to ensure long-term demand for the token, whether that's through mechanisms such as staking rewards, buybacks, or even burning tokens to reduce the supply. In other words, these features are designed to keep adding value to the token, making it more attractive to hold onto rather than sell right away—this is a key ingredient for increasing value accrual and attracting more investors over time. There are several types of token accrual mechanisms; they are as follows:

- **Fee Rebate Mechanisms** - Involves returning a portion of the transaction fees to token holders.
- **Deflationary Mechanisms** - Reduces the token supply over time, thus increasing demand and value of the remaining tokens. Deflationary mechanisms can range from a number of different things, such as
    - **Burn on Transaction** - A proportion of the transaction fees are burned.
    - **Buy-Back and Burn** - The team buys back a portion of the tokens (with money from the treasury) on the market and burns them.
- **Service Mechanisms** - To avail of the core product, the user may be required to pay for that service with tokens. Occasionally, a proportion of the service fee is burned, which helps generate demand.

- **Staking Mechanisms** – Staking involves locking up coins, reducing the circulating supply, which generates demand. Staking rewards are also distributed to holders, proportional to the number of coins staked.
- **Governance Mechanisms** – With the rise of on-chain governance, token holders can vote on protocol decisions and are sometimes rewarded for their efforts. Typically, an investor's voting power is proportional to the tokens they hold, although some protocols curb outsized influence with alternative models—quadratic voting, where each additional vote costs exponentially more tokens; conviction voting, which gives greater weight to votes backed by tokens locked for longer periods; or delegated voting.
- **Lock-Ups Mechanisms** – The team often offers incentives to holders to lock up their tokens for a certain duration. Lock-up mechanisms remove the tokens from circulation, thus generating demand.
- **Discount Utility Mechanism** – Offers users fee or price reductions when they pay with the token, primarily to attract and retain users; any value accrual is indirect, coming from the extra activity these discounts generate.
- **Other Distribution Mechanisms** – These might include airdrops, liquidity bootstrapping, and liquidity mining.

Action Steps

Follow the steps below to identify if the project has effective token accrual processes and mechanisms in place to help ensure sustainable value growth and long-term investor demand.

1) **Identify Token Accrual Processes and Mechanism**
   Perform research to identify the token accrual processes and mechanisms utilized by the project. This information is typically available through the official project documentation, such as the whitepaper, blog, project websites, etc.

2) **Evaluate Token Accrual Processes and Mechanism**

   Evaluate the token accrual process and mechanisms using the below criteria.

   a) **Authenticity of Mechanisms** – Investors should ensure the token accrual process and mechanisms match the project's whitepaper and aren't based on vague promises.

   b) What types of token accrual processes and mechanisms are baked into the token design?

   c) What factors cause the token or coin to rise in value, and why do they have this effect?

   d) What are the underlying drivers of the tokens' value?

   e) Outside of potential price appreciation, in what ways can token holders profit from the token?

   f) Are there any obvious limitations that could negatively impact the token's value?

   g) What protective measures does the team have in place to ensure the intrinsic value of the token?

h) How does the protocol generate revenue (e.g., fees and spreads), and how are those funds retained or distributed between the treasury, the core team, and token holders?

3) **Competitor Research**

Compare the project's token accrual process and mechanisms with other successful competitors and evaluate against the below criteria.

a) Do competitors have the same or different token accrual processes and mechanisms?

b) If the same, how are they performing? Does the token provide a lot of value?

c) If different token accrual processes and mechanisms are used, are they more effective and innovative or performing poorly?

d) Are competitors better at generating and retaining revenue to back token value?

e) Are competitor mechanisms less risky or limited in design?

4) **Take Notes and Document Your Findings in Your Own Style**

5) **Combine the Findings with Other Sections of the Fundamental Evaluation Process**

Evaluation of the Results

This part of the fundamental assessment is favorable if the team has put in place effective token and protocol value accrual strategies and mechanisms—ideally with a proven track record and verifiable performance. On the other hand, exercise extreme caution if the team lacks effective value token and protocol value accrual mechanisms.

CHAPTER 8

Tokenomics

Tokenomics (token + economics) describes the full economic and incentive design of a digital-asset ecosystem—covering supply and demand, behavioral and governance incentives, community reward mechanisms, and utility design. As outlined by Sean Au and Thomas Power in *Tokenomics: The Crypto Shift of Blockchains, ICOs, and Tokens,* tokenomics involves the concept of design and implementation of an economic system to incentivize specific behaviors in a community, using tokens to create a self-sustaining economy. It includes game theory, mechanism design, and incentives governing crypto assets. It also encompasses the entire process of token issuance, token sales, vesting, and investment.

Fact Game theory is the study of how stakeholders make strategic decisions by predicting others' moves, helping them maximize returns while managing risks in competitive markets.

Think of tokenomics as the system of how digital assets operate and function within their own economies. It is not just about supply dynamics; tokenomics also decides the rules that give the token value and utility within the ecosystem. For example, by using game theory and incentives, tokenomics encourages investors to hold tokens and participate in network and product offerings.

P. Garvey, *Blockchain Fundamental Analysis for Digital Asset Investors*,
https://doi.org/10.1007/979-8-8688-1551-5_8

Another very important element to tokenomics is designing and managing the token supply. This involves how tokens are created, distributed, released into circulation, and vested, as well as how many assets are locked or burned through different value-accrual processes and mechanisms. Supply dynamics data such as the circulating supply directly impacts a token's market capitalization and price per coin (or token), which investors care dearly about. Understanding how supply is distributed through staking rewards or early investor allocations helps investors assess the token's long-term potential.

Fact Tokenomics is the study of how digital coins, or tokens, are created and shared. It's like regular economics, where we learn how people make and trade things like money, but with tokenomics, transactions take place on-chain using tokens, reducing reliance on banks or middlemen once the system is stable.

Microtokenomics and Macrotokenomics

Economics, in the traditional sense, is grouped into two main categories: *microeconomics* and *macroeconomics*. While microeconomics focuses on supply and demand concerning individuals and small business owners, macroeconomics addresses the broader economy, including factors like *gross domestic product* (GDP), imports, and exports. Similarly, within the blockchain world, tokenomics can be understood through the lenses of *microtokenomics* and *macrotokenomics*.

Microtokenomics refers to the features that drive the functionality and interactions of participants within a blockchain economy. Factors such as inflation and deflation rates, staking reward adjustments, vesting periods, and token velocity are key components of microtokenomics.

Macrotokenomics captures the broader elements such as governance mechanisms, ecosystem growth, and liquidity provision. The interplay of these variables creates the overall "*token economy*" within a blockchain ecosystem.

Why Are Good Tokenomics Important for Investors?

Well-designed tokenomic structures form the fundamental base on which a successful project is created. Attractive tokenomics are highly desired by investors because of supply and demand characteristics that directly contribute to and influence the value of a token. In addition, understanding the tokenomic structure helps investors predict an asset's worth in the future.

Understanding and analyzing a crypto project's tokenomics is an important part of the fundamental evaluation process. It is a relatively quick and effective process that provides valuable insight that helps gauge a project's chance of success over time. This chapter provides you with the tools and knowledge that are required to evaluate a project's tokenomic structure.

What to Expect in This Chapter

This chapter examines the essential tokenomics elements and the associated metrics that influence the design of the token supply and its behavior within the ecosystem. Supply dynamics—including total supply, circulating supply, and maximum supply—are explained, along with token supply models such as deflationary, inflationary, and fixed models. Token distribution models are also covered, detailing how token allocation impacts market metrics like market capitalization and liquidity. Finally, the chapter explores vesting schedules and their role in creating a sustainable token economy over time.

Fundamentals Discussed in This Chapter:

- *Token Supply Metrics*
- *Token Supply Models*
- *Token Distribution Models*
- *Vesting Schedules*

Token Supply Metrics

Evaluation Objective: Identify and evaluate the total, circulating, and maximum token supply dynamics.

Total supply metrics—including circulating, total, and maximum supply—are key indicators investors use to gauge a digital asset's availability and scarcity. Supply metrics establish how many tokens (or coins) will exist at any particular time. These metrics that are unique to the blockchain world provide insight into how many tokens are currently in circulation, how many exist overall, and how many will eventually be unlocked (released). Unlike fiat currencies—whose supply can be expanded through discretionary monetary policy—many blockchain projects fix a total or maximum supply in the initial token contract, although some protocols retain on-chain or upgradeable mechanisms that let the community change those limits later. However, the circulating supply can fluctuate over time based on on-chain mechanisms like token burns, staking, and vesting schedules. By evaluating these metrics, it helps investors identify tokens with strong growth potential, avoid those prone to extreme inflation, and overall provide an edge in assessing a token's long-term value in the market.

A project's token supply metrics are typically found in the whitepaper, in the tokenomics section. However, in most circumstances, the supply metrics detailed in the whitepaper are outdated. This is because the supply metrics are continually updated as per the predefined token contract parameters. For instance, as time progresses, more coins or tokens are released into circulation based off the predefined token contract parameters until all assets are unlocked as per the initial token allocation schedule set by the project team. Additionally, projects whose tokenomics allow additional minting beyond the originally allocated supply will see the circulating amount keep rising once the genesis tokens are fully distributed. On the other hand, in deflationary models—where tokens are permanently removed from circulation—the circulating supply **tends to decline over time relative to prior periods**, provided there are no other counteracting mechanisms at play. Therefore, due to the dynamic nature of token supply metrics, it is recommended to initially check the project whitepaper; however, for real-time tracking of supply metrics and other related financial data, sources such as CoinMarketCap or CoinGecko are essential for crypto investors.

Figure 8-1 shows Polkadot Networks token supply metrics, including the circulating supply, total supply, and maximum supply on CoinMarketCap.com.

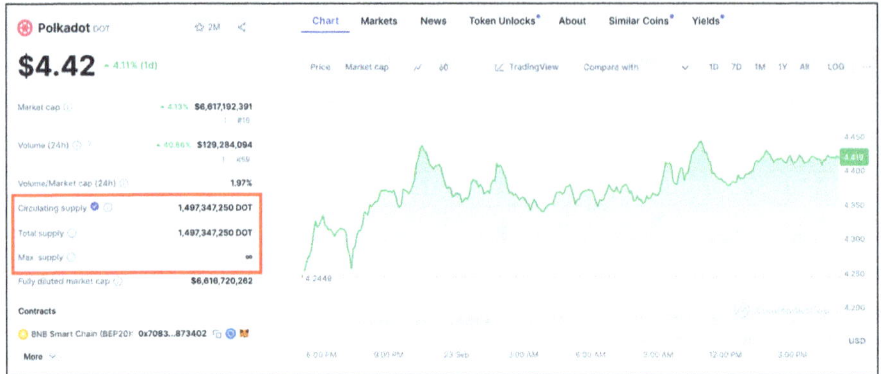

Figure 8-1. *Polkadot Network—circulating, total, and maximum supply (compliments of* `https://coinmarketcap.com/currencies/polkadot-new/`*)*

Total Supply

Total supply refers to the total number of coins or tokens that have been created and are in existence at any one given time. This includes coins or tokens that are in circulation and those that are locked or reserved, minus the total of coins that were burned or destroyed. Note that the total supply excludes coins that will be minted in the future due to inflation.

Figure 8-1 indicates that Polkadot Network has a total supply above of 1,497,347,250 DOT (at the time of this book was written). Also, note that Polkadot's circulating supply of 1,497,347,250 DOT now matches its initially allocated total supply (all large vesting tranches are unlocked; only ongoing inflation can add new DOT), meaning that all DOT that was once locked has now been released into circulation. This is valuable information for investors, as it signals that no further large token unlocks are going to further dilute the supply, often resulting in increased selling pressure, which could push the price per coin down.

Circulating Supply

Circulating supply refers to the total number of tokens or coins currently in circulation, not counting the ones that are locked, reserved, or yet to be released. This metric provides a clearer view of an asset's market availability compared to total supply. While a higher circulating supply generally means the asset is more widely distributed, a lower circulating supply typically creates scarcity, resulting in higher demand and price per asset.

In the case of Polkadot (DOT), the circulating supply matches the total supply of 1,497,347,250 DOT, meaning all tokens are fully unlocked and available in the market. This means no upcoming token unlocks will further dilute the market, driving down the price per coin—this is vital for assessing long-term price stability. Furthermore, it's important to check if the token supply is fixed, deflationary, or inflationary, as they can affect future token supply dynamics and price movements—more on this in the next section titled "Token Supply Models."

Maximum Supply

Maximum supply is the total number of coins or tokens that will ever come into existence. It can be capped, meaning there's a hard limit set on how many can be created, or uncapped, where the supply is unlimited due to inflation. It is important for investors to determine if a token supply is fixed or unlimited, as a capped supply often leads to scarcity, potentially increasing value, while an uncapped supply can dilute value over time. However, some projects also have deflationary mechanisms, such as token burns, to counteract inflation. The Polkadot Network (Figure 8-1), for example, has no maximum supply because it is inflationary; however, it also incorporates deflationary mechanisms, such as burning a portion of transaction fees, which counterbalances the inflation. When a protocol includes both minting and burn mechanisms, investors should compare the annual mint rate with planned burns to determine the net issuance—whether it is inflationary, deflationary, or roughly neutral.

Action Steps

Follow these steps to evaluate a project's circulating supply, total supply, and maximum token supply dynamics.

1) **Whitepaper - Token Supply Check**
   Check the whitepaper, particularly the tokenomics section, to gain an understanding of the initial supply metrics (circulating supply, total supply, and maximum supply). These supply metrics may not be entirely accurate if not updated in real-time, but they will provide a baseline that may help cross-check potential discrepancies with real-time token data sites. For instance, a fixed maximum supply will remain static and should be the same on the whitepaper as displayed on websites such as CoinMarketCap.com.

2) **Circulating Supply Versus Total Supply**
   On CoinMarketCap, compare the circulating supply with the total supply.

   a) If the circulating supply is lower than the total supply, this indicates that more token unlocks are planned. These unlocks can increase selling pressure and further drive down the price per token.

   b) If the circulating supply and the total supply are identical, this indicates that no more token unlocks are planned, reducing the risk of further dilution.

3) **Maximum Supply**
   Verify through the whitepaper and CoinMarketCap if the project has a capped or uncapped maximum supply. Capped supplies often signal scarcity, potentially increasing demand, while uncapped token supplies may face dilution of the supply over time, potentially driving the price per token down.

4) **Take Notes and Document Your Findings in Your Own Style**

5) **Combine the Findings with Other Sections of the Fundamental Evaluation Process**

Evaluation of the Results

There are no right or wrong token supply metrics. A project's total and maximum supply will typically depend on the type, operation, and functionality requirements of the core project or service; therefore, these metrics differ on a case-by-case basis. However, investors should be cautious with respect to the circulating supply, especially if only a small quantity of the supply is released into circulation, as this could have a negative impact on investment down the line as more tokens are unlocked.

Token Supply Models

Evaluation Objective: Identify whether the project adopts a deflationary, inflationary, or fixed supply model and evaluate based on future dilution risks, demand sustainability, and alignment with your investment strategy.

Token supplies are categorized into three primary models or groups: *inflationary*, *deflationary*, and *fixed* supplies. Each model is utilized to suit the specific design and function of a Web3 or blockchain project. Each model type directly impacts token price and total, maximum, and circulating supplies differently. Additionally, the type of consensus mechanism and token accrual mechanism designs in place also dictate whether a token supply is inflationary, deflationary, or fixed. A review of the first twenty networks on StakingRewards.com (a public dashboard that tracks staking yields and token-inflation data) shows that most major protocols target low-single-digit net issuance (roughly 2–5% per year) to balance validator rewards with dilution, while individual projects may aim for much higher inflation—or even net deflation—depending on their protocol design and token-economics goals.

Deflationary Token Supply

A deflationary token supply refers to a tokenomics model where the total supply decreases over time. This reduction can occur through mechanisms like token burns, where a portion of tokens is permanently removed from circulation—see Chapter 7, "Token Design and Use Case," for more details on token deflationary mechanisms. The concept is designed to create scarcity, theoretically driving up the token's value as supply dwindles, assuming demand remains stable or increases. Deflationary systems aim to maintain long-term value growth and, in some cases, counterbalance inflation, making them an attractive option for some investors.

When evaluating deflationary systems, it is recommended for investors to focus on some key elements. Firstly, understanding the burn mechanism, specifically how frequent and significant the burns are, and what triggers them. This is important as it helps to gauge how many tokens will be left in circulation at a specific time period. While some burns may significantly reduce the supply over time, others may have little impact due to low burn rates. Typically speaking, a high burn rate is admirable among investors, as it creates more demand. However, there are many variables that affect demand outside of token scarcity, including the core value of the token and product or service. Therefore, it is vital to be extra vigilant when it comes to burn rate. Some individuals are majorly influenced and blindsided by a deflationary supply and associated burn rate—token scarcity alone will not salvage a flawed project. Creating token scarcity for a product lacking real-world utility or user interest is unlikely to generate meaningful demand. Artificial scarcity can't compensate for fundamental weaknesses in a token's underlying value proposition or adoption potential. Therefore, a deflationary supply is admirable when paired with steady or growing interest.

Pro Tip Smart crypto investors look beyond flashy burn rates, focusing instead on the trifecta of utility, adoption potential, and carefully designed burn schedules to assess a token's true long-term viability.

Examples of Deflationary Projects

BNB Chain **(BNB)** is an algorithmic auto-burn executed quarterly that reduces the supply of BNB coins by automatically removing tokens from circulation and sending them to a burn address.

Ethereum **(ETH)** Ethereum provides an example of how a token supply can adopt both deflationary and inflationary mechanisms. Initially, Ethereum's native currency, ETH, was primarily inflationary, meaning more tokens were regularly introduced into circulation. However, on August 5, 2021, Ethereum implemented a key update called EIP-1559. This update introduced a burn mechanism, which destroys a portion of the transaction fees (known as the "base fee"), reducing the total supply of ETH. Now, the balance between ETH issuance (inflation) and the amount of ETH burned (deflation) determines whether Ethereum experiences deflationary pressure. For example, during times of high network usage, more ETH is burned, and the supply may decrease, creating deflationary effects. On the other hand, during periods of low network activity, the burning mechanism might not outpace the issuance of new ETH resulting from PoS staking rewards, making it inflationary at those times.

Inflationary Token Supply

An inflationary supply is one that creates a larger supply of tokens over time by gradually increasing the number of tokens in circulation. Similar to deflationary token supplies, the reason for incorporating an inflationary token supply system depends on the functionality and design of the product or service. The type of consensus mechanism (e.g., *proof-of-stake* or *proof-of-*stake staking*)* plays a major role in inflationary token supplies. Consensus mechanisms like mining and staking introduce new tokens into circulation, thereby increasing the total token supply. As a result, the supply becomes diluted, which sometimes has a negative effect on the price per coin or token. Therefore, if the demand for the product or service cannot overpower the inflation rate, one's investment may be negatively impacted.

Deflecting the Risk of Inflation

To help reduce the risk of inflation and investment devaluation, investors often stake their digital assets—applicable to PoS (proof-of-stake) consensus mechanisms only. By staking, which involves locking up their holdings, investors earn staking rewards. These rewards can be traded, sold, or re-staked for compound benefits. Restaking for compounded rewards essentially can help mitigate the risk of inflation for investors as they are continuously maintaining or increasing their percentage stake of the entire network supply. In other words, this investor strategy allows an investor's token quantity to grow in parallel with the overall token supply, thus preserving their stake of the supply. However, staking does not come without risk. Depending on the project requirements, staking terms and conditions often incorporate locking periods where investors are unable to unstake their assets until a certain time has elapsed, e.g., a week, a month, etc. These instant withdrawal limitations are dangerous for investors. For example, if the asset value suddenly drops due to negative news about a team member or a hacking incident, investors would be unable to react and would have to wait until the predetermined lock-in period ends. Therefore, it is important to carefully assess which assets to stake in addition to the staking terms and conditions prior to staking any assets.

Example of an Inflationary Project

KILT Protocol (KILT)—KILT Protocol, a decentralized identity blockchain network, has an inflationary supply because of staking to help secure the network. Figure 8-2 shows the relationship between KILT's block rewards, inflation rate, and total distribution of KILT coins over the first 60 years. The reward rate (in purple) gradually decreases, while the total distribution of coins increases over time, indicating more coins entering circulation. However, note that the reward rate is much higher than the initial inflation rate and always remains higher relative to the inflation rate as time progresses. Although this is admirable, unless investors are adopting a reward restaking strategy, as time progresses, they will see their percentage share of the total token supply diminish.

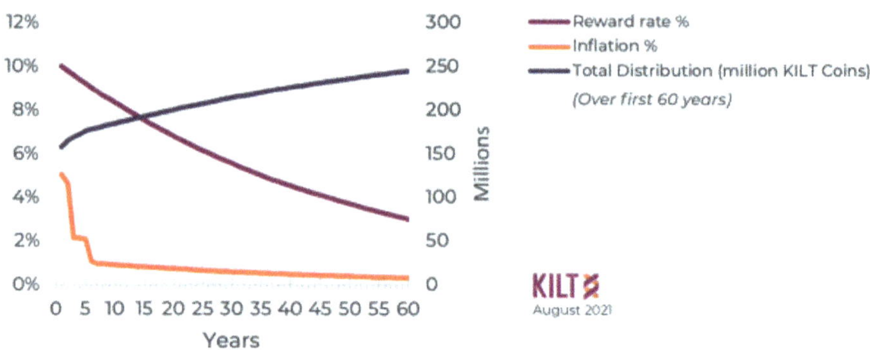

Figure 8-2. *Kilt Protocol block rewards and inflation (compliments of`https://kilt-protocol.org/files/Token-Economy.pdf`)*

Fixed Token Supply

As the name suggests, a fixed supply model is a token supply that has a fixed or total number of tokens that cannot be exceeded. With a fixed supply, no new tokens can be minted after reaching the supply cap, which can create scarcity and may support price if demand remains. Fixed token supplies create a sense of scarcity, as only a finite number of tokens or coins ever exist.

When analyzing fixed token supply, it is important to identify and specifically analyze the projects' circulating and maximum supply metrics—with the maximum being the "fixed" supply value. While the circulating supply metric will provide the number of coins in circulation, maximum supply represents the absolute cap on how many tokens will ever exist. By comparing these two metrics, investors can determine whether more coins are going to be released into circulation, either by token unlocks (through vesting) or by inflation. If the circulating supply matches the maximum supply, no more coins or tokens will be released into circulation. However, if the circulating supply is lower than the maximum supply, then further dilution of the supply is expected, and the severity of this should be evaluated by the investor depending on how low or high the circulating supply is relative to the maximum supply.

Pro Tip When evaluating projects with a fixed token supply, consider their use case and demand growth. Scarcity alone doesn't guarantee price appreciation—real-world utility and adoption matter just as much.

Example of a "Fixed Supply" Project

bitcoin (BTC) is an example of a fixed supply project with a hard (maximum) cap of 21 million coins. As new coins are introduced through mining, bitcoin's supply design transitions from inflationary to disinflationary over time (inflation rate falls toward 0%) until the fixed cap of 21 million coins is reached. bitcoin's halving mechanism, occurring every four years, reduces mining rewards by 50%, gradually decreasing new coin creation. This shifts bitcoin from inflationary to disinflationary, eventually reaching a non-inflationary state with static supply once the cap is hit. At this point, miners will no longer receive block rewards but will solely be incentivized solely through transaction fees paid by users of the bitcoin network.

Figure 8-3 illustrates bitcoin's declining inflation rate and its growing monetary base over time. In the early years, bitcoin's inflation rate was near 100% as new coins were rapidly introduced, but this rate has decreased significantly with each halving event, now approaching zero by the year 2140. Meanwhile, the total number of bitcoins in circulation (the monetary base) rises quickly initially but slows down as it nears the maximum supply of 21 million. This reflects bitcoin's deflationary design, ensuring scarcity and supporting its value proposition as a store of value.

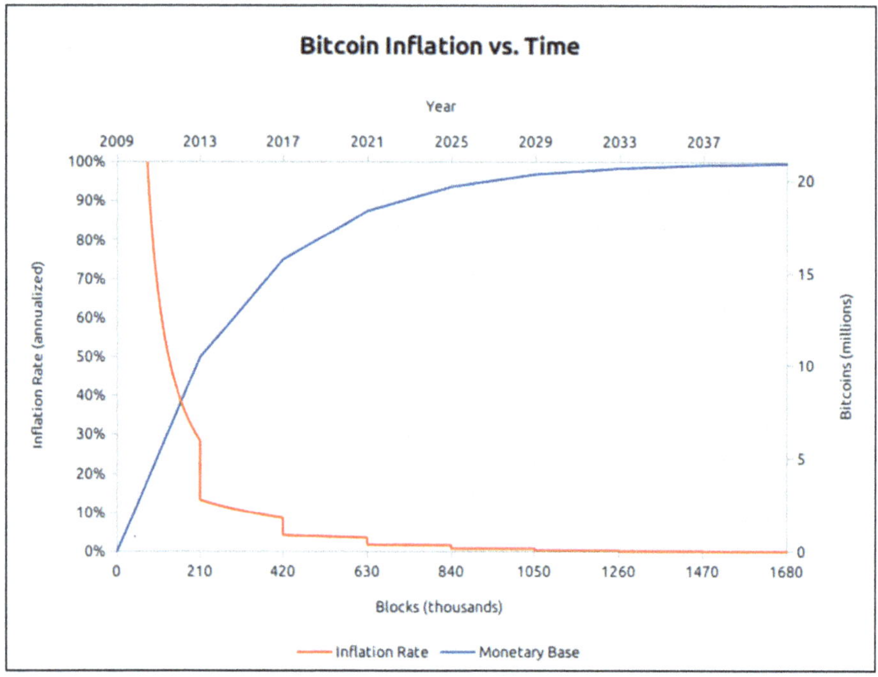

***Figure 8-3.** bitcoin inflation rate versus time (compliments of `https://www.bitcoinblockhalf.com/`)*

Action Steps

Follow these steps to identify whether the project adopts a deflationary, inflationary, or fixed supply model and evaluate based on future dilution risks, demand sustainability, and alignment with your investment strategy.

1) **Token Supply Model**

   Identify the token supply model adopted by the project, whether it is *fixed*, inflationary, or deflationary.

   a) **Fixed Supply** - No new tokens will be created.

   b) **Inflationary Supply** - Adds new tokens regularly.

   c) **Deflationary Supply** - Decreases the token count over time (through burns or similar mechanisms).

2) **Circulating Supply Versus Maximum Supply (Fixed Supply Focus)**

   When evaluating fixed supply models, it is essential to compare the circulating supply to the maximum supply.

   a) It is attractive when the circulating supply and the maximum supply are the same or almost the same, as it removes or minimizes future dilution of the supply.

   b) If a large portion of tokens are not yet in circulation, determine if the level of future dilution is acceptable as per your investment strategy.

      i) Examine investment strategy variables such as it is a short- or long-term investment. How long do you plan on holding? Unless there are aggressive token unlocks planned, supply models, including fixed supply, have less of an impact on short-term investors than long-term investors.

ii) If a long-term strategy is at play, pay particular focus to the other core fundamentals to help determine if you suspect they will overpower future dilution of the token supply.

3) **Inflation Rate (Inflationary Model)**

When evaluating inflationary supply models:

a) Check the inflation rate and how it's distributed (e.g., staking rewards and mining rewards).

b) Predict using other aspects of the fundamental analysis if the project's demand growth can outpace the inflation rate, or if the value of the token could be diluted over time.

c) Is it a short- or long-term investment? Short-term investors have less of an impact than long-term ones?

d) If investing for the long term, do you plan on staking (with PoS-based projects) and restaking for compounded rewards? This helps to retain the same percentage of tokens relative to the total supply and offsets the impact of token dilution for long-term investors.

4) **Burn Mechanisms and Scarcity (Deflationary Model)**

   When evaluating deflationary supply models:

   a) **Do not rely on a deflationary token supply to create demand.** Deflationary supplies are complementary to an existing high fundamental product with visible user growth.

   b) Investigate the burn mechanism:

      i) How frequently do burns happen?

      ii) How much supply is reduced? and

      iii) What triggers the burn mechanism?

      iv) Does the time token burn mechanism end at a certain point?

5) **Take Notes and Document Your Findings in Your Own Style**

6) **Combine the Findings with Other Sections of the Fundamental Evaluation Process**

Evaluation of the Results

There is not really a one-size-fits-all approach to token supply; the project team typically chooses the model that works best for the product. The core design, functionality, and the project's long-term vision and goals will have a direct impact on the selected token model. Ideally, projects that incorporate a fixed supply model or a dominant deflationary mechanism are more attractive to investors. There is a sense of comfort knowing that the token supply is not indefinitely inflated, causing continuous dilution of the supply and, in turn, affecting your investment. However, it is strongly suggested not to focus solely on these aspects. While deflationary or fixed supplies are appealing, they don't guarantee success. Additionally, many projects with inflationary models have thrived, proving that factors like utility, adoption, and overall project fundamentals are significantly important.

Token Distribution Models

Evaluation Objective: Identify a project's token distribution model and determine whether its allocations align with industry benchmarks, ensure fairness, and support long-term growth and community engagement.

A token distribution model is a strategy detailing how a crypto project divides and allocates the token supply among the stakeholders, including the project team, developers, advisors, early backers, and investors. Think of it as slicing up a pie and deciding who gets what. Deciding how many tokens are allocated to each allocation category (including stakeholders) directly impacts investors and the overall long-term viability and success of the project. The design of a token distribution model, including deciding how total and maximum supply quantities are executed by the team with the help of skilled professionals. Many factors are considered during this process, including functionality of the core product, token utility, type of supply model, governance structure, distribution mechanisms, supply and demand, user requirements, and other related areas. Such design detail is out of the scope of this book and not deemed required for this section of the analysis. Instead, token distributions are discussed, including the key elements and red flags that investors need to pay attention to. The main objective is to ensure that the token supply distributions are not heavily distributed to the team or early backers, with a fair distribution having been allocated to the community.

Token Distribution Groups

In the tokenomic design phase, the token supply is split up among different groups to help ensure the project remains successful in the long term. Typically, the project team decides how the token supply is divided and the quantiles given to each allocation category. There is an array of factors that influence this decision, including project funding requirements, developer incentivization, community growth, and future development. Table 8-1 outlines the most common types of allocation categories that typically receive a share of the token supply.

Table 8-1. *Typical token distribution group*

Token Allocation Categories		
Category	**Definitions**	**Allocation Purpose**
Team and Founders	The project's creators, developers, and core team members.	An incentive for their work, dedication, and the project's long-term success.
Accredited Investors	Accredited investors, who invest in early-stage seed, venture capital, and private sale rounds.	Provides adequate funding that's required to help build and grow the project in its early stages.
Partnerships and Advisors	Tokens held for various partnership deals and advisors to help strengthen the project.	Partnerships with blockchain companies. Influencers. Marketing advisors. Technical advisors. Financial advisors.

(continued)

Table 8-1. *(continued)*

Token Allocation Categories		
Category	**Definitions**	**Allocation Purpose**
Community and Ecosystem Incentives	Tokens held for community contribution to incentivize engagement and ecosystem growth.	Airdrops. Ecosystem rewards. Farming and liquidity mining rewards. Community contributor incentivization. Marketing.
Treasury Reserves	Tokens held by the DAO, company, founding institution, or foundation.	Aims to preserve the longevity of the project in the following ways: Operations and maintenance. Uphold security. Ecosystem growth and development. Emergency fund. R&D.
Public Investors	Tokens held for the public, retail investors, and consumers.	Public sales of one or more of the following: Initial coin offerings (ICO). Initial DEX offering (IDO). Initial exchange offering (IEO). Crowdsales.

Example of Uniswap's Token Supply Model

When Uniswap was launched, one billion UNI tokens were minted (created). The tokens were distributed as outlined in Figure 8-4. This is an admirable token distribution model, with the majority share of the tokens allocated to the community incentive programs.

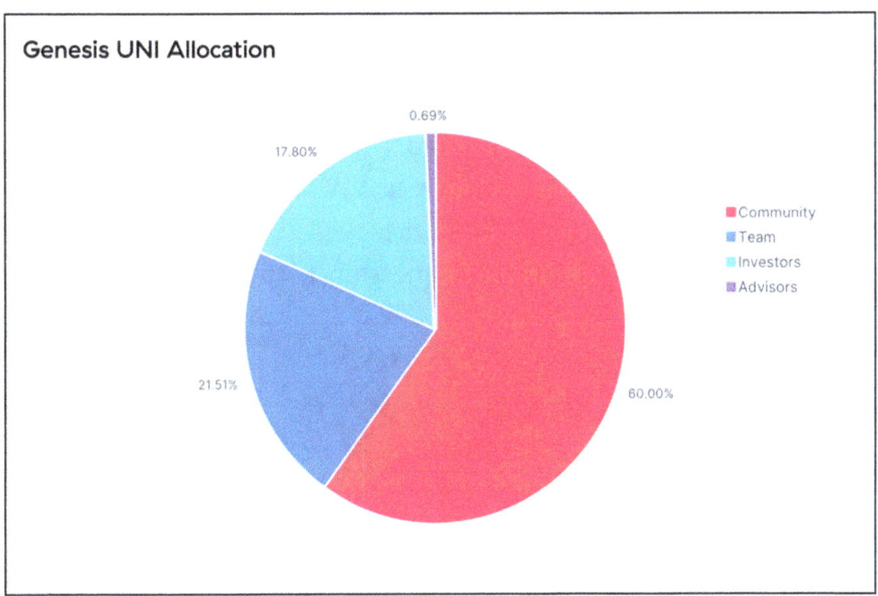

Figure 8-4. *Uniswap (compliments of `https://blog.uniswap.org/uni`)*

From Figure 8-4, 60% (600m UNI) were issued to the community, with the team receiving 21.51% (215.10m UNI) and 17.51% (178m UNI) to early investors, leaving 0.69% (69m UNI) for project advisors. Note that the majority of the tokens went to the community. Almost 60% of UNI tokens are allocated to the Uniswap community to overall drive ecosystem growth and decentralized governance. These tokens were mainly used for rewarding early users through airdrops, supporting liquidity mining initiatives, and empowering community-driven governance.

A significant portion of these tokens is held in a governance treasury to fund community projects, grants, and further incentivize participation in the ecosystem.

Token Distribution Benchmark

When it comes to token distribution, the main goal for investors is to make sure that tokens are allocated in a way that drives growth while also protecting the public investors from the risk of heavy sell-offs by the project team or early seed round investors. A proposed token distribution model benchmark is proposed in Figure 8-5. While the allocation proportions and corresponding percentages will fluctuate from project to project, this structure is admirable for investors for multiple reasons.

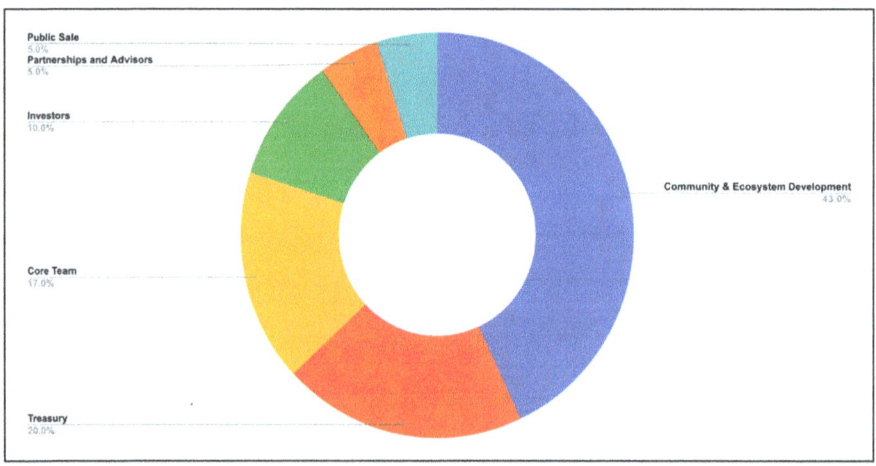

***Figure 8-5.** Token distribution model benchmark for investors*

Community and Ecosystem Development – First, the largest share is reserved for community incentives and ecosystem development. This is crucial for the growth of the project, as it incorporates multiple areas from user rewards, staking, mining, marketing, liquidity, contributor programs, and developer grants—hence the reason why this allocation should be at least 40% or more. Uniswap (Figure 8-4), for example, allocates 60% of its tokens to the community, which plays a crucial role in driving the project's growth. By doing this, they mitigate the risks associated with early token dumping by the project team and seed round investors. With the majority of tokens dedicated to incentivizing the community, any sell-offs by smaller groups have a lesser impact on the overall ecosystem and price per token.

Treasury - Most launches earmark a mid-teens-to-low-20% slice of the initial supply for the treasury (e.g., ≈ 21% in Uniswap, ≈ 20% in Optimism, and ≈ 18% in Polkadot), giving the project 3–5 years of runway for core operations, upgrades, grants, and contingency funding without flooding the circulating float.

Project Team - Anything from 17% to 20% is a standard allocation for the team—provided they earn it!

Investors - Investors' funds are important for startup projects getting established. However, unless early backers are providing extreme value (outside of funding), no more than 10% should be allocated. The bulk of the supply is better allocated to community incentive reserves and the treasury, which will add significantly more value in the long run.

Partnerships and Advisors - Typically allocated about 5% of the supply. Depending on the complexity of the project, this may increase slightly.

Public Sales - Traditionally, public sales—where tokens are sold to the public at the time of launch—were allocated around 3–5% of the total supply. However, there's been a noticeable shift in recent years, with projects moving away from public sales and instead focusing more on community incentive allocations. For example, data from *UnlockInsights.*app historical token launches and the latest figures on *CryptoRank.io* show public-sale allocations sliding from roughly 35% in 2018 to only about 3%–5% by 2025. This shift is for the good of the project, where it helps build strong communities, fueling organic growth of the ecosystem. Additionally, it mitigates the risks associated with large-scale token sell-offs by early investors.

Action Steps

Follow these steps to identify a project's token distribution model and determine whether its allocations align with industry benchmarks, ensure fairness, and support long-term growth and community engagement.

1) **Token Distribution Model Details**
   Review relevant information regarding the project's token distribution model from the whitepaper, official documentation, and other reliable sources.

2) **Benchmark Token Distribution Allocation Model**
   Compare the project's token supply allocations against the benchmark model outlined in this section.

   a) Are there visible concerns regarding excess team or investor token allocations?

   b) Has the community incentives reserve been given the largest allocation? Minimum of 40% is admirable.

   c) Has the treasury been allocated 20% (or more) of the token supply?

   d) Other observations that may be harmful to investors?

3) **Competitor Analysis**
   Compare the project's token supply allocations against that of successful competitors within the same niche.

   a) How do the projects token compare to that of successful investors?

   b) Are there any known issues or pitfalls in the token allocations of these competitors that this project has learned from and addressed?

   c) How transparent are the project's tokenomics compared to its competitors? Greater transparency can be a sign of good governance and a commitment to fair practices.

4) **Take Notes and Document Your Findings in Your Own Style**

5) **Combine the Findings with Other Sections of the Fundamental Evaluation Process**

Evaluating the Results

Distribution of the token supply is a critical fundamental element and carries a lot of weight in the overall fundamental analysis. Therefore, if the team or investor token allocations exceed the allocation of community incentives, it is deemed suspicious and recommended to stay clear of investing.

If there is a significant deviation from the proposed token distribution benchmark, it is recommended to reach out to the project team for advice before investing. Note that there may be nuanced situations where the token allocation categories differ from the benchmark and are acceptable upon further research. For example, in the case of the Moonbeam Network, the unique involvement with the Polkadot's Parachain infrastructure, the token allocation is specifically catered and designed to accommodate some nuanced allocation categories, some including *the take flight community event, the 2021 Moonbeam crowdloan allocation, and the parachain bond reserves.*

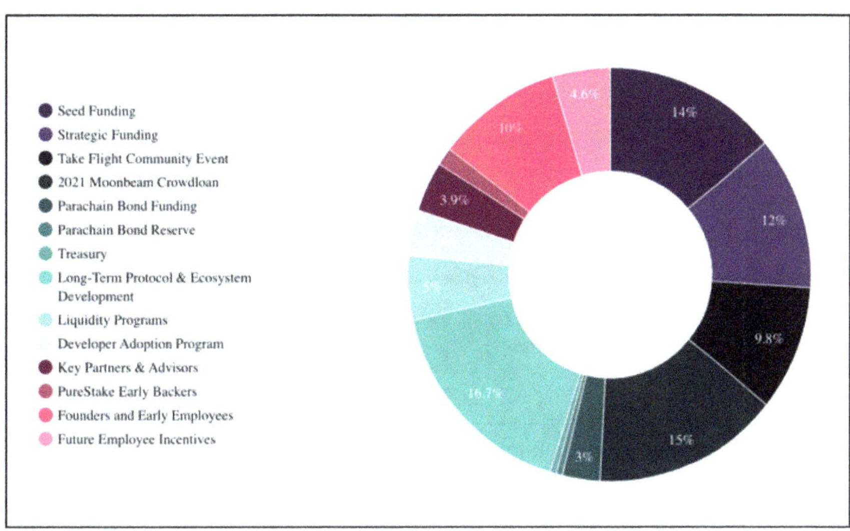

Figure 8-6. *Moonbeam Network, genesis token allocation (compliments of `https://moonbeam.foundation/glimmer-token/`)*

Vesting Schedules

Evaluation Objective: Evaluate a project's vesting schedule to determine its impact on token supply stability, price volatility, and the project team's commitment to long-term success.

Vesting in the crypto space refers to the gradual release of tokens to stakeholders over a set period. When tokens are spread out gradually, it can help reduce sudden price changes, while releasing too many tokens early can instead increase price fluctuations, even if the goal is to show long-term support. For investors, analyzing vesting schedules is a vital part of the fundamental analysis, as it determines if there is potential for heavy token dumping after the project launches or at any period during the early stages of the project lifecycle. Analyzing a vesting schedule can help gauge the project team's level of dedication and commitment, represented by a slow and balanced token release over several years.

Vesting Schedules and Associated Terminology

Understanding the key terms related to vesting is essential for crypto investors. It helps clarify how token distribution works, the conditions under which tokens are released, and how these mechanisms align stakeholder interests with the project's long-term success. Here's a breakdown of the main concepts associated with vesting that every investor should be familiar with:

Table 8-2. *Vesting-related terminology*

Vesting Terminology	
Terminology	**Description**
Vesting Period	The timeframe over which the tokens are gradually released.
Cliff	*Cliff* refers to the initial time period that must elapse before the gradual release of tokens commences. The length of these *cliffs* can differ based on the intended allocation category. For example, a 24-month cliff may apply to project team members or seed round investors, while public sale participants may have a one-month cliff or no cliff in some circumstances.
Linear Vesting	Tokens are released at a constant rate over the vesting period.
Graded Vesting	Tokens are released in increments at specific intervals, rather than uniformly.
Lock-Up Period (Lockups)	The time during which tokens are locked in a smart contract, making them not transferable, even if they are technically vested.
Fully Vested	The point at which all the tokens are entirely owned and can be freely accessed by the holder.

(*continued*)

Table 8-2. (*continued*)

Vesting Terminology	
Terminology	**Description**
Token Unlock	The time when a specific number of tokens are released into circulation as per the vesting schedule.
Vesting Contract	A smart contract that automatically handles the release of tokens according to the vesting schedule.
Milestone-Based Vesting	Token release is triggered upon specific goals or project milestones.

Pro Tip Prior to investing, visit Tokenomist.ai to view detailed data of all upcoming token unlocks. It is advised not to invest before a token unlock; instead, wait until the token unlock has passed and the price per coin or token has settled. This practice will save investors money.

Vesting Schedule Evaluation

In this section, the Immutable X vesting schedule is analyzed and evaluated. Immutable X is a blockchain-based protocol designed for trading and creating non-fungible assets (NFTs). Figure 8-7 shows Immutable X's token supply allocation at genesis, while Figure 8-8 displays the corresponding vesting schedule in a real-time table format.

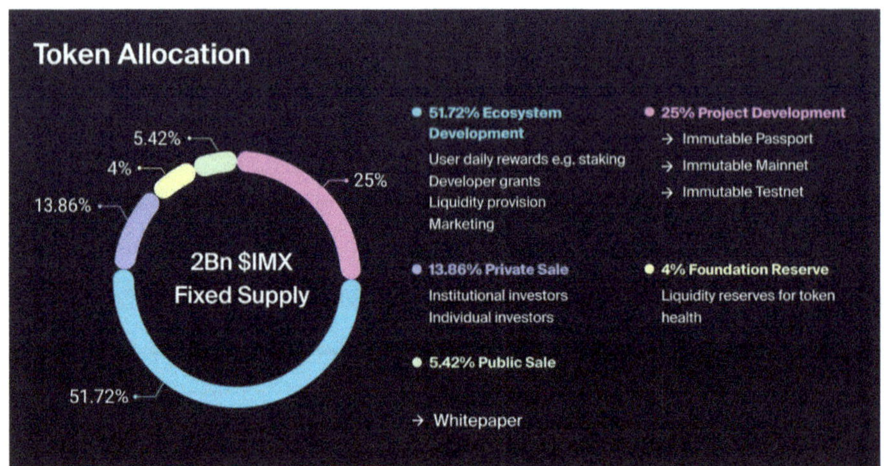

Figure 8-7. *Immutable X token allocation (compliments of `https://imx.community/tokenomics`)*

Vesting Schedule

Table Timeline Chart

Round	TGE Unlock	Cliff	Unlocked	Locked	Next Unlock	Summary
Ecosystem Devel... IMX 1.03B 51.7%	0%	4w	IMX 915.09M Start 2 Dec 2021	IMX 119.33M End 30 Oct 2025	31 Oct 2024 1.54%	then 3.08% daily from 02.12.2021 to 03.11.2022, then 2.31% daily from 01.12.2022 to 02.11.2023, then 1.54%...
Project Developm... IMX 500.00M 25%	0%	1y	IMX 268.16M Start 1 Dec 2022	IMX 231.84M End 30 Oct 2025	31 Oct 2024 3.31%	1 year-cliff, then 1.92% daily from 01.12.2022 to 13.06.2024, then 3.31% daily from 11.07.2024 to 30.10.20...
Private Sale IMX 277.14M 13.9%	0%	11m	IMX 277.14M Start 3 Nov 2022	IMX 0.00 End 18 Apr 2024		1 year-cliff, 03.11.2022 - 40.6%, then 3.13% daily from 01.12.2022 to 18.04.2024
Foundation Reser... IMX 80.00M 4.00%	100%		IMX 80.00M Start 4 Nov 2021	IMX 0.00 End 4 Nov 2021		100% TGE, 52 years-cliff
Public Sale 1 IMX 58.80M 2.94%	0%	4w	IMX 58.80M Start 2 Dec 2021	IMX 0.00 End 27 Jan 2022		33.3% every 28 days for 3 months
Public Sale 2 IMX 49.60M 2.48%	0%	4w	IMX 49.60M Start 2 Dec 2021	IMX 0.00 End 21 Apr 2022		16.7% every 28 days for 6 months
Total	IMX 80.00M		IMX 1.65B 82.4% of Supply	IMX 351.17M 17.6% of Supply		

Figure 8-8. *Immutable X vesting schedule (compliments of `https://cryptorank.io/price/immutable-x/vesting`)*

The first column of the vesting table details the allocation category with the corresponding number of tokens assigned to each distribution (matching Figure 8-7). The column titled "TGE Summary" details the share of the total supply (%) that was unlocked during the token generation event (TGE). TGE is when the tokens (or coins) are publicly released into the market. The set *cliff* for each allocation is outlined in the third column, indicating the waiting period after launch before the tokens are released.

Foundation Reserve Tokens

When evaluating a vesting schedule, start by looking at which allocations and what percentage of those allocations will be released at the token generation event (TGE). This is especially important if the TGE hasn't occurred yet or if you've participated in the public sale. For Immutable X, the foundation reserve was the only allocation released at the TGE and was fully unlocked; because these tokens are designated for long-term project needs rather than immediate liquidity, the risk of a large post-TGE sell-off was greatly reduced. However, investors that are planning to purchase tokens at TGE still need to determine when the next batch of tokens is set for release into circulation and the percentage of them to be released.

Public Sale Tokens

The next tokens set for release are the *public sale* tokens (totaling 5.42% of the supply) and the *ecosystem development* allocation, which are both set to be released four weeks (4-week cliff) after TGE. As noted in the summary column, the public sale tokens are set for release at 33% every four weeks over three months. This release schedule is common practice, according to token-vesting tracker platforms such as CryptoRank.io and Tokenomist.ai; however, this is not always the case, with some projects even releasing their entire public-sale allocation at once. There is no right or wrong; however, spreading the release over three months tends to dampen the wild price movements.

Ecosystem Development Tokens

The *ecosystem development* allocation tokens have a more complex release structure that spans from 2021 to 2025. This release schedule presents no threat for investors, as these tokens have a slow release and are planned for ecosystem development.

Project Development Tokens

The *project development* allocation follows a similar release schedule but has a one-year cliff before any tokens are released. From the "Unlocked-Locked" column, both these allocations are still being distributed until the final distribution is made in October 2025. At the bottom of the table, it indicates the remaining tokens to be distributed equal 351.7 million, or 17.6% of the supply.

Pro Tip Cryptorank.io is a great website to analyze real-time crypto vesting schedules and an array of other financial data. Here, investors can visually see when the next token unlock is so preparations can be made accordingly.

Private Sale Tokens

The release of private and seed round tokens is a threat for most projects. These tokens are typically bought by institutional investors and private equity firms at a very low cost per token. These investors are looking to lock in profits once they gain access to their tokens, and as a result, the market endures high selling pressure, driving down the price per token. Often, these types of investors are always in profit when they sell because of the extremely low cost they purchased the tokens for, compared to public sale participants and those who purchase tokens on the open market. It is common for these high-end institutional investors to lock in anything from 10x to 50x gains depending on the project popularity.

In the case of Immutable X, the *private sale* tokens have an eleven-month cliff after which the release schedule spans from November 2022 to April 2024 (approximately 17 months). Compared to other projects, this cliff and release structure is admirable. Many projects allow a proportion of the private sale and seed round tokens to be released at TGE, which severely impacts public sale participants and buyers on the open market and generally causes severe swings that negatively impact most unexperienced investors and traders. However, IMX public sale participants are comparatively better protected because they receive all their tokens before the private sale tokens, according to their release schedule. Nevertheless, investors holding IMX tokens will typically experience a small dip in price per token coming leading to the release or at the time of release of the private sale tokens. For example, in the immediate days after the release of the batch of private sale tokens (40.60% of 13.90% = 5.64% of the total supply) on November 3, 2022, the price per token dropped over 40% from roughly $0.70 to $0.40. While experienced traders may try to take advantage of these volatile swings or at minimum hold their investment during this time period, most investors panic and sell their tokens even if it means incurring severe losses. Note, about seven weeks later, the IMX token started to increase in price and tripled in value in just 11 weeks. However, this is not always the case, so it is the investors' responsibility to be aware and prepare for such token unlocks.

Project Team Tokens

Due to the fact that the Immutable X team was not issued an allocation, the only potential threat for investors is the release of *private sale* tokens.

Pro Tip Buying at TGE—the moment tokens hit the market and in the subsequent days—often brings wild price swings in both directions; the upside can be huge, but the downside just as brutal, so unless you're genuinely confident (and experienced), it's smarter to wait for things to settle before jumping in.

Vesting Schedule Benchmark

Vesting schedules are not an exact science and will slightly differ based on project requirements and preferences of the project team and advisors. The core objective of an honest and dedicated team is to generate a vesting schedule that helps maintain long-term success of the project while also reducing heavy unwanted selling pressure, resulting in wild price action swings. This entails the team having enough upfront funds for development and operations and also securing the slow and gradual release of tokens into circulation. This type of vesting benchmark structure is reflected in Table 8-3.

Note that the "release schedule" specifies "evenly distributed" for each allocation. This is an ideal situation to help minimize wild price swings (as far as crypto goes). Another popular option is a milestone-based unlock, where new tranches are released only when the project hits specific product or ecosystem goals. That said, it is common for projects to release 10%–40% of allocation for the first release and evenly distribute thereafter. For example, for accredited investors, after the cliff period has ended, 25% may be released and then 75% evenly distributed on a daily, weekly, or monthly basis for the next three years. As previously stated with this, the higher the issue typically is relative to the selling pressure. Therefore, it is admirable for a complete even distribution or, at a minimum, maybe 10% of the 15% initial release.

For investors, vesting schedules are important if the project has not launched or has many tokens yet to be unlocked. However, they tend to be less critical for projects where all tokens or coins have already been fully unlocked. If major deviation from Table 8-3 is experienced, stop, investigate further, and do not proceed with investing until the findings are satisfactory and the concerns are resolved.

Table 8-3. *Admirable vesting schedule and cliff parameters*

Vesting Schedule Benchmark			
Allocations	**TGE Unlock**	**Cliff**	**Release Schedule**
Team and Founders	0–5%	1 or 2 years	4 years minimum (evenly distributed)
Accredited Investors (Private Sale/Seed Round)	0%	1 or 2 years	3 years minimum (evenly distributed)
Partnerships and Advisors	0%	1 year (min)	2 years minimum (evenly distributed)
Community and Ecosystem Development	30%	1 month	4 years minimum (evenly distributed)
Treasury Reserves	20%	2 months	4 years minimum (evenly distributed) (required to maintain stability, support the project's long-term growth, development, and success)
Public Sale Investors	0%	1 month	6 months (evenly distributed)

Pro Tip A constant challenge of investors is the use of different definitions and terminology when evaluating vesting and allocation schedules. If in doubt, reach out to the team for clarity. Remember, projects that have nothing to hide typically have clearly defined supply allocations and vesting schedules.

Action Steps

Follow these steps to evaluate a project's vesting schedule to determine its impact on token supply stability, price volatility, and the project team's commitment to long-term success.

1) **Locate Vesting Schedule**
   Locate the project's vesting schedule. Sometimes this can be hard to find, especially if the project has been launched for many years. First, visit the official project website and blog. Also check out *Cryptorank.io* and *Tokenomist.ai*, compare their data, and cross-check community channels (Discord, Telegram, and governance forums) for the newest info. *CoinGecko.com* and *CoinMarketCap.com* sometimes host vesting schedules if the team has uploaded them.

2) **Evaluate Vesting Schedule**
   Evaluate the condition of the vesting schedule using the vesting schedule analysis technique outlined in the section titled "Vesting Schedule Evaluation." Evaluate the condition of the vesting schedule using the vesting schedule analysis technique outlined in the section titled "Vesting Schedule Evaluation."

a) **TGE %** – Check how much of the token supply will be released at the TGE. Are there any concerning allocations with a high percentage unlock at TGE that could lead to pressure and price drops?

b) Cliff Periods – Review the cliff periods. Are there allocations without cliffs? Or allocations with short cliff periods? Are there multiple cliff periods ending at the same time that may result in volatile price swings and selling pressure?

c) Distribution Schedule – A gradual token release schedule is admirable versus a heavy lump-sum release. Staggered distribution tends to minimize price volatility.

d) Community and Ecosystem Development Allocation – Has a proportion of the ecosystem development tokens been released at TGE or soon after TGE? A slow, gradual token release is admired after the initial token lump sum has been released.

e) Accredited Investor Allocations – Pay close attention to the cliff and vesting schedule of private and seed sale tokens. It is common for early backers to sell at the first opportunity, creating downward pressure on the token's price.

   f) **Teams and Advisor Allocations** - Verify if the project team has a reasonable vesting schedule for their tokens. A long lock-up period shows the team's commitment to the project's long-term success.

3) **Vesting Schedule Benchmark**
   Compare the vesting schedule to that of the vesting schedule outlined in the section titled "Vesting Schedule Benchmark."

4) **Competitor Analysis**
   Compare the vesting schedule to that of successful competitors.
   a) Are there noticeable differences? If so, in what ways will they affect your investment?

5) **Take Notes and Document Your Findings in Your Own Style**

6) **Combine the Findings with Other Sections of the Fundamental Evaluation Process**

Evaluating the Results

If you notice a significant deviation from the vesting schedule benchmark or similar issues as discussed in this section, hold off on making any investment. Only proceed if your concerns are fully addressed and resolved.

CHAPTER 9

Financial Metrics

In this chapter, financial metrics for digital assets, including both on-chain and off-chain financial metrics, are discussed. On-chain metrics refer to information recorded directly on the blockchain, such as total transaction volume, the number of active addresses, and the percentage of the circulating supply currently in profit. On the other hand, off-chain metrics are data typically recorded on central servers—such as price and trading volume from centralized exchanges—and reported to digital asset price-tracking websites such as CoinMarketCap.com. Be aware that reported exchange volumes can be artificially inflated through wash-trading or bot activity, so always cross-check figures with on-chain data and volumes from reputable, regulated venues.

Evaluating a digital asset's historical financial data provides valuable insight into the project's overall performance, fundamental health, and whether it has been losing or gaining movement since its genesis. This also includes its bear and bull market performance, stability, and future potential. Using a variety of on-chain financial metrics, investors can identify and analyze market trends and price action patterns. When analyzing price action, the aim is to identify confluence using one or more metrics, helping to predict the future direction of an asset price per coin. This approach enables investors to strategically plan profit-taking and buying tactics for accumulation and distribution zones and transitional areas where price moves between these zones.

P. Garvey, *Blockchain Fundamental Analysis for Digital Asset Investors*,
https://doi.org/10.1007/979-8-8688-1551-5_9

Using various financial metrics like *market capitalization* (MC), *fully diluted valuation* (FDV), *total value locked* (TVL), and *total value staked* (TVS) allows investors to assess an asset's popularity, trustworthiness, user interaction, economic potential, and overall performance. Combining this data with other on-chain financial metrics and technical analysis significantly enhances an investor's insight, allowing for more efficient risk management and accurate entry and exit points when investing.

Financial Metric Software

A variety of financial metrics software is used throughout this chapter to analyze the financial and fundamental health of digital assets. Such software includes Glassnode, Bitcoin Magazine Pro, CoinMarketCap, and DeFi Lama. Other popular crypto asset financial metric software includes Token Terminal, Messari, Dune Analytics, and Nansen.

Glassnode is the primary software used in this chapter for the in-depth analysis of on-chain metric data, with mostly bitcoin used for illustration purposes. This software is specifically designed for digital asset investors to analyze and evaluate critical on-chain metrics that are not achievable with a standard web-based platform for financial market analysis, e.g., trading charts and price action data. Glassnode offers hundreds of on-chain metric data tools; therefore, only the most relevant metrics are discussed within the scope of this book. It is encouraged that investors research and explore Glassnode and similar sites such as Bitcoin Magazine Pro, CryptoQuant, and CoinMetrics, which provide a broad array of on-chain data-analytic resources—pulled directly from the blockchain. These include detailed metric dashboards, downloadable APIs, quantitative-trading and risk-management tools, and discretionary-trading aids that suit a range of investment strategies.

Fact Quantitative-trading exchange-risk management is the practice of using automated models fed by on-chain analytics—like Glassnode's real-time exchange-flow dashboards and bitcoin Magazine Pro's—to track liquidity and leverage shifts across exchanges and dynamically adjust position size or hedges to limit drawdown risk.

As previously stated, it is important to note that this chapter covers a range of on-chain metrics, many of which are primarily only available for bitcoin and, in some cases, other highly popular coins and tokens. The reason is that newer, less established coins and tokens with lower market capitalizations aren't often tracked; therefore, the level of data is unavailable. However, since bitcoin holds the largest market capitalization and the highest market dominance, understanding its price movements provides investors valuable insights into potential entry and exit points for other altcoins and tokens. Investors are still encouraged to explore different analytical tools, as most DeFi projects offer adequate financial data for evaluation—DeFi Lama is fantastic for all DeFi projects.

Fundamentals Discussed in This Chapter:

- *Market Cap and FDV*
- *Realized Cap*
- *Realized Cap and HODL Waves*
- *Liquidity and Trading Volume*
- *Total Transfer Volume*
- *Total Value Staked (TVS)*
- *Total Value Locked (TVL)*
- *Fees and Revenue*

- *Transaction Count*
- *Inflation Rate*
- *Investor Tool*
- *Percent Supply in Profit*
- *Active Addresses*
- *Number of Addresses with Balance Greater than 10k bitcoins*
- *MVRV Ratio*
- *MVRZ Z-Score*
- *Net Unrealized Profit/Loss (NUPL)*
- *Hash Rate*
- *Network Value to Transactions Signal (NVTS)*
- *Stock-to-Flow Model*

Market Cap and FDV

Evaluation Objective: Evaluate a project's market capitalization and fully diluted valuation (FDV) to determine potential risks, including future token dilution, inflationary impacts, and alignment with your investment strategy.

Identifying and analyzing a project's financial valuation is the first and most critical evaluation step for investors. A project's valuation is assessed by evaluating both the *market capitalization* and *fully diluted valuation (FDV)*. Market capitalization gives a snapshot of the project's current value based on circulating tokens. At the same time, a fully diluted valuation—also known as a fully diluted market cap—looks at its potential future worth if all tokens are in circulation. Both *market capitalization* and *fully diluted valuation* are ultimately calculated by the market consisting of buyers and sellers. However, they are calculated in different ways.

Market Capitalization

Market capitalization, or market cap, is the total market value of a project's circulating supply—see Equation 9-1. It is essential to understand that the market cap does not include tokens (or coins) that are locked, vested, or not yet mined or minted. Since exchanges are sometimes known to inflate volume and data sites can misreport circulating supply, pull the market cap figure from two or three trackers (CoinMarketCap, CoinGecko, and Messari) and sanity-check any big differences before relying on it. A project's market capitalization, or market cap, is calculated by multiplying the circulating supply by the price per token (or coin)—for instance, Figure 9-1 shows the Polkadot Networks financial metrics from CoinMarketCap.com. Polkadot's market cap is calculated as per Equation 9-2.

Market Capitalization = Circulating Supply x Price Per Coin

Equation 9-1. *Formula to calculate market capitalization*

1.51 *billion x* $4.13=$6.22 *billion* (*rounded to* $6.21 *billion by CMC*)

Equation 9-2. *Formula calculating Polkadot Networks market capitalization*

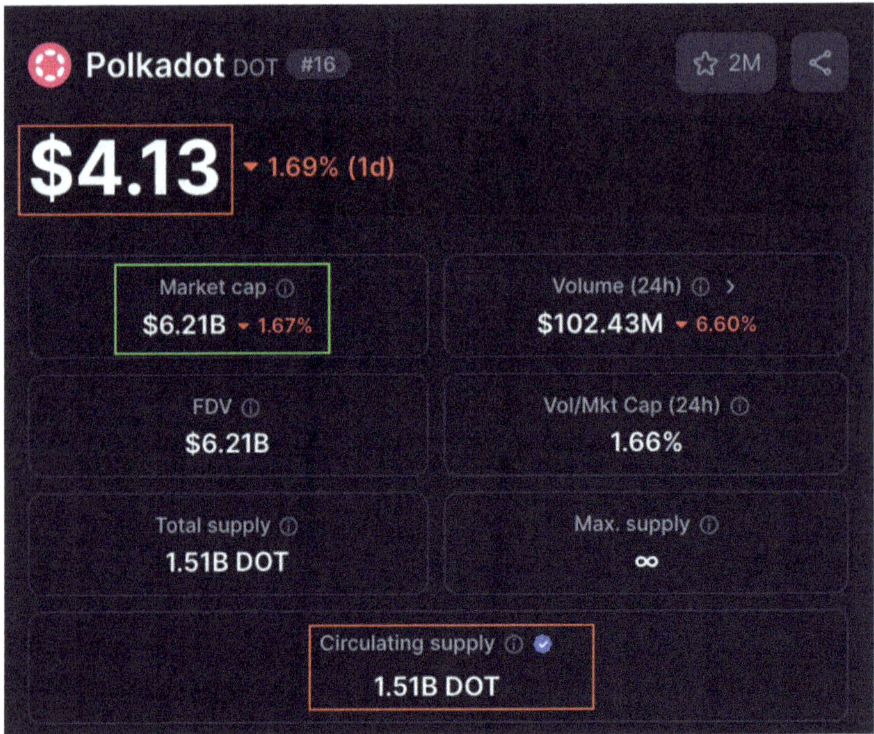

***Figure 9-1.** Polkadot Network financial data on CoinMarketCap (compliments of* `https://coinmarketcap.com/currencies/polkadot-new/`*)*

Fully Diluted Valuation

A *fully diluted valuation* (FDV), or a *fully diluted market capitalization,* is the total market value of a project's entire token supply, including the tokens in circulation and locked and vested tokens. It is calculated by multiplying the maximum supply by the token price—see Equation 9-3. It is vital to understand that while the market capitalization only refers to the tokens in circulation (circulation supply), the FVD refers to all tokens currently in circulation plus the locked tokens yet to be released into circulation (maximum supply)—for instance, Figure 9-2 shows Avalanche blockchain network financial metrics from CoinMarketCap.com. Avalanche's fully diluted valuation is calculated as per Equation 9-4.

Fully Diluted Valuation = Max Supply x Price Per Coin

Equation 9-3. *Formula to calculate fully diluted valuation (FVD)*

715 *million x* $29.28 = $20.957 *billion* (*rounded to* $20.96 *billion by CMC*)

Equation 9-4. *Formula calculating Polkadot Networks fully diluted valuation (FVD)*

Figure 9-2. *Avalanche financial data (compliments of `https://coinmarketcap.com/currencies/avalanche/`)*

Pro Tip Comparing market capitalization to fully diluted valuation reveals if significant token releases are pending, which could impact the token's price.

If no maximum supply is specified, it signifies the supply does not have a fixed cap and, therefore, no limit on how many can exist. If provided, it is better to use the maximum supply in calculations, as it allows for a more accurate result since it accounts for all tokens that will ever be created. However, if no maximum supply is given, use the *total supply* instead.

Accessing Market Cap. and FDV

There is a lot of debate among investors about which metric is more critical: market cap or fully diluted valuation (FDV). It is recommended that both metrics be identified and compared against one another. If the FDV is significantly higher than the current market cap, this indicates that many tokens may be scheduled for release. If there is a small gap between the FDV and the market cap, it suggests there's less risk of future dilution.

Avalanche (Figure 9-2) has an FDV of $20.96B, with a market cap of only $11.91B. This indicates that 43% (1 - (11.91 / 20.96)) of the maximum supply is yet to be released into circulation through unlocks and inflation. As with fundamental supply and demand principles, when a project releases more tokens into circulation and the demand remains static, the price per token will decrease. If the demand for the token increases, the price will increase. Therefore, on the side of caution, checking the corresponding vesting schedule is advised to determine when the next and final unlocks are planned. Note investors must also check when inflation is due to end. Inflation may continue for many years after the last unlock—and in governance-driven networks it can even be extended or adjusted, especially where no fixed supply cap exists. However, this may have less impact on one's investment depending on how long you are planning on holding—it is common for inflation to last up to five years or more before reaching the hard cap, maximum supply value.

Note that the market cap provides the current valuation, while the fully diluted valuation is focused on the future market value. With this, the market cap is more relevant to short-term investors, with FDV more applicable to long-term investors looking one or more years down the line. Nevertheless, checking and analyzing both metrics is relatively fast and should be executed by both short- and long-term investors.

Market Capitalization Ranges

Crypto projects come in all sizes when it comes to market capitalization. Each market cap size comes with its own level of risk, profit potential, volatility, and various other variables. Low market caps are typically riskier and more volatile, with high profit (or loss) potential, while large market caps are deemed more stable with slow, gradual profit (or loss) potential. However, there's no fixed rule for what defines a "small" or "large" market cap.

Table 9-1 outlines how market caps are typically classified in crypto. It is recommended for investors to analyze and understand the advantages and disadvantages of each market cap classification to determine if it meets their investment strategy and lifestyle. **Disclaimer:** These ranges are a rule of thumb drawn from common crypto-market practice; they are not an industry standard and may vary by source.

Table 9-1. *Market capitalization classifications*

Market Capitalization Comparison				
Criteria	**Microcap ($0–$100 million)**	**Small Cap ($100 million to $1 billion)**	**Medium Cap ($1 billion to $15 billion)**	**Large Cap ($15 billion +)**
Project Maturity	Early-stage or start-up.	Early-stage but more mature than microcap.	Mid-stage, semi-established.	Fully established, mature projects.
Popularity	Limited visibility, unknown.	Growing, increasing visibility.	Wide adoption.	Mainstream.
Growth Potential	High room for growth if successful.	Significant room for growth	Moderate room for growth	Limited room for growth.
Volatility	Very high.	High, but more stable than microcap.	Moderate, relatively stable.	Low, but most stable.
Liquidity	Low liquidity.	Moderate liquidity.	Good liquidity.	High liquidity.
Asset Exchange Availability	Limited, often only on smaller exchanges.	Available on smaller and some major exchanges.	Listed on major exchanges.	Widely available on all major exchanges
Investment Monitoring	Requires constant monitoring.	Requires frequent monitoring.	Occasional monitoring.	Minimal monitoring is needed.
Institutional Interest	Very low, mostly retail investors.	Low, some interest from institutions.	Growing interest from institutions.	High, strong institutional backing.

Pro Tip When viewing a project's market capitalizations on CoinMarketCap, always double-check the market capitalization through the applicable blockchain explorer (e.g., BSC SCAN and ETHER SCAN).

Another point is that comparing market capitalizations within the same category is essential when performing competitor analysis. Different categories, such as DeFi, NFTs, gaming, and infrastructure, tend to differ in market cap ranges. Comparing a project's potential market cap to competitors within the same category provides a more accurate view of its growth potential and realistic ROI.

Price Per Coin Versus Market Capitalization

Many newcomers to crypto unintentionally focus on the price per coin rather than the market capitalization when assessing an investment. Price alone doesn't tell the whole story—market cap shows the actual value of a project by accounting for total supply. Investors often tend to shy away from tokens, e.g., \$50.00/token, and instead invest in a token with a price of \$0.10/token. At a glance, it may seem attractive to buy tokens with a low cost per token; however, this type of rationale is setting up for extreme losses.

Figure 9-3 is a snapshot from CoinMarketCap, showing the financial data for Litecoin and Chainlink. Both projects are analyzed with respect to their price per coin and market cap. For this study, it is assumed that both projects have equal fundamental qualities.

Name	Price	Market Cap	Circulating Supply	Last 7 Days	Fully Diluted Mcap
Litecoin LTC	$110.49	$7,706,057,828	69,753,294 LTC		$9,279,975,504
Chainlink LINK	$15.36	$7,165,052,361	467,009,550 LINK		$15,342,410,811

Figure 9-3. *Circulating supply and price per coin (compliments of* *`https://coinmarketcap.com/`)*

There is a noticeable difference between Litecoin (LTC) at $110.49 and Chainlink (LINK) at $15.36. At first glance, LINK might seem more appealing since you could buy around seven LINK tokens for the price of one LTC coin. However, both have market capitalizations close to $7 billion.

Here's the key: price is secondary; the market cap is what truly matters. Even though LINK trades at $15.36 and LTC at $110.49, lifting LINK to $30.72 or LTC to $220.98 would each call for roughly $7 billion in fresh capital—because it's the market cap, not the sticker price, that governs how much new money must flow in—though the exact sum can shift with order-book depth and liquidity. Therefore, looking at the token price alone is misleading. On the other hand, considering financials alone, market capitalization provides a more accurate view of a project's potential growth versus examining the price per token or coin. Projects with smaller market caps (say $1 million) can double far more quickly than billion-dollar projects, which typically grow slower. As an investor, focusing on market cap gives you a clearer picture of a project's room for growth.

Action Steps

Follow the steps below to evaluate a project's market capitalization and fully diluted valuation (FDV) to determine potential risks, including future token dilution, inflationary impacts, and alignment with your investment strategy.

1) **Locate the Market Cap and FDV**

   Identify the project's market cap and FDV by visiting CoinMarketCap (or equivalent).

2) **Evaluate the Market Cap and FDV**

   Evaluate the market cap and FDV against the following:

   a) Compare the current market cap to the FDV. If the FDV is significantly higher, expect future token releases that could dilute the token's price, unless higher demand offsets the extra supply.

   b) If there is a significant difference between the market cap and the FDV, review the vesting schedule to determine when more tokens (or coins) are released into circulation—this could impact long-term investment.

   c) Review inflation rates, durations, and when inflation is due to end. Note some projects have no maximum supply, meaning that inflation is infinite.

3) **Market Cap Comparison**

   Review Table 9-1, "Market Cap Comparison," to determine what size market cap suits your investment strategy and lifestyle.

4) **Take Notes and Document Your Findings in Your Own Style**

5) **Combine the Findings with Other Sections of the Fundamental Evaluation Process**

Evaluation of the Results

For long-term investors, if there is a significant difference between the market cap and FDV, it is imperative that future token dilution and potential selling pressure needs to be taken into consideration before investing. Because FDV has less relevance for the short term, analyzing the market cap is deemed adequate.

The market cap size that suits your investment style will depend on many variables, as outlined in Table 9-1. Always cross-reference the market cap size with your investment goals (risk tolerance and time horizon) to ensure the project aligns with your strategy. This particularly applies to those who are new to the crypto space. Many new and inexperienced investors, chasing quick gains, gravitate toward low-cap “fresh-launch” tokens—which can spike rapidly on hype but often lose steam just as fast if the fundamentals are weak. Many new and inexperienced investors have high profits in mind and, therefore, tend to gravitate toward low-cap projects. In most cases, if unexperienced, this ends in significant losses, not profits. Hence, it is recommended to start with less risky large-cap projects first and then make gradual steps towards adding some lower-cap projects to your portfolio.

Realized Cap

Evaluation Objective: Determine if the average investor has unrealized profit or loss, signaling a potential uptrend, downtrend, or accumulation phase.

The *realized capitalization,* or realized cap, is a variation of market capitalization that values each UTXO (unspent transaction output) based on the price when it was last moved, as opposed to its current value. As such, it represents the *realized* value of all the coins in the network, as opposed to their *market* value. Realized capitalization was first devised for UTXO networks like bitcoin, but on-chain data vendors now apply the same logic to account-based chains such as Ethereum by tagging each account with the price at its last outbound transfer; Glassnode and other on-chain analytics platforms now publish ETH realized-cap series alongside bitcoin.

$$\textbf{\textit{Realized Cap}} = \textbf{\textit{value x price}}_{created}\ [\textbf{\textit{USD}}]\ (\textbf{\textit{of all UTXOs}})$$

Equation 9-5. *Formula to calculate the realized capitalization*

Instead of just looking at today's market cap, the realized cap (Figure 9-4) calculates the value of each coin based on the price at which it was last transacted. This provides a more accurate representation of the actual value users have spent on the coins rather than their current theoretical value. The Realized Cap increases accuracy by reducing the impact of lost and long-dormant coins and weights them according to their actual presence in the economy of a given chain. It is increased when coins last moved at significantly lower prices are spent and repriced at the higher transaction price. On the flip side, realized cap drops only when coins that last moved at higher prices are spent again at a lower transaction price, resetting their cost basis downward.

The primary benefit of this on-chain metric is that assigning value to coins according to their economic active weight mitigates the influence of coins that have been lost or have not moved for an extended period. As a result, by valuing each coin at the price it was last transacted, the realized cap serves as an approximate gauge of the asset's "stored" or "saved" value.

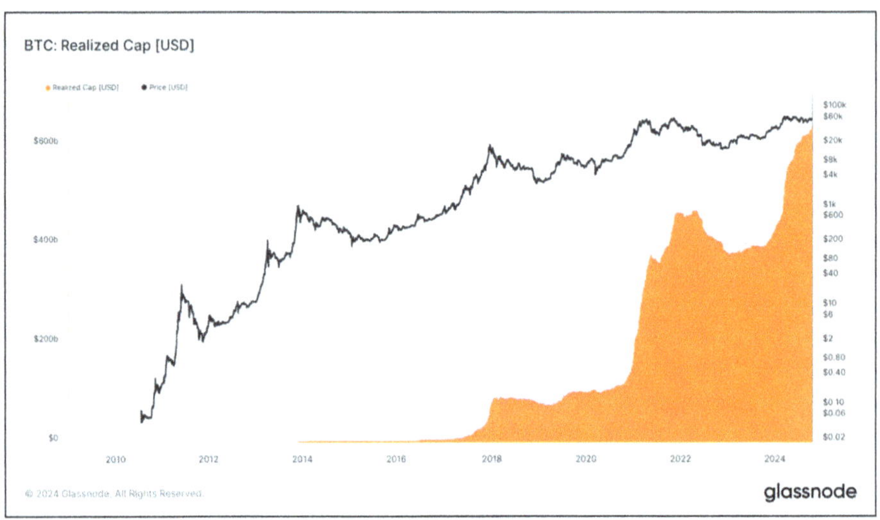

Figure 9-4. *bitcoin realized cap (compliments of `https://studio.glassnode.com/metrics?a=BTC&category=&m=market.MarketcapRealizedUsd`)*

It is important to note that the realized cap is built strictly from on-chain transactions; coins that trade inside a centralized exchange's internal ledger keep the cost basis of their original deposit until they leave the exchange, so CEX-only re-pricing is not reflected. Additionally, the realized cap is not a substitute for the market cap. Instead, it is best used in combination with the market cap. Under this framework, investors can evaluate the percentage of unrealized profit or loss held by the aggregate investor:

- When the market cap trades **above** the realized cap, the average investor holds an **unrealized profit**.
- When the market cap trades **below** the realized cap, the average investor holds an **unrealized loss**.

Figure 9-5 shows bitcoin's market cap versus the realized cap. When the market cap (in black) dips and crosses the realized cap (in orange), it suggests that there may be a potential downtrend at play. Conversely, when the market cap crosses the realized cap to the upside, it indicates a potential uptrend at play. When the market cap is trending below the realized cap, many investors use this buying opportunity to accumulate coins, taking profits (if desired) at various levels when the market cap is trending above the realized cap. Investors must be vigilant and cautious, as a reversal in either a downtrend or uptrend is imminent.

Fact While not all "market cap vs. realized cap" chart data is available for every digital asset, analyzing bitcoin's market-to-realized-cap relationship often serves as a broad gauge of overall market sentiment; always corroborate with asset-specific indicators when possible.

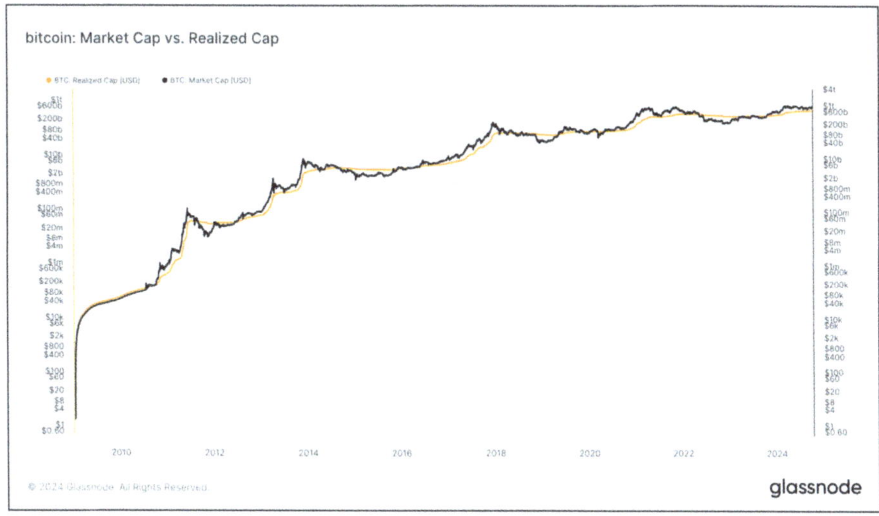

__Figure 9-5.__ bitcoin: Market cap versus realized cap (compliments of `https://studio.glassnode.com/workbench/a402076a-d220-4a8c-6f01-163b529f67ab`)

Action Steps

Follow these steps to determine if the average investor has unrealized profit or loss, signaling a potential uptrend, downtrend, or accumulation phase.

1) **Realized Cap Versus Market Cap**

   Visit Glassnode.com or the equivalent on-chain metric platform to view and compare the realized cap to the market cap.

2) **Unrealized Profit and Loss**

   Use the chart data to determine if the average seller has unrealized profit or loss.

   a) When the market cap trades **above** the realized cap, the average investor holds an **unrealized profit**.

   b) When the market cap trades **below** the realized cap, the average investor holds an **unrealized loss**.

3) **Predicted Movement of Price Action**

   After identifying whether investors hold unrealized profits or losses, use the chart data to assess if the market is entering an accumulation phase, a potential uptrend, or a potential downtrend.

4) **Take Notes and Document Your Findings in Your Own Style**

5) **Combine the Findings with Other Sections of the Fundamental Evaluation Process**

Evaluation of the Results

If the market cap is above the realized cap (indicating unrealized profits), consider taking profits, as the market could be overextended. Conversely, if the market cap is below the realized cap (indicating unrealized losses), consider accumulating assets for potential upside price action.

Realized Cap HODL Waves

Evaluation Objective: Evaluate the Realized Cap HODL Waves metric to help identify accumulation and distribution trends, market sentiment shifts, long-term holding behavior, and potential signals of buying or selling pressure based on coin age dynamics.

The *Realized Capitalization (Cap) HODL Waves* is an on-chain metric primarily used to analyze the transfer and balance of wealth between newer and longer-held digital assets. It presents a macro view of the distribution of age and economic weight of the supply (in USD), where the USD value of the coin is based on when it last moved. This provides a macro gauge on the balance between coin maturation, spending, and "stored value" held by various groups of market participants.

The *Realized Cap HODL Waves* is a variant of HODL Waves that weighs active supply bands by their realized USD value (economic weight) as a proportion of the Realized Cap. This metric provides unique insights such as

- Transfer of wealth (USD) between long-held ("older") coins and recently acquired ("younger") coins. Some analysts read large shifts in these bands as rotation from "smart money" or institutional holders toward retail traders (and vice versa), but the metric itself does not label investor types.

- A true market valuation over time by combining coinage and economic weight into a single metric.
- A true viewpoint that focuses on an active and economically meaningful supply by minimizing the importance of old or lost coins.
- Coin maturation—maturing of new (young) coins into old coins, and vice versa.
- Sentiment of long- and short-term holders.
- Strong accumulation and distribution regions of old and new coins.

How to Read the Realized Cap HODL Waves Chart

Figure 9-6 shows bitcoin Realized Cap HODL Waves chart. The x-axis represents time, the left y-axis represents the percentage of supply (weighted in USD) that each age band possesses, and the right y-axis represents the price per coin. The labels at the top of the chart are color-coded timeframes that indicate how old the coins are to when they were last spent and accumulated—ranging from 24 hours to 10+ years.

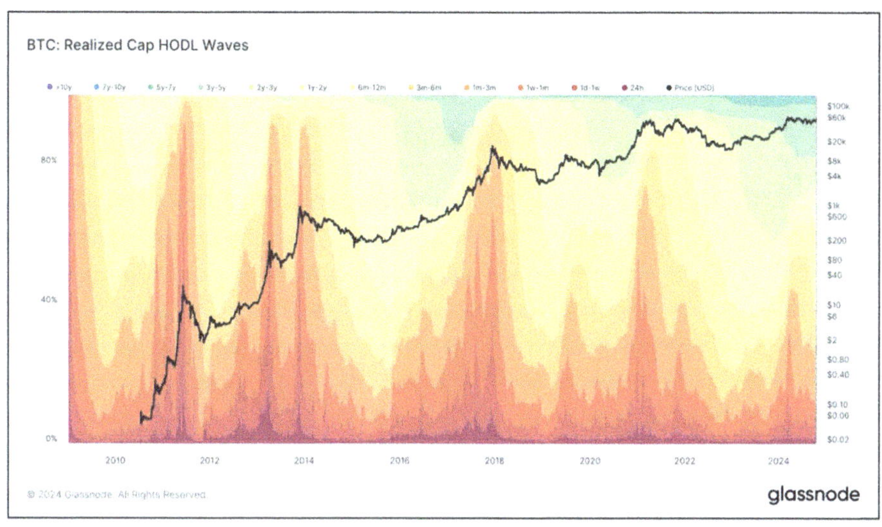

Figure 9-6. *bitcoin: Realized Cap HODL Waves, 24 hours to 10 years plus holders (compliments of `https://studio.glassnode.com/metrics?a=BTC&category=&m=supply.RcapHodlWaves`)*

The chart indicates where the age distribution occurs across the Realized Cap HODL Wave bands. The thickness of the waves represents changes to dormant coins maturing, or when old coins are spent, resetting their age into the youngest category and revaluing to the current price. It also indicates where changes (cross-overs) in this age distribution occur as the thickness of Realized Cap HODL Wave bands changes in response to dormant coins maturing or when old coins are spent, resetting their age into the youngest category, and revaluing to the current price.

Realized Cap HODL Band Waves Indicator Signals

In general, sets of coins are classified on a broad view of age brackets; these are as follows:

Table 9-2. *Coin color sets for HODL band waves*

Coin Color Sets for HODL Band Waves			
Coin Category	**Color**	**Age**	**Description**
Young Coins	Warm Colors	6 months or less	These coins make up the majority of day-to-day transaction volumes. Held by speculative short-term investors/traders, they are the most likely to be re-spent in response to market volatility. These color bands tend to oscillate in reverse to old coins, swelling in bull markets as old coins are spent and shrinking as young coins become dormant and mature during bear markets and accumulation.
Old Coins	Cool Colors	1–5 years	Typically owned by long-term "smart money" investors who accumulate cheap coins in bear markets. These coins are stored in cold storage until they are spent during bull market strength. Older color bands tend to oscillate in thickness over market cycles, swelling after periods of accumulation and thinning out as coins are spent. Additionally, these bands can identify bearish and bullish market cycles as they swell and shrink, respectively.
Lost or Ancient	Dark Cool Colors	5+ years	These coins are rarely spent and, in many instances, are assumed to be either lost or discounted from the freely circulating supply. These bands gradually thin out when long-dormant coins are finally spent, migrating into younger age bands; their cost basis was typically locked in at much lower prices, so spending during higher-price periods reduces the older-band share of realized value. Despite representing large holdings, these coins rarely influence active market dynamics due to their inactivity.

At any point on the Realized Cap HODL Wave chart, each age band displays its share of total realized cap (USD); the bands therefore sum to 100% of the realized value that is currently visible on-chain. This allows investors to see the current distribution trend from old coins to new young coins or vice versa. Depending on the trend direction, investors on a downtrend can clearly see if the percentage of coins is further maturing (increasing % rates for old age ranges) or on an uptrend (increasing % rates for new young coins) as old coins are distributed to the younger age categories.

Figure 9-7 shows a higher percentage of younger coins dominating during bullish markets (large red spikes as price action peaks) as older investors liquidate, transferring wealth to newer, often less experienced holders. Conversely, older coins become more prevalent in bear markets as speculators exit, and long-term investors accumulate more—see Figure 9-8 for reference.

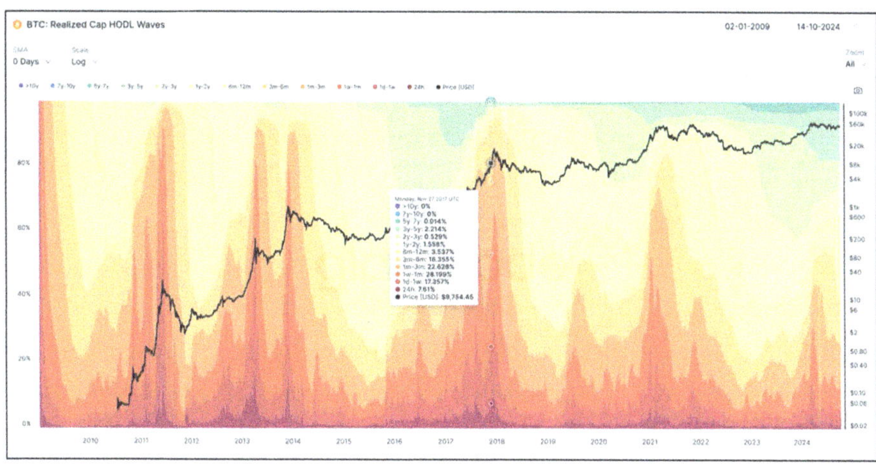

***Figure 9-7.** bitcoin: Realized Cap HODL Waves, showing the younger coins holding the majority share of BTC in the bullish market (compliments of `https://studio.glassnode.com/metrics?a=BTC&category=&m=supply.RcapHodlWaves`)*

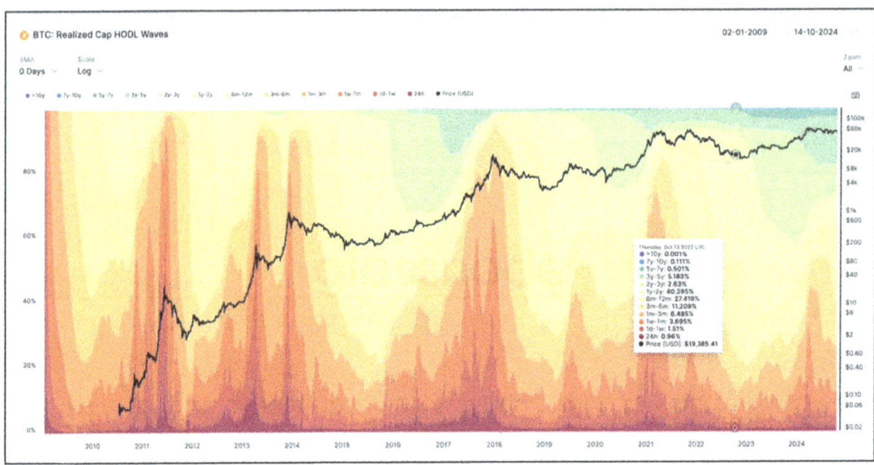

***Figure 9-8.** bitcoin: Realized Cap HODL Waves, showing the older coins holding the majority share of BTC in a bearish market (compliments of `https://studio.glassnode.com/metrics?a=BTC&category=&m=supply.RcapHodlWaves`)*

Maturing Coins

For a more simplistic presentation and more straightforward interpretation of the Realized Cap HODL Waves age categories can be individually switched on and off. Filtering the old age ranges makes it easier to see coin maturation during the bear market, as unmoved coins stand out clearly. As previously discussed, these maturing unspent coins are generally accumulated by smart money, higher conviction buyers. During this period, the economic weight of older coins increases, raising the network's realized price—the aggregate on-chain cost basis of all UTXOs, regardless of whether ownership actually changes. Coins that do move reset their age and appear in the younger bands.

bitcoin Realized Cap HODL Wave (Figure 9-9) shows the coinage ranges from six months to 10+ years. It filters out the younger coins that are frequently bought and sold (24 hours to six months), focusing instead on coins held by larger, long-term holders. In early 2014 and 2015, many coins appeared in the 6–12-month age range (shown in warm yellow). However, as these coins aged beyond one year, they shifted to the cooler yellow range, representing the 1–2-year category. Over time, these coins matured, moving to light green (3-5 years old) and dark green (5-7 years old) before they were spent, instantly resetting into the 24-hour to 6-month age band.

Fact It is important to note that when old coins (e.g., 5 years old) are spent, they are instantly transferred to and classified as new young coins (24-hour age range). However, when young coins (24-hour age range) are accumulated, they take many years to mature into the older coin age ranges.

Notably, strong holders accumulate the most (< 60%) of the realized cap in bear markets. In contrast, during bull markets, these holders distribute their assets, leaving them with minimal holdings (< 20%)—the opposite is true for younger coins (see Glassnode, Realized Cap HODL Waves: `https://docs.glassnode.com/guides-and-tutorials/metric-guides/age-distribution/realized-cap-hodl-waves`).

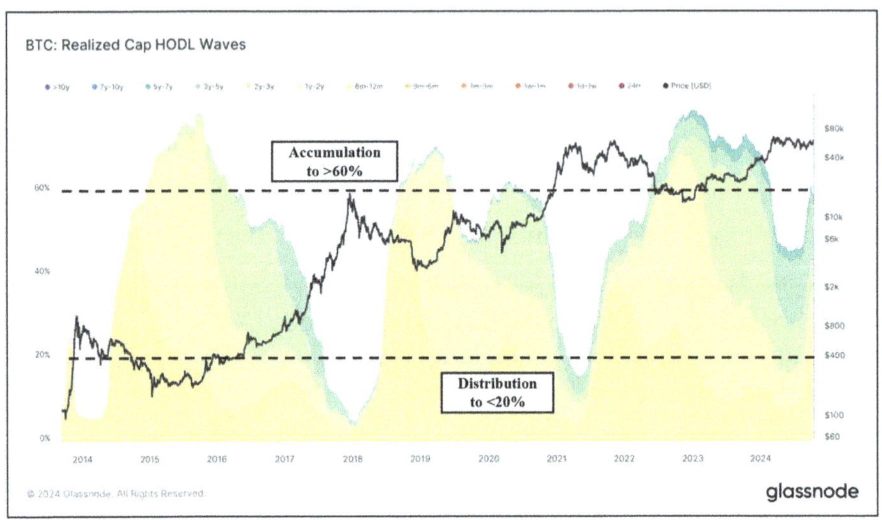

***Figure 9-9.** bitcoin: Realized Cap HODL Waves, transfer of BTC (compliments of `https://studio.glassnode.com/metrics?a=BTC&category=&m=supply.RcapHodlWaves`)*

Younger Coins

Figure 9-10 shows *bitcoin Realized Cap HODL Wave,* where the data is filtered, showing that the coinage ranges from 24 hours to six months. Unlike older coinage (six months to ten years), younger coins typically accumulate during uptrends and distribute on downtrends that slide into bear markets, transferring BTC from weaker to stronger hands. When longer-term, higher-conviction investors accumulate, short-term holders tend to distribute, and vice versa; however, this pattern isn't universal—both groups can move in the same direction for short stretches.

Most of the younger coins are not given a chance to mature. As price action and market cap increase, the long-term investors holding coins for, e.g., six months to five years plus, spend their coins. This results in old coins being converted into young coins with a higher realized price (i.e., the price the coin last moved). During this time, the young coins gradually take the majority share of the supply, while the older coins are increasingly spent and redistributed. This creates a dynamic where short-term holders dominate the market, especially during periods of high price volatility. As these younger coins change hands more frequently, they contribute to heightened market sensitivity, as retail investors tend to react more emotionally to price movements. This redistribution of coins from long-term holders to newer participants (and vice versa) can signal potential market turning points, as seasoned investors often take profits. At the same time, inexperienced traders buy in at peak prices.

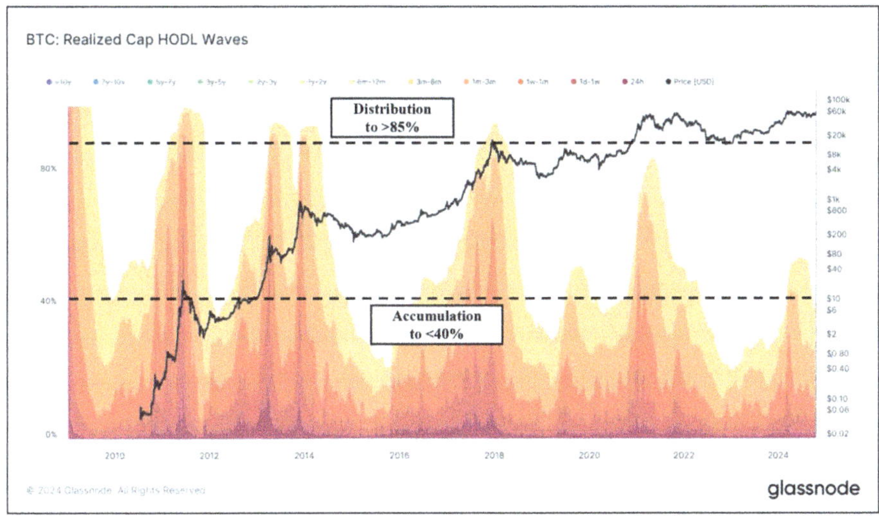

Figure 9-10. *bitcoin: Realized Cap HODL Waves, 24-hour to 6-month holders (compliments of `https://studio.glassnode.com/metrics?a=BTC&category=&m=supply.RcapHodlWaves`)*

Because recently spent coins are now considered “young” coins, they carry greater economic weight than older coins that haven’t moved in years. This increases market liquidity as these younger coins are bought and sold more frequently. Figure 9-10 highlights how short-term coins can dominate during volatile periods, signaling periods of retail participation and potential price fluctuations. Accumulation bottoms occur when young coins (<6 months) are valued at <40% of the value of the realized cap, while distribution tops occur when young coins (<6 months) are valued at 80%+ of the value of the realized cap.

Action Steps

While the Realized Cap HODL Waves is primarily available for major coins like BTC and ETH, coverage and historical depth are far thinner for newly launched or lower-cap coins, so apply the framework cautiously until sufficient on-chain history builds up.

Follow these steps to evaluate the Realized Cap HODL Waves metric to help identify accumulation and distribution trends, market sentiment shifts, long-term holding behavior, and potential buying or selling pressure signals based on coin age dynamics.

1) **Identify Accumulation Versus Distribution Trends**

   Visit Glassnode.com or the equivalent on-chain metric platform to view the Realized Cap HODL Wave.

   a) Analyze the percentage of young coins (< 6 months) in relation to the total realized cap.

2) **Spikes in Younger Coin Activity**

   Analyze the chart by looking for spikes in the young coins (over 70% to 80% +). This often indicates that retail investors may be buying at market peaks. This can be a sign to hold off on investing until the market cools down.

3) **Assess Market Sentiment Through Coin Age**

   Analyze whether old coins (1-5 years) increase in percentage.

4) **Take Notes and Document Your Findings in Your Own Style**

5) **Combine the Findings with Other Sections of the Fundamental Evaluation Process**

Evaluation of the Results

If young coins (<6 months) exceed 80% of the realized cap, it often signals retail buying at market peaks, suggesting long-term holders are selling. This is a good time to consider taking profits and waiting for a clear downtrend. Conversely, if young coins fall below 40% and older coins (1–5 years) are increasing, it indicates long-term accumulation, signaling a potential buying opportunity. Short-term coin dominance often causes volatility, so waiting for market stabilization is advisable unless long-term holders are steadily accumulating.

Liquidity and Trading Volume

Evaluation Objective: Evaluate an asset's liquidity and trading volume to help identify its market activity, trading efficiency, potential risks of slippage, and suitability for investment.

When investing in crypto, liquidity and trading volume are two factors that can make or break your strategy. Liquidity impacts how easily you can buy or sell an asset without shifting its price, while trading volume reveals the level of activity and interest in that asset. These two elements are key because they affect how efficiently investors can move in and out of positions, the price at which the transactions occur, and the overall risk involved.

Liquidity

Liquidity in crypto is simply the ease at which a digital asset can be exchanged for another asset or cash without significantly affecting its price. High liquidity equals the execution of quicker and smoother transactions at prices close to the current market value. bitcoin is an excellent example of a highly liquid digital asset due to its massive volume, which allows investors to buy and sell without having any significant impact on its price—one of the main benefits of a high liquidity market. In markets such as bitcoin, there are lots of buyers and sellers actively trading, which narrows the spread—the difference between the highest price a buyer is willing to pay and the lowest price a seller will accept. This tight spread helps buyers and sellers transact at a price closest to the current market price and with quicker execution times.

On the other hand, in less liquid or more volatile markets, traders may experience *slippage*. Slippage is when a trader receives a different trade execution price than initially intended. This is often the result of several variables, including volatile markets, which cause a change in the price before it is executed, or there may not be enough demand at that price to satisfy large orders, resulting in higher prices (most common with market orders, though very large orders can cause slippage even in deep books). Radical price swings can happen quickly in crypto, especially in illiquid markets. Slippage can be both positive and negative. However, it is typically negative, resulting in traders enduring a worse price than expected.

Pro Tip For small investments, slippage is less of a concern, but for larger amounts, always consider liquidity. High-liquidity assets can absorb big trades without much impact, while low-liquidity ones can cause price shifts, leading to less favorable outcomes.

In decentralized finance (DeFi), "liquidity pools" are essential to the operation of decentralized exchanges (DEXs). Users deposit their assets into smart contracts or "pools," allowing others to trade directly. The larger the pool of an asset, the more liquid that market becomes. In automated market maker (AMM) liquidity pools, liquidity is represented by the pool's total value locked (TVL, i.e., the USD value of all deposited assets). While volume only happens when trades are executed, liquidity reflects the available supply for trading.

Order Book

One way to visualize liquidity is through an open order book—see Figure 9-11 for bitcoin's order book. An order book is a real-time list of buy and sell orders for a specific asset, displayed by price levels. It shows the number of tokens investors are willing to trade at each price point, giving a snapshot of market demand and supply. The buy orders, known as "bids," and the sell orders, called "asks," are continuously updated as traders place or cancel orders.

Order Book Recent Trades

0.1

Price(USDT)	Qty(BTC)	Total(BTC)
108,470.30	0.002	40.688
108,470.20	0.020	40.686
108,470.00	0.454	40.666
108,469.90	0.196	40.212
108,469.00	0.004	40.016
108,468.90	0.007	40.012
108,468.80	0.001	40.005
108,468.70	2.329	40.004
108,468.60	0.151	37.675
108,468.40	1.492	37.524
108,468.30	1.150	36.032
108,468.20	1.003	34.882
108,467.20	1.002	33.879
108,467.10	3.780	32.877
108,467.00	29.097	29.097
↓ 108,466.90	108,466.90	
108,466.90	0.027	0.027
108,466.10	0.002	0.029
108,465.90	0.001	0.030
108,465.00	0.002	0.032
108,464.70	0.009	0.041
108,463.90	0.002	0.043
108,463.20	0.068	0.111
108,463.00	0.004	0.115
108,462.70	0.020	0.135
108,462.20	0.001	0.136
108,460.30	0.001	0.137
108,460.00	0.003	0.140
108,459.10	0.003	0.143
108,459.00	0.001	0.144
108,458.80	0.001	0.145

B 1% 99% S

Figure 9-11. *bitcoin order book (compliments of `https://www.bybit.com/trade/usdt/BTCUSDT`)*

Volume

In crypto, volume, or trading volume, refers to the total number of coins (or tokens) traded over a specific period. Volume is most often shown in fiat terms (e.g., USD) to make market size and liquidity easy to compare, though some platforms also display it in the asset's base units. It provides a good representation of market activity and interest—high volume indicates high interest and participation, while lower volume indicates less activity.

Pro Tip Identify the exchange with the highest trading volume of a particular asset by visiting CoinMarketCap.com, selecting an asset to view the top trading markets, and filtering by highest volume.

Liquidity Versus Volume

Although liquidity and volume are often correlated, they have different meanings. Volume can be a rough indicator of liquidity because rising turnover often attracts market makers and arbitrageurs, which in turn deepens the order book. Generally, high volume typically suggests high liquidity; however, one does not cause the other. For example, high trading volume may boost liquidity because more participants are trading—higher liquidity attracts more volume, and volume spikes often draw fresh capital from market-makers who seek to earn spreads or arbitrage. However, lower liquidity can lead to low volume, as people have less interest in an illiquid asset, resulting in liquidity being pulled from the market.

However, high volume does not always mean high liquidity. Illiquid markets experience periods of high volume, leading to significant price swings, while markets with high liquidity can see low volume during quieter periods. Both liquidity and volume are important. However, liquidity is preferred by long investors who need to enter and exit large trades without significantly affecting the asset's price. As stated, this high liquidity requirement is often accompanied by high trading volume. For short-term investors—those holding positions from a few hours up to several weeks—high volume (e.g., daily turnover above $100 million or more than 5% of circulating supply) is essential, because it lets them enter and exit trades of a few hundred to a few thousand dollars without moving the price and signals strong, broad participation in the market.

Assessing Market Liquidity

There are three key checks to verify if an asset has enough liquidity to meet investor needs: trading volume, bid-ask spread, and order book depth.

Trading Volume

In the blockchain world, volume is the most reliable indicator for gauging the level of liquidity in a crypto asset, as it reflects the number of assets traded (displayed as fiat currency) and market participation. Although it is not perfect, the consistently high volume of a crypto asset typically reflects greater liquidity. Trading volume is available for every tradeable crypto asset on CoinMarketCap.com—see Figure 9-12.

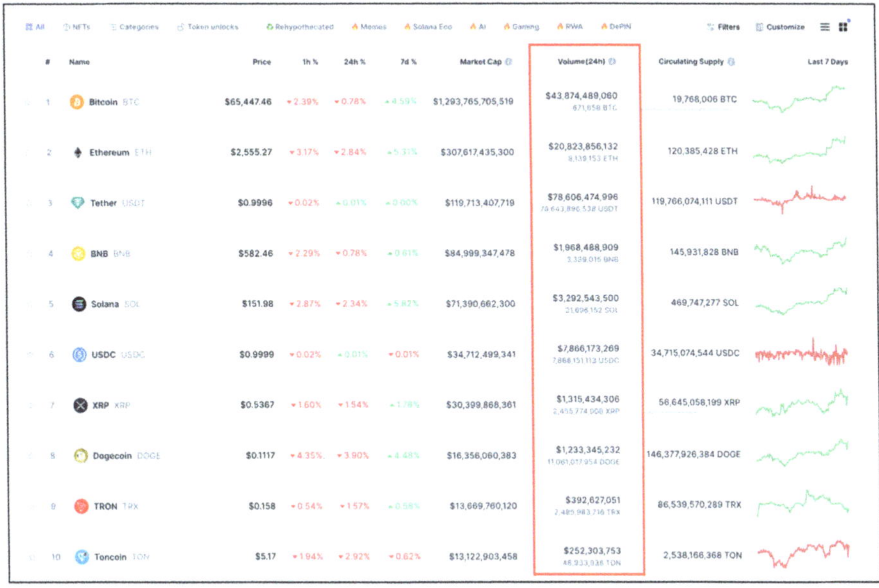

#	Name	Price	1h %	24h %	7d %	Market Cap	Volume(24h)	Circulating Supply	Last 7 Days
1	Bitcoin BTC	$65,447.46	▼2.39%	▼0.78%	▲4.59%	$1,293,765,705,519	$43,874,489,060 671,658 BTC	19,768,006 BTC	
2	Ethereum ETH	$2,555.27	▼3.17%	▼2.84%	▲5.31%	$307,617,435,300	$20,823,856,132 8,139,153 ETH	120,385,428 ETH	
3	Tether USDT	$0.9996	▼0.02%	▲0.01%	▲0.00%	$119,713,407,719	$78,606,474,996 78,643,896,538 USDT	119,766,074,111 USDT	
4	BNB BNB	$582.46	▼2.29%	▼0.78%	▲0.61%	$84,999,347,478	$1,968,488,909 3,339,015 BNB	145,931,828 BNB	
5	Solana SOL	$151.98	▼2.87%	▼2.34%	▲5.82%	$71,390,662,300	$3,292,543,500 21,696,152 SOL	469,747,277 SOL	
6	USDC USDC	$0.9999	▼0.02%	▲0.01%	▼0.01%	$34,712,499,341	$7,866,173,269 7,868,151,113 USDC	34,715,074,544 USDC	
7	XRP XRP	$0.5367	▼1.60%	▼1.54%	▲1.78%	$30,399,868,361	$1,315,434,306 2,455,774,008 XRP	56,645,058,199 XRP	
8	Dogecoin DOGE	$0.1117	▼4.35%	▼3.90%	▲4.48%	$16,356,060,383	$1,233,345,232 11,061,017,954 DOGE	146,377,926,384 DOGE	
9	TRON TRX	$0.158	▼0.54%	▼1.57%	▲0.58%	$13,669,760,120	$392,627,051 2,485,983,716 TRX	86,539,570,289 TRX	
10	Toncoin TON	$5.17	▼1.94%	▼2.92%	▼0.62%	$13,122,903,458	$252,303,753 48,933,938 TON	2,538,166,368 TON	

Figure 9-12. 24-hour volume for the top ten digital assets ranked by market cap (compliments of `https://coinmarketcap.com/`)

Pro Tip Always use limit orders instead of market orders to lock in your desired price and avoid slippage. This secures better pricing and helps you save on transaction fees during volatile market swings.

Unfortunately, there is no trading volume benchmark when investing. It largely depends on the investor's trade size. For instance, a $1,000 buy-in a coin that averages $50 million in daily volume will barely register, but a $50,000 order in a coin trading only $2 million a day could move the price several percent unless you break it into smaller chunks. This requires much higher liquidity and trading volume to avoid price swings and slippage—unless the trade size is broken up over several trades. Nevertheless, for most investors, assets with substantial liquidity, like those in the top fifty assets on CoinMarketCap.com, should not be an issue for larger-size trades. Additionally, by clicking on each asset on CMC, investors can identify the exchanges with the highest liquidity for each asset.

Bid-Ask Spread

Outside of the trading volume, it is also recommended to check the bid-ask spread. While a small spread indicates high liquidity, a large spread suggests poor liquidity. For instance, bitcoin's order book (Figure 9-11) shows a spread of just $0.10 between the best bid and ask. On a BTC priced above $100 000—in this case about $108 467—that's only ≈ 0.00009% of the price, far too small to move the needle on a trade but precisely why it signals deep liquidity. By contrast, thinly traded coins can carry bid-ask gaps of 0.5%–5%, adding hundreds or even thousands of dollars of friction to the same-size order.

Order Book Depth

Analyzing the assets order book provides insight into the availability of buy and sell orders at different price levels. A deep order book with many limit orders signals higher liquidity, while a shallow order book typically entails poor liquidity that can lead to slippage.

Action Steps

Follow these steps to evaluate an asset's liquidity and trading volume to help identify its market activity, trading efficiency, potential risks of slippage, and suitability for investment.

1) **Evaluate Trading Volume**

   Verify the asset's daily trading volume using at least two independent sources (e.g., CoinMarketCap and CoinGecko) to confirm the numbers and ensure sufficient market activity.

2) **Check Bid-Ask Spread**

   Verify that the bid-ask spread in the asset's order book is tight to help confirm adequate liquidity.

3) **Analyze Order Book Depth**

   Assess the depth of the order book by reviewing the number of buy and sell orders at various price points.

4) **Assess Asset's Liquidity Pools (DeFi)**

   Review the liquidity pools associated with the asset when trading on decentralized exchanges (DEXs). Larger pools indicate higher liquidity and less risk of price impact during trades.

5) **Use Limit Orders**

   For more control over trade execution, use limit orders instead of market orders.

6) **Take Notes and Document Your Findings in Your Own Style**

7) **Combine the Findings with Other Sections of the Fundamental Evaluation Process**

Evaluation of the Results

If the results from the action steps show that the asset has high trading volume, tight bid-ask spreads, and a deep order book, it indicates good liquidity—safe for large trades. On the flip side, if the asset shows low volume, wide spreads, or a shallow order book, it is recommended not to invest. There may also be other potential reasons an asset has such poor liquidity and daily trading volume, such as being a newly launched project and having liquidity injection issues; the project may have extremely poor fundamental qualities or be a scam. In any case, it is advised to stay clear of investment due to the high level of risk involved.

Total Transfer Volume

Evaluation Objective: Analyze the total transfer volume to assess network activity, identify growth trends, and pinpoint accumulation or distribution phases.

The *Total Transfer Volume* of a network indicates the total number (or USD value) of coins transferred on-chain over a specific period. This helps investors establish the level of network activity but, more importantly, determine if the transfer volume has increased or decreased over time, indicating if the project is becoming more or less popular.

Note that the on-chain total transfer volume differs from the trading volume discussed in the section titled "Liquidity and Trading Volume." Total transfer volume tracks the number of coins moved on-chain during a set period, while trading volume focuses on off-chain activity, capturing the trades happening on exchanges and reporting through APIs to market data platforms like CoinMarketCap and CoinGecko. Both metrics are essential for investors. Trading volume goes hand-in-hand with liquidity requirements. Total transfer volume provides a clear insight into network growth adoption and provides signals for bull or bear markets, allowing investors to make more informed investment decisions.

The total transfer volume on-chain metric provides key signals for evaluating market trends, as detailed in Table 9-3. Different signals are provided based on how the total transfer volume and price action interact with one another. These signals help investors identify the level of interest in the network, whether the market is in an accumulation and distribution phase, or if a cautious approach is required. bitcoin's total transfer volume

(30-day moving average) from 2010 to 2024, shown in Figure 9-13, is evaluated using this analysis structure, giving a clearer picture of its historical and potential market movements.

Table 9-3. *Total transfer volume and price action signals*

Total Transfer Volume and Price Action Signals				
Transfer Volume	**Price Action**	**Market Activity**	**Signal**	**Investor Opportunity**
Rising	Rising	Strong, suggesting accumulation	Bullish	Buying opportunity
Rising	Falling	Potential distribution or panic selling	Bearish	Consider selling to reduce exposure
Falling	Rising	Speculative price rise	Caution	Monitor for potential market correction
Falling	Falling	Market cooldown or consolidation	Caution/ Bullish for long-term	Accumulation opportunity
Constant	Rising	Off-chain speculation	Caution	Monitor for trend reversal
Constant	Decreasing	Lack of network activity	Bearish	Opportunity for strategic accumulation

Note The patterns in the following chart assume a mature network with sufficient on-chain history; signals can be less reliable for newly launched tokens with thin transfer volume.

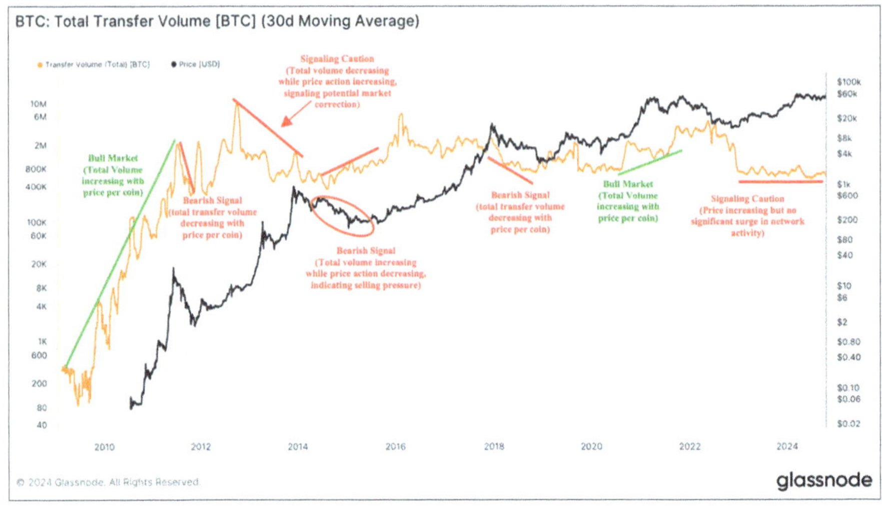

Figure 9-13. *bitcoin: Total transfer volume (compliments of https://studio.glassnode.com/metrics?a=BTC&category=Transactions&m=transactions.TransfersVolumeSum&mScl=log&pScl=log)*

Action Steps

Follow these steps to analyze total transfer volume to assess network activity, identify growth trends, and pinpoint accumulation or distribution phases.

1) **Evaluate Total Transfer Volume**

   Evaluate the total transfer volume using the *Total Transfer Volume & Price Action Signals* as per Table 9-3.

2) **Take Notes and Document Your Findings in Your Own Style**

3) **Combine the Findings with Other Sections of the Fundamental Evaluation Process**

Evaluation of the Results

Evaluate the evaluation results in Table 9-3 under the "Investor Opportunity" column.

Total Value Staked (TVS)

Evaluation Objective: Assess whether the Total Value Staked (TVS) of a digital asset is rising or falling over time, providing insights into market confidence, user engagement, and popularity.

The *total value staked* (TVS) of a particular asset represents the cumulative USD value of tokens actively bonded to that network's native staking contract (e.g., ETH in the Beacon Chain), excluding coins simply "locked" in liquidity or DeFi pools. A higher TVS value typically represents a secure and trusted network by digital asset investors. Conversely, blockchains with a low TVS signify potential issues, skepticism, and unpopularity among investors. TVS is typically expressed in USD; however, some platforms may also be expressed in BTC or ETH.

Figure 9-14 shows the TVS (in blue) for Ethereum from Glassnode.com. It represents the amount of ETH deposited into the ETH 2.0 contract from 2021 to 2024. During this period, regardless of the fluctuation of ETH's price per coin (in black), there has been a steady increase in ETH's TVS. This implies strong support and popularity among investors, coupled with the safety of a highly secure blockchain.

Pro Tip For projects that have a PoS consensus mechanism, it is advised that investors investigate if the TVS has an including or declining value.

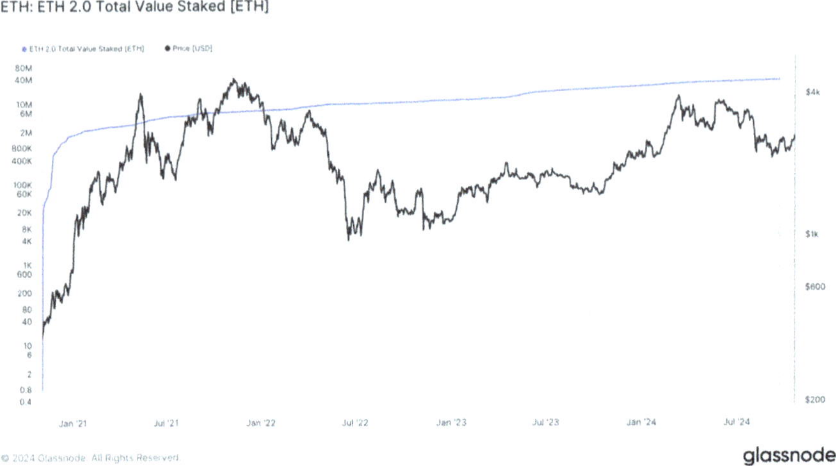

***Figure 9-14.** Ethereum, ETH 2.0 total value staked (compliments of* `https://studio.glassnode.com/metrics?a=ETH&category=&m=eth2.StakingTotalVolumeSum)`

Action Steps

Follow these steps to assess whether a digital asset's total staked value (TSV) rises or falls over time, providing insights into market confidence, user engagement, and popularity.

While Glassnode.com provides advanced data mainly for major coins, platforms such as DeFi Lama and TokenTerminal accommodate a broader range of digital assets.

1) **Evaluate the Total Staked Value**

   Visit Glassnode.com (or DeFi Lama, TokenTerminal) to determine if a digital asset's total staked value increases or decreases over time.

   a) Is the TVS increasing or decreasing over time?

2) **Take Notes and Document Your Findings in Your Own Style**

3) **Combine the Findings with Other Sections of the Fundamental Evaluation Process**

Evaluation of the Results

It is good if the TVS is gradually increasing over time. If decreasing, this may signify a loss of interest in the asset. Note if the TVS is decreasing, it may be an early sign of a price drop (if it has not happened already). Perform more profound research where required.

Total Value Locked (TVL)

Evaluation Objective: Evaluate a DeFi protocol's TVL, analyze its performance over time, and determine whether it is overvalued or undervalued.

Total value locked (TVL) is the total value of digital assets deposited and locked in a DeFi protocol or smart contract. TVL differs from total value staked (TVS), whereby it incorporates not just staked assets, but all assets locked in lending, liquidity pools, yield farming strategies, and other DeFi applications. Many DeFi protocols support these financial services, with some of the more popular ones including Lido, AAVE, and Uniswap.

TVL is commonly used to measure the overall health of the DeFi protocol, where an increasing TVL signifies a rise in liquidity, usability, and popularity that directly impacts the protocol's overall health and success. Tracking TVL in DeFi is commonly done through data aggregators, such as DeFi Lama, and is also available on platforms such as CoinMarketCap and CoinGecko. TVL is typically expressed in USD; however, some platforms may also be expressed in BTC or ETH.

Figure 9-15 is from DeFi Lama, showing the total TVL for all DeFi protocols, which is $90.235b (when writing this book). This provides a good overview of the condition of the market, whether DeFi participants are locking or withdrawing their assets in DeFi protocols. From 2021 to mid-2022, the total TVL increased to $180b, followed by a steep decline into a consolidation period from July 2022 to Jan 2024. There was a rally in early 2024, reaching a TVL of $108b before entering a cool-off period and a slight decline from June 2024. Figure 9-16 shows the TVL breakdown per chain, with Ethereum dominating the DeFi market with 54.79% ($48.51 billion) of assets locked over 1192 DeFi protocols.

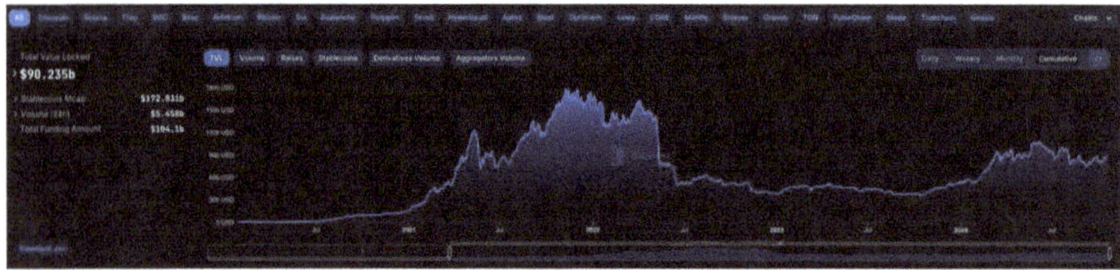

***Figure 9-15.** Total value locked (TVL) for all chains (compliments of `https://defillama.com/`)*

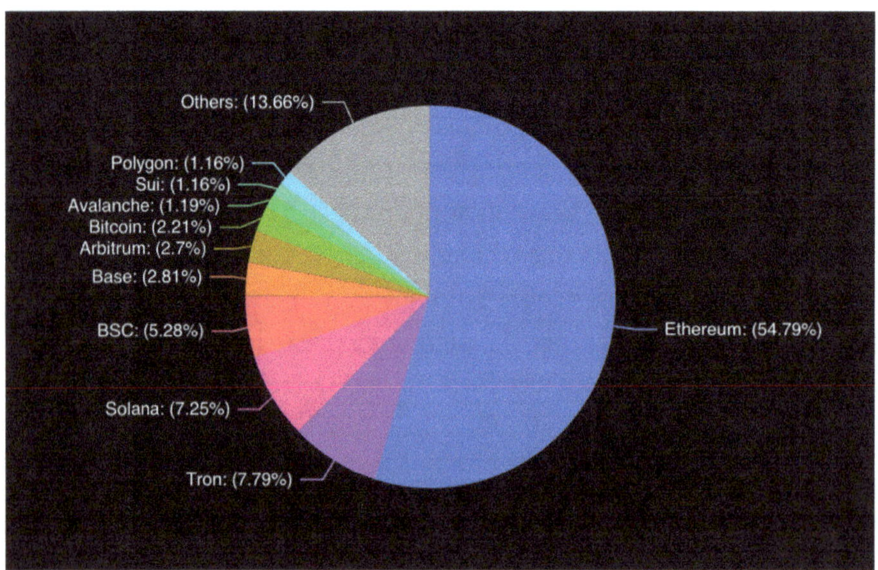

***Figure 9-16.** Break of the TVL for all DeFi blockchains (compliments of `https://defillama.com/chains`)*

How to Evaluate TVL Ratio

The total value locked (TVL) ratio is a metric primarily used to assess whether a DeFi asset is considered overvalued or undervalued. It is calculated by dividing the market capitalization by the TVL. As a general rule of thumb, it is evaluated as follows:

- **TVL Ratio Above 1** – The asset may be overvalued
- **TVL Ratio Below 1** – The asset may be undervalued

Figure 9-17 shows the financial details, including the market capitalization, TVL, and TVL ratio for Compound Finance. Compound Finance is shown to possess a TVL ratio of 0.39. Equation 9-6 and Equation 9-7 show the formula and calculation for compounds TVL ratio.

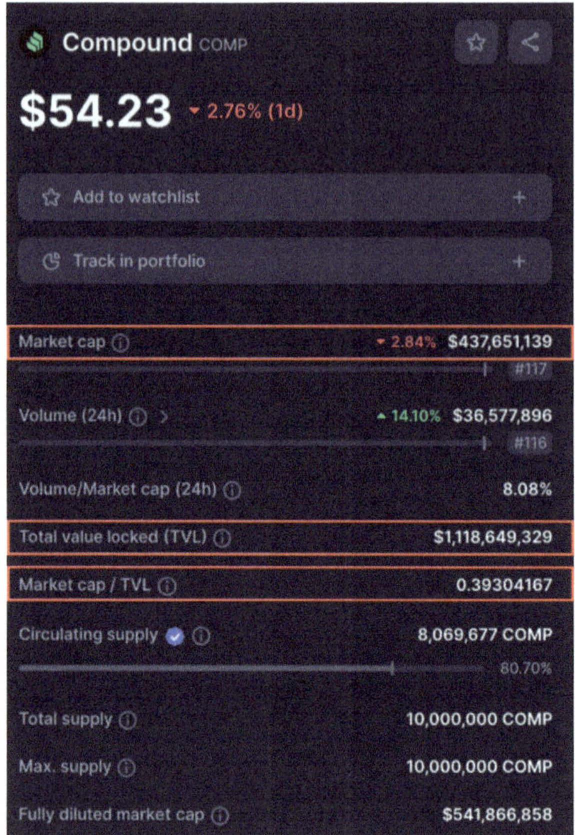

***Figure 9-17.** Financial data, TVL for compound finance (compliments of `https://ccomplimentsp.com/currencies/compound/`)*

$$\textit{TVL Ratio} = \frac{\textit{Market Cap}}{\textit{Total Value Locked (TVL)}}$$

***Equation 9-6.** Formula to TVL Ratio*

$$0.39 = \frac{\$437{,}651{,}139}{\$1{,}118{,}649{,}329}$$

***Equation 9-7.** TVL calculation for Compound Finance*

Pro Tip DeFi-focused platforms such as DeFi Lama and TokenTerminal provide deep financial insight and a range of metrics that allow investors to analyze liquidity, trading volume, and project performance, making it easier to evaluate potential investment opportunities.

TVL Performance History

Analyzing TVL performance over time provides valuable insight into the protocol's popularity and performance in bearish and bullish markets. Figure 9-18 shows a snippet from DeFiLama.com of Ethereum. Ethereum's TVL (in blue) and market capitalization (in green) are shown from April 2018 to October 2024. Note that Ethereum's TVL and market cap are in sync; as the market cap increases, so does the TVL, and the same happens when decreasing. This indicates that Ethereum's TVL is closely linked to market sentiment and demand, with investors locking assets in Ethereum-based DeFi protocols as its price and market cap rise and withdrawing them during declines. When the market cap is climbing, but TVL begins to drop, it may signal an early warning of a trend reversal. Conversely, if TVL rises while the market cap stays stable or begins to increase, this could indicate a potential buying opportunity. However, not all blockchains or DeFi protocols follow the same TVL and market cap patterns, so ideal entry and exit points can vary across projects.

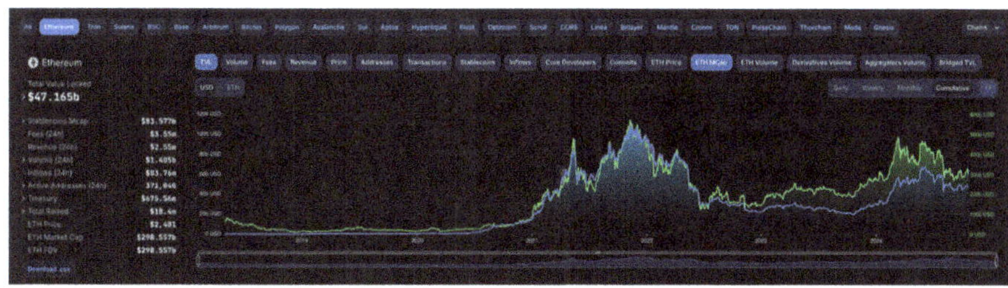

***Figure 9-18.** Ethereum's TVL and market capitalization in sync (compliments of `https://defillama.com/chain/Ethereum?chainTokenMcap=true`)*

Variations in TVL Reporting

Different DeFi protocols have their own way of calculating total value locked (TVL), which is vital to understand when comparing projects. For example, AAVE (Figure 9-19, "Methodology" section) only accounts for the tokens locked in their contracts as collateral or to earn yield—tokens borrowed are not included in their TVL. AAVEs borrowed assets are calculated separately. However, other protocols may include borrowed tokens, staked coins, or yield-bearing assets in their TVL calculation. It is crucial that investors understand how the DeFi protocol calculates TVL, as this is important when performing competitor analysis. Note that borrowed assets are not "locked" in any smart contract and should not be included in a protocol's TVL calculation.

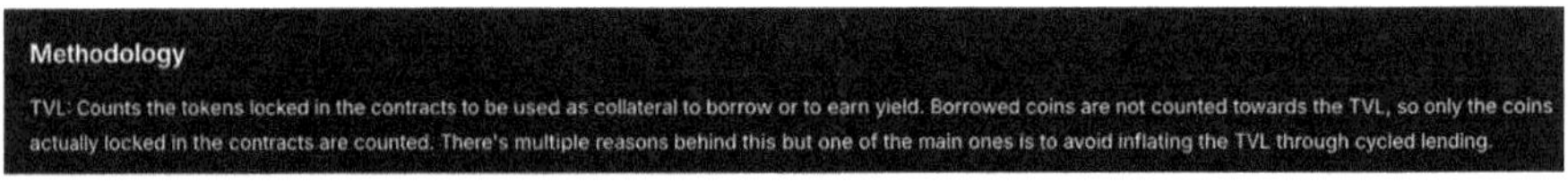

Figure 9-19. *AAVE V3 DeFi protocol TVL reporting methodology (compliments of `https://defillama.com/protocol/aave-v3?events=false`)*

Action Steps

Follow these steps to assess a DeFi protocol's total value locked (TVL), evaluate its performance over time, and determine whether it appears overvalued or undervalued based on its TVL ratio, performance trends, and competitor analysis.

1) **Total Value Locked (TVL) Ratio**

   Visit CoinMarketCap, DeFiLama, or TokenTerminal to view a DeFi asset's TVL.

   a) Calculate the TVL Ratio (M. Cap/TVL)

b) Is the TVL ratio above or under one? (Under one indicates that the DeFi protocol is undervalued, while over one is overvalued.)

2) **TVL Performance**

Analyze the TVL performance.

a) How is the TVL compared with the total TVL for all chains?

i) Has it been outperforming, remaining constant, or in a decline?

b) Does it collate with the market cap?

c) Are there repeating trends with the TVL and the market cap that help identify potential entry and/or exit points?

3) **TVL Reporting**

Determine how the DeFi protocol has calculated their TVL.

a) Have borrowed assets been included in the TVL?

i) Borrowed assets should not be included in a TVL metric.

ii) When performing competitor analysis, always ensure that the projects are calculating TVL in a similar manner. Extra vigilance should be exercised when making project comparisons using more than one DeFi aggregator, as the TVL calculation methods may vary significantly.

4) **Competitor Analysis**

   Perform competitor analysis for TVL, TVL ratio, and past performance.

5) **Take Notes and Document Your Findings in Your Own Style**

6) **Combine the Findings with Other Sections of the Fundamental Evaluation Process**

Evaluation of the Results

If the TVL's on the rise, it's generally a good sign that more investors are interested, liquidity is building, and the project's gaining traction—all positive signals for growth. A steady TVL, even if not growing, still shows stability and reliability. But if you see the TVL dropping, it might be worth investigating what's behind the decline.

A lower TVL ratio (around one or below) can hint that an asset might be undervalued compared to its locked value, possibly signaling a good investment chance. On the flip side, a high TVL ratio could mean the asset is overvalued, so approach it with caution. If the ratio keeps shifting a lot, keep an eye on it to gauge how stable or sustainable the investment is before making any moves.

Fees and Revenue

Evaluation Objective: Evaluate a DeFi protocol's fees, revenue distribution, and earnings to determine its financial health, user demand, and growth potential.

In DeFi, protocol fees and revenue are vital KPIs of a project's financial health, economic activity, and future potential. Understanding a protocol's fee and revenue model is essential for investors. It provides insight into the total fees generated, the portion allocated to liquidity providers, and how much is retained as protocol revenue.

Fees

Like traditional financial services, fees are charged for interacting with DeFi services, such as network fees, and user-based charges for utilizing specific protocol features, including trading, lending, staking, and providing liquidity. Although fees are relatively small, they significantly add up over time. For example, Uniswap, a decentralized exchange (DEX) built on Ethereum, charges only a 0.3% fee for swapping tokens. These fees are distributed to liquidity providers proportional to the amount deposited into the liquidity pools to facilitate trades.

Caution Different data DeFi aggregators sometimes have different methods for calculating generated protocol fees. Therefore, checking the fee calculation method is imperative, especially when comparing data using various aggregators.

Revenue

Revenue is the portion of fees the protocol retains after distributions are made to users, such as liquidity providers, lenders, or staking participants. This retained revenue is critical for the protocol's long-term sustainability, as it funds ongoing development and day-to-day operations. A protocol's revenue depends directly on the fees it generates. Without sufficient user engagement, fee generation suffers, limiting revenue growth. Therefore, when a protocol has a history of earning significant fees, it is a good indication that user engagement is high and, in turn,

---

Fact Fees indicate the demand for a protocol's services, while revenue reflects how well it turns that demand into lasting value.

Evaluating Fees and Revenue

This section analyzes an asset's fees and revenue based on three key criteria: market trends in fees and revenue, the revenue distribution model, and competitor comparisons.

Fees and Revenue Market Trends

Figure 9-20 shows the fees and revenue for Lido, a top-performing liquid staking DeFi protocol built on Ethereum. Lido has an estimated $835.17m in annualized fees with a revenue of $83.52m. Lido monetizes by charging a 10% fee on staking rewards—$83.52m/$835.17m equals 10%. This fee is split between node operators (5%) and the Lido DAO (5%). The remaining 90% is distributed to users using the DeFi platform for staking services.

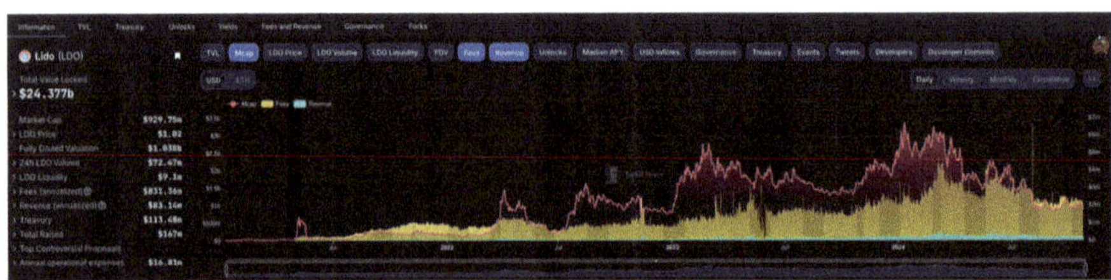

Figure 9-20. *Lido DeFi protocol estimated annual fees and revenue (compliments of `https://defillama.com/protocol/lido?tvl=false&mcap=false&fees=true&revenue=true&events=false&groupBy=daily`)*

Lido had a steady growth of generated fees from mid-2021 to March 2024 (positive indication) before entering a cool-off period from March 2024. This correlates with Lido's market cap (in red) and with the overall crypto market cap (Figure 9-21) entering a daily downtrend at the same time from March 2024 until September 2024. This alignment indicates that Lido's fee and revenue model is responsive to broader market conditions. As with many other protocols, this correlation is typical behavior. However, caution should be exercised with DeFi protocols whose fees and revenue remain constant or decline when the crypto market uptrends. In contrast, when the market is in a downtrend, protocols whose fee and revenue intake remain constant or uptrend are worth investigating. It is also recommended that this data be compared with the protocols TVL and the entire DeFi market TVL, as this may provide additional info that helps with the fundamental evaluation, including entry and exit points.

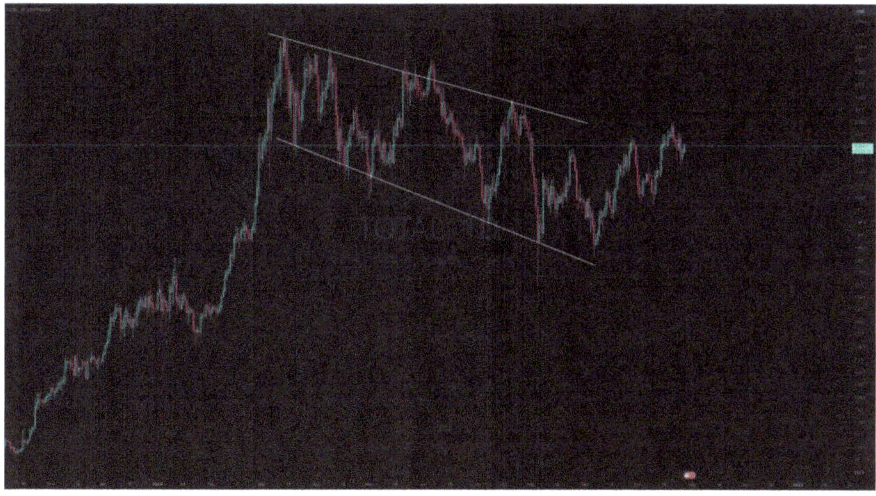

***Figure 9-21.** Total crypto market cap entering a daily downtrend from March 2024 to September 2024 (compliments of `https://www.tradingview.com/x/vgCedYet/`)*

Fees to Revenue Distribution Model

Table 9-4 shows the top five lending platforms (Aave, Just Lend, Compound Finance, Venus Protocol, and Kamino Finance) ranked by total value locked (TVL). It references the total fees collected, the fees distributed to the protocol participants, and the fees retained as revenue. The sum of the fees distributed to the protocol participants and the fees retained as revenue equals the total fees collected by the protocol. Fee distributions range from 64% to 90% of total fees, while the fees retained as revenue range from 10% to 36%. (See TokenTerminal or DeFi Lama protocol dashboards for the underlying data.) Note that both ranges for these lending platforms are significant, but they are still all the most popular as ranked by TVL. Some allocate more fees to revenue, while others allocate more to protocol users.

It is entirely up to the protocol what percentage of fees are distributed back to the protocol participants and allocated as revenue. When evaluating, there is no hard fee distribution to the revenue model benchmark for investors. Instead, and more importantly, focusing on fee, revenue, and TVL history provides more insight into the protocol's financial health and robustness. A DeFi protocol with a steady history of fee intake and revenue generation is considered a positive indicator, especially when there is a history of surviving bear markets.

From Table 9-4, note that Aave, with the highest TVL, distributes the lowest percentage of fees back to lenders and retains the highest revenue from the total collected fees. Unlike protocols that maximize fee distribution to attract users quickly, Aave focuses on sustainable, long-term growth. By retaining a higher revenue percentage, Aave can sustain innovation without relying heavily on external funding. Because of this model, Aave, launched in 2017, has become a reputable DeFi lending platform with an adequate fee and revenue history that users trust. However, this is not insinuating that other lending, liquid staking, DEXs, or similar DeFi platforms that retain a much lower percentage as revenue are any less reputable and trustworthy—each protocol is to be evaluated on a case-by-case basis and compared to other top-performing projects with good fee intake and revenue history.

Table 9-4. *Lending DeFi protocol fee distribution (compliments of `https://defillama.com/`)*

Lending DeFi Protocol Fee Distribution						
Protocol	**TVL**	**Total Fees**	**Fee Distribution to DeFi Participants**		**Fees Retained as Revenue**	
Aave	$13.712b	$398.98m	$254.67m	64%	$144.31m	36%
Just Lend	$4.373b	$2.97m	$2.685m	90%	$284,748	10%
Compound Finance	$2.105b	$10,000,000.000	$8,260,000.000	83%	$1,740,000.000	17%
Venus Protocol	$1.723b	$55.38m	$46.58m	84%	$8.8m	16%
Kamino Finance	$1.606b	61.45m	$49.12m	80%	$12.33m	20%

There are exceptions to a standard fee distribution and revenue model. In the case of Uniswap's decentralized exchange (DEX), 100% of Uniswap's trading fees are distributed to liquidity providers, so the protocol currently retains no revenue for a DAO or treasury. This is because the Uniswap platform is open-source with no direct operational costs; no centralized team runs on Ethereum, and it is managed by smart contracts. Through governance, UNI-token holders and community members—with the aid of Uniswap Labs—vote on proposed protocol decisions, upgrades, and parameter changes. Not all projects are like this; they typically have a team that requires payment and operation costs for a wide range of expenses, including development, marketing, security audits, community building, etc.

Competitor Analysis

To gain a broader view of a wide range of the protocol's total fees and revenue earnings, it is advised to visit DeFi Lama (`https://defillama.com/fees`), select "*Advanced*" mode, and filter by *yearly fee* earnings. The table data is easily filterable to 24-hour, 7-day, and 30-day data. See Figure 9-22 for a list of the top-performing DeFi blockchains and protocols ranked by cumulative fees for the last year. Protocols with consistently high cumulative fees and revenue typically indicate strong user demand, which may qualify for more in-depth research and long-term investment opportunities.

Also, looking at the market capitalization compared to cumulative fees can offer insights into whether a protocol might be over- or undervalued. For example, a protocol with a high market cap but low fee earnings could signal hype without strong fundamentals. On the other hand, a lower market cap with high fee earnings might reveal an undervalued opportunity.

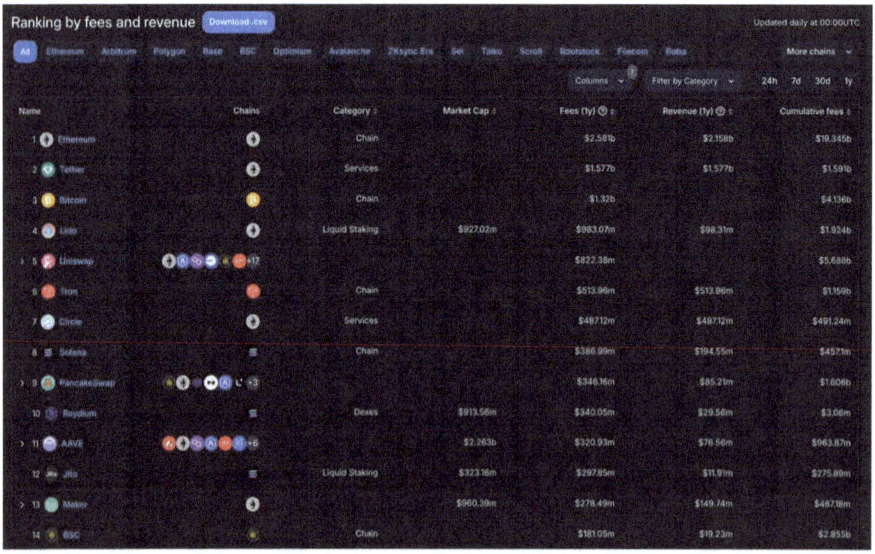
Ranking by fees and revenue
Download .csv
Updated daily at 00:00UTC
All
More chains
Columns
Filter by Category
24h
7d
30d
1y
Name
Chains
Category
Market Cap
Fees (1y)
Revenue (1y)
Cumulative fees
1 Ethereum Chain $2.581b $2.158b $19.345b
2 Tether Services $1.577b $1.577b $1.591b
3 Bitcoin Chain $1.32b $4.136b
4 Lido Liquid Staking $927.02m $983.07m $98.31m $1.924b
5 Uniswap +17 $822.38m $5.686b
6 Tron Chain $513.96m $513.96m $1.159b
7 Circle Services $487.12m $487.12m $491.24m
8 Solana Chain $386.99m $194.55m $457.1m
9 PancakeSwap +3 $346.16m $85.21m $1.606b
10 Raydium Dexes $913.56m $340.05m $29.56m $3.06m
11 AAVE +6 $2.263b $320.93m $76.56m $963.87m
12 Jito Liquid Staking $323.16m $297.85m $11.91m $275.89m
13 Maker $960.39m $278.49m $149.74m $487.18m
14 BSC Chain $181.05m $19.23m $2.855b

Figure 9-22. *DeFi blockchains and protocols ranked by cumulative fees for the last year (compliments of `https://defillama.com/fees`)*

Action Steps

Follow these steps to evaluate a DeFi protocol's fees, revenue distribution, and earnings to determine its financial health, user demand, and growth potential.

1) **Fees and Revenue Data**

   Visit DeFiLama or a similar DeFi data aggregator to view the project's fees and revenue.

2) **Analyze Fee Structure and Revenue Allocation**

   Analyze the fee distribution and revenue allocation with respect to the following:

   a) How does the protocol generate fees and revenue?

   b) Does the DeFi aggregator (e.g., DeFi Lama) calculate the protocol fees accurately?

   c) What percentage of the total fees collected are distributed to protocol users and retained for revenue?

3) **Examine Historical Fee and Revenue Trends**

   On DeFi Lama, filter the protocols chart data showing market cap, fees, and revenue and evaluate with respect to the following:

   a) Review the protocol's fee and revenue trends over time

   b) Is the fee intake in sync with the market cap? If not, is the fee intake increasing, decreasing, or remaining constant relative to the market cap?

c) Is the protocol market cap in sync with the total crypto market cap?

4) **Competitor Analysis**

   Using DeFiLama advanced filtering tools, examine the fee and revenue models of top competitors within the same DeFi sector (e.g., lending, staking, and DEXs) and use this data as a performance benchmark against other protocols.

5) **Take Notes and Document Your Findings in Your Own Style**

6) **Combine the Findings with Other Sections of the Fundamental Evaluation Process**

Evaluation of the Results

If the protocol shows high, stable fees and revenue, it indicates strong demand, trustworthiness, and possibly a solid long-term investment. High fee distribution to users with low revenue retention might signal a focus on growth over sustainability, appealing to short-term participants. However, long-term investors should exercise caution and ensure it looks positive after a complete fundamental evaluation.

A decline in revenue during market downturns indicates market dependence, while stable or growing revenue in such periods signals strong user engagement. Outperforming competitors in fee and revenue metrics could indicate a competitive edge. However, this is more reliable if backed by sufficient market history.

Transaction Count

Evaluation Objective: Analyze the transaction count to help determine whether the market is entering a bull market, bear market, or consolidation phase.

The *Transaction Count* metric signifies the total successful transactions for a digital asset over a specific period. This metric is beneficial for measuring the level of activity of a particular network or digital asset over time. Analyzing transaction count can provide the following insight to investors:

- **Network Growth and Activity** – High and growing transaction counts typically are associated with increased market activity, which signifies a healthy, widely used network with a possible increase in adoption; just note that some of the traffic may come from MEV/arbitrage bots or low-value airdrop-farming transfers on low-fee chains.
- **Trends** – Analyzing the transaction count can help investors identify trends. For example, when the transaction count suddenly spikes, it is often followed by a decrease in price per coin. In contrast, when transaction count drops significantly, it usually signifies an accumulation phase. It could also be an early warning sign of network issues, declining user interest, or even a cyberattack.
- **Interest and Adoption** - The transaction count on-chain metric can be coupled with the Active Address metric to determine if interest and adoption are increasing over time accurately. A growing network (or digital asset) is often a healthy sign of future growth and success.

Figure 9-23 shows bitcoin's number of transactions using a 14-day SMA (simple moving average) for a smoother and clearer understanding of the network activity. From 2016 to the start of 2018, it shows steady growth with an increase in transaction count (or orange) and price action (black line)—a typical indication of a bull market. When the price per coin started to decline rapidly in early 2018, this was accompanied by a steep transaction count fall, signaling a potential bear market. However, as price action continued to decline from 2018 to early 2019, there was a gradual increase in transaction count. This was a clear indication that there was a high interest in bitcoin and possible signs of another rally. This was confirmed when bitcoin rose from roughly $3,500 to $13,000 between February 2019 and June 2019. Another indication of a possible upcoming bull market is when transaction count is consistent while price action is falling. This is visible from 2022 to early 2023, before price action went from roughly $20,000 to $44,000+ by the end of 2023.

Fact Only successful transactions are counted using the transaction count on-chain metric.

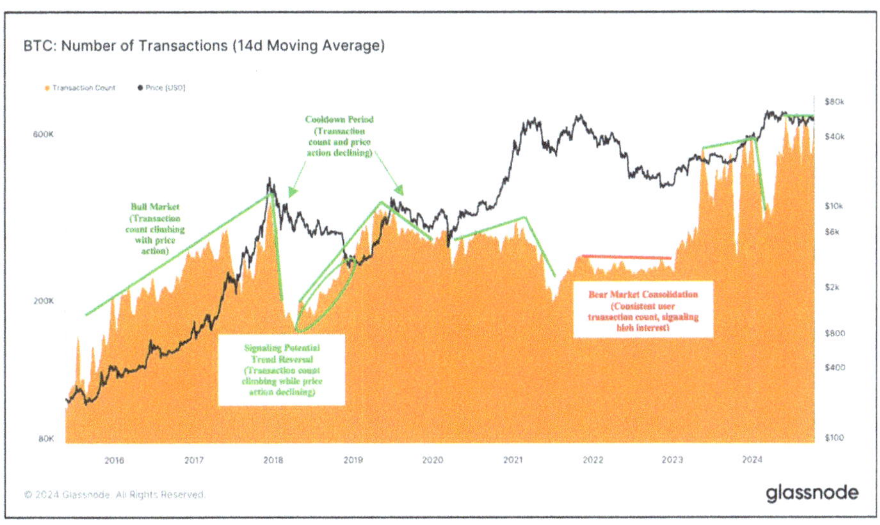

Figure 9-23. *bitcoin: Number of transactions (transaction count) (image compliments of `https://studio.glassnode.com/metrics?a=BTC&category=Transactions&chartStyle=column&ema=0&m=transactions.Count&mAvg=6&mMedian=0&resolution=1month`)*

Action Steps

Follow these steps to analyze the transaction count to help determine whether the market is entering a bull market, bear market, or consolidation phase.

1) **Evaluate Transaction Count On-Chain Metric**

   Visit Glassnode.com (or equivalent) to view the Transaction Count on-chain metric.

   a) Analyze the transaction count metric to better understand the asset's growth, interest, and potential accumulation or distribution opportunities.

2) **Take Notes and Document Your Findings in Your Own Style**

3) **Combine the Findings with Other Sections of the Fundamental Evaluation Process**

Evaluation of the Results

If accumulation or distribution opportunities are presented, it is best to find confluence with other on-chain metrics discussed in this chapter. Never rely on just one or two metrics; higher accuracy is seen in combinations of metrics that all point in the same direction.

Inflation Rate

Evaluation Objective: Track bitcoin's inflation, providing insight into supply dilution and early signs of price increase.

The *inflation rate* metric tracks how much a digital asset's supply is increasing. Note the on-chain metric discussed in this section is specific to bitcoin's inflation, which tends to affect the overall market due to the heavy dominance—please refer to the section "Inflationary Token Supply" in Chapter 8, "Tokenomics," for more detail on inflated token supplies.

Glassnode defines an asset's inflation rate as the net supply change (issuance-burn) divided by the current supply. Many proof-of-stake (PoS) blockchains tend to have inflated token supplies because of how the consensus mechanisms operate. These inflation models can either have an indefinite supply increase or a capped maximum supply, where no more tokens are created once that limit is reached.

bitcoin has an inflated fixed supply, with mining rewards halving after the network mines 210,000 blocks (approximately every 4 years). Figure 9-24 tracks bitcoin's on-chain inflation rate metric (in orange) with the price per coin (in black). In 2012, bitcoin's inflation rate was approximately 44% compared to 2024, where it dropped to roughly 1.8%. Note when bitcoin's inflation rate fell in the years 2012, 2016, and 2020, the price per BTC increased—at the time of writing this, it is too early to confirm this for 2024. bitcoin's mining rewards will continue until roughly 2140, when the proposed limit of 21 million coins is reached. At this time, miners will be rewarded solely by transaction processing fees.

The inflation rate is especially important for long-term investors because a constant token inflation rate leads to significant dilution, reducing the value of each token in circulation. Ideally, the inflation rate should decrease and taper off over time rather than stay constant—or worse, increase.

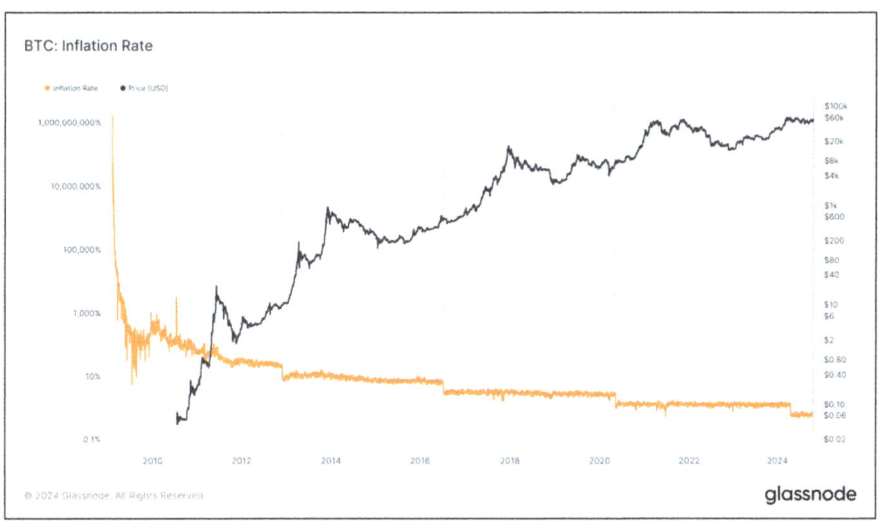

Figure 9-24. *bitcoin: Inflation rate on-chain metric (compliments of* `https://studio.glassnode.com/metrics?a=BTC&category=&m=supply.InflationRate`*)*

Action Steps

Follow the steps below to track bitcoin's inflation, providing insight into supply dilution and early signs of price increase.

1) **Track Inflation Rate**

   Visit Glassnode.com to track bitcoin's inflation details.

   a) Take note of the inflation rate; is it dropping over time or remaining constant?

   b) Are there price action trends when (if) the inflation rate drops? Does this present potential accumulation or distribution (profit-taking) opportunities?

2) **Take Notes and Document Your Findings in Your Own Style**

3) **Combine the Findings with Other Sections of the Fundamental Evaluation Process**

Evaluation of the Results

When bitcoin's inflation rate drops and the price per BTC increases, it indicates potential accumulation opportunities. However, if prices don't react, other market factors might be in play, requiring caution. The results from bitcoin's inflation chart are helpful not only in identifying opportunities in bitcoin but also for other digital assets due to the heavy dominance bitcoin has in the market. This metric is more applicable for long-term investors.

Investor Tool

Evaluation Objective: Utilize the investor tool to identify potential market tops, bottoms, and potential accumulation and distribution zones.

The investor tool was created by Philip Swift as a tool for long-term investors, indicating periods where prices are likely approaching cyclical tops or bottoms. The tool works by utilizing two simple moving averages (a 2-year MA (green) and a 5x multiple of the 2-year MA (red)) with price per coin as the basis for undervalued and overvalued conditions as follows:

- **Price trading below the 2-year MA (moving average)** has often coincided with bear-cycle lows.
- **Price trading above the 2-year MA x5** has frequently aligned with bull-cycle tops and zones where investors de-risk.

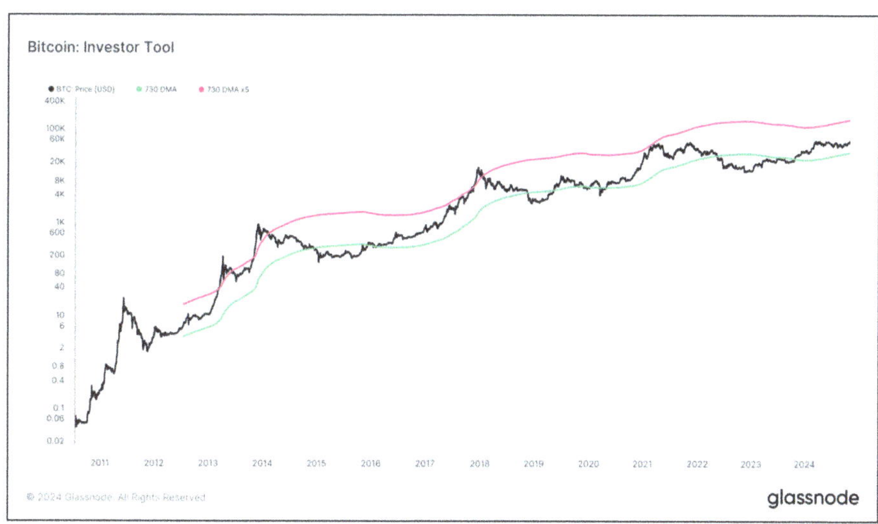

***Figure 9-25.** Glassnode's investor tool (compliments of `https://studio.glassnode.com/workbench/e9e05fce-ce4b-4138-5736-5d2bfadfdf94`)*

Action Steps

Follow these steps to help identify market tops, bottoms, and potential accumulation and distribution zones.

1) **Identify Optimal Entry Points**

   Visit Glassnode.com (or equivalent) to view and use Philip Swift's *Investor Tool.*

   a) Identify where price action lies, either below the 2-year MA (green line), above the 5x multiple of the 2-year MA (red line), or somewhere between.

2) **Take Notes and Document Your Findings in Your Own Style**

3) **Combine the Findings with Other Sections of the Fundamental Evaluation Process**

Evaluation of the Results

If the price dips below the 2-year MA, it's likely undervalued—consider adding to your position. If it's nearing or crossing the 5x multiple of the 2-year MA, that suggests it's overvalued and may be a good time to take profits or reduce risk. Note these levels as guideposts to help decide when to buy, hold, or de-risk, and they should be used with other on-chain market analytics tools.

Percent Supply in Profit

Evaluation Objective: Analyze the "Percent Supply in Profit" metric to assess the current profitability of holders and identify potential accumulation or distribution zones.

A coin is considered "in profit" if its current price is higher than the price at which that coin (or wallet balance, for account-based chains) last moved, and "in loss" if the current price is lower. Understanding how many investors holding an asset are in profit and how many are currently at a loss is invaluable. As a general rule of thumb, a high percentage of holders in profit may signal a potential trend reversal to the downside, while a high rate of holders in loss could be a possible trend reversal to the upside.

The *Percent Supply in Profit* on-chain metric measures the percentage of a total circulating supply in profit—this metric is represented in Figure 9-26 with bitcoin. The x-axis represents time, while the y-axis represents both the percent of the supply in profit and the price per BTC. Generally, when the percent of the supply in profit (orange line) enters the green zone (low % of people in profit), it signals a potential accumulation zone and upcoming trend reversal to the upside. Conversely, when it enters the red zone (high % of people in profit), it signals a potential distribution zone and upcoming trend reversal to the downside.

Although tempting, it is tough to predict the bottom of the market, and relying on this strategy may go against you. Instead, sometimes it is more beneficial to put the dollar cost average into an investment when it is an accumulation zone, thus spreading your risk over time and potentially securing a lower average entry price. The same is true when Percent Supply in Profit enters the red zone. Taking profits at different intervals in the red zone is safer and generally more profitable than trying to sell at the very top.

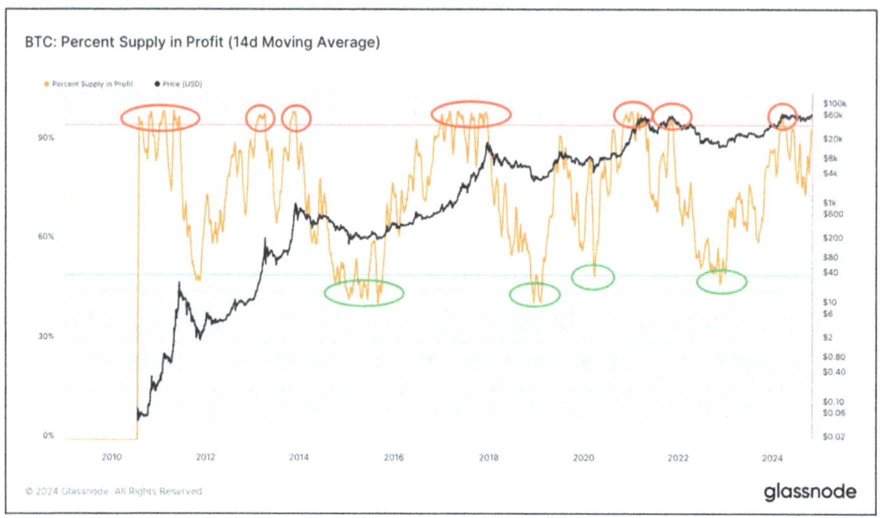

***Figure 9-26.** On-chain metric indicating the percentage of the circulating supply in profit (compliments of `https://studio.glassnode.com/metrics?a=BTC&m=supply.ProfitRelative&utm_source=gn_insights&utm_medium=insights_woc&utm_campaign=woc_25_2024`)*

Action Steps

Follow these steps to analyze the Percent Supply in Profit metric to assess the current profitability of holders and identify potential accumulation or distribution zones.

1) **Analyze the Percent Supply in Profit Metric**

   Visit Glassnode.com (or equivalent) to view and use the *Percent Supply in Profit* on-chain metric.

   a) Check the Percent Supply in Profit to see if the asset is in the green zone (low % in profit), red zone (high % in profit), or somewhere in between.

2) **Take Notes and Document Your Findings in Your Own Style**

3) **Combine the Findings with Other Sections of the Fundamental Evaluation Process**

Evaluation of the Results

If the Percent Supply in Profit is in the green zone (few holders in profit), consider gradually accumulating at various intervals to help spread out the risk over time with the possibility of securing a lower average entry price. The same applies when the Percent Supply in Profit enters the red zone (many holders in profit), so consider gradually distributing your holdings and locking in profits at various intervals.

Active Addresses

Evaluation Objective: Evaluate the Active Addresses metric to determine whether the market is entering a bull phase, bear phase, or consolidation period and to identify potential trend reversals or long-term opportunities.

The Active Address on-chain metric can be described as the number of unique addresses for a digital asset active in the network, either as a sender or receiver. Only addresses that were active in successful transactions are counted and used in this on-chain metric. An increase in active addresses indicates an increase in users on the network, which is also highly admirable for the network and investors. In contrast, a decrease or sudden drop in active addresses suggests the beginning of a bear market. Figure 9-27 shows *bitcoin: Number of Active Addresses (using a 30-day moving average)*. It compares bitcoin's active addresses on the x-axis to the price per BTC on the y-axis. From 2015 to 2018, there has been a steady increase in active addresses, which correlates with the rise in bitcoin's price. However, in early 2018 a sharp drop in active addresses coincided with bitcoin's rapid price decline and the start of a year-long bear market. A similar decline in mid-2021 lined up with the May–July drawdown, although price later set a new all-time high in November 2021—showing that active-address signals can flag interim trend shifts but are not definitive cycle timers.

Strong network growth can be seen by looking at the number of active addresses at the start of each bull market. For instance, if there are more active addresses at the beginning of a new bull market than the previous one, it shows growing interest in the asset over time. On the flip side, if there are fewer active addresses, it may indicate declining interest. Figure 9-27 signifies that since bitcoin's genesis block, there has been a gradual overall increase in the number of active addresses on the network, which is highly admirable for investors. However, there has been a drop in bitcoin's active addresses from early 2024 while the price per coin has increased from roughly $40,000 to $65,000. This is a perfect way to note that using one metric is not enough, and instead, multiple on-chain metrics (as described in this chapter) should be used for a more accurate overall view of the asset and market.

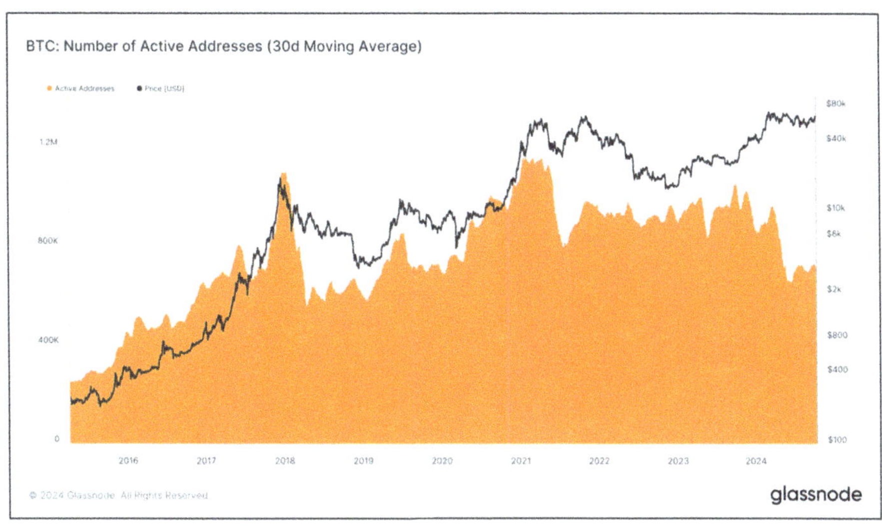

Figure 9-27. *bitcoin: Number of active addresses (compliments of `https://studio.glassnode.com/metrics?a=BTC&category=&chartStyle=line&m=addresses.ActiveCount`)*

Action Steps

While the Active Addresses on-chain metric is primarily available for major coins like BTC and ETH, these top-tier assets dominate the market, making this analysis a practical rough guide for spotting opportunities in other digital assets.

Follow these steps to evaluate the Active Addresses metric to determine whether the market is entering a bull phase, bear phase, or consolidation period and to identify potential trend reversals or long-term opportunities.

1) **Track Active Address Trends**

   Visit Glassnode.com (or equivalent) to view the on-chain metric active addresses for BTC.

a) Does the number of active addresses correlate with the price per coin?

b) Observe how active addresses shift in bull and bear markets to spot potential trend reversals.

c) Are there more or less active addresses at the start of each bull cycle?

2) **Take Notes and Document Your Findings in Your Own Style**

3) **Combine the Findings with Other Sections of the Fundamental Evaluation Process**

Evaluation of the Results

An increase in active addresses signals network growth, while a decline indicates weakening interest and a potential price drop. If active addresses rise but transaction volume is flat, this suggests low engagement. However, if both rise, it confirms strong network activity. In bull markets, increasing addresses align with price growth, and in bear markets, stable addresses suggest a resilient user base, indicating possible long-term opportunities.

Number of Addresses with Balance Greater Than 10k bitcoins

Evaluation Objective: Evaluate the number of BTC addresses that hold more than 10k BTC to help gauge areas of accumulation and distribution.

Glassnode offers a metric that shows the number of addresses that hold a specific number of BTC coins graphed against the price per coin in USD. This metric is provided for bitcoin addresses holding as little as 0.01 BTC; however, viewing the addresses with balances holding 10k (or more) BTC better shows the shift from BTC to USD and vice versa.

Figure 9-28 illustrates the number of bitcoin addresses with balances of 10,000 or more BTC. As the price of BTC (black line) rises, the number of these large-balance addresses (orange line) declines, indicating that whales are selling off their holdings to retail investors during price increases. Conversely, during a price decline, retail investors tend to sell, while long-term holders accumulate more, leading to a rise in the number of addresses holding 10,000+ BTC.

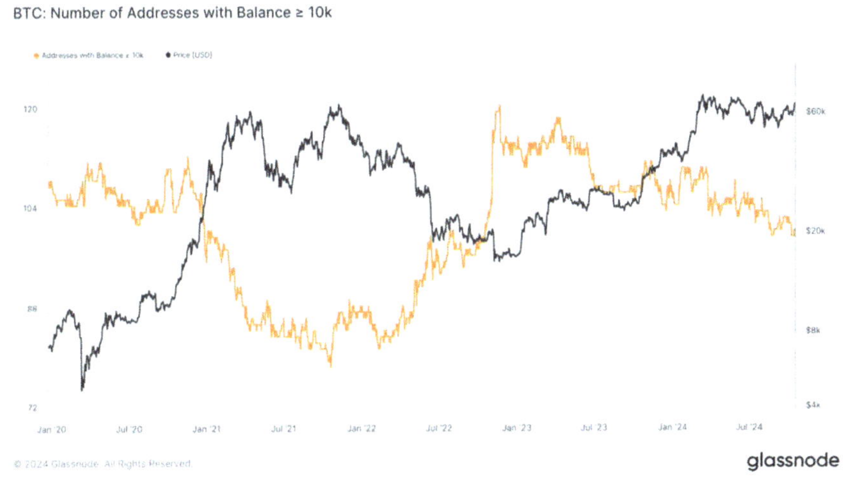

***Figure 9-28.** bitcoin: Number of addresses with balance ≥ 10k (compliments of `https://studio.glassnode.com/metrics?a=BTC&category=Addresses&m=addresses.Min10KCount&s=1518786086&u=1702857600&zoom=`)*

This Glassnode metric provides valuable investor insight into the behavior of large BTC holders (whales), detecting patterns of accumulation or distribution.

- **Selling Opportunity** - When the number of addresses holding 10,000 (or more) BTC decreases as the price rises, it suggests that whales are selling to retail investors, potentially signaling a market top.
- **Buying Opportunity** - When the number of addresses holding 10,000 (or more) BTC increases as the price decreases, it suggests that whales are accumulating from retail investors, potentially signaling a market bottom.

Pro Tip For optimal insight into the shift of supply, use this on-chain metric in conjunction with the Realized Cap HODL Waves on-chain metric.

Action Steps

Follow these steps to determine the number of BTC addresses holding more than 10k BTC, gauging areas of accumulation and distribution.

1) **Number of BTC Addresses Holding More Than 10k BTC**

   Visit Glassnode.com (or equivalent) to view the on-chain metric "Addresses with Balance ≥ 10 k BTC."

   a) Analyze metrics for potential buying or selling opportunities, as discussed in this section.

i) **If the Addresses Decline as BTC Price Rises**:

(1) Indicates whale distribution to smaller retail investors.

(2) A potential market top signal; proceed cautiously with further investment.

ii) **If Addresses Increase as BTC Price Drops**:

(1) Indicates whale accumulation from retail investors

(2) Potential market bottom signal could represent a strategic buying opportunity.

2) **Take Notes and Document Your Findings in Your Own Style**

3) **Combine the Findings with Other Sections of the Fundamental Evaluation Process**

Evaluation of the Results

It is vital for long-term investors not to invest while institutional investors are selling and vice versa. This metric is less applicable for short-term investors who do not plan on holding for long periods. However, investing in the same direction as the whales is still beneficial.

MVRV Ratio

Evaluation Objective: Using the MVRV ratio, determine whether the price per coin is above or below its "fair value," identifying potential buy and sell zones.

The *market value to realized value* (MVRV) ratio is the ratio between market capitalization and realized capitalization, helping to gauge the market sentiment and potential turning points. The MVRV ratio (Equation 9-8) is often used by investors to get a sense of when the price per coin is above or below "fair value" and to assess market profitability. Significant deviations between market value and realized value can signal market tops and bottoms, reflecting periods of extreme unrealized profit (tops) or loss (bottoms) among investors.

$$\boldsymbol{MVRV} = \frac{\textbf{\textit{Market Cap}}}{\textbf{\textit{Realized Cap}}}$$

Equation 9-8. *Formula for MVRV ratio*

Figure 9-29 shows bitcoin's MVRV ratio. Time is represented on the x-axis, with MVRV ratio and price per BTC on the y-axis. When the MVRV (in orange) is below 1 (in green), most holders are at a loss or breaking even—this is typically seen as a buy signal. An MVRV of 1 means the price per coin equals its realized price, or break-even point, showing a balanced market. When the MVRV rises above 3.5 (Glassnode plots 3.5 as the red threshold because every bitcoin cycle top—2011, 2013, 2017, and the February 2021 local high—peaked between 3.5 and 4; it's an empirically observed "danger zone," not a formula-based value), it indicates a possible market top resulting in heavy profit taking—this is seen with bitcoin in early 2021. High MVRV values in an uptrend signal growing unrealized profits, increasing the probability of sell-offs. Conversely, low MVRV values in a downtrend indicate falling market value relative to cost basis, which can either suggest undervaluation or weak demand, depending on other market factors. See Table 9-5 for a further breakdown of MVRV ratio interpretations.

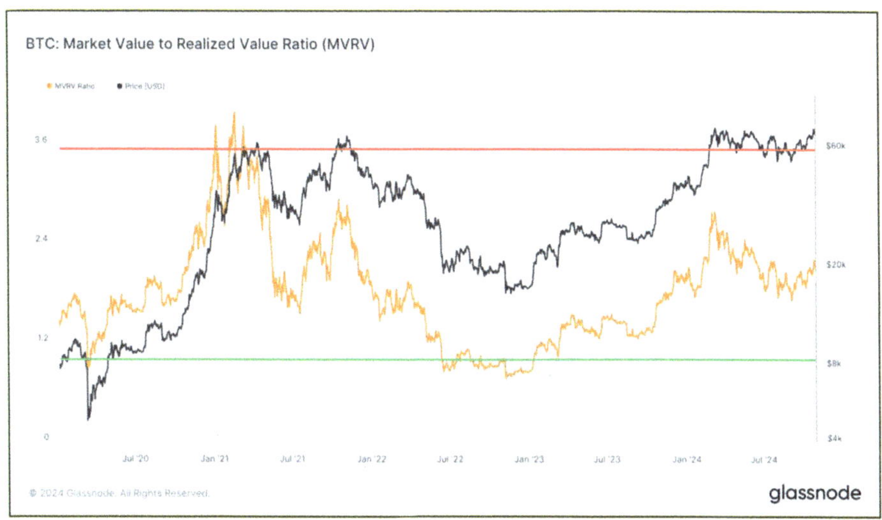

Figure 9-29. *bitcoin: Market value to realized value ratio (MVRV) (compliments of https://studio.glassnode.com/metrics?a=BTC&category=&m=market.Mvrv)*

Fact The MVRV ratio is especially valuable for long-term investors because it highlights big-picture market cycles. However, short-term price swings don't always match up with MVRV signals. To get better timing on when to buy or sell, it is recommended to pair MVRV with other indicators like the Investor Tool, NUPL, Trading Volume, and Realize Cap HODL Waves.

Table 9-5. MVRV ratio interpretations

MVRV Ratio Interpretations	
Ratio Value/ Description	**Ratio Interpretations**
MVRV Values < 1.0	Most holders are at a loss (or breaking even). Signifies market capitulation and late-stage bear accumulation. Often seen as a buy signal.
MVRV = 1	The price per coin is equal to the realized price or break-even.
MVRV > 3.5	Possible market top. Heightened probability of heavy distribution and profit taking.
High Values and Up-Trends	The market value of the coin supply is increasing relative to the realized value (cost basis). Indicates a significant degree of unrealized profit, thus increasing the probability of coin distribution to lock in profits.
Low Values and Down-Trends	The market value of the coin supply is decreasing relative to the realized value (cost basis). Indicates unrealized losses among investors, which may signal undervaluations and poor demand dynamics.

Action Steps

Follow these steps to determine whether the price per coin is above or below its "fair value," identifying potential buy and sell zones.

1) **Identify Buy and Sell Zones Using the MVRV ratio**

   Visit Glassnode.com (or equivalent) to view and use the *MVRV ratio* on-chain metric.

   a) Determine the MVRV ratio of the asset by analyzing the chart data.

2) **Take Notes and Document Your Findings in Your Own Style**

3) **Combine the Findings with Other Sections of the Fundamental Evaluation Process**

Evaluation of the Results

If the MVRV is below 1, consider accumulating at regular intervals; if it is between 1 and 3.5, consider planning for the next entry or exit; and if the MVRV is greater than 3.5, consider taking profits at regular intervals.

MVRV Z-Score

Evaluation Objective: Use the MVRV Z-Score to assess whether an asset is overvalued or undervalued and to pinpoint market tops and bottoms.

As per Glassnode.com, the ***market value to realized value (MVRV) Z-Score*** evaluates whether a digital asset is overvalued or undervalued relative to its "fair value." It is defined as the ratio between the difference of market capitalization and realized capitalization and the standard deviation of market capitalization. Some investors prefer the MVRV Z-Score more than the traditional Z-Score (a statistical measurement that indicates how far a particular price point is from the average price, expressed in terms of standard deviations) because it compares the market value to the realized value. The MVRV Z-Score is calculated by taking the difference between an asset's market value and its realized cap and then dividing it by the standard deviation of the market cap to highlight deviations from the "fair value."

$$\textit{MVRV Z Score} = \frac{\textit{Market Cap} - \textit{Realized Cap}}{\textit{Standard Deviation}\ (\textit{Market Cap})}$$

Equation 9-9. *Formula to calculate MVRV Z-Score*

The MVRV-Z Score is broken up into colored zones. The red zone signifies that the market value (cap) is significantly higher than the realized value (cap). This zone is often associated with heavy distribution and profit-taking. The green zone signifies a considerably lower market value than the realized value, signaling potential market bottoms and buying opportunities.

Figure 9-30 shows bitcoin's MVRV-Z Score data with a 30-day moving average. When the MVRV Z-Score entered the red zone (market peaks) in 2013 and 2017, it was followed by a price decline and a trend reversal. Conversely, when it entered the green zone (market bottoms) in 2011, 2015, 2019, and 2022, it marked the beginning of an accumulation period, followed by an upward trend.

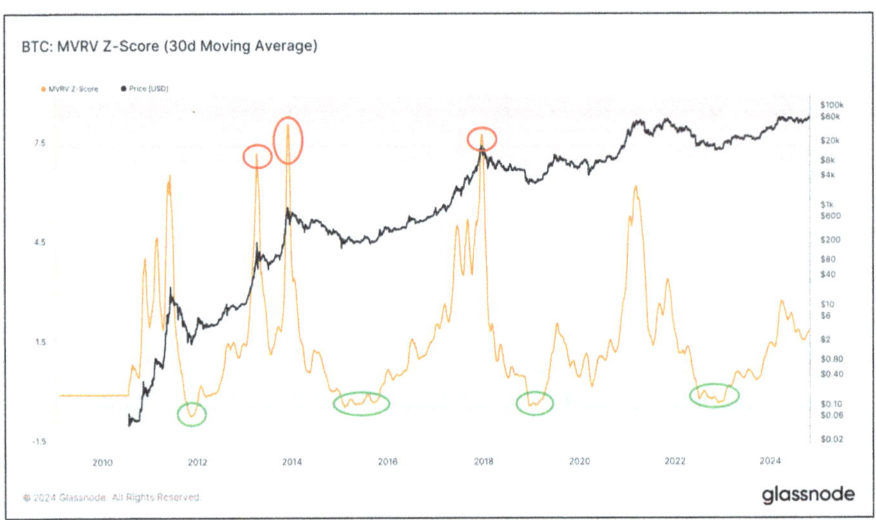

***Figure 9-30.** bitcoin: MVRV Z-Score (compliments of `https://studio.glassnode.com/metrics?a=BTC&category=&m=market.MvrvZScore&zoom=all`)*

Action Steps

Follow these steps to assess whether an asset is overvalued or undervalued and to pinpoint market tops and bottoms.

1) **Identify Buy and Sell Zones Using the MVRV Z-Score**

   Visit Glassnode.com (or equivalent) to view and use the *MVRV Z-Score* on-chain metric.

   a) Determine the MVRV Z-Score of the asset by analyzing the chart data.

2) **Take Notes and Document Your Findings in Your Own Style**

3) **Combine the Findings with Other Sections of the Fundamental Evaluation Process**

Evaluation of the Results

When the MVRV Z-Score enters the red zone, the asset is overvalued; therefore, consider taking profits at regular intervals. In the green zone, this typically means the asset is undervalued; therefore, consider accumulating at regular intervals. Exercise caution between these zones, watch other indicators for clearer trends, and plan for the next entry and exit.

Net Unrealized Profit/Loss (NUPL)

Evaluation Objective: Use the NUPL to access investor emotion, market sentiment, and potential market tops and bottoms, signaling buying and selling opportunities.

Net unrealized profit/loss (NUPL) signifies the difference between a digital asset's **relative unrealized profit** and **relative unrealized loss**. It is a ratio calculated by subtracting the realized market cap (cost basis) from the market cap (current total value) and dividing it by the market cap.

$$NUPL = \frac{Market\ Cap - Realized\ Cap}{Market\ Cap}$$

Equation 9-10. *Formula to calculate the NUPL*

NUPL, which is primarily used for bitcoin, indicates the emotional state of the investor, whether they are in profit or at a loss, and the overall sentiment at various stages throughout the market cycle. It also helps to identify market tops and bottoms that allow investors to plan for entry and exit accordingly.

NUPL contains five horizontal "colored" zones, interpreted from the market psychology perspective. The zones range from the *Capitulation* area (in red) to the Euphoria and greed area (in blue). When the NUPL of a particular asset is in the blue zone, it indicates that most investors are in a state of euphoria and are primarily in profit. Price action typically peaks when NUPL is in this zone. Opposingly, when NUPL is in the red zone, it is said that investors have surrendered to the vicious declining market. During this period, price action has nearly bottomed out, signifying a potential bottom to the bear market with only a few sellers remaining. In other words, NUPL helps investors visualize market cycles in a simplistic color-coded pattern.

Figure 9-31 shows bitcoin's NUPL chart with a seven-day moving average. Time is represented on the x-axis with NUPL, and price per BTC is on the y-axis. Note that bitcoin's price action peaks when the NUPL is green, especially in the blue, often followed by a swift decline and trend reversal. On the other hand, when bitcoin's price action is bottoming out, NUPL dips into the orange and red zones, usually signaling a market bottom and a sharp upward price movement shortly after. See Table 9-6 for a more detailed breakdown and explanation of NUPLs zones.

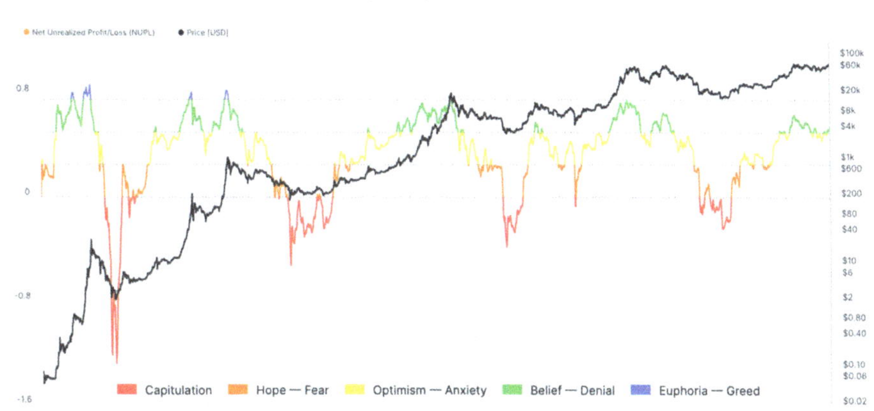

***Figure 9-31.** bitcoin: Net unrealized profit/loss (NUPL) (compliments of `https://studio.glassnode.com/metrics?a=BTC&category=&m=indicators.NetUnrealizedProfitLoss&s=1452251288&u=1702857600&zoom=`)*

***Table 9-6.** Net unrealized profit/loss (NUPL) zones*

Net Unrealized Profit/Loss (NUPL) Zones		
NUPL Zone	**Color**	**Description**
Capitulation (NUPL < 0)	Red	Represents the market bottom, where the majority of investors are holding losses.
Hope/Fear (0 < NUPL < 0.25)	Orange	The transition phase is when the market is recovering from losses, and investors are cautiously optimistic.
Optimism/Anxiety (0.25 < NUPL < 0.5)	Yellow	Investor confidence grows, with market anxiety slowly phasing out.
Belief/Denial (0.5 < NUPL < 0.75)	Green	In the bullish phase, the upward trend is expected to continue with some denial of potential market risks.
Euphoria/Greed (NUPL > 0.75)	Blue	High number of investors in profit and experiencing extreme euphoria. Typically, assets are overvalued in this area, and a trend reversal is imminent.

Action Steps

Follow these steps to access investor emotion, market sentiment, and potential market top and bottom signaling buying and selling opportunities.

1) **Identify Market Sentiment**

   Visit Glassnode.com (or equivalent) to view and use the *NUPL* on-chain metric.

   a) Determine the overall market sentiment and investor emotion by monitoring which color zone bitcoin (or another asset) is in.

   b) Evaluate NUPL zones as described in Table 9-6.

2) **Track Market Cycles**

   a) Observe NUPL's movements across different zones to identify shifts in the market cycle.

3) **Take Notes and Document Your Findings in Your Own Style**

4) **Combine the Findings with Other Sections of the Fundamental Evaluation Process**

Evaluation of the Results

If NUPL is in the blue or green zones, consider securing profits at various levels, as a market peak and trend reversal are likely. Consider accumulating in orange and red zones, as these levels often signal a market bottom.

Hash Rate

Evaluation Objective: Evaluate a PoW network's hash rate to determine trends in network security, miner participation, and their correlation with market conditions and asset performance.

Hash rate is a measure of the computational power (per second) used to validate transactions and secure the network on a proof-of-work (PoW) blockchain during mining. It is generally seen as positive when a network's hash rate increases over time. A high hash rate signifies that a high level of computational power is required to alter or manipulate the blockchain network, making it harder for any single entity to mount a 51% attack. On the other hand, a low hash rate can indicate reduced miner participation, which undermines the network's security by making it easier for malicious entities to control over 50% of the network's computational power—a situation known as a 51% attack. Sudden, sharp drops in hash rate can be red flags, signaling miner shutdowns, regional outages, or profit-driven exodus, and they temporarily erode that security margin.

A network with a decreasing hash rate is a major red flag for long-term investors. A lower hash rate can indicate reduced miner participation, which directly affects the network's security by making it easier for malicious entities to control over 50% of the network's computational power—a situation known as a 51% attack. When this happens, attackers can disrupt and manipulate the blockchain by engaging in double-spending, interfering with the integrity of the network. Furthermore, a low or declining hash rate is often associated with decreasing miner profitability or a lack of incentive to secure the network due to reduced transaction fees or rewards. This is typically the result of low user interaction, which may be rooted in poor fundamental qualities or market conditions.

Hash rate is typically measured in how many hashes are generated per second. Here are the common hash rate measurements, what they mean, and some examples of networks or devices that match each level.

Table 9-7. Hash rate speed

Hash Rate Speed		
Hash Rate Measurements	**Hash Rate per Second**	**Hash Rate Description**
Kilohash	1,000 hashes per second	Extremely slow, potentially one GPU-based miner
Megahash	1 million hashes per second	Very slow, potentially one GPU-based miner
Gigahash	1 billion hashes per second	Small mining pool or potentially cluster of GPUs
Terahash	1 trillion hashes per second	Single ASIC machine or large mining pool.
Petahash	1 quadrillion hashes per second	Large mining pool
Exahash	1 quadrillion hashes per second	A huge mining pool or potentially an entire network
Zetahash	1 sextillion hashes per second	First reached by the entire bitcoin network in 2024; represents ultra-large, global-scale PoW power

Figure 9-32 shows the hash rate for bitcoin. Time is represented on the x-axis, and bitcoin's hash rate and price per coin are represented on the y-axis. As the chart shows, bitcoin's hash rate was on a steep incline from 2010 to roughly 2015 and a steady increase from 2015 to 2024. As bitcoin's hash rate increases, so does its mining difficulty. Although this negatively affects miner profitability, it positively contributes to overall network security and indicates continuous popularity.

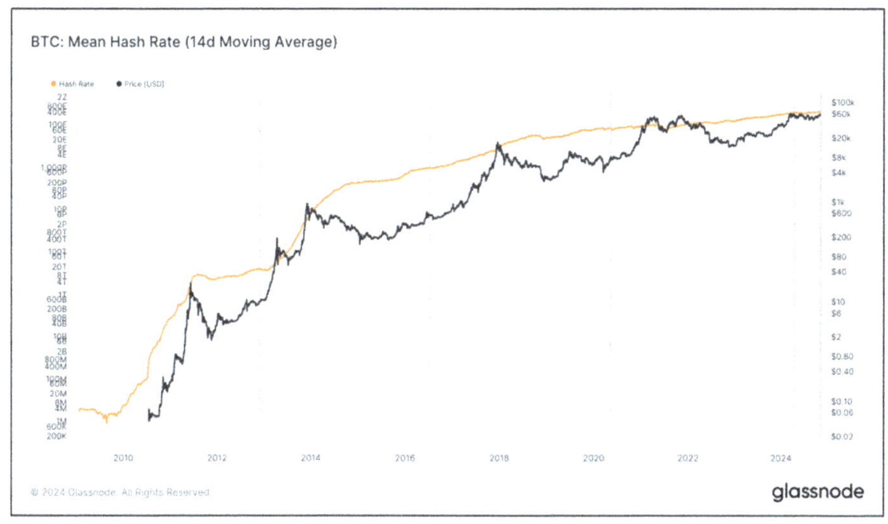

Figure 9-32. *bitcoin hash rate (compliments of `https://studio.glassnode.com/metrics?a=BTC&category=&m=mining.HashRateMean&mScl=log`)*

Figure 9-33. *Ethereum's mean hash rate before it switched to PoS (compliments of `https://studio.glassnode.com/metrics?a=ETH&category=&ema=0&m=mining.HashRateMean&mAvg=14&mMedian=0&mScl=log`)*

Action Steps

Follow these steps to evaluate a PoW network's hash rate to determine trends in network security, miner participation, and their correlation with market conditions and asset performance.

1) **Check Networks Hash Rate**

   Visit Glassnode.com (or equivalent) to view and use the *Hash Rate* on-chain metric.

   a) Track the network's hash rate over time to see if it's trending upwards, stable, or declining.

2) **Analyze Hash Rate Relative to Market Conditions**

   Compare hash rate changes to asset price shifts and overall market conditions.

3) **Take Notes and Document Your Findings in Your Own Style**

4) **Combine the Findings with Other Sections of the Fundamental Evaluation Process**

Evaluation of the Results

An increasing hash rate signals strong network security, miner participation, and popularity. Conversely, a declining hash rate—especially alongside price stagnation or drops—suggests weakening network security and potential miner exits, which may indicate it's time to reassess or reduce exposure.

Network Value to Transactions Signal (NVTS)

Evaluation Objective: Evaluate the NVT signal (NVTS) metric to determine whether an asset appears undervalued or overvalued, identifying potential buying or selling opportunities and possible trend reversals.

The **NVT signal (NVTS)** is an upgraded version of the traditional NVT ratio, providing a more investor-friendly view of a network's valuation than its transaction activity. The traditional NVT uses daily transaction volume, while the NVTS uses a 90-day moving average—dividing the market cap by the 7-day average—to smoothen out short-term swings and make it more reliable for spotting trends.

When the NVTS is high, it indicates that the network's valuation (market cap) is high relative to the transaction volume, suggesting potential overvaluation, as the network's utility (measured by transactions) doesn't justify its price. Investors might interpret this as a warning signal for a possible market correction. Conversely, when the NVTS is low, it indicates that transaction volume is robust relative to the network's valuation, suggesting potential undervaluation and signaling potential buying opportunities if other fundamentals align positively.

Figure 9-34 shows bitcoin's NVTS. Time is represented on the x-axis with NVTS, and price per BTC is on the y-axis. Note that when the NVT Signal plummets (green circles), a price action trend is reversed to the upside. However, caution must be exercised, as this does not always mean it will be a long-term price reversal, as in the case of 2018 (purple circle). On the other hand, when the NVT Signal peaks (red circles), it is typically followed by a steep price decline and trend reversal to the downside.

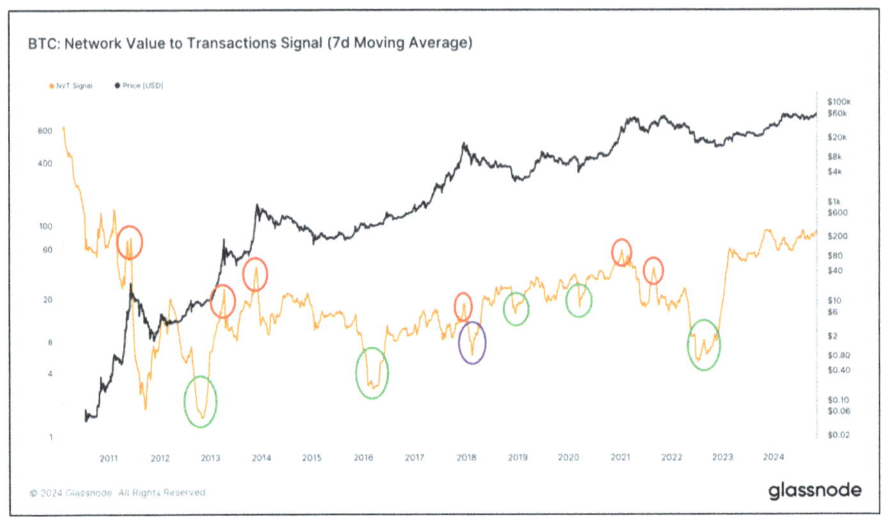

***Figure 9-34.** bitcoin's Network Value to Transactions Signal (7d moving average) (compliments of `https://studio.glassnode.com/metrics?a=BTC&ema=0&m=indicators.Nvts&mAvg=7&mMedian=0&mScl=log&s=1264806612&u=1730505600&zoom=`)*

Action Steps

Follow these steps to evaluate the NVT signal (NVTS) metric to determine whether an asset appears undervalued or overvalued, identifying potential buying or selling opportunities and possible trend reversals.

1) **Identify Overvaluation and Undervaluation**

   Visit Glassnode.com (or equivalent) to view and use the *NVT Signal* on-chain metric.

   a) Check the NVTS reading for the asset you're evaluating.

2) **Analyze for Trend Reversals**

   Identify the possibility of a trend reversal when NVTS is either plummeting or peaking.

3) **Take Notes and Document Your Findings in Your Own Style**

4) **Combine the Findings with Other Sections of the Fundamental Evaluation Process**

Evaluation of the Results

If NVTS is peaking high, the asset might be overvalued—consider reducing managing risk by reducing your position. Conversely, if NVTS is low, it may indicate undervaluation, which could present potential accumulation opportunities. Always validate with recent trend reversals and look for confluence with other on-chain metric indicators.

Stock-to-Flow Model

Evaluation Objective: Evaluate the stock-to-flow model to help predict bitcoin's long-term price movements.

The stock-to-flow (S2F) model is a financial concept initially designed to value scarce resources such as gold and silver by calculating the ratio of an asset's existing supply to its annual production rate. An anonymous figure named Plan B took this S2F model and modified and applied it to bitcoin. In this model, bitcoin's scarcity is assessed by dividing its "stock" (all bitcoins that have been mined and are now in circulation) by its "flow" (the annual number of newly mined bitcoins entering the ecosystem).

Long-term investors use this model to help anticipate bitcoin's—with a capped supply of 21m coin—long-term price movements over time. Because bitcoin's issuance of coins is algorithmically controlled, the S2F model can help estimate the potential future value of BTC compared to other assets such as gold. Through *halving*—a process in which BTC mining rewards are reduced by 50% every four years—bitcoin will become more scarce and harder to obtain, doubling the S2F ratio and potentially increasing its value.

Figure 9-35 shows bitcoin's S2F model as displayed by Bitcoin Magazine Pro. Time is represented on the x-axis with the S2F ratio and the price per BTC on the y-axis. To reduce the effects of market volatility, the S2F ratio line incorporates a 365-day average. The price line is overlaid on top of the S2F ratio line, with colored dots marking the number of days until the next bitcoin halving in 2028 (when writing this book). The theory is that investors can predict where the price may go by observing the projected S2F line. Since 2012, bitcoin's price has generally followed the S2F ratio, fluctuating around it but overall aligning with its upward trajectory. Note how the price increases every four years, as shown in the vertical dotted lines marking bitcoin's halving events. This is due to bitcoin becoming scarcer, with mining rewards cut by 50%.

At the bottom of the S2F chart is a divergence tool, or *Stock-to-flow Deflection bitcoin,* that shows the difference between price and stock-to-flow. It allows investors to quickly see how price interacts with stock-to-flow through market cycles over time. When the price moves above the S2F line, the divergence line turns from green to red. Conversely, the divergence tool turns from red to green when the price moves below the S2F line. The further the divergence line moves away from the S2F level in either direction, the higher the likelihood of a potential price correction, as indicated by the S2F divergence concept.

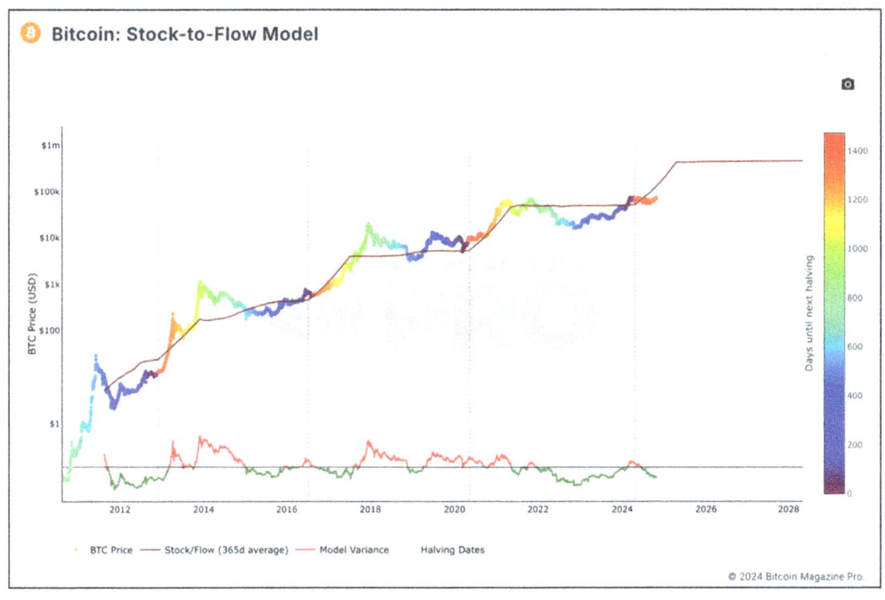

Figure 9-35. *bitcoin stock-to-flow model (compliments of `https://www.bitcoinmagazinepro.com/charts/stock-to-flow-model/`)*

Action Steps

Follow the steps to evaluate the stock-to-flow model to help predict bitcoin's long-term price movements.

1) **Track bitcoin's Price with the Stock-to-Flow Model**

   Visit Bitcoin Magazine Pro, Glassnode.com (or equivalent) to view and use the *S2F* on-chain metric.

   a) Check bitcoin's current alignment with respect to the S2F ratio line.

   b) Use the divergence tool to check whether bitcoin is deemed overvalued or undervalued to the S2F model.

c) Check bitcoin's remaining days until the next halving event.

d) Regularly monitor bitcoin's price in relation to the S2F line.

2) **Use Divergence Tools for Market Sentiment**
Utilize the divergence tool at the bottom of the S2F chart to assess potential buy or sell signals.

3) **Take Notes and Document Your Findings in Your Own Style**

4) **Combine the Findings with Other Sections of the Fundamental Evaluation Process**

Evaluation of the Results

According to the S2F model, if the price increases past the S2F line, it may be overvalued, presenting a potential profit-taking opportunity. On the other hand, if the price dips below the S2F ratio line, it could indicate undervaluation and an attractive investment entry point. Always use the divergence tool when using the S2F model metric.

It is important to note that while some people are skeptical about the S2F model, and outside of expected price fluctuations, it has still proven itself based on historical trends. Nevertheless, it is recommended that this tool be used as a rough guide for assessing long-term investment opportunities. The S2F model should also be used with an array of other off-chain and on-chain metric indicators for greater accuracy.

CHAPTER 10

Project Team

This chapter focuses on one of the most critical—and often overlooked—aspects of crypto project evaluation: the project team. The team is considered a vital driving force for the project and an essential ingredient for long-term success. No matter the project, the core product starts with a few people who share the same vision, and together, they help bring the product to life.

However, no matter how innovative or advanced the technology is, the project will ultimately fail without a dedicated team driving competitiveness, customer engagement, feedback, promotions, partnerships, and daily operations. Note that a team of a decent size consistently working on a product is still not enough. A dedicated team must still possess the right skills, expertise, background, and experience to add meaningful value, not only to develop the core product but also to handle critical aspects such as business development, marketing, financial management, legal compliance, tokenomics, and token design.

Unfortunately, many project teams suffer from a severe lack of transparency that directly lowers investor trust and, more often than not, negatively impacts the project's success and sustainability. Would you stick around if a team refuses to make their identities public or hides internal problems that could directly affect your investment? Probably not—me neither. Another essential element includes the team's level of support and whether they are executing an adequate number of interviews, communicating with the community, and addressing all questions and concerns.

P. Garvey, *Blockchain Fundamental Analysis for Digital Asset Investors*,
https://doi.org/10.1007/979-8-8688-1551-5_10

By the end of this chapter, investors will better understand how the people behind a blockchain project can make or break its success. Investors will learn how to dig into a team's background, skills, public presence, and experience in the blockchain space to spot solid professionals and catch any red flags. Evaluating the team and their performance provides a clearer picture of whether the project has what it takes to go the distance—or if it is better to steer clear.

The evaluation methods discussed in this chapter are designed to be simplistic in nature to provide investors with a straightforward and adequate approach to evaluating a blockchain project team with respect to their experience and technical and non-technical skills.

Fundamentals Discussed in This Chapter:

- Public Identity
- Project Team Members
- Background and Experience
- Developer Team Size
- Project Support
- Team Interviews

Public Identity

Evaluation Objective: Determine if the project team publicly shares their identity or exercises anonymity.

Project teams are considered the initial driving force behind the core product or service and play a vital role in shaping and developing the project from the inside out. Despite their essential role, some project teams remain anonymous, meaning their identity is hidden from the public. There are many reasons for this, including protection from negative backlash, privacy, regulatory compliance issues, or lack of experience and competency in blockchain technology.

Fact The anonymous creator of bitcoin, known only as Satoshi Nakamoto, stands out as an example of how a project with an unknown workforce may achieve outstanding success.

When investing in digital assets, the main objective is reducing risk. However, when a project team remains anonymous, it increases the risk of financial loss because there's no accountability. This lack of transparency makes it easier for fraudulent activity, including scams like rug pulls or price manipulation, to occur. On the other hand, reputable projects typically are open and transparent; showing who's behind them builds immense trust with users and investors. The core advantages of a publicly identifiable team are as follows:

- **Trust** - Investors, network participants, and customers tend to trust an open and transparent team. Trust helps promote credibility and accountability, which is essential for success.
- **Accountability** - With an identifiable team, there is added responsibility. Team members are expected to follow through on their commitments, which boosts reliability.
- **Community Engagement** - Project teams who share their identity can freely interact with the growing community where they share new updates, progress reports, and partnerships; answer questions; and publicly address the potential concerns of the community and blockchain participants.

- **Confidence** – Investor confidence is enhanced when they can freely access and evaluate team members' profiles.
- **Partnerships** – Being present on social media, public events, and Q&As opens the possibility for new partnerships, joint ventures, and other unique opportunities. Visible teams can also build contacts and take advantage of the power of networking on LinkedIn, some of which may blossom into business relationships.
- **Professional Talent** – Public project teams dramatically increase the possibility of seeking experienced talent to form a well-rounded team. Professionals are more inclined to join a team where they can be visibly seen, thus complementing and aiding their careers.
- **Transparency** – One of the key aspects of blockchain technology is transparency. Investors, blockchain users, and customers are more likely to favor fully transparent projects and prove they have nothing to hide.
- **Challenges** – Visible teams are better equipped to overcome obstacles and challenges by personally contacting the community for help.

Pro Tip If some images of team members seem suspicious, perform a reverse Google Image Search to determine if the profile pictures are genuine or stolen from another source.

Action Steps

Follow the steps below to determine if the project team publicly shares their identity or exercises anonymity.

1) **Project Website**

   Check if the team's full names, photos, and job titles are displayed on the project's website. Note that any team profiles on the project website must be validated through LinkedIn. If the team cannot be verified, consider it a red flag.

2) **LinkedIn**

   Search for the project's company page on LinkedIn or follow the links provided on the project's website. Verify that the LinkedIn profiles of team members are available and viewable by the public.

3) **Online Presence**

   Evaluate the team's online presence, transparency, and credibility by checking their activity on social media, project blogs, X, Telegram, and participation in YouTube or podcast interviews.

4) **Run Image and Name Searches**

   Fraudulent images and fake profiles are nothing new within and outside the blockchain world. Use reverse image search to verify profile pictures and search for team members' names to ensure authenticity.

5) **Take Notes and Document Your Findings in Your Own Style**

6) **Combine the Findings with Other Sections of the Fundamental Evaluation Process**

Evaluating the Results

It is advised to avoid projects that do not publicly share their identity. With so many high-quality projects prioritizing team transparency, there's no need to take on the additional risk of an anonymous team.

Project Team Members

Evaluation Objective: Determine if the project team includes the essential professionals to drive success.

A project team can be defined as a group of individuals with the same interest and passion to develop and manage a blockchain-based project. A typical team setup consists of a specific set of professional fields that is essential for delivering a high-quality product and long-term success. There are two types of team structures; they are as follows:

1) **Core Team** - Primary team members who make key decisions, provide strategic insight, and manage the project overall. These team members include founders, co-founders, directors of operations, marketing experts, lead developers, business development, legal experts, financial personnel, and other management roles.

2) **Extended Team** - Individuals who provide support to the core team. These members may include open-source developers, strategic advisors, technical consultants, tokenomic and token design experts, financial consultants, community managers, and influencers.

Note that depending on the size and popularity of the project, some of the extended team may become full-time employees and permanent members of the core team. Additionally, depending on the product use case, some projects may require additional specialists to cater to specific needs. For example, a project that offers decentralized identity solutions may require specialists in cryptographic security or data privacy compliance to address unique challenges in safeguarding user information and adhering to privacy regulations. For most projects, the professionals outlined in Table 10-1 form the base team essential for any successful project.

Table 10-1. Key professionals in a crypto project team

Blockchain Project Core Team Members	
Role	**Responsibility**
Founders/Co-founders and Project Leaders	Responsible for the project's vision, direction, and overall management.
Developers	Skilled in software development, programming, and blockchain architecture. Builds and tests the core product, e.g., a dApp or blockchain infrastructure.
Designers	Responsible for UI/UX design of the core product and project website.
Economists/Financial Experts	Helps design the project's tokenomic structure, token design, and other financial considerations that aim towards a sustainable economic model.
Marketing and PR Specialists	Responsible for promoting the project, managing public relations, and attracting investors and users.
Legal and Compliance Experts	Ensures that the project adheres to relevant regulations and legal requirements.
Business Development	Responsible for developing growth strategies, sourcing new clients, and aiding the project's overall success.
Token Economist/Crypto-Economics	Specializes in designing and optimizing token ecosystems by developing sustainable economic models, incentive structures, and governance frameworks to drive adoption, align stakeholder interests, and ensure long-term ecosystem growth.
Advisors	Offers financial and technical guidance and support to the project.

Action Steps

Follow these steps to determine if the project team includes the essential professionals required to drive success.

1) **LinkedIn Company Page**

   Look for links to the team's LinkedIn company page on the project's website, or search LinkedIn under "Companies" to find it.

2) **Filter by Role**

   On LinkedIn, filter by "People" on the company page. Then, search for the specific roles outlined in Table 10-1.

   a) It is advised to start with the founder, CEO, co-founder, software developers, token economist, business development, marketing, etc.

   b) If the project has a unique product use case, confirm that specialized professionals—such as cryptographic security experts, AI specialists, or data privacy consultants—are part of the team to address its specific needs.

3) **Take Notes and Document Your Findings in Your Own Style**

4) **Combine the Findings with Other Sections of the Fundamental Evaluation Process**

Evaluating the Results

Suppose the project lacks essential team professions that are not visible through the company's profile page on LinkedIn. In that case, proceeding cautiously while contacting the team for clarity is advised. Note these members are highly critical to the project's success, and without them, one or more aspects of the project will suffer depending on what profession the team is lacking.

Background and Experience

Evaluation Objective: Evaluate the legitimacy, background, and experience of the crypto team, ensuring they are qualified and capable of contributing to the project's success.

The project team, more specifically their background, experience, reputation, and skills, is another critical aspect that can make or break a project. As previously discussed, the team is responsible for bringing the project to life, developing the vision, product, or service, and executing the overall strategy. However, even if the essential professions are secured, without each member possessing adequate experience to efficiently perform the tasks at hand, it will harm project performance. Although it is not 100% essential, it is highly admirable if the team members have experience in the blockchain sector, including having worked on past successful projects. Such expertise allows them to refine their skill sets, learn from past mistakes, and gain valuable insights from both their own work and collaboration with other blockchain professionals.

Another critical reason to dig deep into the team's history is to help avoid fraudulent projects and scams. For example, in 2018, an Initial Coin Offering (ICO) was held for a project named Pincoin, where $660 million was raised from approximately 32,000 investors. Soon after, the team disappeared with the money. Another crypto company named LoopX vanished with $4.5 million raised through an ICO and then deleted its entire online presence, leaving investors at a loss.

Fact A well-rounded project team should include a healthy mix of professionals with solid backgrounds in blockchain, software engineering, finance, token and tokenomics design, marketing, and legal.

Evaluate a Team Background and Experience

The primary place to analyze a project team is through LinkedIn. It is highly unusual if the crypto project does not have a LinkedIn page with team members—if this occurs, consider it a red flag. The following procedure outlines the criteria to evaluate the various project team members. Kindly note that the number of team members will vary depending on the project's popularity. For example, while a new startup may only have ten to twenty members, well-known projects such as Ethereum have over a couple hundred members. With that said, it is not necessary to evaluate all members but rather focus on the prominent roles outlined in Table 10-1. Analyzing eight to ten profiles will provide a good overview of the team members' quality, experience, and legitimacy.

1) **LinkedIn Company Page**

   Look for links to the team's LinkedIn company page on the project's website or search LinkedIn under "Companies" to find it.

2) **Filter by Role**

   a) On LinkedIn, filter by "People" on the company page. Then, search for specific roles (e.g., CEO and developers) to see the respective team member profiles.

b) It is advised to start with the Founder, CEO, co-founder, software developers, token economist, business development, marketing, etc.

3) **Review Team Member Profiles**

Evaluate each team member's profile based on the following LinkedIn-specific criteria.

a) **Profile Picture** - Ensure the individual has a profile picture. Perform a "reverse image search" of the image on Google Images to help remove the possibility of a scam.

b) **Followers and Connections** - Does the individual have followers and connections? It is admirable to see 1000+ followers and 500+ connections.

c) **About Section** - This provides a personal summary of the individual's work experience and achievements.

i) Does anything stand out with respect to blockchain technology or being part of past crypto projects?

ii) Any significant achievements?

d) **Activity** - This section simply shows the individual's activity regarding posting, sharing, and interacting with other posts.

i) Has there been adequate activity in recent days, weeks, and months (this helps prove profile legitimacy and credibility).

ii) Has there been interaction on the posts? If so, are the people commenting on legitimate profiles?

e) **Experience**

i) What companies have they worked for before?

ii) How long have they worked there?

iii) Are the previous companies they worked for well-known?

iv) Do the companies have company pages on LinkedIn? If so, do they look legitimate?

v) Did the individual ever own or cofound previous crypto- or financial-based companies? If so, were they successful?

vi) What tasks and responsibilities did the individual have in previous positions?

vii) Do the skills and expertise gained in previous employment complement the current project and position?

viii) Have they been progressing since the beginning of their career?

f) **Education** – This section lists the individual's entire education history. While a full blockchain-related history is admirable, it isn't essential. This applies to various professionals, including web developers, marketing experts, and legal and financial advisors.

i) Has the individual adequate education related to their current or past positions?

ii) Have there been recent courses that the professional has taken to keep up with technology advancements?

iii) Are the professional degrees, masters, and PhDs from accredited institutions and colleges?

g) **Licenses and Certifications** - Any professional licenses and certifications are listed in this section.

   i) Has the individual any professional certifications that complement the project requirements?

   ii) Are the licenses and certifications recent and still valid?

   iii) Are the licenses and certifications accredited?

h) **Skills** - In this profile section, the individual lists their skills.

   i) Evaluate the skills listed, paying the most attention to the skills endorsed by other professionals.

   ii) Do the endorsed skills align with the blockchain project's skills and expertise?

i) **Recommendations** - Here, you'll find endorsements from other professionals, usually people who have worked with the person. Since anyone can give a recommendation, it's a good idea to do a few quick checks:

   i) Check the validity of any "recommendations" by viewing the profile of the individual of the person who made the recommendation.

   ii) Check both work histories to determine if they actually worked together.

j) **Publications** - In this section, any publications are listed.

   i) Check the validity of any publications by clicking on the publication link.

   ii) Are the publication(s) directly related to the professional's position on the project?

Pro Tip Visit the LinkedIn company pages for which the individual previously worked. Visit the profiles of their current employees to ensure legitimacy. Ensure these employees have filled out LinkedIn profiles that can be verified and show their previous employment with legitimate companies.

Action Steps

Follow these steps to evaluate the crypto team's legitimacy, background, and experience, ensuring they are qualified and capable of contributing to the project's success.

1) **Project Teams' Experience and Background Through LinkedIn**

   Evaluate the project team's legitimacy, background, experience, and achievements as outlined in this section.

2) **Verification Through Other Sources**

   Search various sources online for information on the team and their experience, achievements, etc. Check for articles on CoinDesk, The Defiant, Pomp, CoinTelegraph, Decrypt, CryptoSlate, and also social media sites such as X and YouTube.

3) **Take Notes and Document Your Findings in Your Own Style**

4) **Combine the Findings with Other Sections of the Fundamental Evaluation Process**

Evaluation of the Results

It is imperative that the crypto project has a company page on LinkedIn with team members that are legitimate and fully verifiable. If you cannot confirm this, consider it a red flag. At a minimum, the team members—at least the core team members—should have experience in the blockchain or financial world that can help build confidence that helps build confidence in the project's potential for success.

Developer Team Size

Evaluation Objective: Determine the number of developers on a project team to ensure the project has enough talent to build, improve, and scale its product while staying competitive.

Developers are considered one of the core essential building blocks that form the foundation of any blockchain-based project. Without an active developer base, most projects stall and risk stagnation—though a few meme coins or forked chains do persist with minimal ongoing work. The developer's responsibilities range from the development of blockchain infrastructure, decentralized applications (dApps), smart contracts, integration of software applications via APIs, finding and eliminating bugs, product testing, implementation of continuous updates, and much more.

A good-sized developer team is a significant asset for any project. With enough developers, work can be divided efficiently, allowing each developer to focus on their specialties, such as building the blockchain infrastructure, smart contracts, decentralized applications, stress testing, and tackling various technical challenges. Larger teams can also scale with the project, move faster, and prevent burnout by distributing workloads evenly.

In most cases, projects will consist of several core team developers with a higher number of open-source developers from the community that contribute to the project—software such as GitHub is typically used for collaboration. For example, at the time of writing, Polkadot Network lists roughly thirty core developers—an approximate count you can see on LinkedIn, but the more reliable gauge is their GitHub, which shows 409 open-source contributors. For a popular project like Polkadot, this size of the developer team is standard; however, this is not the same for every project.

Crypto projects deviate in team size, including the number of developers, for many reasons, such as the type of project (e.g., dApp or infrastructure), project phase, project budget, level of complexity, and external factors such as market conditions and demand for labor. New-start projects will have significantly fewer developers on the core team and open-source contributors, while popular, successful projects attract more attention among the developer community throughout the space, securing more core teams and open-source developers.

Given all these variables, it is difficult for investors to precisely predict how many developers a project should have. As a general rule of thumb, seeing at least ten developers on the core team is admirable. The number of open-source developers will vary wildly based on how popular the project is; therefore, it is recommended to evaluate direct competitors for accurate insight.

Founded Year

When analyzing the number of developers on a project's core team, it is beneficial to take the founding year into account. For example, suppose a project was launched just a few months ago. In that case, it is reasonable to expect a smaller team, as they are still likely to build momentum and attract new members to the community. However, it is considered a red flag for a project that has been around for a while, e.g., over a year, and still only has a handful of developers. This may indicate that they have a poor product or service, are struggling with funding, have poor community interest, or a combination. Considering the founding year, investors can better judge whether the team size makes sense for its growth stage and what that might mean for its long-term potential.

Action Steps

Follow these steps to determine the number of developers on a project team to ensure the project has enough talent to build, improve, and scale its product while staying competitive.

1) **Determine the Number of Developers on the Project Team**

    a) Visit the project website to find a link to its LinkedIn company page, usually provided under the "Team" or "About" section. If unavailable, search for the project on LinkedIn using the "Companies" filter in the search bar.

    b) Filter by "People."

    c) **Filter per Professional Profession** - Filter by developers' roles (e.g., search for "Developer," "Software Engineer," "Blockchain Engineer," etc.) in the LinkedIn search bar. This will show the number of developers working on the project team.

    d) **Check GitHub Contributors** - Open the project's main GitHub repository and look at the "Contributors" block on the right-hand panel; the figure shown is the total number of individuals who have submitted code, offering a quick gauge of the wider developer community around the project.

2) **Competitor Analysis**

   Compare the number of developers from the core team to that of competitors.

3) **Founded Year**

   Find the crypto company's founding year by visiting its LinkedIn page, navigating to the "About" section, and checking the "Founded" subheading at the bottom. Refer to the section "Founding Year" in Chapter 4, "Core Offering," for more details on the Founding Year.

4) **Take Notes and Document Your Findings in Your Own Style**

5) **Combine the Findings with Other Sections of the Fundamental Evaluation Process**

Evaluating the Results

If the project has been around for over a year and still only has fewer than ten developers, this indicates a lack of growth and success and a potential red flag. It is typical for newer projects—founded only a few months ago—to have 5-10 core developers. However, north of twenty is admirable, as it shows strong activity and popularity.

Project Support

Evaluation Objective: Determine the level of support the team offers to its users, developers, and the broader community.

The provision of adequate project support is critical to every crypto project. Ideally, the core team—or, in more decentralized projects, a well-organized community of contributors—should provide clear resources that help users, developers, and newcomers understand the product, its risks, and the technology it is built on. Projects can struggle to gain traction without adequate support from the team, and it is considered an early warning sign of limited scalability and a lack of long-term commitment from the team.

To help determine if a project team provides a good level of project support, evaluate using the below criteria. The answers to these questions are generally found through the project website, with links to their technical documentation, whitepapers, developer portals, social channels, and other resources such as the project blog. If there is an apparent lack of such information, consider it a red flag and contact the project team for assistance and clarification.

1) **Accessible User Education**

   a) Is there sufficient information available, such as guides, tutorials, and FAQs, for users to quickly understand how to operate the product or service?

   b) Are detailed instructions for node setup, validator participation, or similar technical tasks provided?

   c) Has the team provided technical and non-technical project-related material, including blockchain operation, security, recent developments, staking, farming, mining, node setup, etc.?

2) **Developer Support and Resources**

   a) Does the project offer tools like APIs (application programming interfaces), SDKs (software development kits), other toolkits, libraries, and corresponding technical documentation?

   b) Are there active forums or communication channels where developers can ask for help?

3) **Customer Support Channels**

    a) Is it easy to contact the project team?

    b) Has the team been responsive on platforms such as X, Discord, Telegram, YouTube, or through email? Are there any unanswered questions or concerns?

    c) Analyze community reviews and overall sentiment through the project's social media channels.

4) **Community Engagement**

    a) Check if the team has conducted AMAs (Ask Me Anything sessions). These are particularly helpful at the beginning of the project lifecycle.

    b) Has the team been actively posting on social media?

    c) Has the team been transparent and open regarding technological updates, partnerships, internal and external challenges, other issues, or concerns?

Action Steps

Follow these steps to assess the team's level of support to its users, developers, and the broader community.

1) **Determine the Level of Project Support**

    Using the analysis criteria outlined in this section, evaluate the team's support level to its users, developers, and broader community.

2) **Take Notes and Document Your Findings in Your Own Style**

3) **Combine the Findings with Other Sections of the Fundamental Evaluation Process**

Evaluation of the Results

Consider it a red flag if the project's team does not provide adequate support, such as having no clear resources, poor communication with the community and developer base, or an overall lack of transparency.

Team Interviews

Evaluation Objective: Determine if the project team holds AMAs and if they capture and satisfy community queries and concerns.

Team interviews are vital, as they can help investors and the broader community gain a deeper understanding of the team members, their experience, technical abilities, expertise, professionalism, vision, and how they plan to succeed in a very competitive market. They provide an excellent opportunity for the team to prove their commitment and transparency, which are key success factors in the world of blockchain. Team interviews also help the team build credibility and trust with investors, who are often met with skepticism due to previous instances of scams or frauds. Therefore, team interviews are much more than simple questions and answers; they provide an opportunity to demonstrate accountability and build a strong foundation for a trustful relationship with investors and the broader community.

Ask Me Anything "AMA"

Team interviews are organized events usually hosted on various social media platforms. The attending parties are the team (management and/or developers), the interviewer—the channel moderator—stakeholders, open-source collaborators, and the community members. These interview events are known as **AMAs** (Ask Me Anything). AMA is the term given to a question-and-answers-type interview format that originated on Reddit and is now used within the blockchain world.

Fact AMA events are often hosted pre-launch and around the token-generation event (TGE), especially for marketing-first projects. Build-first teams typically begin holding AMAs later, once a user base has formed, and may continue them periodically to keep the community engaged and informed.

AMAs are typically hosted on social platforms such as Telegram, Discord, and YouTube and are often posted on the project's official blog page or preferred social outlet afterward. AMA invitations are posted on the project's social media pages and usually are well-advertised. During the interview, typical topics and updates related to the core product and value proposition, ongoing development, new features, the roadmap, and partnerships are discussed. Furthermore, AMAs are used to address major concerns or issues surrounding the company, such as a cyberattack, change in management, or regulatory matters. At the end of an AMA, the community is provided the opportunity to ask the team questions with a chance to win a reward for participating.

Action Steps

Follow these steps to determine if the project team holds AMAs and if they capture and satisfy community queries and concerns.

1) **Locate AMA Events**

   Search the project's social media outlets, such as Telegram, X, Medium, and YouTube, for indications of past or present AMAs.

2) **Evaluate AMA Events**

   When participating in or reviewing past AMAs, evaluate the team in the following areas:

a) **Transparency** - Does it seem like the team is completely transparent about the project's current status, future plans, and any challenges they face?

b) **Responsiveness** - How is the team responding to tough and critical questions? Avoiding such critical questions may raise red flags for investors.

c) **Credibility** - Has the team demonstrated adequate credibility in the form of the team's background, including blockchain-related experience and accomplishments?

d) **Vision and Strategy** - Are the team enthusiastic about the long-term vision and goals for the project?

3) **AMA Frequency**

It is considered good practice for a project team to participate in AMAs on a regular basis.

Research how often the team has hosted or taken part in AMA sessions:

a) **Pre-Official Launch** - Some projects schedule bi-weekly AMAs to build community, demonstrate transparency, generate excitement, and clarify the project's roadmap and vision.

b) **Post-Official Launch** - After the product is live and the project is in a stable phase of operation, AMAs are commonly held quarterly or semi-annually to provide updates and address community and investor concerns.

c) **Testnet/Builder Phase** – Builder-first teams often start AMAs when a public testnet or beta goes live, hosting them monthly to answer technical questions and gather feedback before mainnet.

4) **Take Notes and Document Your Findings in Your Own Style**

5) **Combine the Findings with Other Sections of the Fundamental Evaluation Process**

Evaluation of the Results

If the AMA results show strong transparency, responsiveness, and enthusiasm, this tells the investor that the team is committed and builds trust in the project. Poor results, such as vague answers or lack of engagement, indicate potential issues within the project. Too many AMAs without substance can signal noise, while too few suggest disengagement.

If the AMA results show transparency, responsiveness, and enthusiasm, it's a good sign they're committed and trustworthy. On the other hand, vague answers or lack of engagement could point to problems. Also, take note if the AMAs are too frequent, as constant updates might just be noise, while too few can suggest the team isn't fully engaged.

CHAPTER 11

Project Roadmap

A roadmap is a visual representation of a strategic plan. It outlines and defines the plans, goals, and core deliverables, such as the critical milestones that need to be executed to reach a predefined outcome. Think of a roadmap as an efficient and easy-to-understand communication tool that ties together the strategy and includes timelines for all important milestones that align with the corresponding schedule. Moreover, it serves as a guide for the development team, stakeholders, and potential investors, providing them with a clear understanding of the project's direction and progress.

The roadmap presents the project team's vision, serving as a tool to drive conversations and communicate the vision to potential partners, early-stage investors, and public investors. Similar to a project schedule, it is also great for prioritizing critical deliverables, allocating resources, identifying bottlenecks, and tracking vital deadlines. A roadmap is not a static document but instead rather dynamic in nature. Furthermore, it should be flexible enough to accommodate ever-changing market conditions, feature upgrades, milestone completion updates, user demands, and technological innovations. Project roadmaps are typically found through the official project channels such as the company website, whitepaper, social media, and blog.

P. Garvey, *Blockchain Fundamental Analysis for Digital Asset Investors*,
https://doi.org/10.1007/979-8-8688-1551-5_11

Evaluating a project's roadmap is essential for crypto investors, as it indicates whether the team has a solid vision, a clear plan, realistic goals, and the ability to deliver. Roadmaps are not just about timelines; the primary purpose is holding the team accountable to their promises. They allow investors to analyze the project's vision, goals, and objectives and identify potential red flags, like missed milestones or vague promises.

There are many different types of roadmaps in the blockchain world, which will be discussed later in this chapter. Figure 11-1 is an example of a blockchain developer roadmap. This roadmap was created by *https://roadmap.sh/blockchain* as a guide for developers to help identify and navigate the various development regions within the blockchain realm.

Fundamentals Discussed in This Chapter:

- Roadmaps Benefits
- Core Elements of a Blockchain Roadmap
- Roadmap Types
- Evaluating Crypto Roadmaps

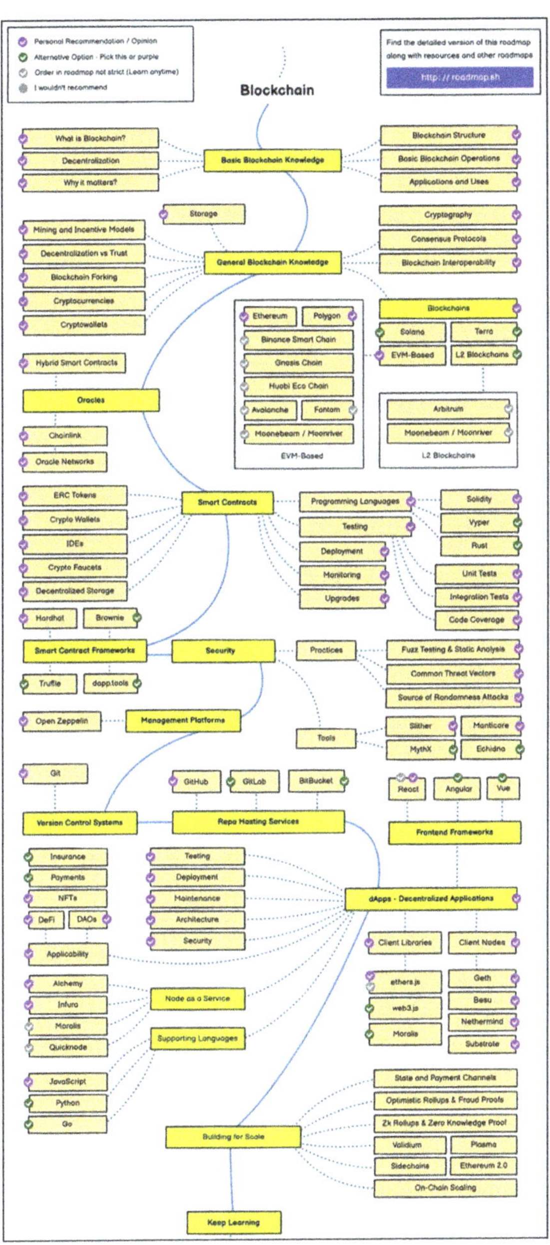

Figure 11-1. *Roadmap to become a blockchain developer (compliments of* `https://roadmap.sh/blockchain`*)*

Roadmap Benefits

There are many benefits associated with a clear and well-structured roadmap. The following are the primary benefits roadmaps offer.

- **Clarity and Direction** – A roadmap outlines the project's vision, goals, and planned milestones that help the project team stay focused and aligned with the project's objectives.
- **Stakeholder Alignment** – A roadmap ensures that all stakeholders, including the project team, core and open-source developers, investors, and community members, are on the same page.
- **Progress Tracking** – A roadmap effectively allows the project team and stakeholders to monitor milestones, track progress, and maintain accountability.
- **Transparency and Trust** – Sharing a detailed and well-structured roadmap shows the public that the project team is serious, has a clear path forward, and is committed to successfully executing their goals and objectives.
- **Investor Confidence** – Investors are more likely to invest in projects with a detailed roadmap that clearly outlines the project's vision, goals, and milestones. This adds credibility and makes the project more appealing to both long- and short-term investors.
- **Community Engagement** – A robust roadmap significantly ignites the community, encouraging them to get involved and engage in upcoming planned events.

Core Elements of a Blockchain Roadmap

In this section, the key elements of a crypto roadmap are broken down, such as the project's goals, vision, and major milestones.

Goals and Objectives

The goals and objectives outlined in a crypto project roadmap help convey the team's actionable steps to be accomplished in order to advance toward the overall project vision. Depending on the type of project and its core value proposition, these goals and objectives can cover a wide range of sectors, including decentralized finance (DeFi), infrastructure, non-fungible assets (NFTs), gaming, Internet-of-Things (IoT), etc. Regardless of the sector, the goals and objectives highlight the project scope regarding various aspects such as technical development, feature implementation, infrastructure upgrades, token distribution, and community engagement. They also help align stakeholders by providing a high-level overview of where the project is headed. Additionally, goals and objectives serve as an excellent way of measuring the team's progress, where each task, goal, milestone, and objective is verifiable by the investor.

SMART Objectives

SMART objectives help the project team and stakeholders set clear, actionable goals that are specific, measurable, achievable, relevant, and time-bound. They keep the project moving forward, help with accountability and timing, and allow the team and stakeholders to easily identify if the objectives are being accomplished. The specified objectives should be aligned with the team's vision and communicated to all stakeholders, including investors, developers, and all network participants. For investors, analyzing the project objectives under the SMART objective framework helps break down the project goals and objectives into clear, realistic steps, making it easier to track progress, spot any red flags, and see if the project is genuinely delivering on its promise.

- **Specific** - Details exactly what the project is trying to achieve. These objectives are clearly written so anyone reading them can understand how they will be executed and who is responsible.
- **Measurable** - Objective includes how the action will be measured, e.g., this could involve numbers, percentages, or other quantifiable metrics. Measuring objectives helps the team and stakeholders determine if progress is being made; thus, it is essential for keeping the project on track and on schedule.
- **Achievable** - Objectives should be realistic and feasible given the internal and external factors. Setting reasonable objectives helps set the project up for success.
- **Relevant** - A relevant objective makes sense if it aligns with the vision and purpose of the project. Objectives should be set for questions such as, "Why are we doing this? And is it actually required?."
- **Time-bound** - Every objective has a specific timeline for completion.

Vision and Purpose

A vision can be described as an aspirational description of what an organization would like to achieve or accomplish in the future. It is intended to serve as a clear guide for choosing current and future courses of action. In the context of a blockchain project, the roadmap captures the team's vision in a high-level overview of the project's long-term desired goals, objectives, unique value proposition, and purpose, which describes the underlying reason for the product offering. It is essential that every project generates and delivers a long-term vision for several reasons, including:

- **Clear Direction** - A clear vision is a guiding star for the project, team, and all stakeholders. It creates a clear direction and focus that keeps all stakeholders aligned toward a common goal.
- **Motivation** - A powerful long-term vision motivates and inspires stakeholders to stay focused while working and supporting each other on their journey.
- **Investor Engagement** - A powerful vision using well-planned goals and objectives helps attract and engage investors and community members.
- **Brand and Identity** - A vision helps the team build out the project's brand and identity, further displaying the true worth of the value offering.

As discussed, a roadmap does not specifically describe the vision of the project word for word. Instead, the vision is conveyed through the project's goals, objectives, value proposition, and core purpose. However, it is critical to validate the vision to ensure the team keeps to their original commitments. Although a whitepaper is primarily technical, many projects still open with a brief section that states the project's vision.

Project Milestone

A milestone is a specific point within a project's life cycle that marks significant progress toward its ultimate goal. These milestones represent critical stages or events, helping teams break down large, complex projects into smaller, manageable phases that can be efficiently tracked and managed. Milestones are also used as a benchmark for payment release based on completed work. Additionally, they are critical to project planning and can contribute to the success of a project in several ways, including

- **Budget Control** – Milestones help prevent projects from going over budget by acting as effective scheduling tools.
- **Project Delivery** – Breaking down large projects into smaller, manageable phases ensures smoother and more predictable delivery.
- **Accurate Timelines** – By marking important milestones, dates, and events, the project team can gauge and provide more accurate timelines with overall enhanced project planning and scheduling.
- **Team Motivation** – Well-defined milestones provide a sense of accomplishment that motivates the team and adds structure to the project's execution.
- **Clear Direction** – Milestones provide clear direction for the team and stakeholders.
- **Resource Management** – By tracking progress through milestones, project managers can allocate resources where they're needed most.
- **Risk Management** – Milestones help identify potential risks early, allowing teams to address them before they escalate.

- **Marketing Impact** - Milestones are a fantastic way to connect and engage with the community.
- **Stakeholder Confidence** - Milestones help align all stakeholders, including investors, partners, and network participants, to help them gauge the project's progress, health, and achievements. This helps instill confidence in the project and the team.

Within the crypto realm, milestones are typically specified on the project roadmap. Similar to goals and milestones, project milestones may include significant development goals, whitepaper release, prototype and beta release, testing phases, token sales, mainnet launch, token launch, regulatory compliance, partnerships, and various continuous feature upgrades and infrastructure improvements.

Fact While it may be somewhat subjective if "milestones" are not clearly labeled in the roadmap, it is common for investors to identify specific goals or achievements highlighted by the team as project milestones.

It is important to note that milestone dates are not always identified on the roadmap or any other related documentation. This may be due to the industry's dynamic nature, which is highly volatile and unpredictable, thus affecting the workforce. Although blockchain technology has been evident since January 3, 2009 (bitcoin's genesis block), it still faces a lot of scrutiny and kickback from regulatory commissions such as the SEC, which in turn has damaging effects on the market, resulting in frustration, negativity, and unwanted bad press. Furthermore, the fact that many projects are open-source introduces a unique challenge when estimating project milestone timelines. Open-source projects allow for worldwide collaboration with varying time zones combined with varying levels of expertise, commitment, and availability. As a result, while many open-source projects maintain disciplined roadmaps, varied time zones and volunteer availability can still cause shifting timelines, so milestone dates are inherently harder to predict.

Feasibility of Deliverables

Promising and delivering milestones are two very different things. It is a relatively easy task to schedule and announce attractive milestones that grab the attention of various stakeholders. However, successfully completing them within specified timeframes is a far more challenging task.

Several factors must be considered when evaluating the feasibility of milestones for a particular project. After assessing these factors, investors should better understand the feasibility level of a project's specified milestones. Additionally, it is important to revisit these assessments periodically because as conditions change, new information or technologies might emerge that can impact a project's milestone feasibility and associated deadlines. There are five key areas to consider when evaluating milestone feasibility in the crypto space; they are as follows:

1) **Technical Complexity**

   a) Do the milestones require advanced technology or cryptographic techniques that have not been seen yet? If so, what edge does the team have to accomplish milestones?

   b) Are the required platform's technological tools available to execute the proposed milestones successfully?

2) **Infrastructure Requirements**

    a) Does the team have adequate testing environments, such as testnets or server setups to help facilitate the ongoing development and milestone accomplishment?

    b) Is the team familiar with and experienced with these infrastructures and testing environments?

3) **Resource Availability**

    a) Does the team have access to the necessary developers or experts with specific skills to execute the known milestones?

    b) Are there sufficient funds to support the development to start and complete each milestone?

4) **Timeline**

    a) Do the set milestones, dates, and timeframes look realistic based on known constraints, challenges, and performance to date?

    b) Have the team backup plans for unexpected delays or challenges?

5) **Performance**

    a) Do future milestones look achievable based on past milestone execution performance?

    b) Is there visible proof of previously completed milestones?

    c) Is there a proven track record of successfully completing milestones spanning a few years?

d) Have there been milestones that the team failed to achieve in the past? Look out for noticeable gaps or delays in the schedule.

e) If past milestones were not completed or not completed on time, was this because of internal or external factors?

Roadmap Types

Many different categories of roadmaps cater to and address specific requirements within the blockchain realm. For instance, an investor roadmap provides a high-level overview of the project's vision, key milestones, and timelines to attract and align investors. In contrast, a developer's roadmap is more relevant to developers as a guide designed to educate and lead them through various skill levels, tools, frameworks, and practices required to become proficient in crypto-related development. Roadmaps that are internal to the team may include regulatory compliance, user adoption strategies, and brand building. For investors, the most common types and relevant roadmaps to focus on are the *investor roadmap* and product *development roadmap.*

Investor Roadmap

Investor roadmaps are one of the most widely used formats—especially around token sales and fundraising rounds. Catered explicitly toward investors, the investor roadmap provides a high-level overview of the project's vision, key milestones, goals and objectives, feature releases, and timelines. The roadmap aims to impress and sway investors by showcasing the projects' specifically designed strategic plan.

Sandbox Roadmap

Sandbox is a decentralized virtual gaming world built on blockchain technology. It allows players to buy, sell, and create digital assets, and it consists of lands represented as non-fungible tokens (NFTs) on the Ethereum blockchain. Originally launched as a 2D mobile game in 2011 by Pixowl, Sandbox was relaunched in 2019 under Animoca Brands, which then began to utilize and implement blockchain technology to elevate the gaming experience to a new level.

Figure 11-2 shows the Sandbox investor roadmap. The roadmap provides investors with an overview of the major deliverables with corresponding timelines, such as LAND sales, gaming platforms, and multiplayer features. It also outlines other key elements, such as new partnership announcements, DAO participation, and various future events.

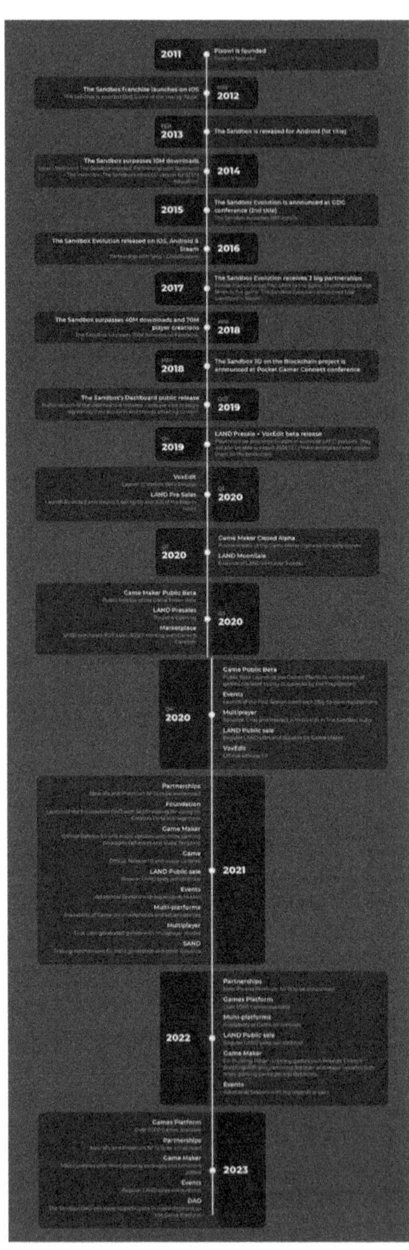

Figure 11-2. *Sandbox (compliments of `https://icodrops.com/the-sandbox/`)*

Factors to Consider

Investors use an investor roadmap—such as Sandbox—to help evaluate the project's progress to date by analyzing what has been achieved to date per the roadmap. If the team has already accomplished significant milestones as promised, there is a high possibility that future objectives, milestones, and innovative feature sets will be executed as promised. This further contributes to the level of professionalism, transparency, trust, and reputation of the project and its associated team members.

Investors need to evaluate the team's planned major deliverables and their respective timelines to ensure that these events align with their investment strategy. For instance, a long-term investment strategy could involve buying an asset that is significantly undervalued, holding that asset, and selling for a profit when major milestones are executed two or three years later. However, this may be unacceptable for short-term holders who may not hold assets for longer than six months and prioritize roadmaps with milestones achievable within their shorter timeframe. This is because short-term strategies focus on quick returns by leveraging near-term developments, such as product launches or partnerships, that can trigger price surges. These investors aim to exit at the peak of market anticipation or immediately after a milestone to maximize gains.

Product Development Roadmap

The product development roadmap focuses on the technical development of the product or service, including the core deliverables outlining the feature set, architecture, and infrastructure-related development. Although the investor roadmap also includes stages, milestones, and deliverables for the product, the product development roadmap primarily focuses on and details the core deliverables of architectural development, upgrades, and enhancements to achieve a particular outcome, such as true decentralization, on-chain governance, or completion of a significant innovative feature.

A product development roadmap is not just used to excite stakeholders; it is often used internally by the team to set goals and coordinate tasks. However, not all deliverables within these roadmaps have designated timelines due to the complexity, open-source nature, and dynamic internal and external factors that can influence the project.

Ethereum's Product Development Roadmap

Figure 11-3 shows Ethereum's product development roadmap. This detailed technical roadmap identifies specific improvements and upgrades. It breaks down into six crucial stages the blockchain makes toward its complete transition from proof-of-work (PoW) to proof-of-stake (PoS) consensus algorithm.

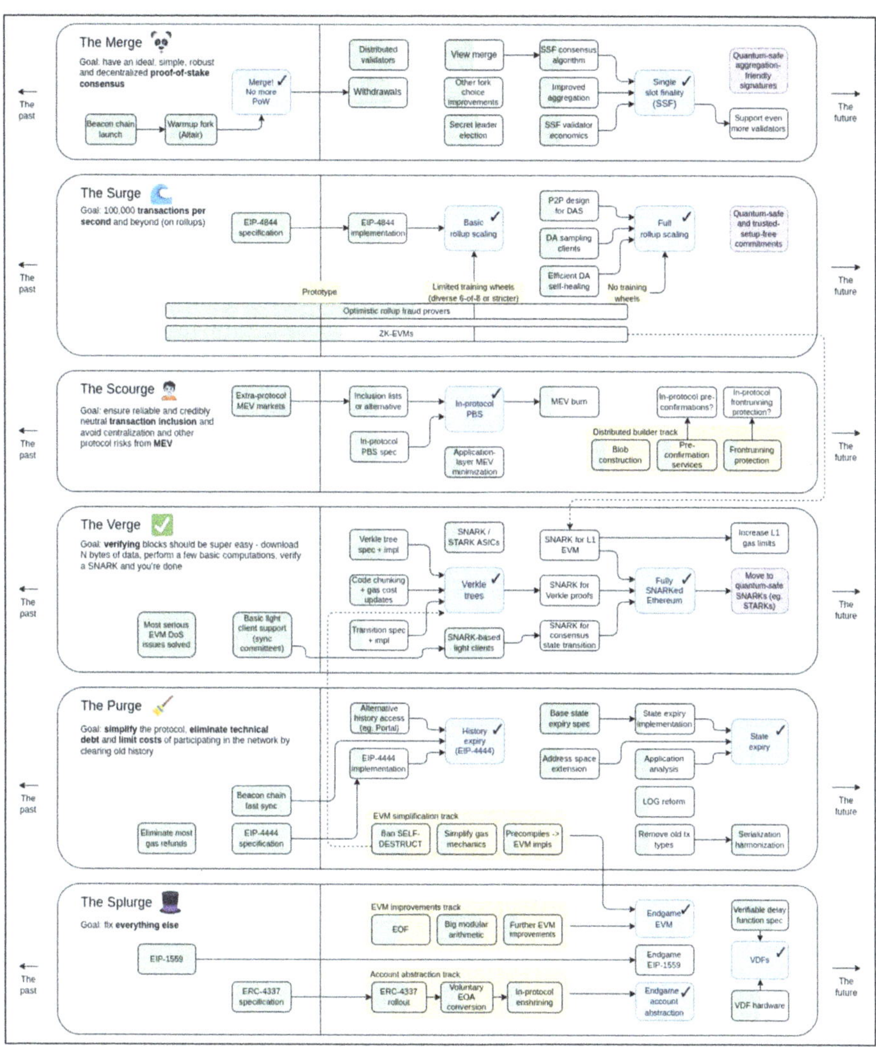

***Figure 11-3.** Ethereum's roadmap containing details (compliments of `https://x.com/VitalikButerin/status/1588669782471368704`)*

Table 11-1 summarizes Ethereum's roadmap in a "non-developer" easy-to-understand approach, including the goals of each corresponding stage.

Table 11-1. *Ethereum's roadmap from PoW to PoS (compliments of https://ethereum.org/en/roadmap/#what-changes-are-coming)*

Ethereum's Product Development Roadmap				
Stage Number	**Stage Name**	**Task**	**Goal**	**Status**
1	The Merge	Upgrades relating to the switch from proof-of-work (PoW) to proof-of-stake (PoS).	Secure PoS consensus by combining the mainnet with the Consensus Layer's Beacon Chain.	Complete
2	The Surge	Upgrades related to scalability by rollups and data sharding.	Rollup-centric scaling to 100,000 + TPS.	In progress
3	The Scourge	Upgrades related to censorship resistance, decentralization, and protocol risks from Maximal Extractable Value (MEV).	Avoid centralization and other protocol risks from MEV.	In progress
4	The Verge	Upgrades related to verifying blocks more quickly.	Easier and more efficient verification of blocks.	In progress
5	The Purge	Upgrades related to reducing the computational and storage costs of running nodes (e.g., state-expiry for old historical data) and simplifying the protocol.	Simplify the protocol and reduce the costs of running network nodes.	In progress
6	The Splurge	Other upgrades that don't fit well into the previous categories.	Fixing of miscellaneous outstanding items.	In progress

---

Pro Tip When a complex roadmap is encountered, it is recommended to break it down in simple terms that make sense to you. Seek help from the community team members if clarification or explanation is required.

Ethereum is a complex and evolving system with many stakeholders, such as developers, researchers, users, and validators. Therefore, providing accurate timelines for each feature or upgrade on the roadmap is challenging. Additionally, elements such as developing, testing, auditing, coordination, consensus, and feedback are primarily managed in an open-source manner, with many participants contributing their time when available. At the time of writing, although several long-term milestones are still ahead, Ethereum has accomplished many major upgrades over the past decade and continues to ship new improvements—although, with a project such as Ethereum, there will always be continuous improvements. For real-time updates on Ethereum's roadmap, check out—`https://ethroadmap.com/`.

Furthermore, Ethereum's roadmap is not a fixed plan, as with many other open-source projects. It is flexible and subject to changes pending new challenges, opportunities, and demands of the network and its users. This construct is designed to support continual innovation while placing a particular emphasis on strengthening the network's security.

Factors to Consider

Several factors contribute to the value of a blockchain project, including the value proposition, token design, tokenomics, programming languages, architecture, project team, and community spirit. Yet these fundamentals carry far less weight if the project's core technical deliverables aren't executed accurately, transparently, and in line with stated goals. Failure to realize these key technical components can negatively impact the core functionality and utility of the product, diminishing the team's reputation and the project's overall long-term success and sustainability. Therefore, investors must allow adequate time to properly understand and evaluate the project's progress to date and future technical deliverables as outlined on the roadmap.

Although unnecessary, some investors align their interest and technical knowledge with their choice of investment category to help reduce risk. For example, infrastructure projects such as Ethereum, Polkadot, Moonbeam, etc., may grab the attention of some investors. In contrast, others may be more knowledgeable in gaming projects like The Sandbox or Axie Infinity. However, this often restricts it to one type of investment category within the crypto world, which may not suit many investors and may miss out on other potential investments. Building the skills and knowledge to evaluate a broad spectrum of projects in the space is more admirable.

Product roadmaps are also used as an excellent comparison tool for competitor analysis. Compare and contrast a roadmap with that of a strong, successful competitor to help identify flaws and benefits that could add to the project's success or contribute to its failure. Some may include:

- What are their unique selling points (USPs), such as features or benefits that could attract a broader audience?
- How does their technology differ, and does it offer any advantages or weaknesses?
- Are their timelines realistic, or do they seem overly aggressive?
- How does their long-term vision compare in terms of sustainability and market trends?
- Are they in compliance with current regulatory requirements?

- Is there any visible lack of professionalism in their roadmap or execution?
- Is the roadmap regularly updated to reflect progress and changes?
- Does the roadmap provide enough detail for investors to truly understand the project's direction?

Evaluating Crypto Roadmaps

Specific roadmap evaluation criteria are used to evaluate real-life crypto project roadmaps. Evaluating crypto roadmaps might seem tricky with all the different types out there. However, in most cases, the same core evaluation criteria can be used across the board. Crucial elements such as clear goals, a strong vision, realistic milestones, and transparency all matter, no matter what kind of roadmap is being evaluated. By focusing on these key areas, investors can get a good feel of whether a project is on the right track or failing to meet their promises.

To begin, locate the project roadmap from the project being evaluated. As previously stated, credible sources where the project roadmap is typically found are the official project channels such as the company website, whitepaper, social media, and blog. It is important to note that a lot of projects update their roadmaps on a yearly basis; always check that you have the most recent and up-to-date one.

Goals and Objectives

Evaluation Objective: Determine if the project roadmap's goals and milestones are clear, realistic, measurable, and aligned with the project's vision.

In this section, the goals and objectives of the BNB Chain are evaluated with the aid of the SMART evaluation parameters. This process helps investors determine if the roadmap's goals and milestones are clearly defined, realistic, measurable, and aligned with the project's vision to ensure the team can execute successfully.

BNB Chain, shown in Figure 11-4, is an example of a product development roadmap. These goals include optimizing the performance, scalability, infrastructure, decentralization, and security of the BNB blockchain. While it is less graphically detailed than Ethereum's product development roadmap, it focuses on high-level deliverables like many other projects. Typically, these visual roadmaps are supplemented by in-depth discussions of each milestone. For BNB Chain, detailed explanations of each deliverable can be found on the official BNB Chain blog: `https://www.bnbchain.org/en/blog/bnb-chain-tech-roadmap-2023`.

The objectives to achieve each goal are written underneath each one of the project's goals. For example, to achieve the first goal, optimize performance, the objective is to increase blockchain speed, reliability, and finality. Again, read the BNB blog for a more detailed description of this goal and objective.

Pro Tip Never solely rely on the high-level overview outlined in the roadmap. Always delve into the documentation surrounding each core deliverable outlined by the team. This provides a clearer and more transparent understanding and may expose information not captured in the visual roadmap.

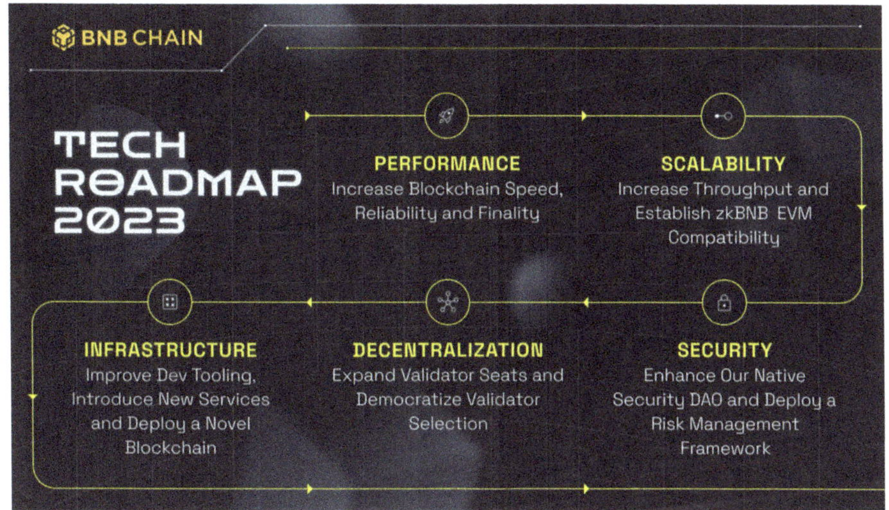

Figure 11-4. *BNB Chain Tech Roadmap 2023 (compliments of `https://www.bnbchain.org/en/blog/bnb-chain-tech-roadmap-2023/`)*

As previously discussed, SMART objectives are critical for the team during the design process and for investors as part of the overall fundamental evaluation. When evaluated against the SMART objectives, BNB Chains had positive results—a summary of the results is shown in Table 11-2.

Table 11-2. *SMART objective analysis of BNB chain (results taken from official roadmap and roadmap details compliments of* `https://www.bnbchain.org/en/blog/bnb-chain-tech-roadmap-2023/`*)*

BNB Chain—SMART Objective Evaluation	
Parameter's	**Findings**
Specific	Each objective, as outlined in the roadmap and detailed on the BNB Chain blog, is clear and understandable. For example, BNB Chain plans to improve scalability by collaborating with the Ethereum community to develop the most performant EVM-compatible client for BSC. Additionally, for added scalability, it plans to leverage emerging technologies, such as ZKP and optimistic rollups, plus modular extensions like opBNB (execution) and BNB Greenfield (data availability), both of which leverage the open-source OP-Stack Bedrock framework to deliver cheaper, scalable, and secure solutions for dApps.
Measurable	Yes, the objectives are measurable. The measurable unit differs from objective to objective. For instance, transactions per second (TPS) is one of the metrics used for measuring performance, while progressive decentralization can be tracked through several validator-related metrics—for example, the number of active validators, their geographic distribution, governance-participation rates, and consensus-layer uptime. Moreover, other objectives are measured as complete, incomplete, or in progress. These include objectives to optimize the BNB Chain infrastructure, such as multiple tools and features to enhance items such as wallet services, messaging and communicating, blockchain data and indexing queries, Web3 identity services, and various types of hybrid applications, including supply chain projects, governance voting, auditing, invoice forwarding, loyalty programs, and medical records.

Achievable	Based on previous goals and objectives set, executed, and completed by BNB Chain, the 2023 objectives working goals, such as enhanced scalability, infrastructure, decentralization, and security, are deemed within reach for the team. For example, see BNB Chain's completed objectives in 2022 below for reference. BNB Chain has proven itself as a quality blockchain infrastructure (although sometimes criticized for being too centralized). Nevertheless, the specified objectives do not seem out of reach for the company.

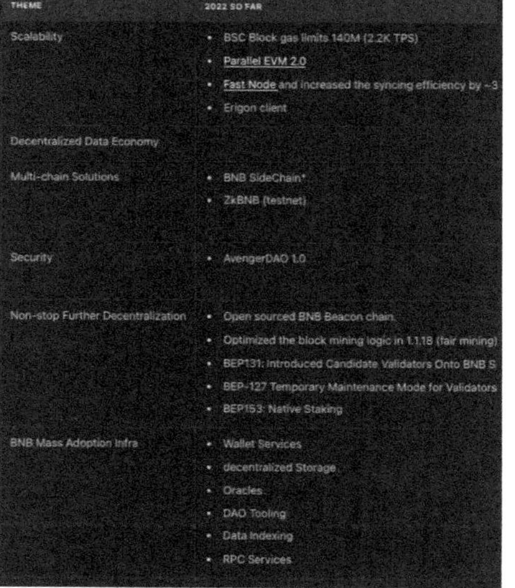

THEME	2022 SO FAR
Scalability	• BSC Block gas limits 140M (2.2K TPS) • Parallel EVM 2.0 • Fast Node and increased the syncing efficiency by ~3 • Erigon client
Decentralized Data Economy	
Multi-chain Solutions	• BNB SideChain* • ZkBNB (testnet)
Security	• AvengerDAO 1.0
Non-stop Further Decentralization	• Open sourced BNB Beacon chain • Optimized the block mining logic in 1.1.18 (fair mining) • BEP131: Introduced Candidate Validators Onto BNB S • BEP-127 Temporary Maintenance Mode for Validators • BEP153: Native Staking
BNB Mass Adoption Infra	• Wallet Services • decentralized Storage • Oracles • DAO Tooling • Data Indexing • RPC Services

(continued)

Table 11-2. (*continued*)

BNB Chain—SMART Objective Evaluation	
Parameter's	**Findings**
Relevant	The objectives are relevant. BNB Chain's vision is to build the infrastructure powering the world's parallel virtual ecosystem. To achieve this, the key elements are the specific goals outlined (*enhanced scalability, infrastructure, decentralization, and security*) on the BNB Chain 2023 roadmap. Thus, the objectives to achieve these goals are relevant and satisfy the company's purpose and vision.
Time-Bound	The essential objectives are time-bound but based on a yearly timeframe, not quarterly or monthly. Given the multi-deliverable roadmap, more granular, feature-by-feature dates are released later.

Action Steps

Follow these steps to assess whether the project roadmap's goals and milestones are clear, realistic, measurable, and aligned with the project's vision.

1) **Goals and Objectives**

   Using the roadmap, read and understand the project's goals and objectives.

2) **SMART Objective Evaluation**

   Using the SMART analysis tool, evaluate the project goals and objectives.

3) **Take Notes and Document Your Findings in Your Own Style**

4) **Combine the Findings with Other Sections of the Fundamental Evaluation Process**

Evaluation of the Results

Suppose the results from the SMART evaluation identify items with vague, unmeasurable, or irrelevant objectives, unrealistic expectations, poorly defined timelines, or somewhat unachievable timelines. In that case, it is advised not to proceed until deeper research is carried out. Depending on what aspect of the evaluation does not meet standard requirements, search for additional information through reliable sources and also reach out to the team if required. It is critical that the goals and objectives are worth the investment. Investing in a project with a poor trajectory is risky and should be avoided at all costs.

Vision and Purpose

Evaluation Objective: Assess whether the project has a clear vision and purpose that addresses real-world problems, aligns with their core objectives, and is deemed high value to the overall growth of the blockchain ecosystem.

This part of the evaluation helps investors determine whether the project has a clear vision and purpose that addresses real-world problems, aligns with their core objectives, and is deemed high value to the overall growth of the blockchain ecosystem.

This section uses Polygon Network as an example to illustrate how a project's vision and purpose are evaluated. Polygon, defined by Polygon as "*an off/side chain scaling solution for existing platforms to provide scalability and superior user experience to dApps/user functionalities.*" Polygon formerly known as Matic Network strives to solve scalability and usability issues while not compromising on decentralization and leveraging the existing developer community and ecosystem.

Polygon's Vision

Polygon's Technology's vision can be found in the project whitepaper. It specifically outlines the project's vision as follows:

> *"The vision behind Polygon as the Value Layer of the Internet is to usher a world in which value can be created and exchanged freely and globally, similarly to how we create and exchange information today. A world which enables new - fairer, more inclusive and more efficient - forms of human organizations and governance. We strongly believe that realizing this vision can significantly advance our society."*

Upon reviewing Polygon's vision, it's evident that the team is passionately pursuing certain goals, such as

1) *"Value can be created and exchanged freely and globally"*—key words here being ***freely*** and ***globally*** indicating the sending of digital assets without any restrictions and intermediaries.

2) *"A world which enables new—fairer, more inclusive and more efficient—forms of human organizations and governance"—the* key words here being, ***fairer, more inclusive,*** *and* ***more efficient****—Polygon strives for cheaper, faster transactions on the network.*

3) *"We strongly believe that realizing this vision can significantly advance our society."*—Polygon wants to add value to the entire blockchain ecosystem that can aid in the further advancement of society.

Polygon's Roadmap and Vision Alignment

Figure 11-5 shows Polygon's technology roadmap. The roadmap highlights four important milestones that Polygon implemented in 2023. These milestones are as follows:

1. ***Polygon PoS to ZK L2***
2. ***Protocol Architecture***
3. ***POL Tokenomics***
4. ***The Three Pillars of Governance***

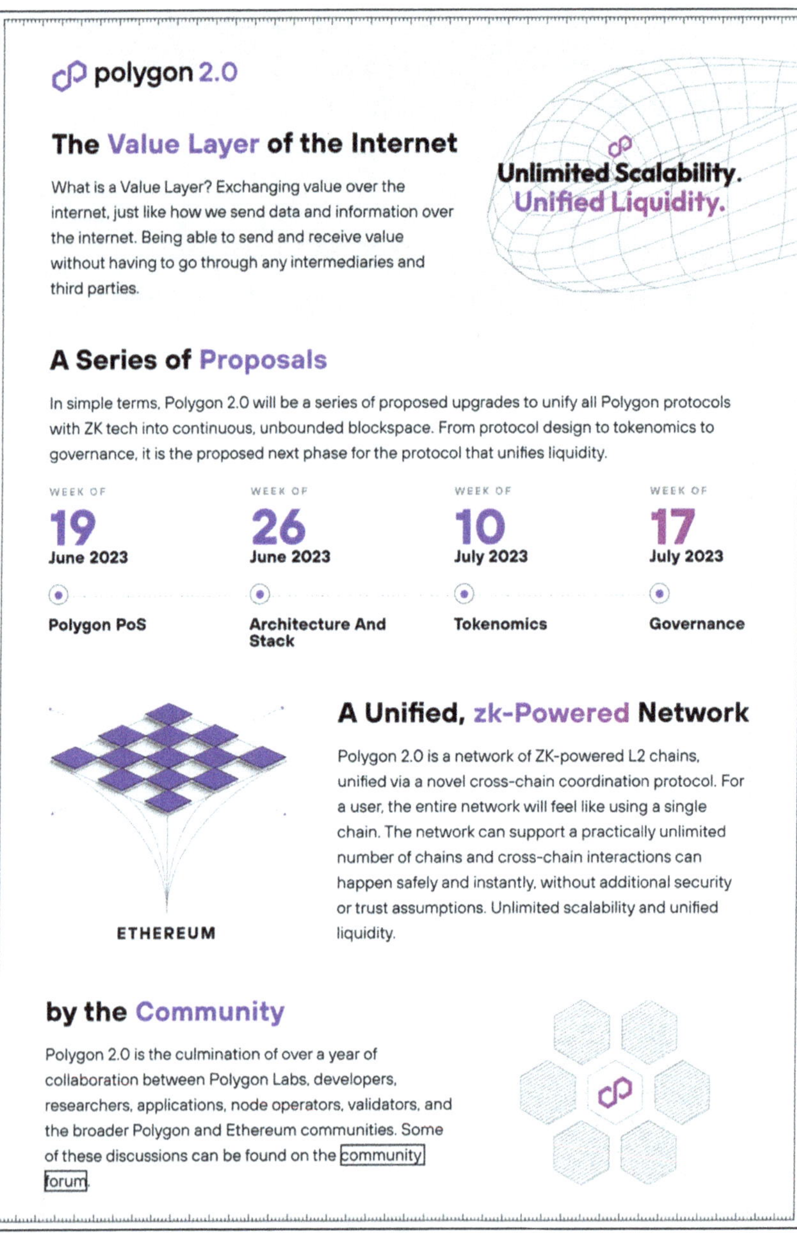

Figure 11-5. *Polygon Technology's Roadmap 2.0 (compliments of* `https://polygon.technology/roadmap`*)*

The Value Layer of the Internet

As described by Polygon, the ***value layer is the Internet,*** which is simply the ability to send and receive value without going through intermediaries and third parties. To enhance this value layer, Polygon plans to improve multiple aspects of its technology by implementing the core deliverables as outlined in the roadmap (*Polygon PoS to ZK L2, protocol architecture, POL tokenomics, and the three pillars of governance*). In the following analysis, these milestones are discussed and compared against Polygon's vision to determine if the project is still aligned with its original vision.

Figure 11-6. *Polygon technology roadmap—key deliverables (compliments of `https://polygon.technology/roadmap`)*

1) ***Polygon PoS to zkEVM Validium*** - As described by Polygon, this is a "proposal to upgrade Polygon PoS to a zkEVM validium, a Validium-type layer-2 that uses zero-knowledge (ZK) proofs while keeping transaction data off-chain, introducing different trust assumptions from roll-ups".

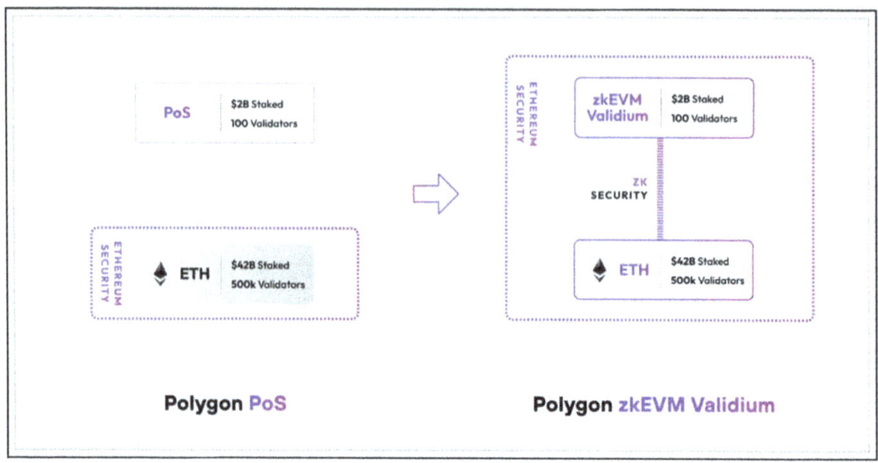

Figure 11-7. *Polygon PoS to zkEVM validium (compliments of `https://polygon.technology/blog/polygon-2-0-polygon-pos-zk-layer-2`)*

Vision Alignment – This milestone deliverable aligns with Polygon's vision by enabling Polygon PoS to become more secure, with low fees and high scalability, thus contributing to an overall more efficient user experience.

2) **Protocol Architecture** – Polygon proposes a four-layer architectural design consisting of *staking, interoperability, execution, and proving* layers. The proposed architecture for Polygon 2.0 is designed to provide unlimited scalability and unified liquidity. Additionally, it realizes the vision of Polygon as the Value Layer of the Internet, which democratizes access to the global economy, allowing for a more decentralized system where value (information or assets) can be exchanged without gatekeepers, rent-seekers, or any form of intermediaries.

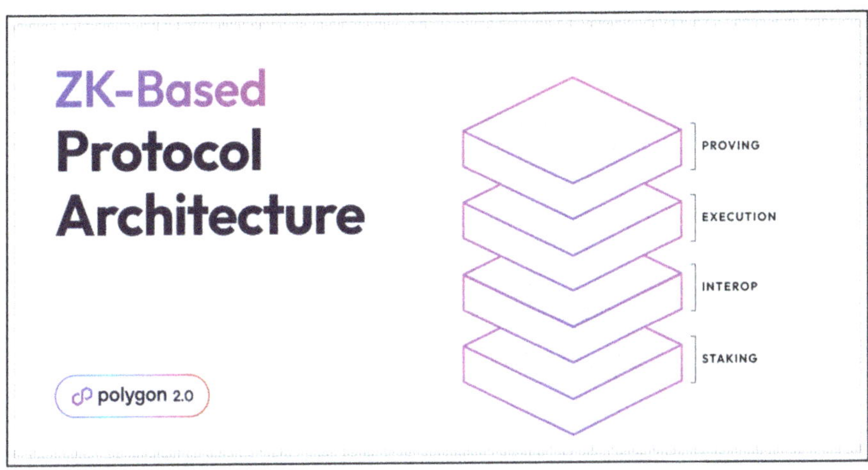

Figure 11-8. *Polygon 2.0 protocol architecture (compliments of `https://polygon.technology/blog/polygon-2-0-protocol-vision-and-architecture`)*

Vision Alignment - This milestone deliverable aligns with Polygon's vision by allowing the free and global exchange of assets while maintaining autonomy. Furthermore, it aids in the further advancement of society by increasing interoperability between blockchains, which will enable individuals the flexibility to use the technology with a higher number of use cases and integrations.

3) **POL Tokenomics** - Polygon, which originally used the MATIC token, has rolled out a technical upgrade that replaces MATIC with POL. POL is the next-generation protocol token, designed to become the major tool for native assets—*hyperproductive tokens. For more detail on this, see* `https://docs.polygon.technology/pos/get-started/matic-to-pol/`.

Similarly to productive tokens, it enables its holders to become validators and receive rewards, but with two game-changing improvements:

- Validators can validate as many chains as they want—"multi-chain validation."
- Every chain can offer multiple roles (and corresponding rewards) to validators.

Vision Alignment – This polygon upgrade and milestone delivery aligns with polygon's vision by altering and improving underlying core technology aspects, significant scalability gains, ecosystem security, ecosystem support, and community ownership.

4) **Polygon 2.0 Governance** – Proposing a forward-looking framework for decentralized ownership and decision-making over all Polygon protocols and the ecosystem. This will give the community full control over the Polygon Network and the final say on all the proposals.

The system involves three governance pillars: *protocol governance, system smart contract governance, and community treasury*. Through decentralized governance, token holders can vote on these three pillars of governance.

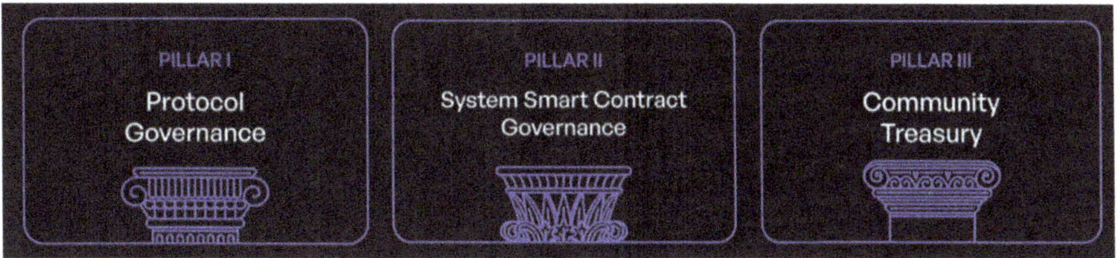

***Figure 11-9.** Polygon's three governance pillars (compliments of `https://polygon.technology/blog/polygon-2-0-governance`)*

Vision Alignment – This milestone deliverable aligns with Polygon's vision by providing true governance features that allow network participants to self-govern their assets and make unified decisions to direct Polygon to long-term success and longevity. This contributes to a fairer world where the power is handed back to the people.

Action Steps

Follow these steps to assess whether the project has a clear vision and purpose that addresses real-world problems, aligns with their core objectives, and is deemed high value to the overall growth of the blockchain ecosystem.

1) **Access the Project Vision and Purpose**

   Using the evaluation procedure executed on Polygon in this section.

   a) Does the project have a clear vision?

   b) Does its vision align with its core objectives?

   c) Does the project's vision contribute and deemed high value to the overall growth of the blockchain realm?

   d) How does the vision relate to other blockchain technologies within the same sector?

   e) Does the vision reward token holders? If so, how is this achieved?

   f) Are there any other observations?

2) **Take Notes and Document Your Findings in Your Own Style**

3) **Combine the Findings with Other Sections of the Fundamental Evaluation Process**

Evaluation of the Results

If the project's vision doesn't align with its goals, that is something to pay close attention to, as it indicates that the team is not even aligned internally. A clear vision usually shows the team knows what they're doing, but if things seem off-track, it might point to poor planning or shifting priorities. Of course, blockchain projects sometimes need to pivot—that's normal in a fast-moving space—and those changes can even be a good thing if they add value or help the project grow. However, significant changes should come with an explanation from the team. If they are not upfront about it, that could be a red flag, and it is fair to wonder if the team is being transparent. Trust matters, and without it, the project could lose support from the community.

Milestones Feasibility

Evaluation Objective: Assess whether the project milestones are feasible and realistic.

This part of the evaluation helps investors determine if the project's milestones are feasible and realistic by evaluating against key metrics such as current milestone status, technical complexity, infrastructure requirements, resource availability, timelines, and overall performance. This section uses Filecoin as an example to show how milestone evaluation can reveal whether a project is on track to deliver value to the blockchain ecosystem. Filecoin is a popular open-source, public blockchain and decentralized file-storage protocol intended to be a blockchain-based cooperative digital storage and data-retrieval method. Filecoin is developed by Protocol Labs and functions as the incentive layer for the *InterPlanetary File System (IPFS)*, allowing users to rent unused hard-drive space.

Why Filecoin? Among the dozens of blockchain roadmaps we reviewed for this book, Filecoin's stood out for its clarity, milestone breakdown, and publicly available progress notes. Many projects publish only high-level bullet points ("Q3 - Mainnet," "Q4 - Partnerships") that offer little substance for an illustrative, step-by-step project milestone feasibility assessment. Filecoin, by contrast, groups its objectives into clearly labelled and dated milestones, explains the technical intent behind each one, and maintains an active trail of development updates, GitHub repositories, Slack channels, and community calls. That level of detail makes it an ideal teaching example for readers who are learning how to evaluate whether milestones are realistic, funded, and technically achievable.

Even with a well-documented project like Filecoin, some milestone-related details can still be tough to track down: team schedules change, roadblocks get sorted in private developer chats, and a few items stay confidential for legal or competitive reasons—pretty normal in crypto. A realistic expectation when you dig into any roadmap is to bump into a mix of solid facts, community chatter, and a few blanks; almost no project lays out everything, so it's important to be aware of this. You may not always be able to confirm if earlier milestones were hit, if all the tools and budget are lined up for what's next, or if the target dates sound reasonable with the information available. Filecoin's roadmap is great for showing how to work through those gaps and reminds us that missing info is part of the game and needs to be weighed carefully before making any call. Big thanks to the Filecoin team for keeping such a detailed roadmap out in the open.

Figure 11-10 shows the *Filecoin Virtual Machine (FVM)* roadmap. The Filecoin Virtual Machine (FVM) is an execution environment for smart contracts on the Filecoin network. It allows anyone to interact with the metadata and transactions stored on Filecoin's storage network, bringing user programmability to Filecoin and unleashing the open data economy. As outlined by Filecoin, the goal of the FVM is to add general programmability to the Filecoin project.

Pro Tip If a project's roadmap doesn't include clear timelines, check whether objectives from previous years were completed. Many projects update their roadmaps annually but often avoid setting specific deadlines for tasks. Reviewing past years' progress can give you valuable insights into how effectively the team delivers on its goals. For example, take a look at BNB Chain's roadmaps:

`https://www.bnbchain.org/en/blog/bnb-chain-tech-roadmap-2023c`

`https://www.bnbchain.org/en/blog/bnb-chain-2024-tech-roadmap`

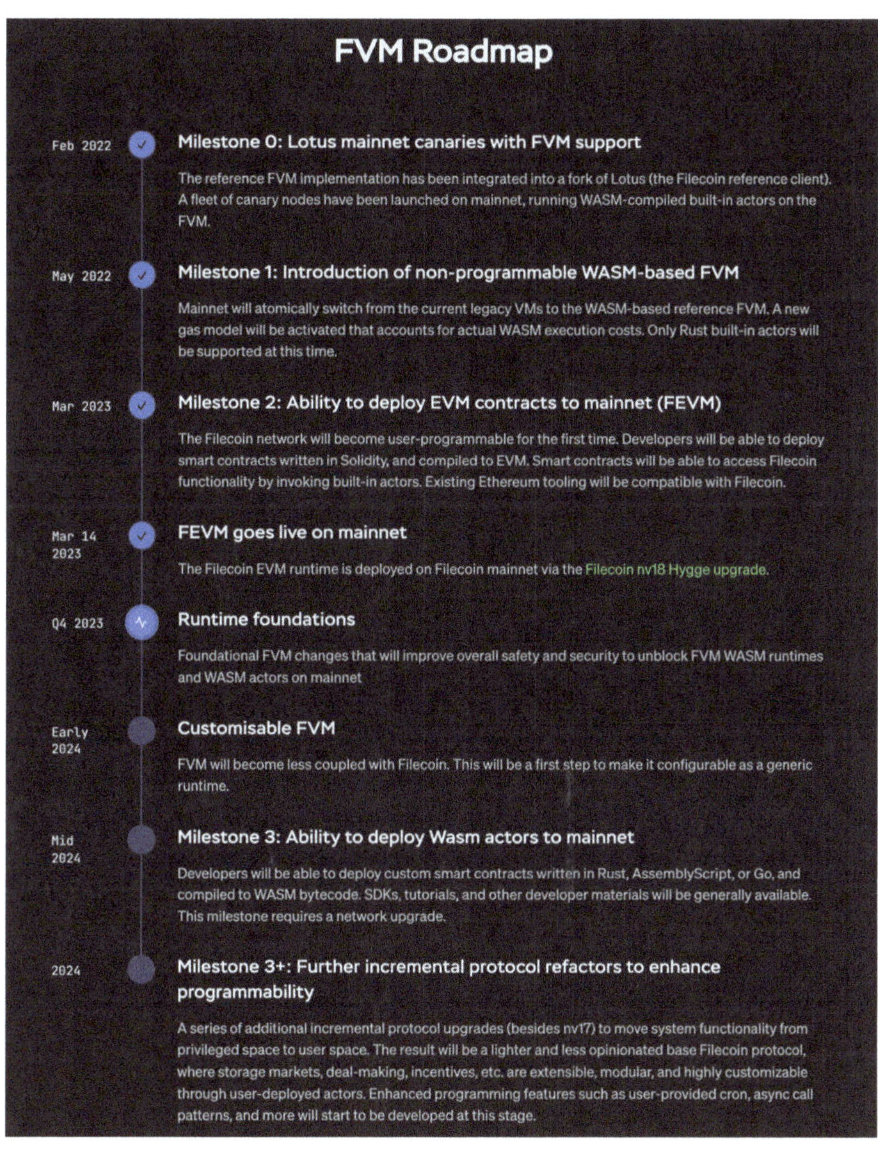

Figure 11-10. *Filecoin roadmap milestones 2022–2024 (compliments of `https://fvm.filecoin.io/`)*

Filecoin's virtual machine (FVM) project milestones are outlined in Table 11-3. This assessment procedure, or evaluation tool, is a means to help investors identify potential risks and gauge the project's milestone feasibility. This evaluation discusses key metrics such as technical complexity, resource availability, infrastructure requirements, performance, and timelines. During this analysis, information for each evaluation metric was sought from multiple locations, such as the whitepaper and official project outlets, such as the project website, GitHub, Slack, and other online resources. Disclaimer: The information below on this project is for illustration purposes only and was updated when writing this book. Additionally, it is essential to note that it is highly likely that Filecoin's milestone status has been updated since the writing of this book.

Table 11-3. *Filecoin roadmap milestone evaluation*

Filecoin FVM—Milestone Evaluation		
Evaluation Parameters	**Evaluation**	**Findings**
Remaining Milestone Status	Determine the remaining number of milestones to be completed as per the roadmap.	Remaining Milestones as per Roadmap: **Milestone 2 (part C): Runtime Foundations**—in progress, advised as nearly complete by the developer team. **Milestone 2 (part D): Customizable FVM**—in progress, advised as nearly complete by the developer team. **Milestone 3: Ability to deploy Wasm actors to mainnet**—in progress. **Milestone 3+: Further incremental protocol refactors to enhance programmability**—in progress.

(*continued*)

Table 11-3. *(continued)*

Filecoin FVM—Milestone Evaluation		
Evaluation Parameters	**Evaluation**	**Findings**
Technical Complexity	Do the milestones look like they require advanced technology or cryptographic techniques that have not been seen in the industry to date? If so, what edge does the team have to accomplish milestones?	From examining the milestones and associated tasks, no technical challenges were suspected. However, upon further research and conversations with the developer team through Slack, it was noted that some technical issues were encountered for Milestone 3, which required additional research and investigations. No technical challenges were publicly documented for milestones 2 or 3+. It's likely the team faced the usual hurdles—most projects do—but any details appear to have stayed inside private developer channels, as no issues were disclosed in the sources available.
	Are the required platform's technological tools available to execute the proposed milestones successfully?	Yes. Filecoin is built on the *InterPlanetary File System (IPFS)*—an advanced distributed file storage protocol that allows computers all over the globe to store and serve files as part of a giant peer-to-peer network. It has been active since 2015 and is considered one of the leading protocols for file storage and sharing.

(continued)

Table 11-3. (*continued*)

Filecoin FVM—Milestone Evaluation		
Evaluation Parameters	**Evaluation**	**Findings**
Infrastructure Requirements	Does the team have adequate testing environments, such as testnets or server setups, to help facilitate the ongoing development and milestone accomplishment?	Yes. Filecoin has many testnet environments, including: Calibration testnet is the most realistic simulation of Filecoin's mainnet, where prospective storage providers can experience more realistic sealing performance and hardware requirements. Spacenet is a Filecoin testnet modified to support Interplanetary Consensus (IPC). Provides developers with a testbed to deploy their FVM use cases and innovate with new Web3 applications that leverage IPC subnets.
Resource Availability	Does the team have access to the necessary developers or experts with specific skills required to execute the known milestones?	Filecoin has 15 direct developers and 26 collaborators visible on GitHub. From speaking with the developer team, I noticed there was a lack of developer resources, and they were currently undergoing a network team restructuring to help allocate resources more efficiently. Note poor market conditions at the time may also affect resources.

(*continued*)

Table 11-3. (*continued*)

Filecoin FVM—Milestone Evaluation		
Evaluation Parameters	**Evaluation**	**Findings**
	Are there sufficient funds to support the development to start and complete each milestone?	Yes. Through Filecoin's Developer Grant System. Filecoin offers grants and rewards for ongoing & existing contributions that add significant value to the Filecoin ecosystem.
Timeline	Do the set milestones, dates, and timeframes look realistic based on known constraints and challenges to date?	Despite a deep dive through Filecoin's blog posts, docs, Discord, Slack, GitHub, and other public channels, not enough hard detail is publicly available to judge whether the upcoming milestone dates are truly achievable. This doesn't imply the team won't deliver—only that key scheduling and resourcing data remains internal (often for legal, competitive, or "work-in-progress" reasons). Such gaps are common across crypto projects, so real-world roadmap analysis must highlight what isn't public just as much as what is.

(*continued*)

Table 11-3. *(continued)*

Filecoin FVM—Milestone Evaluation		
Evaluation Parameters	**Evaluation**	**Findings**
Performance	Do future milestones look achievable based on past milestone execution performance?	Based on previously successfully completed milestones by the dedicated Filecoin team, it is reasonable to say that they can execute the remaining milestone with a new structure of their developer resources.
	Has a visible, proven track record of successfully completed milestones spanning a few years?	This roadmap only details successful milestones back to 2022 (one year ago when writing this). Past roadmaps with milestones seem to be inaccessible.
	Have there been milestones that the team failed to achieve in the past? Look out for noticeable gaps or delays in the schedule.	No official list of missed milestones is published, but community threads hint at a few schedule slips that the team hasn't formally documented.
	If past milestones were not completed or not completed on time, was this because of internal or external factors?	Some milestones are past their roadmap schedule dates. However, work has not stopped. It is suspected that poor market conditions—at the time of writing this book—and lack of developer involvement across the crypto markets are likely contributors.

(continued)

Table 11-3. (*continued*)

Filecoin FVM—Milestone Evaluation		
Evaluation Parameters	**Evaluation**	**Findings**
Final/ Miscellaneous Notes	Filecoin has a history of successfully executing and completing scheduled milestones. Even though they were low on developer resources during this evaluation, the developers and contributors were clearly passionate about the project and fully committed to achieving the planned milestones. The fact that they're so open and transparent builds trust and strengthens the project's credibility. Furthermore, this hidden detail cannot be neglected when evaluating.	

Pro Tip Pay attention to key milestone dates in the project roadmap. The token's value will likely surge before the hype leading to the milestone delivery. Set reminders one to two weeks before these key dates to accommodate a "buy the rumor, sell the news" type scenario.

Action Steps

Follow these steps to assess whether the project milestones are feasible and realistic.

1) **Evaluate Milestone Feasibility**

   a) Review the project roadmap and ensure you understand the milestones and their intended deliverables.

b) Evaluate the project milestones using the criteria and metrics laid out in this chapter.

2) **Take Notes and Document Your Findings in Your Own Style**

3) **Combine the Findings with Other Sections of the Fundamental Evaluation Process**

Evaluation of the Results

If the project milestones do not seem feasible or realistic after being analyzed against the evaluation parameters, it is advised to consult with the team for answers. Investors should be aware that projects often miss milestone deadlines. Given the complex nature of blockchain technology combined with internal and external factors, projects should not be disregarded for missing one or two milestone deadlines. However, this is considered a red flag if the team has a proven track record of multiple missed milestones and timelines and, more importantly, several abandoned milestones.

Transparency and Accountability

Evaluation Objective: Evaluate whether the project team provides clear, timely updates on roadmap milestones and communicates progress openly.

The project team should regularly update and communicate a strong crypto roadmap to investors and the broader community. This holds the team accountable and helps maintain the project's trust, transparency, and confidence. Furthermore, a regularly updated roadmap shows that the team is not hiding anything, being upfront and honest regarding their on-time achievements, where they are falling behind, and any issues encountered.

However, real-time roadmap updates are rare, with many project teams revisiting and manually updating their roadmap once a year or even less frequently. Common reasons for this may be that the team is falling behind on their deadlines, there are no updates to provide, there is a lack of funding and other resources, there is unwanted backlash, there is poor management, or there is simple neglect.

Because roadmap-update frequency varies from project to project and is often sparse, it places more responsibility on the investor to perform research through the project's official channels, such as Discord, GitHub, Slack, X, and Telegram, to speak with team members, including developers, to figure out the current milestone status. If milestone dates have not been met, ask the team for valid reasons why these critical dates have not been met and the planned actions in place to make up for lost time. The team must provide honest answers and feedback, explaining why they are behind schedule, why the roadmap has not been updated, and any other aspects depending on the specific case. Where possible, ask the team to back up their answers with public links or code updates—while recognizing that some progress may stay private for security, legal, or strategic reasons. This is an essential but sometimes tedious task; the time it takes varies depending on the level of support each project provides.

Action Steps

Follow these steps to evaluate whether the project team provides clear, timely updates on roadmap milestones and communicates progress openly.

1) **Evaluate Roadmap Status**

   a) Review the project roadmap and determine if the milestones, goals, and objectives are clearly specified and up to date with the current status.

b) If the roadmap has not been updated, contact the project team for clarification, as outlined in this section.

i) Determine the current status of the milestones.

ii) Determine the reasons for delays, such as technical issues, lack of resources, etc.

iii) Did the reason for the delay seem reasonable and legitimate, or simply an excuse?

iv) Did you get a feeling that the team was hiding information?

v) Did the team have a contingency plan to help make up for time and complete the remaining milestones?

2) **Evaluate Roadmap Transparency and Accountability**

a) Was the roadmap up to date with the current project's status and milestones?

b) Was the team open and honest regarding milestone status and other elements on the roadmap?

c) Has the team agreed to update the roadmap so all stakeholders know the current status?

3) **Take Notes and Document Your Findings in Your Own Style**

4) **Combine the Findings with Other Sections of the Fundamental Evaluation Process**

Evaluation of the Results

Unfortunately, it is common for project roadmaps to be well-defined but lack updates on the progress of individual milestones, leaving it unclear which milestones, goals, and objectives have been completed or are still underway. Therefore, when coming across a roadmap with real-time updates, consider it a clear sign of transparency and accountability—a definite bonus.

If you reach out to a project team about roadmap updates, consider it a positive sign if the team was open, honest, and forthcoming regarding milestones, progress and deadlines, technical challenges, lack of resources, goals, objectives, and overall project performance. Conversely, consider this a red flag if you genuinely tried to reach the team through multiple outlets and received vague, dismissive, or no responses at all. This shows that the team has zero transparency and is not holding themselves accountable, which, in turn, will negatively impact the project's long-term viability and success.

Comparing Competitors' Roadmaps

Evaluation Objective: Compare roadmaps and determine if a project's goals, milestones, and features are realistic, well-executed, and unique while assessing its ability to deliver and innovate.

As part of the roadmap evaluation, it is recommended that the roadmap be compared to that of direct competitors. This helps compare goals, objectives, vision, milestones, transparency, accountability, and technical challenges that sometimes help shed light on various fundamentals that may not have been captured during the complete fundamental analysis. Be vigilant for a lack or addition of certain features, architectural modifications or implementations, and ecosystem integrations that could negatively or positively affect the project. Given that projects have varying levels of maturity, investors must check into already implemented features when comparing roadmaps.

When comparing roadmaps, analyze in terms of feasibility, not only for milestone deadlines but also for the feature set—sometimes roadmaps can be unrealistic without evidence or no clear executing plan. Be vigilant of copies of other roadmaps, not just in terms of design but also milestones, features, goals, objectives, etc. When you line up one project's roadmap against its rivals, focus on the basics—goals, features, and whether deadlines are actually met. If most comparable chains are already rolling out the same bridge or standard and one project keeps falling behind, that's a warning sign. Investigate further to understand why so you have all the essential information for an informed decision.

Action Steps

Follow these steps to compare roadmaps and determine if a project's goals, milestones, and features are realistic, well-executed, and unique while assessing its ability to deliver and innovate.

1) **Locate Competitor Roadmaps**

   Identify the project's competitors and find corresponding roadmaps.

2) **Compare Roadmaps**

   Compare and contrast the project's roadmap to that of competitors, as described in this section.

3) **Take Notes and Document Your Findings in Your Own Style**

4) **Combine the Findings with Other Sections of the Fundamental Evaluation Process**

Evaluation of the Results

If the project's roadmap stands out with realistic goals and unique features, consider it a positive sign and worth a closer look. However, if it mirrors competitors or falls short in feasibility, it might indicate limited originality—or, at worst, something questionable—so proceed with extra caution and conduct further investigation as needed.

CHAPTER 12

Project Codebase

This chapter discusses and evaluates the project codebase in terms of the various programming languages utilized to build the core product and the corresponding performance of the development team executing the development process. A project *codebase* is a complete set of source code files for a software project, including everything needed to build, execute, and maintain an application. In the blockchain world, a project's codebase is typically hosted on platforms like GitHub, a key element that helps development teams and the public collaborate to maximize a project's quality and overall potential.

Analyzing a project's codebase is a critical fundamental element that investors should take seriously. It provides deep insight into the team's performance surrounding the development of the core product. The project team's activity, efficiency, and performance related to the project code are assessed by analyzing code security, commit frequency, programming languages used, types of source code, audits, and other factors. By the end of this chapter, investors will possess the knowledge and skills to quickly evaluate the quality of the project codebase, reflecting the team's performance and commitment.

Fundamentals Discussed in This Chapter:

- Introduction to Programming Languages
- Smart Contracts
- GitHub

P. Garvey, *Blockchain Fundamental Analysis for Digital Asset Investors*,
https://doi.org/10.1007/979-8-8688-1551-5_12

- Open and Closed Source Software
- Programming Languages
- Git Commits
- Git Contributors
- Git Issues
- Code Security Audit
- Bug Bounties
- Source Code

Introduction to Programming Languages

Programming languages are formal languages programmers use to communicate instructions to computers or machines for execution. Each programming language has its own syntax, grammar, and rules, with popular examples including Java, Solidity, Python, C++, JavaScript, Ruby, PHP, and Swift. Programmers (developers) utilize programming languages to build software applications, websites, mobile apps, and other digital products. The choice of programming language typically depends on the software and product requirements, the programmer's expertise, and available resources.

Fact A software program built using code is simply a set of instructions that tells a computer how and when to execute a specific task.

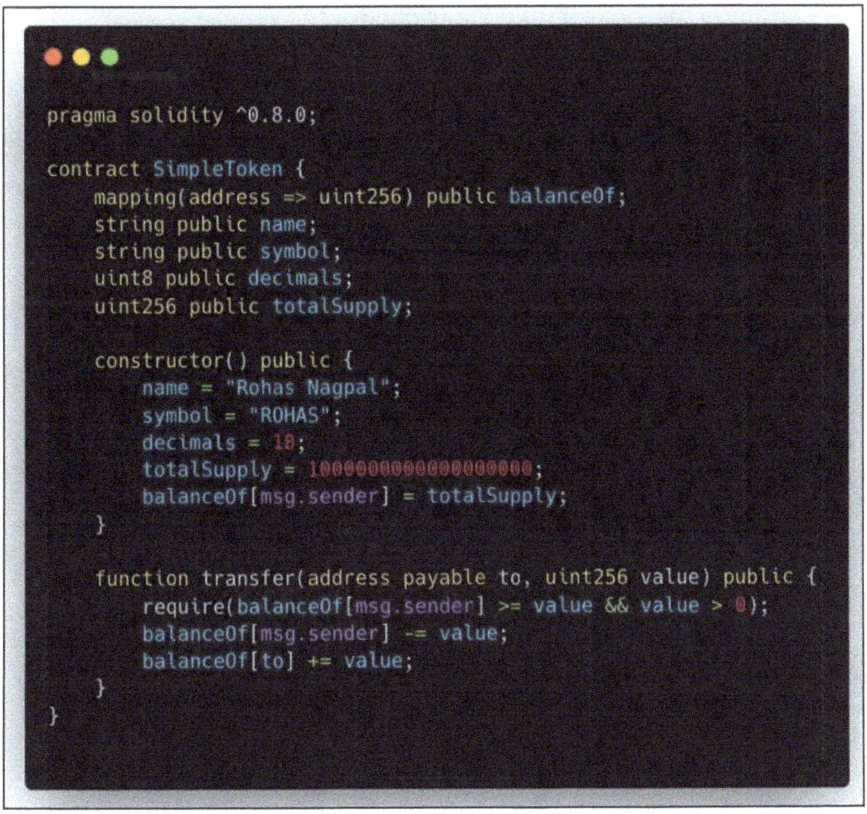

```
pragma solidity ^0.8.0;

contract SimpleToken {
    mapping(address => uint256) public balanceOf;
    string public name;
    string public symbol;
    uint8 public decimals;
    uint256 public totalSupply;

    constructor() public {
        name = "Rohas Nagpal";
        symbol = "ROHAS";
        decimals = 18;
        totalSupply = 1000000000000000000;
        balanceOf[msg.sender] = totalSupply;
    }

    function transfer(address payable to, uint256 value) public {
        require(balanceOf[msg.sender] >= value && value > 0);
        balanceOf[msg.sender] -= value;
        balanceOf[to] += value;
    }
}
```

Figure 12-1. *Solidity code of a simple token (compliments of `https://blockchainblog.substack.com/p/how-to-write-compile-and-deploy-a`)*

In the blockchain sector, different programming languages are used to develop the front and back end of decentralized applications (dApps) and the underlying blockchain infrastructure. Breaking it down further, these languages build essential blockchain-related elements, including distributed ledgers, consensus mechanisms, smart contracts, and network nodes. Furthermore, programming languages define these components' rules, behaviors, interactions, and operations. For instance, Ethereum, one of the most popular blockchain platforms, utilizes Solidity (Figure 12-1), a high-level programming language, for writing smart contracts.

In addition to having a solid knowledge of the various types of programming languages and their applications, a deep understanding of blockchain technology is essential for choosing the most suitable languages for a project. In a typical crypto project, developers utilize a variety of programming languages, each selected based on their application, strengths, and weaknesses.

Figure 12-2 shows Uniswap, a decentralized exchange (DEX) application built primarily from the Solidity programming language.

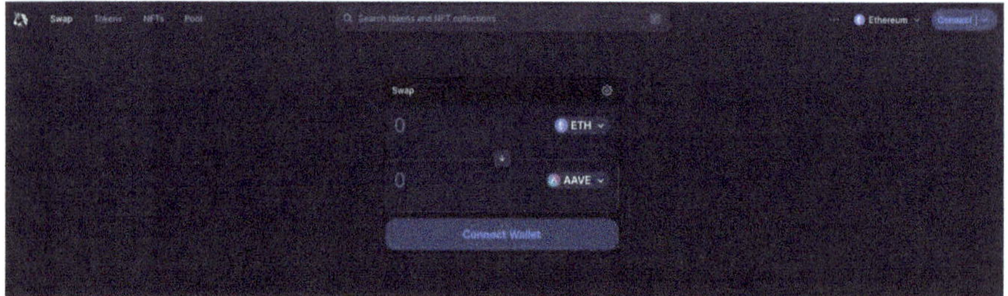

Figure 12-2. *Uniswap decentralized exchange (DEX) application (compliments of `https://app.uniswap.org/#/swap`)*

Smart Contracts

Smart contracts, or self-executing contracts, are digital contracts stored on a blockchain, designed to automatically execute when the terms and conditions of a predetermined agreement are met between two or more parties. They are incredibly reliable, run on a blockchain network, and are recognizable for their ability to self-execute a contract without intermediaries such as banks, lawyers, and other third parties. A smart contract standard defines the rules of how a smart contract operates, interacts, and utilizes the underlying blockchain. An example of a smart contract application would be to automate the payment process between a buyer and a seller, where the funds are automatically released to the seller when the buyer receives the goods or services. As previously stated, smart contracts are written in various programming languages. Solidity is the primary smart-contract language on EVM-compatible chains (e.g., Ethereum, BNB Smart Chain, Polygon, Avalanche, Fantom, Arbitrum, and Optimism). Other networks may use different languages, but Solidity remains widely supported across these ecosystems.

Fact Smart contracts are a computer protocol that digitally facilitates, verifies, and enforces the contracts between two or more parties on blockchain.

Smart Contract Benefits

Smart contracts are typically deployed on and secured by blockchain and have unique characteristics and benefits. They are as follows:

- **Self-executing** - The significant advantage that smart contracts have over traditional contracts is that they are self-executing. Smart contracts are pre-programmed (coded) with the agreement terms. Once these predefined conditions are triggered, an event happens, e.g., the transfer of digital assets.
- **Tamper-Resistant/Immutable** - The entire smart contract, including all agreement terms, is coded and executed on the blockchain, where the immutable nature of a public permissionless blockchain ensures that once the smart contract's code is recorded and verified, it becomes tamper-resistant.

- **No Trusted Authorities Required** - Unlike traditional contracts, smart contracts do not require a legal team or central authority to act as the middleman between the parties involved.
- **Anonymity and Trustless** - Smart-contract participants can remain completely anonymous and do not need to trust each other for a transaction to take place.
- **Transparent** - All smart contract transactions are logged, visible, and traceable on a public blockchain without needing any trusted parties.

Fact Bitcoin transactions are simple smart contracts: each output locks coins under a script condition (e.g., a valid signature, a timelock, or a multi-sig). These limited, non-Turing-complete contracts paved the way for the more expressive, fully programmable smart-contract platforms that began with Ethereum.

Ethereum Virtual Machine (EVM)

Ethereum was the first advanced smart contract development platform. Since Ethereum went live in July 2015, it has remained the most popular among developers and investors. It allows users to completely customize smart contracts, enabling them to create a wide variety of decentralized applications (dApps), some including decentralized exchanges, crowdsourcing platforms, gaming, non-fungible tokens (NFTs), gambling, and decentralized finance (DeFi) applications.

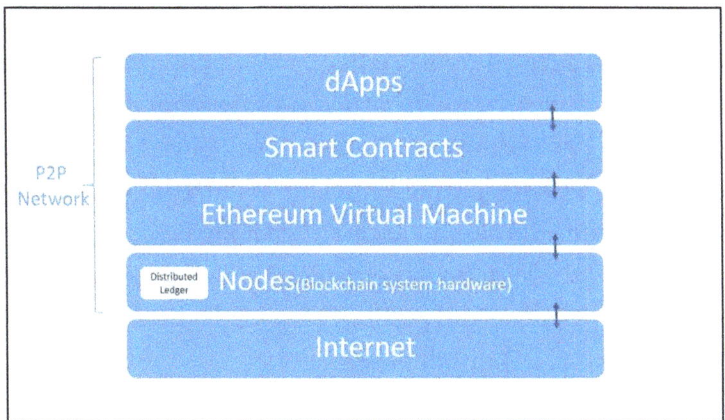

Figure 12-3. *Ethereum virtual machine (EVM) (compliments of https://github.com/LearnWeb3DAO/Sophomore-Track/blob/main/Ethereum-Virtual-Machine.md)*

Ethereum makes this possible through its Turing-complete virtual machine called the *Ethereum Virtual Machine* (EVM). EVM is a virtual and decentralized runtime environment where smart contracts are executed. Think of EVM as Ethereum's computational engine that executes smart contracts and deploys dApps. The smart contracts—written in Solidity—are converted, or compiled, into bytecode, a language that the EVM can understand. A copy of the EVM runs on every full node in the network.

GitHub

Evaluation Objective: Explore and familiarize yourself with the GitHub code repository and collaboration platform.

GitHub is a cloud-based software service that helps programmers and project teams host, collaborate on, store, manage, and control their code repositories. It allows developers worldwide to collaborate simultaneously on single or multiple projects, contributing code, ideas, and feedback to help develop and improve the project. Think of GitHub as an interactive Google Sheets for developers.

Developer teams on GitHub can grant members, collaborators, and the public different access levels to edit and make code contributions. Each user is granted permission to access varying amounts of information and sensitive data depending on the access level. Most crypto projects are open-sourced, which typically allows full visibility of the project code and overall code development progress of the blockchain or dApp. Additionally, open-source allows the public an array of permissions, such as viewing the project code and pulling requests, code issues, and latest code commits—this is important for investors!

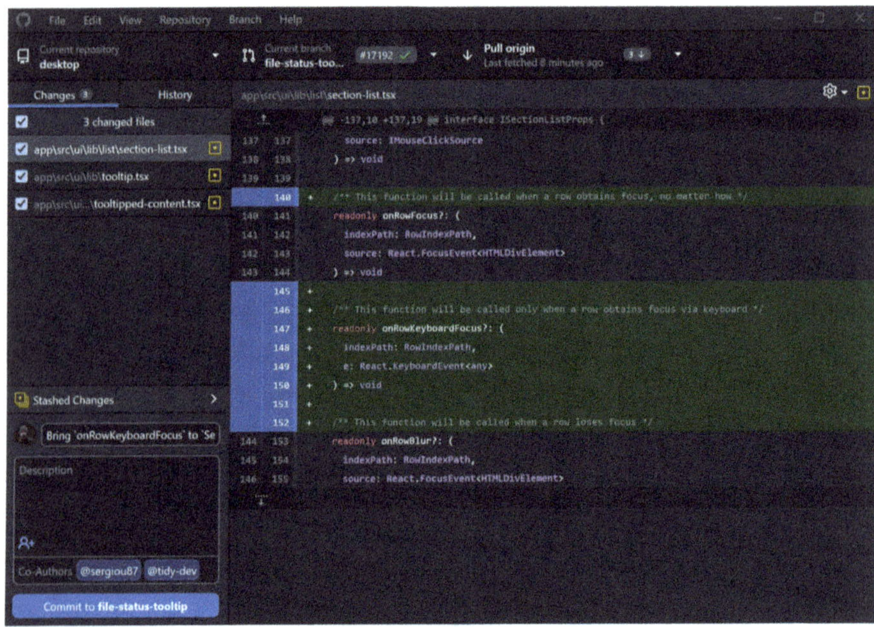

Figure 12-4. *GitHub desktop interface for developers (compliments of* `https://github.com/apps/desktop`*)*

Another fantastic feature of GitHub is that it allows for *open-source* and *closed-source* projects. Developers can create public and private code repositories for open-source or closed-source projects. This enables development teams to let the public view, interact, and contribute to the project code or keep it private in case of private, sensitive, or patented material such as traditional financial banking entities.

Why Is GitHub Important for Investors?

Software services like GitHub provide investors with deep insight into the development of the core product, including project activity, performance, and overcompetence. This is important because investors can get a true feel for the team's commitment to the project. For example, a code repository with frequent code commits (submissions) and a low number of issues encountered indicates the team is working diligently and making a genuine effort towards achieving their goals and deadlines.

Another core benefit of GitHub is its level of transparency and accountability. The open nature of the software enables the general public, community, and potential investors to scrutinize a project's codebase, revealing any vulnerabilities or security issues. Fast resolution of outstanding bugs and vulnerabilities is another clear and positive sign. GitHub also has functionality that allows the community to participate in code reviews, where they can offer up their findings, including proposed improvements and bug fixes. Opposingly, projects with closed or inactive repositories raise red flags, as they may be less transparent, or worse, potentially abandoned or fraudulent.

Action Steps

The following sections of this book require a basic understanding of GitHub, explicitly navigating the project interface to analyze various aspects of the team's performance and activity surrounding the project code.

1) **GitHub Familiarization and Navigation**

   Familiarize yourself with the GitHub.com interface and navigational menus. There are multiple videos on YouTube.com that help get a feel for the application. For example, please see an example with this link: `https://www.youtube.com/watch?v=w3jLJU7DT5E`

2) **Take Notes and Document Your Findings in Your Own Style**

3) **Combine the Findings with Other Sections of the Fundamental Evaluation Process**

Evaluation of the Results

There is no requirement for results to be evaluated.

Open and Closed Source Software

Evaluation Objective: Determine if a crypto project is open-source or closed-source to assess its level of transparency, accountability, and associated risks if there is limited access to its codebase.

Source code is simply a list of human-readable instructions (code), the building blocks written to control the operations of software applications. Every piece of software in the blockchain realm is built using code from an array of different programming languages. This software is classified into two groups: *open-source software* and *closed-source software*. Table 12-1 compares the core differences between open- and closed-source software.

Table 12-1. *Open-source versus closed-source software*

	Open-Source Versus Closed-Source Software	
Aspect	**Open-Source Code**	**Closed-Source Code**
Definition	Open-source code refers to software whose source code is available to the public. This allows anyone to view, modify, and distribute the code.	Closed-source code refers to software whose source code is kept private. Only those with access may view, modify, and distribute the code.
Security	High security due to scrutiny of the code by the community, the general public, and paid third-party code audit firms.	Depends solely on internal code reviews and that of paid third-party code audit firms.
Community Involvement	Strong community participation	Not open to the community
Developer Goals and Motivation	Driven by innovation, learning, self-accomplishment, and contributing to the broader community.	Typically driven by profit and corporate goals.
Code Improvement and Effective Debugging	Continuous improvement through community feedback and collaboration.	Improvement is internal and may be slower due to fewer reviewers.
Code Reliability	Very reliable and widely tested by the community.	Reliability depends on internal testing and resources.
Trust	High community trust due to a high level of transparency.	Trust is dependent on the reputation of the company.

(*continued*)

Table 12-1. *(continued)*

	Open-Source Versus Closed-Source Software	
Aspect	**Open-Source Code**	**Closed-Source Code**
Innovation	Rapid innovation is due to the diverse community and developer base.	Innovation is dependent directly on the company's resources.
Control	Less control, as the community can modify the code, often resulting in forks.	Complete control over the project code.
Legal Use and Compliance	Individuals are free to copy, modify, and use the code as their own, provided they comply with the open-source license, which may require attribution and sharing modifications.	Code use is restricted by the company's licensing terms, often prohibiting copying or modification without permission.

Fact The term "source" code serves as the primary source from which all other forms of the software are derived.

Open-Source Licenses

A license is a contract between the author and the user of a software component that declares where the software can be used, modified, or distributed in commercial applications under specific conditions. An open-source license grants other users the permission and rights to use or repurpose the code for new applications or to include the code in different projects. The software program is unusable without an open-source license—even if the codebase is posted on GitHub—because, in most jurisdictions, code without an explicit license is automatically "all rights reserved," so others have no legal right to copy, modify, or redistribute it. There are over eighty different types of open-source licenses, each with different permissions and restrictions. Open-source licenses are categorized into two main groups: *copyleft* and *permissive* licenses.

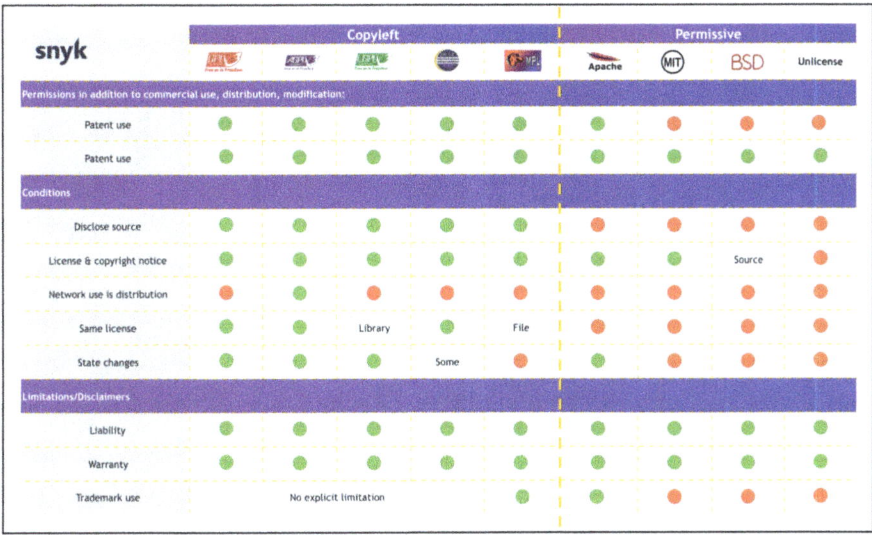

***Figure 12-5.** Open-source licenses—copyleft and permissive (compliments of* `https://snyk.io/learn/open-source-licenses/`*)*

Copyleft Licenses

Copyleft licenses are open-source licenses that provide the right for anyone to reuse, modify, and distribute intellectual property (software), provided that any changes made are shared under the same license and anyone who uses the software thereafter is granted the same freedoms. Common examples of copyleft licenses are the following:

- **GNU General Public License (GPL)** - Requires that any software using GPL code must make its entire source code available under the same GPL license.
- **GNU Lesser General Public License (LGPL)** - Allows smaller components to be used in larger projects without requiring the entire project to be distributed under the same license.
- **Affero General Public License (AGPL)** - Extends the GPL by ensuring that software offered over a network must also release its source code under the GPL.
- **Eclipse Public License (EPL)** - Permits combining EPL-licensed code with non-EPL code, as long as modifications to EPL code are released under the EPL.
- **Mozilla Public License (MPL)** - Allows MPL-licensed code to be used in proprietary software, provided it remains in separate files and includes patent grants and copyright notices.

By law and under the terms and conditions for using open-source software, a license (copyleft or permissive) must be provided and made visible to users, typically through inclusion in the distributed software or documentation. Figure 12-6 shows an image of Moonbeam Networks visible open-source GNU General Public License v3.0 from Moonbeam's official codebase on GitHub.com.

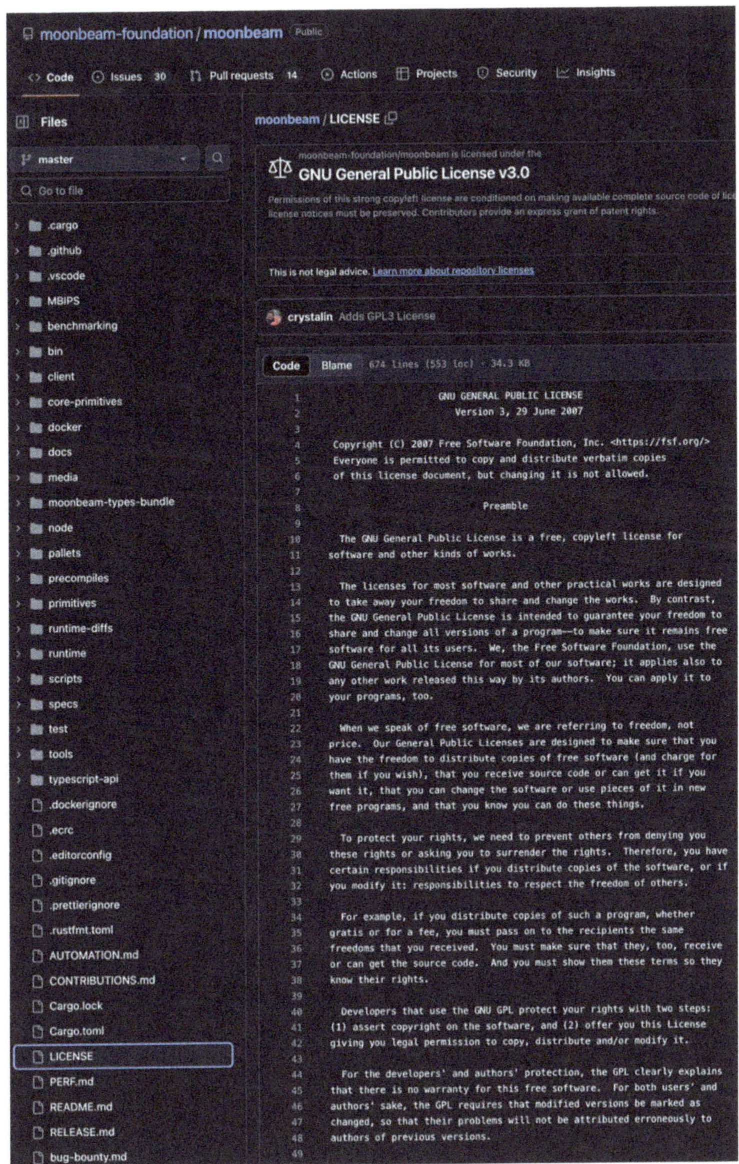

***Figure 12-6.** Moonbeam Network, open-source GNU general public license visible on Moonbeam Network's official project codebase on GitHub (compliments of `https://github.com/moonbeam-foundation/moonbeam/blob/master/LICENSE`)*

Permissive Licenses

Permissive licenses are open-source licenses that allow anyone to use, modify, and distribute the software with only minimal conditions—usually keeping the original copyright notice and license text (and, for Apache 2.0, an attribution NOTICE file). This means the software and its derivatives can be incorporated into proprietary or closed-source products without disclosing the source code or sharing the modifications. Some examples of permissive licenses are

- **Apache License** - Allows modifications and derivative works under different licenses, with required license notifications and a patent grant included.
- **MIT License** - Permits unrestricted use of the code as long as the original copyright and license notice are retained, without any liability for authors.
- **BSD License** - Similar to MIT, it allows code to be used under different licenses without requiring source code distribution. However, the restrictions vary depending on the specific version of the BSD License.
- **Unlicense** - Places the code in the public domain with no conditions, allowing complete freedom of use and distribution under any terms.

What Does This Mean for Investors?

Although closed-source has some positives around privacy, these are only advantageous for organizations prioritizing control over their codebase, proprietary advantages, and the ability to protect sensitive information from public scrutiny. Closed-source code offers little to no benefits for investors in the crypto space. From a crypto investor standpoint, the transparency aspect is critical. Open-source projects provide transparency that enables investors to evaluate the team's performance for the codebase. When investing in a project, investors inherit significant financial risk, not knowing anything about the codebase or the team's track record in managing it. Additionally, as per Table 12-1, open-source code promotes higher levels of community trust in the core product, innovation, collaboration, and security through the code's scrutiny by the developers' community. For these reasons, it is advised that digital asset investors focus on crypto investments that are open-source in nature.

Action Steps

Follow the steps below to determine if a crypto project is open-source or closed-source and assess its level of transparency, accountability, and associated risks if there is limited access to its codebase.

1) **Project Code Repository**

   Locate the official link to the project code repository.

   a) Visit the official project website and search for a link to the codebase on GitHub.

   b) In some unlikely cases, some projects may use GitLab or Bitbucket instead of GitHub.

2) **Locate Open-Source License**

   Once the project's codebase repository on GitHub (or other), check the project has an open-source license. This is typically located in the project code repository, as in the case of Moonbeam Network, as shown in Figure 12-6.

a) The open-source license file is typically labeled as "LICENSE." Always perform a quick keyword search if it is not clearly visible.

b) Once the license has been located, clicking on the file opens another page where the license type will be visible.

c) Validate and confirm that the license is in fact open source by visiting `https://choosealicense.com/appendix/` and checking if the license is listed. Note—Most open-source licenses used in the crypto world are typically the ones mentioned in Section 2.4.1 "Open-Source Licenses."

If you can't find a license, the project is likely closed-source. If this situation occurs, contact the project team and ask for clarification with reference URLs for backup and evidence for answers provided. If a repository is advertised as open-source but no license file is present, the code is legally all rights reserved—treat this as a serious red flag and ask the team to provide a proper open-source license.

3) **Project Whitepaper**

The project whitepaper is an excellent source for technical information and typically defines whether the project is open or closed source. See Moonbeam Network continued in Figure 12-7, where it is noted that the project is open-source with a link to their codebase on GitHub, where the open-source license file is found—as specified in Step 2.

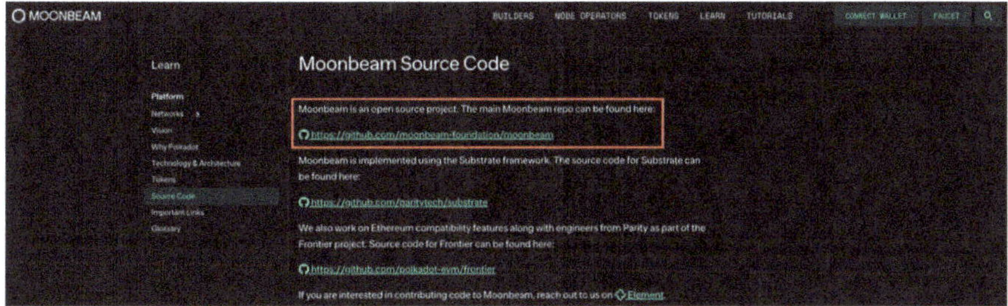

Figure 12-7. *Moonbeam open-source code outlined in the project whitepaper (image compliments of `https://docs.moonbeam.network/learn/platform/code/`)*

4) **Take Notes and Document Your Findings in Your Own Style**

5) **Combine the Findings with Other Sections of the Fundamental Evaluation Process**

Evaluating the Results

Blockchains and Web3 dApps that are open-sourced are highly admired. Closed-source projects are considered high-risk investments due to the lack of transparency and project team accountability—these should be avoided unless a very nuanced situation is encountered.

Programming Languages

Evaluation Objective: Confirm if the project uses a variety of well-known programming languages with specific strengths that cater to the particular needs of the product or service.

This section covers popular programming languages used in the blockchain industry for building blockchains, decentralized applications, and related software. Although digital asset investors are not required to have "developer" level knowledge, it is important to confirm that known and popular programming languages are being utilized, as this helps mitigate unforeseen risks related to the core product or service down the line. Additionally, it is essential that developer teams are using a variety of programming languages with strengths that cater to the specific piece of software or application being developed. For example, while Solidity is primarily used for writing smart contracts, its qualities and strengths do not compare to languages such as Python for data analysis and machine learning tasks. Each programming language has unique strengths and weaknesses, depending on what's needed, whether for visuals, speed, security, or ease of use.

Table 12-2 shows the most popular programming languages used in blockchain development.

Table 12-2. Popular programming languages used in blockchain development

Popular Blockchain Programming Languages				
Language	**Adoption Status**	**Type**	**Description**	**Typical Blockchain Use Cases**
Solidity	Mainstream	Smart Contract (EVM = Ethereum Virtual Machine)	Purpose-built language (looks a bit like JavaScript) for programs that live inside blocks.	• Create tokens and on-chain assets • Run voting or treasury rules • Automate DeFi actions
C++	Mainstream	General Purpose (Systems)	A very fast compiled language that lets programmers manage computer memory directly.	• Build full blockchain nodes • Code consensus algorithms • Write crypto libraries
Python	Mainstream	General Purpose (Scripting)	Easy-to-read scripting language with huge library support—great for quick jobs.	• Automate chain interactions • Analyze blockchain data • Prototype smart-contract logic
Java	Mainstream	General Purpose (JVM = Java Virtual Machine)	Object-oriented language that runs the same on Windows, macOS, and Linux.	• Enterprise middleware that talks to chains • JVM-based node software • Integration tools for contracts

(*continued*)

Table 12-2. (*continued*)

Popular Blockchain Programming Languages				
Language	**Adoption Status**	**Type**	**Description**	**Typical Blockchain Use Cases**
Rust	Mainstream	General Purpose (Systems)	Modern systems language: C-level speed plus built-in memory safety.	• High-performance runtimes • Web Assembly (WASM) smart contracts • Secure cryptography code
JavaScript	Mainstream	General Purpose (Scripting)	The language of the web; it runs in every browser and on servers via Node.js.	• Build decentralized-app (dApp) front-ends • Create client libraries • Write lightweight back-end services
Go (Golang)	Mainstream	General Purpose (Systems)	Compiled language from Google with simple syntax and easy concurrency.	• Stand-alone node software • Chaincode for private ledgers • Scalable back-end tooling
C#	Mainstream (niche)	General Purpose (.NET)	Microsoft's .NET language—strong typing and automatic garbage collection.	• Cross-platform nodes on .NET • Enterprise APIs for contracts • Desktop wallets or tools
Erlang	Mainstream (niche)	General Purpose (Functional)	Functional language built for huge numbers of simultaneous tasks that "never crash."	• Always-on node back-ends • Real-time messaging between peers • Fault-tolerant modules

TypeScript	Mainstream	General Purpose (Scripting)	JavaScript plus static types—catches many errors before code runs.	• Type-safe DApp user-interfaces • Test suites for contracts • Developer tooling
Ruby	Mainstream (minor in blockchain)	General Purpose (Scripting)	Very readable scripting language with a rich "gem" package system.	• Quick blockchain prototypes • Small web services • Command-line utilities
SQL	Mainstream	Domain-Specific (Query)	Declarative language for asking questions of relational databases.	• Query off-chain blockchain data • Build analytics dashboards • ETL (Extract-Transform-Load) pipelines
Vyper	Experimental	Smart Contract (EVM)	Python-like contract language that removes complex features to aid audits.	• Security-critical contracts • Reduce hidden bugs • Enable simpler formal reviews
Rholang	Experimental	Smart Contract (Concurrency)	Language based on process calculus; excels at parallel, message-passing logic.	• Contracts that run many tasks at once • Safe on-chain coordination • Model complex workflows

(continued)

Table 12-2. (continued)

Popular Blockchain Programming Languages				
Language	**Adoption Status**	**Type**	**Description**	**Typical Blockchain Use Cases**
OCaml	Experimental	General Purpose (Functional)	Fast functional language with a strong static type system.	• Prove protocol correctness • Research-grade node code • Formally verified contracts
Scilla	Experimental	Smart Contract (Safety-Focused)	Contract language that forces a clear state-machine structure to avoid pitfalls.	• Safer contract development • Formal analysis of state changes • Prevent reentrancy bugs
Simplicity	Experimental	Smart Contract (Formal DSL = Domain-Specific Language)	Minimal, non-Turing-complete language whose programs can be proven correct.	• Contracts with predictable cost • Mathematical proofs of behavior • Advanced payment conditions
Michelson	Experimental (industry-wide)	Smart Contract (Stack-Based)	Stack-machine language with strict types that supports formal proofs.	• Resource-predictable on-chain logic • Mathematically verified contracts • Upgradeable governance code
Haskell	Experimental (growing use)	General Purpose (Functional)	Pure functional language with a powerful type system and lazy evaluation.	• High-assurance blockchain protocols • Create contract DSLs • Verify complex algorithms

Investor Analysis of Programming Languages

It is recommended that investors perform the following programming language checks to confirm if the project is utilizing multiple, well-known, and popular languages with specific strengths to build the core product or service.

Evaluating Unusual Coding Languages

Table 12-2 lists the most popular programming languages in blockchain development. However, investors may occasionally encounter projects that use a language not mentioned in this table. There are many potential reasons for this, such as the language may be in its infancy, of poor quality, rarely used in blockchain development, or used for a specific nuance case or feature that is rare or new in the blockchain world. The level of risk and severity of this project depends on several factors. For instance, if the language is only used for 1% of the codebase, it will not typically raise red flags. However, suppose the particular language encountered accounts for a large proportion of the project code. In that case, more research is required to determine if the language does not threaten the project. This research will involve checking if the language has been used on other crypto projects and if these projects are successful with no history of attacks or crashes.

Figure 12-8 is a screenshot from Moonbeam Networks codebase showing the programming languages used at the bottom right of the image. Programming languages, including TypeScript, Rust, and Solidity—all used specifically for high-performing and highly secure blockchain development, dApps, and smart contracts—make up 99.6% of the code, with only 0.3% written in the Shell programming language. The Shell language is simply used to automate tasks and interact with the operating system, as well as to handle build, configuration, and deployment workflows. The remaining 0.1% is shown as a *Dockerfile,* a tool developers use to create a *Docker image,* a packaged version of the software that ensures it runs consistently in different environments such as computer systems, servers, or cloud platforms. While a Dockerfile is primarily a developer tool, its presence can signal reproducible build processes and team maturity—factors that can matter to technically oriented investors.

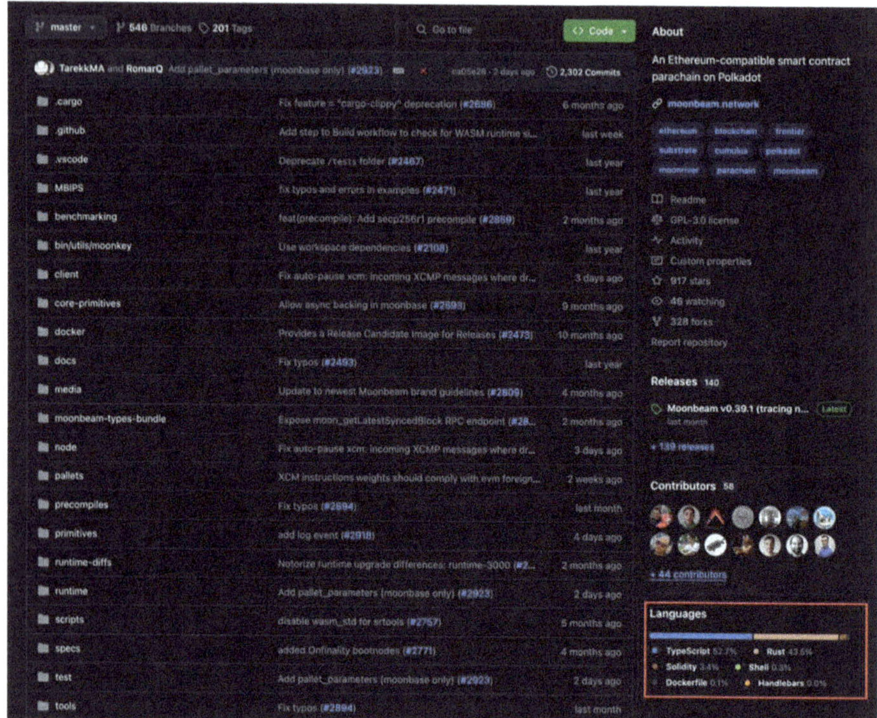

Figure 12-8. *Moonbeam Network programming languages (compliments of* `https://github.com/moonbeam-foundation/moonbeam`*)*

Programming Language Variety

As mentioned earlier, developer teams employ a range of programming languages when creating blockchain projects or dApps, each chosen for its specific strengths relevant to the software or application. As investors, verifying that the codebase encompasses multiple languages is important, as is ensuring the product is being developed with the appropriate tools. This also helps to identify potential scams, where developers might flood a project with code in just one or two languages to create the illusion of a legitimate product.

As per Figure 12-8, Moonbeam Network has a total of four programming languages. In comparison, GitHub language statistics for each network's primary client repository show about five dominant languages for Ethereum, five for Cosmos, and six for bitcoin. This illustrates a rough average range of four to six top programming languages per project and is seen as typical. Note that smaller projects, mainly dApps, may only utilize two to three programming languages on average. However, extreme caution should be taken if a project only employs one programming language. It is recommended to reach out to the project team and the community for clarity and, more importantly, compare against successful competitors in the same niche.

Caution This fundamental is only applicable to open-source projects. The analysis cannot be performed if the project is closed-source unless the development team grants you GitHub access.

Action Steps

Follow the steps below to determine if the project's codebase encompasses credible and a variety of programming languages that cater to the specific needs and requirements of the core product or service.

1) **Determine the Programming Languages Utilized**

   a) Locate the link for the project's GitHub or respective codebase software (usually in the footer of the project's website).

   b) View the project's programming languages in the "Languages" section on GitHub.

2) **Programming Language Fit of Use Case**

   a) Review the languages utilized by the project and confirm whether they match the application features of the projects or service. For example, in the case of Moonbeam Network, a blockchain infrastructure, the programming languages for blockchain development, Rust and TypeScript, are used and make up 96.2% of the project codebase. These languages are correct for Moonbeams blockchain service.

3) **Evaluating Unusual Coding Languages**

   a) If you encounter a programming language that accounts for a significant portion of the project and is not discussed in Table 12-2, research it and consider evaluating it against the following criteria.

      i) Why is the language used instead of traditional established programming languages?

      ii) How long has the programming language been released?

iii) Has the programming language been used on other cryptocurrency or Web3 projects? If so, are these projects successful in terms of performance, scalability, and speed? Were there successful attacks due to bugs and vulnerabilities?

iv) If the language has not been utilized within the blockchain world, determine if it is used to build centralized systems. If so, what is the overall feedback from developer communities?

4) **Programming Language Quantity**

   a) Review the number of programming languages utilized by the project team. While blockchain networks may employ four to six languages, dApps may only use two to three programming languages.

   b) If a project only utilizes one programming language, proceed with caution. Reach out to the team and community for clarity and compare against successful competitors in the same niche.

5) **Take Notes and Document Your Findings in Your Own Style**

6) **Combine the Findings with Other Sections of the Fundamental Evaluation Process**

Evaluating the Results

Suppose the programming languages utilized by the project have been selected based on application requirements and have a strong reputation and proven track record in the blockchain space. In that case, it is considered a positive indication. If not, it is recommended not to invest until any doubts or concerns have been satisfied through adequate research.

Git Contributors

Evaluation Objective: Determine the number of open-source contributors, ensure the development team remains active, and confirm ongoing progress is being made in the background.

A *contributor*—on GitHub—is someone who contributes to an open-source project by submitting code, documentation, or other technical resources to one or more repositories. On GitHub, a contributor is anyone whose commit has been merged into the repository—typically via a pull request—regardless of whether they currently hold collaborator (read-write) permissions. Depending on an open-source project's size and popularity, there could be anything from just a couple to a few hundred contributors continuously adding value to the core product. The type of contributions varies from person to person. Still, they are related to code development, underlying infrastructure, governance, user experience, new innovations, security audits, testing and quality, documentation, and research. Furthermore, increased global contributions boost visibility and credibility, leading to a stronger community, reduced development costs, and mainstream adoption.

Open-source contributions are crucial to a blockchain project's development, long-term success, and sustainability. Contributions are made globally by developers with diverse perspectives, strengths, and skill sets. This worldwide collaboration helps accelerate the growth and quality of the product or service. Additionally, due to the number of contributors, the project undergoes heavy scrutiny, filtering, and resolving of bugs and code vulnerabilities that were found.

Figure 12-9 shows Moonbeam Networks official GitHub; the contributor count—58 in the bottom-right corner—includes only developers whose commits were merged into the repository's default branch (main), so other Moonbeam repos may list additional contributors.

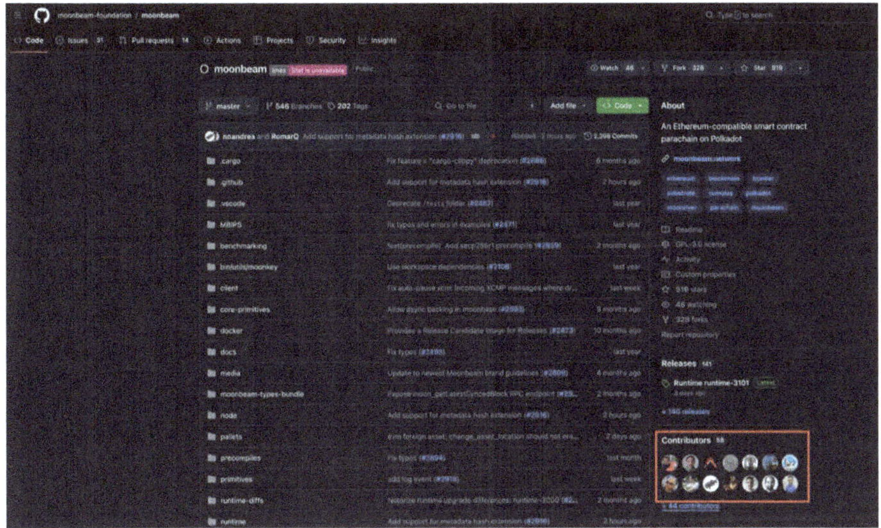

Figure 12-9. *Moonbeam Network—contributors (compliments of `https://github.com/moonbeam-foundation/moonbeam`)*

Action Steps

Follow the steps below to determine the number of open-source contributors, ensure the development team remains active, and confirm ongoing progress is being made in the background.

1) **Project Code Repository**

   Locate the official link to the project's code repository.

   a) Visit the official project website and search for a link to the codebase on GitHub.

      i) Some projects may sometimes use GitLab or Bitbucket instead of GitHub.

2) **Number of *Contributors***

   a) On the main code repository page, navigate to the bottom right to view the number of contributors.

   b) Take note of the number of project contributors.

3) **Take Notes and Document Your Findings in Your Own Style**

4) **Combine the Findings with Other Sections of the Fundamental Evaluation Process**

Evaluating the Results

It is admirable to see a large number of active open-source contributors adding value to a project. However, the number of contributors will vary from project to project depending on whether it is a small, medium, or large project when it was launched, popularity, use case, and many other variables. For better comparison criteria, comparing the number of contributors against successful competitors is recommended, confirming that the number of commits has remained constant or increased during the specified period.

Git Commits

Evaluation Objective: Determine the level of developer activity, productivity, and long-term interest in the project by analyzing the number of contributor code commits on GitHub.

This section aims to validate if the project team is progressing with building, updating, and enhancing the core product or service. Many project teams claim to be making progress behind the scenes with false impressions through social media or other channels. Although not every team is a scam, some projects lack transparency and have come to a semi-

or complete halt for several different reasons, such as abandonment, lack of funding, or even being a scam from the start. It is the investor's responsibility to validate whether the team's claims are accurate or if there are underlying issues causing the lack of progress.

An effective way to verify the progress of a project on the core product or service is to analyze the number of *commits* per month on GitHub. A "commit" is a fundamental concept in Git, representing a snapshot of the entire project at a particular time. This means every commit records the exact state of every file at that point in time—Git simply reuses unchanged file blobs under the hood to avoid duplication. For example, when a developer modifies, renames, deletes, or adds to the project source code, the developer can submit a commit—which includes a brief message outlining the changes—that updates every project file, thus providing a new snapshot of the entire project. This action is recorded as a commit in the project's GitHub repository. Any changes made can be compared against the previous (parent) submission.

By analyzing these commits, investors can determine if a project continues to be actively developed, even when its progress is not immediately evident from an external perspective. Additionally, a project in its early stages tends to be more active, with a higher number of commits than projects launched five years ago. Regardless, for a project to ensure long-term success and longevity, continuous "commits" incorporating new features and innovations are deemed essential.

Admirable Monthly Commit Contributions

There is no right or wrong number of commits per month that is deemed acceptable. It depends on variables such as the project lifecycle stage and its popularity. A popular open-source permissionless blockchain project will have a significant number of monthly commits compared to another less well-known and fundamentally strong project. As an indicator, from Sept 2023 to Sept 2024, the main branch of each project's primary repository averaged roughly 257 monthly commits for bitcoin, 224 for Chainlink, and 24 for Moonbeam Network—see Figure 12-10 for reference. From an investor standpoint, anything over roughly 15 monthly commits shows that the team and community are still progressing in the background.

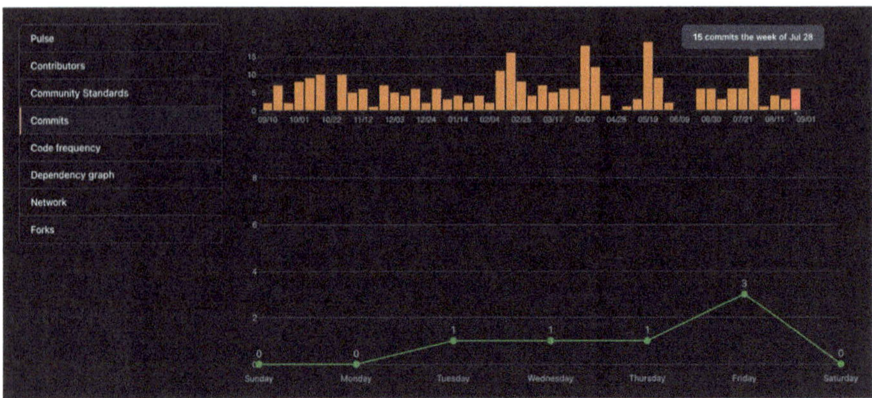

Figure 12-10. *Moonbeam Network code commits (compliments of* *`https://github.com/moonbeam-foundation/moonbeam/graphs/commit-activity`)*

It is also recommended that investors gauge the developer interest level in the project by checking whether the average number of commits in the primary repository has increased, decreased, or stayed the same over time—bearing in mind that commit volume can fluctuate with the project's roadmap and planned milestones. This can be achieved by going to the project's code repository and navigating to "Contributors"—as seen in Figure 12-9—which directs you to the "Contributors," as seen in Figure 12-11 with Moonbeam Network. At the top of the page, Moonbeams' date range is displayed, from February 2020 to December 2024, representing the number of commits made from the project launch to the current date. The graph for Moonbeam shows a consistent number of commits throughout these years, which is a positive sign of ongoing interest in the project.

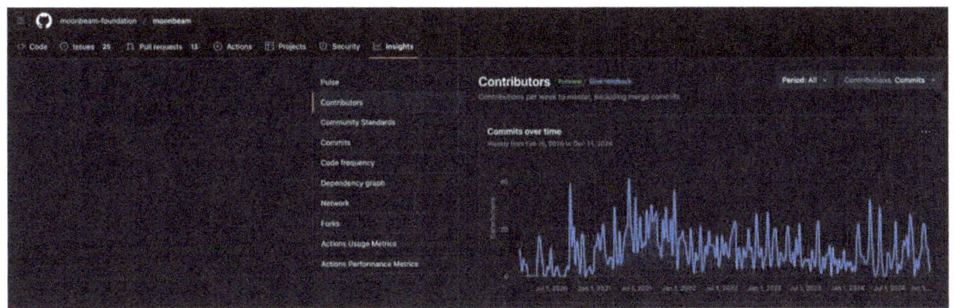

***Figure 12-11.** Contributors to the Moonbeam Network (compliments of `https://github.com/PureStake/moonbeam/graphs/contributors`)*

Action Steps

Follow the steps below to determine the level of developer activity, productivity, and long-term interest in the project by analyzing the number of contributor code commits on GitHub.

1) **Project Code Repository**

   Locate the official link to the project's code repository.

   a) Visit the official project website and search for a link to the codebase on GitHub.

      i) Some projects may sometimes use GitLab or Bitbucket instead of GitHub.

2) **Analyze the "Commits" in GitHub**

   a) Locate the Commits - From the project's Home Page in GitHub, navigate to "Insights" ➤ "Commits"—see Figure 12-10 for reference.

b) Count the Number of Commits – The orange bars at the top of the graph represent the number of commits for each week of the year (Figure 12-10).

   i) Click on each week (orange bar) to view the commits per day of the week.

   ii) To find the average number of commits per month, count the number per week for the whole year and divide by twelve.

3) **Evaluate the Contributor "Commit" Graph**

   Check if the average number of commits since the project launched has increased, decreased, or stayed the same over time.

   a) On the project's Home Page in GitHub, navigate to the bottom right to view the number of contributors.

   b) Click on "Contributors" to navigate to the Contributor page.

   c) Review the period to determine how long the open-source developer community has contributed to the project.

   d) Review the contributor/commit graph to determine if the number of contributor commits has increased, remained constant, or tapered off since the project's inception. Notethat while the "Y" axis represents the number of commits, the "X" axis represents time.

4) **Take Notes and Document Your Findings in Your Own Style**

5) **Combine the Findings with Other Sections of the Fundamental Evaluation Process**

Evaluating the Results

Seeing an average of fifteen commits in the past month is reassuring. A smaller number of commits, particularly less than ten, may raise questions about the work behind the scenes. When there are fewer than five commits, it should be viewed as a red flag.

From a long-term perspective, the number of commits over a few-year period should preferably increase or, at a minimum, remain constant, as this shows there is excitement among the developer community surrounding this project. It is not a hard deal breaker if this metric is tapering off. However, there must be a reason for this—exercise caution until a clearer picture has been obtained.

Git Issues

Evaluation Objective: Evaluate a project's open and closed issues on GitHub to assess development progress, team responsiveness, and overall project health.

On GitHub, every project has a repository named "Issues," where all open and closed issues relating to bugs, feature requests, tasks, improvements, design innovations, documentation, and concerns are logged. Most of these issues are related to the project code in some way or format. Anyone with access to this repository, meaning contributors, project maintainers, and even users who encounter bugs or have feature requests can create issues to report problems, suggest enhancements, or ask questions.

Open-source projects typically allow anyone with a GitHub account to create and submit a new *issue*. Once an issue has been generated, it is reviewed, categorized, managed, and assigned to contributors based on the required skill set and level of importance. Figure 12-12 shows a screenshot of Moonbeam Network's Git Issue repository. When working on this book, Moonbeam had 435 total issues captured by the open-source community and the project team—410 are closed (some marked resolved, others closed as duplicates or "won't-fix"), and only 25 remain open. This is considered excellent, as only 5.75% (25/435) of the Issues remain open, and 94.25% (410/435) have been resolved.

Also, by viewing the closed issues (Figure 12-13), investors can gauge if the team and community have made recent progress by viewing the date that the last issues were resolved. In the case of Moonbeam Network, multiple issues were resolved in the previous two weeks (at the time of writing this book).

Projects with a high percentage of open, unresolved issues may signal weak code quality, limited resources, or poor community support—but heavy-use projects also accumulate issues simply because more users are filing them, so context and activity levels must be considered before judging overall health.

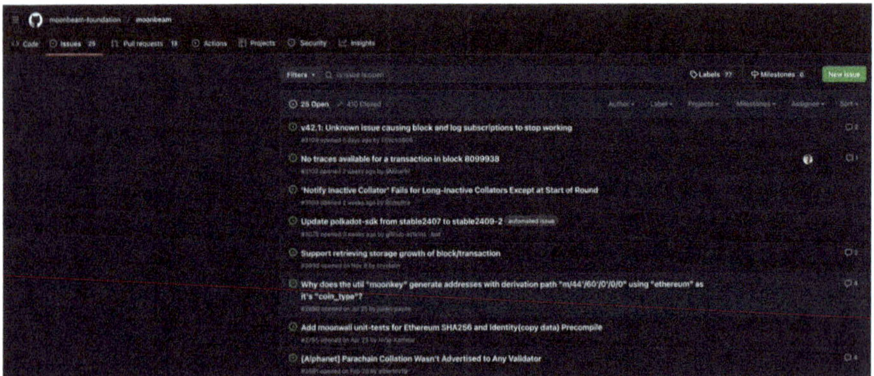

Figure 12-12. *Moonbeam Network—outstanding open issues (compliments of* `https://github.com/moonbeam-foundation/moonbeam/issues`*)*

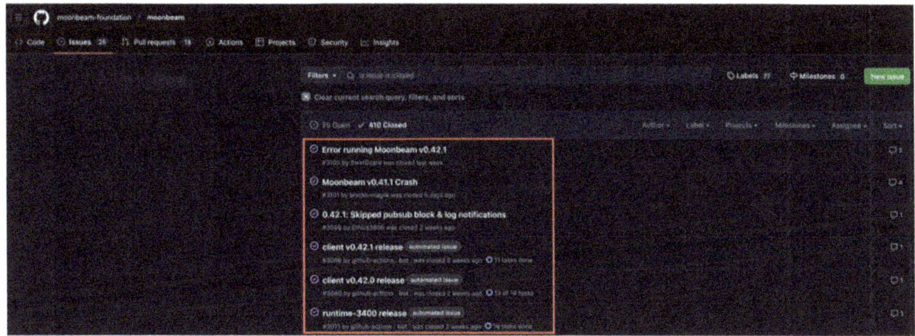

Figure 12-13. *Moonbeam Network—closed issues (compliments of https://github.com/moonbeam-foundation/moonbeam/issues?q=is%3Aissue+is%3Aclosed)*

Evaluating a project's open and closed issues on GitHub is a worthwhile and essential exercise, as it can shed light on performance metrics relating to the development, responsiveness, user experience, and potential risks involved. These performance metrics are as follows.

- **Development Progress** - Examining the percentage of open to closed issues and when the last issues were resolved provides investors a decent understanding of how the development team is progressing.
- **Team Responsiveness** - Opening and viewing several *issues* and reading the dialogue between the team and the contributor, including the dates the responses were generated, provides investors with a good indication of the team's responsiveness.
- **Risk Versus Reward** - By analyzing the problems and feedback on several *issues*, investors can better gauge if there is greater risk or reward than expected.

- **User Experience** – By evaluating several open and closed *issues* in terms of potential complaints, problems, negative feedback, and overall dissatisfaction, investors can get a feel of how the users and community are finding their experience.

Action Steps

Follow these steps to evaluate a project's open and closed issues on GitHub to assess development progress, team responsiveness, and overall project health.

1) **Project Code Repository**

   Locate the official link to the project's code repository.

   a) Visit the official project website and search for a link to the codebase on GitHub.

      i) Some projects may sometimes use GitLab or Bitbucket instead of GitHub.

2) ***Issues* Repository**

   a) Search and open the "Issues" repository at the top of the page.

      i) If the "Issues" tab is not visible, it means the repository owner has disabled the Issues feature. If visible but no issues are listed, this could mean that no issues have been created, or the owner has restricted visibility to specific groups (this is rare).

3) **Evaluate the Open and Closed *Issues***

   Evaluate the open and closed issues against the following criteria, as discussed in this section.

   a) Development Progress

   b) Team Responsiveness

   c) Risk versus Reward

   d) User experience

4) **Take Notes and Document Your Findings in Your Own Style**

5) **Combine the Findings with Other Sections of the Fundamental Evaluation Process**

Evaluating the Results

It is admirable to see a low percentage of open issues compared to closed ones—ideally keeping open issues below ~20% in mature projects (new launches can run higher until early backlogs clear). However, it should be considered an early warning sign if the team consistently fails to address issues. Such situations often lead to a growing backlog of open issues, negatively impacting user experience. However, if the team is responding to contributors, has a low ratio of open to closed items, and has recently closed out various issues, this is seen as a positive sign.

Code Security Audit

Evaluation Objective: Determine if the project has conducted a code security audit to ensure its codebase is secure and vulnerabilities are addressed, providing adequate protection from attacks.

A code security audit in the blockchain realm is a complete analysis of the project's codebase to identify potential bugs, vulnerabilities, weaknesses, or possible exploits. This security check encompasses the project's codebase, including smart contacts, protocols, consensus mechanisms, dApps, third-party services, etc. The end goal of the audit is to ensure that the project's codebase is secure, robust, efficient, and free from any malicious bugs that might try to exploit the system.

Caution It is crucial that every project has its entire codebase—smart contracts, protocol logic, and supporting libraries—audited by a professionally recognized auditing firm.

Why Execute a Code Security Audit?

While decentralization and strong consensus mechanisms help protect against attacks, no blockchain or dApp is completely protected with a zero percent chance of being exploited. Many projects are subjected to attacks more often than one may think. For example, in recent years, there have been dozens of attacks, including projects such as Ronin Network ($625 million stolen), Poly Network ($611 million), Penpie ($27 million), Binance BNB Bridge ($569 million), Bitmart ($196 million), Multichain ($125 million), and Coincheck (532 million). Therefore, it is essential for every project, no matter the size, to undergo a rigorous code security audit. Failing to do so often results in a catastrophic financial loss for the project team and investors.

Pro Tip To see if a project has had past security issues, check out the following:

Rekt `https://rekt.news/`

Cointelegraph `https://cointelegraph.com/tags/security`

Cryptoslate `https://cryptoslate.com/hacks/Substack`

Substack `https://substack.com/@blockthreat`

Web3 Is Going Great `https://web3isgoinggreat.com`

On the other hand, conducting a code audit has many benefits, including minimizing the risk of exploitation, optimizing the codebase for faster and more efficient performance, reducing cost and effort to maintain the product, enhancing user satisfaction, protecting sensitive data, and promoting code consistency. As a result, projects that have engaged professional code security firms to review their codebase and implement their recommendations face a much lower risk of successful attacks. This added layer of security is a significant advantage for investors, as it reduces the potential for security breaches that could harm the project's reputation and value.

Code Security Audit Execution

Crypto-project code audits are typically carried out by third-party firms specializing in code security. There are dozens of blockchain code audit firms, with most offering the same core services and varying degrees of professionalism and reputation. Some of the more popular blockchain code audit firms are, but not limited to, Hacken, Certik, Quanstamp, and Trail of Bits.

A standard code security audit typically involves the following steps:

1) **Scope** - Define the objectives and the areas of the codebase that need auditing. This may include auditing various smart contracts, protocols, blockchain infrastructure, and a combination of all or specific customer requirements.

2) **Planning** - Plan the stages of the audit from start to finish with the project team.

3) **Gathering Information** - Gather the relevant information about the blockchain, or dApp, and its respective codebase and corresponding documentation to understand the system thoroughly.

4) **Code Analysis** - First run automated scanners—community or commercial—to flag common issues, then scan the codebase for bugs, vulnerabilities, and weaknesses through various tools and techniques, including static analysis, dynamic analysis, and manual review of code.

5) **Risk Assessment** - Prioritize identified bugs, vulnerabilities, and weaknesses based on severity and likelihood.

6) **Reporting** - After completion of the audit, a detailed audit report is presented to the project team. This report includes all identified bugs and vulnerabilities, their potential impact, and recommendations on how to eliminate them.

7) **Remediation** - The developers collaborate with the auditors to fix the identified bugs, vulnerabilities, and weaknesses.

8) **Re-testing** - Once all the identified issues are corrected, the codebase is retested (where applicable) to ensure the system is bug-free.

9) **Post Audit Support** - Often, the auditing firm offers ongoing guidance and support to help maintain high security. This may include post-audit monitoring to track the effectiveness of the implemented fixes and identify any new potential threats.

Investor Code Security Audit Checks

Unfortunately, some project teams are relatively relaxed regarding code security, and it is not taken seriously until an attack occurs and the project's reputation is tarnished. Therefore, it is the investor's responsibility to ensure that a code security audit has been conducted, and, at a minimum, the critical bugs, vulnerabilities, and weaknesses have been resolved. If the project team does not address the issues identified by the auditing firm, this is considered a significant red flag that leaves the project exposed and vulnerable to attacks.

Pro Tip Investors can view a list of projects that claim to have undergone code audits, along with the respective auditing firms, by visiting CoinMarketCap.com and selecting Filters ➤ Add Filter ➤ Audited; because this tag is self-reported, always confirm the audit with the project's published report or team.

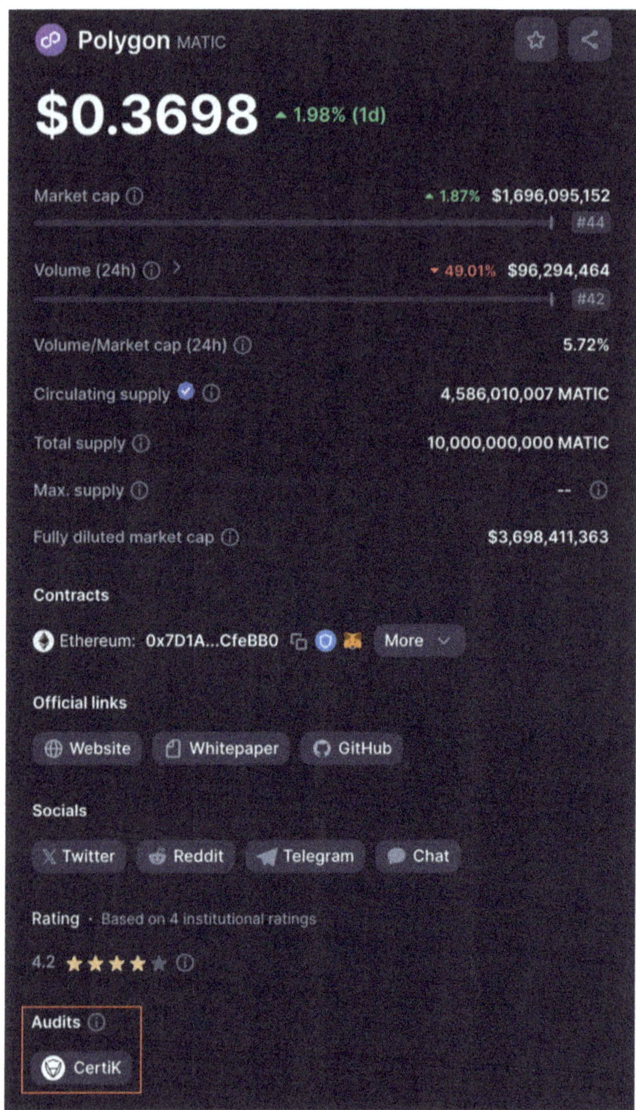

Figure 12-14. *Polygon Network on CoinMarketCap.com, showing the code security audit performed by the CertiK auditing firm (compliments of `https://coinmarketcap.com/currencies/polygon/`)*

CertiK is a leading code security firm that provides a comprehensive suite of tools to monitor and help secure the blockchain sector—including investors. Figure 12-15 and Figure 12-16 show code security audit report summaries for Polygon (MATIC). Based on Polygon's code audits executed by CertiK, a score of 95.44 out of 100 has been provided, deemed excellent in terms of secure source code. Two different code audits were carried out for Polygon by CertiK. While Figure 12-15 displays the code audit summary for Polygon's "*MATIC Staking Contract*," Figure 12-16 shows the code audit for *MATIC*'s smart contracts that power MATIC's PoS (proof-of-stake) based bridge. Although this specific scope of work for MATIC's PoS-based bridge is not visible in the code audit summary, it is found within the full code security audit report, accessible through the "View PDF" button in the code summary. This report is available for both of Polygon's audits executed by CertiK. The detail in the report is detailed and is worth reading to understand the scope of work performed and the associated findings.

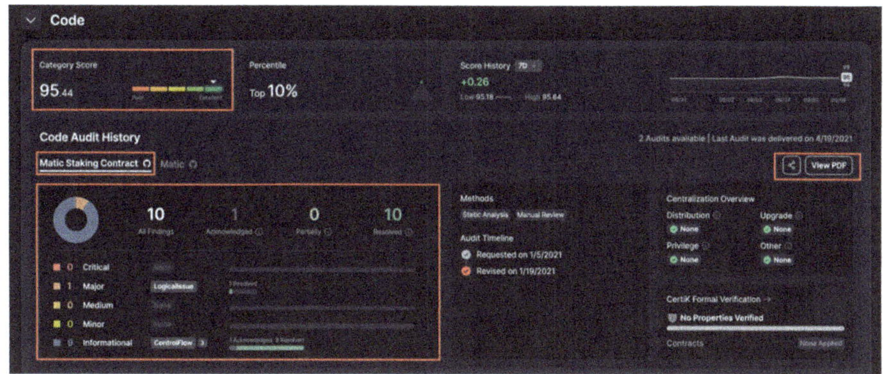

***Figure 12-15.** Polygon Network security code audit for "MATIC Staking Contract" through Certik (compliments of `https://skynet.certik.com/projects/polygon`)*

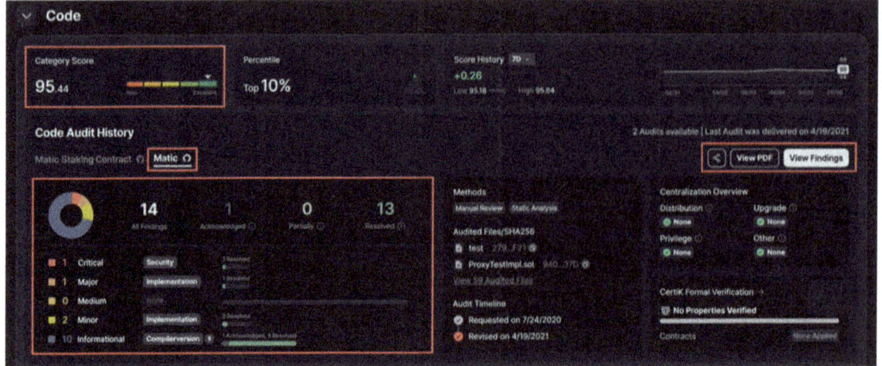

Figure 12-16. *Polygon Network security code audit for "MATIC" through Certik (compliments of* `https://skynet.certik.com/projects/polygon`*)*

CertiK categorizes identified issues by severity—from *informational, minor, medium, major,* to *critical*—though other audit firms may use slightly different labels for equivalent risk levels. While the score provided by CertiK reflects the overall condition of the source code, investors need to verify whether any issues classified as *critical* or *major* were identified during the code audit and have been either resolved or, at a minimum, the risk mitigated. In auditing Polygon's "MATIC" smart contracts for the PoS-based bridge, CertiK identified fourteen code issues: one *critical,* one *major,* two *minor,* and ten *informational* —see Figure 12-16 and Figure 12-17. Although the *medium, minor,* and *informational* categories of issues must be addressed for any project, the project team must deal with the *critical* and *major* issues immediately. The corresponding status of each issue is visible on Polygon's full and summarized code reports. For instance, thirteen of Polygon's fourteen reported code issues have been resolved, including the *critical* and *major* issues. This is an excellent sign that the codebase is secure, and the project team is working diligently to keep the project codebase free from bugs, vulnerabilities, and weaknesses. Consider it a red flag if any *critical* or *major* categorized issues have been found to have a status of "*Acknowledged*" for more than a few days.

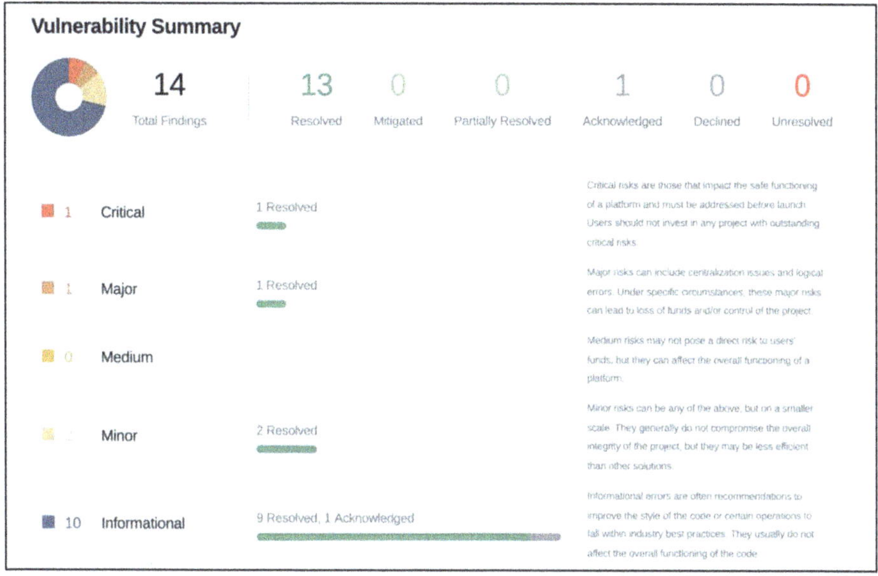

***Figure 12-17.** Polygon's "MATIC" code audit report from CertiK, indicating the finding of the code audit (compliments of `https://skynet.certik.com/projects/polygon`)*

***Figure 12-18.** Polygon's "MATIC" code audit report from CertiK, indicating the specific scope of the audit; smart contracts that power the PoS-based bridge for the MATIC Network (compliments of `https://skynet.certik.com/projects/polygon`)*

As previously discussed, many other code security audit firms service the blockchain sector. While CertiK was used as the example in this section, most code security audit firms produce similarly formatted audit reports. For example, see the code security audit for the **Binance Proof of Reserves (PoR)** verification system (`https://audits.hacken.io/binance/por-binance-por-code-audit-feb2023/`), executed by Hacken.

Continuous Improvement Code Monitoring

Once the initial code security audits are completed and any identified issues have been resolved, many firms provide ongoing code monitoring services, either monthly or annually. Although these services are deemed not as critical as the primary code security audit, continuous improvement monitoring helps ensure that, moving forward, any new vulnerabilities, updates, or changes to the codebase are caught early, minimizing the risk of security breaches and maintaining the integrity of the software over time. This proactive approach allows projects to stay ahead of potential threats.

Figure 12-19 shows a screenshot from the Aave DeFi project audit report through CertiK. This indicates that Aave has Certik-powered active monitoring on its website, codebase on GitHub, and social media. Projects with active code security monitoring have a slightly lower chance of getting hacked. Most code security audit firms offer post support, such as active monitoring. Therefore, investors are advised to check if the project utilizes this service with any code security auditing firm as part of the fundamental evaluation.

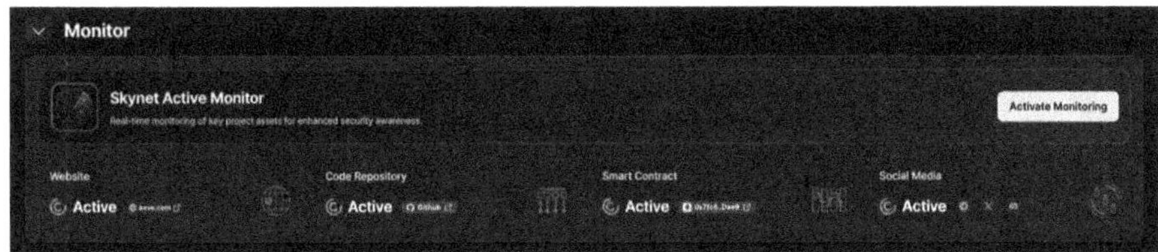

***Figure 12-19.** Active security monitoring of Aave DeFi project on CertiK (compliments of `https://skynet.certik.com/projects/aave?utm_source=CMC&utm_campaign=AuditByCertiKLink`)*

Action Steps

Follow these steps to determine if the project has conducted a code security audit to ensure its codebase is secure and vulnerabilities are addressed, providing adequate protection from attacks.

1) **Code Security Audit**

   Determine if the project's codebase has successfully undergone a code security audit. There are several ways this can be accomplished.

   a) Contact the project team through official channels and request a link to the report. The URL to the audit report must be provided as confirmation via message or email, as this is not sufficient.

   b) Visit the homepage of CoinMarketCap.com, select *Filters* ➤ *Add Filter,* and then toggle *Audited*. This will show the list of the projects that have reported audits of their codebases to CoinMarketCap.

   c) A simple search through your preferred browser can help determine if a code security audit was executed for a particular project, including links to the code audit report—please ensure URL legitimacy.

2) **Code Audit Firm Credibility**

   Perform research to verify that a professional, accredited, certified, and reputable firm conducted the code audit. Also, review the other projects they have audited.

3) **Resolution of Found Code Issues**

   Code issues ranked as critical and major must be resolved or, at a minimum, mitigated.

   a) Check the project's code audit report to determine if any *critical* and *major* ranked code errors have a *Resolved* or *Mitigated* status.

      i) Always check to see if the audit report is regularly updated. In most cases, it is; however, if not, reach out to the project team for clarification.

4) **Post Audit Support Audit**

   Regular security monitoring of the project codebase after the initial audit reduces hacking risks.

   a) Check with the project team to verify if they are availing of post-audit security monitoring.

5) **Take Notes and Document Your Findings in Your Own Style**

6) **Combine the Findings with Other Sections of the Fundamental Evaluation Process**

Evaluating the Results

Investors should prioritize projects with thorough code audits, with all *critical* and *major* ranked code errors resolved. Investing in a project that has not undergone a code audit from a professional code audit security firm is not recommended. Not only is the project codebase at a higher potential risk of attack, but it also reflects poorly on the project team.

Bug Bounties

Evaluation Objective: Determine if a project has issued, completed, or planned a bug bounty program to evaluate its commitment to code security.

As an additional measure to help secure the project codebase, crypto projects run bug bounties programs—an approach long used by major tech companies such as Google, Microsoft, and Meta–where developers and community members throughout the blockchain industry are incentivized to help identify bugs, vulnerabilities, or weaknesses in the project code. Details such as how the bug was caught, the severity of the issues, and recommendations on how to remediate are detailed in the report sent to the project team. Like a professional security audit, bug bounties usually focus on a project's highest-value components—smart contracts, bridges, wallets, or other critical modules—although some well-funded teams extend the bounty's scope to cover their entire codebase. Bug bounties are recognized as a collaborative community approach that helps maintain and improve the blockchain's or dApp's overall code security.

Fact Bug bounties are typically executed by "white hat hackers" whose expert knowledge and skills are used to identify and fix bugs, vulnerabilities, and weaknesses in a project's codebase. Conversely, "black hat hackers" exploit these vulnerabilities for personal gain or malicious purposes.

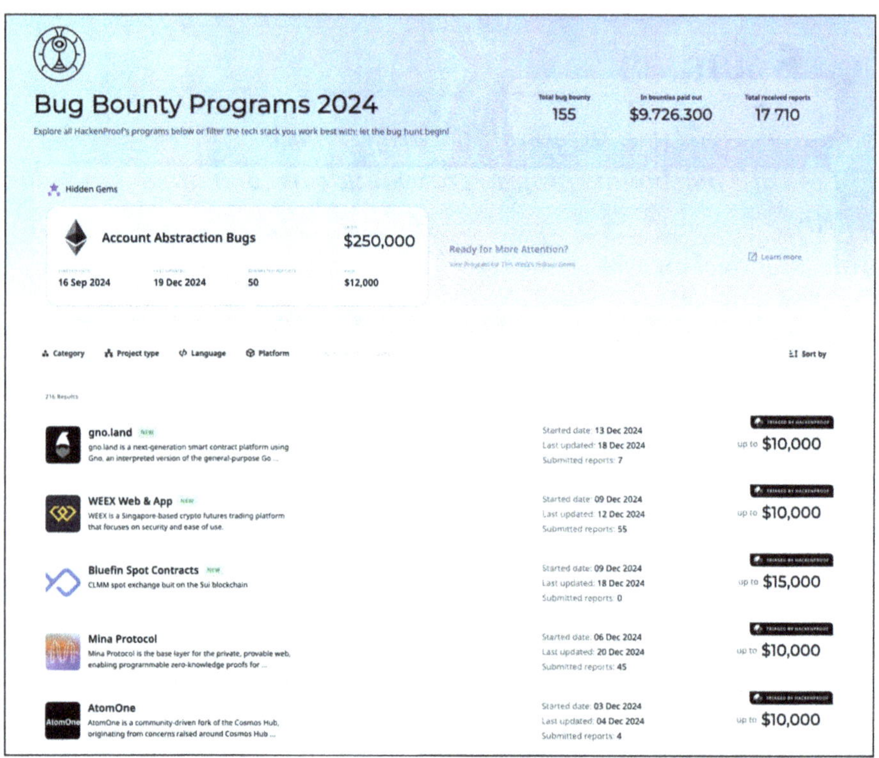

***Figure 12-20.** HackenProof bug bounties programs started in December, including for Mina Protocol 2024 (compliments of `https://hackenproof.com/programs`)*

Bug bounties are important for trust and transparency between the project team and its community outside code security. It also encourages active community engagement, thus contributing to more visibility and credibility. It is recommended for investors to determine if bug bounties have been scheduled, are in progress, or have been completed for the project being evaluated. Several websites allow investors to see past, current, and future planned bug bounties within the crypto space. These are as follows:

HackenProof—`https://hackenproof.com/programs`

CertiK—`https://skynet.certik.com/leaderboards/bug-bounty`

Immunefi—`https://immunefi.com/bug-bounty/`

Bug Bounty Radar—`https://bbradar.io/`

Bugcrowd—`https://www.bugcrowd.com/bug-bounty-list/`

Action Steps

Follow the steps below to determine if a project has issued, completed, or planned a bug bounty program to evaluate its commitment to code security.

1) **Project Bug Bounty**

   Check whether the project team has finished a bug bounty program, if it is ongoing, or if it has been planned.

   a) Reach out to the project team for information on their bug bounty (if any). Ensure they provide links so all information provided to you can be verified.

b) Research popular bug bounty websites and platforms—specifically those mentioned in this section—to review bug bounty data for a particular project (if available).

2) **Bug Bounty Findings**

   If bug bounty results are available:

   a) Determine if the project team has acknowledged and resolved the identified critical and major code issues.

      i) For security reasons, some projects tend to keep any findings private to help maintain security and prevent potential exploitation of disclosed vulnerabilities.

3) **Take Notes and Document Your Findings in Your Own Style**

4) **Combine the Findings with Other Sections of the Fundamental Evaluation Process**

Evaluating the Results

It is a positive sign if a bug bounty program was performed on the blockchain or dApp. Although somewhat unfavorable, it is not necessarily a red flag, provided a bug bounty has not been issued as long as a professional code auditing firm has performed a code security audit.

CHAPTER 13

Incentivization and Rewards

Crypto asset-based incentives and rewards are crucial for many reasons, including driving user participation, securing the network, providing liquidity, network growth, community, behavior engagement, governance participation, economic stability, and contributing to a more attractive ecosystem. These are integral to many blockchain networks and decentralized applications' functionality, growth, and sustainability.

For investors, understanding these incentive structures is key to evaluating a project's sustainability and growth potential. This chapter is also beneficial for investors interested in participating in decentralized finance (DeFi) reward protocols, as it discusses the pros and cons of each type of DeFi yield-earning protocol and the type of investor they may be suited to. High-yield rewards may seem appealing but often carry underlying risks, such as unsustainable rewards, token inflation, centralization, or scams.

Incentive mechanisms attract participants by paying a reward—commonly called "yield" in DeFi but distinct from proof-of-work "mining"—for participating in various yield-earning activities and other contributions to the network. The payout rates depend on the magnitude of different factors, such as the type of incentive mechanism, digital asset stability, supply and demand metrics, and associated risk. Yield-earning processes are vital components for **many** blockchain networks and

P. Garvey, *Blockchain Fundamental Analysis for Digital Asset Investors*,
https://doi.org/10.1007/979-8-8688-1551-5_13

DeFi-focused dApps, acting as prime motivators for attracting investors and network participants. They provide the opportunity to make money outside of traditional trading or investing. Unlike traditional markets, blockchain technology has created a variety of specially designed yield-earning processes that put digital assets to work to generate a steady flow of passive income with little effort.

Yield earning processes fall under the categories of blockchain security and the umbrella of DeFi. The combination of these incentive processes helps create a more secure, efficient, and liquidity-rich blockchain ecosystem where participants are financially motivated to act in the network's best interest. Various yield-earning processes are available, such as staking, liquidity mining, and various DeFi yield farming processes.

Terminology associated with DeFi yield farming, including the naming conventions for various processes, remains subject to misuse due to the absence of proper clarity. For example, some people define yield farming and liquidity mining as separate processes. However, some conclude that since "yield" is also generated from liquidity mining, it falls under the "yield farming umbrella." Staking and mining also generate a "yield"; however, some do not refer to these processes as a typical "yield"-bearing process. As time passes, the distinction between these classifications will become clearer and more distinguished. Nevertheless, the classification or labeling of such practices is somewhat irrelevant, provided the concept of each process is understood. Moreover, in this book and in the interest of clarifying, incentive mechanisms are broken into two main categories: *primary incentive mechanisms* and *secondary incentive mechanism*s.

It is highly recommended that adequate time be taken when evaluating the primary and secondary incentive mechanisms. Although lucrative, most yield-earning processes come at a high risk compared to financial markets. Therefore, it is imperative for investors, particularly those looking for long-term gains, to comprehend these processes thoroughly. This understanding will help select a suitable yield-generating process(es) that aligns with the investor's risk tolerance, time commitment, and technical skill requirement. Additionally, analyzing these yield-bearing mechanisms also unfolds important information that helps investors understand the level of network security, liquidity resources, level of volatility, and community trust and faith in the network or dApp.

Fundamentals Discussed in This Chapter:

- Primary Incentive Mechanisms
    - Staking
    - Mining Rewards
    - Yield Farming
    - Yield Aggregators
    - Governance Rewards
    - Play-to-Earn-Rewards
- Secondary Incentive Mechanisms
    - Airdrops
    - Platform Incentives
    - Beta Testing Rewards
    - Referral Programs
    - Loyalty Rewards

Pro Tip Incentive mechanisms aren't just about profits; they often signal a project's maturity and alignment with user interests. Look for projects with sustainable reward structures, as overly generous incentives may indicate unsustainable tokenomics.

Primary Incentive Mechanisms

Primary incentive reward systems are yield-earning processes whereby rewards are often generated and automatically distributed on-chain in a decentralized manner, although some staking or yield-farming schemes route payouts through custodial or semi-centralized services. This is accomplished through mining, staking, or smart-contract-controlled systems, including DeFi yield-earning mechanisms and play-to-earn incentives in decentralized gaming. In most cases, due to the benefits of decentralization and open-source permissions, these award mechanisms do not require a centralized authority. However, in most circumstances, transaction fees are required. Primary reward incentive mechanisms include

- **Staking**
- **Mining**
- **Liquidity Mining**
- **Yield Farming**
- **Yield Aggregators**
- **Governance Participation**
- **Play-to-Earn**

Staking

Staking refers to the process where an individual receives rewards for locking their assets (coins) on-chain to help support the security of a blockchain network. The rate at which staking participants receive new rewards is called the *reward rate,* and it is measured as a percentage of how many rewards are earned throughout a given year.

Staking is possible with proof-of-stake (PoS) blockchain and PoS blockchain variants supporting validation, security, and maintenance operations. Digital assets (native coins or tokens) from PoS-based blockchains are "*staked*," acting as insurance to help keep validators from acting maliciously. Staking motivates users to lock up (stake) their coins, offering "staking" rewards based on the amount each investor stakes. The more coins staked, the higher the potential rewards. Examples of PoS-based blockchains are Ethereum (ETH), Solana (SOL), and Cosmos (ATOM). The staking reward rate is indicated as an APY (annual percent yield) percentage value. APY values differ from protocol to protocol; however, a typical reward rate for mature projects is between 2% and 6%.

Many different staking processes are available, with slightly different steps to stake an asset. However, the most common fundamental steps to staking a digital asset are as follows:

1) **Select a PoS Digital Asset** – Choose a suitable PoS digital asset to stake based on variables such as involved risk, asset stability, annual reward percentage, etc.

2) **Select a Staking Service** – Run your own validator (self-host) or use a reputable third-party staking service for your PoS asset.

3) **Stake Assets** – Stake your assets. This may be directly from a wallet or through a third-party staking service.

4) **Monitor Rewards and Asset Value** – Keep track of the distributed rewards and asset market value.

5) **Restake or Claim Rewards** – Choose whether to reinvest the staking rewards or withdraw them based on protocol guidelines.

6) **Unstake Assets** – Unstake and withdraw your assets (if required). Note that there may be an unlock period before assets can be withdrawn.

Various staking variations and processes are discussed in the following sections. The pros and cons of each staking process provide investors with a more thorough understanding that aids in selecting a staking process that aligns with the investor's risk tolerance and time commitment. Furthermore, critical factors for evaluating long-term success, such as adjusted staking rewards, transaction fee-based earnings, staking ratio, and circulation versus maximum supply, are discussed.

Validator Staking

Examples: Polkadot Network, Ethereum, and Avalanche Network
As discussed in the section "Proof-of-Stake (PoS)" in Chapter 6, "Blockchain Architecture," validators, also known as *block creators*, help maintain security and system efficiency by validating transactions on the blockchain. Validators stake a significant amount of digital assets (e.g., 32 ETH in the case of Ethereum) as collateral, from which a portion may be slashed—up to the full stake only in severe or repeated offenses—if the validator acts dishonestly or negligently. The validator is responsible for checking (signing) that new blocks (containing transactions) propagated over the network are valid and occasionally creating and propagating new blocks themselves.

Advantages

- **Maximum Rewards** - Earn maximum rewards directly from the protocol without intermediary fees.
- **Full Control** - Running a full node provides.
    - **Private Key Security** - By using their own private key, validators can secure their staked assets directly, which adds an extra layer of security because they don't need to trust a third party with their assets.

    - **Direct Transaction Validation** – The ability to validate transactions directly without relying on third parties.

- **Voting Rights** – In most PoS blockchains, validators have the right to participate in governance processes, allowing them to vote on various aspects and directions of the network.

- **Network Security** – Validators help strengthen network security.

- **Transparency and Trust** – Running a node allows validators to manage and monitor their own funds without the requirement of intermediaries.

Disadvantages

- **Technical Knowledge** – Requires a high level of technical expertise to set up a node.

- **Operating Costs** – Running a node requires the following:

    - High-speed internet.

    - High-powered, efficient operating system.

    - **Hardware** – Maintain hardware that runs an Ethereum execution client and consensus client while connected to the internet.

    - Sufficient amount of computer SSD disk storage. For example, to run an Ethereum node, it is recommended to have at least 2TB of SSD storage with an additional 0.5TB to 1TB as a precaution.

    - Increased electricity costs because the node must be constantly active (online) without disruptions or downtime.

- **Active Participation** – Requires constant monitoring to ensure the node is always online and behaving accordingly.
- **Minimum Stake** – Running validator nodes comes with minimum stake requirements, which can discourage and hinder many individuals with lesser funds. The minimum requirement varies widely from network to network.
- **Slashing** – Malicious behavior can result in the "slashing" of larger amounts of the staked asset.

Liquid Staking

Examples: Lido and Stader

In a traditional staking (*hard staking*) process, the user's assets are locked up for a set period and cannot be easily accessed or traded. This reduces investor liquidity, which prevents trading or using assets as collateral until the locking period elapses or the user initiates an early withdrawal. A prime example of this is Ethereum 2.0, where users are required to stake 32 Ether (ETH) on the network. While the staking participant's 32 ETH is locked, they will continue to receive rewards as long as there is no malicious activity. However, they cannot use these funds while their funds are staked. The issue is that not every investor has 32 ETH; therefore, they do not qualify to participate in Ethereum's staking process. Liquid staking platforms help alleviate this problem with partial stake opportunities.

A liquid staking (*soft staking*) protocol combats the issues associated with traditional staking by providing the staking party with a synthetic, *liquid staking derivative* (LSD) in return for their staked assets. This LSD, also known as a liquid staking token (LST), is programmatically minted by the protocol when the user stakes. LSTs represent the value of the staked assets, an IOU that provides further investment opportunity, increased liquidity, and capital efficiency for the user. These LSTs are liquid in design, enabling users to trade or put them to work in DeFi applications as part of a strategy to earn additional passive income.

An example of a well-known decentralized liquid staking provider is Lido. Lido allows users to stake Ethereum, and in return, users are provided with an LST, stETH (staked ETH). These stETH synthetic tokens mirror the value of the user's staked ETH balance on the Ethereum Beacon Chain at a target 1:1 ratio (including any staking rewards or penalties), though the market price can drift above or below 1 ETH during periods of heavy demand or limited liquidity. are free to use stETH derivative tokens as part of additional DeFi strategies, trade, or simply hold in case sudden liquidity is required. The Lido user can trade in (burn) the stETH tokens to retrieve their staked assets.

Lido's protocol consists of a staking pool that aggregates user stakes and delegates them to independent validators, stETH tokens, and a DAO for governance. The staking pool employs an oracle contract to monitor the DAO's validator balances. The DAO is crucial for governance, providing a decentralized layer of security that reduces the risk of a single point of failure in maintaining the ETH-to-stETH peg. It also oversees protocol updates and selects an insurance provider, with its treasury funded by staking rewards earned through the Lido smart contract.

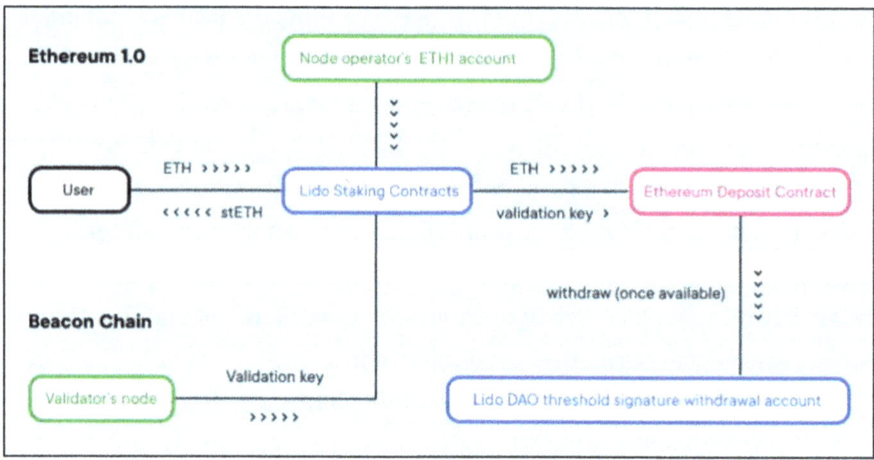

Figure 13-1. *Staking framework for Ethereum on Lido staking platform provider (compliments of `https://blog.lido.fi/how-lido-works/`)*

On liquid staking platforms, users continue to earn staking rewards based on the original staked tokens. These rewards may be "baked into" the value of the derivative token, or they may be distributed separately.

Advantages

- **Liquidity** – Unlike traditional staking, liquid staking provides liquidity to staking participants in the form of derivative digital assets.
- **Increased Capital Efficiency** – LSDs provide an increased opportunity to earn additional rewards by utilizing the synthetic assets in different DeFi protocols in return for extra yield.
- **Lower Entry Barrier** – Through liquid staking providers, participants with fewer assets can earn rewards by entering various staking pools where the rewards are distributed proportionally to one's stake.

- **Price Drop Protection** – Allows staking derivative holders to instantly sell their assets in the case of a severe price crash versus being bound to an unlock period while the assets continue to decrease in value.

Disadvantages

- **Security Risk** – Participants are at a higher risk of the multiple moving parts associated with liquid staking, such as various staking and liquidity pools, smart contracts, derivative assets, and validators. Any bugs or vulnerabilities in the code may cause participants to lose some or all of their assets.
- **Complexity** – The liquid staking process is more difficult to understand than traditional staking; therefore, additional care and understanding are required before staking.
- **Slashing Risk** – Liquid staking processes are also subject to *slashing*. Any validator misbehavior or malicious activity can lead to punishment whereby some or all of the staked assets are deducted.

Staking-as-a-Service (SaaS)

Examples: BloxStaking and Ethpool
Staking as a service (SaaS) is a software service offered by various blockchain-based companies that enables users to participate in the staking processes without owning or maintaining the hardware and software required to run validator nodes. This process usually involves being guided through the initial setup, including key generation and deposit, or keeping them locally while the operator connects via a

non-custodial remote-signing setup. This allows the service to operate your validator on your behalf, usually for a monthly fee—Blox Staking is a prime example of this type of setup.

As outlined by Ethereum.org, before utilizing a SaaS company, it is vital to consider the following attributes:

1. **Open-Source** – Ensure that the code is open-source and available to the public to fork and use.
2. **Audited** – The essential code has undergone formal auditing, and results have been published and made available publicly.
3. **Bug Bounties** – A public bug bounty has been performed on any essential code to reward users for safely reporting and/or fixing vulnerabilities.
4. **Battle Tested** – Service has been available and used by the public for a minimum of six months, but preferably over one year.
5. **Permissionless** – Users do not require special permission, account signup, or *know-your-customer* (KYC) verification to participate in the service.
6. **Execution Diversity** – Service should not run more than 50% of their aggregate validators with a majority execution client.
7. **Consensus Diversity** – The service should not run more than 50% of their aggregate validators with a majority consensus client.
8. **Self-Custody** – User maintains custody of any validator credentials, including signing and withdrawal keys.

Advantages

- **Maintenance** - SaaS platforms ensure optimal staking conditions by ensuring server requirements such as software and updates.
- **Ease of Use** - Simplified staking process, no need for heavy technical knowledge.
- **Reduced Start-Up Costs** - No need to purchase hardware, including a high-powered operating system and adequate storage space.
- **Reliable** - Continuous and reliable service with no downtime.

Disadvantages

- **Control Limitations** - With some SaaS companies, you may not have full control of the validation node.
- **Auditable Restrictions** - Some SaaS platforms use proprietary, closed-source code, limiting transparency and suitability for users requiring fully auditable systems for compliance or security.
- **Custodial Risk** - The risk of losing staked assets if the service provider is hacked. Therefore, non-custodial service providers are favored.
- **Slashing** - Malicious behavior can result in the "slashing" of larger amounts of the staked asset.

Centralized Staking Platforms

Examples: Bybit, Coinbase, Binance, and Kraken
Centralized staking platforms run by centralized entities enable users to stake PoS-based digital assets in return for rewards. Users can deposit their assets or purchase them directly on the platform, where they are then staked and locked for a predetermined timeframe.

Advantages

- **User-Friendly** – Simple and straightforward
- **Accessibility** – No technical knowledge required
- **Reduced Risk** – Reduces risk of slashing, thus protecting user's staked assets

Disadvantages

- **Centralization** – Risk of attacks from hackers due to centralization
- **Limited Control** – Less control over their staked assets
- **Governance** – May not be allowed to participate in governance votes on the network
- **Fees** – Reduced rewards due to centralized platform fees

Staking Through Decentralized Wallets

Examples: Lido, Trust Wallet, Trezor, Exodus, and MetaMask
Decentralized staking-based wallets and providers enable users to stake their PoS digital assets to earn rewards. Staking functionality is provided either natively within the wallet or by connecting the wallet to a decentralized staking protocol, so no centralized governing body is involved, and users keep full control of their assets and keys.

Advantages

- **Self-custody -** Full user control over digital assets and private keys.
- **Security -** Less risk of attack due to direct staking participation with no intermediary.
- **Transparency -** All staking operations are open for audit by the community.
- **Lower Fees -** Fees may be lower due to having no centralized intermediary.

Disadvantages

- **Complexity** - May present technical challenges for those without an understanding of blockchain basics.
- **No Customer Support** - Most decentralized staking providers lack adequate customer support.
- **Responsibility** - Users bear full responsibility for the safety and security of their staked assets, requiring constant vigilance.

Staking Considerations for Investors

When participating in staking on a Proof of Stake (PoS) blockchain, investors can earn rewards from two primary sources: *newly minted coins* or *transaction fees*, or a combination of both. Each method has distinct implications for the token's supply, inflation, and potential value stability. This section breaks down these reward types and other key staking factors like real reward rate and optimal staking ratio to help investors make informed decisions.

Staking Rewards: Minting Versus Transaction Fees

When network participants (e.g., validators) participate in a PoS (or a PoS variant, e.g., DPoS and LPoS) consensus mechanism, they provide a service that validates transactions and secures the network. In return, they are rewarded with "staking" rewards for their efforts. These rewards, also referred to as *yield*, can originate from two primary sources: transaction fees and newly minted coins.

Rewards from Minted Coins

In this type of staking reward model, staking rewards are generated by the creation of new native coins that are minted on the blockchain. These newly minted coins are distributed to validators for their work done. This type of inflationary reward mechanism is the primary method used in PoS blockchains.

Advantages

- **Encourages Participation** – A constant flow of rewards incentivizes more network participants to stake their assets, thus further securing the network.
- **Consistent Reward Supply** - Steady, consistent, and predictable rewards for validators and *stakers* with little fluctuations.

Disadvantages

- **Diluted Token Supply** - The most significant drawback to this approach is the constant dilution of the supply caused by creating new tokens and introducing them into the circulating supply. This may further devalue the token price if the inflation rate surpasses the pace of network expansion or adoption, which can be detrimental for long-term investors.

- **Discourage Investors** - Heavily inflated supplies caused by the minting of new tokens may discourage new investors from investing, thus further devaluating the project's worth and reputation.

Rewards from Transaction Fees

Staking rewards can also be derived from transaction fees, meaning that the transaction fees paid in the blockchain's native currency (e.g., BNB) are used to reward the validators and staking participants for their efforts in validating transactions and maintaining blockchain security. The rate at which validators can earn rewards via transaction fees is typically weighed against the number of coins staked, the network protocol, and the number of transactions processed.

The core benefit of this method is that the digital asset used to pay transaction fees already exists in the total supply. Therefore, the process is a simple reallocation of the coins from the hands of the "senders" to the validators and staking participants. There is no requirement for the creation of new coins. Therefore, the process is inflation-free with no further dilution of the supply.

Advantages

- **Inflation Control** - This method enables the payment of validators and staking participants without inflating the supply.
- **Attracts Investors** - Investors tend to gravitate towards projects not subject to inflated token supplies.

Disadvantages

- **Unpredictable Rewards** - Rewards can fluctuate depending on the transaction volume and network usage. This can cause periods of high rewards and times where validators and staking participants earn little rewards.
- **Barrier to Adoption** - Transaction fees need to be controlled so that they do not hinder the growth of the blockchain. High transaction fees can discourage network users, while low transaction costs promote highly incentivized opportunities for validators and network users.

Although staking can be lucrative, it does not come without risk. *Slashing* is a PoS mechanism where validators are penalized for failing to meet specific requirements, acting maliciously, failing to meet certain conditions, or acting in a way that harms the network. Additionally, it is crucial to monitor the price per coin to ensure that it is not only still worth the effort of staking but also because it can impact the total yield.

Real Reward Rate

When staking digital assets, it is vital to understand the asset's inflation rate and its effect on the net staking rewards. As discussed in the section "Inflationary Token Supply" in Chapter 8, "Tokenomics," with an inflationary token supply, more tokens are continuously added into circulation, increasing the total supply over time. This dilutes each token holder's share of the total supply, meaning your proportion of ownership decreases unless you are compensated with an equivalent amount of newly minted tokens. Therefore, when staking, investors need to focus on the *real reward yield* versus receiving more newly minted tokens that are continuously diluting the token supply.

Pro Tip Long-term investors should always stake their assets to prevent their share of the total supply from shrinking due to inflation. Compounding (or re-staking) rewards further offset dilution, helping to maintain value while earning additional rewards.

Unlike the standard "gross" reward rate, the *real reward rate* (formerly known as the "adjusted staking reward") represents the actual "net" staking yield, showing the true rewards—indicated as a percentage—an investor receives after accounting for inflationary or deflationary factors. This helps determine if they are gaining real value or simply holding more, yet diluted, tokens. A positive real reward rate indicates that the distributed staking rewards exceed the inflation rate, with the investor earning true net staking rewards. Conversely, a negative real reward rate means that, after accounting for inflation, the value of the staking rewards falls short, and the investor may be gaining more tokens in number but with diminished overall purchasing power. Therefore, it is strongly recommended to consider the real reward rate before investing in an asset, especially if the intention is to earn passive rewards from staking. However, if invested in an asset because of its highly admirable fundamentals and it has a negative real reward rate, staking may still be worthwhile—this is a nuanced situation. Without staking, your holdings would likely lose purchasing power as inflation dilutes the token supply. In this case, staking to at least break even or reduce losses is a preferable choice to letting inflation gradually erode the value of your investment.

The real reward rate is calculated as per Equation 13-1. The nominal staking rate is the staking reward before considering inflation, while the inflation rate is the rate at which the token supply increases annually.

$$\textit{Real Reward Rate} = \left(\frac{1 + \textit{Nominal Reward Rate}}{1 + \textit{Inflation Rate}} \right) - 1$$

Equation 13-1. *Formula to calculate the real reward rate*

Figure 13-2 shows Ethereum and Solana's staking reward data from StakingRewrds.com, a platform for crypto staking and real-time reward analytics. Ethereum has a reward rate of 3.39%, an inflation rate of 0.38%, and a real reward rate of 3%. This indicates that Ethereum's inflation rate is practically zero; therefore, the 3% real reward rate is generated from transaction fees and not inflation, which is highly admirable for investors. Since Ethereum transitioned to a proof-of-stake model and implemented EIP-1559, a portion of transaction fees is burned, while another portion is used to support the network, including staking rewards.

On the other hand, Solana has a reward rate of 6.31%, an inflation rate of 5.32%, and a real reward rate of 0.93%. This indicates that when staking SOL, even though it has a high inflation rate (6.31%), it is being neutralized with the high inflation rate (5.32%), with investors only truly earning a 0.93% yearly reward rate. Unlike Ethereum, Solana's rewards are generated from newly minted coins, not transaction fees. As a result, the supply is being continuously diluted. However, without staking, investors will continue to lose their percentage stake in the supply as time passes. Solana's final inflation supply is expected to be 1.5% in 2031.

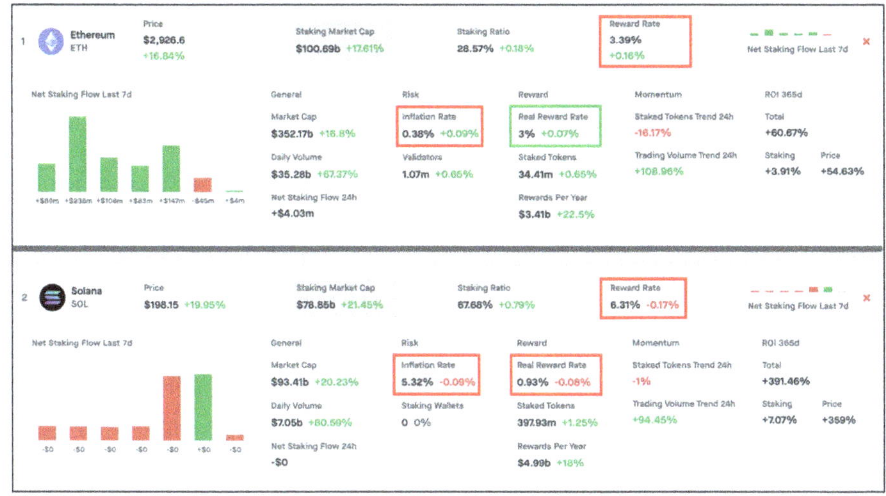

***Figure 13-2.** Ethereum and Solana staking data from StakingRewards.com showing reward rate, inflation rate, and real reward rate (compliments of `https://www.stakingrewards.com/assets/proof-of-stake?sort=staking_marketcap&timeframe=7d&order=desc&byChange=false&columns=reward_rate%2Cprice%2Cstaking_marketcap%2Cstaking_ratio%2Cinflation_rate%2Creal_reward_rate`)*

The following four conditions can define an ideal staking opportunity:

1) *When the "real reward rate" value is higher than the "reward rate" value.*

2) *When the staking rewards originate from transaction fees versus minting on new coins.*

3) *When the circulating supply is close to the maximum supply, indicating there is little inflation left.*

4) *When a burning mechanism is in place, the overall token supply decreases.*

Staking Ratio

A key element to consider is the *staking ratio,* which is indicated as a percentage. The staking ratio can be defined as the aggregate tokens staked in the economy to the total quantity of tokens in supply. A higher staking ratio generally indicates a higher level of trust in the project by the community, as more users are willing to lock their tokens for a certain period.

At the network level, there is typically an inverse relationship between the overall staking ratio and the reward earned per staked token—as more tokens are staked, the same reward pool is shared among a larger set of participants. As the number of tokens staked increases, individual staking rewards tend to decrease, given the distribution of rewards among a larger pool. On the other hand, as the quantity of unstaked tokens decreases, meaning fewer tokens are staked, individual staking rewards increase because they are divided among fewer participants. However, regardless of the APY, the more tokens an individual stakes, the greater the rewards they will receive in return. This naturally attracts and leads to more overall staking activity, creating a higher staking ratio in aggregate and for individuals.

$$\textbf{\textit{Staking Ratio}} = \left(\frac{\textbf{Total Staked Token}}{\textbf{Total Token Supply}} \right) \boldsymbol{x}\ \mathbf{100}$$

Equation 13-2. *Formula to calculate Staking Ratio*

For example, *Project X has 250 million staked tokens and a total supply of one billion tokens.*

$$\left(\frac{\mathbf{250,000,000}}{\mathbf{1,000,000,000}} \right) \boldsymbol{x}\ \mathbf{100 = 25\%}$$

Equation 13-3. *Staking ratio example calculation for fictitious Project X*

Optimal Staking Ratio

An optimal staking ratio is one that balances security, liquidity, profitability, volatility, and trust in the project. A high staking ratio possesses increased network security and faith in the project, resulting in increased volatility and low staking APY. On the other hand, a project with a low number of staked coins—i.e., a low staking ratio—tends to have low volatility and excellent staking APY but may harm network security and raise questions regarding investor sentiment in the project. Table 13-1 further simplifies the advantages and disadvantages of low and high staking ratios.

Table 13-1. *Consequences of low and high staking ratios*

Staking Ratio—Low and High Consequences		
	Low Staking Ratio(e.g., 0–5%)	**High Staking Ratio(e.g., 95–100%)**
Network Security	Poor	Excellent
Liquidity	Excellent	Poor
Rewards (APY)	Excellent	Poor
Faith/Trust	Poor	Excellent

A staking ratio either too high or too low may significantly negatively impact the project's success. Therefore, as a general rule of thumb, a staking ratio between 30% and 70% helps balance essential elements such as security, liquidity, profitability, volatility, and trust in the project. This is especially relevant for projects with a low staking market cap to help maintain network security. Large-cap networks can remain secure with just 20–30% staked because the bonded value is enormous—Ethereum, for example, locks about $87 B at 29%, and BNB Chain secures roughly $19 B with only 21% staked—all while preserving liquidity and keeping inflation modest.

From an investor standpoint, an ideal staking opportunity is one with a high APY without the drawbacks typically associated with a high staking ratio.

Figure 13-3 shows the top ten staking assets ranked by staking market capitalization, compliments of stakingrewards.com on November 09, 2024. The staking ratio for each project is outlined in red. Table 13-2 lists these staking ratios and their respective real reward rates and shows the average of each.

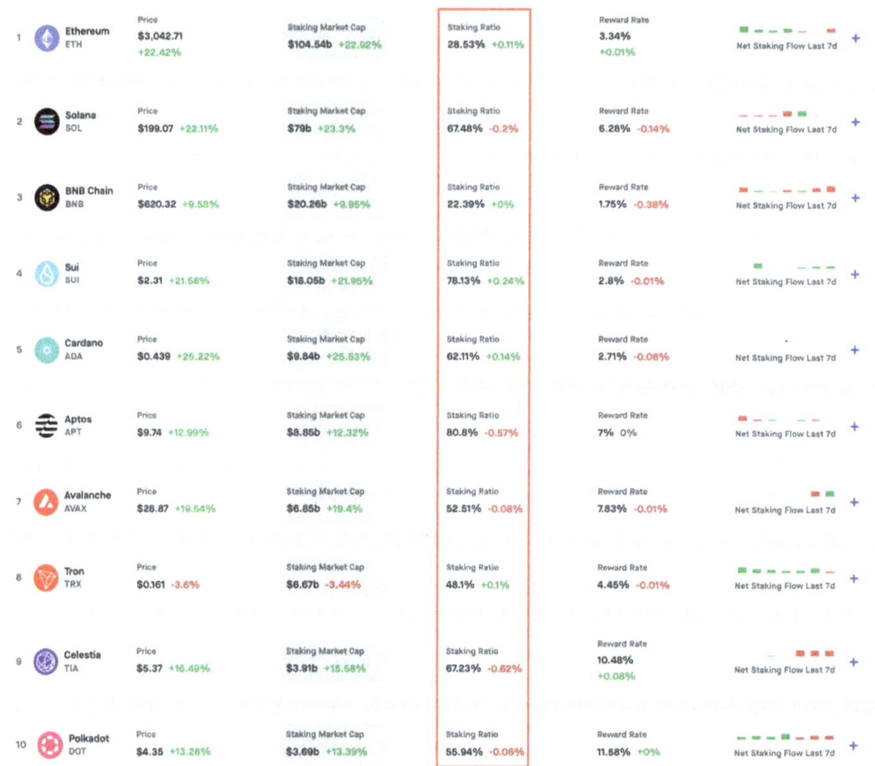

#	Asset	Price	Staking Market Cap	Staking Ratio	Reward Rate	
1	Ethereum ETH	$3,042.71 +22.42%	$104.54b +22.92%	28.53% +0.11%	3.34% +0.01%	Net Staking Flow Last 7d
2	Solana SOL	$199.07 +22.11%	$79b +23.3%	67.48% -0.2%	6.28% -0.14%	Net Staking Flow Last 7d
3	BNB Chain BNB	$620.32 +9.58%	$20.26b +9.95%	22.39% +0%	1.75% -0.38%	Net Staking Flow Last 7d
4	Sui SUI	$2.31 +21.68%	$18.05b +21.95%	78.13% +0.24%	2.8% -0.01%	Net Staking Flow Last 7d
5	Cardano ADA	$0.439 +25.22%	$9.84b +25.53%	62.11% +0.14%	2.71% -0.06%	Net Staking Flow Last 7d
6	Aptos APT	$9.74 +12.99%	$8.85b +12.32%	80.8% -0.57%	7% 0%	Net Staking Flow Last 7d
7	Avalanche AVAX	$28.87 +19.54%	$6.85b +19.4%	52.51% -0.08%	7.83% -0.01%	Net Staking Flow Last 7d
8	Tron TRX	$0.161 -3.6%	$6.67b -3.44%	48.1% +0.1%	4.45% -0.01%	Net Staking Flow Last 7d
9	Celestia TIA	$5.37 +16.49%	$3.91b +15.58%	67.23% -0.62%	10.48% +0.08%	Net Staking Flow Last 7d
10	Polkadot DOT	$4.35 +13.28%	$3.69b +13.39%	55.94% -0.06%	11.58% +0%	Net Staking Flow Last 7d

Figure 13-3. *Top ten voted assets ranked by market capitalization (July 29, 2023) (compliments of `https://www.stakingrewards.com/assets/proof-of-stake`)*

Table 13-2. Optimal staking ratio

Optimal Staking Ratio			
No	**Digital Asset**	**Real Reward Rate (%)**	**Staking Ratio (%)**
1	Ethereum	2.94%	28.53%
2	Solana	0.93%	67.48%
3	BNB Chain	6.34%	22.39%
4	Sui	-4.54%	78.13%
5	Cardano	0.59%	62.11%
6	Aptos	-5%	80.80%
7	Avalanche	3.13%	52.51%
8	Tron	7.36%	48.10%
9	Celestia	-7.16%	67.23%
10	Polkadot	2.79%	55.94%
Average	–	**0.74%**	**56.32%**

Leaving aside project fundamentals for all projects, Tron and BNB Chain stand out as top staking projects, with real reward rates of 7.36% and 6.34%, respectively—followed closely by Ethereum and Polkadot. Tron's staking ratio of 48.10% represents a good balance of tokens staked, supporting network security while maintaining adequate liquidity. BNB Chain has a lower staking ratio of 22.39%, contributing to its high and attractive reward rate. Even with its low staking ratio, its large $20.26 billion staking market cap makes it a highly secure network, reducing the risk of attack. To maintain network security, achieving a moderate staking ratio is vital for projects with smaller staking market caps.

Solana and Cardano have high staking ratios with low real reward rates. In contrast, Aptos and Celestia have moderate to high staking ratios with negative real reward rates due to immense inflation, 12.24%

and 18.94%, respectively. Assets with solid reward rates and high staking market caps with low to moderate staking ratios offer investors the best mix of profitability, security, and liquidity.

Mining Rewards

As discussed in the section "Proof-of-Work (PoW)" in Chapter 6, "Blockchain Architecture," *mining* is validating and recording blockchain transactions by creating a valid block—known as block creation—through generating a cryptographic solution that meets specific criteria. When *miners* solve this complicated mathematical puzzle, they mint (create) new bitcoins and collect the transaction fees included in that block. Note only the miner who solves the mathematical puzzle first gets to keep the rewards—this is known as a proof-of-work (PoW) consensus mechanism. bitcoin is a prime example of a PoW blockchain, where miners are incentivized for their computational work.

Advantages

- **Rewards** - Depending on the digital asset, mining can be very profitable, with miners not only earning mining rewards but also transaction fees, e.g., bitcoin.
- **Asset Appreciation** - If the value of the cryptocurrency being mined appreciates over time, the rewards earned by miners could be worth significantly more in the future.
- **Network Contribution** - Miners help maintain the security of the blockchain network, enhancing the project's reputation and investor confidence, which may indirectly support long-term token value.
- **Decentralization** - Solo miners add to the overall decentralization of the network.

Disadvantages

- **Energy Consumption** – Electricity costs can be extreme due to the high-powered ASIC (*application-specific integrated circuit*) mining machines, which may outweigh the profits from mining rewards.
- **Startup Costs** – Initial startup costs can be costly, mainly due to the setup of the ASIC mining rig. Typically, the more efficient the ASIC rig, the higher the price.
- **Maintenance** – Setup and maintenance of a mining rig can be technically challenging for someone not new to PoW mining.
- **Technology Advancements** – Due to rapid advancements in technology, mining rigs are quickly being replaced with more powerful technology, which hinders the profit rating of old rigs unless more money is spent updating to the latest technology.
- **Operating Requirements** – Mining equipment is generally noisy and expels significant heat. Therefore, a secluded, controlled environment may be required depending on living arrangements.
- **Competition** – Large, centralized mining farms make it difficult for solo miners or smaller pools to compete for profits.
- **Technical Knowledge** – Complex for many without prior experience because of the technical nature of setting up, maintaining, and upgrading mining hardware and software.

Liquidity Mining

Examples: Uniswap, PancakeSwap, Balancer, and Curve
Liquidity mining is a DeFi process whereby users can earn passive income by providing liquidity to decentralized finance (DeFi) protocols. Decentralized exchanges (DEX) such as Uniswap and Curve are AMMs (automated market makers) that facilitate the swap of digital assets without the involvement of a third-party trading platform. For token swaps to take place, there has to be adequate liquidity.

Highly liquid digital assets have many buyers and sellers, facilitating fast-execution trades at a minimal cost. In contrast, low-liquidity assets often lead to slower trades, potential price slippage, and higher fees. To combat this, AMMs incentivize users, known as liquidity providers (LPs), to deposit their digital assets into liquidity pools. LPs earn rewards for helping maintain liquidity, which benefits all DEX users by facilitating faster and cheaper swaps.

For example, an LP providing liquidity to accommodate swaps between ETH and USDT (and vice versa) would deposit an equal dollar value worth of ETH and USDT in an ETH/USDT liquidity pool. In return, the LP earns rewards, often a share of the transaction fees generated by trades in that pool. Some projects also offer additional token rewards to encourage more liquidity, especially for new or lesser-known tokens, which can be less liquid early on.

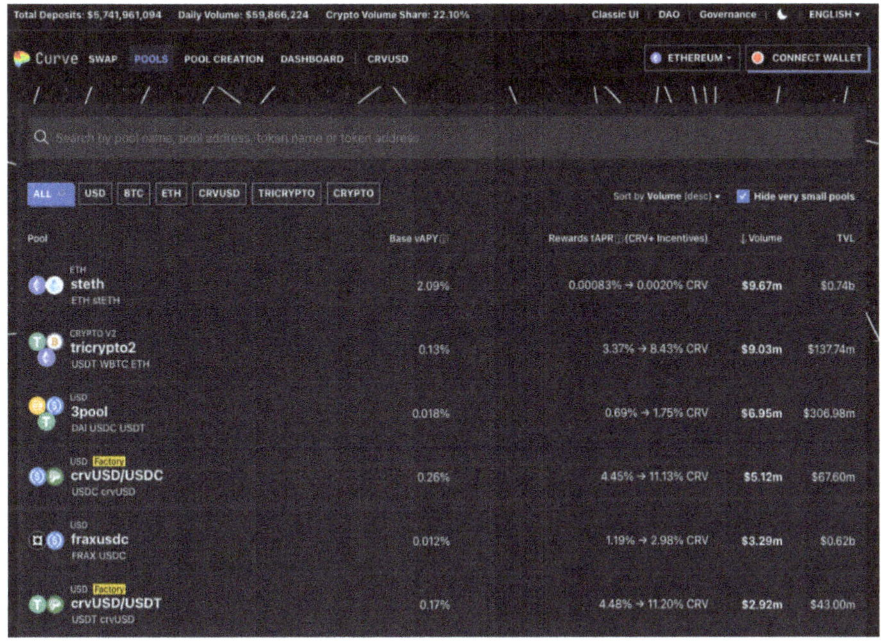

***Figure 13-4.** Curve DAO, liquidity pools (compliments of `https://curve.fi/#/ethereum/pools`)*

LPs receive automatically minted liquidity-pool tokens (LP tokens) that track their share of the pool and entitle them to a proportionate cut of trading fees, plus any extra incentives the AMM provides. Some examples of LP tokens can be seen on platforms like Balancer and SushiSwap. On Balancer, these tokens are referred to as *Balancer Pool Tokens* (BPT), whereas on SushiSwap, they are named *SushiSwap Liquidity Provider* (SLP) tokens. These LP tokens are integral to most DEX providers and represent proof (receipt) of the participant's stake in the liquidity pool and interest earned. LP tokens act as a receipt for assets that remain locked in the pool's smart contract, letting providers withdraw their original stake (and fees) whenever the protocol allows. LP tokens enable liquidity providers to access crypto loans, transfer ownership of the staked liquidity, and earn compound interest in yield farming if desired. It is common for most liquidity mining platforms to allow participants to withdraw their LP tokens at any time and redeem the fees and rewards earned.

For new projects, liquidity rewards typically start out with liquidity providers (LPs) earning high rewards (yield). However, as more LPs add liquidity to the pool, the rewards are spread out among all LP participants, thus diluting the incentives. Furthermore, other factors such as the type of protocol, specific liquidity pool, and market conditions all impact liquidity mining rewards.

Although lucrative, liquidity mining does not come without risk. Impermanent loss (IL) occurs when the price ratio between the two tokens in a liquidity pair moves away from the ratio at deposit—regardless of whether their fiat prices rise or fall—so the LP position ends up worth less than simply holding the tokens outright. The spread between these two values dictates the size of the loss incurred: the bigger the spread, the bigger the loss.

Pro Tip Exercise extreme caution where very high LP yields are offered. These are often associated with token pairings that involve smaller, early startup projects with minute market capitalizations that carry high risk and excessive volatility.

Since impermanent loss results from volatility within a trading pair, liquidity pools containing at least one stable asset (USDC, USDT, or DAI) are less vulnerable. Similarly, for liquidity pairs composed of two stablecoins, the impermanent loss risk is further minimized; however, so is the level of incentivization. In some cases, the rewards provided to liquidity providers within the pool can potentially offset the impermanent loss over time while still providing profits.

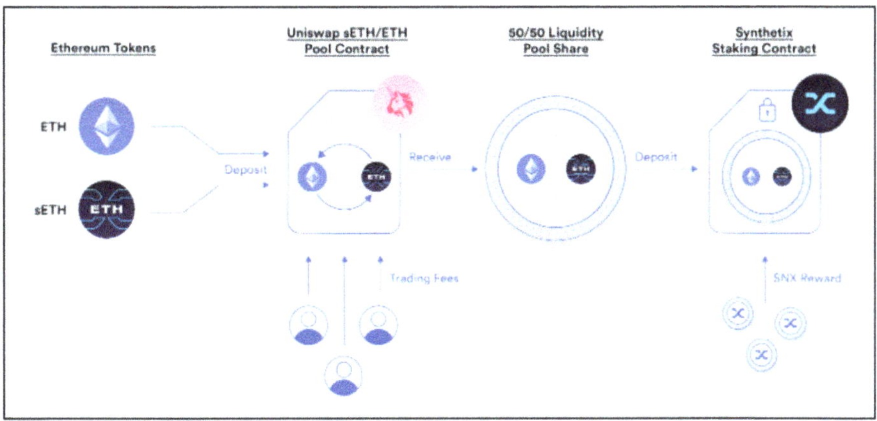

Figure 13-5. *Liquidity farming process for Uniswap decentralized exchange (`https://academy.shrimpy.io/lesson/what-is-liquidity-mining`)*

Advantages

- **Potential for High Yield** – Investors can earn high annual percentage yields (APYs).
- **Low Barrier to Entry** – No requirement for expensive hardware or software.
- **Project Support** – By providing liquidity, users support and contribute to the project's success.
- **Access to New Projects** – Liquidity providers can earn tokens from new emerging and promising projects that may increase in value over time.

Disadvantages

- **Risk of Impermanent Loss** – Potential for substantial losses due to changes in token values within liquidity pools.

- **Rug-Pulls** – Early-stage projects often attract liquidity providers with high returns. However, sometimes, fraudulent teams suddenly withdraw all the liquidity, leaving investors with worthless tokens. This scam is commonly referred to as a "rug pull."
- **Code Vulnerabilities** – Any bugs or code vulnerabilities in the liquidity present an opportunity for hackers that may result in permanent losses for liquidity providers.

Yield Farming

Examples: Compound Finance and Aave
Yield farming is the process where DeFi users stake or lend their digital assets to earn passive income. Protocols such as Compound Finance and Aave attract liquidity providers by offering incentives to lend or lock their assets in smart contract-powered liquidity pools. Typically, these rewards come from a mix of transaction fees, interest from borrowers, and sometimes platform-specific tokens. In the case of Aave, for example, users who stake AAVE in the Safety Module receive "stAAVE" tokens, representing their contribution to the protocol's security.

Yield farming participants typically stake or lend stablecoins such as USDC, USDT, or DAI, as these assets help mitigate the risk of IL. Recently, yield farmers have also started staking LP tokens earned from liquidity mining, allowing them to maximize returns by providing liquidity and re-staking rewards for additional yield. Yield farming returns are typically expressed as APY, accounting for compounding interest. However, these rates are subject to frequent fluctuations due to changes in pool demand, protocol incentives, and asset prices.

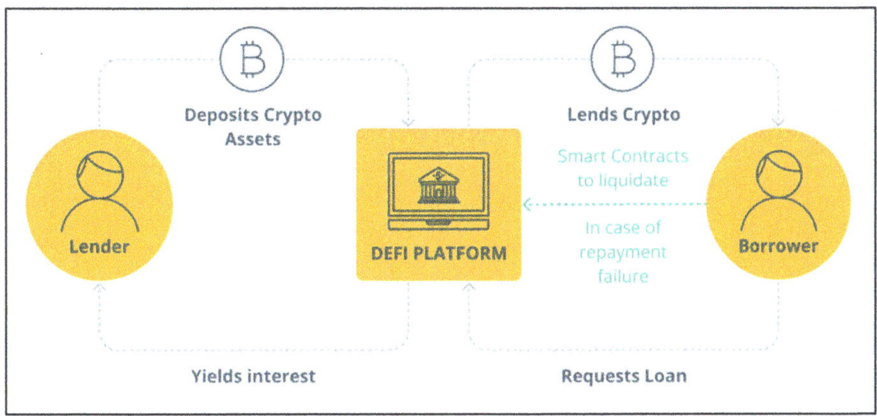

Figure 13-6. *Typical yield farming process (compliments of `https://cointelegraph.com/learn/what-are-defi-yield-aggregators-and-how-do-they-work`)*

Many yield farming platforms implement a "cooldown period" after unstaking, requiring users to wait before fully withdrawing their tokens. This measure protects the protocol from disruptions caused by sudden, large withdrawals. For example, Aave enforces a ten-day cooldown in its Safety Module to help maintain stability.

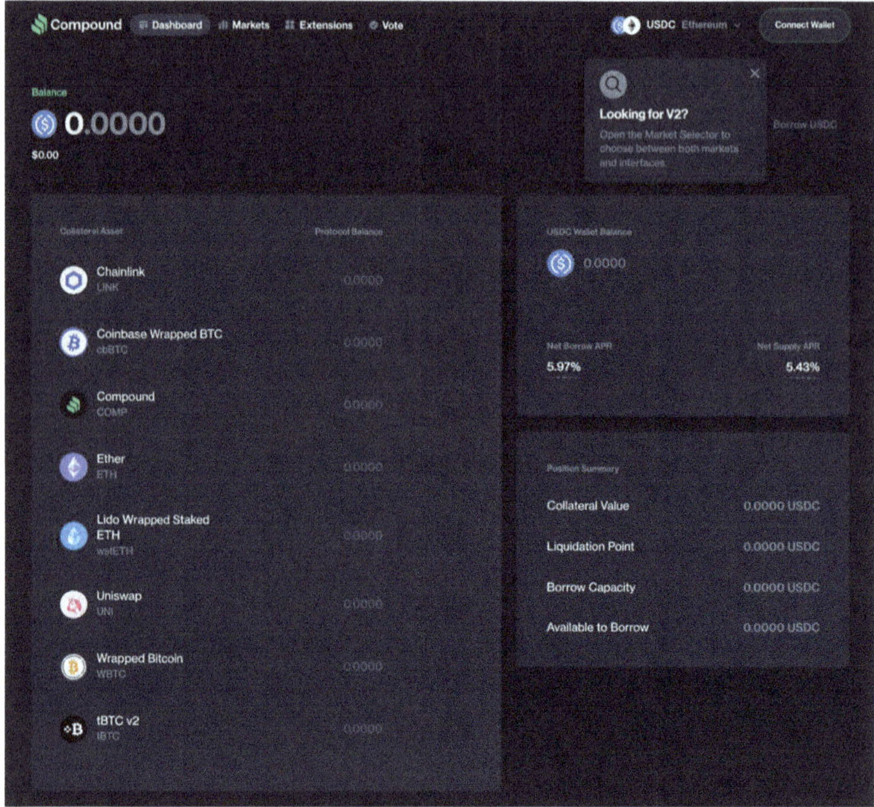

Figure 13-7. *Compound finance dashboard (compliments of `https://app.compound.finance/?market=usdc-mainnet`)*

Advantages

- **High Returns** – Potential for significant profits compared to traditional staking.
- **Enhanced Liquidity** – Yield farmers contribute to sufficient market liquidity to balance supply and demand.
- **Platform Tokens** – Many platforms reward liquidity providers with native tokens. If these tokens increase in value, they can significantly boost overall returns.

Disadvantages

- **High Fees** – Yield farmers may face substantial ongoing fees depending on the network and strategy.
- **Impermanent Loss** – Exposure to price-ratio swings in the AMM pair; LPs may end up with less value than simply holding the two tokens.
- **High Risk** – Bugs or vulnerabilities in smart contracts can lead to significant losses.
- **Complexity** – Yield farming can be complex and requires a decent understanding of the protocol, impermanent loss, strategies, and risk levels.

Yield Aggregators

Examples: Yearn Finance and Beefy Finance
DeFi yield aggregators, also named *yield optimizers*, are a specific type of DeFi protocol that helps maximize investor profits by combining and automating the process of yield farming protocols and strategies. Aggregators achieve this by pooling users' digital assets together and investing them in a selection of portfolios of high-paying yield products and services through automated yield-generating smart contracts.

The main drawback with yield farming is that the above process needs to be manually executed by the investors, which takes time and effort. For a fee, yield aggregators take the above example of a typical yield farming process and completely automate it on behalf of the investor. This removes a lot of unwanted stress and time consumption. Another issue with yield farming strategies is the associated fees. Investors may incur fees when they first redeem their LP tokens for the underlying assets (or sell any separate reward tokens) and again when they reinvest those newly earned tokens into a fresh staking or liquidity position. However, since yield aggregators pool a large number of assets together from different investors, the fees incurred are spread out across all liquidity providers (LP) and staking participants. This shared cost approach typically minimizes the effect of fees, often bringing them close to negligible. Another significant benefit of yield aggregators is that they generate passive income by automatically compounding rewards, reducing transaction costs, and managing the entire process on behalf of investors.

Yield Aggregator Architecture

A typical yield aggregator pool operation can be summarized into three to four stages, depending on the specific protocol.

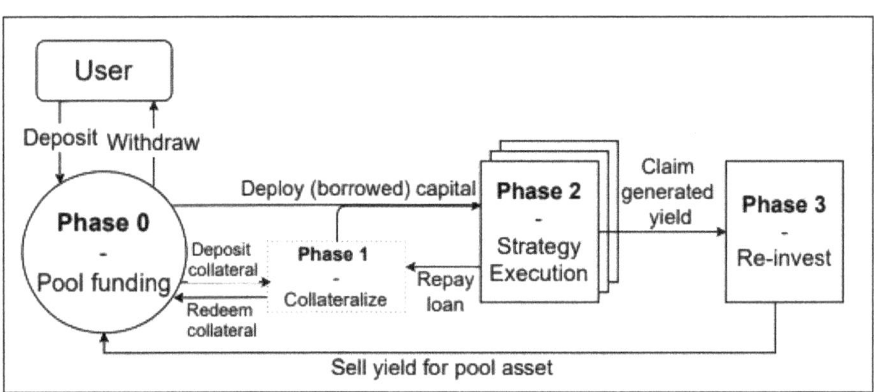

***Figure 13-8.** Stylized yield aggregator mechanism (compliments of Sok: Yield aggregators in DeFi–`https://arxiv.org/pdf/2105.13891.pdf`)*

Phase 0

a) A yield farming strategy is proposed, created, and deployed on the blockchain.

b) Through governance or internal team voting, the yield farming strategy is either approved or rejected.

c) Once approved, a pool is created for this specific yield farming strategy. Yield farmers can now deposit funds into this pool.

d) Upon depositing, yield farmers receive pool shares in the form of "liquidity tokens."

e) When exiting the strategy, farmers surrender their liquidity tokens to redeem funds proportionate to their shares.

Phase 1

a) Funds pooled in Phase 0 are used as collateral to borrow another asset through lending platforms (e.g., Aave, Compound).

b) Depending on the strategy, the pooled assets may first be swapped into another token (often a stablecoin) before Phase 2; many vault-style strategies keep the original asset or LP tokens and skip this step entirely.

c) In the background, the yield aggregator manages the collateralized assets to avoid liquidation by directing the flow of funds between smart contracts used in Phase 0 and Phase 1.

Phase 2

a) Assets from Phase 0 and/or Phase 1 are utilized in preprogrammed strategies that start generating yield. These strategies yield strategies such as lending, borrowing, or liquidity strategies.

b) If the assets deposited in the pool in Phase 1 are the yield-earning tokens (such as LP tokens), then Phase 1 can be skipped, and the pooled assets flow directly from Phase 0 to Phase 2.

c) It is possible for borrowed assets to flow back to Phase 1 to pay back part of the loan in case of a relatively big fund withdrawal from the original pool.

There are many advantages and disadvantages associated with yield aggregators; they are as follows:

Advantages

- **Increased Profits** - Potential for high returns compared to traditional yield-generating DeFi services due to reduced fees and optimal automated strategies.
- **Token Rewards** - Common for yield farming participants to earn participation rewards.
- **Flexibility** - Greater choice of investment strategies.
- **Increased Liquidity** - Provides excellent market liquidity for all DeFi users.

Disadvantages

- **High Risk** - Smart contract bugs and code vulnerabilities, impermanent loss (IL), and potential liquidation—if when availing of collateralized positions—can severely impact investors.
- **Complexity** - Managing risk and avoiding financial loss requires a solid understanding of the intricate risk factors and strategic variables.
- **Volatility** - A drop in token price can significantly reduce the value of earned rewards.

Governance Rewards

Governance rewards—which in most cases are automatically issued on-chain—are incentives for users that participate in the decision-making process of a decentralized protocol or platform. Governance tokens grant asset holders the right to vote on proposals for improving the network in a variety of ways. For example, Uniswap (UNI) enables holders to govern the Uniswap decentralized exchange, and Maker (MKR) holders are responsible for governing the Maker Protocol, which includes adjusting policy for the Dai stablecoin, choosing new collateral types, and improving governance itself.

Play-to-Earn Rewards

Gaming platforms offer play-to-earn rewards to incentivize players to participate in the gaming experience. These rewards are generally provided in the form of digital assets. For example, when a player hits a specific goal or milestone, wins a battle, or completes a particular task, they can collect an in-game NFT asset. Depending on the theme of the game, the NFT (non-fungible tokens) could be assets such as customized skins for avatars, weapons, vehicles, land plots, collectibles, or art. It is common for individuals within the gaming world to earn some extra income by playing play-to-earn games. Some of the core benefits of play-to-earn games include

- Top players can enter gaming contests where they can earn significant cash prizes.
- Opportunities for dedicated players to earn a sizeable income.
- Players own the NFTs or tokens that represent their in-game assets on-chain, though the game studio can still limit how those assets function inside the game.

- Potential to reinvest earnings back into the gaming platform or withdraw to other platforms or markets.
- Incentives engage with other players and the broader community, which helps boost adoption.

One of the most popular examples of a play-to-earn game is Axie Infinity, which allows players to breed, raise, and battle digital creatures called Axies.

***Figure 13-9.** Axie Infinity—Battle, collect, and trade collectible NFT creatures (compliments of`https://axieinfinity.com/`)*

Secondary Incentive Mechanisms

Secondary incentive mechanisms refer to token rewards managed off-chain, often controlled and distributed manually in a centralized manner. There are many types of reward processes, from airdrops and referral incentives to contributor and loyalty rewards. The project team issues these rewards to specific individuals and community members who support the project's growth by raising awareness, testing new features, identifying code vulnerabilities, creating content, and fostering engagement. These reward mechanisms include:

- **Platform Incentives**
- **Beta Testing Incentives**
- **Referral Incentives**
- **Loyalty Incentives**

Airdrops

Airdrops are a token distribution method where free tokens or coins are distributed to individuals who meet specific criteria, such as promoting the project through social media. Usually, these rewards are manually distributed, but they are sometimes automatically distributed on-chain via self-executing smart contracts. Airdrops are generally categorized into types, including

- **Standard Airdrop** – New startups sometimes issue airdrops for new users registering their wallet address with the projects dApp, e.g., Uniswap issued 400 UNI tokens for those who used their platform before September 2020.
- **Bounty Airdrops** – Bounty airdrops are another way of making money inside the blockchain realm besides trading and investing. They are designed to reward participants (*bounty hunters*) who execute specific tasks that contribute to the success and longevity of the project. These tasks include creating awareness around ICOs, creating value by writing blog posts, creating videos, attending virtual events, code development,

promoting a project on social media, or translating website copy, whitepaper, or other content into different languages.

Furthermore, as described in the section "Bug Bounties" in Chapter 12, "Project Codebase," bug bounties are programs issued by projects to help overcome cyberattacks and security issues. These bug bounty airdrops are used to incentivize and attract external developers, community members, and hackers to identify and disclose any valid security vulnerabilities, glitches, and errors in the code. Bug bounty hunters also suggest solutions that help enhance the security and reliability of their blockchain or dApp.

- **Forked Airdrop** - As described in the section "Forking" in Chapter 6, "Blockchain Architecture," when a blockchain undergoes a hard fork, it splits into two incompatible versions. Investors holding the blockchain's native digital assets before the split are airdropped new tokens from the newly created blockchain. For example, Bitcoin Cash forked from bitcoin in 2017; it issued BCH to BTC holders at a 1:1 ratio—but the drop was credited mainly to self-custody wallets; many centralized exchanges did not distribute the new coins.
- **Holder Airdrop** - To qualify for a "holder" airdrop, investors must hold a specific number of tokens at a set time indicated by the team. Snapshots are used to verify if the minimum number of tokens is present in the investor's wallet.

Platform Incentives

Decentralized applications (dApps) offer attractive incentives for investors to hold native assets and avail of features the project provides—sometimes distributed automatically on-chain, but this depends on the protocol rules. Outside of previously discussed DeFi incentives such as staking, yield farming, and provision of liquidity, some platform reward incentives include:

- **Transaction Fee Discounts** - Some platforms incentivize investors by offering discounts on transaction fees and, in some cases, even earning a proportion of the transaction fees.
- **Revenue Sharing** - It is common for platforms to share a percentage of their revenue with token holders, incentivizing users to hold tokens and use the platform's services; note that regulators in some jurisdictions may classify such revenue-sharing tokens as securities, adding compliance risk.
- **Access to Premium Features** - It is common for projects to incentivize investors by offering premium dApp features or services, including advanced trading features on a decentralized exchange (DEX), discounts to subscriptions, and early access to new features.
- **Early Access to New Projects** - IDO (initial decentralized offering) launchpads are platforms that offer crowdfunding opportunities to token holders. These platforms, such as Polkastarter, Synapse Network, and Launchpool crowdfund, help provide liquidity for new startup projects by allowing IDO launchpad token holders to invest in the early stages of the project lifecycle.

Beta Testing Rewards

Beta testing is a process where the product (e.g., DeFi dApp and NFT marketplace) is tried and tested by the development team and often the broader community through incentivized public testnets. The aim is to identify potential bugs, glitches, and code vulnerabilities so the project team can make changes where applicable. The community members participating in this process are rewarded with native digital assets for their efforts.

Referral Programs

Referral programs are marketing tools used by blockchain-related communities such as exchanges, DeFi platforms, and blockchain providers to incentivize existing users and secure new customers or participants. The end goal of a referral program is to drive growth and adoption of the specific platform or project. The rewards for successful referrals are usually paid out in the form of digital assets. Traditional Web-2 referral programs may pay out in gift cards or vouchers (e.g., Amazon credits and ride-share coupons), but blockchain projects generally avoid those real-world rewards and instead give on-platform perks such as fee rebates or free trading tiers. The following are two examples of referral programs with the blockchain within the blockchain realm (at the time of writing this book):

- **Bybit:** Referrers can earn up to 30% commission on their referees' trading fees, and referees can receive up to 1,025 USDT in bonuses by completing specific tasks.
- **Coinbase:** Both referrer and referee receive $10 in bitcoin when the referee signs up using the referrer's link and buys or sells at least $100 worth of cryptocurrency within 180 days.

Loyalty Incentives

Loyalty incentives are rewards issued by blockchain companies and offered to loyal customers in recognition of their continued long-term support and custom. The goal of a loyalty-based program is to increase customer retention and satisfaction. Rewards are typically paid in the form of digital assets. However, similar to referral programs, rewards may be offered in vouchers, coupons, free products or services, or access to premium services. The following are two examples of loyalty incentive programs (at the time of writing this book):

- **Binance:** Offers tiered discounts on trading fees through its VIP Program and up to 8% cashback on eligible purchases with the Binance Card.
- **Crypto.com:** Provides up to 5% cashback on purchases with its Visa Card, along with rebates on services like Spotify, Netflix, and Amazon Prime.

Action Steps

It is common for projects to sway investors into purchasing digital assets by promising an attractive yield-earning process. However, investors soon discover that these processes carry incredibly high risk and volatility, are only available for a limited time, and require holding a specified number of tokens to participate. It is imperative for investors to possess the skills to identify and avoid these situations and, more importantly, find and evaluate legitimate projects with long-term incentive mechanisms that offer sustainable rewards. It is recommended to adhere to the following key considerations and action steps before committing to these investments.

Considerations and Actions Steps When Determining a Suitable Reward-Based Strategy

1. **Risk Versus Reward** - Evaluating the most suitable reward-based strategy that works best for you is highly advised before investing. For most investors, risk plays a major role in choosing a reward-based strategy. For PoS-based blockchain projects, traditional staking is the safest and most attractive choice for long-term investors. However, short-term investors may gravitate towards high-risk-high-reward strategies such as complex yield farming strategies through yield aggregators. Nevertheless, the pros and cons of each reward strategy should be weighed against the incentive rates offered, associated risk, and type of investment (long/short term) and combined with the other aspects of the overall fundamental analysis.

2. **Level of Expertise** - Assess your knowledge and time to learn before selecting a reward-based strategy. For example, suppose it is not feasible for investors to set aside adequate time to deep dive into the technical setup of PoS validator nodes or a PoW node for mining purposes. In that case, choosing a strategy that aligns with your current skill level is advised.

   Given the intricate nature and complexity of some yield farming strategies, it is imperative to invest sufficient time and proceed with caution. It is very common for investors to lose money due to impermanent loss (IL).

3. **Time and Commitment** - Assess how much time you can realistically commit and compare it to the time required to understand and engage in a specific reward strategy. For example, a traditional staking process with a decentralized wallet provider or centralized exchange requires little time or commitment. All that is needed is intermittent price monitoring, market sentiment, and project progress. However, more intricate reward strategies demand additional time and commitment, such as multiple yield farming strategies where constant monitoring is required on a daily basis. Validator and node staking and mining strategies demand regular oversight to keep nodes online—ideally near-continuous unless a third-party SaaS provider is used, which can shoulder some of the monitoring burden for a fee.

4. **Reward Strategies** - A critical aspect of any reward-based strategy is that it engages and maintains its users and stakeholders. Projects are specifically strategized to suit different types of investors. In doing so, this creates a clear focus that targets a specific investor type. For instance, some projects reward users for completing tasks, winning battles, or creating content, while some projects offer high rewards to users for holding and using their tokens on the associated platforms, e.g., DeFi. Whatever the reward mechanics, it should stand out as the best in its space, beating the competition, ensuring user safety, and providing real value to its users.

In the case of Axie Infinity, with a dedicated followership and high engagement rate, the reward structure and incentive mechanisms should be evaluated against similar popular projects. This may help investors determine if the proposed reward strategy is strong or weak compared to its competitors and if it is aligned with other successful projects. However, please remember that this should be combined with many other fundamental aspects discussed throughout this book to ensure a well-rounded evaluation.

5. **Unique Reward Strategies** – Examine any out-of-the-box rewards offered by the project that offer attractive rewards. These may include enticing platform-based rewards or new and improved yield farming strategies. Before participating, it is vital to fully understand the terms, conditions, risks, active periods, and the internal and external factors affecting profitability.

6. **Investor and Community Engagement** – Attractive reward systems help build and encourage community participation that, in turn, helps lure more investors. These reward systems should be evaluated with respect to long-term sustainable yield versus short-term incentives. For example, assume ***Project X*** offered yield farming incentives at 40% APY to all participants. This automatic red flag indicates either a) unsustainable rewards that a new startup is offering early participants for a limited period or b) that it is a scam. Rewards typically vary depending on price volatility, quality, and

reputation of the project, with less stable, low-value projects offering higher yields in compensation for higher risk. More stable projects with large market capitalizations and adequate credibility tend to offer an average of 10% to 15% for yield farming and between 2% and 7% APY for staking.

7. **Staking Ratio** - Many successful proof-of-stake networks aim for a staking ratio of about 30%–70%. Data from the ten largest staking networks on StakingRewards.com show that this range usually locks in enough tokens to protect the network while still leaving plenty in circulation for trading and keeping new-token inflation manageable. Very large chains—such as Ethereum or BNB Chain—can remain secure even when only 20%–30% is staked, because the total dollar value already bonded to the network is so high. To calculate the staking ratio, visit CoinMarketCap or CoinGecko and extract the information for the following formula: ***Staking Ratio = (Total Staked Tokens / Total Token Supply) * 100***. Alternatively, visit StakingRewards.com, where the staking ratios for a large quantity of digital assets are precalculated.

8. **Real Reward Rate** - To maintain the same percentage stake of the supply and ensure that the staking returns are net positive. It is vital that the real reward rate is a positive value and meets investor requirements as per the top ten staking assets ranked by market capitalization on StakingRewards.com. The average real reward rate is roughly 0.74%. However, many top-tier projects like Ethereum, BNB

Chain, and Avalanche have significantly higher than average real reward rates. At a minimum, investors must combine the staking ratio and real reward rate results to ensure all factors, such as liquidity and network security, are not sacrificed.

9. **Secondary Inventive Mechanisms** - Incentive mechanisms such as airdrops, platform rewards, play-to-earn rewards, beta testing rewards, referrals, and program rewards need to be evaluated on a case-by-case basis. While these incentives benefit investors, they are not considered "passive income" like primary mechanisms such as staking. Investors typically want their money to work for them versus the alternative unless the aim is to build a reputation and rapport with project teams with long-term goals of securing a permanent position within the team. Rewards from primary incentive mechanisms are relatively consistent, unlike the more irregular rewards from secondary mechanisms like airdrops or referral programs. With that said, whether passive or earned, any additional incentives should be viewed as a bonus.

Evaluation of the Results

The most critical aspect of this analysis is ensuring that the investor does not suffer any losses with the chosen incentive mechanism(s). In most cases, there is no wrong or right yield-bearing process, provided it is evaluated and seen as legitimate and lies within the investor's level of risk. The results of this analysis should satisfy the following items:

1) The risk factor aligns with the investor's risk tolerance, time, and technical expertise.

2) The incentive mechanism aligns with the investor's strategy and overall goals over a specific timeframe and whether they are long- or short-term goals.

3) The type of yield flow aligns with the investor's strategy, e.g., passive income or mostly active participation, such as play-to-earn incentives.

4) The incentive structure is well-aligned with fundamental aspects of the project, including blockchain architecture, token design, tokenomics, team quality, roadmap, funding, and partnerships. (Excludes stablecoins.)

5) The incentive mechanism is resilient to market conditions. If it is influenced by the market, create a clear entry and exit strategy.

6) The project is not a scam.

In most circumstances, inventive mechanisms that carry less risk are coupled with low to medium rewards. Conversely, high-yield mechanisms carry high risk. Most investors, as with human nature, seek attractive rewards without wanting to accept increased levels of risk. Therefore, in most circumstances, unless the investor is in acceptance of a high-risk incentive strategy, it is advised to limit the expectations and set rewards targets based on current averages from top-tier projects and relevant competitors.

CHAPTER 14

Community and Social Media

In the crypto space, a strong community and a well-managed and active social media presence indicate a project's commitment and potential long-term success. A community is not just a group of followers; it is a core driving force that helps attract more interest and pushes the project on the path to success. Through social media outlets and other official channels such as project blogs, GitHub repositories, and governance forums, communities gather to share knowledge, answer questions, offer advice, generate momentum, participate in technical and non-technical discussions, and learn about new updates from the project's teams.

Projects with engaged communities and an active presence on social media show the public, dApp users, network participants, investors, and alike that the team is committed to the project's success, is transparent, and wants the trust of the broader community. Conversely, if the team is inactive and has a poor social presence, resulting in a lack of communication with the community, it indicates their heart is not in it. So, short- or long-term success is severely jeopardized.

Fundamentals Discussed in This Chapter:

- Importance of Social Media
    - Beta Testing
    - Code Collaboration

P. Garvey, *Blockchain Fundamental Analysis for Digital Asset Investors*,
https://doi.org/10.1007/979-8-8688-1551-5_14

    - Network Effects
    - Continuous Feedback
    - Spreading Awareness
    - Governance
    - Mainstream Adoption and Acceptance
- Social Media and Community Evaluation
    - Social Platforms for Blockchain Communities
    - Follower Count
    - Post Frequency
    - Content Engagement
    - Community Moderators

Social Media

The word "social" refers to the interactions, communication, and connections between members of a group, community, or society. Popular social media platforms such as Facebook, X, Instagram, TikTok, and LinkedIn have enabled people from all over the world to interact with each other in a social manner. Moreover, these social media platforms are not just for the general public. They also cater to small businesses, massive companies, and organizations for marketing and promotional purposes.

What Is a Community?

A community can be described as a group of individuals with common interests interacting with each other in a shared environment. Many communities include cultural, professional, heritage, technology, sports, animals, music, and various blockchain communities. Community members typically share some main characteristics, such as a shared value, mutual respect, a sense of belonging, and bonding relationships. It is common for community members to support others by contributing information and providing assistance when necessary. This helps build a stronger, more robust, meaningful community with a positive knowledge-sharing atmosphere.

Communities come in two primary forms: physical and virtual. In a physical, in-person type community, each community member meets in a physical location. These communities are typically geographical, where people with shared interests from towns, cities, or villages gather to interact. As the name suggests, "online" communities are held online, where each community member meets and interacts through the internet. It is typical for the majority of the community members never to meet each other—in most cases. Many social media platforms aid online social interactions. It is important to note that sometimes, in-person communities may also have an online presence where they interact outside of their physical meet-ups. Additionally, depending on the type of community and the location of its members, it is common for online communities to arrange physical meet-ups and events.

In the blockchain world, there are three primary types of online communities; they are categorized as follows:

1) **Development Communities** - Consisting of many developers collaborating in unity to help and share ideas and knowledge, contributing to overall advancements in blockchain technology.

2) **Informational Communities** - Consisting of people from all sectors learning about all aspects of blockchain technology.

3) **Investment Communities** - Consisting of investors of all levels sharing and explaining investment and profit-taking advice.

Importance of Blockchain Project Communities

The community is not just important; it is essential. Think of a blockchain community as a decentralized, multi-functional marketing weapon that aids the project in various ways, influencing the overall sentiment, growth, and long-term success of the project. The community achieves this through several different ways, such as beta testing, code collaborations, network effects, spreading feedback, and much more. The following section delves deeper into these roles and highlights how communities contribute to blockchain projects.

Beta Testing

As discussed in the section "Product Testing" in Chapter 4, "Core Offering," beta testing is a safety technique used by crypto projects utilizing their community to test their product or service before its official launch. During this process, the product (e.g., DeFi dApp or NFT marketplace) is tried and tested by several community members who are typically incentivized for their efforts. The community helps uncover glitches, bugs, and vulnerabilities in the product. Each and every feature is tested, including the feature set, user interface, network transactions, smart contracts, and overall security and performance. This information is fed back to the team, and all the data and test reports are compiled. Updates and changes are implemented to correct the found bugs, glitches, and code vulnerabilities.

Code Collaboration

Open-source project community members are vital to the core and heart of the project—the code. They actively work together to contribute to the overall development of the project. This entails developing, evaluating, and altering code to help optimize the project's overall value.

Network Effects

"Network effects" is a term used to describe when a product or service increases in size and value due to an increasing number of users—where existing users attract new users, who attract even more users, which helps exponentially grow the product at a multiplying rate. In crypto, increased user interaction on a platform, dApp, or protocol typically leads to greater growth and expansion of the network. The community helps drive this interaction by posting and promoting the project through social media. This, in turn, creates demand for additional programmers that help to scale the protocol accordingly in a powerful collaboration-type environment.

Continuous Feedback

Throughout the project's life cycle, the team must be aware of any glitches, bugs, or vulnerabilities in the code that may affect the protocol. This is accomplished through a continuous feedback loop between the project and community members. In addition to identifying vulnerabilities in the code, feedback loops also collect valuable input and suggestions from the community members. This includes feedback on community pain points, feature requests, or related items. This insight helps the team identify, improve, and implement new features that increase the project's overall value.

Spreading Awareness

A project's success is determined by its value proposition and ability to gain traction, attract users, and build a powerful ecosystem. Community members spread awareness that helps generate interest, drive adoption, increase network effects, organize collaborations, and secure partnerships.

Governance

Blockchain governance is the term whereby various decisions are made through structured collective processes and mechanisms. These decisions help establish and implement rules for a blockchain network's development, direction, and management. Community members who hold governance tokens can vote on proposals and influence decisions, but voting power is often concentrated in the hands of large holders (whales, VCs, or core teams), which may limit how much impact the broader community ultimately has.

Mainstream Adoption and Acceptance

Blockchain communities play a significant role in informing and teaching the masses about blockchain technology, including its operation, decentralization benefits, and impactful use cases, enabling more efficient and better-informed participants and more reputable projects. In doing so, communities help foster an impactful learning environment, allowing mainstream adoption.

Social Media and Community Evaluation

Understanding and interpreting social media metrics is critical to any project evaluation process. It can provide investors with insight into how well the project is operating from popularity and engagement perspectives, in addition to how well the social content is performing with respect to competitors.

Social media evaluation allows investors to understand the overall sentiment of the community, where each post provides a snapshot of the general attitude and emotional reaction toward the project, whether it's a negative, neutral, or positive environment. Furthermore, sentiment analysis can help identify potential trends and forecast market movement. For example, if there is a lot of positivity surrounding a particular project, it may generate more interest and, in turn, cause the price of the digital asset to increase.

Social Platforms for Blockchain Communities

Evaluation Objective: Determine if the project team utilizes an adequate number of social platforms to optimize communication, awareness, collaboration, and support with the community.

There are seven primary media platforms available that projects primarily utilize in today's world. Crypto projects utilize these platforms to help communicate with the public and market their product or service. Moreover, these platforms are also home to empowering community members who help promote a magnitude of project ecosystems and drive blockchain adoption on a broader scale. Projects should aim to utilize most of the social media platforms outlined in this section—selecting those that fit their size, resources, and stage of development—to help optimize communication, awareness, collaboration, and support with the community.

- X - It is a type of "micro-blogging" and social networking platform. It allows people to post "tweet" messages containing photos, videos, links, and text. X, also formally known by blockchain enthusiasts as "Crypto Twitter—'CT,'" is home to some of the most influential people within the blockchain world. Organically grown blockchain communities on X voice their opinions, knowledge, and information on new and exciting projects.

- YouTube – It is a video-sharing platform where users can watch, like, share, comment, and upload their own videos online. It is used widely by blockchain projects to provide updates and informational tutorial videos for the team. YouTube is extremely beneficial for those who want to learn about blockchain technology, news, and information about existing and upcoming feature-rich projects.
- Discord – It is a free communications application enabling users to share voice, video, and text. Due to its easy-to-use, feature-rich user interface, it is widely used by blockchain projects and enthusiasts worldwide. Discord is highly admired by project teams because they can create independent channels (chats) within their official server, with each chat catering to different aspects of the project. These chats will vary in nature from project to project; typical chats may include new announcements, main chats, media, help, and developer chats.
- Telegram – It is a secure messaging and audio-calling cloud-based application that allows users to send messages, photos, videos, and files. Blockchain developers, cryptocurrency traders, and entrepreneurs utilize Telegram for its feature-rich user interface. It includes and promotes privacy, multi-platform availability, automated bots and RSS feeds, and price bots. While not a native feature, Telegram's open API lets traders run custom bots that push real-time cryptocurrency price alerts and other data to their channels.

- Reddit – It is an American social news aggregation, content rating, and discussion website. It prioritizes the feedback of its users when it comes to what it shows first. With its unique upvote and downvote system, it can identify not just what people like but also what they don't want in a timely and accurate manner. Blockchain projects utilize Reddit to build strong and powerful communities.
- Medium – It is a publishing "blog" platform where people can post and read important, insightful articles on the topics that matter most to them. Blockchain projects utilize Medium to distribute updates, ideas, technical documentation, news, and announcements to the community. Due to the blogging-type functionality, it is perfect for educating users and investors about their product and blockchain technology as a whole.
- LinkedIn – It is the world's largest online professional network. It is used to find the right job or internship, connect, and strengthen professional relationships. LinkedIn is particularly important for blockchain projects to help secure new client partnerships and build a broad network of professionals that may benefit the project.
- Substack – It combines a blog with an email newsletter, so every post lands directly in a subscriber's inbox. Project teams use it for long-form updates—think developer diaries, governance explainers, or monthly recaps—without relying on social media algorithms.

Because followers get an email notification, they're less likely to miss critical announcements. Projects can also add paid tiers for premium research or early-access content, creating an optional revenue stream.

Action Steps

Follow these steps to determine if the project team utilizes an adequate number of social platforms to optimize communication, awareness, collaboration, and support with the community.

1) **Social Media Platform Check**

   Check if the project utilizes an adequate number of social media platforms such as X, YouTube, Discord, Telegram, Medium, Reddit, and LinkedIn.

2) **Take Notes and Document Your Findings in Your Own Style**

3) **Combine the Findings with Other Sections of the Fundamental Evaluation Process**

Evaluation of the Results

Ideally, the project should maintain an active presence on several social media outlets, as outlined in this section. If not, it is advised to exercise caution and determine if there are underlying issues, such as understaffing, inadequate funding, or poor team commitment.

Follower Count

Evaluation Objective: Evaluate the popularity of a project by comparing their social following across multiple social platforms to that of competitors.

A project's number of followers—or subscribers—on its social media platforms is often the most obvious metric for evaluating its online presence. However, it is not always the most critical. Generally, a large follower base suggests high visibility, popularity, interest in the project, and confidence in its community. That said, there is no definitive benchmark for what constitutes a "good" follower count, as many factors come into play. Watch for red flags like sudden follower-count spikes, very low likes or comments per post, or many blank profiles—these can signal bot-farm or fake-engagement activity. Therefore, investors need to analyze follower counts by considering the following elements:

1) **Founding Year** - As discussed in the section titled "Founding Year" in Chapter 4, "Core Offering," the company's founding year is vital information. Analyzing the follower count in conjunction with the company's founding year is advised for a more accurate understanding. In most circumstances, a project founded five years ago is naturally more likely to have more followers than a project founded a few months ago.

2) **Competitor Follower Count** -Investors should only compare the follower count within the same crypto niche, e.g., DeFi, blockchain networks, gaming, decentralized exchanges (DEX), etc.

3) **Social Media Platform** - Always compare competitor follower counts on the same platform, e.g., X vs. X or Discord vs. Discord.

Pro Tip To comprehensively analyze cryptocurrency projects' social media followings, including Twitter, Discord, and Telegram, utilize platforms like AlphaGrowth.

Action Steps

Follow these steps below to evaluate the popularity of a project by comparing their social following across multiple social platforms to that of competitors.

1) **Social Media Following**

   a) Identify the project's presence on X, YouTube, Discord, Telegram, Medium, Reddit, and LinkedIn platforms.

   b) Visit the project's official website to find links to their social media accounts.

   c) Note the number of followers on each platform.

2) **Competitor Analysis**

   a) Visit CoinMarketCap.com—or a similar platform such as CoinGecko or AlphaGrowth—and select the category that the project falls under, e.g., Layer 1 blockchain projects.

   b) Select three competitors with similar market capitalizations.

   c) Visit each competitor's social media platforms and record their follower counts.

   d) Compare these follower counts and consider the founding years of each project for context.

3) **Take Notes and Document Your Findings in Your Own Style**

4) **Combine the Findings with Other Sections of the Fundamental Evaluation Process**

Evaluation of the Results

A large follower count is admirable but does not guarantee quality or success. It indicates that the project is not a scam, is popular, and has adequate community support. This metric should be used in conjunction with the fundamental social media metrics in this chapter. If the follower count is significantly lower than competitors across multiple platforms, it could signal a poor product use case, poor marketing, insufficient visibility, inadequate content quality, and a poorly managed project team. Further investigation is required.

Post Frequency

Evaluation Objective: Evaluate the project team's social media activity to help determine if the team members are still active.

Post frequency refers to how often a company or individual publishes new content within a specific timeframe, whether through social media platforms, blogs, newsletters, or podcasts. This metric shows the activity level of the project team across different social media channels. At a minimum, the project's leaders and key team members should maintain a strong social media presence for many reasons, such as

- **Activity** – Posting frequently shows the community that the company is active and still working diligently.
- **Credibility** – Posting quality content regularly helps promote expertise in a specific field, which helps build credibility.
- **Social Engine Optimization (SEO)** – By posting frequently, the company's page will likely be ranked higher through SEO, making it more visible in search results.

- **Reach** - Regularly posting helps reach more people, which helps grow a wider audience.
- **Audience Engagement** - Posting regularly helps to keep the audience engaged.

Pro Tip When analyzing a project's posting activity, it is advised to quickly scan through each post to ensure the content is specific to the team's core product or service. Many projects post a lot of "fluff," which has no connection to the actual value offering but instead focuses on market conditions or blockchain-related material on a broader scale.

Action Steps

Follow these steps to evaluate the project team's social media activity to help determine if the team members are still active.

1) **Determine Post Frequency**

   Determine the project team's post frequency across different social media platforms.

   a) Visit the project's official website.

   b) Navigate to the project's social media icons.

   c) Visit each of the major social media platforms utilized by the team, e.g., X, Telegram, and Blog (Medium).

   d) On each platform, tally the number of posts made by the team over the past 30 days to measure their activity level.

2) **Competitor Analysis**

   Compare the data to that of popular and direct competitors.

3) **Take Notes and Document Your Findings in Your Own Style**

4) **Combine the Findings with Other Sections of the Fundamental Evaluation Process**

Evaluation of the Results

The main objective is determining whether the project team is active and engaged in the product. It is admirable to see roughly fifteen to twenty posts every month for each social media platform, or at least the leading platforms utilized by the team.

Content Engagement

Evaluation Objective: Determine if the team shares quality, engaging content and how the community reacts.

Evaluating a project's social media posts is not just about quantity; community engagement is also essential, if not more critical. The level of engagement depends on how well the project team can connect with its community through meaningful, impactful, quality content. To get a feel for how engaged the community is, investors can evaluate metrics like likes, comments, shares, reach, and impressions—these give you a quick snapshot of how healthy and active the community is.

In any social media post, no matter the platform, each post can be engaged with through *likes*, *shares*, or *comments* (replies). At the same time, *reach* is used to identify the number of unique people who saw the posted content. Figure 14-1 is a post from the Polkadot Network on X. This particular post got 80.4k views (reach), 151 comments, 480 reshares, and 823 likes.

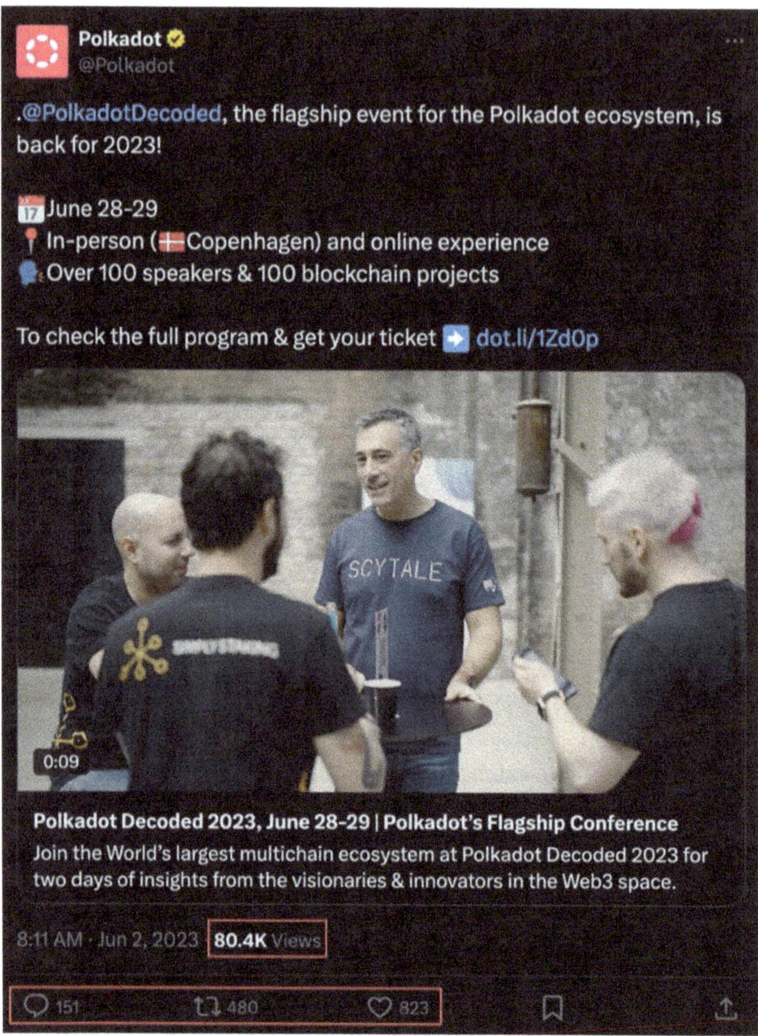

Figure 14-1. *Polkadot Network post on X, highlighting the number of comments, shares, likes, and views (reach) (`https://x.com/Polkadot/status/1664620666690351105`)*

Engagement Rates

Engagement rate (ER) measures the amount of interaction content generated relative to the number of likes, reactions, shares, comments, clicks, votes, and brand mentions. A high ER represents strong engagement and interaction, while a low ER represents poor interaction.

The engagement rate is expressed as a percentage; the higher the percentage is, the more ER there is, and vice versa. Each social media platform has different ERs. For example, Table 14-1 shows engagement rates from poor to excellent for X, YouTube, and LinkedIn. These ranges draw on the 2024–2025 engagement benchmarks compiled by Rival IQ and SocialInsider, which analyze millions of brand posts on each platform. However, due to the dynamic nature of social media development, algorithms, and strategies, engagement scoring rates continuously fluctuate. Therefore, checking for the most current ERs for each platform is encouraged when performing a fundamental analysis.

Table 14-1. *Social media engagement rates for X, YouTube, and LinkedIn*

	Engagement Rates		
Platform	**Poor ER**	**Good ER**	**Excellent ER**
X	Below 0.02%	0.02%–0.09%	Above 0.09%
YouTube	Below 1%	1%–3%	Above 3%
LinkedIn	Below 0.5%	0.5%–1.5%	Above 1.5%

There are several ways to calculate engagement rates, depending on whether it's measured against reach, posts, impressions, views, followers, or daily activity. However, we will focus on one primary method for calculating ER: *engagement rate by reach* (ERR).

Engagement Rate by Reach (ERR)

The engagement rate by reach (ERR) formula measures the percentage of people interacting with content on a per-post basis compared to those who have viewed it. This approach is more accurate than the engagement rate by follower (ERF) because it measures engagement relative to actual reach rather than total follower count, which can include users who never see the content.

$$ERR = \frac{Total\ Number\ of\ Engagements\ Per\ Post}{Reach\ Per\ Post} * 100$$

Equation 14-1. *Formula to calculate engagement rate by reach (ERR)*

Example Calculation:

Using post data from the Polkadot Network (Figure 14-1).

- Total Number of Engagements Per Post:

151 (comments) + 480 (reshares) + 823 (likes) = 1454

- Reach (views) = 80,400

Polkadot's Post ERR is calculated as follows:

$$\textbf{Polkadot Post ERR} = \frac{1454}{80400} * 100 = 1.81\%$$

Equation 14-2. *ER for Polkadot Network social media post on X*

Pro Tip Calculate the average ERR over twenty recent posts for more accurate and balanced results.

Action Steps

Follow these steps to see if the team shares quality, engaging content and how the community reacts. Calculate the engagement rate on a few posts to get a clear picture.

1) **Calculate Post Engagement Rate**

   Determine the project's average engagement rate over ten to fifteen posts.

   a) Navigate to one or more of the project's social media channels by accessing official links through the project website.

   b) Calculate the engagement rate by reach (ERR) for the 10–15 most recent posts. Add up the total number of engagements across these posts, divide by the total number of posts, and multiply by 100 to get the percentage.

2) **Analyzer Against Platform Engagement Ratings**

   Compare the calculated ERR to the current engagement rating specific to each social media platform.

3) **Competitor Analysis**

   Compare the ERR results to those of popular and direct competitors.

4) **Take Notes and Document Your Findings in Your Own Style**

5) **Combine the Findings with Other Sections of the Fundamental Evaluation Process**

Pro Tip When determining ERR and AVERR, take some time to read each post and comment to determine if there is good sentiment toward the project. A positive sentiment is always admirable; however, try to identify any negative comments that may provide an opening for further investigation.

Evaluation of the Results

A high engagement rate is highly admirable, especially when the project outperforms competitors. However, some projects take some time to gain momentum, especially new startups; therefore, checking when the project was launched is important. While engagement rate is an important metric, it shouldn't carry too much weight. Investors should always be coupled with other aspects of the fundamental analysis of social media discussed in this chapter.

Community Moderators

Evaluation Objective: Gauge the team's commitment to supporting its community by evaluating the quality and performance of their social media moderators.

As the name suggests, the role of a community moderator is to moderate, maintain, and oversee discussions within a community. A moderator ensures that conversations remain respectful, organized, and aligned with the community's goals and rules. In doing so, they help create an environment where members can effectively share information, exchange ideas, voice concerns, and express views without the disruption of spam, misinformation, or conflict. In the blockchain space, community moderators are essential to project-based communities, promoting meaningful interactions on platforms like X, Telegram, Discord, and subreddits.

Community moderators have some specific tasks and responsibilities that aid a stable, efficient, friendly, and information-sharing environment, such as

- **Enforcing Rules** - Moderators help ensure community members adhere to the rules and guidelines.
- **Facilitating Discussions** - Moderators ensure that the discussions are aligned and relevant to the set-out topic.
- **Conflict Resolution** - Moderators help control and mediate any disagreements, arguments, and conflicts in the community in a friendly manner.
- **Spam Removal** - Moderators quickly identify and remove any non-relevant or harmful spam.
- **Educating** - Moderators relay official updates from the core team, answer questions, and help newcomers understand basic blockchain and project concepts.
- **Content Approval** - Moderators decide what content is allowed on the channel.
- **Management** - Moderators often organize and manage on-platform events such as interviews (known as Ask Me Anything (AMAs)) with other team members or influential individuals in the blockchain space.

Regardless of the social platform, investors must examine moderators' performance, quality, and efficiency. It is considered a red flag if the moderators seem absent, are slow to respond, give vague or false information, or fail to eliminate spam threats. This may be because of a lack of staffing, funding, or poor team commitment; either way, it is not a good sign and not worth your investment.

Action Steps

Follow these steps to gauge the team's commitment to supporting its community by evaluating the quality and performance of their social media moderators.

1) **Moderator Quality and Performance**

   a) Visit one or more of the project's social media channels, such as Telegram, by following the official links on the project's website.

   b) Scan and evaluate the moderators, channel, and chat history with the following criteria in mind:

      i) Are the moderators answering community questions in a timely fashion?

      ii) Is moderator coverage reasonably spread across key time zones—providing timely responses during peak community hours, even if not strictly 24/7?

      iii) Is the community provided with consistent project updates?

      iv) Are quality responses being provided?

      v) Are the moderators answering questions and concerns in an easy-to-understand manner?

      vi) Is the channel being managed in a professional manner?

      vii) Are the moderators kind and pleasant toward the community?

      viii) Are the moderators filtering spam advertisements and non-project-related material?

2) **Take Notes and Document Your Findings in Your Own Style**

3) **Combine the Findings with Other Sections of the Fundamental Evaluation Process**

Evaluation of the Results

The moderators' image directly reflects on the project and the individuals running it. Therefore, the moderators must be professional, courteous, responsive, and professionally doing their job, thus building trust and adding credibility. However, if they fail at their duty, it is recommended to exercise caution and see how the project performs in the rest of the fundamental evaluation.

CHAPTER 15

Funding and Partnerships

Similar to traditional companies, crypto projects also require funding to pay for expenses to fuel the growth of the product or service and grow their user base, security, day-to-day operations, and salaries for team members and various experts within the blockchain world. Therefore, without funding, most projects would not exist.

Funding takes many forms, from large institutions and private investors to public token sales like ICOs. This chapter breaks down funding into simple terms, including where funding comes from, why projects are funded, and the benefits of financing, all while providing an easy-to-follow evaluation structure to analyze the risks for retail investors and determine the credibility and reputation of funding entities. Additionally, this chapter includes an essential checklist for investors participating in public offerings, offering guidance on minimizing risks and avoiding potential scams or losses.

Partnerships in the crypto space are also discussed. Partnerships occur between crypto projects "crypto-to-crypto" or "crypto-to-enterprise" where blockchain projects collaborate with traditional companies. Both types of partnerships are important and allow companies to combine resources, technical expertise, and technology, which increases the project's value output and helps drive adoption and innovation. For example, crypto-to-crypto partnerships often focus on interoperability, liquidity, or cross-chain functionality, while crypto-to-enterprise

P. Garvey, *Blockchain Fundamental Analysis for Digital Asset Investors*,
https://doi.org/10.1007/979-8-8688-1551-5_15

partnerships bring blockchain solutions into real-world industries. However, it is the investor's responsibility to verify if the partnerships claimed by the project team are strong, valid, and credible—an evaluation procedure is presented to help achieve this.

Understanding the effects of funding and partnerships on crypto projects is essential for investors. Adequate financing of entities and private investors helps ensure that a project can meet development milestones. At the same time, the funding source can add extreme credibility to investor confidence and increase the project's overall long-term potential. Projects backed by reputable institutions or strong strategic partners often feel more trustworthy than those relying on unverified sources. Taking the time to examine the credibility of funding entities and genuine value-adding partnerships provides investors with a clearer picture of the potential future value of the project and, more importantly, the risks involved.

Note that this chapter is written for everyday investors; therefore, experience in the financial sector is not required to follow along. Instead, this straightforward approach outlines easy-to-follow evaluation steps for the investor.

Fundamentals Discussed in This Chapter:

- Institutional Investing
- Private Funding
- Public Funding
- Partnerships

Fact Over 50% of blockchain projects—much like early-stage tech start-ups—fail within their first year because they run out of funding. By understanding where the money comes from and how it's used, you're already ahead of most investors.

Institutional Investing

Evaluation Objective: Evaluate potential institutional investments to assess whether the project gains added credibility and strengthened fundamentals from institutional backing.

Institutional investing in blockchain companies refers to the practice of large financial institutions, such as hedge funds, investment banks, pension funds, and other major financial entities, investing in blockchain-based technology and digital "crypto" assets. Regardless of the uncertainty and high volatility, there has been a significant rise in institutional involvement in the blockchain realm in recent years. The forces driving institutions towards digital assets include the potential for high returns, diversification, hedging, growing market acceptance and legitimacy, institutional infrastructures (e.g., regulated exchanges), competitive pressure, investor demand, and long-term investment potential. bitcoin is still the usual entry point, and Ethereum a close second, but many institutional products now add other large-cap altcoins—for example, Solana or Avalanche—giving investors broader exposure. However, recently, some investment firms, such as Grayscale Investments, have been investing and adding a diverse range of digital assets to their portfolios.

Unlike individual or retail investors, these institutions inject massive amounts of capital and are considered the largest investors in the blockchain industry. Millions to billions of dollars have been and continue to be invested by institutions, significantly leveraging market control. Institutions have the money to increase the price and market capitalization of major digital assets such as bitcoin, thus increasing the portfolio value of retail investors. They also have the power to apply tremendous selling pressure, which often results in devastating market conditions. An example was when Tesla sent bitcoin surging after buying $1.5 billion in BTC on February 8, 2021. However, Tesla sold 10% in 2021 and the remaining 75% in July 2022. Although Tesla made a profit of $936 million, the sell-off sent the "crypto" into turmoil financially, destroying many unexperienced retail investors.

Nevertheless, these investment institutions also positively impact the "crypto" markets. While a larger institutional base can dampen day-to-day volatility by adding liquidity, an outsized buy or sell from one of these players can still trigger sharp price swings in either direction. Investment institutions also have various trading and investment strategies that aid liquidity for retail investors and vice versa. Additionally, institutional investment attracts significant interest in the blockchain, which adds credibility and legitimacy. Institutions invest in digital assets in many different ways, including

- **Balance Sheets** - Holding digital assets on their balance sheets is the most common and direct way for institutions to invest in cryptocurrency.
- **Exchange-Traded Funds (ETFs)** - Several ETFs now track the price of bitcoin, Ethereum, and other digital assets. This allows institutions to invest in digital assets without buying and selling the underlying assets directly.
- **Payment for Goods and Services** - More businesses now accept BTC, ETH, or stablecoins at checkout—either directly on-chain via processors such as BitPay or Coinbase Commerce, or through off-chain conversion services offered by PayPal, Stripe, and similar gateways. This gives institutions the option to spend digital assets when paying suppliers or settling invoices.

Why Institutions Favor bitcoin and Ethereum

Institutional investors are very conservative when investing in digital assets. In fact, in companion to the 16,300 active projects (when writing this book), outside of Grayscale's diverse digital asset portfolio and other lesser-known institutions, most major institutions solely invest in bitcoin and Ethereum. There are four core reasons for this type of institutional investment strategy:

1) **Liquidity** – Institutional investment firms buy and sell large sums of assets when rebalancing their portfolios, making sufficient liquidity critical for such transactions. bitcoin, followed by Ethereum, is best suited for this due to its high market capitalization and substantial daily trading volumes. For example, when writing this, bitcoin has a market capitalization of $1.9 trillion with a daily trading volume of $60 billion.

2) **Reduced Volatility** – Due to the massive market capitalizations of bitcoin and Ethereum, the volatility is significantly reduced compared to the rest of the "crypto" market. This makes bitcoin and Ethereum more stable investments that will help mitigate aggressive swings in institutional investment portfolios.

3) **Reduced Risk** – Because bitcoin and Ethereum are blue-chip mainstream crypto assets, the risk of total collapse or extreme overnight losses is significantly reduced compared to other digital assets.

4) **Fundamental Acceptance** – Institutional investors perform rigorous, detailed fundamental and technical analyses to ensure assets meet their portfolio and strategy requirements. These evaluations may contain special criteria and requirements (e.g., regulatory or legal compliance) that a particular asset has to comply with, disqualifying many crypto projects from consideration.

As the blockchain sector evolves and matures, wider adoption of digital assets and blockchain technology is expected, potentially paving the way for more structured regulations in the blockchain space. This could result in more diversified institutional portfolios. Therefore, it is crucial to validate institutional investments by ensuring the project team is transparent and trustworthy.

Types of Institutional Investing

There are many different flavors of institutional investment companies. The core institutional investment groups are identified in Table 15-1.

Table 15-1. *Types of institutional funding in blockchain*

Institutional Investing	
Investment Vehicles	**Description**
Corporate Investment (MicroStrategy, Google Ventures, Intel Capital, IBM Blockchain, Fidelity)	Corporate investment companies are large enterprises that invest their profits or surplus cash instead of using it as income or holding it in a bank account. They achieve this by direct investing or else through a venture capital firm. Corporate investment is an attractive way to withdraw money from a company due to its tax advantages. For example, MicroStrategy, a business intelligence (BI) software company, increased its bitcoin holdings to 386,700 BTC as of November 24, 2024.
Investment Trusts (Grayscale Investments)	Investment trusts are financial products that receive funds from investors and invest in different assets on their behalf. Investment trusts, also called closed-end trusts, allow investors to trade their shares on the open market. An example of an investment trust is the Grayscale Bitcoin Trust (GBTC). It allows investors to trade shares in trusts that hold large pools of bitcoin. The GBTC is the world's largest bitcoin fund and the first publicly traded trust with a digital currency as its underlying value. The GBTC fund enables investors to gain exposure to BTC through security while directly avoiding the challenges of buying, storing, and safekeeping BTC.

(*continied*)

Table 15-1. *(continied)*

Institutional Investing	
Investment Vehicles	**Description**
Exchange Traded Funds (ARK Invest, Amplify Transformational Data Sharing ETF (BLOK), VanEck Bitcoin Strategy ETF (XBTF), ProShares Bitcoin Strategy ETF (BITO))	Exchange-traded funds (ETFs) are SEC-registered investment companies that offer investors a way to pool their money in a fund that invests in stocks, bonds, or other digital assets. As this implies, ETFs are traded on an exchange, much like equities, and track the performance of an underlying asset. Additionally, investors may also receive dividends from the fund. Most ETFs are professionally managed by investment advisers. When investors purchase a share of an ETF, they become a partial fund owner. ETFs can focus on a specific sector or industry, such as an energy sector ETF. In the case of the blockchain sector, the following are the three types of EFTs: 1. **Blockchain ETFs** – Blockchain ETFs are thematic exchange-traded funds that own the stocks of companies that focus on developing blockchain technology. Example: Amplify Transformational Data Sharing ETF (BLOK) 2. **Physical Digital Asset ETFs** – A physical bitcoin ETF is a type of ETF that offers exposure to the price of spot digital assets. As of January 2024, the SEC has approved several spot bitcoin (physical) ETFs—e.g., BlackRock iShares Bitcoin Trust (IBIT) and Fidelity Wise Origin Bitcoin Fund (FBTC)—giving US investors regulated access to the underlying asset. 3. **Digital Asset Futures ETFs** – An exchange-traded fund that tracks the performance of digital asset futures contracts. They are a type of derivative investment security that allows investors to speculate on the future price of a particular asset. For example, by investing in a bitcoin futures ETF, investors can gain exposure to the price movements of bitcoin without holding the digital currency itself. Examples: VanEck Bitcoin Strategy ETF (XBTF) and ProShares Bitcoin Strategy ETF (BITO)

Exchange Traded Products (Fidelity Wise Origin Bitcoin Fund (FBTC))	Exchange-traded products (ETPs) are a category of financial securities that trade on exchanges. ETPs track the performance of an underlying asset or index. An example is the Fidelity Wise Origin Bitcoin Fund (FBTC). FBTC is 100% physically backed by bitcoin held in custody provided by Fidelity Digital Assets and trades on US (Cboe BZX) and European exchanges.
Government Grants (EU Blockchain Observatory, National Science Foundation (NSF) grants)	Government grants are non-equity contributions from government bodies to support and promote blockchain research and development. The European Blockchain Observatory and Forum is a European Commission initiative to accelerate blockchain innovation and the development of the blockchain ecosystem within the EU and help cement Europe's position as a global leader in this transformative new technology.
Bank Loans (JPMorgan Chase, Bank of America, Wells Fargo)	Banks give traditional loans to blockchain companies to aid the development of blockchain technology and new startup "crypto" projects.

Institutional Investment Advantages

- **Credibility** - The extensive due diligence in the form of advanced long-term investment strategies, fundamental and technical analysis including market research, risk management, macroeconomic trends, and institutional-grade tools carried out by institutional investors adds credibility and legitimacy to the project and asset. This helps attract a significant number of retail investors and encourages further investment.
- **Institutional Adoption** - The rise of institutional investors is driving higher compliance standards, boosting transparency, market integrity, and investor confidence.
- **Access to Capital** - Through significant institutional investment, projects can scale more quickly and efficiently by hiring top talent, speeding up development and operations, and funding extensive marketing campaigns.
- **Large Sums** - Institutional investors can invest significant sums of money that help reduce volatility while increasing stability.
- **Liquidity** - Institutional investors bring sophisticated trading strategies to the blockchain market that aid liquidity and market efficiency.
- **Visibility and Interest** - Institutional investment draws and attracts more professional investment firms and traditional market investors to the crypto space.

Institutional Investment Disadvantages

- **Regulatory Scrutiny** – The involvement of institutional investors may attract increased attention from regulators, bringing additional scrutiny and compliance challenges to the project.
- **Dependence on Few Investors** – If a project becomes overly reliant on institutional funding, the withdrawal or failure of these investors can jeopardize the entire project.
- **Project Reputation** – If an institutional investor sells their token holdings, it could damage the project's reputation, resulting in uncertainty among the project team and all other stakeholders.
- **Limited Risk Tolerance** – Most institutional investors avoid very early-stage or high-risk projects, whereas dedicated crypto VCs and specialized funds may still allocate to them.
- **Investment Constraints** – Institutional investors may be restricted from investing in specific projects depending on where the project is registered.

Pro Tip Visit the websites of reputable institutional and private investment firms and research the projects in which they have invested. These investment firms carry out professional fundamental and technical analyses before investment.

Institutional Investment Evaluation

Institutional investments outside of bitcoin and Ethereum are rare, which is precisely why they are worth paying attention to. Consider it a strong positive signal when a major institution invests in an alternative digital asset, as this confirms that the project has passed rigorous evaluations and meets strict criteria. Spotting these assets can be a significant advantage for investors since institutional involvement indicates solid fundamentals, regulatory compliance, and strong long-term potential.

Verification of Institutional Investment

Institutional funding from corporations, venture capitalists, hedge funds, banks, and government authorities adds extreme credibility to blockchain projects versus projects solely funded through public offerings. Therefore, while not critical, it is advantageous if reputable investment institutions have invested in the project.

Investors can assess a project's institutional backing by visiting its official website and verifying claimed investments through online research. For example, in the instance of Aave, browser results showed that Aave is one of the underlying assets held in a Grayscale investment product, giving investors indirect exposure through the fund. was verified through the official Grayscale website (Figure 15-1) and also shown as part of the Grayscale DeFi Fund (Figure 15-2).

Financials *Includes crypto assets that seek to deliver financial transactions and services*	Aave (AAVE) MakerDao (MKR) Synthetix (SNX) Uniswap (UNI)	Aerodrome (AERO) Ethena (ENA) Injective Protocol (INJ) Jupiter (JUP)* Mantra (OM) Ondo Finance (ONDO) Pendle (PENDLE) THORChain (RUNE)

***Figure 15-1.** Grayscale digital assets portfolio 2025 (compliments of `https://grayscale.com/assets-under-consideration-and-current-products/`)*

Number of Holdings: 5 — As of 11/27/2024

NAME	ASSETS/SHARE	WEIGHT
UNI Uniswap	1.12405750	59.03%
AAVE Aave	0.02202522	17.72%
MKR Maker	0.00130034	9.48%
LDO Lido DAO	1.31388674	9.09%
SNX Synthetix	0.48249713	4.68%

***Figure 15-2.** Grayscale DeFi Fund (compliment of `https://grayscale.com/products/grayscale-decentralized-finance-fund/`)*

Action Steps

Follow these steps to evaluate potential institutional investments to assess whether the project gains added credibility and strengthened fundamentals from institutional backing.

1) **Determine If Institutional Investment**

   Visit the project's website and determine if the project has any form of institutional investment. Companies that invested in the project are typically listed on the main pages—especially if they are known, credible institutional investors.

2) **Verification of Institutional Investment**

   Verify any stated institutional investment by checking the institution's official website. Look for confirmation that the institution has indeed invested in the project.

3) **Take Notes and Document Your Findings in Your Own Style**

4) **Combine the Findings with Other Sections of the Fundamental Evaluation Process**

Evaluation of the Results

While institutional investment offers many advantages, many successful projects have thrived without it—therefore, it is not critical for project success. However, if the project has institutional investment, it should be considered a major positive. This represents that the project will likely have strong fundamentals because it passed the investment firm's rigorous fundamental and technical evaluations.

Private Funding

Evaluation Objective: Validate and evaluate a project's private funding, including assessing the reputation and expertise of the investment firms involved.

Private funding in blockchain refers to investments made by private bodies such as venture capital firms, angel investors, private equity firms, or high-net-worth individuals into blockchain projects and Web3-based companies. While it can sometimes include institutional investments, it differs from public funding methods like token offerings or sales, where retail investors contribute smaller amounts. Private funding often involves larger investment sums and may come with specific terms, like equity ownership, voting rights, a proportion of the token supply, or convertible debt.

Types of Private Funding

There are many different flavors of private funding companies—these groups are identified in Table 15-2.

Table 15-2. *Types of private funding schemes in the blockchain industry*

Private Funding	
Type of Funding	**Description**
Angel Investors (Naval Ravikant, Tim Draper)	An angel investor is a successful entrepreneur, business professional, or wealthy individual who provides capital for early-stage startup projects or companies, usually in exchange for equity. Angel investors often invest in high-risk ventures; outside of capital investment, they typically offer mentorship. Tim Draper is a famous angel investor who has invested in many blockchain companies. Outside of bitcoin and Ethereum, Tim Draper also invested in other projects, including Bitcoin Cash (BCH), Tezos (XTZ), Ripple (XRP), Polygon (POL), and $1 million in a new start-up named Aragon (ANT).

Hedge Funds (Valmar Capital, Bluesky Capital)	Hedge funds are private investment vehicles that pool money from both private and institutional investors. They gather investments from various sources and then implement trading strategies across different asset classes, such as securities, futures contracts, options, bonds, currencies, and digital assets, and across the financial markets. Hedge funds generate revenue by charging a management fee for their services and a percentage of the profits earned for their investors. Most US blockchain-focused hedge fund advisers register with the SEC, but the funds themselves typically operate under private fund exemptions (e.g., 3(c)(1) or 3(c)(7)), meaning they are not subject to the full Investment Company Act regime. Although many hedge fund strategies target shorter holding periods, investors' capital can still be subject to lock-up periods and scheduled redemption windows, so liquidity is not always immediate. "*Hedge funds are often known as the institutional gateway to digital assets*" They are managed by industry investment experts and professional traders who deploy various strategies to help maximize returns and reduce risk for their investors. At a bare minimum, these strategies typically consist of fundamental and technical analysis while utilizing market volatility and executing both long and short positions. There are different types of hedge funds for various investors. Hedge funds mainly invest in currencies, commodities, public equities, and, in recent times—digital assets. Valmar Capital is an example of a digital asset hedge fund geared towards institutional investors. The platform operates by allocating capital to multiple trading strategies and trading styles (systematic and fundamental) that help form a well-rounded, diversified portfolio that helps reduce and mitigate risk for investors.

(*continied*)

Table 15-2. *(continied)*

Private Funding	
Type of Funding	**Description**
Venture Capital Firms (Polychain Capital, Coinbase Ventures, Pantera Capital, Blockchain Capital)	Venture capital (VC) firms are investors that fund new startups, early-stage companies, and entrepreneurial pursuits in exchange for equity, assets, and possibly board seats. VCs typically invest in private companies that may or may not generate a profit but can see long-term profit potential. Therefore, VC investment strategies are considered high-risk compared to hedge funds, where investments are made in more established companies. Furthermore, Venture Capital investments are long-term investments where investors' money is locked up for long periods and considered illiquid. The main goal of venture capital financing is to give high-potential-growth businesses financial support, knowledge and industry expertise, strategic direction, and resources to help these companies grow. Additionally, VCs help handle regulatory obstacles, business development, marketing, community building, and token listings. This enables the new startups and early-stage companies to escalate development and scale operations that allow for rapid expansion. A well-known example of a VC firm is Polychain Capital. Polychain Capital analyzes and invests in cutting-edge blockchain companies in their early stages, including Parity Technologies, 0(1) Labs, and Web3 Foundation.

Private Equity (Franklin Templeton Blockchain Fund II, L.P.)	As the name suggests, private equity is the investment of equity capital in private companies. In a typical private equity deal, capital is gathered from high-net-worth individuals, large companies, and institutions to buy stakes in private companies with the hope of ultimately realizing an increase in the value of that stake. Private equity investments are long-term strategies ranging from two to ten years plus. Due to the lengthy lock-ups, investors' capital is considered illiquid. Private equity firms are more commonly associated with making investments in established businesses. However, these firms have begun showing an increased interest in the startup sector, with a number of them allocating funds to early-stage investments. Furthermore, in recent years, private equity firms have started to invest in more mature blockchain companies, often buying a significant stake. Private equity and venture capital funds both buy stakes in private companies, but they differ in more than just timing: VC typically funds early-stage growth through smaller, milestone-driven rounds, while PE deploys larger pools of capital into later-stage or mature firms, often using buyout or scale-up strategies and distinct deal-sourcing channels. Private equity funds invest in companies that are much more mature than the stage at which a venture capital fund would enter. Private equity funds invest in the companies at a much later stage to ensure that the technology or applications promised by the company have been proven to work and that the company is ready to scale, thereby reducing the risk exposure of the fund. When writing this book, Franklin Templeton, a private equity investment company, had filed with the SEC for a private equity fund called "*Franklin Templeton Blockchain Fund II, L.P.*" This Blockchain Fund II is a private equity fund. It will carry a minimum investment sum of $100,000.

(continied)

Table 15-2. *(continied)*

Private Funding	
Type of Funding	**Description**
Bootstrapping (Self-funded Startups)	The term "bootstrapping" refers to the process of how an individual starts and builds a company from personal finances or the operating revenues of the new company. Bootstrapped founders do not utilize any form of outside investment but instead self-fund the business by using sweat equity, personal savings, including borrowed or invested funds from family or friends, and income from initial sales. Blockchain projects often bootstrap to boost growth and expansion. Bootstrapped launches aren't rare—bitcoin (2009, no premine or outside funding) and Monero (2014, no ICO or VC backing) both started on founder sweat equity and community miners, proving a project can grow without external capital.
Strategic Investment and Partnership	A strategic partnership is a relationship between two or more companies that agree to support each other to help both parties succeed. Although the partners remain independent, the collaboration and partnership aim to achieve mutual benefits, synergies, long-term benefits, risks, and control over joint actions. Unlike purely financial investments, which aim simply to realize a return on investment (ROI), strategic partnerships are often established when companies need to acquire new capabilities within their existing business. Examples of this within the blockchain sector may include "crypto" projects investing in other projects that provide complementary services, such as interoperability, scalability, security, or innovation. An example of a strategic partnership in the blockchain sector is the Immutable and Polygon Labs partnership. Immutable and Polygon Labs partnered to build a dedicated gaming blockchain using zero-knowledge technology to accelerate decentralized game development and bring Web3 closer to mass adoption.

Pro Tip Projects funded by the blockchain research and development company Web3 Foundation are highly deemed admirable for investors. The Web3 Foundation is at the forefront of blockchain technology and the decentralized web (Web3), which selects high-quality projects to nurture cutting-edge applications for decentralized web software protocols.

Private Funding Advantages

- **Early-Stage Support** - Private funding firms are more willing to take risks on earlier-stage startups than institutional investors, who often prefer more established projects.
- **Investment Flexibility** - Certain private vehicles, such as crypto hedge funds, can run both long- and short-side strategies, whereas PE and VC funds are typically long-only. Even so, private vehicles in general face fewer portfolio-mandate restrictions than most traditional institutional funds.
- **Speed** - Private funding rounds are faster to complete than institutional investment, which usually involves more red tape and due diligence.
- **Stronger Relationships** - Angel investors and other private funders often promote closer personal relationships, leading to more trust, better communication, and consensus.

- **Credibility** - Private funding adds credibility and legitimacy to the projects, as private funding firms typically conduct thorough technical and fundamental analysis.
- **Fast Access Capital** - Through private funding, projects can scale quickly by hiring top talent, speeding up development and operations, and funding extensive marketing campaigns.
- **High-Risk Investments** - Private investors, especially those with a high-risk tolerance, are more open to backing high-risk projects than institutional investors.
- **Strategic Partnerships** - Aside from capital, private funding firms tend to offer strategic guidance, operational expertise, and contacts such as other investors, potential clients, and partners that may help secure high-value strategic partnerships for the project.
- **Regulatory Push** - When sizeable private capital flows into a blockchain project, it can put the project—and sometimes the wider sector—on regulators' radar, potentially accelerating the development of clearer compliance and disclosure rules.
- **Increased Liquidity** - Hedge funds and similar private investors often adopt short-term strategies that enhance market liquidity, benefiting both retail and institutional participants.
- **Expertise and Experience** - Private funding firms often bring specialized knowledge, operational experience, and strategic expertise, helping projects overcome complex challenges.

Private Funding Disadvantages

- **Market Volatility** - If an adequate vesting schedule is not in place, large withdrawals of capital by private equity firms can negatively impact retail investors, leading to token price drops and increased market volatility.
- **Limited Funds** - Private funding typically offers less capital than institutional investments, which may not suffice for large-scale projects.
- **Regulatory Scrutiny** - Private funding may attract increased attention from regulators, leading to added compliance requirements and scrutiny.
- **High Equity Stakes** - Depending on the level of risk, private investors often demand high equity stakes or a large proportion of the token supply.
- **Legal Risks** - Informal or improperly structured private funding deals may result in legal actions, particularly if regulatory compliance is not addressed.

Private Investment Evaluation

Private funding can be highly beneficial for projects, especially when sourced from funding firms with a pristine reputation. However, some crypto projects falsely claim backing from well-known private funding firms to boost their credibility. Therefore, the investor must verify any claims of private funding made by the project team and their track record, reputation, and capabilities before investing.

Verification of Private Funding

Investors should verify any claims of private funding by confirming directly with the funding source. This aims to determine if the team is trustworthy, transparent, and honest. A simple check can verify whether a private funding body has funded a project. For example, Figure 15-3 shows Acala Network claiming Polychain Capital as a private investor in their project. This is verified through the official Polychain Capital website (Figure 15-4), which shows Acala as part of their portfolio.

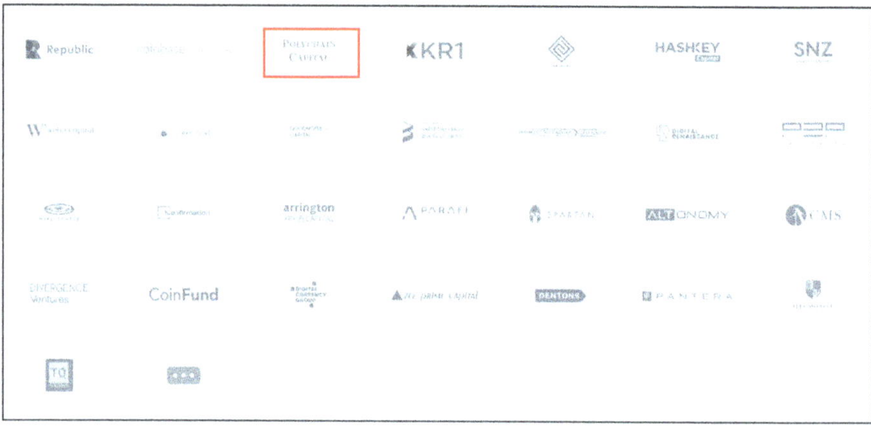

***Figure 15-3.** Acala Network investors (compliments of `https://acala.network/`)*

***Figure 15-4.** Polychain Capital—Confirming Acala Network on their portfolio (compliments of `https://jobs.polychain.capital/companies`)*

Crunchbase

Investors can verify whether a reputable venture capital firm has invested in a project by using Crunchbase. Crunchbase is a platform that provides real-time company data for sales professionals, CEOs, VCs, and investors. For example, by utilizing Crunchbase, investors can verify any funding projects claimed to have been received, how much was raised, and where the funds originated. In the example of Acala Network receiving funding from Polychain Capital—this has been verified through the Crunchbase platform; see Figure 15-5.

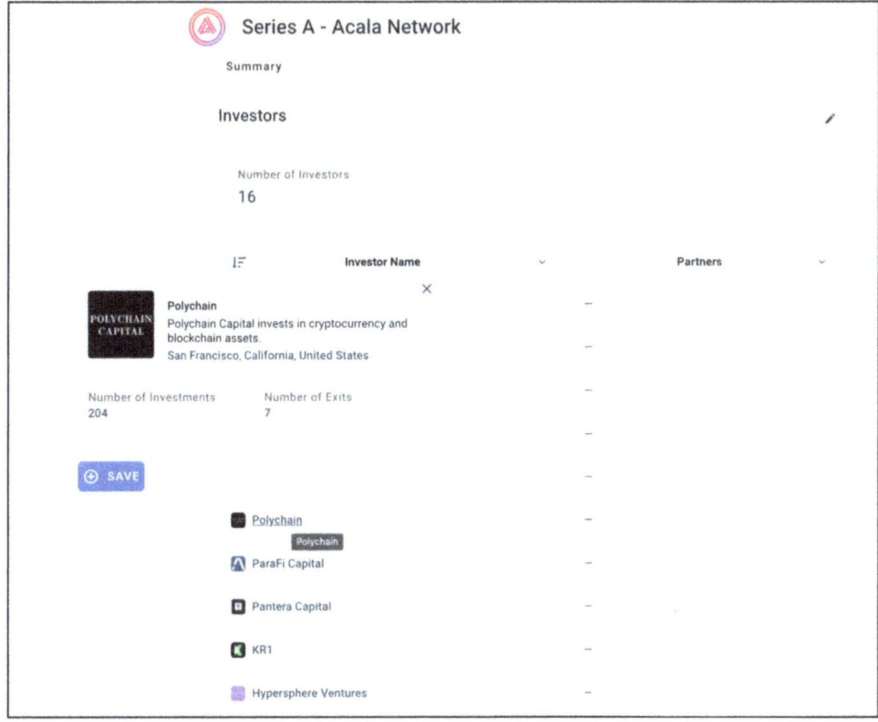

***Figure 15-5.** Verifying Acala Network funding through Polychain Capital (compliments of `https://www.crunchbase.com/funding_round/acala-network-series-a--bf148606`)*

Reputation and Role of Private Investors

Projects often secure funding from multiple private investment firms, some of which may not be as well-known as prominent names like Polychain Capital, Coinbase Ventures, Pantera Capital, or Blockchain Capital. Therefore, it is critical, especially for long-term investors, to research and evaluate these lesser-known firms' reputations and blockchain experience.

Furthermore, it is common for private investors to provide more value than capital alone. As previously discussed, new startups require and benefit immensely from experienced private investment firms that offer value in the form of quality guidance, expertise, and access to professional contacts to help the project grow to its full potential.

When analyzing private funding firms, it is recommended that the evaluation be done using the following analysis criteria. Reliable information about these firms can often be found through online research, including their official websites and various blockchain community forums.

1) **Track Record**

    a) What blockchain projects have they previously funded?

    b) Were their previously funded projects successful?

2) **Investment Approach**

    a) How long do they typically stay invested in a project?

3) **Reputation**

    a) Is there any negative or positive feedback about the funding firm found online?

    b) Do they have good or bad rapport within the blockchain community?

4) **Value Beyond Capital**

   a) Outside of capital, do they provide guidance and technical expertise?

   b) Do their advisors have a good, credible reputation in the blockchain realm?

5) **Partnerships and Networks**

   a) Do they bring strategic connections and professional networks?

Action Steps

Follow these steps to validate and evaluate a project's private funding, including assessing the reputation and expertise of the investment firms involved.

1) **Private Investor Firms**

   Scan official project outlets such as the project website and blog to obtain a list of the private funding firms claimed by the team.

2) **Verification of Funding**

   Verify any funding the projects claim to have acquired.

   a) Visit the private investing firm's website and verify project funding by viewing their investment portfolio.

   b) Further, verify any funding through the Crunchbase platform.

3) **Research**

   Investigate each private investment firm with respect to the evaluation criteria outlined in the section titled "***Reputation and Role of Private Investors.***"

4) **Take Notes and Document Your Findings in Your Own Style**

5) **Combine the Findings with Other Sections of the Fundamental Evaluation Process**

Evaluation of the Results

It is admirable for private investors to have a good reputation, a proven track record, and high-level expertise in the blockchain sector from which the project can benefit. However, it is not a hard requirement for the project to have private funding, provided it has adequate funds from other sources, enough professional connections, and in-house technical expertise to execute its vision.

Public Funding

Evaluation Objective: Evaluate the project's public sale funding model as a potential investment opportunity.

Public funding in the blockchain world typically refers to the process of raising capital from the sale of digital tokens to the public. These token sales are executed through various public sale models that crypto projects utilize to gain funding for the development value offering. The type of public funding scheme a project team selects is influenced by several factors, ranging from funding amounts, funding caps, development stage, regulatory considerations, complexity, credibility, and trust.

Types of Public Funding Models

This section explores the different types of public funding models. It is advantageous for investors to understand each funding model's risks, drawbacks, and limitations to help make informed investment decisions when participating in public token sales.

Initial Coin Offering (ICO)

Examples: Ethereum ICO and IOTA ICO

An Initial Coin Offering (ICO) is a process whereby an entrepreneurial venture raises funds in exchange for cryptographically secured digital assets intended to be the sole means of payment for the venture's future products or services on a decentralized application (dApp). In an ICO, the project team organizes and manages the entire token offering from start to finish. This also includes directly distributing the tokens (or coins) to ICO participants after the token sale, handling regulatory issues (if any), and developing and executing marketing strategies through official outlets such as the project website, blog, or third-party ICO advertising websites.

ICOs are typically aimed at retail investors, providing the opportunity to gain early exposure to a particular project during the early stages of development. ICO participants invest in digital assets such as bitcoin (BTC), Ethereum (ETH), Tether (USDT), and sometimes fiat currency in exchange for tokens from the project. These tokens (or coins) may represent various rights or benefits for the holders, such as access to a product service, governance rights, or some form of utility and participation in a network. However, from an investor standpoint, one of the core reasons for investing in ICOs is for short- or long-term financial gain.

Although ICOs can sometimes be lucrative, it is essential to note that they are considered high-risk investments compared to already established projects. Most "crypto" projects raising funds through ICOs do not yet have a working product or service. This essentially means ICO participants are mainly betting on the team behind the project. Moreover, unless high-end institutional or private investment firms have already funded ICO projects, it is highly unlikely they have faced professional, rigorous, complex, and expensive auditing, which adds extreme risk for ICO participants. With ICOs, there is no guarantee of the quality or legitimacy of the project or company or the value of the tokens or coins. It is common for "scam" projects to fundraise through ICOs with little or no intention of delivering on their promises. As a result of widespread fraud concerns, regulators have cracked down—the US SEC, for instance, has repeatedly ruled in enforcement actions that many ICOs were unregistered securities offerings and has brought cases against several issuers.

Know Your Customer (KYC) is a process that financial institutions and businesses use to verify the identity of potential investors to prevent illegal activities such as money laundering or fraud. Many ICOs impose KYC restrictions on investors. This can reduce the number of potential investors due to the additional steps involved, increase the time it takes to raise funds from the ICO, and potentially influence its overall performance. Investors can locate and find information on ICO listings through websites such as ICO Drops, CryptoRank, and ICO Holder. ICO participation is typically done through the project website.

Successful ICOs Include

Ethereum ICO - Ethereum is a platform for smart contracts and decentralized applications. It raised approximately $16 million in its ICO in 2014, selling its tokens for $0.31 each. Ethereum reached an all-time high of $4,878 in 2021.

NEO ICO - NEO is a Chinese blockchain project that aims to create a smart economy with digital assets, digital identity, and smart contracts. NEO raised approximately $5.05 million between its 2015 and 2016 ICOs, selling tokens for $0.032 each. The tokens reached an all-time high of $196 in 2018.

IOTA ICO - IOTA is an open-source distributed ledger and cryptocurrency designed for the Internet of Things, raised approximately $590,000 in 2015. The IOTA price hit an all-time high of $5.69.

Initial Exchange Offering (IEO)

Examples: Binance Launchpad, OKEx Jumpstart, and Gate.io
An initial exchange offering (IEO) is a digital asset fundraising event where a blockchain project (new or established) raises capital via a trading platform, selling tokens directly to investors through the exchange. IEOs are similar to Initial Coin Offerings (ICOs), but in an IEO, the exchange administers and organizes the entire token sale on behalf of the startup. Tokens from fundraising are issued to investors through the exchange versus an ICO, which is issued directly to investors. With respect to marketing, IEO benefits include community management, SEO optimization, influencer marketing, multiple marketing strategies, and PR outreach, compared to an ICO where the project is responsible and accountable for everything.

IEOs have become more prevalent in recent years as ICOs have lost their appeal. One of the core reasons is due to the reduced level of risk with an IEO. In an IEO, professional digital asset analysts from the exchange perform detailed audits and analyses of the project wanting to raise funds on their platform. Major digital asset exchanges have a reputation to uphold and generally screen out scams or poor-quality projects—though a few can still slip through their due-diligence net. Another reason why projects are leaning towards IEOs is because there is a higher chance of getting listed on the exchange after the token offering. This is extremely important for projects, as it provides more opportunity and access for investors worldwide to gain exposure to the digital asset.

A challenge that most new startups and IEO platforms face is geographical restrictions, where certain investors, depending on their location, may be restricted from investing in a particular IEO. Additionally, unlike ICOs, all investors must be registered with the IEO exchange, which may further limit the investment amount. As the blockchain sector further matures, more IEOs are being launched. Some popular IEO platforms include Binance Launchpad, OKEx Jumpstart, and Gate.io. The IEO funding method creates a unique collaboration environment between exchanges and promising blockchain startups that helps ensure transparency, liquidity, and trust. Examples of successful projects that utilized and received funding through IEOs are Band Protocol and Polygon (Matic) Network, which took advantage of the Binance Launchpad.

Initial DEX Offering (IDO)

Examples: PancakeSwap and TrustSwap, Polkastarter
An Initial DEX Offering (IDO) is a fundraising technique that utilizes a decentralized exchange (DEX) to facilitate the token sale for a new startup "crypto" project. IDOs offer a fast and efficient way for projects to raise capital. They also provide access to a large pool of potential investors and the ability to establish a loyal community. IDOs eliminate the need for a centralized exchange and permission to launch the fundraising event. They also have low fees. Project teams typically pay only the gas fee to deploy a new smart contract, although many launchpads also impose extra listing fees or require a small share of the raise/tokens. The IDO process is best described as having two phases:

Phase 1 - IDO Launchpad and Incubation
The fundraising project submits a *listing request* to an IDO Launchpad platform with specific information (whitepaper, tokenomics, capital requirements, etc.). The IDO Launchpad (e.g., TrustSwap, Polkastarter, PancakeSwap) will review the submitted information, and if approved, the project team needs to fulfill specific demands from the platform. These demands may include some type of staking and whitelist requirements. It is important to understand that these "ecosystem-specific launchpads" incubate the projects and help nurture them to increase the chances

of the project's long-term success. Marketing is carried out, and all IDO information, including project-specific fundamental details, is made available to the public. On the day of the IDO, through the IDO Launchpad, investors pay for their tokens in advance by entering a pool, committing their money for essentially IOUs (IOU-style tokens). The funds collected from investors are sent to the project team, and they will use them to help develop the project. Next, a *token generation event (TGE)* is held, during which the tokens are generated and sent to all IDO participants.

Phase 2 - IDO Token Listing

Once the IDO is successfully concluded and the TGE takes place, the token is listed for trading on decentralized exchanges (DEX)—automated market makers (AMM) include Sushiswap or PancakeSwap.

IDOs are an alternative to ICOs and IEOs; however, although they have some advantages, they also have limitations. Upon launch, no requirement for centralized exchanges means instant liquidity through the IDO platform (e.g., PancakeSwap). This means that investors on the IDO platform have the option to start trading instantly. Furthermore, launching through an IDO Launchpad and automated market makers eliminates hefty listing fees that projects incur through IEOs.

However, extreme caution must be exercised when interacting and investing through IDO launchpads and automated market makers. Investors must be extra vigilant when evaluating suitable IDO launchpads and fundraising projects through these platforms. Also, in many circumstances, especially for large and hyped projects, it is challenging for investors to secure participation. IDOs often have "anti-whale" measures, meaning no single investor can buy many tokens.

Examples of successful projects fundraised through IDO Launchpads and listed directly on IDO trading platforms are Astar Network, Mantra DAO, and Ferrum Network.

Initial Farm Offering (IFO)

Example: PancakeSwap

There is another version of an IDO called an Initial Farm Offering (IFO). This is essentially the same thing as an IDO except that in an IFO, rather than investors locking their tokens directly, they must first stake (farm—provide liquidity) in a DeFi Liquidity Pool (LP) to earn LP tokens. On PancakeSwap, for instance, a project that wants to raise BNB in an IFO requires users to stake (deposit) BNB-CAKE LP tokens; when the sale concludes, the CAKE portion is permanently burned, the BNB portion goes to the project team as the raise, and participants receive the newly issued tokens.

Security Token Offering (STO)

Examples: Polymath, Securitize, and Tokensoft

A Security Token Offering (STO) is the procedure where the sale of real-world assets through financial instruments, represented by digital tokens, is offered to KYC-approved (qualified) investors. A security token simply acts as a digital representation of an underlying real-world asset that may include art, shares, bonds, gold, derivatives, or property. Therefore, security token offering services enable asset tokenization for many businesses. Additionally, security tokens provide the same rights to profit participation, dividends, and voting in important management decisions. Investors buying security tokens mainly aim to generate profits through cash flows or asset appreciation. Companies can issue security tokens following the standard procedure for issuing financial instruments to the public. Similar to traditional markets, a certificate of ownership is recorded for all security token holders. However, as with conventional asset ownership recording procedures, security token ownership is recorded on the blockchain versus entered into a document as an official certificate of ownership.

A Security Token Offering (STO) is a process of selling security tokens through a specific platform. These securities are issued on a platform that is registered with (or otherwise complies with) applicable securities-market regulations—such as an SEC-registered alternative trading system (ATS) in the United States—similar to a traditional stock exchange, and the sale is conducted as a Security Token Offering (STO). Similar to ICOs, STOs enable founders to raise funds for new ventures. Unlike ICOs, these fund-raising events are accompanied by strict government regulations. Nevertheless, getting an STO approved is a relatively fast and cost-efficient process compared to traditional "security" funding processes. STOs uniquely combine blockchain technology with the requirements of regulated securities markets to facilitate asset liquidity and finance accessibility. Smart contract automation promotes and incorporates securities regulatory disclosure objectives, market integrity, fairness, innovation, and efficiency. This, in turn, enables investors both inside and outside the blockchain realm to invest in regulated financial securities in a tokenized form—similar to that of conventional financial instruments.

Although STOs are still in their infancy, they are a fast-emerging fundraising process that allows small and medium-sized companies to fundraise without significant cost impacts. Additionally, due to the high level of regulation and scrutiny surrounding STOs, they are considered less risky than ICOs, IDOs, and IEOs. STO platforms were developed to simplify the token generation process and be more accessible. Investors can find information on various STO listings through websites such as Polymath, Securitize, and Tokensoft.

Digital assets that the SEC has alleged are unregistered securities in ongoing or recent enforcement actions include Cardano (ADA), Solana (SOL), Polygon (MATIC), Cosmos (ATOM), NEAR Protocol (NEAR), Binance Coin (BNB), Filecoin (FIL), and Algorand (ALGO).

Crowdloans

Examples: Polkadot Network and Kusama Network

Crypto crowdloans are a new method for blockchain projects to raise funds and gain support from the community. Unlike traditional fundraising events such as ICOs, IEOs, and IDOs, where new startups essentially sell tokens to investors, in a crowdloan, projects borrow tokens (or coins) from the broader community and then utilize the collected funds to add value to the project. In return, community members who lend their tokens are rewarded with the project's native tokens or other incentives—think of these rewards as interest from a typical loan. Predetermined terms and conditions outlined by the project will specify such criteria as the start and finish dates of the crowdloan, how to participate, the reward structure, and when borrowers will have their initial contributed funds returned to them.

Examples of well-known projects that utilized the crowdloan funding mechanism are Moonbeam Network and Moonriver Network. Both networks borrowed funds (DOT, KSM) from the greater community and used the contributed funds to bid for and win parachain slots on the Polkadot Network and Kusama Network, respectively. The contributed funds were also used to cover the cost of each parachain lease, which is approximately two years long. They achieved this by locking up the contributed tokens for the length of the parachain lease. Therefore, the contributed tokens are locked in the crowdloan module for the full parachain lease period and cannot be spent or moved by the project; at the end of the lease period, all participants who contributed funds get their contributions returned to them. At the end of the lease period, all participants who contributed funds get their contributions returned to them. Additionally, all contributors receive rewards (GLMR and MOVR) distributed linearly as recognition for their efforts.

One of the core advantages of Polkadot's digital auction process is the unique *"candle auctions"* process. Traditional open digital actions are prone to "auction sniping," where bidders wait until the last minute when they try to "snipe" the bid. However, with Polkadot's *"candle auctions"* process, the Verifiable Random Function (VRF) determines when the auction actually ended during the seven days towards the end of the action period. This encourages bidders to place sincere, early bids, making the process fairer and less susceptible to manipulation.

DAICO Funding

Examples: Aragon and MolochDAO
In 2018, Vitalik Buterin, the creator of Ethereum, proposed a Decentralized Autonomous Initial Coin Offering (DAICO). The DAICO is a fundraising model that aims to increase investor trust in ICOs by locking an ICO's proceeds into a decentralized autonomous organization (DAO) smart contract. Investors are given voting rights, giving contributors voting power to adjust or halt the "tap" (a per-second trickle of funds) if key milestones aren't met—rather than approving every individual expense.

The DAICO is a unique merge of the best ideas and concepts from ICOs and DAOs that aims to protect investor money from scams and poor project performance. Similar to ICOs, DAICOs start by initiating a fundraiser in which investors contribute (e.g., ETH, USDT) in return for native tokens from the project. However, unlike an ICO, the DAICO possesses a "tap" mechanism. The sole purpose of the "tap" is to allow the DAO to control the amount of money (funding allocation) made available to the project team on a second-to-second basis. Therefore, the team is limited to the amount of funds available at any given point in time.

The funds are raised through a DAICO; a portion is reserved for the team, development, marketing, treasury, rewards, liquidity, etc. If, for example, payments are made to developers gradually (e.g., once a month) and the developers need more funds than the tap is currently delivering, they must ask token holders to vote on raising the tap rate; governance cannot approve one-off lump-sum disbursements—only adjust (or stop) the continuous stream. The DAO has the opportunity to restrict access to funds, which helps reduce the risk of the team manipulating tokens and funds. This synergistic model allows collecting and allocating funds to be as transparent and safe as possible. Additionally, it gives token holders power and control, thus protecting their investments.

In the DAO governance structure, shareholders can vote on specific token-related resolutions, including raising the "tap" (increasing money flow to the team) or permanently self-destructing the contract, where the token holders would proportionately withdraw the remaining funds. This aims to prevent the team's manipulation of tokens and funds, hold them accountable for quality workmanship and progression, and commit to their promises and milestones defined in the whitepaper and roadmap.

The DAICO funding and governance model is still largely theoretical—only a few projects have experimented with it, and no large-scale, long-running implementation exists yet. However, it is expected to make the governance of ICO funds more democratic and offer investors a degree of protection from fraud.

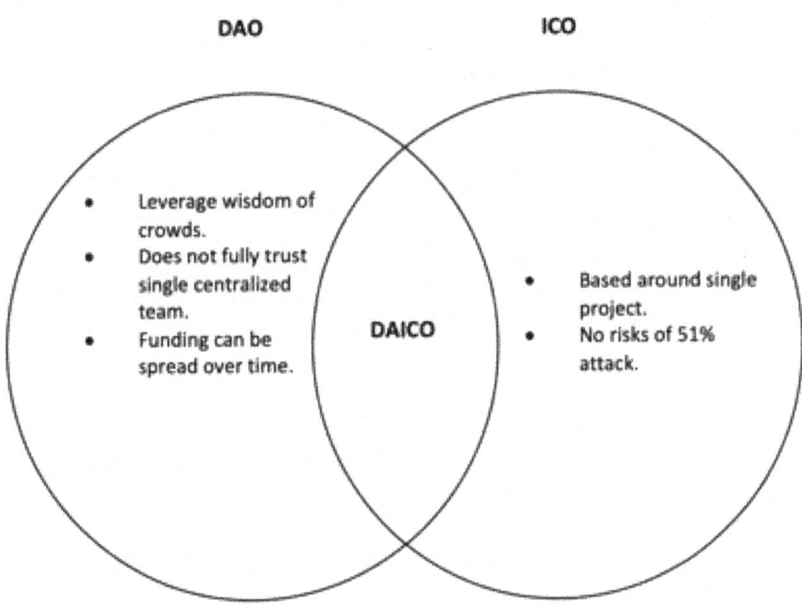

Figure 15-6. *DAO-ICO combination model (compliments of DAO-ICO combination:* `https://www.garbcan.com/blockchain/developing-better-initial-coin-offerings-icos-an-overview-of-daicos/#:~:text=DAICOs%2C%20like%20ICOs%2C%20are%20based,to%20be%20a%20typical%20ICO`

Advantages

- **Democratization** – Allows non-accredited investors to participate in token sales, promoting a more inclusive and democratic token sale.
- **Trust and Transparency** – Projects that hold public token sales often undergo public scrutiny, and due diligence can gain increased trust and credibility.

- **Community Spirit -** Allowing the public to participate in token sales generates a positive and exciting environment in the community.
- **Balanced Token Distribution** - Public token sales help ensure a more balanced and decentralized distribution of tokens, thus contributing to network security and stability.
- **Public Awareness** - A more expansive selection of investors can increase project awareness.
- **Flexibility** - Allows the team, including developers, to make more efficient decisions without being bound or limited by large private or institutional investors.
- **Insight and Innovation** - A broad selection of public investors can increase the level of innovation by receiving insight, views, and opinions from many different people from different sectors.

Disadvantages

- **Lack of Accountability** - Because there is less oversight, accountability, and focus on funds collected from public token sales, this often leads to misuse of funds.
- **Project Feasibility** - When relying solely on public funding, the project may not get a professional evaluation from private or institutional investment firms, thus lowering the credibility factor.
- **Scale and Growth** - Generally, public funding cannot provide enough capital for the project to grow and reach its full potential.

- **Regulatory Scrutiny** – Various public funding methods (e.g., ICOs) have faced intense scrutiny and regulatory challenges, leading to uncertainty and potential legal issues for projects.
- **Strategic Guidance** – When relying solely on public funding, projects do not receive the added support and mentorship from private or institutional investment firms.

Public Sale Model Summary

Table 15-3 summarizes various types of public funding models. Note that there is no right or wrong model type; it solely depends on the project scope and requirements. However, each funding model has many distinct advantages and disadvantages. The project team and stakeholders are responsible for choosing a model that aligns with the project's funding goals and public and sale regulatory restrictions that may restrict certain public investors from participating.

Table 15-3. *Public sale ICO, IEO, IDO, STO, and crowdfunding comparison*

	Summary of Public Funding Methods						
Criteria	**Initial Coin Offering (ICO)**	**Initial Exchange Offering (IEO)**	**Initial DEX Offering (IDO)**	**Initial Farm Offering (IFO)**	**Security Token Offering (STO)**	**Crowd Loans**	**DAICO Funding**
Fundraising Hosting Platform	Project Website	Centralized Exchange (Binance Launchpad, Gate.io)	Decentralized Exchange (PancakeSwap, TrustSwap Polkastarter)	Decentralized Exchange (Pancake-Swap)	Regulated Platforms (Polymath, Securitize, Tokensoft)	Polkadot, Kusama	BUIDL-1
Project Examples	Ethereum ICO, IOTA ICO)	Band Protocol, Polygon Network	Astar Network, Mantra DAO, Ferrum Network.	Duet Protocol, Horizon Protocol	tZERO (TZROP), INX Limited (INX Token)	Moonbeam Network, Acala Network	The Abyss (DAICO-like model)
Regulation	Usually unregulated	Usually unregulated	Unregulated	Unregulated	Highly Regulated	Unregulated	Unregulated
Screening Intensity	Low (by the community)	High (by the exchange)	Medium (by IDO Launchpad)	Medium (by IDO Launchpad)	Medium (community, platform)	Low (by the community)	Medium (by the DAO)

Accessibility	Public	Users of the Specific Exchange	Public	Public	Accredited Investors Often Required	Public	Public
KYC/AML	Varies	Required	None	None	Required	Varies	Required
Fundraising Costs	Low	Medium	Low	Low	Medium	Low	Low
Marketing Responsibility	Project Team	Project Team & Exchange (joint marketing)	Project Team & IDO Launchpad	Project Team & IDO Launchpad	Project Team	Project Team	DAO
Automatic Token Listing	No (exchange reach-out required)	Yes	Yes	Yes	Varies (depends on the STO platform)	No (exchange reach-out required)	No (exchange reach-out required)
Liquidity Level	Medium (varies)	High	Medium to High (depends on no. of LPs)	High	High (may have some restrictions)	Medium (varies)	Low-Medium
Investor Protection	Low (limited)	Medium (exchange insurance, KYC & AML)	None	None	High	Low (limited)	Medium

(continued)

Table 15-3. *(continied)*

	Summary of Public Funding Methods						
Criteria	**Initial Coin Offering (ICO)**	**Initial Exchange Offering (IEO)**	**Initial DEX Offering (IDO)**	**Initial Farm Offering (IFO)**	**Security Token Offering (STO)**	**Crowd Loans**	**DAICO Funding**
Cost for Issuers/ Projects	Moderate	High (Listing Fee)	Low	Low	High (Legal & Compliance Cost)	Low	Low
Complexity	Moderate	Moderate	Low	Medium	High	Medium	Medium
Speed of Execution	Moderate to Slow (depends on the product & marketing)	Moderate to Fast (high user reach, some restrictions)	Fast (wide reach, no restrictions)	Fast (wide reach, no restrictions)	Slow (due to regulations)	Moderate to Fast (depending on the funding model)	Moderate to Fast (depends on DAO efficiency and structure)
Centralization Level	Low to Medium	High	Decentralized	Decentralized	High	Medium to High	Mostly Decentralized

Public Sale Evaluation

Institutional and private investors perform sophisticated evaluations and due diligence before investing in any project. Their team of experts deep dives into every aspect and detail of the project before making an investment decision. However, with public funding, the onus is on the general public, community, and retail investors. Investors can also apply specific checks to evaluate public token sales, as outlined in the following sections. First, it's essential to identify the token allocation model. There are two methods, or models, to allocate public sale tokens: fair *launch* and *premine* token models.

Fair Launch and Premine Models

There are two ways token allocations can be issued: Fair *Launch* or *Pre-mined*. Depending on the type of model utilized by the project will affect how the public sale tokens are distributed. For example, in a Fair Launch, tokens are allocated to active protocol participants who provide value. On the other hand, the Premine model distributes tokens through more common methods such as ICOs, IEOs, IDOs, or crowdloans.

Fair Launch

Examples: bitcoin, Litecoin, Yearn Finance, and Cryptex Finance
Fair launch projects do not have any specific "traditional" token allocation model before launch. Instead, the project's native assets are earned, owned, and governed by the users who actively participate and add value to the product or service. The goal of a fair launch is simply to level the playing field so that every investor can obtain tokens (or coins) at the same price, at the same time, and without any price discrepancies—hence the term a "*fair launch.*"

Depending on the value offering, the native assets can be earned in a variety of ways, including increasing the security of the blockchain by mining or staking, providing liquidity, code contribution, identification and resolution of bugs, or even through centralized activities such as marketing, creating awareness, and other related activities. A prime and most noticeable example of a fair launch project is bitcoin. Since bitcoin genesis block in 2009, when the first 50 BTC were mined, bitcoin miners have been generating—mining—BTC while enhancing blockchain security and decentralization.

Another core feature and commitment of fair launches is eradicating traditional funding methods and eliminating team incentives. The idea is to restrict projects from issuing tokens before public access, including issuing tokens for product development. This is to avoid any form of initial concentration of tokens among a select few.

Advantages

- **Highly Decentralized** - Currently the most decentralized token distribution mechanism available.
- **Increased Transparency** - Since a fair launch is carried out in a decentralized manner, the distribution of tokens is transparent and publicly documented.
- **Equality** - Everyone has an equal opportunity to attain tokens or coins from Genesis.
- **Reduced Manipulation** - Less chance of market manipulation due to the reduced concentration of digital assets like traditional (pre-mined) token allocation models.
- **Investor Appeal** - Increased level of trust among the community and investors due to the highly decentralized token distribution model and reduced chance of market manipulation.

- **Return of Investment** - Although fair launch projects are rare and hard to find, they are often more rewarding compared to traditional (pre-mined) token allocation models.
- **Increased Accessibility** - A fair launch is designed to be open to anyone who wants to participate, without any restrictions or barriers to entry.

Disadvantages

- **Poor Tokenomics** - Although the project team has some control, fair launches strongly emphasize community input and consensus. This puts significant responsibility on the community to generate an effective and powerful tokenomic structure that satisfies all project requirements.
- **Funding Restrictions** - Developers may be starved of funds necessary to bring the project to life and heightened optimization.
- **Difficulty of Execution** - A fair launch can be difficult and time-consuming, as it requires a deep understanding of the process and technical expertise in delivery and execution.

Pro Tip Excellent resources to locate fair launches are websites such as YouTube, X, Reddit, and Bitcoin Talk.

Premine Launch

Examples: Ripple and Stellar

In contrast to a fair-launch model, most projects launched today use a pre-allocated (often called "pre-mine") approach. As the name suggests, in a premine launch, a set percentage of the total native assets are pre-mined and allocated to specific groups (e.g., the founding team, advisors, ecosystem development, investors, private and public investors, etc.) pre-launch. Although this approach has many benefits, it often results in a high initial concentration of tokens among a select few, depending on the token distribution structure, which can lead to centralized control. See the section "Token Distribution Models" in Chapter 8, "Tokenomics," for more details on tokenomic allocations.

Advantages

- **Project Initiation** – The project team can efficiently sell pre-mine assets to kick-start the project in key areas, including marketing, partnerships, developments, etc., facilitating a more efficient project initiation.
- **Incentivization for Developers** – Pre-mine assets allocated to developers can help incentivize ongoing development.
- **Private Funding Benefits** – Funding from private investment firms can properly financially prepare and provide the project team with expert advice and strategies to complement a successful launch.

Disadvantages

- **Risk of Collapse** – Without a proper token allocation model, projects face a high risk of failure due to the concentration of tokens among a select few, leading to excessive centralization and governance issues.

- **Community Distrust** - May lead to a lack of trust in the community, especially if there is a perception of unfairness or lack of transparency.
- **Market Manipulation** - High risk of significant selling pressure by large token holders at launch and the following subsequent weeks.

Streamlined Filtering of Public Offerings

The most efficient way to view active and scheduled public token sales, including ICOs, IDOs, and IEOs, is by searching through dedicated cryptocurrency market insight and analytics platforms such as ICO Drops, CryptoRank, and ICO Holder. While public sale offerings are enticing, do not take anything for granted and assume that just because they are advertised and held on legitimate platforms, the risk is reduced, because it isn't. These sites are largely listing aggregators and do not perform full due diligence on the projects. A constant flow of new crypto startups is advertised on these platforms, promising to be the next big project. However, given that new crypto startups carry the highest risk, and most fade in the shadows once the initial hype is over, it is essential to perform adequate due diligence before investing in any public sale (ICO, IEO, IDO, IFO, etc.). Investors are responsible for avoiding public sales scams while identifying fundamentally strong projects with minimal risk and maximum return on investment.

In this section, you will find a list of quick fundamental checks designed to help you filter the scams and fundamentally poor projects. The purpose of this is to help streamline your public sale selection by highlighting investments that are worth a closer look. However, note that these checks are just the starting point, and once the shortlisted potential public sale investments are identified, a full, detailed fundamental evaluation—as discussed in this book—is required.

Project Summary

Every public sale website advertising an ICO, IDO, IEO, etc., for a particular project always includes a summary of the value offering. For example, Figure 15-7 shows various details for the *Patex Network* taken from CryptoRank. At a minimum, these details should include the type of public offering (e.g., IDO), the hard cap ($450k), project classification (e.g., blockchain infrastructure), and a summary of the project and its value offering.

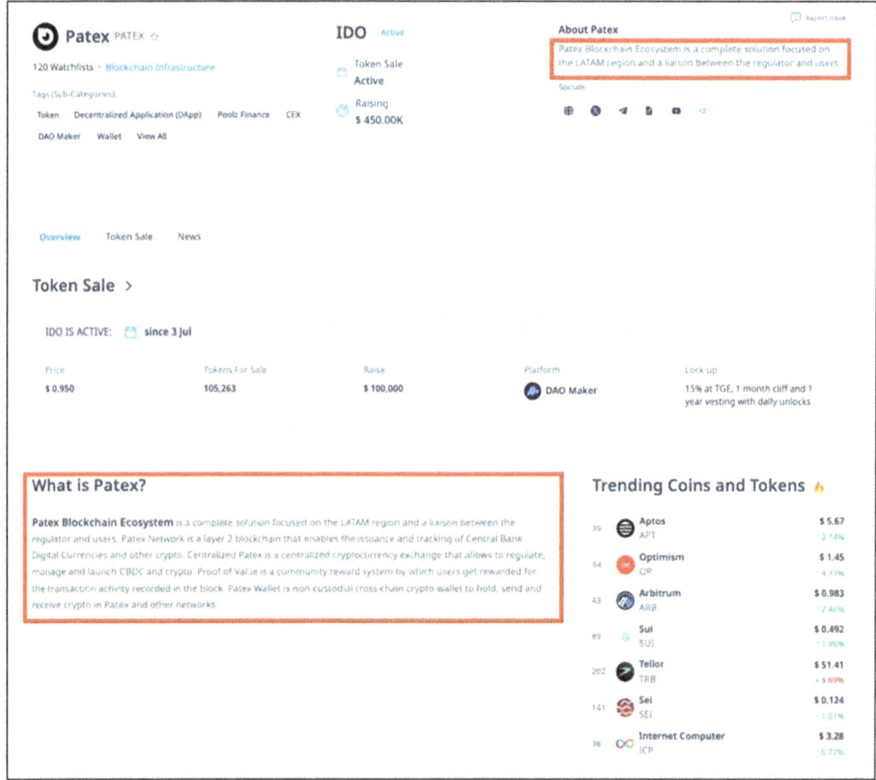

Figure 15-7. *Patex Network —Project summary on CryptoRank.io (compliments of* `https://cryptorank.io/ico/patex`*)*

Caution Influencers with poor technical evaluation skills are sometimes manipulated into promoting public sales projects with poor fundamentals and are usually fraudulent in nature. Investors must execute their own fundamental evaluation and not rely on secondhand information from influencers with no credibility.

As the name suggests, the project summary is an outlined summary of the project's value offering. A good summary should be precise and to the point. It should capture essential information that includes a short description of a unique use case and the problem it solves. In a nutshell, high-quality use cases solve known issues—for crypto projects or traditional centralized companies—or provide some value offering that complements major projects such as Ethereum and bitcoin, adding value to the overall blockchain ecosystem. Investors must be aware of the following red flags when reviewing summary sections of public sale offerings.

- **Vague Detail** - Lacks specific technical information about the product or service and corresponding value proposition.
- **Unspecified Fund Allocation** - Unclear hard cap or no explanation of how funds will be utilized within the project.
- **Unclear Timelines** - No clear timelines with respect to token generation events, product release, or other critical milestones.
- **Imitation Projects** - The use case or product description sounds similar to major projects such as bitcoin or Ethereum.

- **Anonymous Teams** - No visible information or credentials provided on the team (founders, developers, etc.), or the team explicitly states it will remain pseudonymous.
- **No Regulatory Compliance** - Ignores KYC/AML requirements or other legal guidelines—a major red flag for regulated offerings (e.g., STOs) but still worth noting even in permissionless sales such as many ICOs or IDOs.
- **Poor Grammar** - Misspellings or poor grammar indicate a lack of professionalism.

Caution When I started investing in digital assets, I sent one ETH to a scam ICO (initial coin offering). I was influenced by flashy, devious marketing, and my emotions took over. Only after I found out I was scammed did I have a proper look at the website. I noticed many spelling mistakes, poor-quality images, fake LinkedIn profiles, and poorly written whitepapers. Valuable lessons learned. Research and due dilligence are key.

Soft and Hard Cap

When crypto projects acquire funding through public token sales, specific financial parameters are used, known as *soft cap* and *hard cap*. The soft and hard caps represent the minimum and maximum amounts of funds that a project aims to raise.

Soft Cap is the minimum amount a project aims to raise to allow it to proceed or continue with development. It is considered the minimum viable funding for a project to achieve the basic fundamental goals in its roadmap. The funds are typically returned to participants if the soft cap isn't reached—but only if the token-sale smart contract is written to enable refunds, so investors should always review those terms before contributing.

Hard Cap is the maximum amount the project aims to raise. The project resource requirements determine the hard cap and typically include funding for development, marketing, operations, legal compliance, and other areas. Once the sale reaches the maximum number of tokens or raises a target amount of funds (e.g., USD 1 million), no more contributions are accepted, and the public funding round will close. For example, suppose a team decides to set a 30 million token hard cap and manages to sell this amount before the official end date of the public sale. In that case, the token sale will end regardless of continued interest from investors. The collected funds allow the team to continue with development in full force. The core purpose of the hard cap is to prevent over-funding of a project, which can be as detrimental as under-funding since it may distort the tokenomics and lead to mismanagement or waste.

Hard Cap Analysis

It is highly admirable if the hard cap for public token sales has been reached. This indicates that early-stage investors are interested in the project. For example, Figure 15-8 shows the public sale details for a project called Neon Labs—an Ethereum Virtual Machine (EVM) on Solana that enables dApp developers to use Ethereum tooling to scale and access Solana's liquidity. Neon Labs set a hard cap of $45 million and fully reached this goal. The fact that the Neon Labs hard cap was reached indicates significant early-stage interest in this project, which is a positive sign. Additionally, not only was the hard cap reached, but it is also considered high at $45 million compared to other projects funded through public sales—indicating severe interest.

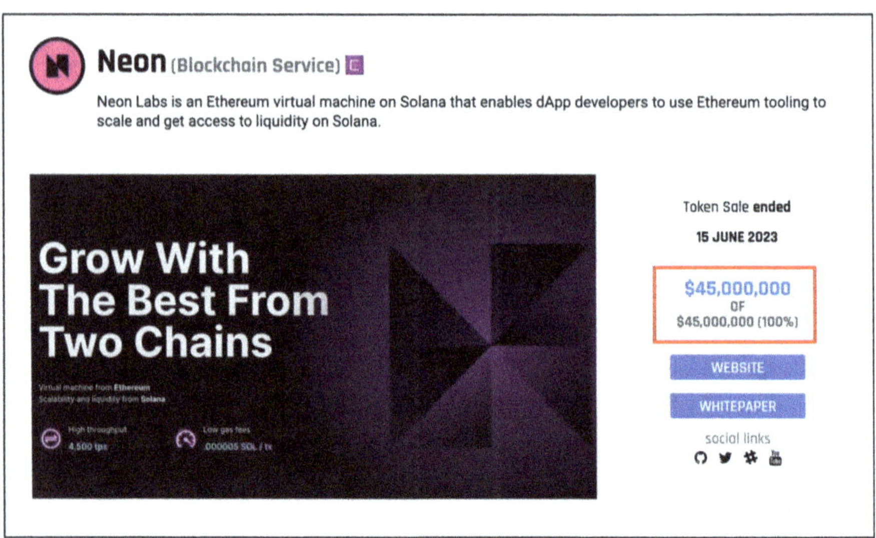

Figure 15-8. *Neon Labs ICO on ICO Drops: $45 million hard cap reached (compliments of* `https://icodrops.com/sophiaverse/`*)*

Pro Tip Verify the legitimacy of the specified funding hard cap by evaluating whether the project is already profitable and requires additional funding. Are there significant development requirements and milestones outlined on the roadmap? Is the funding being used to enhance the value of the company? Will the company survive without funding rounds? Can the team be trusted with the gathered funds? Who controls the collected funds: the team, a DAICO, or others? Compare this against past funding rounds from competitors.

Token Standard

Checking the token standard can reveal valuable insight into the development team's effort and expertise. For example, ERC-20 tokens are easy to create with minimal technical skill. However, coins created and issued on a project's native blockchain require significant effort, commitment, and expertise. Suffice it to say that on a grand scale, projects that dedicate considerable time, effort, and resources to their development tend to be more genuine and trustworthy—at least at the ICO stage. In contrast, projects that aim to deceive or scam individuals usually do so by expending the least amount of effort and resources possible, seeking quick and easy gains at the expense of others. Therefore, extra caution and a more in-depth initial screening are advised with public sales involving ERC-20 or similar easily created token standards. These are simple to develop and often used by projects looking to cut corners or make quick profits. Investors can also find details of the token standard on the project whitepaper.

Price Per Coin

When evaluated alone, the price per coin (or token) is somewhat misleading. For example, *Project A*, with a public sale price per coin of $0.50 USD with a total supply of 30 million coins, has greater ROI potential than *Project B*, with a price per coin of $ 0.50 USD but with the total supply of ten billion coins. Based on supply and demand, *Project A*—with the lower token supply—possesses much greater profit potential due to scarcity, demand, and a lower market cap, making it easier for both the **price** and **market cap** to double more quickly.

Project A: Market Cap = $0.50 x 30 million = $15 million

Project B: Market Cap = $0.50 x 10 billion = $5 billion

Therefore, it is advised to properly evaluate the price per coin for the project's tokenomics, including the number of coins or tokens released at launch and associated vesting schedules—refer to the section "Market Cap and FDV" in Chapter 9, "Financial Metrics," where this is discussed in more detail.

Figure 15-9 shows scheduled IDOs for Patex Network token (PATEX) with price per token ranging from $0.95USD to $1.00USD. Considering that Patex Network has a limited maximum token supply of 8,000,000 (PATEX) and allocates 13.25% of the supply to IDO participants (Figure 15-10), it is worthy of further investigation. More specifically, given these details, including the attractive vesting schedule (Figure 15-11), the IDO price per token is considered attractive.

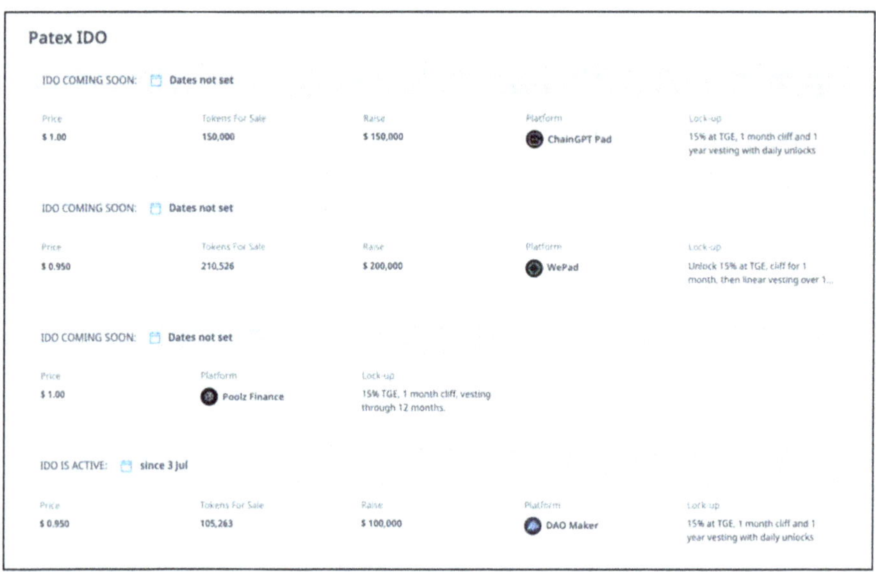

Figure 15-9. *Patex Network—IDO details and price per coin on CryptoRank.io (compliments of `https://cryptorank.io/ico/patex`)*

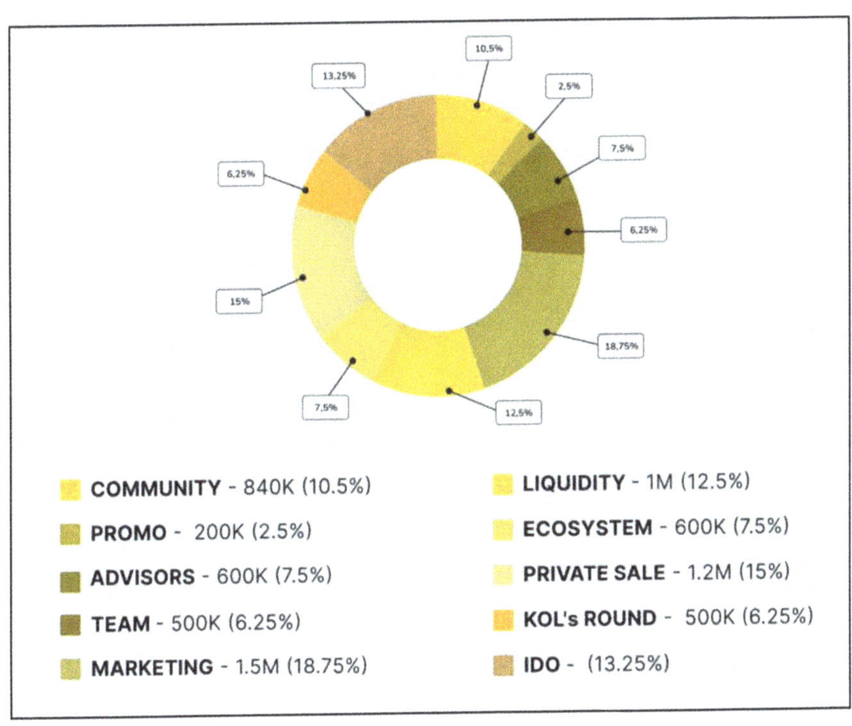

Figure 15-10. Patex Network—token allocation (compliments of https://patex.io/docs/Patex%20WP.pdf)

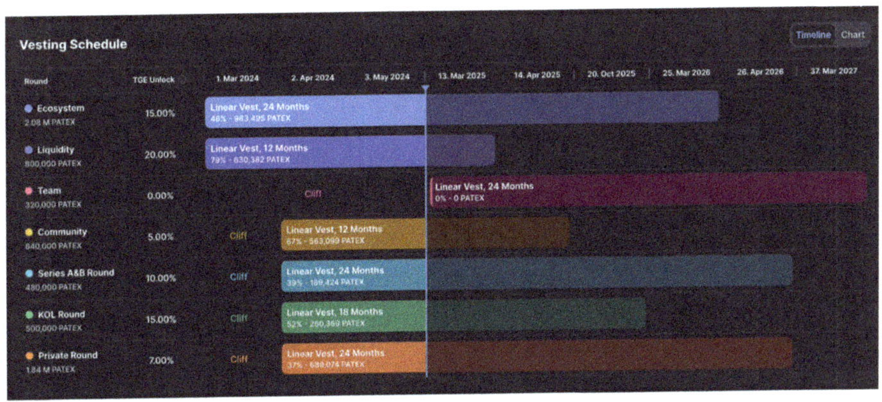

Figure 15-11. Patex Network—PATEX token vesting schedule (compliments of https://dropstab.com/coins/patex/vesting)

Caution Never rely on or assume the information on a project token sale on any third-party website is accurate. Always verify any project data through official resources such as the project's website, GitHub, blog, or social media channels.

Project Whitepaper

Do not invest in a public sale if the project does not have a whitepaper or a litepaper at a very minimum. Poor whitepapers filled with buzzwords and cheap websites can be easily generated for a mere few thousand dollars. Refer to Chapter 3, "Project Documentation," for detailed whitepaper evaluation steps.

Action Steps

Follow these steps to determine the project's public sale funding model and evaluate it as a potential investment opportunity. Note this is primarily for investors who plan to invest through scheduled public sale events. Investors can view active and scheduled public sale offerings by visiting crypto market insight and analytics platforms such as ICO Drops, CryptoRank, and ICO Holder.

1) **Fair Launch of Premine**

   Determine if the project utilizes a *fair launch* or a *pre-mined* token allocation model.

   a) Details for each model will typically be found in one or more official outlets, including the project's website, whitepaper, blog, and social media outlets.

2) **Public Sale Funding Models**

   If the premine model is adopted, determine the type of public sale funding model the project utilizes.

   a) Examine the public sale funding models and comparison summary outlined in Table 15-3 respectively.

   b) Does the model type meet your investment requirements, such as public sale accessibility, KYC/AML, screening intensity, regulation, investor protection, centralization level, etc.?

3) **Streamlined Filtering of Public Offerings**

   Filter for high-profit potential public offering opportunities through quick evaluation steps discussed in this chapter and summarized below.

   a) **Project Summary** - Review the project summary for a clear product description, value proposition, specific technical details, and any potential red flags such as vague descriptions, an anonymous team, or a lack of compliance.

   b) **Soft and Hard Caps** - Examine the soft and hard cap details to help determine if funding goals are realistic and aligned with the work scope on the project roadmap. Additionally, determine if there is a hard cap limit and if it was reached.

   c) **Token Standard** - Identify the type of token standard the project has adopted. Projects that create their own blockchain with native tokens are less likely to be scams due to the level of work involved.

d) **Price Per Coin** - Evaluate the price per coin alongside the tokenomics, including total supply, market cap, and vesting schedules, to determine realistic profit potential.

e) **Project Whitepaper** - Determine if the project has a whitepaper and if it is of good quality.

f) **Risk Tolerance** - Assess your risk tolerance, and do not invest unless you are comfortable with the fact that you could lose your money.

4) **Full Fundamental Evaluation**

   Perform a complete fundamental evaluation of the projects that made it through the public sale streamlined filtering process.

5) **Take Notes and Document Your Findings in Your Own Style**

6) **Combine the Findings with Other Sections of the Fundamental Evaluation Process**

Evaluation of the Results

Investing in public offerings is extremely risky. The team has not yet proven their capabilities or overall potential at this early stage. In many cases, there is not even a proven concept of a product or beta version available for testing. Therefore, investors are essentially betting on the team to deliver on their promises. Since fifty percent of new projects fail after the first year, extreme caution and adequate research are advised before participating in public offerings. Investors should carefully assess their risk tolerance based on their knowledge, experience, and financial situation before participating in public sales. Additionally, when you have pre-selected a public sale investment, conducting a complete, in-depth fundamental evaluation is strongly recommended, as detailed in this book.

Partnerships

Evaluation Objective: Determine and evaluate the project's public sale funding model as a potential investment opportunity.

A partnership is an agreement between two or more parties to work together to achieve something that benefits everyone involved. Partnerships typically form between companies or individuals whose interests overlap to a certain degree, thus helping to improve each other's performance, share resources, and create measurable value for all parties involved. However, in the blockchain space, some partnerships are often more about optics than substance.

For example, while some partnerships deliver actual value—like improving products, expanding ecosystems, or solving real problems—others are just for show and a means to grab the attention of investors. Additionally, many companies claim the title "partnership" when just availing of services from another company—this is not a partnership. As an investor, it is vital to determine which partnerships are legitimate and provide actual value and which ones are not.

There are many types of partnership formations within the blockchain world, ranging from crypto-to-crypto, blockchain-based centralized-to-centralized, and crypto-to-centralized partnerships. In this section, the various types of partnerships are discussed, as well as the ones that actually provide value.

Crypto-to-Crypto (C2C) Business Partnerships

Crypto-to-crypto (C2C) partnerships refer to partnerships that are formulated directly between two crypto projects within the blockchain space. These types of partnerships increase the value of crypto products and services by enabling platform integration, shared infrastructures, enhanced liquidity, and ecosystem expansion. Legitimate C2C partnerships also help both projects grow by introducing them to each other's communities, which means more users, developers, and opportunities overall.

Caution To help boost awareness, it is common for projects to sponsor various events. Examples include Crypto.com sponsoring the 2022 FIFA World Cup and the Ultimate Fighting Club (UFC). Although this is perfectly acceptable, be aware that this is not a partnership but simply a sponsorship deal. Although not Crypto.com, some projects portray sponsorship deals as partnerships, which is incorrect and misleading.

An example of a C2C partnership is the Immutable and Polygon Labs collaboration. Immutable, a leading Web3 gaming company partnered by Polygon Labs, a major Layer 2 (L2) blockchain scaling platform in the crypto space, where they launched Immutable zkEVM, an Ethereum-compatible L2 scaling solution for gaming. For the gaming community, this is a dream come true, as it enhances the gaming experience by increasing scalability, speed, and security, reducing transaction costs, adding new in-game functionalities, and overall making the gaming experience smoother and more enjoyable.

The partnership between Immutable and Polygon Labs also benefited each company directly. For example, the gaming advancements achieved by this partnership attracted more developers and gamers to the Immutable ecosystem. At the same time, Polygon strengthened its reputation in the gaming sector, gaining increased exposure and credibility, which boosted the adoption of Polygon's zkEVM and opened doors to new partnerships.

Pro Tip When evaluating and validating partnerships, it is advised to consider all claimed partnerships non-existent or poor at best—"guilty until proven innocent."

Crypto-to-Traditional (C2T) Business Partnerships

Crypto-to-traditional (C2T) partnerships are collaborations between crypto projects and blockchain-focused traditional companies. C2T partnerships aim to integrate blockchain technology with traditional businesses, thus offering a range of benefits to both sectors. For example, crypto projects partnering with well-known, established traditional companies help to increase adoption and credibility in the blockchain realm. Traditional companies often complement blockchain companies by providing various integrations, financial resources, and industry expertise. On the other hand, implementing blockchain solutions can increase operational efficiency, help streamline processes, reduce costs, and automate processes using smart contracts in a trustless manner. Combining blockchain with traditional companies leads to overall increased innovation and product development by leveraging the fundamental qualities of blockchain.

An example of a C2T partnership is the Solana Pay and Shopify collaboration. Solana Pay, a partially decentralized payment protocol built on the Solana blockchain, partnered with Shopify, a large e-commerce platform, allowing merchants to accept payments in USDC (a stablecoin pegged to the US dollar). This provides a seamless and cost-effective alternative to traditional credit card payments, where merchants and customers can transact without intermediaries at lower costs. Customers enjoy privacy as no sensitive financial info is shared, and payments are settled instantly through crypto payment integrations without worrying about exchange rates or extra fees. As a result, this type of partnership offers immense value for platforms such as Shopify and their customers and for driving widespread blockchain exposure and adoption.

Caution To gain visibility and credibility, crypto projects might include in their marketing strategy the initiative to be featured in articles by well-known and respected publications such as Forbes, Bloomberg, or The New York Times. Although these features may attract a wider audience and potential investors, they are not genuine publications and are better classified as paid promotions.

Traditional-to-Traditional (T2T) Business Partnerships

Traditional-to-traditional (T2T) partnerships are where two crypto-focused traditional companies partner to further their shared interests and objectives. These partnerships are crucial for making blockchain technology practical in the real world, as they help build trust and create accessible entry points for individuals outside the crypto space to engage with digital assets.

An example of a crypto-related T2T partnership is Paxos and PayPal. Paxos, an NYDFS-regulated (licensed and supervised by the New York Department of Financial Services) payments company, offers the underlying custody and liquidity support for PayPal users who buy, sell, and hold various digital assets. Additionally, PayPal's digital dollar "PayPal USD" (PYUSD) stablecoin is backed by US Treasury reverse repurchase agreements with "backed by US dollar deposits, short-term US Treasuries, and similar cash equivalents. Note that this type of partnership actually offers significant value that helps spread the adoption of blockchain technology and digital assets regardless of the market conditions.

Fact The strongest partnerships are those that positively affect and add significant value to the product or service. Any other partnership can be considered weak or non-relevant.

Examples of Non-Partnerships

Spotting scams or low-quality partnerships is just as important as identifying high-value ones. Fraudulent projects often claim partnerships with reputable companies to boost their credibility, even when no real association exists or when they misrepresent the use of a company's service as a genuine partnership. These claims must be carefully scrutinized to verify their legitimacy.

Therefore, verifying the type of partnership presented and whether each partner is helping one another is essential. This information should always be verified from official pages of each company involved, press releases, or other trusted sources. Investors must remain cautious until there is clear evidence and justification that the two companies are connected and leveraging their strengths to enhance their products and value offerings. Always verify these partnerships through official channels or press releases from the purported partner companies. Be cautious of projects that cannot provide clear evidence of their claimed collaborations. The following are some *fictitious examples* of scams related to low-quality partnerships.

1) **Google Cloud and PlasmaPenguin Partnership**

   Blockchain project Plasma Penguin partnered with Google Cloud to integrate and host parts of its permissioned blockchain. This allows Plasma Penguin to scale its blockchain, providing rapid transactions and low costs.

   Reasons Why This Is Not a Legitimate Partnership

   a) Plasma Penguin is simply availing of Google Cloud's services as a paying customer, as do thousands of other companies. Google Cloud is not a strategic partner contributing to mutual interest or shared benefits.

   b) No official releases from Google Cloud have been found online claiming such a partnership.

2) **CactusSquid and PortGlobal Partnership**

   Blockchain project CactusSquid announces a strategic partnership with PortGlobal, a well-known worldwide leader in supply chain operations, by creating a secure, transparent ledger for tracking goods, reducing fraud, and overall improving supply chain efficiency throughout the process.

   Reasons Why This Is Not a Legitimate Partnership

   a) After taking a closer look, it was discovered that PortGlobal is only running a small pilot program to test the CactusSquids blockchain in their supply chain management system—no long-term commitment was made.

b) No evidence was even found that PortGlobal implemented the blockchain into their supply chain system. Therefore, the announcement was based on pure speculative outcomes versus actual actions taken.

c) PortGlobal did not invest any or share any other resources with CactusSquid. PortGlobal simply agreed to try out their service and product like any other customer. Therefore, it does not qualify as a true partnership.

3) **Amazon Web Services (AWS) and FusionFerret Partnership**

Blockchain project FusionFerret partnered with AWS to offer various blockchain solutions through the AWS Marketplace. This allows immense exposure to all AWS users to avail of unique applications for their business and personal needs.

Reasons Why This Is Not a Legitimate Partnership

a) The AWS marketplace is open to any business, entity, or individual that wants to sell their software products. FusionFerret is just another vendor selling their product on the AWS platform—nothing special.

b) AWS is not collaborating with FusionFerret to co-develop new innovations or share resources towards a mutual interest.

c) FusionFerret is just using AWS's tools, like thousands of other companies do.

d) No official releases from AWS have been found online claiming such a partnership.

Caution Fake or misleading partnerships signal a lack of transparency and honesty within the project team, raising serious red flags.

Action Steps

Follow these steps and considerations to help evaluate whether partnerships are legitimate and genuinely beneficial for both companies involved.

1) **Identify Partnerships**

   Make a list of the project's claimed partnerships, typically found on their website. Proceed cautiously, assuming all claimed partnerships are non-existent or blown out of proportion.

2) **Check for Official Announcements**

   Official partnership announcements for each party are essential.

   a) Search for official press releases or partnership confirmations from each company involved. It is important that both companies involved have released official announcements detailing the same type of partnership, value interests, and benefits through their official channels.

   b) Verify that information from multiple trusted sources aligns and confirms the partnership details.

3) **Determine the Type of Partnership**

   Determine the type of partnership in question and if it provides value for both parties involved.

   a) **Crypto-to-Crypto** - Look for mutual benefits such as shared infrastructure, technology, professional networks, and other related resources.

   b) **Crypto-to-Traditional** - Verify how blockchain improves traditional business operations or increases exposure and adoption.

   c) **Traditional-to-Traditional** - Ensure the collaboration generates significant blockchain adoption and usability in the crypto space.

4) **Check for Deliverables and Resource Sharing**

   Clear partnership deliverables must be stated.

   a) Identify measurable outcomes regarding the mutual benefits or increased value offering because of the partnership. This may be a new innovative product or specific value-added that complements existing users or ecosystems.

   b) Check for shared resources such as network integrations, technical infrastructure (e.g., oracles, APIs, and Layer 2 scaling solutions), technology, ecosystem tools, user base, liquidity, financial capital, human capital and expertise, etc.

5) **Value and Benefits**

   Determine if the partnership benefits and creates value for each partner.

a) For example, a "crypto-to-crypto" partnership like that of the Graph and Fantom Network facilitates cross-chain interoperability. This partnership adds significant value by enabling *The Graph* to support querying data across multiple blockchains. At the same time, Fantom developers gain access to these tools for building applications and facilitating cross-chain swaps with Ethereum.

6) **Investigate the Credibility of Partners**

   Research the track record of the partners involved to determine if they are legitimate and have a good track record. Legitimate partnerships are open about their terms and benefits. If details are vague or overly hyped, dig deeper or steer clear.

7) **Take Notes and Document Your Findings in Your Own Style**

8) **Combine the Findings with Other Sections of the Fundamental Evaluation Process**

Evaluation of the Results

If the evaluated partnership is legitimate—both partners have confirmed it, there is clear mutual value, and there are clear deliverables—it is considered a green light. On the other hand, if there is no actual value for both parties, a lack of evidence found online, or vague deliverables, it is advised to stay clear of investment until more profound research has been executed. If projects try to trick investors into believing they have secured legitimate partnerships, the real question is, what other things are they lying about? Consider this a red flag. It is the investor's responsibility to determine that all partnerships the project team claims are strong, valid, and credible.

Quick Glossary

This quick glossary contains the terms used in relation to the fundamental analysis of a blockchain or dApp-based project in the crypto realm. These terms are used throughout the book; therefore, bookmark the following pages as a quick reference.

51% Attack

A 51% attack, in the context of proof-of-work (PoW) based blockchain, refers to a situation where an entity or group gains control of more than 50% of a network's mining power—also known as the hash rate.

Architecture Layers

Blockchain architecture is structured in layers—distinct levels of code or protocol design—each built to handle a specific role. Layers 0, 1, 2, and 3 work together to improve a network's security, speed, efficiency, interoperability, and overall user experience across blockchains and decentralized applications (dApps).

Accrual Mechanism

Token accrual mechanisms are specifically designed strategies that are built into the token design that aim to increase the value of the token over time. These methods and techniques include staking distributions, buyback-and-burn, fee rebates, and governance rewards.

P. Garvey, *Blockchain Fundamental Analysis for Digital Asset Investors*,
https://doi.org/10.1007/979-8-8688-1551-5

bitcoin

bitcoin is the first decentralized digital currency and payment system that operates on a secure, peer-to-peer blockchain, enabling trustless transactions without the need for intermediaries.

Block Explorer

A blockchain explorer—or a *block explorer*—is a web-based tool to view and track transactional data, including addresses, tokens, smart contracts, source codes, wallet addresses, prices, and other activities on a blockchain in real-time and through historical (archival) records.

Blockchain

A blockchain is a decentralized, immutable digital ledger that records transactions across a network of computers, ensuring transparency, security, and trust without intermediaries.

Blockchain Trilemma

Every blockchain has three paramount characteristics: decentralization, scalability, and security—the *blockchain trilemma* refers to the challenge of achieving all three simultaneously at an optimal level without compromising one for the other.

Circulating Supply

Circulating supply refers to the total number of tokens or coins currently available in the market and actively traded, excluding those locked, reserved, or set aside for future release or development.

Closed-Source

"Closed-source" refers to software whose source code is proprietary and not publicly accessible, restricting modifications or redistribution to authorized parties only.

Codebase

A project *codebase* is a complete set of source code files for a software project, including everything needed to build, execute, and maintain an application.

Coin

A cryptocurrency—also known as a "coin"—is a native *protocol coin* issued directly by the blockchain protocol on which it runs, which is why it is often referred to as a blockchain's native currency.

Consensus

Consensus is the process by which blockchain network participants agree on the validity of transactions inside a block and the ledger's state, ensuring accuracy and trust without a central authority.

Consensus Mechanism

A consensus mechanism is a protocol that ensures all participants in a blockchain network agree on the validity of transactions and the state of the ledger.

Cryptography

Cryptography in blockchain secures data, protects user identities, and ensures transactions are tamper-proof using mathematical techniques like hashing and digital signatures.

Cryptocurrency

Cryptocurrency, also referred to as crypto or a coin, is a digital asset secured by cryptography, operating on decentralized blockchain technology, with its primary purpose being to secure the network by incentivizing validators or miners to maintain consensus and protect against attacks. It also is used as a medium for exchange and peer-to-peer transactions.

Cross-Chain Interoperability

Cross-chain interoperability refers to a blockchain's ability to freely communicate with other blockchains, thus aiding a frictionless transfer of information, assets, and data with one another.

Decentralization

Decentralization is defined as the process by which the activities of an organization, particularly those regarding planning and decision-making, are distributed or delegated away from a central authoritative location or group.

Decentralized Application (dApp)

A decentralized application (dApp) is a type of app (software application) that runs on a blockchain instead of a central server. It uses smart contracts to work automatically, allowing users to interact directly without needing a company or third party in the middle.

Deflationary Supply

Deflationary supply refers to a tokenomics model where the total supply of a cryptocurrency decreases over time due to deflationary mechanisms such as burning tokens, reducing the circulating amount, and potentially increasing value.

Digital Asset

A digital asset, such as a cryptocurrency "coin" or token, is typically a blockchain-based project's financial or utility instrument. Digital assets represent a specific value, access, or participation within the project's blockchain ecosystem.

Digital Asset Exchange

A digital asset exchange is an online platform where users can buy, sell, and trade cryptocurrencies, tokens, and other digital assets, such as tokens or non-fungible tokens (NFTs).

Distributed Ledger Technology

Distributed ledger technology (DLT) is a type of technological infrastructure that allows for simultaneous access, validation, and recording and updating across a network of interconnected nodes (computers), ensuring transparency and security.

Double Spending

Double spending is the risk of using the same cryptocurrency in multiple transactions, which blockchain prevents through consensus mechanisms and transaction validation.

End-User

An end-user in blockchain is the individual that directly interacts with blockchain and associated applications such as decentralized applications (dApps), wallets, etc.

Fees

Fees in blockchain are small payments paid to miners or validators as a reward for processing transactions and securing the network.

Financial Metrics

Financial metrics in blockchain are key indicators, such as market capitalization, trading volume, and token supply, used to evaluate a project's performance, value, and market position.

Fundamental Analysis

Fundamental Analysis (FA) is a method investors use to determine an asset's actual or "fair market" value, such as a stock or digital asset.

Fully Diluted Valuation

A *fully diluted valuation* (FDV), or a *fully diluted market capitalization*, is the total market value of a project's entire token supply, including the tokens in circulation and locked and vested tokens. It is calculated by multiplying the maximum supply by the token price.

Genesis Block

The genesis block is the first block of a blockchain, establishing the foundation of the network—often, it may include a meaningful message or data from its creator.

GitHub

GitHub is a cloud-based software service that helps programmers and project teams host, collaborate, store, manage, and control their code repositories.

Governance

Governance refers to the structures and processes that ensure accountability, transparency, responsiveness, stability, inclusiveness, empowerment, and broad-based participation.

Hard Fork

A hard fork is a blockchain update that introduces changes incompatible with the previous version, creating two separate networks if not all nodes or participants adopt the new rules.

Hash Rate

Hash rate is the measure of computational power miners use to solve cryptographic puzzles and validate transactions, with increases in hash rate leading to greater mining difficulty to maintain consistent block creation times.

Immutability

Immutability in blockchain refers to the inability of transactional or other data to be manipulated, modified, or deleted once recorded on the blockchain network.

Inflationary Supply

An inflationary supply is one where the supply gradually increases due to the creation of newly minted coins. This creates an abundance of tokens over time by slowly increasing the number in circulation.

Latency

Latency, often referred to as *finality*, is a measure of the time (in seconds (s) or milliseconds (ms)) from when a transaction is requested to when it is confirmed on the blockchain.

Ledger

A ledger in blockchain is a decentralized digital record that stores all transactions and data across a network, ensuring transparency and tamper-resistance.

Liquidity

Liquidity in blockchain is the ease at which a digital asset can be exchanged for another asset or cash without significantly affecting its price. While high liquidity allows for quicker and smoother transactions at prices close to the current market value, illiquid markets result in higher volatility and larger spreads in the order book, resulting in traders experiencing slippage.

Liquidity Mining

Liquidity mining is a decentralized finance (DeFi) process whereby users can earn passive income by providing liquidity to DeFi protocols.

Litepaper

The litepaper, also known as a lightpaper, is simply a concise, less detailed, simplified version of the whitepaper detailing a range of fundamental aspects relating to the project.

Mainnet

The mainnet is the primary blockchain network where live transactions occur, and coins or tokens with actual economic value are used instead of testnet tokens (dummy tokens), which are solely for testing purposes.

Market Capitalization

Market capitalization, or market cap, is the total market value of a project's circulating supply. It is calculated by multiplying the circulating supply by the price per token (or coin).

Maximum Supply

Maximum supply is the total number of coins or tokens that will ever exist. It can be capped, meaning there's a hard limit on how many can be created or uncapped, where the supply is unlimited due to inflation.

Mining

Mining is the process of using computational power to validate transactions, solve cryptographic puzzles, and add new blocks to the chain.

Minimum Viable Product

A minimum viable product (MVP) is a product with the minimum necessary features required to validate an idea or concept and meet the initial needs of end-users.

Network Effects

Network effects in blockchain occur when a network's value grows as more users, developers, and participants join, creating a virtuous cycle where increased participation enhances the network's value and fosters even greater engagement.

Network Participants

Encompasses anyone who interacts or adds value to a blockchain network or dApp—including developers, miners, validators, senders, receivers, liquidity providers, governance participants, etc.

NFT

Non-fungible tokens (NFTs) are unique, indivisible digital assets with distinct identifiers and characteristics, making them non-interchangeable and transferable. They are often tied to metadata for added functionality or representation.

Node

A node is a computer or device that participates in a blockchain network by storing, validating, and sharing a copy of the distributed ledger. Each node on the network contributes to maintaining the integrity and security of the blockchain.

On-Chain

"On-chain," or "on the blockchain," refers to any activity, process, or transaction carried out directly on the blockchain, such as governance, liquidity management, or asset transfers.

On-Chain Metrics

On-chain metrics refer to information recorded directly on the blockchain, such as total transaction volume, the number of active addresses, and the percentage of the circulating supply currently in profit.

Open-Source

Open-source in blockchain refers to software with publicly available code that anyone can view, modify, and distribute.

Permissionless

A permissionless blockchain is an open public blockchain, meaning anyone on the open internet can run a node and participate in the consensus validation.

Private Blockchain

A *private* blockchain is a centralized distributed ledger that operates as a closed "database catering to organizational privacy requirements." The nodes are restricted from the public, and only those with permission rights from the organization can run a full node, make transactions, or validate/authenticate the blockchain changes.

Public Blockchain

A *public blockchain* is an open, permissionless, transparent, and decentralized blockchain ledger. It allows all network participants to check and verify transactions on the blockchain and participate in the consensus process.

Private Key

A private key, also known as a *secret key*, is a cryptography variable used with an algorithm to encrypt and decrypt data. It is used to verify one's digital asset ownership on-chain using digital signatures.

Product or Service

In blockchain, a product or service refers to any application, platform, or solution built on blockchain technology that delivers user value.

Product Use Case

A product use case refers explicitly to applying blockchain technology to solve a particular problem or enhance a specific process within the blockchain world or of a traditional company.

Proof-of-Stake

Proof-of-Stake (PoS) is a consensus mechanism to validate incoming transactions and add them as new blocks on the blockchain. Ethereum is an example of a PoS-based blockchain.

Proof-of-Work

Proof-of-Work (PoW) is a consensus algorithm used in blockchain networks to confirm transactions and add new blocks to the blockchain. bitcoin is an example of a PoW-based blockchain.

Public Address

A public address can be considered equivalent to a typical bank account number. It is used to receive digital assets. It is auto-derived via your personal/private key.

Public Blockchain

A *public blockchain* is an open, permissionless, transparent, and decentralized blockchain ledger that allows all network participants to check and verify transactions and participate in the consensus process.

Public Key

In asymmetric cryptography, the public key is used to encrypt messages, thus only allowing the individual to use the corresponding and cryptographically linked public key.

Pseudonymous

Pseudonymous in blockchain means operating under a digital identity, or address, that conceals the user's real-world identity while still allowing their transactions to be publicly visible on the ledger.

Roadmap

A roadmap is an efficient and easy-to-understand communication tool that ties together the strategy and includes timelines for all crucial milestones that align with the corresponding schedule. It guides the development team, stakeholders, and potential investors, providing them with a clear understanding of the project's direction and progress.

Satoshi Nakamoto

Satoshi Nakamoto is the pseudonymous creator of bitcoin and its original whitepaper.

Scalability

Blockchain scalability refers to a blockchain's ability to scale and maintain user efficiency under increased load.

Smart Contracts

Smart contracts, or self-executing contracts, are digital contracts stored on a blockchain, designed to automatically execute when the terms and conditions of a predetermined agreement are met between two or more parties.

Soft Fork

A soft fork is a backward-compatible update to a blockchain protocol. It introduces new rules that do not require all nodes to upgrade, allowing non-upgraded nodes to continue participating in the network.

Stable Token

Stable tokens are a type of digital asset designed to maintain a consistent value with minimal fluctuation. For example, USDT (USD Tether) is an ERC-20 stable token pegged to the US dollar, typically fluctuating by approximately one percent on average.

Staking

Staking refers to the process where an individual receives rewards for locking their assets (coins) on-chain to help support the security of a blockchain network.

Token

Tokens, or application-type tokens, are created on top of existing blockchain Layer 0 and Layer 1 networks such as Polkadot Network and Ethereum. They represent the fundamental building block of Web3, overseen by a distributed ledger representing anything from digital assets to specific permissions, whether in the real world, digital space, or even legal agreements.

Token Design

Token design refers to the process of structuring a token's purpose, use case, functionality, and economic model, including supply, utility, and incentives, to align with the project's goals and product requirements.

Token Supply

A token supply refers to how many tokens will exist at any given time; it can be the circulating supply, the maximum supply, or the total supply, depending on the current state of issuance and distribution within the network.

Throughput

Throughput, in blockchain, refers to the average measure of how many transactions can be processed at any given time. It is measured in transactions per second (TPS) or sometimes in transactions per minute (TPM).

Transaction

A blockchain-based transaction refers to the transfer of data or digital assets, such as cryptocurrency, tokens, and NFTs, between one or more parties.

Trading Volume

In crypto, volume, or trading volume, refers to the total number of coins (or tokens) traded over a specific period. It is displayed in fiat units (e.g., USD) to provide a clearer picture of the market activity and liquidity, which is a good representation of the level of interest in an asset.

Validator

A validator in the proof-of-stake (PoS) blockchain is a network participant responsible for verifying transactions and maintaining the network's integrity.

Vesting

Vesting in the crypto space refers to the gradual release of tokens to stakeholders over a set period, safeguarding against significant price swings and market volatility whicle also encouraging long-term commitment.

Wallet

A wallet is a digital interface or application that allows users with access rights to access their digital assets stored on the blockchain, enabling them to send, receive, and manage their funds securely.

Web3

Web3 refers to the evolution of the internet using blockchain technology to enable decentralized applications, user-controlled data, and peer-to-peer interactions. While many decentralized applications remove the requirement for many central authorities, Web3 still relies on centralized infrastructure like internet providers for connectivity.

Whitepaper

In blockchain, a whitepaper is a comprehensive document that provides stakeholders with detailed technical and non-technical information about the core product or service. It identifies the problem, the solution to that problem, details about the underlying technology, the project's goals, tokenomics, the development roadmap, and a range of other fundamental aspects.

References and Further Reading

Chapter 1—Introduction to Blockchain Technology

35 Top Blockchain Applications to Know for 2024, Built In. (n.d.). Retrieved March 22, 2024, from https://builtin.com/blockchain/blockchain-applications

Andola, N., Raghav, Yadav, V. K., Venkatesan, S., & Verma, S. (2021). Anonymity on blockchain based e-cash protocols—A survey. *Computer Science Review, 40,* 100394. https://doi.org/10.1016/J.COSREV.2021.100394

Anonymity vs. Pseudonymity In Crypto, Gemini. (n.d.). Retrieved August 20, 2022, from https://www.gemini.com/cryptopedia/anonymity-vs-pseudonymity-basic-differences

Antonopoulos, A., & Harding, D. (2017). *Mastering Bitcoin—Programming the Open Blockchain.* https://books.google.com/books?hl=en&lr=&id=3zfhEAAAQBAJ&oi=fnd&pg=PT7&dq=mastering+Bitcoin&ots=mYlkWaPw4e&sig=bLOy8DyoQLYwPmVs3Jvu1lNwwR4#v=onepage&q=mastering%20Bitcoin&f=false

Asymmetric Cryptography In Blockchains, HackerNoon. (n.d.). Retrieved February 14, 2024, from https://hackernoon.com/asymmetric-cryptography-in-blockchains-d1a4c1654a71

P. Garvey, *Blockchain Fundamental Analysis for Digital Asset Investors,*
https://doi.org/10.1007/979-8-8688-1551-5

Bashir, I. (2020). *Mastering Blockchain: A deep dive into distributed ledgers, consensus protocols, smart contracts, DApps, cryptocurrencies, Ethereum, and more.* https://books.google.com/books?hl=en&lr=&id=ZZ_6DwAAQBAJ&oi=fnd&pg=PP1&dq=mastering+blockchain+imran+bashir&ots=dwbRn3gESK&sig=PfB7xH2wfZEOPO3wdNh8-sfvK84

bitaddress.org. (n.d.). Retrieved February 17, 2024, from https://www.bitaddress.org/bitaddress.org-v3.3.0-SHA256-dec17c07685e1870960903d8f58090475b25af946fe95a734f88408cef4aa194.html

Bitcoin—Open source P2P money. (n.d.). Retrieved February 10, 2024, from https://bitcoin.org/en/

Blockchain in Government Examples to Know, Built In. (n.d.). Retrieved March 22, 2024, from https://builtin.com/blockchain/blockchain-in-government

Blockchain Infrastructure for the Decentralised Web, Parity Technologies. (n.d.). Retrieved September 2, 2023, from https://www.parity.io/

Buldas, A., Draheim, D., Gault, M., & Saarepera, M. (2022). Towards a Foundation of Web3. *Communications in Computer and Information Science, 1688 CCIS*, 3–18. https://doi.org/10.1007/978-981-19-8069-5_1

Cascading Style Sheets—What Is CSS?—Moralis Web3, Enterprise-Grade Web3 APIs. (n.d.). Retrieved March 7, 2024, from https://moralis.io/cascading-style-sheets-what-is-css/

Cloudflare. (n.d.). *What is HTTP?, Cloudflare.* Retrieved March 3, 2024, from https://www.cloudflare.com/learning/ddos/glossary/hypertext-transfer-protocol-http/

CoinLedger — The #1 Free Crypto Tax Software. (n.d.). Retrieved February 9, 2024, from https://coinledger.io/

CoinTracking · The leading Crypto Portfolio Tracker & Tax Calculator. (n.d.). Retrieved February 9, 2024, from https://cointracking.info/

Darcy DiNucci—Wikipedia. (n.d.). Retrieved March 5, 2024, from https://en.wikipedia.org/wiki/Darcy_DiNucci

Decentralized Governance in Web3: Real-World Examples, by Giakaaweb3 Medium. (n.d.). Retrieved March 10, 2024, from https://medium.com/@sm_28205/decentralized-governance-in-web3-real-world-examples-d05e786e22d9

Encryption: Symmetric and Asymmetric—Practical Cryptography for Developers. (n.d.). Retrieved February 12, 2024, from https://cryptobook.nakov.com/encryption-symmetric-and-asymmetric

Encryption: Symmetric and Asymmetric—Practical Cryptography for Developers. (2020). https://cryptobook.nakov.com/encryption-symmetric-and-asymmetric

Ether.js. (n.d.). Retrieved March 8, 2024, from https://docs.ethers.org/v6/

Gavin Wood—Wikipedia. (n.d.). Retrieved March 9, 2024, from https://en.wikipedia.org/wiki/Gavin_Wood

Halak, B., Yilmaz, Y., & Access, D. S.-I. (2022). Comparative analysis of energy costs of asymmetric vs symmetric encryption-based security applications. *Ieeexplore.Ieee.Org.* https://ieeexplore.ieee.org/abstract/document/9835713/

Hardjono, T., Lipton, A., & Pentland, A. (2020). Toward an Interoperability Architecture for Blockchain Autonomous Systems. *IEEE Transactions on Engineering Management, 67*(4), 1298–1309. https://doi.org/10.1109/TEM.2019.2920154

Home, ethereum.org. (n.d.). Retrieved September 7, 2023, from https://ethereum.org/en/

Home, Monero—Secure, private, untraceable. (n.d.). Retrieved February 10, 2024, from https://www.getmonero.org/

Home—Truffle Suite. (n.d.). Retrieved March 8, 2024, from https://archive.trufflesuite.com/

How Google uses cookies—Privacy & Terms—Google. (n.d.). Retrieved March 5, 2024, from https://policies.google.com/technologies/cookies?hl=en-US

InterPlanetary File System—Home. (n.d.). Retrieved March 8, 2024, from https://www.ipfs.com/

Johnson, L. (2016). *Security Controls Evaluation, Testing, and Assessment Handbook: Chapter 11—Security Component Fundamentals for Assessment.* O'Reilly. https://learning.oreilly.com/library/view/security-controls-evaluation/9780128025642/B9780128023242000117/B9780128023242000117_1.xhtml

Kaushal, R. K., Kumar, N., Narayan, S., Hsien, K., Chung, Y., Adriaens, P., Adeeb, N., Abdu, A., Wang, Z., Zhai, S., Yang, Y., Li, J., Qiu, C., & Zhao, J. (2019). *Research on the Application of Cryptography on the Blockchain Blockchain technology for pay-for-outcome sustainable agriculture financing: implications for governance and transaction costs Blockchain for Healthcare Sector-Analytical Review Research on the Application of Cryptography on the Blockchain.* 32077. https://doi.org/10.1088/1742-6596/1168/3/032077

Keys and Addresses: Private Keys, Saylor Academy. (n.d.). Retrieved February 17, 2024, from https://learn.saylor.org/mod/book/view.php?id=36350&chapterid=18931

Koinly: Free Crypto Tax Software. (n.d.). Retrieved February 9, 2024, from https://koinly.io/

Kusama, Polkadot's Canary Network. (n.d.). Retrieved March 9, 2024, from https://kusama.network/

Marengo Vincenzo, L. D. (2018). *History and Evolution of the main Cryptocurrencies.* http://tesi.luiss.it/23488/1/680091_D%27ANDREA_VINCENZO_History%20and%20evolution%20of%20the%20main%20cryptocurrencies.pdf

Mohammed, M., Rohiem, A., & ... A. E.-I. J. of. (2103). Chaotic Encryption Based PGP Protocol. *Citeseer, 4.* https://citeseerx.ist.psu.edu/document?repid=rep1&type=pdf&doi=0592529b2a7ace93d17bfe6da7b2ef817d788674

Naik, R., & ... N. C.-S. D. of C. (2013). Optimising the sha256 hashing algorithm for faster and more efficient bitcoin mining. *Nicolascourtois. Com.* http://nicolascourtois.com/bitcoin/Optimising%20the%20SHA256%20Hashing%20Algorithm%20for%20Faster%20and%20More%20Efficient%20Bitcoin%20Mining_Rahul_Naik.pdf

Next.js by Vercel—The React Framework. (n.d.). Retrieved March 8, 2024, from https://nextjs.org/

Polkadot: Web3 Interoperability, Decentralized Blockchain. (n.d.). Retrieved September 9, 2023, from https://www.polkadot.network/

Production, P. D. F.-J. of P., & Issue, undefined. (2016). The interplay between decentralization and privacy: the case of blockchain technologies. *Papers.Ssrn.Com.* https://papers.ssrn.com/sol3/papers.cfm?abstract_id=2852689

Sheridan, D., Harris, J., Wear, F., Cowell, J., Wong, E., & Yazdinejad, A. (n.d.). Web3 challenges and opportunities for the market. *Arxiv.Org.* Retrieved February 25, 2024, from https://arxiv.org/abs/2209.02446

Singh, M., & computers, S. K.-A. in. (2019). Blockchain technology for decentralized autonomous organizations. *Elsevier.* https://www.sciencedirect.com/science/article/pii/S0065245819300257

Stackpole, T., Lopez, M., & Belmont Creative, (2022). What is web3. *Curator.Diplomacy.Edu.* https://curator.diplomacy.edu/wp-content/uploads/2022/07/What-is-Web3.pdf

Sunny, J., Undralla, N., & Madhusudanan Pillai, V. (2020). Supply chain transparency through blockchain-based traceability: An overview with demonstration. *Computers & Industrial Engineering, 150,* 106895. https://doi.org/10.1016/J.CIE.2020.106895

Svetlin Nakov. (2018). *Welcome—Practical Cryptography for Developers.* https://github.com/nakov/Practical-Cryptography-for-Developers-Book/blob/master/SUMMARY.md

Tim Berners-Lee—Biography. (2024). https://www.w3.org/People/Berners-Lee/

TokenTax—Crypto Tax Software the Pros Use. (n.d.). Retrieved February 9, 2024, from https://tokentax.co/?gclid=CjwKCAiA2pyuBhBKEiwApLaIO7zk7CUJ7GBNrEAv3xopO_8Y9lxlauis3B_aWvisTBW7EvIxlbRISRoCToQQAvD_BwE

W3F Web3 Foundation. (n.d.). Retrieved March 9, 2024, from https://web3.foundation/

web3.js—Ethereum JavaScript API — web3.js 1.0.0 documentation. (n.d.). Retrieved May 9, 2024, from https://web3js.readthedocs.io/en/v1.10.0/

Welcome to Web3: How NFTs Are Revolutionizing Ownership LinkedIn. (n.d.). Retrieved March 9, 2024, from https://www.linkedin.com/pulse/welcome-web3-how-nfts-revolutionizing-ownership-nftpay-sd8mc/

What are public keys, private keys and wallet addresses? — Bitpanda Academy. (n.d.). Retrieved February 10, 2024, from https://www.bitpanda.com/academy/en/lessons/what-are-public-keys-private-keys-and-wallet-addresses/

What is asymmetric encryption? — Bitpanda Academy. (n.d.). Retrieved February 15, 2024, from https://www.bitpanda.com/academy/en/lessons/what-is-asymmetric-encryption/

What is Web 1.0, Web 2.0, and Web 3.0? Definitions, Differences & Similarities. (n.d.). Retrieved March 3, 2024, from https://www.simplilearn.com/what-is-web-1-0-web-2-0-and-web-3-0-with-their-difference-article

What is Web 2.0?, Definition from TechTarget. (n.d.). Retrieved May 9, 2024, from https://www.techtarget.com/whatis/definition/Web-20-or-Web-2

What is Web3?, Chainlink. (n.d.). Retrieved March 2, 2024, from https://chain.link/education/web3

Who Is Satoshi Nakamoto, Inventor of bitcoin? (n.d.). *Fortune.* Retrieved February 15, 2024, from https://en.wikipedia.org/wiki/Satoshi_Nakamoto

Yu, G., Wang, X., Yu, K., Ni, W., Zhang, J. A., & Liu, R. P. (2020). Survey: Sharding in Blockchains. *IEEE Access, 8,* 14155–14181. https://doi.org/10.1109/ACCESS.2020.2965147

Zarrin, J., Hao, Phang, W., Lakshmi, Saheer, B., & Zarrin, Bahram. (2021). Blockchain for decentralization of internet: prospects, trends, and challenges. *SpringerJ Zarrin, H Wen Phang, L Babu Saheer, B ZarrinCluster Computing, 2021 Springer, 24*(4), 2841–2866. https://doi.org/10.1007/s10586-021-03301-8

Zcash: Privacy-protecting digital currency. (n.d.). Retrieved February 10, 2024, from https://z.cash/

Chapter 2—Investing in Digital Assets

A Guide to Cryptocurrency Fundamental Analysis, Binance Academy. (n.d.). Retrieved September 5, 2023, from https://academy.binance.com/en/articles/a-guide-to-cryptocurrency-fundamental-analysis

Baresa, S., Bogdan, S., & Economics, Z. I.-U. J. of. (n.d.). Strategy of stock valuation by fundamental analysis. *Econstor.Eu, 4*(1), 45–51. Retrieved April 12, 2024, from https://www.econstor.eu/handle/10419/105304

Baresa, S., Bogdan, S., Economics, Z. I.-U. J. of, & 2013. (n.d.). Strategy of stock valuation by fundamental analysis. *Econstor.Eu, 4*(1), 45–51. Retrieved April 12, 2024, from https://www.econstor.eu/handle/10419/105304

Brennan, M., & economics, A. S.-J. of financial. (n.d.). Investment analysis and price formation in securities markets. *Elsevier*. Retrieved March 29, 2024, from https://www.sciencedirect.com/science/article/pii/0304405X9400811E

Bybit. (2021, June 16). *How to Analyze a Cryptocurrency Using Fundamental Analysis—Bybit Learn*. Bybit. https://learn.bybit.com/investing/how-to-analyze-a-cryptocurrency-using-fundamental-analysis/

Edwards, R. D., Magee, J., & Bassetti, W. H. C. (2018). Technical analysis of stock trends, Eleventh edition. *Technical Analysis of Stock Trends, Eleventh Edition*, 1–638. https://doi.org/10.4324/9781315115719/TECHNICAL-ANALYSIS-STOCK-TRENDS-BASSETTI-ROBERT-EDWARDS-JOHN-MAGEE

Fundamental Analysis in Crypto Trading—LCX. (n.d.). Retrieved September 5, 2023, from https://www.lcx.com/fundamental-analysis-in-crypto-trading/

Giudici, G., Milne, A., & Vinogradov, D. (2020). Cryptocurrencies: market analysis and perspectives. *Journal of Industrial and Business Economics*, *47*(1), 1–18. https://doi.org/10.1007/S40812-019-00138-6/FIGURES/1

Glaser, F., on, L. B.-23rd E. conference, & 2015. (n.d.). Beyond cryptocurrencies-a taxonomy of decentralized consensus systems. *Papers.Ssrn.Com*, 5–29. Retrieved September 2, 2022, from https://papers.ssrn.com/sol3/papers.cfm?abstract_id=2605803

Hougan, M., & Lawant, D. (2021). *Cryptoassets: The guide to bitcoin, blockchain, and cryptocurrency for investment professionals*. https://books.google.com/books?hl=en&lr=&id=M3cSEAAAQBAJ&oi=fnd&pg=PT3&dq=Why+Should+Anyone+Invest+in+Crypto%3F&ots=Sz196nRyEV&sig=cA-lUYXOBLOjRtxaLFqNlQFIUgI

Hromov, M. (2022). Incubation of crypto projects in marketing: analysis of digital marketing tools. *Digikogu.Taltech.Ee*. https://digikogu.taltech.ee/en/Download/2e2db198-cebe-4df1-8143-dcafb4b20894/Krptoprojektideinkubatsioonturundusesdigitaal.pdf

Investment Analysis: Definition, Types, and Importance. (n.d.). Retrieved March 29, 2024, from https://www.investopedia.com/terms/i/investment-analysis.asp

Kolb, J., Abdelbaky, M., Katz, R. H., & Culler, D. E. (2020). Core Concepts, Challenges, and Future Directions in Blockchain. *ACM Computing Surveys (CSUR), 53*(1). https://doi.org/10.1145/3366370

Park, C. H., & Irwin, S. H. (2007). What do we know about the profitability of technical analysis? *Journal of Economic Surveys, 21*(4), 786–826. https://doi.org/10.1111/J.1467-6419.2007.00519.X

policy, P. S.-J. of public, & 1986. (n.d.). Top-down and bottom-up approaches to implementation research: a critical analysis and suggested synthesis. *Cambridge.Org, 6*(1), 21–48. Retrieved April 13, 2024, from https://www.cambridge.org/core/journals/journal-of-public-policy/article/topdown-and-bottomup-approaches-to-implementation-research-a-critical-analysis-and-suggested-synthesis/2100355E461CC28D75C42AF64A4083D9

Schwager, J. (1995). *Technical analysis.* https://books.google.com/books?hl=en&lr=&id=hOAfBRLrkJYC&oi=fnd&pg=PA1&dq=what+is+technical+analysis&ots=FfccBuNmHA&sig=xDwbZcESViREPFvYqt4N92GFrcI

SCIENCES, H. H.-S., AND, M., & 2019. (2019). The importance of regulations on cryptocurrency transactions. *Drhulya.Com, 1*(2). http://drhulya.com/images/Regulations_on_Cryptocurrency.pdf

Top Projects by Market cap, AlphaGrowth. (n.d.). Retrieved June 5, 2024, from https://alphagrowth.io/projects/top-all-projects-on-all-by-market-cap-value

Toygar, A., Jr, C. R., & of, J. Z.-J. (2013). A new asset type: digital assets. *Scholarworks.Lib.Csusb.Edu, 22.* https://doi.org/10.58729/1941-6679.1024

TradingView — Track All Markets. (n.d.). Retrieved April 13, 2024, from https://www.tradingview.com/

What is Fundamental Analysis (FA)?, Binance Academy. (n.d.). Retrieved September 5, 2023, from https://academy.binance.com/en/articles/what-is-fundamental-analysis-fa

What Is Technical Analysis?, Binance Academy. (n.d.). Retrieved September 5, 2023, from https://academy.binance.com/en/articles/what-is-technical-analysis

Why Should Anyone Invest in Crypto? (n.d.). Retrieved March 23, 2024, from https://www.investopedia.com/tech/question-why-should-anyone-invest-crypto/

Xi, D., O'Brien, T. I., & Irannezhad, E. (2020). Investigating the investment behaviors in cryptocurrency. *Journal of Alternative Investments, 23*(2), 141-160. https://doi.org/10.3905/JAI.2020.1.108

Zaghloul, E., Li, T., Member, S., Mutka, M. W., & Ren, J. (2020). Bitcoin and Blockchain: Security and Privacy. *IEEE INTERNET OF THINGS JOURNAL, 7*(10). https://doi.org/10.1109/JIOT.2020.3004273

Chapter 3—Project Documentation

Aave. (2017, January 1). *Flashpaper—Aavenomics*. Aave. https://docs.aave.com/aavenomics/flashpaper

Bureau, C. (2022, February 9). *Reading Crypto White Papers: How To Find GEMS!!💎 —YouTube* . https://www.youtube.com/watch?v=j63BIvOoQjg

Buterin, V. (2015). *Ethereum: A Next-Generation Smart Contract and Decentralized Application Platform.*

Contributing to Open-Source Crypto Projects by Mark Mathis Coinmonks Medium. (n.d.). Retrieved August 27, 2022, from https://medium.com/coinmonks/contributing-to-open-source-crypto-projects-7532273062a

Cosmos Network. (n.d.). *Whitepaper—Resources—Cosmos Network*. Cosmos. Retrieved April 19, 2022, from https://v1.cosmos.network/resources/whitepaper

Feng, C., Li, N., Wong, M. H. F., & Zhang, M. (2019). Initial Coin Offerings, Blockchain Technology, and White Paper Disclosures. *SSRN Electronic Journal*. https://doi.org/10.2139/SSRN.3256289

Filecoin FIL whitepapers—whitepaper.io. (n.d.). Retrieved May 3, 2024, from https://whitepaper.io/coin/filecoin

Footnotes for white papers 101—That White Paper Guy. (n.d.). Retrieved May 5, 2024, from https://thatwhitepaperguy.com/footnotes-for-white-papers-101/

KILT Protocol KILT whitepapers—whitepaper.io. (n.d.). Retrieved May 3, 2024, from https://whitepaper.io/coin/kilt-protocol

Moonbeam Cross-Chain Connected Smart Contract Platform. (n.d.). Retrieved May 3, 2024, from https://moonbeam.network/

Nebulas Mauve Paper: Developer Incentive Protocol. (n.d.). Retrieved May 4, 2024, from https://www.nebulas.io/docs/NebulasMauvepaper.pdf

Polkadot Protocol Information · Polkadot Wiki. (n.d.). Retrieved July 22, 2023, from https://wiki.polkadot.network/docs/build-protocol-info

Polkadot: Vision For A Heterogeneous Multi-Chain Framework. (n.d.). Retrieved May 4, 2024, from https://github.com/ethereum/wiki/wiki/Chain-Fibers-Redux

polkadot-light-paper/Polkadot-lightpaper.pdf at master · w3f/polkadot-light-paper · GitHub. (n.d.). Retrieved May 4, 2024, from https://github.com/w3f/polkadot-light-paper/blob/master/Polkadot-lightpaper.pdf

Reading Crypto White Papers: How To Find GEMS!! (n.d.). Retrieved March 11, 2022, from https://www.youtube.com/watch?v=j63BIvOoQjg

Satoshi Nakamoto—Wikipedia. (n.d.). Retrieved May 4, 2024, from https://en.wikipedia.org/wiki/Satoshi_Nakamoto

White paper—Wikipedia. (n.d.). Retrieved April 28, 2024, from https://en.wikipedia.org/wiki/White_paper

Wood, G. (2016). Polkadot Lightpaper: An Introduction to Polkadot. *Polkadot*. https://assets.polkadot.network/Polkadot-lightpaper.pdf

Wood, G., & Buterin, V. (2015a). Ethereum 2.0 Mauve Paper Minimal Proof of Stake. *Ethereum*. https://cdn.hackaday.io/files/10879465447136/Mauve%20Paper%20Vitalik.pdf

Wood, G., & Buterin, V. (2016). Ethereum: A Secure Decentralized Generalised Transaction Ledger EIP-150 Revision. *Polkadot*. https://gavwood.com/paper.pdf

Wood, G., & Buterin, V. (2015b, January 1). *An Ethereum Technical Specification—Beigepaper*. Ethereum. https://github.com/chronaeon/beigepaper/blob/master/beigepaper.pdf

Chapter 4—Core Offering

Adams, H., Zinsmeister, N., Salem moody, M., River Keefer, uniswaporg, & Robinson, D. (2021). *Uniswap v3 Core*. https://uniswap.org/whitepaper-v3.pdf

Berneis, M., & Winkler, H. (2021). Value Proposition Assessment of Blockchain Technology for Luxury, Food, and Healthcare Supply Chains. *Logistics 2021, Vol. 5, Page 85*, *5*(4), 85. https://doi.org/10.3390/LOGISTICS5040085

Bitcoin Average Transaction Fee Daily Insights: Bitcoin Statistics YCharts. (n.d.). Retrieved December 11, 2024, from https://ycharts.com/indicators/bitcoin_average_transaction_fee

Blemus, S., Journal, D. G.-C. M. L., & 2020. (2018). Initial crypto-asset offerings (ICOs), tokenization and corporate governance. *Academic.Oup.Com*. https://academic.oup.com/cmlj/article-abstract/15/2/191/5825337

Capturing the Value of Blockchain. (n.d.). Retrieved May 11, 2024, from https://www.bcg.com/publications/2019/capturing-blockchain-value

Chainlink price today, LINK to USD live price, marketcap and chart CoinMarketCap. (n.d.). Retrieved June 4, 2024, from https://coinmarketcap.com/currencies/chainlink/

Chainlink: The Industry-Standard Web3 Services Platform. (n.d.). Retrieved June 4, 2024, from https://chain.link/

Cryptocurrency Prices, Charts, and Crypto Market Cap CoinGecko. (n.d.). Retrieved June 4, 2024, from https://www.coingecko.com/

Cryptocurrency Prices, Charts And Market Capitalizations CoinMarketCap. (n.d.). Retrieved May 18, 2024, from https://coinmarketcap.com/

Domain Age checker, check Registrar, Server, IP, and History of Domain. (n.d.). Retrieved June 29, 2024, from https://www.duplichecker.com/domain-age-checker.php

Ethereum Compatibility Moonbeam Docs. (n.d.). Retrieved May 17, 2024, from https://docs.moonbeam.network/learn/features/eth-compatibility/

Ethereum Sepolia Faucet. (n.d.). Retrieved June 1, 2024, from https://www.alchemy.com/faucets/ethereum-sepolia

Goerli Testnet. (n.d.). Retrieved June 1, 2024, from https://goerli.net/

Home ethereum.org. (n.d.). Retrieved May 18, 2024, from https://ethereum.org/en/

Home Uniswap Protocol. (n.d.). Retrieved May 11, 2024, from https://uniswap.org/

How does Uniswap work?—Uniswap Labs. (n.d.). Retrieved May 11, 2024, from https://support.uniswap.org/hc/en-us/articles/8671577468813-How-does-Uniswap-work

How Uniswap works Uniswap. (n.d.). Retrieved May 11, 2024, from https://docs.uniswap.org/contracts/v2/concepts/protocol-overview/how-uniswap-works

Injective The Blockchain Built For Finance. (n.d.). Retrieved May 18, 2024, from https://injective.com/

Klein, S., Prinz, W., Blockchain, W. G.-P. of 1st E., & 2018. (n.d.). A use case identification framework and use case canvas for identifying and exploring relevant blockchain opportunities. *Academia.Edu.* Retrieved May 11, 2024, from https://www.academia.edu/download/81621926/blockchain2018_02.pdf

List of 4 Testnets on Ethereum (2024). (n.d.). Retrieved June 1, 2024, from https://www.alchemy.com/list-of/testnets-on-ethereum

Moonbeam Network (@MoonbeamNetwork) / X. (n.d.). Retrieved June 29, 2024, from https://x.com/MoonbeamNetwork

Mina Protocol: Lightest Blockchain for Secure DApps. (n.d.). Retrieved May 18, 2024, from https://minaprotocol.com/

NEAR Blockchains, Abstracted. (n.d.). Retrieved May 18, 2024, from https://near.org/

Networks · Polkadot Wiki. (n.d.). Retrieved June 1, 2024, from https://wiki.polkadot.network/docs/maintain-networks

TESTNET Moonbase Alpha (DEV) Blockchain Explorer. (n.d.). Retrieved June 2, 2024, from https://moonbase.moonscan.io/

Token Unlocks—Your Unlock Schedule & Tokenomics Data. (n.d.). Retrieved May 11, 2024, from https://token.unlocks.app/

Uniswap 101: What is Uniswap? Uniswap Labs. (n.d.). Retrieved May 11, 2024, from https://blog.uniswap.org/what-is-uniswap

Uniswap Proposal: An Alternative Use-Case for the Fee Switch—Uniswap Governance. (n.d.). Retrieved May 11, 2024, from https://gov.uniswap.org/t/uniswap-proposal-an-alternative-use-case-for-the-fee-switch/20779

Uniswap (UNI) Up 20% as Token Reward Scheme Gets Overwhelming Support. (n.d.). Retrieved May 11, 2024, from https://www.coindesk.

com/markets/2024/03/06/uniswaps-uni-gains-20-as-token-reward-proposal-inches-closer-to-approval/

Uniswap Use Case CryptoWallet.com . (n.d.). Retrieved May 11, 2024, from https://cryptowallet.com/academy/uniswap-use-case/

Web3 Infrastructure for Everyone Solana. (n.d.). Retrieved June 3, 2024, from https://solana.com/

What is the Sepolia testnet? (n.d.). Retrieved June 1, 2024, from https://www.alchemy.com/overviews/sepolia-testnet

Chapter 5—End-User Experience

Niji Oni & Co. (2021). Regulation of Cryptocurrency in Various Jurisdiction across the World. *SSRN Electronic Journal.* https://doi.org/10.2139/SSRN.3841589

3 Gwei Ethereum Gas Tracker Etherscan. (n.d.). Retrieved June 22, 2024, from https://etherscan.io/gastracker

Moonbeam Network (@MoonbeamNetwork) / X. (n.d.). Retrieved June 29, 2024, from https://x.com/MoonbeamNetwork

30-30 Gwei POLY Gas Tracker PolygonScan. (n.d.). Retrieved June 22, 2024, from https://polygonscan.com/gastracker/

Bitcoin—Open source P2P money. (n.d.). Retrieved June 22, 2024, from https://bitcoin.org/en/

Blockchain.com Charts—Median Confirmation Time. (n.d.). Retrieved June 22, 2024, from https://www.blockchain.com/explorer/charts/median-confirmation-time

Buy & Sell Bitcoin, Ether Cryptocurrency Exchange Bybit. (n.d.). Retrieved June 28, 2024, from https://www.bybit.com/en/

Carson, B., Romanelli, G., Walsh, P., Company, A. Z.-M. &, & 2018. (2018). Blockchain beyond the hype: What is the strategic business value. *Caba.Org.* https://www.caba.org/wp-content/uploads/2020/04/IS-2018-209.pdf

ChainSecurity. (2019, June 5). *Zero Gas Price Transactions — what they do, who creates them, and why they might impact Scalability.* ChainSecurity.

Coinbase—Sign In. (n.d.). Retrieved June 28, 2024, from https://login.coinbase.com/signin?client_id=258660e1-9cfe-4202-9eda-d3beedb3e118&oauth_challenge=91d2f029-c3dc-4942-b80b-4cdb50539d0e

Coinbase Advanced: Trading platform for sophisticated crypto traders. (n.d.). Retrieved June 28, 2024, from https://www.coinbase.com/advanced-trade/spot/BTC-USD

Conway, L. (2021, November 8). *Best Crypto Exchanges of 2022.* Investopedia. https://www.investopedia.com/best-crypto-exchanges-5071855

Crypto Exchange Bitcoin Exchange Bitcoin Trading KuCoin. (n.d.). Retrieved June 28, 2024, from https://www.kucoin.com/

dYdX—Trade Perpetuals on the most powerful trading platform. (n.d.). Retrieved June 28, 2024, from https://dydx.exchange/

Finance, P. (2022, February 2). *Cryptocurrency exchange license in USA Prifinance Company.* Private Finance. https://prifinance.com/en/cryptocurrency-license/usa/

FinCEN. (2022, January 1). *United States Department of the Treasury Financial Crimes Enforcement Network FinCEN.gov.* FinCEN. https://www.fincen.gov/

Fridgen, G., Lockl, J., Radszuwill, S., Rieger, A., Schweizer, A., & Urbach, N. (2018). A Solution in Search of a Problem: A Method for the Development of Blockchain Use Cases. *Fim-Rc.De.* https://www.fim-rc.de/Paperbibliothek/Veroeffentlicht/751/wi-751.pdf

Global Legal Insights. (2022). *Blockchain & Cryptocurrency Laws and Regulations USA GLI.* Global Legal Insights. https://www.globallegalinsights.com/practice-areas/blockchain-laws-and-regulations/usa

Gov, B. (n.d.). *Registering your crypto service company with DNB Business.gov.nl.* 2022. Retrieved March 10, 2022, from https://business.gov.nl/starting-your-business/registering-your-business/registering-your-crypto-service-company-with-dnb/

Gwei 125–125 Gwei MOONBEAM Gas Tracker Moonbeam. (n.d.). Retrieved June 22, 2024, from https://moonscan.io/gastracker

GWEI to USD Price Converter & Calculator, Live Exchange Rate CoinBrain. (n.d.). Retrieved June 22, 2024, from https://coinbrain.com/converter/eth-0x29e683aeafd03bb6c02055c3ca8b6edb4bb9bae5/usd

Hazari, S. S., & Mahmoud, Q. H. (2019). A parallel proof of work to improve transaction speed and scalability in blockchain systems. *2019 IEEE 9th Annual Computing and Communication Workshop and Conference, CCWC 2019,* 916–921. https://doi.org/10.1109/CCWC.2019.8666535

Home PancakeSwap. (n.d.). Retrieved June 28, 2024, from https://pancakeswap.finance/

Home Uniswap Protocol. (n.d.). Retrieved June 28, 2024, from https://uniswap.org/

Kraken The crypto platform for smarter investing. (n.d.). Retrieved June 28, 2024, from https://www.kraken.com/

Lightning Network. (n.d.). Retrieved June 21, 2024, from https://lightning.network/

Moonbeam Cross-Chain Connected Smart Contract Platform. (n.d.). Retrieved June 22, 2024, from https://moonbeam.network/

Moonbeam Dapps—Interface. (n.d.). Retrieved June 10, 2024, from https://apps.moonbeam.network/moonbeam/staking

Newbery, E. (2021, October 3). *Why Are So Many Crypto Exchanges Unavailable in the U.S.?* Fool. https://www.fool.com/the-ascent/cryptocurrency/articles/why-are-so-many-crypto-exchanges-unavailable-in-the-us/

Olinga, L. (2022, January 22). *Here Are Countries Where Crypto Are Illegal—TheStreet.* The Street. https://www.thestreet.com/investing/russia-wants-to-ban-crypto-these-countries-outlaw-crypto

Pierro, G. A., Tonelli, R., & Marchesi, M. (2020). An Organized Repository of Ethereum Smart Contracts' Source Codes and Metrics. *Future Internet 2020, Vol. 12, Page 197, 12*(11), 197. https://doi.org/10.3390/FI12110197

Polkadot price today, DOT to USD live price, marketcap and chart CoinMarketCap. (n.d.). Retrieved June 28, 2024, from https://coinmarketcap.com/currencies/polkadot-new/

Reiff, N. (2021, November 3). *Cryptocurrency Exchanges: What They Are and How to Choose.* https://www.investopedia.com/tech/190-cryptocurrency-exchanges-so-how-choose/

Sunny, J., Undralla, N., & Madhusudanan Pillai, V. (2020). Supply chain transparency through blockchain-based traceability: An overview with demonstration. *Computers & Industrial Engineering, 150,* 106895. https://doi.org/10.1016/J.CIE.2020.106895

Szczerbowski, J. J. (2018). Transaction Costs of Blockchain Smart Contracts. *Law and Forensic Science, 16*(2). https://ssrn.com/abstract=3258285

Top 5 Enterprise Blockchain Protocols You Must Know by Amarpreet Singh Brandlitic Medium. (n.d.). Retrieved August 9, 2022, from https://medium.com/brandlitic/top-5-enterprise-blockchain-protocols-you-must-know-4e9903d812aa

Top Cryptocurrency Exchanges Ranked By Volume CoinMarketCap. (n.d.). Retrieved June 28, 2024, from https://coinmarketcap.com/rankings/exchanges/

Web3, Aggregated. (n.d.). Retrieved June 22, 2024, from https://polygon.technology/

What Are the Customer Support Strategies for Cryptocurrency Exchange Software Development? by Albert Peter NFT Daily Dose Medium. (n.d.). Retrieved June 23, 2024, from https://medium.com/nftdailydose/

what-are-the-customer-support-strategies-for-cryptocurrency-exchange-software-development-8f014ae09a42

What is User Experience? Definition and Overview. (n.d.). Retrieved June 15, 2024, from https://www.productplan.com/glossary/user-experience/

Yano, M., Dai, C., Masuda, K., & Kishimoto, Y. (n.d.). *Economics, Law, and Institutions in Asia Pacific Blockchain and Crypt Currency Building a High Quality Marketplace for Crypt Data.* Retrieved September 11, 2022, from http://www.springer.com/series/13451

Chapter 6—Blockchain Architecture

N. P.-T. S. P. O. B., & 2018. (2018). An Architectural, Ideological, and Economic Analysis of Key Cryptocurrency Projects. *Business.Wisc.Edu.* https://business.wisc.edu/wp-content/uploads/2020/03/Nicholas-Center-Cryptocurrencies-Papers-December-2018.pdf#page=36

8 best practices for blockchain security. (n.d.). Retrieved August 12, 2022, from https://www.techtarget.com/searchsecurity/tip/8-best-practices-for-blockchain-security

A comparison of blockchain network latencies by Klaytn Klaytn Medium. (n.d.). Retrieved August 3, 2024, from https://medium.com/klaytn/a-comparison-of-blockchain-network-latencies-7508509b8460

A Comparison of Heterogeneous Blockchain Networks by Burak Arikan Medium. (n.d.). Retrieved August 25, 2022, from https://medium.com/@arikan/a-comparison-of-heterogeneous-blockchain-networks-4bf7ff2fe279

AAVE & AAVE Token Crypto Analytics & User Data AlphaGrowth. (n.d.). Retrieved July 19, 2024, from https://alphagrowth.io/aave

Aave—Open Source Liquidity Protocol. (n.d.). Retrieved October 14, 2023, from https://aave.com/

Akash Network—Decentralized Compute Marketplace. (n.d.). Retrieved July 31, 2024, from https://akash.network/

All About the Bitcoin Cash Hard Fork. (n.d.). Retrieved August 19, 2024, from https://www.investopedia.com/news/all-about-bitcoin-cash-hard-fork/

Anonymity vs. Pseudonymity In Crypto Gemini. (n.d.). Retrieved August 20, 2022, from https://www.gemini.com/cryptopedia/anonymity-vs-pseudonymity-basic-differences

Arbitrum — The Future of Ethereum. (n.d.). Retrieved August 9, 2024, from https://arbitrum.io/

Aru, I. (2021, March 4). *The Danger of Centralization That [Still] Exists in the Blockchain Ecosystem.* CNN. https://www.ccn.com/the-dangerous-threat-of-centralization-that-exists-in-the-blockchain-ecosystem/

Athanere, S., & Thakur, R. (2022). Blockchain based hierarchical semi-decentralized approach using IPFS for secure and efficient data sharing. *Journal of King Saud University—Computer and Information Sciences, 34*(4), 1523–1534. https://doi.org/10.1016/J.JKSUCI.2022.01.019

B. Rawat, D., Chaudhary, V., & Doku, R. (2021). Blockchain Technology: Emerging Applications and Use Cases for Secure and Trustworthy Smart Systems. *Journal of Cybersecurity and Privacy, 1*(1), 4–18. https://doi.org/10.3390/JCP1010002

Band Protocol. (n.d.). Retrieved July 12, 2024, from https://www.bandprotocol.com/

Bashir, I. (2020). *Mastering Blockchain: A deep dive into distributed ledgers, consensus protocols, smart contracts, DApps, cryptocurrencies, Ethereum, and more.* https://books.google.com/books?hl=en&lr=&id=ZZ_6DwAAQBAJ&oi=fnd&pg=PP1&dq=mastering+blockchain+imran+bashir&ots=dwbRn3gESK&sig=PfB7xH2wfZEOPO3wdNh8-sfvK84

Bitcoin—Open source P2P money. (n.d.). Retrieved August 30, 2024, from https://bitcoin.org/en/

Bitcoin Cash—Peer-to-Peer Electronic Cash. (n.d.). Retrieved August 9, 2024, from https://bitcoincash.org/

Bitcoin Core :: Compact Blocks FAQ. (n.d.). Retrieved August 9, 2024, from https://bitcoincore.org/en/2016/06/07/compact-blocks-faq/

Bitcoin Decentralization and Where to Find It—Bitcoin Magazine—Bitcoin News, Articles and Expert Insights. (n.d.). Retrieved July 29, 2024, from https://bitcoinmagazine.com/technical/bitcoin-decentralization-and-where-to-find-it

Bitcoin Gold Make Bitcoin decentralized again. (n.d.). Retrieved August 17, 2024, from https://bitcoingold.org/

Bitcoin [TPS, Max TPS, Block Time & TTF] Chainspect. (n.d.). Retrieved August 16, 2024, from https://chainspect.app/chain/bitcoin

Blockchain interoperability and how does it work? (Part 75) by Techskill Brew Blockchain 101 by Techskill Brew Medium. (n.d.). Retrieved February 19, 2023, from https://medium.com/techskill-brew/blockchain-interoperability-and-how-does-it-work-part-75-f5d0a70d12b0

Blockchain Interoperability Solutions—Examples. (n.d.). Retrieved February 23, 2023, from https://lisk.com/blog/posts/blockchain-interoperability-solutions-examples

Blockchain technology is based on a mutual distributed network,... Download Scientific Diagram. (n.d.). Retrieved February 9, 2024, from https://www.researchgate.net/figure/Blockchain-technology-is-based-on-a-mutual-distributed-network-allowing-high-level-trust_fig3_368230430

Blockchain Vs. Distributed Ledger Technology—Blockchain Council. (n.d.). Retrieved July 24, 2024, from https://www.blockchain-council.org/blockchain/blockchain-vs-distributed-ledger-technology/

Blockchain vs. Distributed Ledger Technology: Differences. (n.d.). Retrieved February 9, 2024, from https://imiblockchain.com/blockchain-vs-distributed-ledger-technology/

BNB Chain—Build Web3 dApps on the Most Popular Blockchain. (n.d.). Retrieved July 12, 2024, from https://www.bnbchain.org/en

BNB Smart Chain (BSC): Bring Smart Contracts to BNB Chain. (n.d.). Retrieved July 13, 2024, from https://www.bnbchain.org/en/bnb-smart-chain

Bring the World to Ethereum Polygon—Polygon. (n.d.). Retrieved February 23, 2023, from https://polygon.technology/

Centralized vs Decentralized vs Distributed Systems · Berty Technologies. (n.d.). Retrieved April 26, 2022, from https://berty.tech/blog/decentralized-distributed-centralized

Centrifuge The platform for onchain finance. (n.d.). Retrieved July 31, 2024, from https://centrifuge.io/

Cloud Computing Services—Amazon Web Services (AWS). (n.d.). Retrieved July 30, 2024, from https://aws.amazon.com/

Coinbase—Buy and Sell Bitcoin, Ethereum, and more with trust. (n.d.). Retrieved July 29, 2024, from https://www.coinbase.com/

Coinbase Global, Inc. (n.d.). Retrieved July 29, 2024, from https://www.sec.gov/Archives/edgar/data/1679788/000162828021003168/coinbaseglobalincs-1.htm

Cointelegraph. (n.d.). *A beginner's guide to understanding the layers of blockchain technology.* Cointelegraph. Retrieved April 19, 2022, from https://cointelegraph.com/blockchain-for-beginners/a-beginners-guide-to-understanding-the-layers-of-blockchain-technology

Cosmos: The Internet of Blockchains. (n.d.). Retrieved July 12, 2024, from https://cosmos.network/

Crypto Investing Checklist. How to Analyze Layer 1 & 2 Cryptos- (Ethereum, Hex, Cardano, XRP...!)—YouTube. (n.d.). Retrieved September 4, 2023, from https://www.youtube.com/watch?v=Rd4glmNOY8I

Crypto.com. (2020, January 3). *A Deep Dive Into Blockchain Scalability.* Crypto.Com. https://crypto.com/university/blockchain-scalability

Cryptopedia. (2021, July 12). *Networks: Decentralized, Distributed, & Centralized Gemini.* Cryptopedia. https://www.gemini.com/cryptopedia/blockchain-network-decentralized-distributed-centralized#section-what-is-a-centralized-network

Dasgupta, D., Datta Gupta, K., Shrein, J. M., Kishor, ·, & Gupta, D. (2019). A survey of blockchain from security perspective. *Springer, 3*(1), 1–17. https://doi.org/10.1007/s42786-018-00002-6

Decred Politeia Overview—Decred Documentation. (n.d.). Retrieved June 14, 2025, from https://docs.decred.org/governance/politeia/overview/

Developer learning tools ethereum.org. (n.d.). Retrieved July 13, 2024, from https://ethereum.org/en/developers/learning-tools/

Developer Report: Analysis of Open-Source Crypto Developers by Electric Capital. (n.d.-a). Retrieved July 13, 2024, from https://www.developerreport.com/developer-report?s=developer-report

Developer Report: Analysis of Open-Source Crypto Developers by Electric Capital. (n.d.-b). Retrieved July 13, 2024, from https://www.developerreport.com/

Digitale, J., Martin, J., Epidemiology, M. G.-J. of C., & 2022. (n.d.). Tutorial on directed acyclic graphs. *Elsevier.* Retrieved July 24, 2024, from https://www.sciencedirect.com/science/article/pii/S0895435621002407

Distributed Ledger Technology (DLT): Definition and How It Works. (n.d.). Retrieved July 21, 2024, from https://www.investopedia.com/terms/d/distributed-ledger-technology-dlt.asp#citation-2

Distributed VS Decentralized: What's The Difference?—Zipmex. (2020, December 1). Zimpex. https://zipmex.com/learn/distributed-vs-decentralized/

DOT token Polkadot Tokens. (n.d.). Retrieved August 24, 2024, from https://polkadot.com/get-started/dot-token

Electric Capital. (n.d.). Retrieved July 13, 2024, from https://www.electriccapital.com/

Ethereum 2.0 staking: A beginner's guide on how to stake ETH. (n.d.). Retrieved July 1, 2023, from https://cointelegraph.com/learn/ethereum-2-0-staking-a-beginners-guide-on-how-to-stake-eth

Ethereum Classic. (n.d.). Retrieved August 17, 2024, from https://ethereumclassic.org/

Ethereum: Understanding Post-Merge Rewards—Figment. (n.d.). Retrieved July 1, 2023, from https://figment.io/insights/ethereum-understanding-post-merge-rewards/

Ethereum, & Wackerow, P. (2024, January 25). *Plasma chains.* https://ethereum.org/en/developers/docs/scaling/plasma/

Ewing, M. (2021, November 29). *Horizen and the Importance of Layer-0 Blockchains.* Dapp Radar. https://dappradar.com/blog/horizen-and-the-importance-of-layer-0-blockchains

Fantom. (n.d.). Retrieved July 24, 2024, from https://fantom.foundation/

Fantom Network. (n.d.). Retrieved August 3, 2024, from https://fantom.foundation/

Fantom [TPS, Max TPS, Block Time & TTF] Chainspect. (n.d.). Retrieved August 3, 2024, from https://chainspect.app/chain/fantom

Filippi, P. de. (2016). The Interplay between Decentralization and Privacy: The Case of Blockchain Technologies by Primavera De Filippi :: SSRN. *Journal of Peer Production.* https://papers.ssrn.com/sol3/papers.cfm?abstract_id=2852689

Gandal, N., & Hałaburda, H. (2014). A Service of zbw Competition in the cryptocurrency market. *Bank of Canada.* http://hdl.handle.net/10419/103022www.econstor.eu

Geeks for Geeks. (2021, September 13). *Comparison—Centralized, Decentralized and Distributed Systems—GeeksforGeeks.* Geeks for Geeks. https://www.geeksforgeeks.org/comparison-centralized-decentralized-and-distributed-systems/

GitHub—bitcoin/bips: Bitcoin Improvement Proposals. (n.d.). Retrieved June 14, 2025, from https://github.com/bitcoin/bips

Google Authenticator—Apps on Google Play. (n.d.). Retrieved August 22, 2024, from https://play.google.com/store/apps/details?id=com.google.android.apps.authenticator2&hl=en_GB&gl=US&pli=1

Griffith, K., & Grigg, I. (n.d.). *Bitcoin Verification Latency The Achilles Heel for Time Sensitive Transactions.* http://iang.org/papers/mutual_funds.html

Gross domestic product (GDP) Definition & Formula Britannica Money. (n.d.). Retrieved July 19, 2024, from https://www.britannica.com/money/gross-domestic-product

Guy. (2022, May 17). Decentralization: Which Crypto's Aren't Centralized?! Let's Find Out!—YouTube. In *Coin Bureau.* Coin Bureau. https://www.youtube.com/watch?v=9ybYhv_VFaE

Hafid, A., Hafid, A. S., & Samih, M. (2020). Scaling Blockchains: A Comprehensive Survey. *IEEE Access, 8,* 125244–125262. https://doi.org/10.1109/ACCESS.2020.3007251

Handbook of Research on Blockchain Technology. (2020).

Hardware Wallet & Crypto Wallet—Security for Crypto Ledger. (n.d.). Retrieved August 2, 2024, from https://www.ledger.com/

Hayat Mosakheil, J. (2018). *Security Threats Classification in Blockchains. 48.* https://repository.stcloudstate.edu/msia_etdshttps://repository.stcloudstate.edu/msia_etds/48

Home Ethereum Improvement Proposals. (n.d.). Retrieved June 14, 2025, from https://eips.ethereum.org/

Home ethereum.org. (n.d.). Retrieved July 12, 2024, from https://ethereum.org/en/

Home IOTA. (n.d.). Retrieved August 6, 2024, from https://www.iota.org/

Home LayerZero. (n.d.). Retrieved July 12, 2024, from https://layerzero.network/

Home Solidity Programming Language. (n.d.). Retrieved July 13, 2024, from https://soliditylang.org/

Home Tezos. (n.d.). Retrieved August 24, 2024, from https://tezos.com/

Home Uniswap Protocol. (n.d.). Retrieved July 12, 2024, from https://uniswap.org/

Homepage Celo. (n.d.). Retrieved July 13, 2024, from https://celo.org/

How to write, compile & deploy a simple Solidity smart contract. (n.d.). Retrieved August 29, 2024, from https://blockchainblog.substack.com/p/how-to-write-compile-and-deploy-a

Hussein, Z., Salama, M. A., & El-Rahman, S. A. (2023). Evolution of blockchain consensus algorithms: a review on the latest milestones of blockchain consensus algorithms. *Cybersecurity, 6*(1), 1–22. https://doi.org/10.1186/S42400-023-00163-Y/TABLES/7

Hyperledger—The Open Global Ecosystem for Enterprise Blockchain. (n.d.). Retrieved August 23, 2024, from https://www.hyperledger.org/

Hyperledger Fabric. (n.d.). Retrieved June 13, 2025, from https://www.lfdecentralizedtrust.org/projects/fabric

IBM Supply Chain Intelligence Suite—Food Trust. (n.d.). Retrieved August 23, 2024, from https://www.ibm.com/products/supply-chain-intelligence-suite/food-trust

IBM Supply Chain Intelligence Suite—Food Trust IBM. (n.d.). Retrieved February 25, 2023, from https://www.ibm.com/products/supply-chain-intelligence-suite/food-trust

Immutable Powering The Next Generation Of Web3 Games. (n.d.). Retrieved July 12, 2024, from https://www.immutable.com/

In Defence of Polkadot's Governance Mechanism by Gilbert Bassey Coinmonks Medium. (n.d.). Retrieved July 12, 2024, from https://medium.com/coinmonks/in-defence-of-polkadots-governance-mechanism-83db6558e33f

Information, G. C.-, & 2021. (2021). Wrapping Trust for Interoperability: A Preliminary Study of Wrapped Tokens. *Mdpi.Com.* https://doi.org/10.3390/info13010006

Introduction to Blockchain Security Issues & Vulnerabilities Blockchain Security Explained—YouTube. (n.d.). Retrieved August 9, 2022, from https://www.youtube.com/watch?v=dl8Hl91siM8

IOTA. (2021, November 5). *Sharding: Throughput, Scalability and Why We Need Them.* IOTA. https://blog.iota.org/sharding-throughput-scalability-and-why-we-need-them/

IPFS—Home. (n.d.). Retrieved July 31, 2024, from https://www.ipfs.com/

Iredale, G. (2021, November 24). *6 Key Blockchain Features You Need to Know Now.* 101 Blockchains. https://101blockchains.com/introduction-to-blockchain-features/

Is Bitcoin ACTUALLY Decentralized?—YouTube. (n.d.). Retrieved July 25, 2024, from https://www.youtube.com/watch?v=cOyLiOuwjHQ

Jaggi, H., & Jha, R. (n.d.). *Blockchain Interoperability (Part 1).*

Jennings, M. (n.d.). *Principles & Models of Web3 Decentralization.* A16zcrypto. Retrieved May 19, 2022, from https://a16z.com/wp-content/uploads/2022/04/principles-and-models-of-decentralization_miles-jennings_a16zcrypto.pdf

Johnson, S., Robinson, P., & Brainard, J. (2019). *Sidechains and interoperability.*

Joseph Poon Golden. (n.d.). Retrieved August 11, 2024, from https://golden.com/wiki/Joseph_Poon-6XDWEM

Karame, G., Androulaki, E., Archive, S. C.-C. Ep., & 2012. (n.d.). Two bitcoins at the price of one? double-spending attacks on fast payments in bitcoin. *Eprint.Iacr.Org.* Retrieved August 9, 2022, from https://eprint.iacr.org/2012/248

Khan, D., Jung, L., Sciences, M. H.-A., & 2021. (2021). Systematic Literature Review of Challenges in Blockchain Scalability. *Mdpi.Com.* https://doi.org/10.3390/app11209372

Kolb, J., Abdelbaky, M., Katz, R. H., & Culler, D. E. (2020). Core Concepts, Challenges, and Future Directions in Blockchain. *ACM Computing Surveys (CSUR), 53*(1). https://doi.org/10.1145/3366370

Latency and Throughput in Blockchain Technology Shardeum. (n.d.). Retrieved August 15, 2024, from https://shardeum.org/blog/latency-throughput-blockchain/

Layer 1 vs. Layer 2: The Difference Between Blockchain Scaling Solutions. (n.d.). Retrieved August 5, 2024, from https://www.investopedia.com/what-are-layer-1-and-layer-2-blockchain-scaling-solutions-7104877

Lee, D. K. C., Guo, L., & Wang, Y. (2017). Cryptocurrency: A New Investment Opportunity? *The Journal of Alternative Investments, 20*(3), 16–40. https://doi.org/10.3905/JAI.2018.20.3.016

Lightning Network. (n.d.). Retrieved July 12, 2024, from https://lightning.network/

Litecoin—Open source P2P digital currency. (n.d.). Retrieved August 9, 2024, from https://litecoin.org/

Lu, Y. (2018). Blockchain and the related issues: a review of current research topics. *Journal of Management Analytics, 5*(4), 231–255. https://doi.org/10.1080/23270012.2018.1516523

MetaMask—The Ultimate Crypto Wallet for DeFi, Web3 Apps, and NFTs MetaMask. (n.d.). Retrieved July 31, 2024, from https://metamask.io/

Mining Dashboard—mempool—Bitcoin Explorer. (n.d.). Retrieved July 25, 2024, from https://mempool.space/mining

Mohanty, D., Anand, D., Aljahdali, H., Sustainability, S. V.-, & 2022. (2022). Blockchain Interoperability: Towards a Sustainable Payment System. *Mdpi.Com.* https://doi.org/10.3390/su14020913

Moonbeam Chain Top Accounts by GLMR Balance Moonbeam. (n.d.). Retrieved August 2, 2024, from https://moonscan.io/accounts

Moonbeam [TPS, Max TPS, Block Time & TTF] Chainspect. (n.d.). Retrieved August 3, 2024, from https://chainspect.app/chain/moonbeam

Muneeb, M., & Raza, Z. (2021). Tree-Based Blockchain Architecture for Supply Chain. *Article in International Journal of Blockchains and Cryptocurrencies, 2*(2), 143–160. https://doi.org/10.1504/IJBC.2021.10038698

OpenSea, the largest NFT marketplace. (n.d.). Retrieved July 12, 2024, from https://opensea.io/

Optimism—Home. (n.d.). Retrieved August 9, 2024, from https://www.optimism.io/

Orbs: Bringing CeFi-level execution to DeFi. (n.d.). Retrieved July 12, 2024, from https://www.orbs.com/

Osanaiye, O., Choo, K. K. R., & Dlodlo, M. (2016). Distributed denial of service (DDoS) resilience in cloud: Review and conceptual cloud DDoS mitigation framework. *Journal of Network and Computer Applications, 67*, 147–165. https://doi.org/10.1016/J.JNCA.2016.01.001

Paper, V. B.-R. R., & 2016. (2016). Chain interoperability. *Allquantor.At.* https://allquantor.at/blockchainbib/pdf/buterin2016chain.pdf

Parachains · Polkadot Wiki. (n.d.). Retrieved July 12, 2024, from https://wiki.polkadot.network/docs/learn-parachains

Permissioned and Permissionless Blockchains Blockchain Technology. (n.d.). Retrieved August 13, 2022, from https://freemanlaw.com/permission-and-permissionless-blockchains/

Phantom — Crypto & NFT Wallet — Solana Ethereum Polygon. (n.d.). Retrieved August 9, 2024, from https://phantom.app/

Pirate Chain 🔒 The No. 1 Private, Fungible Cryptocurrency. (n.d.). Retrieved June 13, 2025, from https://piratechain.com/

Plasma chains ethereum.org. (n.d.). Retrieved July 12, 2024, from https://ethereum.org/en/developers/docs/scaling/plasma/

Polkadot 1.0 · Guide. (n.d.). Retrieved July 12, 2024, from https://guide.kusama.network/docs/polkadot-v1/

Polkadot: Web3 Interoperability Decentralized Blockchain. (n.d.). Retrieved July 12, 2024, from https://polkadot.network/

Polygon PoS The most efficient blockchain protocol. (n.d.). Retrieved July 12, 2024, from https://polygon.technology/polygon-pos

Polygon [TPS, Max TPS, Block Time & TTF] Chainspect. (n.d.). Retrieved August 16, 2024, from https://chainspect.app/chain/polygon

Polygon zkEVM Scaling for the Ethereum Virtual Machine. (n.d.). Retrieved July 12, 2024, from https://polygon.technology/polygon-zkevm

Poon, J., & Buterin, V. (2017). *Plasma: Scalable Autonomous Smart Contracts.* https://plasma.io/

Production, P. D. F.-J. of P., Issue, & 2016. (2016). The interplay between decentralization and privacy: the case of blockchain technologies. *Papers.Ssrn.Com.* https://papers.ssrn.com/sol3/papers.cfm?abstract_id=2852689

Proof of Work (PoW) Definition. (n.d.). Retrieved August 21, 2022, from https://www.investopedia.com/terms/p/proof-work.asp

Proof-of-Stake (PoS) vs Delegated Proof-of-Stake (dPoS) CoinMarketCap. (n.d.). Retrieved August 2, 2024, from https://coinmarketcap.com/academy/article/proof-of-stake-pos-vs-delegated-proof-of-stake-dpos

Pros and Cons of Running Your Own Node. (n.d.). Retrieved July 7, 2023, from https://www.alchemy.com/overviews/running-your-own-node

Punathumkandi, S., Modi, C., & Patel, D. (2019). Preventing Sybil Attack in Blockchain using Distributed Behavior Monitoring of Miners; Preventing Sybil Attack in Blockchain using Distributed Behavior Monitoring of Miners. *2019 10th International Conference on Computing, Communication and Networking Technologies (ICCCNT).* https://doi.org/10.1109/ICCCNT45670.2019.8944507

Quorum Blockchain Build & Deploy Networks Quickly. (n.d.). Retrieved August 23, 2024, from https://www.kaleido.io/blockchain-platform/quorum

Raikwar, M., & Gligoroski, D. (2022). DoS Attacks on Blockchain Ecosystem. *Lecture Notes in Computer Science (Including Subseries Lecture*

Notes in Artificial Intelligence and Lecture Notes in Bioinformatics), 13098 LNCS, 230–242. https://doi.org/10.1007/978-3-031-06156-1_19

Router Chain. (2023).

Router Protocol: Powering Cross-chain Liquidity & Interoperability with Chain Abstraction. (n.d.). Retrieved August 24, 2024, from https://www.routerprotocol.com/

Runtime Upgrades Polkadot Developer Docs. (n.d.). Retrieved June 14, 2025, from https://docs.polkadot.com/develop/parachains/maintenance/runtime-upgrades/

Rutland, E. (n.d.). *Blockchain Byte The Blockchain Byte features a question from the distributed ledger space R3 Research*. Retrieved July 21, 2024, from https://r3-cev.atlassian.net/wiki/x/HgEwAw

Sai, A. R., Buckley, J., Fitzgerald, B., & Gear, A. le. (2021). Taxonomy of centralization in public blockchain systems: A systematic literature review. *Information Processing & Management, 58*(4), 102584. https://doi.org/10.1016/J.IPM.2021.102584

SCIENCES, H. H.-S., & AND, M. (2019). The importance of regulations on cryptocurrency transactions. *Drhulya.Com, 1*(2). http://drhulya.com/images/Regulations_on_Cryptocurrency.pdf

Segregated Witness (SegWit) Definition CoinMarketCap. (n.d.). Retrieved August 19, 2024, from https://coinmarketcap.com/academy/glossary/segregated-witness-segwit

Serasinghe, H. (2022, January 20). *What are Layer 0, 1 & 2 Blockchains? by Harshana Serasinghe Medium*. Medium. https://harshanas.medium.com/what-are-layer-0-1-2-blockchains-7bc819a9336f

Singh, M., computers, S. K.-A. in, & 2019. (n.d.). Blockchain technology for decentralized autonomous organizations. *Elsevier*. Retrieved February 11, 2024, from https://www.sciencedirect.com/science/article/pii/S0065245819300257

Soft fork vs. hard fork: Differences explained. (n.d.). Retrieved August 9, 2022, from https://cointelegraph.com/blockchain-for-beginners/soft-fork-vs-hard-fork-differences-explained

Standard Allocation: Trends and Industry. (n.d.). Retrieved June 14, 2025, from https://insights.unlocks.app/tokenunlocks-standard-allocation/

StarkWare Bringing Scalability, Security and Privacy to Blockchai. (n.d.). Retrieved July 12, 2024, from https://starkware.co/

Sushi partners with ZetaChain for first native BTC support Sushi . (n.d.). Retrieved July 13, 2024, from https://www.sushi.com/blog/sushi-partners-with-zetachain

SushiSwap. (n.d.). Retrieved July 12, 2024, from https://www.sushi.com/swap

Swap—Curve. (n.d.). Retrieved July 12, 2024, from https://curve.fi/#/ethereum/swap?from=0xdac17f958d2ee523a2206206994597c13d831ec7&to=0xeeeeeeeeeeeeeeeeeeeeeeeeeeeeeeeeeeeeeeee

The Amendment (and Voting) Process — Octez & Protocol products documentation. (n.d.). Retrieved June 14, 2025, from https://octez.tezos.com/docs/active/voting.html

The Beacon Chain ethereum.org. (n.d.). Retrieved August 2, 2024, from https://ethereum.org/en/roadmap/beacon-chain/

The Complete Guide for Types of Blockchain! Simplilearn. (n.d.). Retrieved February 24, 2023, from https://www.simplilearn.com/tutorials/blockchain-tutorial/types-of-blockchain

The Game-Changing Technology Behind Layer 0 Blockchains: Explained!—YouTube. (n.d.). Retrieved September 4, 2023, from https://www.youtube.com/watch?v=2G1KreaGhjM

Thibault, L., Sarry, T., Access, A. H.-I., & 2022. (n.d.). Blockchain scaling using rollups: A comprehensive survey. *Ieeexplore.Ieee.Org*. Retrieved August 3, 2024, from https://ieeexplore.ieee.org/abstract/document/9862815/

Token Metrics. (2022, April 13). *What are Layer 0 Blockchain Protocols?—Token Metrics Blog*. Token Metrics. https://blog.tokenmetrics.com/layer-0-blockchain-protocols/

Tongia, R., & Iii, E. J. W. (2011). The Flip Side of Metcalfe's Law: Multiple and Growing Costs of Network Exclusion. *International Journal of Communication, 5*, 665–681. http://ijoc.org.

Top 5 Enterprise Blockchain Protocols You Must Know by Amarpreet Singh Brandlitic Medium. (n.d.). Retrieved August 9, 2022, from https://medium.com/brandlitic/top-5-enterprise-blockchain-protocols-you-must-know-4e9903d812aa

Top Projects by Market cap on Cosmos AlphaGrowth. (n.d.). Retrieved July 13, 2024, from https://alphagrowth.io/projects/top-all-projects-on-cosmos-by-market-cap-value

Top Wallets Projects by Market cap on Ethereum AlphaGrowth. (n.d.). Retrieved July 13, 2024, from https://alphagrowth.io/projects/top-wallets-projects-on-ethereum-by-market-cap-value

Trezor Hardware Wallet (Official) Bitcoin & Crypto Security. (n.d.). Retrieved August 2, 2024, from https://trezor.io/

Understanding a 51% Attack on the Blockchain Engineering Education (EngEd) Program Section. (n.d.). Retrieved August 11, 2022, from https://www.section.io/engineering-education/understanding-the-51-attack-on-blockchain/

Uniswap price today, UNI to USD live price, marketcap and chart CoinMarketCap. (n.d.). Retrieved August 24, 2024, from https://coinmarketcap.com/currencies/uniswap/

Verge Currency. (n.d.). Retrieved August 17, 2024, from https://vergecurrency.com/

Vertical Scaling—FasterCapital. (n.d.). Retrieved August 9, 2024, from https://fastercapital.com/keyword/vertical-scaling.html

Vitalik Buterin—Wikipedia. (n.d.). Retrieved August 11, 2024, from https://en.wikipedia.org/wiki/Vitalik_Buterin

Web3 and Polkadot Governance—Polkadot Wiki. (n.d.). Retrieved June 14, 2025, from https://wiki.polkadot.network/general/web3-and-polkadot/

What Are Layer-0 Protocols? Infrastructure for Customised Blockchains. (n.d.). Retrieved July 12, 2024, from https://crypto.com/university/what-are-layer-0-protocols

What Are Sidechains? Scaling Blockchain on the Side. (n.d.). Retrieved July 12, 2024, from https://crypto.com/university/what-are-sidechains-scaling-blockchain

What Is a 51% Attack? (n.d.). Retrieved August 7, 2022, from https://www.coindesk.com/learn/what-is-a-51-attack/

What is a DDoS Attack? How Can it Affect Crypto? by CertiK Medium. (n.d.). Retrieved August 19, 2024, from https://certik.medium.com/what-is-a-ddos-attack-how-can-it-affect-crypto-4f62cc1cad8c

What is a fork? Coinbase. (n.d.). Retrieved August 9, 2022, from https://www.coinbase.com/learn/crypto-basics/what-is-a-fork

What Is an Oracle in Blockchain? » Explained Chainlink. (n.d.). Retrieved July 12, 2024, from https://chain.link/education/blockchain-oracles

What Is Blockchain Interoperability?—Chainlink Blog. (n.d.). Retrieved February 23, 2023, from https://blog.chain.link/blockchain-interoperability/

What is blockchain interoperability: A beginner's guide to cross-chain technology. (n.d.). Retrieved February 19, 2023, from https://cointelegraph.com/blockchain-for-beginners/what-is-blockchain-interoperability-a-beginners-guide-to-cross-chain-technology

What is Cosmos: A beginner's guide to the 'Internet of Blockchains.' (n.d.). Retrieved August 28, 2024, from https://cointelegraph.com/learn/what-is-cosmos-a-beginners-guide-to-the-internet-of-blockchains

What is Distributed Ledger Technology DLT Explained Blockchain Technology 101 Blockchains—YouTube. (n.d.). Retrieved July 22, 2024, from https://www.youtube.com/watch?v=P27GqazhH24

What is Sharding? Sharding's potential challenges and risks. (n.d.). Retrieved August 10, 2024, from https://bho.network/what-is-sharding

What is the Secret to Building Valuable Tokens?—Outlier Ventures. (n.d.). Retrieved July 12, 2024, from https://outlierventures.io/research/what-is-the-secret-to-building-valuable-tokens/

Wheatstones. (2010, December 10). *Polkadot. Connecting the World of Blockchains. by Wheatstones Coinmonks Medium.* Coinmonks. https://medium.com/coinmonks/polkadot-connecting-the-world-of-blockchains-d4136bae1265

WIPRO. (2019, November). *Improving performance & scalability of blockchain networks—Wipro.* WIPRO. https://www.wipro.com/blogs/hitarshi-buch/improving-performance-and-scalability-of-blockchain-networks/

XDC Network. (n.d.). Retrieved June 13, 2025, from https://xdc.org/

Xu, X., Weber, I., Staples, M., Zhu, L., Bosch, J., Bass, L., Pautasso, C., & Rimba, P. (2017). A Taxonomy of Blockchain-Based Systems for Architecture Design. *Proceedings—2017 IEEE International Conference on Software Architecture, ICSA 2017,* 243–252. https://doi.org/10.1109/ICSA.2017.33

Yu, G., Wang, X., Yu, K., Ni, W., Zhang, J. A., & Liu, R. P. (2020). Survey: Sharding in Blockchains. *IEEE Access, 8,* 14155–14181. https://doi.org/10.1109/ACCESS.2020.2965147

Zaghloul, E., Li, T., Member, S., Mutka, M. W., & Ren, J. (2020). Bitcoin and Blockchain: Security and Privacy. *IEEE INTERNET OF THINGS JOURNAL, 7*(10). https://doi.org/10.1109/JIOT.2020.3004273

Zarrin, J., Wen Phang, H., Babu Saheer, L., & Zarrin, B. (2021). Blockchain for decentralization of internet: prospects, trends, and challenges. *Cluster Computing, 24*(4), 2841–2866. https://doi.org/10.1007/S10586-021-03301-8/FIGURES/9

Zheng, Z., Xie, S., Dai, H., ... X. C.-I. journal of web, & 2018. (2018). Blockchain challenges and opportunities: A survey. *Allquantor.At, 14*(4), 352-375. https://doi.org/10.1504/IJWGS.2018.10016848

Zhou, Q., Huang, H., Zheng, Z., & Bian, J. (2020). Solutions to Scalability of Blockchain: a Survey. *IEEE Access, 8,* 16440–16455. https://doi.org/10.1109/ACCESS.2020.2967218

Zilliqa The Zilliqa platform. (n.d.). Retrieved August 6, 2024, from https://www.zilliqa.com/our-platform

Chapter 7—Token Design and Use Case

N. P.-T. S. P. O. B., & 2018. (2018). An Architectural, Ideological, and Economic Analysis of Key Cryptocurrency Projects. *Business.Wisc.Edu.* https://business.wisc.edu/wp-content/uploads/2020/03/Nicholas-Center-Cryptocurrencies-Papers-December-2018.pdf#page=36

Alpos, O., Cachin, C., Marson, G. A., & Zanolini, L. (n.d.). On the Synchronization Power of Token Smart Contracts. *Ieeexplore.Ieee.Org.* Retrieved September 1, 2022, from https://ieeexplore.ieee.org/abstract/document/9546529/

Bakos, Y., & Halaburda, H. (2019). *The role of cryptographic tokens and ICOs in fostering platform adoption.* https://papers.ssrn.com/sol3/papers.cfm?abstract_id=3426940

Caldarelli, G. (2021). Wrapping Trust for Interoperability: A Preliminary Study of Wrapped Tokens. *Information 2022, Vol. 13, Page 6, 13*(1), 6. https://doi.org/10.3390/INFO13010006

Chainlink: What It Is and How It Works. (n.d.). Retrieved September 19, 2024, from https://www.investopedia.com/chainlink-link-definition-5217559

Ciaian, P., Markets, M. R.-J. of I. F., & 2018. (n.d.). Virtual relationships: Short-and long-run evidence from BitCoin and altcoin markets. *Elsevier.*

Retrieved September 8, 2022, from https://www.sciencedirect.com/science/article/pii/S1042443117302858

Coin Desk. (n.d.). *Security Tokens Are Back and This Time It's Real Janine Yorio—CoinDesk.* Retrieved August 30, 2022, from https://www.coindesk.com/business/2021/06/30/security-tokens-are-back-and-this-time-its-real/

CoinMarketCap. (n.d.). *Security Token Alexandria.* Retrieved August 30, 2022, from https://coinmarketcap.com/alexandria/glossary/security-token

Compound Crypto Proof of Stake Coins Staking Rewards. (n.d.). Retrieved July 20, 2024, from https://www.stakingrewards.com/assets/proof-of-stake

Cong, L. W., & Xiao, Y. (2021). Categories and Functions of Crypto-Tokens. *The Palgrave Handbook of FinTech and Blockchain,* 267–284. https://doi.org/10.1007/978-3-030-66433-6_12

Crypto Coin vs. Token: Understanding the Difference. (n.d.). Retrieved September 6, 2022, from https://blog.liquid.com/coin-vs-token

di Angelo, M., & Salzer, G. (n.d.). *Tokens, Types, and Standards: Identification and Utilization in Ethereum.* https://doi.org/10.1109/DAPPS49028.2020.00-11

Ferrari, V. (2020). The regulation of crypto-assets in the EU—Investment and payment tokens under the radar: https://doi.org/10.1177/1023263X20911538, *27*(3), 325–342. https://doi.org/10.1177/1023263X20911538

Freni, P., Ferro, E., & Moncada, R. (2022). Tokenomics and blockchain tokens: A design-oriented morphological framework. *Blockchain: Research and Applications, 3*(1), 100069. https://doi.org/10.1016/J.BCRA.2022.100069

Gandal, N., & Hałaburda, H. (2014). A Service of zbw Competition in the cryptocurrency market. *Bank of Canada.* http://hdl.handle.net/10419/103022www.econstor.eu

GeeksforGeeks. (n.d.). *What is a Cryptographic Token?—GeeksforGeeks.* Retrieved September 1, 2022, from https://www.geeksforgeeks.org/what-is-a-cryptographic-token/

Hacker, P., & Thomale, C. (2018). Crypto-securities regulation: icos,token sales and cryptocurrencies under eu financial law. *European Company and Financial Law Review, 15*(4), 645–696. https://doi.org/10.1515/ECFR-2018-0021/HTML

Härdle, W. K., Yanan, W., Kee, S., Harvey, C. R., & Reule, R. C. G. (2020). Understanding cryptocurrencies. *Academic.Oup.Com.* https://academic.oup.com/jfec/article-abstract/18/2/181/5735422

Henderson, M., Rev., M. R.-Colum. Bus. L., & 2019. (n.d.). A regulatory classification of digital assets: toward an operational Howey test for cryptocurrencies, ICOs, and other digital assets. *HeinOnline.* Retrieved September 1, 2022, from https://heinonline.org/hol-cgi-bin/get_pdf.cgi?handle=hein.journals/colb2019§ion=14

Home · sherminvo/TokenEconomyBook Wiki · GitHub. (n.d.). Retrieved September 14, 2024, from https://github.com/sherminvo/TokenEconomyBook/wiki

Investopedia. (n.d.). *What Crypto Users Need to Know: The ERC20 Standard.* Retrieved September 8, 2022, from https://www.investopedia.com/tech/why-crypto-users-need-know-about-erc20-token-standard/

Lee, D. K. C., Guo, L., & Wang, Y. (2017). Cryptocurrency: A New Investment Opportunity? *The Journal of Alternative Investments, 20*(3), 16–40. https://doi.org/10.3905/JAI.2018.20.3.016

Motley Fool. (n.d.). *Utility Tokens vs. Security Tokens: What's the Difference? The Motley Fool.* Retrieved August 30, 2022, from https://www.fool.com/investing/2021/11/16/utility-tokens-vs-security-tokens-whats-the-differ/

paper, V. B., & 2014. (n.d.). A next-generation smart contract and decentralized application platform. *Nft2x.Com.* Retrieved September

10, 2022, from https://nft2x.com/wp-content/uploads/2021/03/EthereumWP.pdf

PAX Gold—Paxos. (n.d.). Retrieved September 18, 2024, from https://paxos.com/paxgold/

Regner, F., Schweizer, A., & Urbach, N. (2019). *NFTs in Practice-Non-Fungible Tokens as Core Component of a Blockchain-based Event Ticketing Application Completed Research Paper.* 1. https://www.researchgate.net/publication/336057493_NFTs_in_Practice_-_Non- Fungible_Tokens_as_Core_Component_of_a_Blockchain-based_Event_Ticketing_Application

RSK Developers. (n.d.). *The Difference between a Cryptocurrency and a Token—RSK Developers Portal.* Retrieved September 5, 2022, from https://developers.rsk.co/guides/get-crypto-on-rsk/cryptocurrency-vs-token/

Sazandrishvili, G. (2020). Asset tokenization in plain English. *Journal of Corporate Accounting and Finance, 31*(2), 68–73. https://doi.org/10.1002/JCAF.22432

Token Standards ethereum.org. (n.d.). Retrieved September 8, 2022, from https://ethereum.org/en/developers/docs/standards/tokens/

Token Standards OpenTezos. (n.d.). Retrieved September 8, 2022, from https://opentezos.com/defi/token-standards/

Value Accrual. The Super Duper Meme Edition… by Nick Metzler Medium. (n.d.). Retrieved September 20, 2024, from https://medium.com/@metzlernick2/value-accrual-000b8813a065

Victor, F., … B. L.-C. on F. C. and D., & 2019. (2019). Measuring ethereum-based erc20 token networks. *Springer, 11598 LNCS*, 113–129. https://doi.org/10.1007/978-3-030-32101-7_8

What are Token Standards? An Overview. (n.d.). Retrieved September 8, 2022, from https://crypto.com/university/what-are-token-standards

What Is Chainlink & How Does It Work? Who Created LINK? (n.d.). Retrieved September 19, 2024, from https://kriptomat.io/cryptocurrency-prices/chainlink-link-price/what-is/

Yano, M., Dai, C., Masuda, K., & Kishimoto, Y. (n.d.). *Economics, Law, and Institutions in Asia Pacific Blockchain and Crypt Currency Building a High Quality Marketplace for Crypt Data.* Retrieved September 11, 2022, from http://www.springer.com/series/13451

Yilmaz, N., and, H. H.-J. of E. F., & 2018. (2018). Predicting future cryptocurrency investment trends by conjoint analysis. *Dergipark.Org.Tr, 5*(4), 321–330. https://doi.org/10.17261/Pressacademia.2018.999

Zaghloul, E., Li, T., Mutka, M. W., & Ren, J. (2020). Bitcoin and Blockchain: Security and Privacy. *IEEE Internet of Things Journal, 7*(10), 10288–10313. https://doi.org/10.1109/JIOT.2020.3004273

Chapter 8—Tokenomics

A Walkthrough of Polkadot's Governance. (n.d.). Retrieved May 27, 2023, from https://polkadot.network/blog/a-walkthrough-of-polkadots-governance

Bashir, I. (2020). *Mastering Blockchain: A deep dive into distributed ledgers, consensus protocols, smart contracts, DApps, cryptocurrencies, Ethereum, and more.* https://books.google.com/books?hl=en&lr=&id=ZZ_6DwAAQBAJ&oi=fnd&pg=PP1&dq=mastering+blockchain+imran+bashir&ots=dwbRn3gESK&sig=PfB7xH2wfZEOPO3wdNh8-sfvK84

Bitcoin Block Reward Halving Countdown. (n.d.). Retrieved September 27, 2024, from https://www.bitcoinblockhalf.com/

Bitcoin Halving: What It Is and Why It Matters for Crypto Investors. (n.d.). Retrieved September 27, 2024, from https://www.investopedia.com/bitcoin-halving-4843769

Blockchain, S. K.-T. J. of T. B., & 2022. (2020). Auditing Tokenomics: A Case Study and Lessons from Auditing a Stablecoin Project.

Jbba.Scholasticahq.Com. https://jbba.scholasticahq.com/article/34696.pdf

CoinMarketCap. (n.d.). *Total Value Locked (TVL) Definition CoinMarketCap.* Retrieved July 7, 2023, from https://coinmarketcap.com/alexandria/glossary/total-value-locked-tvl

Cong, L., Li, Y., Studies, N. W.-T. R. of F., & 2021. (2020). Tokenomics: Dynamic adoption and valuation. *Academic.Oup.Com.* https://academic.oup.com/rfs/article-abstract/34/3/1105/5891182

Cryptex Finance. (n.d.). Retrieved September 29, 2023, from https://cryptex.finance/

Crypto token supplies explained: Circulating, maximum and total supply. (n.d.). Retrieved September 23, 2024, from https://cointelegraph.com/explained/crypto-token-supplies-explained-circulating-maximum-and-total-supply

Cryptocurrency Prices, Charts, and Crypto Market Cap CoinGecko. (n.d.). Retrieved September 22, 2024, from https://www.coingecko.com/

Cryptocurrency Prices, Charts And Market Capitalizations CoinMarketCap. (n.d.). Retrieved September 22, 2024, from https://coinmarketcap.com/

EIP-1559: Fee market change for ETH 1.0 chain. (n.d.). Retrieved September 27, 2024, from https://eips.ethereum.org/EIPS/eip-1559

Fellowship of Ethereum Magicians. (n.d.). *EIP-1238: Non-Transferable Tokens—Tokens—Fellowship of Ethereum Magicians.* Retrieved September 8, 2022, from https://ethereum-magicians.org/t/eip-1238-non-transferable-tokens/9044

Gandal, N., & Hałaburda, H. (2014). A Service of zbw Competition in the cryptocurrency market. *Bank of Canada.* http://hdl.handle.net/10419/103022www.econstor.eu

How is the Immutable X Team involved in the IMX Token distribution?—Immutable. (n.d.). Retrieved October 8, 2024, from https://support.immutable.com/hc/en-us/articles/9439196375823-

How-is-the-Immutable-X-Team-involved-in-the-IMX-Token-distribution

How to choose a vesting and lockup schedule for crypto tokens. (n.d.). Retrieved October 8, 2024, from https://www.liquifi.finance/post/what-vesting-and-lockup-schedule-should-i-use

Immutable (IMX) Token Unlocks and Vesting: Schedule and Tokenomics CryptoRank.io. (n.d.). Retrieved October 9, 2024, from https://cryptorank.io/price/immutable-x/vesting

Immutable's Tokenomics and Staking Principles Immutable Blog. (n.d.). Retrieved June 15, 2025, from https://www.immutable.com/blog/immutables-tokenomics-and-staking-principles

Introducing UNI. (n.d.). Retrieved October 8, 2024, from https://blog.uniswap.org/uni

Liquifi. (n.d.). *Token Vesting and Allocations Industry Benchmarks.* Retrieved September 21, 2024, from https://www.liquifi.finance/post/token-vesting-and-allocation-benchmarks

PixelPlex. (n.d.). *Best Token Distribution Models: What Are They? PixelPlex.* Retrieved March 25, 2023, from https://pixelplex.io/blog/best-token-distribution-models/

Standard Allocation: Trends and Industry. (n.d.). Retrieved June 14, 2025, from https://insights.unlocks.app/tokenunlocks-standard-allocation/

Steis, M. (2021, February 21). *What is the Secret to Building Valuable Tokens? Outlier Ventures.* Medium. https://outlierventures.io/research/what-is-the-secret-to-building-valuable-tokens/

Tezos. (n.d.). *Tezos Improvement Process (TZIP) Tezos Wiki.* Retrieved September 8, 2022, from https://wiki.tezos.com/learn/governance/tezos-improvement-process-tzip

Tokenomics $IMX Token. (n.d.). Retrieved October 8, 2024, from https://imx.community/tokenomics

Tokenomics: The Crypto Shift of Blockchains, ICOs, and Tokens—Sean Au, Thomas Power—Google Books. (n.d.). Retrieved September 21, 2024, from https://books.google.com/books?hl=en&lr=&id=hCdyDwAAQBAJ&oi=fnd&pg=PP1&dq=Sean+Au+and+Thomas+Power+The++vs,+ICOs,+and+Tokens&ots=j_KbGmCCan&sig=fIEDzIa5YN5srn8QUIaC167EPZE#v=onepage&q=Sean%20Au%20and%20Thomas%20Power%20The%20%20vs%2C%20ICOs%2C%20and%20Tokens&f=false

What is the Secret to Building Valuable Tokens? Part 2—Outlier Ventures. (n.d.). Retrieved September 21, 2024, from https://outlierventures.io/research/what-is-the-secret-to-building-valuable-tokens-part-2/

What is tokenomics?—Tokenomics [Book]. (n.d.). Retrieved September 21, 2024, from https://www.oreilly.com/library/view/tokenomics/9781789136326/ch01s02.html

Chapter 9—Financial Metrics

Trade BTCUSDT Bybit Perpetual Contracts. (n.d.). Retrieved October 14, 2024, from https://www.bybit.com/trade/usdt/BTCUSDT

A Beginner's Guide To The Bitcoin Stock-To-Flow Model. (n.d.). Retrieved November 3, 2024, from https://www.ccn.com/education/a-beginners-guide-to-the-bitcoin-stock-to-flow-model/

A Guide to Cryptocurrency Fundamental Analysis Binance Academy. (n.d.). Retrieved September 5, 2023, from https://academy.binance.com/en/articles/a-guide-to-cryptocurrency-fundamental-analysis

Aave. (n.d.). Retrieved October 28, 2024, from https://aave.com/

AAVE V3—DefiLlama. (n.d.). Retrieved November 6, 2024, from https://defillama.com/protocol/aave-v3?events=false

All Chains TVL—DefiLlama. (n.d.). Retrieved November 6, 2024, from https://defillama.com/chains

Assessing The Teams Behind Cryptocurrencies And Blockchain Projects by Team Luno Luno Publication Medium. (n.d.). Retrieved April 7, 2023, from https://medium.com/luno/assessing-the-teams-behind-cryptocurrencies-and-blockchain-projects-b8ccfae455fa

Avalanche: Create Without Limits dApp Platform. (n.d.). Retrieved October 13, 2024, from https://www.avax.network/

Avalanche price today, AVAX to USD live price, marketcap and chart CoinMarketCap. (n.d.). Retrieved October 13, 2024, from https://coinmarketcap.com/currencies/avalanche/

Bitcoin Goes Beast Mode—Mining Power Tops 1 Zetahash in First-Ever Surge. (n.d.). Retrieved June 15, 2025, from https://www.newsbtc.com/news/bitcoin/bitcoin-goes-beast-mode-mining-power-tops-1-zetahash-in-first-ever-surge/

Bitcoin Realized Cap HODL Waves—An Essential Tool for Studying Supply Dynamics (On-chain 101)—YouTube. (n.d.). Retrieved December 21, 2023, from https://www.youtube.com/watch?v=8rY8GAvR2Ts

BTC: Active Addresses—Glassnode Studio. (n.d.). Retrieved November 6, 2024, from https://studio.glassnode.com/metrics?a=BTC&category=&chartStyle=line&m=addresses.ActiveCount

BTC: Addresses with Balance ≥ 10k—Glassnode Studio. (n.d.). Retrieved November 6, 2024, from https://studio.glassnode.com/metrics?a=BTC&category=Addresses&m=addresses.Min10KCount&s=1518786086&u=1702857600&zoom=

BTC: Inflation Rate—Glassnode Studio. (n.d.). Retrieved November 6, 2024, from https://studio.glassnode.com/metrics?a=BTC&category=&m=supply.InflationRate

BTC: Net Unrealized Profit/Loss (NUPL)—Glassnode Studio. (n.d.). Retrieved November 6, 2024, from https://studio.glassnode.com/metrics?a=BTC&category=&m=indicators.NetUnrealizedProfitLoss&s=1452251288&u=1702857600&zoom=

BTC: NVT Signal—Glassnode Studio. (n.d.). Retrieved November 2, 2024, from https://studio.glassnode.com/metrics?a=BTC&ema=

0&m=indicators.Nvts&mAvg=7&mMedian=0&mScl=log&s=1264806612&u=1730505600&zoom=

BTC: Percent Supply in Profit—Glassnode Studio. (n.d.). Retrieved November 6, 2024, from https://studio.glassnode.com/metrics?a=BTC&m=supply.ProfitRelative&utm_source=gn_insights&utm_medium=insights_woc&utm_campaign=woc_25_2024

BTC: Realized Cap—Glassnode Studio. (n.d.). Retrieved November 6, 2024, from https://studio.glassnode.com/metrics?a=BTC&category=&m=market.MarketcapRealizedUsd

BTC: Stock-to-Flow Deflection—Glassnode Studio. (n.d.). Retrieved November 2, 2024, from https://studio.glassnode.com/metrics?a=BTC&category=Market+Indicators&ema=0&m=indicators.StockToFlowDeflection&mAvg=14&mMedian=0&mScl=log

BTC: Stock-to-Flow Ratio—Glassnode Studio. (n.d.). Retrieved October 15, 2024, from https://studio.glassnode.com/metrics?a=BTC&m=indicators.StockToFlowRatio

BTC: Transaction Count—Glassnode Studio. (n.d.). Retrieved November 6, 2024, from https://studio.glassnode.com/metrics?a=BTC&category=Transactions&chartStyle=column&ema=0&m=transactions.Count&mAvg=6&mMedian=0&resolution=1month

BTC: Transfer Volume (Total)—Glassnode Studio. (n.d.). Retrieved November 6, 2024, from https://studio.glassnode.com/metrics?a=BTC&category=Transactions&m=transactions.TransfersVolumeSum&mScl=log&pScl=log

Can On-chain Data Help Us Spot Fake Exchange Trading Volumes?—Chainalysis. (n.d.). Retrieved October 17, 2024, from https://www.chainalysis.com/blog/fake-trade-volume-cryptocurrency-exchanges/

Chainlink: The Industry-Standard Web3 Services Platform. (n.d.). Retrieved October 13, 2024, from https://chain.link/

Compound Finance. (n.d.). Retrieved January 27, 2024, from https://compound.finance/

Compound price today, COMP to USD live price, marketcap and chart CoinMarketCap. (n.d.). Retrieved January 27, 2024, from https://coinmarketcap.com/currencies/compound/

Cryptex Finance. (n.d.). Retrieved September 29, 2023, from https://cryptex.finance/

CRYPTOCAP:TOTAL Chart Image by paulgarvey — TradingView. (n.d.). Retrieved November 6, 2024, from https://www.tradingview.com/x/vgCedYet/

CryptoQuant Actionable On-chain market intelligence. (n.d.). Retrieved December 26, 2023, from https://cryptoquant.com/

CryptoQuant On-Chain Actionable Insights. (n.d.). Retrieved June 15, 2025, from https://cryptoquant.com/

DefiLlama—DeFi Dashboard. (n.d.). Retrieved November 6, 2024, from https://defillama.com/

Definition of crypto onchain metrics PCMag. (n.d.). Retrieved December 15, 2023, from https://www.pcmag.com/encyclopedia/term/crypto-onchain-metrics

Dune Analytics. (n.d.). Retrieved December 15, 2023, from https://dune.com/home

ETH: ETH 2.0 Total Value Staked—Glassnode Studio. (n.d.). Retrieved November 6, 2024, from https://studio.glassnode.com/metrics?a=ETH&category=&m=eth2.StakingTotalVolumeSum

ETH: Hash Rate—Glassnode Studio. (n.d.). Retrieved November 2, 2024, from https://studio.glassnode.com/metrics?a=ETH&category=&ema=0&m=mining.HashRateMean&mAvg=14&mMedian=0&mScl=log

Ethereum—DefiLlama. (n.d.). Retrieved November 6, 2024, from https://defillama.com/chain/Ethereum?chainTokenMcap=true

Explained: What Is a Fair Launch Crypto? Bybit Learn. (n.d.). Retrieved September 29, 2023, from https://learn.bybit.com/crypto/what-is-a-fair-launch-crypto/

Fees Uniswap. (n.d.). Retrieved October 26, 2024, from https://docs.uniswap.org/contracts/v2/concepts/advanced-topics/fees

Fees—DefiLlama. (n.d.). Retrieved November 6, 2024, from https://defillama.com/fees

Glassnode Studio—On-Chain Market Intelligence. (n.d.-a). Retrieved November 6, 2024, from https://studio.glassnode.com/workbench/e9e05fce-ce4b-4138-5736-5d2bfadfdf94

Glassnode Studio—On-Chain Market Intelligence. (n.d.-b). Retrieved December 15, 2023, from https://studio.glassnode.com/home

Glassnode Studio—On-Chain Market Intelligence—BTC: Percent Supply in Profit. (n.d.). Retrieved October 16, 2024, from https://studio.glassnode.com/metrics?a=BTC&m=supply.ProfitRelative&s=1230940800&u=1729036800&utm_campaign=woc_25_2024&utm_medium=insights_woc&utm_source=gn_insights&zoom=

Hash Rate: How It Works and How to Measure. (n.d.). Retrieved January 20, 2024, from https://www.investopedia.com/hash-rate-6746261

Home Bitcoin Magazine Pro. (n.d.). Retrieved November 3, 2024, from https://www.bitcoinmagazinepro.com/

Home—Coin Metrics. (n.d.). Retrieved June 15, 2025, from https://coinmetrics.io/

How to Measure Crypto Liquidity. (n.d.). Retrieved October 14, 2024, from https://calebandbrown.com/blog/crypto-liquidity/

How to track DeFi protocol fees and revenues—DL News. (n.d.). Retrieved October 25, 2024, from https://www.dlnews.com/articles/llama-u/how-to-track-defi-protocol-fees-and-revenues-with-defillama/

JustLend DAO JustLend DAO is the first official lending platform on TRON where users can borrow, lend, deposit assets and earn interests. (n.d.). Retrieved October 28, 2024, from https://justlend.org/

Lending Kamino Finance. (n.d.). Retrieved October 28, 2024, from https://app.kamino.finance/

Lido—DefiLlama. (n.d.). Retrieved October 26, 2024, from https://defillama.com/protocol/lido?tvl=false&mcap=false&fees=true&revenue=true&events=false&groupBy=daily

Lido Finance Review 2024: Largest ETH Liquid Staking Platform. (n.d.). Retrieved October 25, 2024, from https://coinbureau.com/review/lido-finance-review/

Lido Liquid Staking. (n.d.). Retrieved October 26, 2024, from https://lido.fi/

Litecoin—Open source P2P digital currency. (n.d.). Retrieved October 13, 2024, from https://litecoin.org/

Market Cap vs Realized Cap. (n.d.). Retrieved October 15, 2024, from https://docs.amberdata.io/docs/market-cap-vs-realized-cap

MVRV Ratio—Glassnode Academy. (n.d.). Retrieved December 20, 2023, from https://academy.glassnode.com/market/mvrv/mvrv-ratio

Nansen Onchain Insights for Crypto Investors & Teams. (n.d.). Retrieved December 15, 2023, from https://www.nansen.ai/

Opinion: The Importance of Revenue/Fee Analysis in Cryptocurrencies by Caner Can Medium. (n.d.). Retrieved October 25, 2024, from https://medium.com/@skatistic888/opinion-the-importance-of-revenue-fee-analysis-in-cryptocurrencies-068baec58e7a

Over 75% of Bitcoin's On-Chain Volume Doesn't Change Hands. (n.d.). Retrieved October 17, 2024, from https://insights.glassnode.com/true-bitcoin-volume/

PlanB (@100trillionUSD) / X. (n.d.). Retrieved November 3, 2024, from https://x.com/100trillionUSD

Polkadot price today, DOT to USD live price, marketcap and chart CoinMarketCap. (n.d.). Retrieved October 13, 2024, from https://coinmarketcap.com/currencies/polkadot-new/

Realized Cap HODL Waves—Glassnode Academy. (n.d.). Retrieved December 21, 2023, from https://academy.glassnode.com/supply/hodl/realized-cap-hodl-waves

SECRETS To Finding a 100x Token Sale!!—YouTube. (n.d.). Retrieved September 29, 2023, from https://www.youtube.com/watch?v=4c4wlSgsQ2A

Stock-to-Flow Model BM Pro. (n.d.). Retrieved November 3, 2024, from https://www.bitcoinmagazinepro.com/charts/stock-to-flow-model/

Stylianou, K., Economics, N. C.-J. of C. L. &, & 2020. (n.d.). The size of the crypto economy: Calculating market shares of cryptoassets, exchanges and mining pools. *Academic.Oup.ComK Stylianou, N CarterJournal of Competition Law & Economics, 2020, academic.Oup.Com.* https://doi.org/10.1093/joclec/nhaa016

The Beacon Chain ethereum.org. (n.d.). Retrieved July 3, 2023, from https://ethereum.org/en/roadmap/beacon-chain/

Token Terminal Dashboard. (n.d.). Retrieved November 6, 2024, from https://tokenterminal.com/terminal

Uniswap Trade crypto and NFTs safely on the top DeFi platform. (n.d.). Retrieved October 20, 2024, from https://app.uniswap.org/

Valuing Crypto Assets: Navigating The New Financial Frontier. (n.d.). Retrieved October 14, 2024, from https://www.forbes.com/sites/roomykhan/2024/06/29/valuing-crypto-assets-navigating-the-new-financial-frontier/

Venus Protocol. (n.d.). Retrieved October 28, 2024, from https://venus.io/

Volume (Market Pair, Cryptoasset, Exchange, Aggregate)—CoinMarketCap. (n.d.). Retrieved October 17, 2024, from https://support.coinmarketcap.com/hc/en-us/articles/360043395912-Volume-Market-Pair-Cryptoasset-Exchange-Aggregate

Web3 Operating Metrics: Fees, Revenue, and Profitability of Protocols. (n.d.). Retrieved October 26, 2024, from https://www.linkedin.com/

pulse/web3-operating-metrics-fees-revenue-profitability-protocols-kumar-

Yearn Finance. (n.d.). Retrieved January 27, 2024, from https://yearn.fi/

Chapter 10—Project Team

15 ways crypto companies can be more transparent with customers. (n.d.). Retrieved May 21, 2023, from https://cointelegraph.com/innovation-circle/15-ways-crypto-companies-can-be-more-transparent-with-customers

A step-by-step framework for evaluating crypto projects. (n.d.). Retrieved July 29, 2023, from https://cointelegraph.com/news/a-step-by-step-framework-to-evaluating-crypto-projects

Assessing The Teams Behind Cryptocurrencies And Blockchain Projects by Team Luno Luno Publication Medium. (n.d.). Retrieved April 7, 2023, from https://medium.com/luno/assessing-the-teams-behind-cryptocurrencies-and-blockchain-projects-b8ccfae455fa

Catalini, C., ACM, J. G.-C. of the, & 2020. (2020). Some simple economics of the blockchain. *Dl.Acm.Org*. https://dl.acm.org/doi/fullHtml/10.1145/3359552

Dewasiri, N., Karunarathne, K., ... S. M.-... the S. of, & 2023. (2023). Fusion of Artificial Intelligence and Blockchain in the Banking Industry: Current Application, Adoption, and Future Challenges. *Emerald.Com*, 293–307. https://doi.org/10.1108/978-1-80262-277-520231021

Dorfleitner, G., & Braun, D. (2019). *Fintech, Digitalization and Blockchain: Possible Applications for Green Finance*. 207–237. https://doi.org/10.1007/978-3-030-22510-0_9

Eskandari, S., Moosavi, S., & Clark, J. (2020). SoK: Transparent Dishonesty: Front-Running Attacks on Blockchain. *Lecture Notes in Computer Science (Including Subseries Lecture Notes in Artificial*

Intelligence and Lecture Notes in Bioinformatics), 11599 LNCS, 170–189. https://doi.org/10.1007/978-3-030-43725-1_13

Ethereum: About LinkedIn. (n.d.). Retrieved November 15, 2024, from https://www.linkedin.com/company/ethereum/about/

Exit scammers run off with $660 million in ICO earnings TechCrunch. (n.d.). Retrieved November 11, 2024, from https://techcrunch.com/2018/04/13/exit-scammers-run-off-with-660-million-in-ico-earnings/?guccounter=1&guce_referrer=aHR0cHM6Ly93d3cuZ29vZ2xlLmNvbS8&guce_referrer_sig=AQAAACtX5mBmXxM-LnsPnkC1WOps3ERcpzVUZFnL7k_R-E1vsWzYTjUHaK7ugKOUiiyddZ-w6OkUbi2BNl7R7kfZrvKVm2qBKtZWUovJh68roCzR6naR6oqNvfqMGQ4gDyLUjkV3BgscQGUWuohArO6y84jdGZ1wt5T7wFymQ4obgVGI

Faria, I. (2021). When tales of money fail: the importance of price, trust, and sociality for cryptocurrency users. https://doi.org/10.1080/17530350.2021.1974070, *15*(1), 81–92. https://doi.org/10.1080/17530350.2021.1974070

GitHub—paritytech/polkadot-sdk: The Parity Polkadot Blockchain SDK. (n.d.). Retrieved November 13, 2024, from https://github.com/paritytech/polkadot-sdk

LinkedIn: Log In or Sign Up. (n.d.). Retrieved April 7, 2023, from https://www.linkedin.com/home

LoopX pulls exit scam, walks away with $4.5m in investor cryptocurrency ZDNET. (n.d.). Retrieved November 11, 2024, from https://www.zdnet.com/article/loopx-pulls-exit-scam-walks-away-with-4-5m-in-investor-funds/

Tezel, A., Papadonikolaki, E., Yitmen, I., & Bolpagni, M. (2022). Blockchain Opportunities and Issues in the Built Environment: Perspectives on Trust, Transparency and Cybersecurity. *Structural Integrity, 20,* 569–588. https://doi.org/10.1007/978-3-030-82430-3_24

Why a Crypto Project's Team Is Critically Important—American Institute for Crypto Investors. (n.d.). Retrieved April 7, 2023, from https://

aicinvestors.com/article/why-a-crypto-projects-team-is-critically-important/

Xu, W., Wang, T., Chen, R., & Zhao, J. L. (2021). Prediction of initial coin offering success based on team knowledge and expert evaluation. *Decision Support Systems, 147,* 113574. https://doi.org/10.1016/J.DSS.2021.113574

Chapter 11—Project Roadmap

6 Blockchain Use Cases in 2023: Learn Blockchain Today—Berkeley Boot Camps. (n.d.). Retrieved August 5, 2023, from https://bootcamp.berkeley.edu/blog/blockchain-use-cases/

6 Ways To Evaluate a Crypto Project .cult by Honeypot. (n.d.). Retrieved February 19, 2023, from https://cult.honeypot.io/reads/6-ways-to-evaluate-a-crypto-project/

A Complete Roadmap to Blockchain Development Engineering Education (EngEd) Program Section. (n.d.). Retrieved July 29, 2023, from https://www.section.io/engineering-education/the-complete-roadmap-to-blockchain-development/

A step-by-step framework for evaluating crypto projects. (n.d.). Retrieved April 7, 2023, from https://cointelegraph.com/news/a-step-by-step-framework-to-evaluating-crypto-projects

Best Practices For Creating A Blockchain Roadmap—101 Blockchains. (n.d.). Retrieved July 29, 2023, from https://101blockchains.com/blockchain-roadmap/

Blockchain Developer Roadmap: Learn to become a blockchain developer. (n.d.). Retrieved July 29, 2023, from https://roadmap.sh/blockchain

Blockchain Development Roadmap > 7 Great Questions to Consider. (n.d.). Retrieved July 29, 2023, from https://chainwave.io/blockchain-development-roadmap/

BNB Chain—Build Web3 dApps on the Most Popular Blockchain. (n.d.). Retrieved August 12, 2023, from https://www.bnbchain.org/en

BNB Chain 2024 Outlook—The "One BNB" Multi-chain Paradigm—BNB Chain Blog. (n.d.). Retrieved November 22, 2024, from https://www.bnbchain.org/en/blog/bnb-chain-2024-tech-roadmap

BNB Chain Tech Roadmap 2023. (n.d.). Retrieved August 12, 2023, from https://www.bnbchain.org/en/blog/bnb-chain-tech-roadmap-2023/

Clavin, J., Duan, S., Zhang, H., Janeja, V. P., Joshi, K. P., Yesha, Y., Erickson, L. C., & Li, J. D. (2020). Blockchains for government: Use cases and challenges. *Digital Government: Research and Practice, 1*(3). https://doi.org/10.1145/3427097

Crypto Roadmap Design 101: The Guide. (n.d.). Retrieved November 23, 2024, from https://www.growthchain.io/blog/crypto-roadmap

ESSENTIAL ELEMENTS OF A STRONG CRYPTO ROADMAP — CRYPTORSY BLOG. (n.d.). Retrieved July 29, 2023, from https://cryptorsy.io/blog/roadmap

Ethereum 2.0 Updates: Ethereum PoS Roadmap Gemini. (n.d.). Retrieved July 30, 2023, from https://www.gemini.com/cryptopedia/ethereum-2-0-blockchain-roadmap-proof-of-stake-pos#section-serenity-phase-0-beacon-chain-and-po-s-framework

Ethereum Roadmap. (n.d.). Retrieved November 22, 2024, from https://ethroadmap.com/

Filecoin Grants. (n.d.). Retrieved August 19, 2023, from https://grants.filecoin.io/#learnmore

FVM Filecoin Virtual Machine. (n.d.). Retrieved November 23, 2024, from https://fvm.filecoin.io/

Goals vs milestones—Definitions, meanings, differences Termscompared. (n.d.). Retrieved August 11, 2023, from https://www.termscompared.com/goals-vs-milestones/

How to Create Compelling Product Roadmaps 280 Group. (n.d.). Retrieved July 29, 2023, from https://280group.com/product-management-blog/compelling-product-roadmaps-tips-best-practices/

How To Define & Track Project Milestones (Complete Guide). (n.d.). Retrieved August 14, 2023, from https://toggl.com/blog/project-milestones

How to distinguish a good crypto project from a bad one. (n.d.). Retrieved July 29, 2023, from https://cointelegraph.com/innovation-circle/how-to-distinguish-a-good-crypto-project-from-a-bad-one

How to Evaluate a Roadmap Before Investing in a Crypto Project. (n.d.). Retrieved July 29, 2023, from https://cryptoadventure.com/how-to-evaluate-a-roadmap-before-investing-in-a-crypto-project/

How to Write and Format a White Paper (With Examples). (n.d.). Retrieved July 30, 2023, from https://www.foleon.com/topics/how-to-write-and-format-a-white-paper

Introducing BNB Chain: The Evolution of Binance Smart Chain Binance Blog. (n.d.). Retrieved August 12, 2023, from https://www.binance.com/en/blog/ecosystem/introducing-bnb-chain-the-evolution-of-binance-smart-chain-421499824684903436

IT Roadmaps Explained with Examples—BMC Software Blogs. (n.d.). Retrieved July 29, 2023, from https://www.bmc.com/blogs/it-roadmaps/

K. Blaine Lawlor. (n.d.). Smart goals: How the application of smart goals can contribute to achievement of student learning outcomes. *Absel-Ojs-Ttu.Tdl.Org.* Retrieved August 11, 2023, from https://absel-ojs-ttu.tdl.org/absel/article/view/90

Management, O. O.-B. J. of H., & 2017. (2017). Why written objectives need to be really SMART. *Magonlinelibrary.Com, 23*(7), 324–336. https://doi.org/10.12968/bjhc.2017.23.7.324

Migrate to POL—Polygon Knowledge Layer. (n.d.). Retrieved June 16, 2025, from https://docs.polygon.technology/pos/get-started/matic-to-pol/

Moonbeam DeFi Ecosystem on Polkadot Moonbeam Network. (n.d.). Retrieved August 5, 2023, from https://moonbeam.network/networks/moonbeam/defi/

Networks—Filecoin Docs. (n.d.). Retrieved August 19, 2023, from https://docs.filecoin.io/basics/what-is-filecoin/networks/

opBNB: Scaling Economically for Developers—BNB Chain Blog. (n.d.). Retrieved June 16, 2025, from https://www.bnbchain.org/en/blog/opbnb-scaling-economically-for-developers?utm_source=chatgpt.com

Parachain Crowdloans · Polkadot Wiki. (n.d.). Retrieved July 30, 2023, from https://wiki.polkadot.network/docs/learn-crowdloans

PathDAO—Bringing millions to the metaverse. (n.d.). Retrieved August 3, 2023, from https://pathdao.io/

Polygon 2.0—One-Pager.pdf—Google Drive. (n.d.). Retrieved August 10, 2023, from https://drive.google.com/file/d/1ZhutWNWDtEmmSxpMfHhjf1M71ZXeTrWA/view?pli=1

Polygon 2.0: Polygon PoS -> ZK L2. (n.d.). Retrieved August 11, 2023, from https://polygon.technology/blog/polygon-2-0-polygon-pos-zk-layer-2

Polygon 2.0 Roadmap. (n.d.). Retrieved August 10, 2023, from https://polygon.technology/roadmap

Project roadmap or token price — Which is most important? (n.d.). Retrieved July 29, 2023, from https://cointelegraph.com/news/project-roadmap-or-token-price-which-is-most-important

Project roadmap: What it is and why it is important—Twproject: project management software,resource management, time tracking, planning, Gantt, kanban. (n.d.). Retrieved July 29, 2023, from https://twproject.com/blog/project-roadmap-important/

Protocol Architecture One pager.pdf—Google Drive. (n.d.). Retrieved August 11, 2023, from https://drive.google.com/file/d/1frnn7VVBTMbgIx8wQzhgp-lXGdkEBFwf/view

Roadmap—Filecoin Docs. (n.d.). Retrieved August 12, 2023, from https://docs.filecoin.io/smart-contracts/fundamentals/roadmap/

Roadmapping Starter Guide: Roadmaps Made Easy With Templates Aha! software. (n.d.). Retrieved July 29, 2023, from https://www.aha.io/roadmapping/guide/roadmap/ultimate-guide

Roadmaps—A Complete Guide with Examples, Tools & Tutorials. (n.d.). Retrieved July 29, 2023, from https://www.officetimeline.com/roadmaps

Setting Goals and Developing Specific, Measurable, Achievable, Relevant, and Time-bound Objectives. (n.d.). Retrieved December 8, 2023, from https://www.samhsa.gov/sites/default/files/nc-smart-goals-fact-sheet.pdf

The Filecoin Virtual Machine has Arrived Filecoin Foundation. (n.d.). Retrieved November 23, 2024, from https://www.fil.org/blog/the-filecoin-virtual-machine-has-arrived

What are Business Roadmaps? Definitions and Examples Indeed.com. (n.d.). Retrieved July 29, 2023, from https://www.indeed.com/career-advice/career-development/roadmap-examples

Whitepaper—POL: One token for all Polygon chains. (n.d.). Retrieved August 9, 2023, from https://polygon.technology/papers/pol-whitepaper

Chapter 12—Project Codebase

5 Best Programming Languages for Blockchain Development. (n.d.). Retrieved February 27, 2023, from https://blaize.tech/article-type/5-best-programming-languages-for-blockchain-development/

Aave. (n.d.). Retrieved September 7, 2024, from https://aave.com/

Aave GitHub Repositories. (n.d.). Retrieved September 9, 2024, from https://github.com/orgs/aave/repositories

Advantages of Functional Programming for Blockchain Protocols HackerNoon. (n.d.). Retrieved March 4, 2023, from `https://hackernoon.com/advantages-of-functional-programming-for-blockchain-protocols-1ca2d4ac1033`

Advantages Of Open Source & Closed Source In Cryptocurrency by Damilola Stephen Debel AirGap Medium. (n.d.). Retrieved August 26, 2022, from `https://medium.com/airgap-it/advantages-of-open-source-closed-source-in-cryptocurrency-e14abab57a24`

Aergo—The Blockchain for the WORLD. (n.d.). Retrieved August 31, 2024, from `https://www.aergo.io/`

æternity—Blockchain for scalable, secure, and decentralized æpps. (n.d.). Retrieved August 31, 2024, from `https://aeternity.com/`

Appendix Choose a License. (n.d.). Retrieved August 30, 2024, from `https://choosealicense.com/appendix/`

Barnaby, C., Coblenz, M., Etzel, T., Kanal, E., Sunshine, J., Myers, B., & Aldrich, J. (n.d.). Fact: A flexible, constant-time programming language. *Ieeexplore.Ieee.Org.* Retrieved August 25, 2022, from `https://ieeexplore.ieee.org/abstract/document/8077809/`

Best Practices for a Smart Contract Audit Rather Labs Blog. (n.d.). Retrieved September 6, 2024, from `https://www.ratherlabs.com/blog/best-practices-for-a-smart-contract-audit`

Binance audit by Hacken. (n.d.). Retrieved September 6, 2024, from `https://audits.hacken.io/binance/por-binance-por-code-audit-feb2023/`

Bitbucket Git solution for teams using Jira. (n.d.). Retrieved August 30, 2024, from `https://bitbucket.org/product/`

Bitcoin—Open source P2P money. (n.d.). Retrieved August 31, 2024, from `https://bitcoin.org/en/`

Bitcoin GitHub Repositories. (n.d.). Retrieved September 9, 2024, from `https://github.com/orgs/bitcoin/repositories`

BitMart—Cryptocurrency Exchange Buy & sell Bitcoin, Ethereum, Tether instantly. (n.d.). Retrieved September 5, 2024, from https://www.bitmart.com/en-US

Blockchain Security Services Company—Web3, Crypto, DeFi Hacken. (n.d.). Retrieved September 6, 2024, from https://hacken.io/

BNB Chain Bridge Cross-Chain Transfer. (n.d.). Retrieved September 5, 2024, from https://www.bnbchain.org/en/bnb-chain-bridge

Bug Bounty Program List Bugcrowd. (n.d.). Retrieved September 7, 2024, from https://www.bugcrowd.com/bug-bounty-list/

Bug Bounty Programs: Most Rewarding Web3 Bug Bounties of 2024 Immunefi. (n.d.). Retrieved September 7, 2024, from https://immunefi.com/bug-bounty/

Buy, sell & trade Ethereum and other top tokens on Uniswap. (n.d.). Retrieved August 31, 2024, from https://app.uniswap.org/swap

C# Guide—.NET managed language Microsoft Learn. (n.d.). Retrieved August 31, 2024, from https://learn.microsoft.com/en-us/dotnet/csharp/

C Plus Plus. (n.d.). Retrieved August 31, 2024, from https://cplusplus.com/

C Programming Language Tutorial—GeeksforGeeks. (n.d.). Retrieved August 31, 2024, from https://www.geeksforgeeks.org/c-programming-language/

CertiK—Securing The Web3 World. (n.d.). Retrieved September 6, 2024, from https://www.certik.com/

CertiK Bug Bounty Leaderboard. (n.d.). Retrieved September 7, 2024, from https://skynet.certik.com/leaderboards/bug-bounty

CertiK Skynet—Web3 Security, Due Diligence and Insights. (n.d.). Retrieved September 6, 2024, from https://skynet.certik.com/

Choose an open source license Choose a License. (n.d.). Retrieved August 30, 2024, from https://choosealicense.com/

Coblenz, M., Aldrich, J., Myers, B. A., Sunshine, J., & Sun, J. (2018). Interdisciplinary Programming Language Design. *Proceedings of the 2018*

ACM SIGPLAN International Symposium on New Ideas, New Paradigms, and Reflections on Programming and Software, 14. https://doi.org/10.1145/3276954

Coincheck—The easiest way to buy and sell Bitcoin and cryptocurrency. Coincheck. (n.d.). Retrieved September 5, 2024, from https://coincheck.com/

Combining C# with Blockchain for Development TechnoBrains. (n.d.). Retrieved August 31, 2024, from https://technobrains.io/the-reasons-for-combining-c-with-blockchain-for-development/

Commit Activity · bitcoin/bitcoin · GitHub. (n.d.). Retrieved September 1, 2024, from https://github.com/bitcoin/bitcoin/graphs/commit-activity

Commit Activity · ethereum/solidity · GitHub. (n.d.). Retrieved September 1, 2024, from https://github.com/ethereum/solidity/graphs/commit-activity

Commit Activity · moonbeam-foundation/moonbeam · GitHub. (n.d.). Retrieved September 1, 2024, from https://github.com/moonbeam-foundation/moonbeam/graphs/commit-activity

Compound. (n.d.). Retrieved August 31, 2024, from https://compound.finance/

Consensys—A complete suite of trusted products to build anything in web3. (n.d.). Retrieved August 31, 2024, from https://consensys.io/

Contributing to Open-Source Crypto Projects by Mark Mathis Coinmonks Medium. (n.d.). Retrieved August 27, 2022, from https://medium.com/coinmonks/contributing-to-open-source-crypto-projects-7532273062a

Crypto Bug Bounty Programs 2024 HackenProof. (n.d.). Retrieved September 7, 2024, from https://hackenproof.com/programs

Dannen, C. (2017). *Introducing Ethereum and solidity*. https://link.springer.com/content/pdf/bfm%253A978-1-4842-2535-6%252F1.pdf

Development—Rchain network. (n.d.). Retrieved August 31, 2024, from https://rholang.io/

Documentation page for Rholang 🎓—Rchain network. (n.d.). Retrieved March 3, 2023, from https://rholang.io/

Elements elementsproject.org. (n.d.). Retrieved August 31, 2024, from https://elementsproject.org/

EOS Network—Home. (n.d.). Retrieved August 31, 2024, from https://eosnetwork.com/

erlang-and-elixir-blockchain-tech-deep-dive. (n.d.). Retrieved August 31, 2024, from https://www.erlang-solutions.com/blog/erlang-and-elixir-blockchain-tech-deep-dive/

Ethereum Virtual Machine (EVM) ethereum.org. (n.d.). Retrieved August 31, 2024, from https://ethereum.org/en/developers/docs/evm/

Fantom. (n.d.). Retrieved August 31, 2024, from https://fantom.foundation/

GitHub Desktop Simple collaboration from your desktop · GitHub. (n.d.). Retrieved August 30, 2024, from https://github.com/apps/desktop

Global Payments & Financial Solutions for Businesses Ripple. (n.d.). Retrieved August 31, 2024, from https://ripple.com/

Haskell Language. (n.d.). Retrieved August 31, 2024, from https://www.haskell.org/

Helium—Introducing The People's Network. (n.d.). Retrieved August 31, 2024, from https://www.helium.com/

Home cardano.org Cardano. (n.d.). Retrieved August 31, 2024, from https://cardano.org/

Home ethereum.org. (n.d.). Retrieved August 31, 2024, from https://ethereum.org/en/

Home go-ethereum. (n.d.). Retrieved August 31, 2024, from https://geth.ethereum.org/

Home Internet Computer. (n.d.). Retrieved August 31, 2024, from https://internetcomputer.org/

Home IOTA. (n.d.). Retrieved August 31, 2024, from https://www.iota.org/

Home Solidity Programming Language. (n.d.). Retrieved August 31, 2024, from https://soliditylang.org/

Home Tezos. (n.d.). Retrieved August 31, 2024, from https://tezos.com/

How to write, compile & deploy a simple Solidity smart contract. (n.d.). Retrieved August 30, 2024, from https://blockchainblog.substack.com/p/how-to-write-compile-and-deploy-a

Hyperledger Fabric. (n.d.). Retrieved August 31, 2024, from https://www.hyperledger.org/projects/fabric

IBM—United States. (n.d.). Retrieved August 31, 2024, from https://www.ibm.com/us-en?ar=1

Index—Erlang/OTP. (n.d.). Retrieved August 31, 2024, from https://www.erlang.org/

Introduction to Linux Shell and Shell Scripting—GeeksforGeeks. (n.d.). Retrieved September 1, 2024, from https://www.geeksforgeeks.org/introduction-linux-shell-shell-scripting/

Java Oracle. (n.d.). Retrieved August 31, 2024, from https://www.java.com/en/

Kyber Network Liquidity Hub for Crypto Trading and DeFi. (n.d.). Retrieved August 31, 2024, from https://kyber.network/

Learn JavaScript Online—Courses for Beginners—javascript.com. (n.d.). Retrieved August 31, 2024, from https://www.javascript.com/

Lisk. (n.d.). Retrieved August 31, 2024, from https://lisk.com/

Lombardi, R., de Villiers, C., Moscariello, N., & Pizzo, M. (2022). The disruption of blockchain in auditing—A systematic literature review and an agenda for future research. *Accounting, Auditing and Accountability Journal, 35*(7), 1534–1565. https://doi.org/10.1108/AAAJ-10-2020-4992/FULL/HTML

Loom Network—Production-Ready, Multichain Interop Platform for Serious Dapp Developers. (n.d.). Retrieved August 31, 2024, from https://loomx.io/

Magpie XYZ. (n.d.). Retrieved September 5, 2024, from https://www.pendle.magpiexyz.io/stake

Michelson Tezos Developer Documentation. (n.d.). Retrieved August 31, 2024, from https://docs.tezos.com/smart-contracts/languages/michelson

Michelson —The Language of Tezos smart-contracts. (n.d.). Retrieved August 31, 2024, from https://www.michelson.org/

Moonbeam-Foundation GitHub Repositories. (n.d.). Retrieved September 9, 2024, from https://github.com/orgs/moonbeam-foundation/repositories

MultiChain Enterprise blockchain platform. (n.d.). Retrieved September 5, 2024, from https://www.multichain.com/

MySQL. (n.d.). Retrieved August 31, 2024, from https://www.mysql.com/

NEAR Blockchains, Abstracted. (n.d.). Retrieved August 31, 2024, from https://near.org/

Near Protocol GitHub Repositories. (n.d.). Retrieved September 9, 2024, from https://github.com/orgs/near/repositories

Neo Smart Economy. (n.d.). Retrieved August 31, 2024, from https://neo.org/

Open Source Helium Documentation. (n.d.). Retrieved August 31, 2024, from https://docs.helium.com/faq/open-source/

Open Source Licenses: Types and Comparison Snyk. (n.d.). Retrieved August 30, 2024, from https://snyk.io/learn/open-source-licenses/

Parizi, R. M., Amritraj, & Dehghantanha, A. (2018). Smart contract programming languages on blockchains: An empirical evaluation of usability and security. *Lecture Notes in Computer Science (Including Subseries Lecture Notes in Artificial Intelligence and Lecture Notes in Bioinformatics), 10974 LNCS*, 75–91. https://doi.org/10.1007/978-3-319-94478-4_6/FIGURES/6

Polkadot. (n.d.). Retrieved August 31, 2024, from https://polkadot.com/

Polygon Technology. (n.d.). Retrieved August 31, 2024, from https://polygon.technology/

PolyNetwork. (n.d.). Retrieved September 5, 2024, from https://www.poly.network/#/

Pros and cons of programming in Erlang—Sebastian Borrazas. (n.d.). Retrieved March 4, 2023, from http://sborrazas.com/blog/pros-cons-programming-erlang

Quantstamp: Securing the Future of Web3. (n.d.). Retrieved September 6, 2024, from https://quantstamp.com/

RChain · GitHub. (n.d.). Retrieved August 31, 2024, from https://github.com/rchain

Ronin Network. (n.d.). Retrieved September 5, 2024, from https://roninchain.com/

Ruby is a Multi-paradigm programming language by Tech—RubyCademy RubyCademy Medium. (n.d.). Retrieved March 4, 2023, from https://medium.com/rubycademy/ruby-is-a-multi-paradigm-programming-language-49c8bc5fca80

Rust Programming Language. (n.d.). Retrieved August 31, 2024, from https://www.rust-lang.org/

Scilla in Depth — scilla-doc 0.11.0 documentation. (n.d.). Retrieved August 31, 2024, from https://scilla.readthedocs.io/en/latest/scilla-in-depth.html

Secinaro, S., Mas, F. D., Accounting, V. B.-, & A., & 2021. (2021). Blockchain in the accounting, auditing and accountability fields: a bibliometric and coding analysis. *Emerald.Com, 35*(9), 168–203. https://doi.org/10.1108/AAAJ-10-2020-4987

Simplicity Bitcoin Optech. (n.d.). Retrieved June 17, 2025, from https://bitcoinops.org/en/topics/simplicity/

Sophomore-Track/Ethereum-Virtual-Machine.md at main · LearnWeb3DAO/Sophomore-Track · GitHub. (n.d.). Retrieved August 30, 2024, from https://github.com/LearnWeb3DAO/Sophomore-Track/blob/main/Ethereum-Virtual-Machine.md

The benefits of Erlang & Elixir for blockchain—DEV Community. (n.d.). Retrieved August 31, 2024, from https://dev.to/erlang_solutions/the-benefits-of-erlang-elixir-for-blockchain-4hjk

The Bug Bounty Radar—The Latest Public Bug Bounty Programs. (n.d.). Retrieved September 7, 2024, from https://bbradar.io/

The Go Programming Language. (n.d.). Retrieved August 31, 2024, from https://go.dev/

The Largest Cryptocurrency Hacks So Far. (n.d.). Retrieved September 5, 2024, from https://www.investopedia.com/news/largest-cryptocurrency-hacks-so-far-year/

The most-comprehensive AI-powered DevSecOps platform GitLab. (n.d.). Retrieved August 30, 2024, from https://about.gitlab.com/

The Top 21 Blockchain Programming Languages, Explained. (n.d.). Retrieved February 26, 2023, from https://supraoracles.com/academy/the-top-21-blockchain-programming-languages-explained/#Obsolete-Languages

TypeScript: JavaScript With Syntax For Types. (n.d.). Retrieved August 31, 2024, from https://www.typescriptlang.org/

Uniswap GitHub Repositories. (n.d.). Retrieved September 9, 2024, from https://github.com/orgs/Uniswap/repositories

Visual Studio: IDE and Code Editor for Software Developers and Teams. (n.d.). Retrieved September 9, 2024, from https://visualstudio.microsoft.com/

Vyper documentation. (n.d.). Retrieved August 31, 2024, from https://docs.vyperlang.org/en/stable/toctree.html

Wang, S., Ouyang, L., Yuan, Y., Member, S., Ni, X., Han, X., Wang, F.-Y., Yuan Wang, Y. S., Ouyang, L., Yuan, Y., Ni, X., & Han, X. (2019). Blockchain-Enabled Smart Contracts: Architecture, Applications, and Future Trends. *SYSTEMS*, *49*(11). https://doi.org/10.1109/TSMC.2019.2895123

Web3 Infrastructure for Everyone Solana. (n.d.). Retrieved August 31, 2024, from https://solana.com/

Web3 is Going Just Great. (n.d.). Retrieved June 17, 2025, from https://www.web3isgoinggreat.com/

Welcome to a World of OCaml. (n.d.). Retrieved August 31, 2024, from https://ocaml.org/

Welcome to Python.org. (n.d.). Retrieved August 31, 2024, from https://www.python.org/

What is Blockchain Security Audit and How to do it? (n.d.). Retrieved September 6, 2024, from https://www.uscsinstitute.org/cybersecurity-insights/blog/what-is-blockchain-security-audit-and-how-to-do-it

What is copyleft? Opensource.com. (n.d.). Retrieved August 30, 2024, from https://opensource.com/resources/what-is-copyleft

What is "open source" and why is it important?—Coin Center. (n.d.). Retrieved August 26, 2022, from https://www.coincenter.org/education/advanced-topics/open-source/

What is Vyper?—GeeksforGeeks. (n.d.). Retrieved August 31, 2024, from https://www.geeksforgeeks.org/what-is-vyper/

Worldcoin GitHub Repositories. (n.d.). Retrieved September 9, 2024, from https://github.com/orgs/worldcoin/repositories

Zilliqa. (n.d.). Retrieved August 31, 2024, from https://www.zilliqa.com/

Chapter 13—Incentivization and Rewards

2024 Social Media Industry Benchmark Report Rival IQ. (n.d.). Retrieved June 18, 2025, from https://www.rivaliq.com/blog/social-media-industry-benchmark-report-2024/

Alam, M., Ahad, A., … S. Z.-… and B., & 2020. (2020). A neoteric smart and sustainable farming environment incorporating blockchain-based artificial intelligence approach. *Wiley Online Library*, 197–213. https://doi.org/10.1002/9781119621201.ch11

Augustin, P., Chen-Zhang, R., 4063228, D. S.-A. at S., & 2022. (2022). Yield farming. *Papers.Ssrn.Com.* https://papers.ssrn.com/sol3/papers.cfm?abstract_id=4063228

Beginner's Guide: What is a Bounty?—101 Blockchains. (n.d.). Retrieved June 24, 2023, from https://101blockchains.com/what-is-bounty/

Best Crypto Staking Strategy for 2023!!—YouTube. (n.d.). Retrieved July 3, 2023, from https://www.youtube.com/watch?v=F8zht_HXYB4

Binance Academy on Binance Feed: What Is BNB Auto-Burn? Binance Feed. (n.d.). Retrieved June 30, 2023, from https://academy.binance.com/en/articles/what-is-bnb-auto-burn

Cong, L., He, Z., 4059460, K. T.-A. at S., & 2022. (2023). Staking, token pricing, and crypto carry. *Papers.Ssrn.Com.* https://papers.ssrn.com/sol3/papers.cfm?abstract_id=4148899

Cousaert, S., Xu, J., … T. M. B. and C., & 2022. (n.d.). Sok: Yield aggregators in defi. *Ieeexplore.Ieee.Org.* Retrieved July 16, 2023, from https://ieeexplore.ieee.org/abstract/document/9805523/

Crypto Referral Program 101: The Basics and How It Works—Cryptoflies News. (n.d.). Retrieved July 22, 2023, from https://blog.cryptoflies.com/crypto-referral-program-101-the-basics-and-how-it-works/

Crypto Rewards: Using Tokens to Get People to do What You Want. (n.d.). Retrieved June 24, 2023, from https://beincrypto.com/crypto-rewards-using-tokens-to-get-people-to-do-what-you-want/

Crypto Staking Explorer Staking Rewards. (n.d.). Retrieved July 28, 2023, from https://www.stakingrewards.com/

Cryptocurrency Airdrop: What Is It and How Does It Work. (n.d.). Retrieved July 21, 2023, from https://www.investopedia.com/terms/a/airdrop-cryptocurrency.asp

Decentralized protocol for launching new ideas. (n.d.). Retrieved July 21, 2023, from https://polkastarter.com/

Explore the world of decentralized finance Synapse Network. (n.d.). Retrieved July 21, 2023, from https://synapse.network/

He, P., Tang, D., 3609817, J. W.-A. at S., & 2020. (n.d.). Staking pool centralization in proof-of-stake blockchain network. *Papers.Ssrn.Com.* Retrieved July 7, 2023, from https://papers.ssrn.com/sol3/papers.cfm?abstract_id=3609817

Home Substack. (n.d.). Retrieved June 18, 2025, from https://substack.com/home

How Crypto Incentives Work, Explained. (n.d.). Retrieved June 24, 2023, from https://cointelegraph.com/explained/how-crypto-incentives-work-explained

Inflation Schedule Solana Validator. (n.d.). Retrieved November 8, 2024, from https://docs.solanalabs.com/implemented- proposals/ed_overview/ed_validation_client_economics/ed_vce_state_validation_protocol_based_rewards

Khan, I. A. (2021). *Blockchain technology and its implementation with a staking application in an Ethereum network.* https://www.theseus.fi/handle/10024/507708

L., N. G.-F. J. Corp. & Fin., & 2022]. (n.d.). Does Cryptocurrency Staking Fall under SEC Jurisdiction? *HeinOnline, 27.* Retrieved July 7, 2023, from https://heinonline.org/hol-cgi-bin/get_pdf.cgi?handle=hein.journals/fjcf27§ion=22

Launchpool Egalitarian Investing in Blockchain projects. (n.d.). Retrieved July 21, 2023, from https://launchpool.xyz/

Liquid staking—Wiki Golden. (n.d.). Retrieved July 3, 2023, from https://golden.com/wiki/Liquid_staking-X9GXDZ8

Price, T. (2017). *Predictive Cryptocurrency Mining and Staking.* https://www.tdcommons.org/dpubs_series/889/

Real Reward Rate Staking Data. (n.d.). Retrieved November 7, 2024, from https://docs.stakingrewards.com/staking-data/metrics/real-reward-rate

Safety Module Aave Protocol Documentation. (n.d.). Retrieved November 8, 2024, from https://aave.com/docs/primitives/safety-module

Safety Module / stkAAVE—Developers. (n.d.). Retrieved July 8, 2023, from https://docs.aave.com/developers/v/1.0/developing-on-aave/the-protocol/safety-module-stkaave

Scharnowski, S., 4180341, H. J.-A. at S., & 2022. (n.d.). Liquid staking: Basis determinants and price discovery. *Papers.Ssrn.Com.* Retrieved July 7, 2023, from https://papers.ssrn.com/sol3/papers.cfm?abstract_id=4180341

Social Media Benchmarks For 2025. (n.d.). Retrieved June 18, 2025, from https://www.socialinsider.io/social-media-benchmarks

Staking as a service ethereum.org. (n.d.). Retrieved July 7, 2023, from https://ethereum.org/en/staking/saas/

The Latest Trends and Innovations in Loyalty and Reward Programs Tied to Payments. (n.d.). Retrieved July 22, 2023, from https://www.financemagnates.com/cryptocurrency/education-centre/the-latest-trends-and-innovations-in-loyalty-and-reward-programs-tied-to-payments/

The Use of Incentives in Crypto—AIER. (n.d.). Retrieved June 24, 2023, from https://www.aier.org/article/the-use-of-incentives-in-crypto/

Top Proof of Stake Tokens Staking Rewards. (n.d.-a). Retrieved June 18, 2025, from https://www.stakingrewards.com/assets/proof-of-stake?sort=staking_marketcap&timeframe=7d&order=desc&byChange=false&columns=reward_rate%2Cprice%2Cstaking_marketcap%2Cstaking_ratio%2Cinflation_rate%2Creal_reward_rate

Top Proof of Stake Tokens Staking Rewards. (n.d.-b). Retrieved November 7, 2024, from https://www.stakingrewards.com/assets/proof-of-stake

Top-10 IDO launchpads for Web3 projects and investors—Hacken. (n.d.). Retrieved July 21, 2023, from https://hacken.io/discover/top-10-ido-launchpads-for-web3-projects-and-investors/

What are DeFi yield aggregators, and how do they work? (n.d.). Retrieved July 6, 2023, from https://cointelegraph.com/learn/what-are-defi-yield-aggregators-and-how-do-they-work

What are liquidity provider (LP) tokens, and how do they work? (n.d.). Retrieved July 8, 2023, from https://cointelegraph.com/explained/what-are-liquidity-provider-lp-tokens-and-how-do-they-work

What is Axie Infinity game? How to get started [Beginner guide]—Zipmex. (n.d.). Retrieved July 22, 2023, from https://zipmex.com/learn/axie-infinity-game-explained/

What Is Liquid Staking? Chainlink. (n.d.). Retrieved July 3, 2023, from https://blog.chain.link/liquid-staking/

What is liquid staking? · Liquid Collective. (n.d.). Retrieved July 3, 2023, from https://liquidcollective.io/liquid-staking/

What Is Staking—Forbes Advisor. (n.d.). Retrieved July 28, 2023, from https://www.forbes.com/advisor/investing/cryptocurrency/crypto-staking-basics/

What Is Yield Farming? CoinMarketCap. (n.d.). Retrieved July 8, 2023, from https://coinmarketcap.com/alexandria/article/what-is-yield-farming

Xu, J., Service, Y. F.-I. T. on N. and, & 2022. (n.d.). Reap the harvest on blockchain: A survey of yield farming protocols. *Ieeexplore.Ieee.Org.*

Retrieved July 8, 2023, from https://ieeexplore.ieee.org/abstract/document/9953979/

Chapter 14—Community and Social Media

5 reasons why Telegram is so popular with cryptocurrency communities. (n.d.). Retrieved May 27, 2023, from https://www.coininsider.com/5-reasons-why-telegram-popular-with-cryptocurrency-communities/

6 Ways To Evaluate a Crypto Project .cult by Honeypot. (n.d.). Retrieved February 19, 2023, from https://cult.honeypot.io/reads/6-ways-to-evaluate-a-crypto-project/

10 Crypto Marketing Metrics to Measure for Social Media Growth. (n.d.). Retrieved May 27, 2023, from https://influencermarketinghub.com/crypto-marketing-metrics/

16 Key Social Media Metrics to Track in 2023 [BENCHMARKS]. (n.d.). Retrieved June 8, 2023, from https://blog.hootsuite.com/social-media-metrics/#1_Reach

18 Essential Cryptocurrency Stats for 2023. (n.d.). Retrieved May 27, 2023, from https://influencermarketinghub.com/crypto-stats/

Aggarwal, S., Chaudhary, R., Aujla, G., ... N. K.-J. of N. and, & 2019. (n.d.). Blockchain for smart communities: Applications, challenges and opportunities. *Elsevier.* Retrieved May 26, 2023, from https://www.sciencedirect.com/science/article/pii/S1084804519302231

Engagement Rate Calculator. (n.d.). Retrieved June 9, 2023, from https://www.omnicalculator.com/other/engagement-rate

Engagement vs. Reach vs. Impressions : Understanding Social Media Analytics. (n.d.). Retrieved June 9, 2023, from https://allegiantmedia.com.au/engagement-vs-reach-vs-impressions-understanding-social-media-analytics/

How to Calculate Engagement Rate Socialinsider. (n.d.). Retrieved June 9, 2023, from https://www.socialinsider.io/blog/engagement-rate/#c4

How to Calculate Engagement Rate I Improve Your Campaigns—YouTube. (n.d.). Retrieved June 9, 2023, from https://www.youtube.com/watch?v=UxyxyWPZBkk

Kimani, N. (2021). *Bitcoin adoption in South Africa, an end user perspective*. https://open.uct.ac.za/handle/11427/35756

Ku-Mahamud, K., Omar, M., … N. B.-I. J. on, & 2019. (n.d.). Awareness, trust, and adoption of blockchain technology and cryptocurrency among blockchain communities in Malaysia. *Academia.Edu*. Retrieved May 26, 2023, from https://www.academia.edu/download/70084071/2034.pdf

Martínez-Cámara, E., … M. M.-V.-N. language, & 2014. (2016). Sentiment analysis in Twitter. *Cambridge.Org*, *49*(2). https://doi.org/10.1145/2938640

Review, M. F.-T. P., & 1919. (n.d.). Community is a process. *JSTOR*. Retrieved May 31, 2023, from https://www.jstor.org/stable/2178307

Shahbaznezhad, H., Dolan, R., & Rashidirad, M. (2021). The Role of Social Media Content Format and Platform in Users' Engagement Behavior. *Journal of Interactive Marketing*, *53*, 47–65. https://doi.org/10.1016/J.INTMAR.2020.05.001

Syrdal, H. A., & Briggs, E. (2018). ENGAGEMENT WITH SOCIAL MEDIA CONTENT: A QUALITATIVE EXPLORATION. *Journal of Marketing Theory and Practice*, *26*(1–2), 4–22. https://doi.org/10.1080/10696679.2017.1389243

The Reddit Experts' Guide to Building a Crypto Community. (n.d.). Retrieved May 27, 2023, from https://www.meetbunch.com/the-reddit-guide

The Role of Community Manager and Community Moderator—Lunarstrategy. (n.d.). Retrieved June 16, 2023, from https://www.lunarstrategy.com/article/the-roles-in-a-thriving-community

Twitter Engagement Calculator (Free Tool). (n.d.). Retrieved June 8, 2023, from https://mention.com/en/twitter-engagement-calculator/

Twitter engagement rate calculator. (n.d.). Retrieved June 8, 2023, from https://getmashhor.com/en/twitter-engagement-calculator

What Are Crypto Communities and How Do They Boost Adoption? (n.d.). Retrieved May 27, 2023, from https://www.makeuseof.com/what-are-crypto-communities/

What Is a Good Engagement Rate (and How To Calculate It). (n.d.). Retrieved June 9, 2023, from https://napoleoncat.com/blog/what-is-a-good-engagement-rate/#ig

Why Engagement Rate is More Important than Likes on Your Facebook Social Media Today. (n.d.). Retrieved June 8, 2023, from https://www.socialmediatoday.com/content/why-engagement-rate-more-important-likes-your-facebook

Xu, R., Lin, X., Dong, Q., International, Y. C.-P. of the 15th E., & 2018. (n.d.). Constructing trustworthy and safe communities on a blockchain-enabled social credits system. *Dl.Acm.Org*. Retrieved May 26, 2023, from https://dl.acm.org/doi/abs/10.1145/3286978.3287022

Zhang, L., Wang, S., Data, B. L.-W. I. R., & 2018. (2018). Deep learning for sentiment analysis: A survey. *Wiley Online Library*, *8*(4). https://doi.org/10.1002/widm.1253

Chapter 15—Funding and Partnerships

10 Largest Venture Rounds In Crypto And Blockchain. (n.d.). Retrieved August 26, 2023, from https://www.forbes.com/sites/ninabambysheva/2021/04/03/10-largest-venture-rounds-in-crypto-and-blockchain/?sh=534a14f83ce8

12 Largest Venture Rounds In Crypto History. (n.d.). Retrieved September 3, 2023, from https://www.forbes.com/sites/ninabambysheva/2021/05/28/440-million-circe-investment-is-the-largest-crypto-round-in-history/?sh=6a41b0cc379f

A decentralized, permissionless, and open-source payments protocol Solana Pay. (n.d.). Retrieved October 14, 2023, from https://solanapay.com/

About Us Polygon. (n.d.). Retrieved December 1, 2024, from https://polygon.technology/about

Abyss Finance. (n.d.). Retrieved June 18, 2025, from https://abyss.finance/

accounting, A. W.-C. J. of finance &, & 2018. (n.d.). The initial coin offering–challenges and opportunities. *Apcz.Umk.Pl*. https://doi.org/10.12775/CJFA.2018.011

Active IDO/IEO/ICO CryptoRank.io. (n.d.). Retrieved September 7, 2023, from https://cryptorank.io/active-ico

Algorand Foundation Launches $300 Million USD Viridis Fund to Support DeFi Innovation Algorand Foundation News. (n.d.). Retrieved September 2, 2023, from https://www.algorand.foundation/news/viridis

Algorand Foundation Launches $300M DeFi Fund—Blockworks. (n.d.). Retrieved November 28, 2024, from https://blockworks.co/news/algorand-foundation-launches-300m-defi-fund

Amplify ETFs—BLOK. (n.d.). Retrieved August 31, 2023, from https://amplifyetfs.com/blok/

Astar Network—The Future of Multichain Smart Contracts. (n.d.). Retrieved September 8, 2023, from https://astar.network/

Bakos, Y., & Halaburda, H. (2019). *The role of cryptographic tokens and ICOs in fostering platform adoption*. https://papers.ssrn.com/sol3/papers.cfm?abstract_id=3426940

Band Protocol—Company. (n.d.). Retrieved September 7, 2023, from https://www.bandprotocol.com/company

Best Blockchain ETFs of September 2023—Forbes Advisor. (n.d.). Retrieved August 31, 2023, from https://www.forbes.com/advisor/investing/cryptocurrency/best-blockchain-etfs/

Binance Launchpad Binance. (n.d.). Retrieved September 7, 2023, from https://launchpad.binance.com/en

Blockchain and Private Equity. (n.d.). Retrieved September 2, 2023, from https://www.linkedin.com/pulse/blockchain-private-equity-chirantha-ambepitiya

Blockchain Capital. (n.d.). Retrieved September 5, 2023, from https://www.blockchaincapital.com/

Blockchain Infrastructure for the Decentralised Web Parity Technologies. (n.d.). Retrieved September 2, 2023, from https://www.parity.io/

Blockchain Interoperability 2.0 Pioneer Ferrum Network. (n.d.). Retrieved September 8, 2023, from https://ferrum.network/

Bootstrapping Definition, Strategies, and Pros/Cons. (n.d.). Retrieved September 2, 2023, from https://www.investopedia.com/terms/b/bootstrapping.asp

buidl1: web3 integrable protocol for private launchpad and controllable investments. (n.d.). Retrieved September 25, 2023, from https://buidl.one/#Purposes

Catalini, C., & Gans, J. S. (2018). *Initial coin offerings and the value of crypto tokens.* https://www.nber.org/papers/w24418

Chainflip. (n.d.). Retrieved September 29, 2023, from https://chainflip.io/

Chainflip (FLIP)—All information about Chainflip ICO (Token Sale)—ICO Drops. (n.d.). Retrieved September 29, 2023, from https://icodrops.com/chainflip/

Comments of David A. Vaughan for the SEC Roundtable on Hedge Funds. (n.d.). Retrieved August 31, 2023, from https://www.sec.gov/spotlight/hedgefunds/hedge-vaughn.htm

Companies Polychain Capital Talent network. (n.d.). Retrieved September 30, 2023, from https://jobs.polychain.capital/companies

Companies—Draper Associates. (n.d.). Retrieved August 31, 2023, from https://www.draper.vc/companies

Crowdloan DEXTools. (n.d.). Retrieved September 8, 2023, from https://info.dextools.io/crypto-glossary/crowdloan/

Crowdloan Definition CoinMarketCap. (n.d.). Retrieved September 8, 2023, from https://coinmarketcap.com/alexandria/glossary/crowdloan

Crunchbase: Discover innovative companies and the people behind them. (n.d.). Retrieved September 30, 2023, from https://www.crunchbase.com/

Crypto Brokerage—Paxos. (n.d.). Retrieved October 14, 2023, from https://paxos.com/crypto-brokerage/

Crypto Solutions for Business Ripple. (n.d.). Retrieved September 30, 2023, from https://ripple.com/

Crypto.com's sports sponsorships persist: "Business as usual." (n.d.). Retrieved December 15, 2023, from https://www.sportsbusinessjournal.com/Daily/Issues/2022/11/16/Marketing-and-Sponsorship/Crypto-dotcom-says-sports-deals-are-fine.aspx

Cryptocurrency Private Equity—eToroX. (n.d.). Retrieved September 2, 2023, from https://etorox.com/about-etorox/glossary/cryptocurrency-private-equity/

Debunking the narratives about cryptocurrency and financial inclusion. (n.d.). Retrieved December 5, 2024, from https://www.brookings.edu/articles/debunking-the-narratives-about-cryptocurrency-and-financial-inclusion/

Developing Better Initial Coin Offerings (ICOs): An Overview of DAICOs—Garbage Can Lab. (n.d.). Retrieved September 9, 2023, from https://www.garbcan.com/blockchain/developing-better-initial-coin-offerings-icos-an-overview-of-daicos/

Difference between: ICO / IEO / STO / IDO EDSX—European Digital Assets Exchange. (n.d.). Retrieved September 7, 2023, from https://www.edsx.ch/blognews/difference-between-ico-ieo-sto-ido-eto

Digital Wallets, Money Management, and More PayPal US. (n.d.). Retrieved September 5, 2023, from https://www.paypal.com/us/home

Do Private Equity Firms Invest in Startups? (n.d.). Retrieved August 31, 2023, from https://stachecow.com/do-private-equity-firms-invest-in-startups-212#stories

DODO Home. (n.d.). Retrieved September 8, 2023, from https://dodoex.io/en

Duet Protocol. (n.d.). Retrieved September 8, 2023, from https://duet.finance/

Elon Musk's Tesla Didn't Buy or Sell Any Bitcoin for Fourth Straight Quarter in Q2. (n.d.). Retrieved August 25, 2023, from https://www.coindesk.com/business/2023/07/19/tesla-didnt-buy-or-sell-any-bitcoin-for-fourth-straight-quarter-in-q2/

ERC-20 Token Standard. (n.d.). Retrieved June 18, 2025, from https://ethereum.org/en/developers/docs/standards/tokens/erc-20/

Ethereum (ETH)—All information about Ethereum ICO (Token Sale)—ICO Drops. (n.d.). Retrieved September 7, 2023, from https://icodrops.com/ethereum/

Exchange-Traded Fund (ETF) Investor.gov. (n.d.). Retrieved August 31, 2023, from https://www.investor.gov/introduction-investing/investing-basics/glossary/exchange-traded-fund-etf

Fantom. (n.d.). Retrieved October 17, 2023, from https://fantom.foundation/

Feng, C., Li, N., Wong, M. H. F., & Zhang, M. (2019). Initial Coin Offerings, Blockchain Technology, and White Paper Disclosures. *SSRN Electronic Journal.* https://doi.org/10.2139/SSRN.3256289

Fidelity® Wise Origin® Bitcoin Fund (FBTC) Fidelity Institutional. (n.d.). Retrieved November 28, 2024, from https://institutional.fidelity.com/advisors/investment-solutions/asset-classes/alternatives/fidelity-wise-origin-bitcoin-fund

Fidelity Investments® Launches Spot Bitcoin Exchange-Traded Product, Fidelity® Wise Origin® Bitcoin Fund (FBTC). (n.d.). Retrieved November

28, 2024, from https://newsroom.fidelity.com/pressreleases/fidelity-investments--launches-spot-bitcoin-exchange-traded-product--fidelity--wise-origin--bitcoin-/s/02f9b68a-de40-41c5-baab-584ef8510471?utm_source=chatgpt.com

Fidelity Physical Bitcoin ETP. (n.d.). Retrieved August 31, 2023, from https://www.fidelity.lu/funds/fidelity-physical-bitcoin-etp

Franklin Templeton. (n.d.). Retrieved September 2, 2023, from https://www.franklintempleton.com/

Franklin Templeton Blockchain Fund II, L.P.—SEC FORM D. (n.d.). Retrieved September 2, 2023, from https://www.sec.gov/Archives/edgar/data/1974921/000197492123000001/xslFormDX01/primary_doc.xml

Franklin Templeton Files for Blockchain Fund Targeting Institutional Investors Looking at Crypto. (n.d.). Retrieved September 2, 2023, from https://www.coindesk.com/business/2023/05/11/franklin-templeton-to-list-blockchain-fund-targeting-institutional-investors/

Friedlmaier, M., … A. T.-… distribution of blockchain, & 2018. (n.d.). Disrupting industries with blockchain: The industry, venture capital funding, and regional distribution of blockchain ventures. *Papers.Ssrn.Com*. Retrieved August 23, 2023, from https://papers.ssrn.com/sol3/papers.cfm?abstract_id=2854756

Giudici, G., Milne, A., & Vinogradov, D. (2020). Cryptocurrencies: market analysis and perspectives. *Journal of Industrial and Business Economics*, *47*(1), 1–18. https://doi.org/10.1007/S40812-019-00138-6/FIGURES/1

Glimmer (GLMR) & Moonriver (MOVR) Utility Token Moonbeam Network. (n.d.). Retrieved September 9, 2023, from https://moonbeam.network/tokens/

Grayscale®—Assets Under Consideration and Current Products. (n.d.). Retrieved August 26, 2023, from https://grayscale.com/assets-under-consideration-and-current-products/

Grayscale® DeFi Fund—Grayscale®. (n.d.). Retrieved August 27, 2023, from https://grayscale.com/products/grayscale-decentralized-finance-fund/

Grayscale 485a. (n.d.). Retrieved August 31, 2023, from https://www.sec.gov/Archives/edgar/data/1540305/000089418921007886/grayscale485a.htm

Hacker, P., & Thomale, C. (2018). Crypto-securities regulation: icos,token sales and cryptocurrencies under eu financial law. *European Company and Financial Law Review, 15*(4), 645–696. https://doi.org/10.1515/ECFR-2018-0021/HTML

Hassija, V., Chamola, V., Society, S. Z.-S. C. and, & 2020. (n.d.). BitFund: A blockchain-based crowd funding platform for future smart and connected nation. *Elsevier.* https://doi.org/10.1016/j.scs.2020.102145

Home ethereum.org. (n.d.). Retrieved September 7, 2023, from https://ethereum.org/en/

Home IOTA. (n.d.). Retrieved September 7, 2023, from https://www.iota.org/

Home PancakeSwap. (n.d.). Retrieved September 8, 2023, from https://pancakeswap.finance/

Homepage—tZERO.com. (n.d.). Retrieved June 18, 2025, from https://tzero.com/#home

How Are Institutions and Companies Investing in Crypto? (n.d.). Retrieved August 25, 2023, from https://www.coindesk.com/learn/how-are-institutions-and-companies-investing-in-crypto/

How Do Cryptocurrency Exchange-Traded Funds (ETFs) Work? (n.d.). Retrieved August 31, 2023, from https://www.investopedia.com/investing/understanding-cryptocurrency-etfs/

How Paxos Works with PayPal to Build Innovative Crypto Products—Paxos. (n.d.). Retrieved October 14, 2023, from https://paxos.com/2022/08/23/how-paxos-works-with-paypal-to-build-innovative-crypto-products/

ICO Drops—Calendar of active and upcoming ICO & IEO. Complete list with Token Sales. (n.d.). Retrieved September 6, 2023, from https://icodrops.com/

ICOholder Ultimate Rated ICO & IEO List. (n.d.). Retrieved September 7, 2023, from https://icoholder.com/

ICOmarks—6000+ ICOs with Ratings (Initial Coin Offering) 2020. (n.d.). Retrieved September 6, 2023, from https://icomarks.com/

ICOs vs. STOs vs. IPOs in crypto: Key differences explained. (n.d.). Retrieved September 7, 2023, from https://cointelegraph.com/learn/icos-vs-stos-vs-ipos-in-crypto-key-differences-explained

Immutable Powering The Next Generation Of Web3 Games. (n.d.). Retrieved December 1, 2024, from https://www.immutable.com/

Immutable and Polygon Labs are partnering to build a dedicated gaming blockchain using zero-knowledge technology to accelerate decentralized game development and bring Web3 a step closer to mass adoption. . (n.d.). Retrieved September 3, 2023, from https://polygon.technology/blog/introducing-immutable-zkevm-powered-by-polygon-the-home-of-gaming-in-web3-in-partnership-with-immutable

Immutable and Polygon Labs Partner to Create the New Home for Web3 Gaming Immutable Blog. (n.d.). Retrieved December 1, 2024, from https://www.immutable.com/blog/immutable-and-polygon-labs-partner-to-create-the-new-home-for-web3-gaming

Initial Farm Offering PancakeSwap. (n.d.). Retrieved September 8, 2023, from https://pancakeswap.finance/ifo

Institutional Investors & Traders in the Crypto Market: Insights and Actions. (n.d.). Retrieved August 26, 2023, from https://coindcx.com/

blog/cryptocurrency/rise-of-institutional-involvement-and-traders-in-crypto-market/

Institutional Money Is Pouring Into The Crypto Market And Its Only Going To Grow. (n.d.). Retrieved August 24, 2023, from https://www.forbes.com/sites/lawrencewintermeyer/2021/08/12/institutional-money-is-pouring-into-the-crypto-market-and-its-only-going-to-grow/?sh=10ce2f6a1459

Introducing Immutable zkEVM Powered by Polygon: the Home of Gaming in Web3 in Partnership with Immutable. (n.d.). Retrieved December 1, 2024, from https://polygon.technology/blog/introducing-immutable-zkevm-powered-by-polygon-the-home-of-gaming-in-web3-in-partnership-with-immutable

JUMPSTART OKX. (n.d.). Retrieved September 7, 2023, from https://www.okx.com/jumpstart

Kusama, Polkadot's Canary Network. (n.d.). Retrieved September 9, 2023, from https://kusama.network/

Lyandres, E., Palazzo, B., & Rabetti, D. (2022). Initial Coin Offering (ICO) Success and Post-ICO Performance. *Management Science, 68*(12), 8658–8679. https://doi.org/10.1287/MNSC.2022.4312

Lynn, T., Mooney, J. G., Rosati, P., & Cummins, M. (n.d.). *PALGRAVE STUDIES IN DIGITAL BUSINESS AND ENABLING TECHNOLOGIES SERIES EDITORS: Disrupting Finance FinTech and Strategy in the 21st Century.* Retrieved September 7, 2023, from http://www.palgrave.com/gp/series/16004

MEDIA Private equity: a Brief Overview. (n.d.). Retrieved September 2, 2023, from https://www.law.du.edu/documents/registrar/advassign/Yoost_PrivateEquity%20Seminar_PEI%20Media's%20Private%20Equity%20-%20A%20Brief%20Overview_318.pdf

MicroStrategy Bitcoin Holdings Chart & Purchase History. (n.d.). Retrieved November 28, 2024, from https://treasuries.bitbo.io/microstrategy/

MolochDAO: The Original Grant Giving DAO. (n.d.). Retrieved November 29, 2024, from https://molochdao.com/

Monero (XMR) Review: A Coin that Offers Complete Privacy and Anonymity Chainbits. (n.d.). Retrieved June 18, 2025, from https://www.chainbits.com/reviews/monero-review/

Moxotó, A. C., Melo, P., & Soukiazis, E. (2021). *Initial Coin Offering (ICO): a systematic review of the literature.* https://scholarspace.manoa.hawaii.edu/handle/10125/71124

NEO (NEO)—All information about NEO ICO (Token Sale)—ICO Drops. (n.d.). Retrieved September 7, 2023, from https://icodrops.com/neo/

Neo Smart Economy. (n.d.). Retrieved September 7, 2023, from https://neo.org/

Neon EVM—Grow with the Best from Two Chains. (n.d.). Retrieved September 29, 2023, from https://neon-labs.org/

Neon (NEON)—All information about Neon ICO (Token Sale)—ICO Drops. (n.d.). Retrieved September 29, 2023, from https://icodrops.com/neon-labs/

Nor, R., Rahman, M., ... T. R.-P. of the 6th, & 2017. (2017). Blockchain sadaqa mechanism for disaster aid crowd funding. *Soc.Uum.Edu.My.* https://soc.uum.edu.my/icoci/2023/icoci2017/Pdf_Version_Chap07e/PID211-400-405e.pdf

O(1) Labs. (n.d.). Retrieved September 2, 2023, from https://o1labs.org/

Parachains · Polkadot Wiki. (n.d.). Retrieved September 9, 2023, from https://wiki.polkadot.network/docs/learn-parachains

Partners and integrations Fantom. (n.d.). Retrieved October 17, 2023, from https://fantom.foundation/partners/

PATEX—Patex Network. (n.d.). Retrieved September 30, 2023, from https://patex.io/

Patex Network—Tokenomics. (n.d.). Retrieved October 13, 2023, from https://patex.io/docs/Patex%20WP.pdf

Patex (PATEX) IDO, Token Sale Review & Tokenomics Analysis CryptoRank.io. (n.d.). Retrieved September 30, 2023, from https://cryptorank.io/ico/patex

Patex (PATEX) Unlocking Progress DropsTab. (n.d.). Retrieved December 5, 2024, from https://dropstab.com/coins/patex/vesting

PayPal Cryptocurrency Terms and Conditions. (n.d.). Retrieved October 13, 2023, from https://www.paypal.com/us/legalhub/cryptocurrencies-tnc

PayPal USD (PYUSD)—Paxos. (n.d.). Retrieved October 14, 2023, from https://help.paxos.com/hc/en-us/articles/18082790045972-PayPal-USD-PYUSD-

Polkadot: Web3 Interoperability Decentralized Blockchain. (n.d.). Retrieved September 9, 2023, from https://www.polkadot.network/

Polygon Pledges $100 Million To Bootstrap Growth, But Co-Founder Also Expresses Caution About Crypto Projects Having Too Much Money. (n.d.). Retrieved September 2, 2023, from https://www.forbes.com/sites/stevenehrlich/2022/04/22/polygon-pledges-100-million-to-bootstrap-growth-but-co-founder-also-expresses-caution-about-crypto-projects-having-too-much-money/?sh=5f1e6d2cfb88

Polygon Technology—Web3, Aggregated. (n.d.). Retrieved December 1, 2024, from https://polygon.technology/

Polymath One platform powering a smart future. (n.d.). Retrieved September 7, 2023, from https://polymath.network/

Private Capital And Institutions Are Piling Into Bitcoin And Other Digital Assets But You Need To Know Where To Look. (n.d.). Retrieved August 24, 2023, from https://www.forbes.com/sites/lawrencewintermeyer/2020/09/03/private-capital-and-institutions-are-piling-into-bitcoin-and-other-digital-assets-but-you-need-to-know-where-to-look/?sh=66ce30d55359

Private Equity vs Hedge Funds vs Venture Capital... How to tell them apart.—YouTube. (n.d.). Retrieved September 2, 2023, from https://www.youtube.com/watch?v=w83OAMVcrrk&t=1s

Ripple Labs Unlocks 1 Billion XRP Tokens in Monthly Distribution—DailyCoin. (n.d.). Retrieved September 30, 2023, from https://dailycoin.com/ripple-labs-unlocks-1-billion-xrp-tokens-in-monthly-distribution/

SEC Crypto Regulation—Forbes Advisor. (n.d.). Retrieved September 7, 2023, from https://www.forbes.com/advisor/investing/cryptocurrency/sec-crypto-regulation/

SECRETS To Finding a 100x Token Sale!!—YouTube. (n.d.). Retrieved September 29, 2023, from https://www.youtube.com/watch?v=4c4wlSgsQ2A

Securitize Unlocking Access to Alternative Assets. (n.d.). Retrieved September 7, 2023, from https://securitize.io/

Securrency Global Liquidity and Financial Freedom for All. (n.d.). Retrieved September 7, 2023, from https://www.securrency.com/

Solana Web3 Infrastructure for Everyone. (n.d.). Retrieved September 8, 2023, from https://solana.com/

Solana Pay Integrates with Shopify as New Payment Option to Transform Commerce Solana. (n.d.). Retrieved October 14, 2023, from https://solana.com/news/solana-pay-shopify

Startup- high-quality blockchain startup projects -Gate.io. (n.d.). Retrieved September 7, 2023, from https://www.gate.io/startup

Stellar A Blockchain Network for Payments and Tokenization. (n.d.). Retrieved September 30, 2023, from https://stellar.org/

SushiSwap. (n.d.). Retrieved September 8, 2023, from https://www.sushi.com/swap

Takahashi, K. (2019). *Jurisdiction in Securities Regulations: Transformation from the ICO (Initial Coin Offering) to the STO (Security Token Offering) and the IEO (Initial Exchange Offering)*. *45*, 31–50. https://doi.org/10.35148/ilsilr.2020..45.31

Tapscott, A., Review, D. T.-H. B., & 2017. (2017). How blockchain is changing finance. *Capital.Report*. https://capital.report/Resources/

Whitepapers/40fc8a6a-cdbd-47e6-83f6-74e2a9d36ccc_finance_topic2_source2.pdf

The 13 Banks Investing the Most in Crypto and Blockchain to Date. (n.d.). Retrieved August 24, 2023, from https://markets.businessinsider.com/news/currencies/13-top-banks-investing-cryptocurrency-blockchain-technology-funding-blockdata-bitcoin-2021-8

The Abyss—Play and Get Rewarded! (n.d.). Retrieved September 25, 2023, from https://www.theabyss.com/

The Best IDO & IGO Launchpad for Crypto Projects DAO Maker. (n.d.). Retrieved September 8, 2023, from https://daomaker.com/

The Future Of Crypto And Blockchain: Fintech 50 2022. (n.d.). Retrieved August 26, 2023, from https://www.forbes.com/sites/ninabambysheva/2022/06/07/the-future-of-crypto-and-blockchain-fintech-50-2022/?sh=653a39fb60cc

The Graph. (n.d.). Retrieved October 17, 2023, from https://thegraph.com/

The Most Successful ICOs of All Time. (n.d.). Retrieved September 7, 2023, from https://www.investopedia.com/tech/most-successful-icos-all-time/

The Value Layer of the Internet. (n.d.). Retrieved September 7, 2023, from https://polygon.technology/

The world's first fully regulated platf—INX One Platform. (n.d.). Retrieved June 18, 2025, from https://www.inx.co/

Tokensoft Over $1B Raised by Customers. (n.d.). Retrieved September 7, 2023, from https://www.tokensoft.io/

Top 30 Crypto VC Investment Funds: List of the Best Crypto Venture Capital Firms. (n.d.). Retrieved September 3, 2023, from https://ninjapromo.io/top-30-crypto-vc-investment-funds

Top Physical Bitcoin ETFs. (n.d.). Retrieved August 31, 2023, from https://etfdb.com/themes/physical-bitcoin-etfs/

Trusted & Compliant DeFi Ecosystem MANTRA. (n.d.). Retrieved September 8, 2023, from https://www.mantraomniverse.com/

TrustSwap—Accelerating the Global Transition to Web3. (n.d.). Retrieved September 8, 2023, from https://trustswap.com/

Understanding the Different Types of Cryptocurrency SoFi. (n.d.). Retrieved September 6, 2023, from https://www.sofi.com/learn/content/understanding-the-different-types-of-cryptocurrency/

Valmar Capital. (n.d.). Retrieved August 31, 2023, from https://www.valmar.io/

Valmar Capital at Coherra—23rd of August, 2023. (n.d.). Retrieved September 2, 2023, from https://explorer.coherra.com/video/4ce56433-4060-4432-888e-a650a5de910e

Venmo—Share Payments. (n.d.). Retrieved September 5, 2023, from https://venmo.com/

Venture capital financing in crypto, explained. (n.d.). Retrieved August 31, 2023, from https://cointelegraph.com/explained/venture-capital-financing-in-crypto-explained

Victor, F., ... B. L.-C. on F. C. and D., & 2019. (2019). Measuring ethereum-based erc20 token networks. *Springer, 11598 LNCS,* 113–129. https://doi.org/10.1007/978-3-030-32101-7_8

W3F Web3 Foundation. (n.d.). Retrieved September 2, 2023, from https://web3.foundation/

What Are Parachain Slot Auctions and Crowdloans? CoinMarketCap. (n.d.). Retrieved September 8, 2023, from https://coinmarketcap.com/alexandria/article/what-are-parachain-slot-auctions-and-crowdloans

WHAT Is a Bitcoin Futures ETF? (n.d.). www.cftc.gov/bitcoin

What Is a Crowdloan? Benefits & Explanation Moonbeam Network. (n.d.). Retrieved September 9, 2023, from https://moonbeam.network/education/what-is-a-crowdloan/

What Is an IEO? Initial Exchange Offerings & IDOs. Gemini. (n.d.). Retrieved September 8, 2023, from https://www.gemini.

com/cryptopedia/ieo-crypto-ido-crypto-initial-exchange-offering#section-initial-dex-offering-ido

What Is Crowdloan? Definition & Meaning Crypto Wiki. (n.d.). Retrieved September 8, 2023, from https://www.bitdegree.org/crypto/learn/crypto-terms/what-is-crowdloan

What Is PayPal USD (PYUSD)? (n.d.). Retrieved October 14, 2023, from https://www.paypal.com/us/cshelp/article/what-is-paypal-usd-pyusd-HELP1005

Index

P. Garvey, *Blockchain Fundamental Analysis for Digital Asset Investors*,
https://doi.org/10.1007/979-8-8688-1551-5

B

C

F

G

H

I

M

N

O

P, Q